THE HISTORY AND PHILOSOPHY OF EDUCATION

VOICES OF EDUCATIONAL PIONEERS

Madonna M. Murphy
University of St. Francis, Joliet, Illinois

PEARSON

Merrill
Prentice Hall

Upper Saddle River, New Jersey
Columbus, Ohio

Library of Congress Cataloging in Publication Data

Murphy, Madonna M.
    Readings in the history and philosophy : voices of educational pioneers / Madonna M. Murphy.
      p. cm.
    Includes bibliographical references and index.
    ISBN 0-13-095550-7
    1. Education—Philosophy. 2. Education—History. I. Title.
    LB14.7.M875 2006
    370'.1'09—dc22

                2005016530

Vice President and Executive Publisher: Jeffery W. Johnston
Executive Editor: Debra A. Stollenwerk
Senior Editorial Assistant: Mary Morrill
Assistant Development Editor: Elisa Rogers
Senior Production Editor: Linda Hillis Bayma
Production Coordination: Mike Remillard, Pine Tree Composition
Design Coordinator: Diane C. Lorenzo
Photo Coordinator: Lori Whitley
Cover Designer: Jason Moore
Cover image: Corbis
Production Manager: Susan Hannahs
Director of Marketing: Ann Castel Davis
Marketing Manager: Darcy Betts Prybella
Marketing Coordinator: Brian Mounts

This book was set in Berkeley by Pine Tree Composition. It was printed and bound by Hamilton Printing. The cover was printed by The Lehigh Press, Inc.

Photo Credits: akg-images, London, p. 104; Art Museum, Basel, Switzerland/A.K.G., p.137; Bettmann/Corbis, p. 143; Sappho, Greek lyric poet, © Bettmann/Corbis, p. 17; MS Harley, 4431 f4 (min) "Christine de Pisan In Her Study", by Permission of the British Library, p. 128; Corbis/Bettmann, pp. 5, 31, 59, 79, 98, 112, 150, 290, 328, 368; Special Collections Research Center, The University of Chicago Library, portrait by Ansel Adams, p. 352; Courtesy of the Instituto Paulo Freire Archives, p. 383; Getty Images, Inc., p. 375; Courtesy of Hampton University Archives, p. 219 (right); Courtesy of the Library of Congress, pp. 24, 53, 72, 163, 171, 186, 194, 201, 227, 235, 242, 259, 266, 296, 303, 310; Special Collections Research Center, Morris Library, Southern Illinois University Carbondale, p. 345; North Wind Picture Archives, p. 179; Rauner Special Collections Library, Dartmouth College, p. 219 (left); The Schlesinger Library, Radcliffe Institute, Harvard University, p. 274; Science Resource/Photo Researchers, Inc., p. 39; © Carl Van Vechten/Courtesy of the Library of Congress, p. 336.

Pearson Prentice Hall™ is a trademark of Pearson Education, Inc.
Pearson® is a registered trademark of Pearson plc
Prentice Hall® is a registered trademark of Pearson Education, Inc.
Merril® is a registered trademark of Pearson Education, Inc.

Pearson Education Ltd.
Pearson Education Singapore Pte. Ltd.
Pearson Education Canada, Ltd.
Pearson Education–Japan

Pearson Education Australia Pty. Limited
Pearson Education North Asia Ltd.
Pearson Educación de Mexico, S.A. de C.V.
Pearson Education Malaysia Pte. Ltd.

    10 9 8 7 6 5 4 3 2 1
    ISBN: 0-13-095550-7

To my past, present, and future students
at the University of St. Francis

ABOUT THE AUTHOR

Madonna Murphy is a professor of education at the University of St. Francis in Joliet, Illinois where she teaches History and Philosophy of Education, Teaching in a Diverse Society, and Character Education for Teachers to graduate and undergraduate students. She has traveled throughout the United States and to various countries in Europe and Latin America, visiting schools and speaking with teachers.

She is the author of *Character Education in America's Blue Ribbon Schools,* now in its second edition. She serves as the character education consultant for Capstone Press. To date they have published forty books on character education for elementary school children.

A graduate of the University of Chicago and Loyola University, Murphy is also a member of the Philosophy of Education Society, the History of Education Association, Phi Delta Kappa, Kappa Delta Phi, the Association for Supervision and Curriculum Development, the Association of Moral Education, and the Character Education Partnership.

PREFACE

This is a core textbook for courses in the history and philosphy of education. Uniquely offering both concepts and primary source readings, this book takes a biographical approach in tracing the development of educational innovations. It explores a collection of the original works of Eastern, Western, and American educators who helped shape educational theory and practice, from the ancient civilizations to the twenty-first century. The readings are presented in chronological order, and are organized around the theme that key people in each main historical period have developed ideas about education that still affect us today.

Some of these people were professional educators, but others were not; they include politicians, reformers, psychologists, sociologists, religious leaders, and public speakers. They represent the voices of men and women in different countries through many different time periods who have each made a significant contribution to educational history and philosophy and have left a written record of the contribution. This book is unique in that it includes a significant number of women educators from the time of the Greeks to current day America as well as Native-American, African-American, and Hispanic educators and their writing.

All of the educators in this book had definite ideas about who should be taught and by whom, what should be taught and how, and why education is important. Readers can develop their own philosophy of education by examining these diverse philosophies. By exploring the ideas of these leading figures from around the world, this book seeks to illustrate the perennial nature of education and the strong connection between educational practices today and ideas from the past. The writings of these great thinkers include the key ideas which are attributed to them today as their main contribution to educational thought. Some key educators are not included because they did not leave a written account of their ideas, or (if they did) it is no longer available. Currently living educators are not included because of the lack of biographical material on them, since they are still making their mark in history. This allows each instructor to choose the current educators with whom to conclude the course.

Teachers and teacher candidates need to have a professional preparation that includes an understanding of the historical development of educational thought. Developments in educational history and philosophy often rise out of the milieu in which they occur. This book places a special emphasis on the history of reform movements in education, including the development of the character education movement and the importance of creating caring and safe classrooms. Issues of gender, ethnicity, religion, and race are also highlighted as they gradually take on more importance in education in order to ensure equity and equal opportunity for all. Schools are a reflection of society, and education has not only a social but also a cultural and political purpose. Many look to the schools today, as they have in the past, to help build a better society and future.

Organization of the Book

The book is organized chronologically. Each chapter focuses on a major historical period (Ancient Civilizations, Greeks, Romans, Medieval, Renaissance, Enlightenment, American Colonial, Antebellum America, Twentieth-Century America, and Education in the Twenty-First Century) with the key educators from each period included in sections of the chapter.

Each section contains the following components:

- **A short biography** of the person's life, positioning each in a historical milieu. Examining the early lives of these educators can reveal the cause or explanation for the remarkable contributions they made. Often, as a result of a difficult early life where the only joy that was found was through learning, these people were convinced of the importance of the school. Historically one sees that they were the right person in the right place at the right time with exactly the qualities of mind, personality, and background to meet the challenges of the time.
- **A summary of the main contributions** that this person has made to educational thought. This introductory section is meant to assist students in reading the primary sources. After first considering the historical situation in which the person lived, one can then see the influence these factors had in the development of the person's philosophic ideas with the connection to the corresponding educational ideas proposed.
- **Questions to guide your reading.** These knowledge-level questions are presented before each primary source reading. They are intended to help the reader discern the important points in the document, since reading primary sources can be challenging. Students are asked to reflect on these main points in light of current education and schooling.
- **Primary source readings.** These readings were chosen for their expression of the educator's philosophy of education and his or her main pedagogical contribution to educational history. These primary sources are intended to help students develop critical thinking skills and skills of analysis, synthesis, and evaluation. They encompass a wide range of genres including poems, letters, speeches, book excerpts, and journal articles.
- **Discussion questions** follow each reading. These are meant to promote higher-level thinking about the ideas presented in the reading, applying these ideas to current educational issues.
- **Internet sites and bibliography.** Each section ends with Internet sites and a bibliography of books for further research on the educator.

Each chapter ends with "Chapter Activities" to relate the educational contributions made in each section to current educational practice. These include activities for linking past educational ideas to present-day teaching and learning and for connecting theory to practice, ideas for developing one's philosophy of education, and a chart summarizing the main contributions of the educators featured in the chapter.

Use in Course Development

Because there are more educators featured in this textbook than can be covered in a one-quarter or one-semester course, instructors can choose those that best complement their course objectives. For example:

- A complete survey of the development of educational thought can be achieved by choosing a few educators from each chapter.
- An American survey can be realized by starting with Chapter 8 and including all the subsequent educators. Some may like to include the immediate predecessors to American educational thought by also studying Chapter 7 educators.
- A unique feminist survey of educational philosophy can be accomplished by including all of the women featured in the book.

The author welcomes comments from readers and any suggestions for educators to add to subsequent chapters. E-mail your ideas to her at mmurphy@stfrancis.edu

Acknowledgments

I would like to acknowledge those who were my mentors as I learned about these philosophers of education. First, Dorothy Murphy, my mother, a teacher of the deaf who loved the Montessori philosophy of education. Then my collegiate study at the University of Chicago was done under the guidance of the late Patricia Luecke, my graduate study continued under the expertise of Gerald Gutek at Loyola University, and my research was finalized through post-doctoral study with Concepción Naval of the University of Navarra.

I would like to thank the Teaching and Professional Growth Committee and Dr. John Gambro, the Dean of the College of Education, for supporting my research by granting me both a faculty scholarship and a semester sabbatical to work on this book. Mary Yahnke, Director of the U.S.F. Bookstore, is greatly appreciated for her expertise in procuring copyright permissions and custom publishing this manuscript for use in my classes.

My colleagues at the University of St. Francis were a continuous source of support and assistance. Dan Hauser first encouraged me to write this book of readings in education, so appropriate for the liberal arts study of education students. Jeff Chamberlain, Karen Duys, Vin Katilius-Boydston, Janet Luecke, Susan Mangels, Marcia Marcez, Cathy Schultz, Mark Schultz, and Madonna Wojtaszek-Healy each assisted me in various chapters of the book, sharing their areas of expertise.

I would like to acknowledge the wonderful assistance of the USF librarians, Julie Dahl, Gail Gawlik, Carolyn Gudgeon, Marianne Kobe, Joan Koren, and Lucia Testin, who skillfully obtained books from around the country through inter-library loan, and which Tony Zordan generously picked up for me on the days he was on campus and I was not.

Thanks to Pat Joho and the student workers for their help with so many things, and to Mike Kustra, Chris Marks and Gina Stevens for their continuous help with computer problems.

I would like to acknowledge the assistance of my students in writing and piloting discussion questions, Internet sites, and chapter activities. A special thanks to Jason Blust, Linda Bowers, Shannon Ceh, Angela Cipolla, Mary Lou del Rosario, Beth Van Duyne, Michele Galvin, Melissa Maher, Tina Markum, Ann Ongenae, Kathleen Reid, Jean La Rocco, Dawn Sakanis, Tim Sawyer, and Annmarie Zan.

Many thanks to Alta Cameron, Karen Johnson, Linda Motz, and Amanda Murphy for their assistance in editing the book and Krista Franklin and Jan Whitten for their typing assistance. Thank you also to Meghan and Dorothy Murphy for typing the index and to Amy Reiner for her graphic design of the cover.

I appreciate the support and patience of Debbie Stollenwerk, my editor at Merrill/Prentice Hall, for understanding how long it takes to write a book while teaching and doing all the other things expected of professors at a university.

Finally, I would like to thank the reviewers of this book for their many fine suggestions: Henry C. Amoroso, Jr., University of Southern Maine; Mauria R. Berube, Old Dominion University; Richard Brosio, University of Wisconsin–Milwaukee; Malcolm B. Campbell, Bowling Green State University; Gloria J. Crawford, University of West Alabama; Mary Ann Clark, Brown University; Richard Farber, The College of New Jersey; Catherine M. Finnegan, Greenfield Community College; Louise E. Fleming, Ashland University; John Georgeoff, Purdue University; Shirley Jacob, Southeastern Louisiana University; Elizabeth A. McAuliffe, St. Mary Academy–Bay View; Vincent R. McGrath, Mississippi State University; Stephen D. Oates, Northern Michigan University; Patrick Socoski, University of Florida; Roberto L. Torres, Texas A&M University–Kingsville; Robert E. Vadas, State University of New York–Potsdam; Penelope Wong, California State University–Chico; and Carol A. Winkle, Aquinas College.

LETTER TO THE READER

Sometimes students wonder why they must take a course in the history and philosophy of education. They do not see it as practically related to what they will need to know as teachers in the field. As part of their professional knowledge base, preservice teachers need to understand how education and schooling originated and developed to realize its purpose of preparing youth to be productive, caring citizens of the future.[1] It is hoped that you will see, through the readings in this book, that many contemporary educational issues are the same as they have been throughout history. To solve these problems today, students should study the historical roots to understand the issue in depth. Educational theory is the application of philosophy to the classroom. The way the curriculum is organized, how it is taught, the manner in which students are graded (assessed), organized, and disciplined all reflect a philosophic view.[2] Each student of education needs to develop his/her own philosophy of education and his/her own view on these educational issues.

This book will allow you to read the educational views of many great thinkers. These readings contain aspects of their philosophy of education, that is, their view of the role of the student and that of the teacher, what they think is important to learn, how this should be taught and, finally, what they think is the main purpose of education. Through an analysis and synthesis of these ideas you should be able to construct your own philosophy of education that will guide you as you begin your career as an educator.

A teacher must have a very strong liberal arts background in order to successfully teach in a truly interdisciplinary manner. Thematic instruction helps students to seek the linkages in subjects that lead to wisdom or knowledge of the truth. According to Leo Strauss, "Liberal education is education in culture. Liberal education reminds us of our human greatness, of our call to live a life of virtue. Liberal education consists in reading the great books and having a conversation with these great minds about the most important issues in life."[3]

Developing Your Philosophy of Education

This book consists of selections from the original writings of great thinkers on educational issues throughout time. Reading these primary sources will allow you to have that conversation or dialogue about these ideas according to the perspective of our current concerns in education. The questions put to these educators will be broad ones, dealing with the very nature of teaching and learning which form the foundation of one's philosophy of education. For example: What is knowledge? What is education? What is the role of the teacher? What is the purpose of the school? Who should attend school? How should one teach so that students learn effectively? Can virtues and pro-social values be taught to students in schools, or is this the role of the home? The conversation that will pursue between you and these great thinkers will be one you will never forget. It will help to transform you from a student into a teacher.

Undergraduate students will find this textbook valuable for helping them to write a philosophy of education for their portfolio as an artifact under Standard 9 of the Interstate New Teacher Assessment and Support Consortium (INTASC) Standards to show that they are reflective practitioners. Graduate students pursuing administrative and/or supervisory certification will also find this textbook a valuable resource for meeting Standard 1 G of the Interstate School Leaders Licensure Consortium (ISLLC) Administrative standards, helping them to articulate their philosophy of educational leadership. This book aims to help graduate and undergraduate students gain knowledge and understanding of the history and philosophy of education.

Notes

1. Edward Power, *Philosophy of Education: Studies in Philosophies, Schooling and Educational Policies.* (Prospect Heights, IL: Waveland Press, 1990), p. 13.

2. Jill Stamm and Caroline Wactler, *Philosophy of Education Workbook: Writing a Statement of Beliefs and Practices* (New York: McGraw-Hill, 1997), p. 4.

3. Leo Strauss, "What is Liberal Education?" in *Liberalism Ancient and Modern* (New York: Basic Books, 1968), p. 4.

BRIEF CONTENTS

CONTENTS

Chapter 3
Roman Educational Contributions   49

Chapter 6
*Education in the Renaissance and
  the Reformation*   121

Chapter 7
New Educational Ideas in the Enlightenment   159

Chapter 9
Developing an American Educational System: Education in the New Nation   251

Chapter 10
Education for All? 283

Chapter 12
Education for a Global World   363

Note: Every effort has been made to provide accurate and current Internet information in this book. However, the Internet and information posted on it are constantly changing, and it is inevitable that some of the Internet addresses listed in this textbook will change.

MAPS

FIGURES

PICTURES

TABLES

TIMELINES

THE HISTORY
AND PHILOSOPHY
OF EDUCATION

CHAPTER 1

Education in the Early Cultures

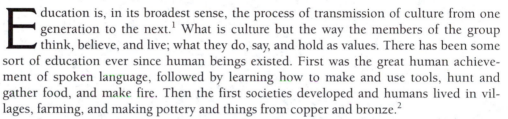

Education is, in its broadest sense, the process of transmission of culture from one generation to the next.[1] What is culture but the way the members of the group think, believe, and live; what they do, say, and hold as values. There has been some sort of education ever since human beings existed. First was the great human achievement of spoken language, followed by learning how to make and use tools, hunt and gather food, and make fire. Then the first societies developed and humans lived in villages, farming, and making pottery and things from copper and bronze.[2]

Education in primitive society was informal. It consisted of teaching the young to survive by hunting for food and (eventually) by planting crops; to secure shelter; to make tools and other utensils; and to learn the tribes' values and rules. Boys learned to make tools, to hunt, and fish. Girls learned to gather and prepare food. Primitive education knew nothing of books and schools. It was motivated by the need for self-preservation; it was direct and effective; and it was carried on by the active participation of the learner as he imitated adult activities or was shown how to make tools, engage in the hunt, or fish. Parents were, from the beginning, the primary educators of their children. They were helped by other members of their tribe who taught children the practical skills needed, and who told them stories that explained the customs (mores) of the tribe.[3] Moral education was thus an integral part of the educative process from the beginning.

Language: The Mark of Civilization

Language, the ability to communicate orally, is the mark of civilization. Education emphasized language learning by using songs, stories, and rituals that formed the groups' cultural inheritance. Unique to human beings is the ability to use abstract thought, conceptualize, and communicate in oral and written language; this has tremendous educational consequences. As primitive man began to scratch rough pictures of the world around him on the walls of caves, he was laying the basis for a process that would later culminate in written symbols of communication.

Education in the Near East

It is impossible to determine the exact date that schools first came into existence. However, we know that written language was developed around 4000 B.C. Once there was a written language, there was a need for a more formal kind of education.[4] The earliest civilizations that left records were a group of city-states formed in the Tigris-Euphrates River valley in Mesopotamia (now Iraq; see Map 1.1 of the Near East). Known as Sumeria, these city states became the basis for later social and educational developments in China, India, and Egypt. Although the Sumerians did not have an alphabet, they developed symbols that came to be known as *cuneiform* that were made by pressing a wedge-shaped stylus into a soft clay tablet. In Babylon (and later in Egypt), this process at first took the form of *picture writing* or *pictograms*. The picture referred not only to the object portrayed but also had meaning beyond the actual object.

Recent discoveries in Iraq have turned up cuneiform mathematics textbooks used by schoolboys in Sumeria as early as 2000 B.C.[5] One can assume that some form of schools probably existed at that time. There is considerable evidence that by the time of Hammurabi (1792–1750 B.C.) there was an elaborate system of schools for the elite, devoted to

Map 1.1 Ancient Civilizations and Trade Routes of the Near East

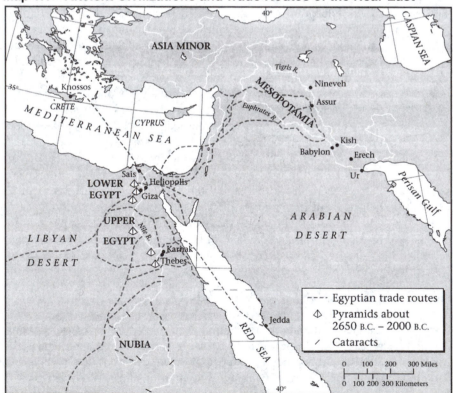

Source: From Anthony Esler, *The Human Venture, Combined Volume: From Prehistory to the Present,* 5th edition, 2004. Reprinted by permission of Pearson Education.

the education of priests, scribes, and civil servants. The Phoenicians developed a system of 22 signs, each of which represented a consonant sound, around 1000 B.C. This was the beginning of the development of an alphabet as we know it today.

Females could attend school and a woman could manage her husband's business and household affairs when he was away. In the Old Babylonian period, women could act as witnesses and be scribes. There are even reports of women physicians.

Earliest Written Literature

By 2700 B.C., cuneiform was also used for works of literature. *The Epic of Gilgamesh* is the earliest known written work of literature. It deals with the profound themes of friendship, the reality of death, and the quest for eternal life.

Education in China

China has also been a civilized society for a very long time. There is evidence to suggest that formal schools existed in China during the Hsia and Shang dynasties, perhaps as early as 2000 B.C.[6] (see Map 1.2 of China). Religion has always been one of the fundamental factors in Chinese life and education. The Chinese have a great devotion to tradition. This in evident in the family, where the father has absolute power to enforce obedience to himself as the carrier of tradition. The state was but an enlargement of the family, and the

Map 1.2   China

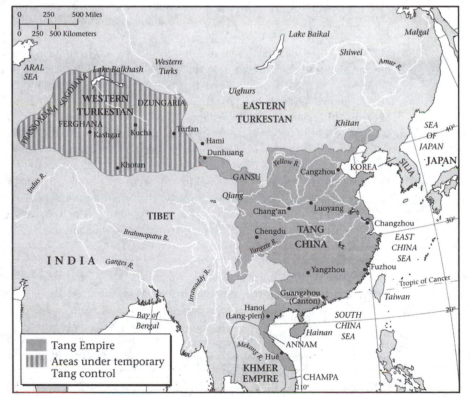

Source: From Anthony Esler, *The Human Venture, Combined Volume: From Prehistory to the Present,* 5th edition, 2004. Reprinted by permission of Pearson Education.

emperor functioned as the Great Father of all the people. Filial piety was important, as was dedication to the country. Chinese education aimed to conserve the past and maintain things as tradition dictated.

The Chinese Curriculum

Around the seventh century B.C., we see the Chinese curriculum leaning heavily on tradition. Classical subjects were studied in a prescribed curriculum: history, poetry, literature of antiquity, government documents, and law. China had no state system of schools nor public education. Formal education was strictly for men, and only those men who could pay for it. In general, the education of women was limited to that which they needed in order to be polished in social situations, but there are reported incidents of women receiving some formal education. They, like men, were able to quote from the *Book of Poetry* and other books. Some even participated in public affairs. Wives of kings held the reins of power when their husbands were away.[7]

Chinese Educational Institutions

There were three levels of ancient Chinese education: elementary, academies, and examinations. The elementary school met in the teacher's house. The hours were long and the work severe. The private academies were more like "cram" or "drill" schools in which the youth studied the Chinese classics, grammar, and prose in order to pass the examinations. The methodology at every level of Chinese education was extremely formal, emphasizing memorization and an exact reproduction of textual material. The classroom was a scene of confusion and ear-splitting noise as the children studied their lessons and recited aloud. To motivate students to this rote memory and absolute imitation, the teacher had to exert harsh discipline.

Chinese education has always been characterized by tradition, morality, and conformity—all designed to help the students to become the kind of human person envisioned by oriental thought. We traditionally credit the philosophers and thinkers of Greece and Rome with establishing the foundations of our intellectual educational thought. However, it is interesting to study Eastern thought to see that, in the same time period, a similar system of ideas was established in China. Eastern thought is different from Western thought in that it is cyclical, emphasizing harmony while also juxtaposing opposites.

Confucius was the first private teacher in China who taught men the value of teaching itself. It will do us well, therefore, to begin this book of educational writings with a work from one of China's great thinkers, the famous philosopher Confucius, who wrote about the importance of education for society. This will help us to see that educational issues are perennial and cross cultures, civilizations, and time periods.

For Further Research on the Internet

Site with information on ancient Babylonia, Egypt, and other ancient civilizations. **http:// home.echo-on.net/~smithda/**

Information on the Sumerians of Babylonia and other ancient civilizations. **http://www .eliki.com/ancient/civilizations/**

Lesson plans on the ancient civilizations. **http://lessonplans.com**

Many links to ancient China, Egypt, and India. **http://www.crystalinks.com/ancient.html**

Notes

1. Edward Power, *Philosophy of Education: Studies in Philosophies, Schooling and Educational Policies* (Prospect Heights, IL: Waveland Press, 1990).
2. Marvin Perry et al., *Western Civilization: Ideas, Politics & Society* (Boston: Houghton Mifflin Company, 2000).
3. Tim Megarry, *Society in Prehistory: The Origin of Human Culture* (New York: New York University Press, 1996).
4. Yun Lee Too, *The Pedagogical Contract: The Economies of Teaching and Learning in the Ancient World* (Ann Arbor: University of Michigan Press, 2000).
5. Eleanor Robson, *Mesopotamian Mathematics, 2100–1600 B.C.* (Oxford: Clarendon Press, 1999).
6. Ray Huang, *China: A Macro History* (Armonk, N.Y.: M.E. Sharpe, 1997).
7. Conrad Schirokaurer, *A Brief History of Chinese Civilization* (New York: Harcourt Brace Jovanovich, 1991).

Section 1.1: Confucius (552–479 B.C.)

Proverbs and maxims are one of the most effective ways of teaching moral principles because when learned young, they stick with you all your life. We all remember our parents' quoting: "Early to bed, early to rise, makes a man healthy, wealthy, and wise." Confucius was the great moral teacher who taught using maxims.

Confucius' Life and Times

Confucius (born Kung Chiu, meaning Chiu of the Kung family, later stylized as Chung-ni meaning "second son") was born to a poor but noble aristocratic family in the country of Lu in 552 B.C. His father was a distinguished soldier who died in battle when Confucius was only three years old. Confucius' mother was diligent in her drive to provide a sound education for her four sons.

His Education

It was the custom of the times to appoint a private tutor to educate the sons of the noble classes.[1] Confucius was, therefore, well trained in the great classics of Chinese literature as well as in history, poetry, music, and archery. Poetry and music were to have a special influence on him. At the age of fifteen, he entered a local school in his village where he was taught by his elders the etiquette of respectful service and good morals as well as the course of studies.[2] As a young adult, he quickly earned a reputation for fairness, politeness, and love of learning. After studying in the village school, he went to the establishment for higher learning in the Lu imperial capital of Zhou where he met and spoke with Lao Zi, the founder of Taoism. He traveled extensively. Confucius married at the age of nineteen. He had at least one son, Li Poyu, and a daughter.[3] (See the timeline of Confucius' life shown in Figure 1.1.)

Confucius, the Great Teacher

Upon his return to Lu at the age of thirty, Confucius began his career in teaching. Tradition tells us that he used his own house as a school and charged small fees for his students whom he instructed in his favorite subjects: history, poetry, government, morality, and music. He taught the art of thinking through conversation with his students about their own opinions on important matters, much in the style of Socrates. Beginning with just a few students, Confucius rapidly developed a reputation as a great teacher. He had an incredible ability to inspire others to see the truths of the great ideas. He loved learning and he sought out pupils who shared this love. By the time he died, he had mentored more than 3,000 male students who carried on his teachings as his disciples.

His success as a teacher led to his receiving a major civil appointment. During Confucius' reign as minister of justice, society ran very smoothly and the crime rate dropped substantially. This was attributed to Confucius' principle of "rule by good example" rather than "strong fisted force." When other nobles began plotting against Confucius' position, he retired from public life to concentrate on teaching and studying. He spent the rest of his years teaching and writing, dying in 479 B.C at the age of 72.[4]

Confucius' Importance for Educational Thought

Prior to the time of Confucius, all branches of learning had been in the official custody of hereditary aristocrats. Except for schools of archery, there were no schools in China to provide what we consider a basic education. Reading and writing were learned at home. Confucius was the first to offer to instruct private individuals and to set up a sort of school for all young men, irrespective of their social status and means.

Confucius' Philosophy of Education

Confucius' aim was to provide all students with an education that would be both practical and moral; an education that would "cultivate the person" and teach them to solve the daily problems of governmental service and bring the best benefits to the people they served. Confucius saw his role as a teacher to be a "transmitter of knowledge," one who should inspire students with the truths of the great ideas. His method of instruction consisted of conversation and dialogue; sometimes he would question his students and comment on their answers, like Socrates. Confucius expected his students to be motivated and active learners who would take the initiative in their learning. He established the curriculum of reading and studying the six Chinese classics instead of acquiring practical

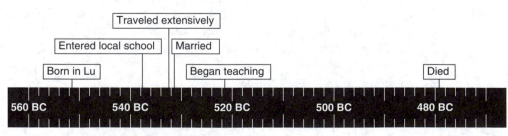

Figure 1.1 Confucius' Life and Times

knowledge. His emphasis on liberal instead of vocational education had significant influence on the history of Chinese education.[5]

Moral Role of Education. Confucius was deeply convinced that learning and morality were inseparable. Education, he felt, improved the moral character of a person as well as the intellect. Morality needs good education, and a good education is one based on the moral principles. Confucius set up a universal ethical system.[6]

Confucius taught that there were key cardinal virtues that all people needed to develop. However, all virtues are interrelated because the human being is an interrelational creature. The development of virtues brought harmony. Students should be taught filial piety and fraternal love. Education is central to building up a strong society. The dream of Confucius was a world as it *should* be.

Confucius and his followers have had a tremendous impact on Chinese society and education. The traditional values advocated by Confucius—filial respect, moderation, and truthfulness—still play an important part in Chinese people's lives as does the principle that education should be for all as it has a social purpose. According to Confucius, "Those who excel in office should learn; those who excel in learning should take office."[7]

For Further Research on the Internet

A short biography of Confucius with an explanation of Chinese characters. **http://www.friesian.com/confuci.htm**

A publishing company concentrating on disseminating the work of Confucius. **http://www.confucius.org/maine.htm**

A site dedicated to Confucius and his writings. **http://www.cifnet.com/~geenius/kongfuzi/**

Notes

1. Shigeki Kaizuka, *Confucius: His Life and Thought* (Mineola, NY: Dover Publications, 2002), pp. 42, 62.
2. Ibid., p. 64.
3. Paul Strathern, *The Essential Confucius* (London: Virgin Publications, 2002), p. 20.
4. Kaizuka, p. 45.
5. Jianping Shen, *Confucius* (New York: Routledge, 2001), pp. 2–3.
6. Strathern, p. 30.
7. Shen, pp. 3–4.

Questions to Guide Your Reading

1. Diagrams help us to understand the logic of arguments. See if you can diagram Confucius' explanation of *The Great Learning* and *The Doctrine of the Mean* as you read these selections.

2. Of what well-known literary form found in the *Bible* do *The Analytics* remind you? Why is the use of maxims an effective learning device? Can you mention some maxims that hold true in both Eastern and Western societies?

3. Can you find Confucius' version of *The Golden Rule?* Using the Internet, see if you can research other versions of the Golden Rule as found in different cultures and religions.

READING 1.1:
CONFUCIUS, THE MASTER TEACHER

The Great Learning

1. What the Great Learning teaches, is to illustrate illustrious virtue; to renovate the people; and to rest in the highest excellence.

2. Things have their root and their branches. What is first and what is last will lead near to what is taught in the *Great Learning*.

3. The ancients who wished to illustrate illustrious virtue throughout the kingdom, first ordered well their own States. Wishing to order well their States, they first regulated their families. Wishing to regulate their families, they first cultivated their persons. Wishing to cultivate their persons, they first rectified their hearts. Wishing to rectify their hearts, they first sought to be sincere in their thoughts. Wishing to be sincere in their thoughts, they first extended to the utmost their knowledge. Such extension of knowledge lay in the investigation of things.

4. Things being investigated, knowledge became complete. Their knowledge being complete, their thoughts were sincere. Their thoughts being sincere, their hearts were then rectified. Their hearts being rectified, their persons were cultivated. Their persons being cultivated, their families were regulated. Their families being regulated, their States were rightly governed. Their States being rightly governed, the whole kingdom was made tranquil and happy.

5. From the Sun of Heaven down to the mass of the people, all must consider the cultivation of the person the root of everything besides.

6. It cannot be, when the root is neglected, that what should spring from it will be well ordered. It never has been the case that what was of great importance has been slightly cared for, and, at the same time, that what was of slight importance has been greatly cared for.

Source: The Four Books. James Legge, ed., trans. *The Chinese Classics*, Vol. I (Oxford: Clarendon, 1893).

Chapter VII

7. What is meant by, 'The cultivation of the person depends on rectifying the mind,' *may be thus illustrated:* If a man be under the influence of passion, he will be incorrect in his conduct. He will be the same if he is under the influence of terror, or under the influence of fond regard, or under that of sorrow and distress.

8. When the mind is not present, we look and do not see; we hear and do not understand; we eat and do not know the taste of what we eat.

9. This is what is meant by saying that the cultivation of the person depends on the rectifying of the mind.

Confucian Analects

2:11 The Master said, 'If a man keeps cherishing his old knowledge, so as continually to be acquiring new, he may be a teacher of others.'

2:15 The Master said, 'Learning without thought is labor lost; thought without learning is perilous.'

2:17 The Master said, 'Yu, shall I teach you what knowledge is? When you know a thing, to hold that you know it; and when you do not know a thing, to allow that you do not know it;—this is knowledge.'

4:16 The Master said, 'The mind of the superior man is conversant with righteousness; the mind of the mean man is conversant with gain.'

4:17 The Master said, 'When we see men of worth, we should think of equaling them; when we see men of a contrary character, we should turn inwards and examine ourselves.'

7:1 The Master said, '[I am a] transmitter and not a maker, believing in and loving the ancients. . . .'

7:8 The Master said, 'I do not open up the truth to one who is not eager to get knowledge, nor help out any one who is not anxious to explain himself. When I have presented one corner of a subject to anyone, and he cannot from it learn the other three, I do not repeat my lesson.'

7:19 The Master said. 'I am not one who was born in the possession of knowledge; I am one who is fond of antiquity, and earnest in seeking it there.'

7:21 The Master said, 'When I walk along with two others, they may serve me as my teachers. I will select their good qualities and follow them, their bad qualities and avoid them.'

7:24 There were four things which the Master taught,—letters, ethics, devotion of soul, and truthfulness.

9:4 There were four things from which the Master was entirely free. He had no foregone conclusions, no arbitrary predeterminations, no obstinacy, and no egoism.

12:16 The Master said, 'The superior man seeks to perfect the admirable qualities of men, and does not seek to perfect their bad qualities. The mean man does the opposite of this.'

15:23 Tsze-kung asked, saying, 'Is there one word which may serve as a rule of practice for all one's life?' The Master said, 'Is not reciprocity such a word? What you do not want done to yourself, do not do to others.'

17:2 The Master said, 'By nature, men are nearly alike; by practice, they get to be wide apart.'

The Doctrine of the Mean

1:4 While there are no stirrings of pleasure, anger, sorrow, or joy, the mind may be said to be in the state of EQUILIBRIUM. When those feelings have been stirred, and they act in their due degree, there ensues what may be called the state of HARMONY. This EQUILIBRIUM is the great root from which grows all the human acting in the world, and this HARMONY is the universal path which they all should pursue.

1:5 Let the states of equilibrium and harmony exist in perfection, and a happy order will prevail throughout heaven and earth, and all things will be nourished and flourish.

2:3 The Master said, 'Perfect is the virtue which is according to the Mean! Rare have they long been among the people, who could practice it!'

8:3 [The Master said] 'When one cultivates to the utmost the principles of his nature, and exercises them on the principle of reciprocity, he is not far from the path. What you do not like done to yourself, do not do to others.'

15:5 The Master said, 'In archery we have something like the way of the superior man. When the archer misses the center of the target, he turns round and seeks the cause of his failure in himself.'

20:11 [The Master said] 'He who knows these three things [knowledge, magnanimity, and energy], knows how to cultivate his own character. Knowing how to cultivate his own character, he knows how to govern other men. Knowing how to govern other men, he knows how to govern the kingdom with all its States and families.'

21:21 [The Master said] 'When we have intelligence resulting from sincerity, this condition is to be ascribed to nature; when we have sincerity resulting from intelligence, this condition is to be ascribed to instruction. But given the sincerity, and there shall be intelligence; given the intelligence, and there shall be the sincerity.'

25:1 Sincerity is that whereby self-completion is effected and its way is that by which man must direct himself.

25:2 Sincerity is the end and beginning of things; without sincerity there would be nothing. On this account, the superior man regards the attainment of sincerity as the most excellent thing.

25:3 The possessor of sincerity does not merely accomplish the self-completion of himself. With this quality he completes other men and things also. The completing of himself shows his perfect virtue. The completing of other men and things shows his knowledge.

Discussion Questions

1. Oriental thought is cyclical. Confucius sees a perfect relationship between the values of the family, the state and the person. How would Confucius solve the problem we face today in our schools when the values of a student's family clash with the values of the school and society?

2. Confucius says the "the cultivation of the person is the root of everything besides." Do you think that this is the main goal of education today? If not, what do schools today say is their mission toward students?
3. What is *The Doctrine of the Mean* according to Confucius? Is this similar or different from Western philosophy's understanding of virtue as a mean between two defects, one of excess and the other of deficiency? What do you think Confucius would say about the current character education movement in schools and their definition of virtue? (Look at the *character.org* site to help you answer this question.)
4. Confucius explains his philosophy of the teacher as "[I am] a transmitter and not a maker. . . ." Is this an accurate metaphor to use to describe the teacher in today's schools? If not, can you propose a more accurate metaphor? What do you think Confucius would say about the status, prestige, and role of teachers in the schools today? Do you think they are given the respect they were given in Chinese society?
5. The Chinese were one of the first groups to extensively use examinations and tests to measure learning. Compare and contrast their use of tests to our current use of standardized tests in the "No Child Left Behind" legislation. In what ways does this show that some educational issues are perennial?
6. Contrast the political ideas of Confucius with those of a later Chinese ruler, Mao Tse-Tung, who led the Communist revolution and created a new China based on Marxist ideology.

For Further Research on the Internet

Internet site with pictures of Confucius and links to Chinese history. **http://www. crystalinks.com/confucius.html**

A publishing company dedicated to the writings of Confucius. **http://www. confucius.org/index.html**

An interactive site on ancient China, Confucius, and Chinese literature. **http://www. wsu.edu:8080/~dee/ANCCHINA/ANCCHINA.HTM**

Suggestions for Further Reading

Confucius. *The Wisdom of Confucius.* New York: Partridge Green Citadel, 2001.
Kaizuka, Shigeki. *Confucius: His Life and Thought.* Mineola, NY: Dover Publications, 2002.
Shen, Jianping. "Confucius." In Joy Palmer, *Fifty Major Thinkers on Education: From Confucius to Dewey.* New York: Routledge Publishers, 2001.
Strathern, Paul. *The Essential Confucius.* London: Virgin Publications, 2002.

CHAPTER ACTIVITIES

Linking the Past to the Present

Compare and contrast aspects of education in early cultures to education in modern times (See Table 1.1). What components of early educational practice would help us to make education more meaningful and relevant to students in schools in the twenty-first century? What would be needed in order to actualize these changes? Imagine what schools could be like. Write about your utopian educational world.

**TABLE 1.1   Education in Early Society Compared to Education
in Modern Society**

Education in Early Society	Education in Modern Society
Simple, homogeneous, integrated	Complex, diverse, dispersed
Daily experience is educational	Only schools educate (businesses now educating too)
Objectives self-evident—survival	Students unable to see the importance of the curriculum
The family is always an important educational agent	The breakdown of the family
Education serves to prepare for important roles in society	Education may not get you a job in the current job market
Each generation accepts the standards and values of its predecessors	Generation gap—rejection of norms and mores of parents
Security, survival	Confusion, lack of aims

Developing Your Philosophy of Education

Reflect on the importance the family had in Confucius' educational system and in Chinese society. Write about the role the family will have in your educational philosophy. How will you interact with the parents of the children you educate? How will you communicate with them? Will you invite them into your classroom? For what purposes? What will you do if the parents of your students subscribe to different values than those of the school?

Connecting Theory to Practice

1. In your classroom clinical experience, observe the teacher-student relationship. How are the students taught appropriate behaviors? Does the teacher emphasize the development of virtues in the students? Do the students respect the teacher? Is there a general atmosphere of harmony in the classroom and school?
2. Can you give three reasons why the study of the history and philosophy of education will help you as a teacher?
3. Give two examples of how knowledge of the history of education will assist you in solving modern educational problems and prevent you from "reinventing the wheel" or repeating the errors of the past.

Educators' Philosophies and Contributions to Education

1. Using Table 1.2 of educational contributions from the various early cultures, make a list of current educational contributions made by the modern American culture.

TABLE 1.2   Educational Contributions from Early Cultures

Sumerians	Egyptians
First written language around 4000 B.C.	Invented papyrus (paper)
Developed cuneiform writing with stylus in clay	Created hieroglyphic writing system
Invented picture writing or pictograms	Started first libraries
First cuneiform math books	Developed a complete school system and curriculum
Babylonians	**Chinese**
Earliest written literature—*Gilgamesh*	Invented gunpowder, compass
Elaborate system of schools for the elite	Developed first "universities"/schools of higher learning
	Developed printing
	First to use "standardized tests"

2. What contribution does Confucius make to modern-day educators? Review Table 1.3 for ideas.

TABLE 1.3   Confucius' Philosophy of Education

Educator	Role of Teacher & Learner	View of Curriculum & Methodology	Purpose or Goal of Education	Major Contribution
Confucius	The teacher is "The Master"—a transmitter of knowledge—and the student is an active learner who takes the initiative in learning	*The Liberal Arts: The Five Classics and the Four Books* (ethics, wisdom, spirit, truthfulness) are taught using the informal method of conversation and dialogue	Transmit a cultural heritage in order to cultivate the moral person that knows how to solve the problems of society and government	An ethics and value system that still inspires people today

CHAPTER 2

Education in Ancient Greece

We turn to Greece to find the origins of many of our educational policies and systems. Greece is the originating source of Western civilization. Greek ideas about education and their educational practices have been very influential on other cultures. We will see that Rome's greatest service to mankind is that it carried the Greek tradition to all the Western lands.

Greek civilization developed between 1200 and 490 B.C. From the fifth century to the third century B.C. Greece, and particularly Athens, enjoyed a flourishing level of culture and education. They colonized much of the Mediterranean area, including towns in Italy and along the French borders during these years. It is in the Age of Pericles, around 500 B.C., that we see the first organized effort in a Western society toward formal education.[1]

Education in Sparta

It was in Sparta, a city in the mountains of Greece, cut off from others, that the concept of the state's (or polis') obligation for the proper training of its citizens was first developed. Previous to this, in other Greek states and other countries, families educated their children. In Sparta, every detail of the child's life, and of adult life, was controlled by the State. The State needed well-trained warriors who could defend their country against invaders. A distinctive feature of the Spartan system was the attention paid to the training of women. (Elsewhere in Greece girls were brought up in the seclusion of the home and only received domestic training.) Spartans had a clear view of the value of education for all. They educated their women because they had to become worthy mothers who would be the primary educators of their sons from birth to age seven. The mothers taught the young children at home, while the father was busy with the duties of citizenship. At about age 7, young boys began their education under the tutorship of older males. As far back as we can trace the history of Greek culture, schoolmasters appear as a regular feature of Greek social life. The Spartan model of an educated man was a brave warrior whose goal was to become a courageous military hero.[2] (See Map 2.1 of ancient Greece.)

Education in Athens

In Athens, the education of the young was looked at as a public rather than a private matter and was entrusted exclusively to professional hands. Athenian citizens were expected to be able to read and write, to count, and sing or play the lyre. Education began in Athens around 640–550 B.C. with Solon's edict that every boy should be taught to swim and to read in schools and *palaestrae,* or gymnastic schools. Solon did not define the curriculum or the methods but only the age and rank of students and the qualifications of the **pedagogues,** that is, the slaves who tutored each student. Today, when we use the word pedagogy we are referring to its Greek derivation from "piad" + "agoge" that meant "the leading of the child/slave." Using the term pedagogy instead of education specifically refers to this social process of teaching and learning in recognition of that fact that education is a political process.[3] Schools in Athens were not a creation of the state but a private enterprise with the teacher supported by tuition payments. The Greek style of education tended to be a male-to-male tutorial, often involving a close personal relationship between the older and younger male. School was not compulsory in Athens, nor was it open to all, but only to the male children of the citizens. Between the ages of eight and sixteen some Athenian boys attended a series of public schools.

The Greek School System

The Greek schools included a grammar school or **grammatica** to learn reading, writing, and counting, a gymnastic school (**palaestra**) to learn sports and games, and a music school, or **cithara,** that taught history, drama, poetry, speaking, and science as well as music. By 335 B.C., political and social changes lead to the requiring of compulsory military training for all Athenian males ages eighteen to twenty before they were granted full citizenship.[4] The Athenian educated ideal was a well-rounded, liberally educated individual who was capable in politics, military affairs, and general community life and could take part in the direct participatory democracy.

Education of Athenian Women

The aim of education for Athenian women was more at the level of training, enabling them to master domestic tasks rather than intellectual. Most Athenian girls were only educated in the home. However, a few women's schools did exist. Sappho of Lesbos, most notably, operated a school that taught women of rank such subjects as singing, music, dancing, and sports.[5] Greek women may have lacked the breadth and cultural value given to boys in their education, but they learned more than the home crafts of spinning, weaving, and embroidery; they were also familiar with the rich folk lore of their people, which was culture itself, and their music and dances. Most characteristic of Athenian life was the general opinion that education—cultural and civic education—was an art to be learned by each individual.[6]

Map 2.1 Ancient Greece

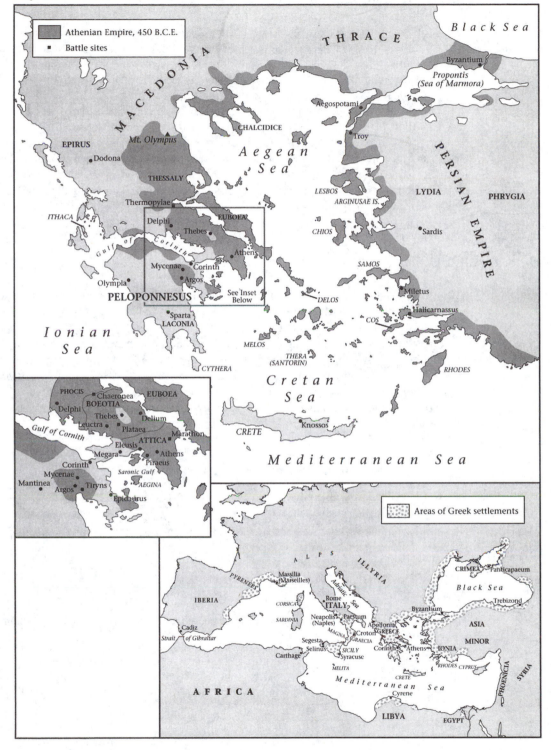

Source: From Anthony Esler, *The Human Venture, Combined Volume: From Prehistory to the Present,* 5th edition, 2004. Reprinted by permission of Pearson Education.

Sophism, Stoicism, and Epicureanism

The Sophists flourished from 470–370 B.C. in Athens and sought an education that would lead to political power and social status by emphasizing rhetoric, or persuasive speech, as practical education.[7] Socrates and Plato did much to discourage the Athenian youth from seeking this practical, utilitarian education and instead encouraged them to seek the truth, or true education, i.e., the love of wisdom or philosophy.

The conquests of Alexander the Great in the fourth century extended the Greek culture to much of the eastern Mediterranean, Asia Minor, and northern Africa. The Hellenistic philosophies of Stoicism and Epicureanism challenged the Athenian ideas. Epicurus had a materialistic view of life with its only goal being to avoid pain and secure pleasure. Stoicism was a contrary philosophy that saw the body as unimportant, so one should free themselves from their passions. Both Plato and Aristotle challenged these two world views with their philosophy of life.

A Greek Philosophy of Education

The study of ancient Greek civilization provides valuable lessons on citizenship and civic education that illustrate the important role of education in shaping good citizens. In these next selections, we will be presented with the Greek thinkers' views on the purpose of education, what it is that should be taught to others, and how the teacher should impart this knowledge. The study of Greek educational thought illuminates many problems today's educators face: Who are worthy models for children to imitate? How does education help to shape good citizenship? How does education serve humankind's search for truth? Sappho, Socrates, Plato and Aristotle each dealt with these questions and their ideas are relevant to us today as we too search for answers for our schools.

For Further Research on the Internet

The Classics Page has information about life, literature, art, and archeology in ancient Greece. **http://www.classicspage.com/**

This site has many links to ancient Greek resources on line. **http://www.webcom.com/ shownet/medea/grklink.html**

Notes

1. Mark Griffin, *Public and Private in Early Greek Education* (Leiden, Netherlands: Koninklijke Brill, 2001), pp. 66–67.
2. Ibid., pp. 46–47, Aubrey Gwynn, *Roman Education from Cicero to Quintillian* (London: Oxford University Press, 1926), pp. 26–29; Sara Pomeroy, *Spartan Women* (New York: Oxford University Press, 2002).
3. Yun Lee Too, *Education in Greek and Roman Antiquity* (Leiden, Netherlands: Koninklijke Brill, 2001), pp. 13–14.
4. Griffin, pp. 46–47; Gerald Gutek, *A History of the Western Educational Experience* (Prospect Heights, IL: Waveland Press, Inc., 1995), p. 29; H. I. Marrou, *A History of Education in Antiquity* (Madison: University of Wisconsin Press, 1982), p. 63.
5. Anne Haward, *Penelope to Poppaea: Women in Greek and Roman Society* (Surrey, England: Nelson, 1992).
6. Josiah Ober, The Debate over Civic Education in Classical Athens, in *Education in Greek and Roman Antiquity* (Leiden, Netherlands: Koninklijke Brill, 2001), p. 179.
7. Gutek, p. 35.

Section 2.1: Sappho (630?–572? B.C).

Most of us probably learned music in school and maybe we even learned to play an instrument. Sappho was the first female music teacher we know of who also wrote poetry and read it to the accompaniment of her lyre. In addition, she was the first health and physical education teacher for girls.

Sappho, Greek lyric poet. © Bettmann/Corbis

Sappho's Life and Times

Sappho was born around 630 B.C. in either the city of Mytilene or Eresus, both located on the island of Lesbos, to an aristocratic family (see the timeline of Sappho's life shown in Figure 2.1). The oldest bibliographical source in existence, the Byzantine Encyclopedic work *Suda* written about 100 A.D., gives us this fact and what little else we know about Sappho. From this and what Sappho tells us in her poems, we believe that her father was Scamandronymous and her mother was Cleis of Mytilene, and that she had three brothers.[1]

From ancient art, especially decorated vases with portraits of Sappho, we know that she played a type of lyre called a "barbito." Sappho enjoyed immense popularity for the beauty of her language and the directness and power of her expression, but to the fourth century Athenian, the most remarkable thing about her was that she was a woman.[2]

Her Family and "Friends"

It seems that Sappho married Cercylas of Andros, a very wealthy man who traded from Andros, and had one child by him, a daughter names Cleis (named after Sappho's mother). Sappho was from a family of some social prominence and an aristocratic world view is represented in her poetry. In fact, it is this status that enabled her to dedicate herself to her work, and gave her the leisure for music-making and for having her work valued and preserved.

According to the *Suda*, Sappho had three companions and friends, and "acquired a bad reputation for her shameful friendship with them."[3] Sappho, although married, had other male lovers; Archilocus and Hipponaxare are two mentioned in her poems. Fragments of Greek biography found on papyrus from the second and third century state that Sappho was accused by some of being irregular in her ways and a woman lover.[4] Some find it hard to reconcile Sappho's involvement in the institution of marriage with the passionate love

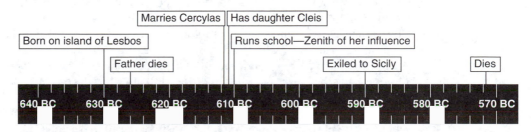

Figure 2.1   Sappho's Life and Times

poetry she addresses to other women. It seems that Sappho herself did not regard marriage and lesbianism as mutually exclusive; in other words, the two could co-exist in her world.[5] An inscription on a marble from the island of Paros records that Sappho fled from Mytilene to Sicily some time between 605 and 590 B.C., probably for these social and political reasons.[6] Others maintain that Sappho was not bi-sexual, but had deep relations with both men and women as was common in the Greek culture of her time.

Seventh Century Greece

The time in which Sappho lived, the seventh century B.C., was the archaic Greek period characterized by the lively interchange of people, products, and ideas. This was a period of great change with efforts being made to colonize other areas and to expand trade. In this climate of economic and social change, the women of Lesbos enjoyed a freedom similar to that of the women in Sparta, giving them the opportunity for self-development. They were known not only for their beauty and culture but also for their skill in the art of heterosexual love-making. Sappho was an educated woman who wrote about love.[7]

Sparta's educational system had spread throughout the Greek world. Although it included education for both boys and girls, they were segregated from one another. This reflected the Greek societal norms; men and women usually separated into groups according to both gender and status and those groups were divided by age; boys in a group separate from men, girls from women.[8]

Sappho's School for Girls

Tradition has Sappho as the head of a girls' school. The *Suda* names some of her pupils and fragments of poetry list other names; nineteen different students in all.[9] As Jane McIntosh Snyder states, she "must have been a model of purity for no one would send young women from a distance to study under a woman unless she had a wonderful reputation."[10] The institution that she headed trained young women according to the customs of the time. They studied poetry and music, chorus dancing, and singing under Sappho's guidance. However, one day they do "go away again" and return to their homes to marry; now cultured women.

The issues raised by her school regarding the relationship of the pupil and the instructor remain relevant to our current concerns.[11] The relationship between Sappho and her students was similar to that of Socrates and his disciples, that of a mentor with followers (see the next section of this chapter). Sappho foreshadows the development of mentoring as an important way to help teachers develop their practical teaching skills.

Sappho's Poetry

Sappho composed lyric poetry, that is, songs with lyre accompaniment. According to the *Suda*, "she invented the plectrum. She wrote epigrams, elegiacs, iambics and solo songs."[12] (The plectrum is like a guitar pick; the epigram, a short poem used for commemorative purposes, is a genre popular at this time; the elegiac is poetry written in couplets.) Sappho is best known for the poem meter named after her: a "Sapphic" poem is made up of stanzas consisting of three lines of eleven syllables followed by a single line of five syllables, the syllables follow a formal pattern of "long" and "short".[13] The circumstances for which Sappho's poems were written are shrouded in mystery as we are not sure who heard them or performed them. Sappho herself may have performed her poems, but perhaps they were not written down until after her death. As far as we know, writing was only in limited use in Sappho's lifetime and for some time afterwards. It was, nevertheless, customary for the upper class to be accomplished in the art of music and to have a repertoire of songs memorized. Like others of her time period, Sappho may have written copies of her poems in lead or gold and dedicated them in the temple. Using an image of female creativity, Sappho's poems are called her "daughters."[14] Sappho's "Hymn to Aphrodite" is her only complete poem that has been widely translated, for in 1073 authorities in Rome and Constantinople publicly burned all known poems by Sappho due to their homoeroticism. About one hundred years ago, archeologists discovered fragments of her poems while excavating some coffins at Oxyrhnchus, Egypt, renewing research and translations of this ancient poet.[15]

Sappho was one of the first to write using the first person, describing her feelings about love and loss from her perspective. In addition, she is the first woman we know of who defined women in terms of themselves rather than in terms of men.[16] We will see that her work will influence other important women writers and educators such as Hildegard and Christine de Pizan (see sections 5.2 and 6.1). Sappho could be considered the first liberated woman and feminist; she is certainly the first female independent thinker. Plato called her "the tenth muse" and throughout the history of western literature, women who write, and especially those who write in Latin and Greek, are celebrated as "the tenth muse" or "another Sappho."[17] Sappho lived on in later literature as the main character in Greek comedies and dramas, popular plays, and even a French opera was named for her, *Sapho,* in 1851.

It is said that Sappho has inspired the work of the following modern poets: Michael Field, Pierre Louys, Renee Vivien, Marie Madeleine, Amy Lowell, and H.D.[18] (Hilda Doolittle).

Legends About Sappho

Now we get into the world of legend that has Sappho doing many different things. Supposedly after marrying Cercylas and having a child, Sappho fell in love with Phaon, the handsome ferryman on the island of Lesbos, but when he spurned her love she leapt to her death by jumping off the cliff, or White Rock of Leukas, off the west coast of Greece. Works of literature, art, and history refer to this legend of her suicidal leap in various ways, saying that it signifies all sorts of things from guilty despair, passionate abandon, and poetic inspiration.[19] Other traditions build upon what is said in poem Fragment #99 and say that Sappho died peacefully in bed, tended by her daughter Cleis.[20]

Sappho's Importance for Educational Thought

Sappho of Lesbos is important in western civilization both as an author and as an educator. She is the most highly regarded woman poet of Greek and Roman antiquity. Her work is the earliest literature by a woman writer that has survived the passage of time and the perhaps willful attempts to silence the voices of women. Sappho is the first voice of a woman speaking about her own sex.[21]

Sappho, the Music Teacher

It is difficult to separate legend from truth in describing Sappho's actual role in education as it has changed throughout the ages. Some see Sappho as a music teacher, others as a sex educator or a physical education instructor, others see her as the head of her school.[22] All of these roles were important, especially that of head of the girls' school that she began on the island of Lesbos. It was one of the first of its kind, and certainly one of the most elite, for she had many different students, all from aristocratic parents. According to the *Suda,* Sappho educated nobly born girls, not only from local families but also from Ionia. It was more than a school, it was a house for those who cultivated the Muses, and together they formed a *thiasos* in which they bound themselves to each other and to their leader by ties of great strength and intimacy. The young women studied with her, learning poetry and music, chorus dancing and singing. Their parents sent them to study with the most celebrated lyricist of the day, who accepted them as her students and companions. Sappho's school was a kind of boarding school, similar to a finishing school, that prepared girls for marriage. Culture, deportment, and dress were all matters for study among Sappho's girls, but music was at the core of the curriculum.[23]

Sappho, the Dance Teacher

For over two centuries, choral dancing was recognized as central to the educational process. The circumstances for which Sappho's poems were composed have been a matter of controversy, but one theory sees them composed for girls' choruses. Sappho is thus allowed an educational role, leading groups of *parthenoi*, or young women, in the prime of their life before they are married. It is this aspect of her role that has given her the description as a sex education instructor.

Sappho, the Reading Teacher

Sappho's poems, once written down, were probably used as reading and writing exercises when, probably shortly after her lifetime, literacy started to become a standard part of education. We might imagine a generation of school children (girls as well as boys) learning to read aloud from texts of Sappho or laboriously incising them on their own waxed tablets. By the fifth century, it is likely that Sappho's texts found a more permanent state in the standard form of books of that time: the papyrus roll. By far the most important scholarly endeavor relating to the study of Sappho was that of the librarians at Alexandria, for without them we might have none of Sappho's poetry today. Since Sappho was considered one of the nine great lyric poets, they collected her work into nine books and later transformed them from papyrus to parchment, and then to the codex (most like the modern book). The work of other poets was not considered as "popular," was not transcribed, and thus was lost.[24]

Sappho's Philosophy of Education

Sappho believed in the education of the whole student and so she gave equal importance to all the areas of education. She developed human virtues and social graces in her students; cared for their intellectual development by having them memorize and write poetry; promoted their physical development by teaching them to dance; and their spiritual development by teaching them to sing to the muses. Sappho emphasized the important role of the teacher as a mentor for her students for the goal of education was to help these girls develop and mature so that they could marry and become outstanding Greek women. Sappho also speaks to us today about the importance of the teacher–learner relationship.

Sappho saw the purpose of education as a finishing school to help these young aristocratic girls develop their social, physical, and emotional potential so as to prepare them for marriage and for taking their place as contributing members of high Greek society.

Sappho wrote, "I say that even later someone will remember us."[25]

Notes

1. *Suda*, cited in Margaret Williamson, *Sappho's Immortal Daughters* (Cambridge: Harvard University Press, 1995), p. 1.
2. Jane McIntosh Snyder, *The Woman and the Lyre: Women Writers in Classical Greece and Rome* (Carbondale: Southern Illinois University Press, 1989), p. 8.
3. *Suda*, cited in Williamson, p. 2.
4. Margaret Williamson, *Sappho's Immortal Daughters* (Cambridge: Harvard University Press, 1995), p. 28.

5. Snyder, p. 33.
6. Williamson, p. 65.
7. Ibid., p. 23, Snyder, p. 2.
8. Williamson, pp. 76–77.
9. Margaret Reynolds, *The Sappho Companion* (New York: Palgrave for St. Martin's Press, 2001), p. 4.
10. Snyder, p. 12.
11. L. Glenn Smith and Joan K. Smith. *Lives in Education: A Narrative of People and Ideas,* 2nd ed. (New York: St. Martin's Press, 1994), p. 8.
12. *Suda,* cited in Williamson, p. 2.
13. Alison Sharrock and Rhiannon Ash, "Sappho," in *Fifty Key Classical Authors,* edited by A. Sharrock and R. Ash (New York: Routledge, 2002), p. 25.
14. Williamson, pp. 15, 37.
15. Smith and Smith, p. 8.
16. Ibid., p. 8.
17. Sharrock and Ash, p. 26.
18. URL: http://www.sappho.com/poetry/sappho.html, p. 2, accessed 10/16/03.
19. Williamson, p. 9.
20. Mary Barnard, *Sappho: A New Translation* (Los Angeles: University of California Press, 1958), p. 97.
21. Verna Zinserling, *Women in Greece and Rome,* translated by L. A. Jones (New York: Abner Schram, 1973), p. 8.
22. Holt Parker, "Sappho Schoolmistress," in *Re-Reading Sappho: Reception and Transmission,* edited by E. Green (Berkeley: University of California Press, 1996), p. 149ff.
23. Ibid., pp. 151–52.
24. Williamson, pp. 38–42.
25. Sappho in Fragment 147, cited in Snyder, *The Woman and the Lyre: Women Writers in Classical Greece and Rome* (Carbondale: Southern Illinois University Press, 1989).

Questions to Guide Your Reading

An effective way to read poetry is to read it out loud. It is also helpful to work in groups in which you can pair-share your understanding of the poem. Try first to understand the text of the poem itself, then relate the text to yourself, and finally, see how/if the text can relate to the world of education. Use these questions to guide your discussion.

1. What kind of school does Sappho run according to the poem *The Show Pupil?* Is it like today's magnet schools with selective admissions or is it more like a private school?

2. Some think that Fragment #94 explains Sappho's school. What kinds of things did they do in the school? In what ways does this fragment show the whole purpose of Sappho's school: getting a girl ready for marriage? In what way is Fragment #94 a farewell poem? What has changed that they must part?

3. The *Hymn to Aphrodite* is the one complete poem that we have of Sappho's. It is a celtic hymn: the speaker calls on the goddess with several epithets. Can you find and list some of them? Can you also find "epic language" used? What do you think it symbolizes? Do you think that the *Hymn to Aphrodite* is a prayer? Is the goddess being invoked to help Sappho or does she exert some kind of power over her?

READING 2.1:
THE SONGS OF SAPPHO

The Show Pupil

You seek through Mica entrance to my school,
The House of Song, but this I must deny.
A Penthilus* pupil taught to write by rule!
Would play the mischief with my girls.

For I have taught them to sing as does the nightingale,
That, hid in leafy nook of dewy green,
Pours forth his unpremeditated tale,
"Show Pupil?" Poets should be heard, not seen.

(*Mica is shortened for Mnasidca;
House of Penthilus refers to a rival school or Thiasoso)

#94- Lament for a Lost Student

No MORE returns my Atthis dear
    Since to Andromeda she fled,
And ne'er will come again I fear
    Ah me! I wish that I were dead.

Yet on her parting from me-still
    I see her bosom heave with strain
Of sobbing, eyes with tear-drops fill
    From springs of seeming grief; again

I hear her trembling voice-she cried,
    "Sappho, how terribly we grieve
I swear" (with oaths have ever lied)
    "Wantons against my will I leave."

And I, poor dupe, made brave essay
    To stop my tears, and with a smile
Replied, "Rejoicing go your way,
    Dear, but remember me the while."

For well you know I love you. Yet,
    Even should you doubt me, still recall
That which you seemingly forget,
    Our deeds of dalliance, graven all

On my heart's 'tablet: When a chain
    Of myriad blossoms you entwined
To throw around my neck, as fain
    Me captive of your love to bind.

When with a zone of roses red
    And violets blue you girdled me,
My long locks bound therein, and said,
    "Were but Alcreus here to see!"

When royal myrrh from dainty vase
    You took, and rubbed my cheeks aglow,
And cried, "Come, Cypris, on her gaze
    If you would beauty's secret know!"

When, as we'lay in fond embrace
    Upon a couch mid nibbled cates
And cups half-drained, to Muse and Grace'
    You called, "Thus Sappho passion sates"

All this you may forget, or, worse,
    Remember but to turn to jest,
Saying, "Twill serve for Sappho's verse
    I hope she tells how I was dressedl"

Hymn to Aphrodite

Throned in splendor, beauteous maid of mighty Zeus,
wile-weaving, immortal Aphrodite,
Smile again; thy frowning so affrays me
Woe overweighs me.

Come to me now; if ever in the olden!
Days thou didst hearken afar, and from the golden
Halls of thy Father fly with all speeding
Unto my pleading.

Down through midaether from Love's empyral regions
Swan-drawn in car convoyed by lovely legions
Of bright-hued doves beclouding with their pinions
Earth's broad dominions,

Quickly thou camest; and, Blessed One, with smiling
Countenance immortal my heavy heart beguiling,
Askedst the cause of my pitiful condition
Why my petition:

Source: Robinson, David M. and Miller, Marion Mills, translator. 1925. *The Songs of Sappho: Including the Recent Egyptian discoveries*. The Maxwelton Co., Lexington, Kentucky.

What most I craved in brain-bewildered yearning;
Whom would I win, so winsome in her spurning;
"Who is she, Sappho, evilly requiting
Fond love with slighting?

"She who flees thee soon shall turn pursuing,
Cold to thy love now, weary thee with wooing,

Gifts once scorned with greater gifts reclaiming
Unto her shaming."

Come thus again; from cruel cares deliver;
Of all that my heart wills graciously be given
greatest of gifts, thy loving self and tender
To be my defender.

Discussion Questions

1. Sappho had a school just for girls. What does some of the current research on single-sex schools show? What does Sappho say to us today about the education of women and the role of women in education?
2. Sappho was the first sex and health educator. What do you think she would do or say today about the spreading of AIDS, the rising number of teen-aged, unwed mothers, and other issues regarding sexuality?
3. What do you think is Sappho's major contribution to education? What does she say to us about the teacher–student relationship? Do you think you should befriend your students? Why or why not?

For Further Research on the Internet

A biography of Sappho with links to her poems. **http://www.sappho.com/poetry/sappho.html**

A site dedicated to understanding Sappho's poetry with links to her poetry and pictures of her. **http://www.temple.edu/classics/sappho.html**

Suggestions for Further Reading

Barnard, Mary. *Sappho: A New Translation.* Los Angeles: University of California Press, 1958.

Parker, Holt. "Sappho Schoolmistress." In *Re-Reading Sappho: Reception and Transmission,* edited by E. Green. Berkeley: University of California Press, 1996.

Reynolds, Margaret. *The Sappho Companion.* New York: Palgrave for St. Martin's Press, 2001.

Reynolds, Margaret. *The Sappho History.* New York: Palgrave Macmillan, 2003.

Sharrock, Alison, and Rhiannon Ash. "Sappho." In *Fifty Key Classical Authors,* edited by A. Sharrock and R. Ash. New York: Routledge, 2002.

Smith, L. Glenn, and Joan K. Smith. *Lives in Education: A Narrative of People and Ideas;* 2nd ed. New York: St. Martin's Press, 1994.

Snyder, Jane McIntosh. *The Woman and the Lyre: Women Writers in Classical Greece and Rome.* Carbondale: Southern Illinois University Press, 1989.

Williamson, Margaret. *Sappho's Immortal Daughters.* Cambridge: Harvard University Press, 1995.

Zinserling, Verna. *Women in Greece and Rome.* Translated by L. A. Jones. New York: Abner Schram, 1973.

Section 2.2: Socrates (470–399 B.C.)

Don't you enjoy classes where you discuss the material read? A skilled teacher will ask provocative questions and have the students analyze the reading through their answers. We have Socrates to thank for popularizing this method that now bears his name—the Socratic Method.

Socrates' Life and Times

Socrates was a native-born Athenian. He was the son of Sophroniscus, a well-known stonemason and a respected Athenian citizen, and Phaenarete, a midwife. Socrates' early years were typical of other Athenian youth: he received an 'elementary' education and became well-versed in mathematics and astronomy, a capable athlete, and a distinguished member of the city's military corps.

Socrates continued in his father's profession as a sculptor, cutting and shaping stone; it is said that he also continued his mother's profession as a midwife of ideas. At age 35, he fought with exceptional courage and distinction in the Peloponnesian War, saving Xenophon's and Alcibiades' life. Socrates married Xanthippe and they had three sons. Socrates' wife had a difficult temper but he knew how to humor her.[1]

Socrates is described in *Meno* as "an ugly man with a snub nose and pop eyes" and in *Symposium* as having wide nostrils, protruding eyes, thick lips, and a paunch.[2] He traveled barefoot, wore simple clothes, and strutted like a pelican. People called him a torpedo fish because he benumbed everyone that came near him with his questions.

Socrates, the Philosopher

After the war, Socrates gave up his trade and devoted himself wholly to teaching the youth of Athens because he heard an "inner voice" from the gods that told him to seek the good.[3] Socrates felt that he was the only wise man he could find because he was the only one who knew that he did not know anything. Socrates could be found in the **palaestrae**, in the market place, in the gymnasium, or in the streets asking people questions and probing for answers. He believed that there was a moral truth that held for all human beings and that if one did not live by it, one acted wrongly.[4] Socrates was not a relativist and was very much against the sophists of his time that believed only in the logic of their arguments and not the reality of what they were saying.

Socrates taught primarily by asking questions and inducing his listeners to answer, challenging their beliefs. Socratic education is based on the principle that both the teacher and the student harbor knowledge as well as ignorance within themselves. Socrates did not teach by inculcating his own ideas and views into another, but by guiding and questioning and leading others to recollect what is in some way already within them. In his role as teacher, he tried to nourish the seeds of knowledge within his students.[5]

Socrates' *Apology* and Death

Socrates was loyal to his principles and his mission to arouse his fellow citizens out of their lethargic acceptance of previously accepted beliefs about man's place in the world. In 406 B.C. Socrates angered the oligarchic rulers who had overthrown the democratic government and passed the power to a junta of thirty.[6] (See the timeline for Socrates' life in Figure 2.2.) In 399 B.C., when Socrates was 70 years old, he was put on trial for corrupting the youth and not believing in the gods. The *Apology* is a dialogue in which Socrates gives a defense of his life. He could have been exiled, but he felt that exile for an Athenian was to be a non-person, so he chose to accept his sentence and drink the hemlock. Plato was so moved by the death of his teacher that he dedicated much of his life to writing down the lessons he had learned in dialogues with Socrates. In Plato's opinion, Socrates was "the best man of his time as well as the wisest and most just."[7]

Socrates' Importance for Education

Socrates was one of the first Greek philosophers. Socrates' philosophy was a simple ethic that held that man's only reason for being was to develop moral excellence. The man who is excellent as a human being is one whose actions are governed by reason.

Although Socrates is the central figure in *Meno* and the other dialogues, he left no actual writings; what we have is a transcription of Socrates' words by his dedicated student, Plato. Socrates dialogued with his students using leading questions that were meant to stimulate the student to examine and ponder basic human concerns. Socrates called his method *elenchos* (pronounced eh-lenk-us) which means *to examine*. The technique of question and answer, or dialogue, between teacher and student is known today as the *Socratic Method*. Socrates is one of the most important philosophers in history because he taught us how to examine, analyze, and dissect ideas using this method of inquiry.[8]

Socrates' Philosophy of Education

Socrates is important in educational history because he developed an explicit educational theory that, in a way, was the very first philosophy of education. He has clear opinions on the role of the teacher, the student, the curriculum, the method, and the reason for teaching. He had a unique concept of teacherless education in which the teacher's role was to draw the knowledge out of the student. He firmly defended the teacher's academic freedom to think, question, and teach. He believed that knowledge could not be transmitted from a teacher to the students, but that the students had to discover the knowledge that

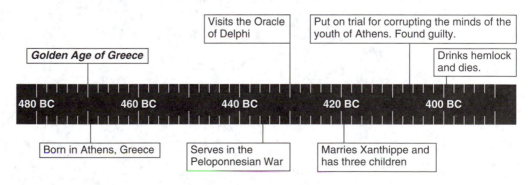

Figure 2.2   Socrates' Life and Times

was within them. The teacher's role was to ask the right question so that the students would think about the issue and solve the problem themselves. Use of the *Socratic Method* requires skillful questioning on the part of the teacher. It is still used today in education but is often referred to as *higher order questioning* or *developing higher order thinking skills and stimulating critical thinking.* Socrates stressed that the purpose of genuine education was to cultivate morally excellent people.[9]

Socrates believed that moral education is the only defensible educational objective for any society and that knowledge was to be sought for the good of the person and the state. Socrates is important because he began the dialogue on "virtue ethics" that has continued to intrigue educational philosophers (including Plato and Aristotle) through the ages.[10]

In the reading from *Meno,* some of Socrates' key doctrines are revealed regarding virtue, knowledge, and teaching men to do good. Meno is a wealthy young Thessalian who spends some time with Socrates on a visit to Athens.[11] They discuss virtue and how it comes to be as they follow Socrates guiding principle "Know thyself. The unexamined life is not worth living."

Notes

1. C. C. W. Taylor, *Socrates: A Very Short Introduction* (Oxford: Oxford University Press, 2000), p. 5.
2. Gary Allan Scott, *Plato's Socrates as Educator* (Albany: State University of New York, 2000), p. 11.
3. Colin Davies, *Socrates* (New Delhi: Deep & Deep Publications Pvt., Ltd., 2000), p. 71.
4. Hope May, *On Socrates* (Belmont, CA: Wadsworth/Thomson Learning, Inc., 2000), p. 2.
5. Scott, pp. 44–47.
6. Taylor, p. 11.
7. Davies, p. 78.
8. May, p. 57.
9. Paul Woodruff, *Socratic Education* (London: Routledge, 1998).
10. Mark Lutz, *Socrates' Education to Virtue* (Albany: State University of New York, 1998), pp. 50–51, 182–183.
11. Christopher Bruell, *On the Socratic Education* (Lanham, MD: Rowman & Littlefield Publishers, Inc., 1999), p. 164.

Questions to Guide Your Reading

1. Read out loud at least pages 29 and 30 of this selection with a classmate. As you role play Socrates and Meno, experience the Socratic method of questioning.

2. As you read, try to make an outline of the logic of Socrates' three main arguments found in the *Meno.* (*Socrates helps you to do this at the end of the selection.*)

3. List the different definitions of virtue as they are presented in the dialogue. Which one(s) does Socrates seem to like?

4. Why does Meno call Socrates a "torpedo fish"?

READING 2.2:
MENO

by Plato

Persons of the Dialogue:

- **Meno**
- **Socrates**
- **A Slave of Meno**
- **Anytus**

Meno. Can you tell me, Socrates, whether virtue is acquired by teaching or by practice; or if neither by teaching nor practice, then whether it comes to man by nature, or in what other way?

Socrates. O Meno, there was a time when the Thessalians were famous among the other Hellenes only for their riches and their riding; but now, if I am not mistaken, they are equally famous for their wisdom ... I am certain that if you were to ask any Athenian whether virtue was natural or acquired, he would laugh in your face, and say: "Stranger, you have far too good an opinion of me, if you think that I can answer your question. For I literally do not know what virtue is, and much less whether it is acquired by teaching or not." And I myself, Meno, living as I do in this region of poverty, a man poor as the rest of the world; and I confess with shame that I know literally nothing about virtue; and when I do not know the "quid" of anything how can I know the "quale"?

Men. But are you in earnest, Socrates, in saying that you do not know what virtue is? And am I to carry back this report of you to Thessaly?

Soc. Not only that, my dear boy, but you may say further that I have never known of any one else who did, in my judgment ...

Soc. By the gods, Meno, be generous, and tell me what you say that virtue is; for I shall be truly delighted to find that I have been mistaken, and that you and Gorgias do really have this knowledge; although I have been just saying that I have never found anybody who had.

Men. There will be no difficulty, Socrates, in answering your question. Let us take first the virtue of a man—he should know how to administer the state, and in the administration of it to benefit his friends and harm his enemies; and he must also be careful not to suffer harm himself. A woman's virtue, if you wish to know about that, may also be easily described: her duty is to order her house, and keep what is indoors, and obey her husband. Every age, every condition of life, young or old, male or female, bond or free, has a different virtue: there are virtues numberless, and no lack of definitions of them; for virtue is relative to the actions and ages of each of us in all that we do. And the same may be said of vice, Socrates.

Soc. How fortunate I am, Meno! When I ask you for one virtue, you present me with a swarm of them, which are in your keeping. Suppose that I carry on the figure of the swarm, and ask of you, What is the nature of the bee? and you answer that there are many kinds of bees, and I reply: But do bees differ as bees, because there are many and different kinds of them; or are they not rather to be distinguished by some other quality, as for example beauty, size, or shape? How would you answer me?

Men. I should answer that bees do not differ from one another, as bees.

Soc. And if I went on to say: That is what I desire to know, Meno; Tell me what is the quality in which they do not differ, but are all alike;—would you be able to answer?

Men. I should.

Soc. And so of the virtues, however many and different they may be, they have all a common nature which makes them virtues; and on this he who would answer the question, "What is virtue?" would do well to have his eye fixed: Do you understand?

Men. I am beginning to understand; but I do not as yet take hold of the question as I could wish.

....

Soc. Now, in your turn, you are to fulfill your promise, and tell me what virtue is in the universal; and do not make a singular into a plural, as the facetious say of those who break a thing, but deliver virtue to me whole and sound, and not broken into a number of pieces: I have given you the pattern.

Men. Well then, Socrates, virtue, as I take it, is when he, who desires the honorable, is able to provide it for himself; so the poet says, and I say too—*Virtue is the desire of things honorable and the power of attaining them.*

Soc. And does he who desires the honorable also desire the good?

Source: Translated by Benjamin Jowett. From *Dialogues of Plato*, New York, P. F. Collier & Son. Copyright 1900. The Colonial Press.

Men. Certainly.

Soc. Then are there some who desire the evil and others who desire the good? Do not all men, my dear sir, desire good?

Men. I think not.

Soc. There are some who desire evil?

Men. Yes.

Soc. Do you mean that they think the evils that they desire, to be good; or do they know that they are evil and yet desire them?

Men. Both, I think.

Soc. And do you really imagine, Meno, that a man knows evils to be evils and desires them notwithstanding?

Men. Certainly I do.

Soc. And desire is of possession?

Men. Yes, of possession.

Soc. And does he think that the evils will do good to him who possesses them, or does he know that they will do him harm?

Men. There are some who think that the evils will do them good, and others who know that they will do them harm.

Soc. And, in your opinion, do those who think that they will do them good know that they are evils?

Men. Certainly not.

Soc. Is it not obvious that those who are ignorant of their nature do not desire them; but they desire what they suppose to be goods although they are really evils; and if they are mistaken and suppose the evils to be good they really desire goods?

Men. Yes, in that case. That appears to be the truth, Socrates, and I admit that nobody desires evil.

· ·

Soc. Then begin again, and answer me, What, according to you and your friend Gorgias, is the definition of virtue?

Men. O Socrates, I used to be told, before I knew you, that you were always doubting yourself and making others doubt; and now you are casting your spells over me, and I am simply getting bewitched and enchanted, and am at my wits' end. And if I may venture to make a jest upon you, you seem to me both in your appearance and in your power over others to be very like the flat torpedo fish, who torpifies those who come near him and touch him, as you have now torpified me, I think. For my soul and my tongue are really torpid, and I do not know how to answer you; and though I have been delivered of an infinite variety of speeches about virtue before now, and to many persons—and very good ones they were, as I thought—at this moment I cannot even say what virtue is. And I think that you are very wise in not voyaging and going away from home, for if you did in other places as you do in Athens, you would be cast into prison as a magician . . .

Soc. Then, as we are agreed that a man should enquire about that which he does not know, shall you and I make an effort to enquire together into the nature of virtue?

Men. By all means, Socrates. And yet I would much rather return to my original question, Whether in seeking to acquire virtue we should regard it as a thing to be taught, or as a gift of nature, or as coming to men in some other way?

Soc. Had I the command of you as well as of myself, Meno, I would not have enquired whether virtue is given by instruction or not, until we had first ascertained "what it is." . . . At any rate, will you condescend a little, and allow the question "Whether virtue is given by instruction, or in any other way," to be argued upon hypothesis? . . . And we too, as we know not the nature and qualities of virtue, must ask, whether virtue is or not taught, under a hypothesis: as thus, if virtue is of such a class of mental goods, will it be taught or not? Let the first hypothesis be that virtue is or is not knowledge; in that case will it be taught or not? or, as we were just now saying, "remembered"? For there is no use in disputing about the name. But is virtue taught or not? or rather, does not everyone see that knowledge alone is taught?

Men. I agree.

Soc. Then if virtue is knowledge, virtue will be taught?

Men. Certainly.

Soc. Then now we have made a quick end of this question: if virtue is of such a nature, it will be taught; and if not, not?

Men. Certainly.

Soc. The next question is, whether virtue is knowledge or of another species?

Men. Yes, that appears to be the question that comes next in order.

Soc. Do we not say that virtue is a good? This is a hypothesis that is not set aside.

Men. Certainly.

Soc. Now, if there be any sort of good which is distinct from knowledge, virtue may be that good; but if knowledge embraces all good, then we shall be right in thinking that virtue is knowledge?

Men. True.

Soc. And virtue makes us good?

Men. Yes.

....

Soc. But if the good are not by nature good, are they made good by instruction?

Men. There appears to be no other alternative, Socrates. On the supposition that virtue is knowledge, there can be no doubt that virtue is taught.

Soc. I will try and tell you why, Meno. I do not retract the assertion that if virtue is knowledge it may be taught; but I fear that I have some reason in doubting whether virtue is knowledge: for consider now, and say whether virtue, and not only virtue but anything that is taught, must not have teachers and disciples?

Men. Surely.

Soc. And conversely, may not the art of which neither teachers nor disciples exist be assumed to be incapable of being taught?

Men. True; but do you think that there are no teachers of virtue?

Soc. I have certainly often enquired whether there were any, and taken great pains to find them, and have never succeeded; and many have assisted me in the search, and they were the persons whom I thought the most likely to know....And these are the sort of men from whom you are likely to learn whether there are any teachers of virtue, and who they are. Please, Anytus, help me and your friend Meno in answering our question, Who are the teachers?

....

Soc. If neither the Sophists nor the gentlemen are teachers, clearly there can be no other teachers?

Men. No.

Soc. And if there are no teachers, neither are there disciples?

Men. Agreed.

Soc. And we have admitted that a thing cannot be taught of which there are neither teachers nor disciples?

Men. We have.

Soc. And there are no teachers of virtue to be found anywhere?

Men. There are not.

Soc. And if there are no teachers, neither are there scholars?

Men. That, I think, is true.

Soc. Then virtue cannot be taught?

Men. Not if we are right in our view. But I cannot believe Socrates, that there are no good men: And if there are, how did they come into existence?

Soc. Seeing then that men become good and useful to states, not only because they have knowledge, but because they have right opinion, and that neither knowledge nor right opinion is given to man by nature or acquired by him (do you imagine either of them to be given by nature?)

Men. Not I.

Soc. Then if they are not given by nature, neither are the good by nature good?

Men. Certainly not.

Soc. And nature being excluded, then came the question whether virtue is acquired by teaching?

Men. Yes.

Soc. If virtue was wisdom [or knowledge], then, as we thought, it was taught?

Men. Yes.

Soc. And if it was taught it was wisdom?

Men. Certainly.

Soc. And if there were teachers, it might be taught; and if there were no teachers, not?

Men. True.

Soc. But surely we acknowledged that there were no teachers of virtue?

Men. Yes.

Soc. Then we acknowledged that it was not taught, and was not wisdom?

Men. Certainly.

Soc. And yet we admitted that it was a good?

Men. Yes.

Soc. And the right guide is useful and good?

Men. Certainly.

Soc. And the only right guides are knowledge and true opinion—these are the guides of man; for things that happen by chance are not under the guidance of man: but the guides of man are true opinion and knowledge.

Men. I think so too.

Soc. But if virtue is not taught, neither is virtue knowledge.

Men. Clearly not.

Soc. Then of two good and useful things, one, which is knowledge, has been set aside, and cannot be supposed to be our guide in political life.

Men. I think not.

Soc. And therefore not by any wisdom, and not because they were wise, did Themistocles and those others of whom Anytus spoke govern states. This was the reason why they were unable to make others like themselves—because their virtue was not grounded on knowledge.

Men. That is probably true, Socrates.

Soc. But if not by knowledge, the only alternative which remains is that statesmen must have guided states by right opinion, which is in politics what divination is in religion; for diviners and also prophets say many things truly, but they know not what they say.

Men. So I believe.

. . . .

Soc. To sum up our enquiry—the result seems to be, if we are at all right in our view, that virtue is neither natural nor acquired, but an instinct given by God to the virtuous. Nor is the instinct accompanied by reason, unless there may be supposed to be among statesmen someone who is capable of educating statesmen. . . .

Men. That is excellent, Socrates.

Soc. Then, Meno, the conclusion is that virtue comes to the virtuous by the gift of God. But we shall never know the certain truth until, before asking how virtue is given, we enquire into the actual nature of virtue. I fear that I must go away, but do you, now that you are persuaded yourself, persuade our friend Anytus. And do not let him be so exasperated; if you can conciliate him, you will have done good service to the Athenian people.

Discussion Questions

1. From where do you think virtue comes? Are we born with it or are we taught it? There is a movement in the schools today to teach character education. Do you think that virtue can be taught in schools? Why or why not?

2. Do you think that the Socratic method of teaching through questioning is effective with all students or only with some students? Explain your reasoning.

3. Socrates says that the unexamined life is not worth living. Through a series of questions, Socrates encourages his students to examine their ideas. How can this type of self-examination be implemented in today's classrooms?

4. Do you agree with Socrates that everyone in the world desires to do good? How would he explain the bad and/or evil things that people do? Can education in the good and the virtuous solve all of these problems?

5. In *Meno* Socrates presents his philosophy of education. Explain his view of the teacher and the student, what he thinks the curriculum should be and how it should be taught, and what he thinks is the purpose of education.

For Further Research on the Internet

A brief discussion of the life and works of Socrates, with links to electronic texts. **http://www.philosophypages.com/ph/socr.htm**

Richard Hooker's site on Socrates with links to major Greek historical events. **http://www.wsu.edu/~dee/GREECE/SOCRATES.HTM**

Suggestions for Further Reading

Bruell, Christopher. *On the Socratic Education.* Lanham, MD: Rowman & Littlefield Publishers, Inc., 1999.

Davies, Colin. "Socrates." In *Socrates (469–399 B.C.),* edited by S. Mukherjee and S. Ramaswamy. New Delhi: Deep & Deep Publications Pvt., Ltd., 2000.

Lutz, Mark. *Socrates' Education to Virtue: Learning the Love of the Noble.* Albany: State University of New York, 1998.

May, Hope. *On Socrates.* Belmont, CA: Wadsworth/Thomson Learning, Inc., 2000.

Scott, Gary Allan. *Plato's Socrates as Educator.* Albany: State University of New York, 2000.

Taylor, C. C. W. *Socrates: A Very Short Introduction.* Oxford: Oxford University Press, 2000.

Woodruff, Paul. "Socratic Education." In *Philosophers on Education: New Historical Perspectives,* edited by A. O. Rorty. London: Routledge, 1998.

Section 2.3: Plato (427–347 B.C.)

Do you think students should be tracked according to their ability into basic, vocational, and college preparatory courses in high school? Well, Plato thought that each person (including women) should be given all the education they were capable of receiving and needed in order to do the job for which they were suited in the Republic. According to Plato, those who ruled the country should receive education in philosophy until they were fifty years old!

Plato's Life and Family

We know about Plato and his family from the comments he makes in his dialogues. Plato was born in 427 B.C., the son of Ariston and Perictione, both of whom were descended from distinguished Athenians of royalty. His father died when Plato was a few years old and his mother remarried. Plato was the youngest of four children. In *The Republic,* he mentions his brothers, Glaucon and Adeimantus, and his sister, Potone, who became the mother of Speusippus, who succeeded his uncle Plato as the head of the Academy, the school of philosophy Plato established in Athens.[1]

In *The Republic,* Plato outlines the normal education of a Greek boy, which he also received—learning to read and write and study the poets. Plato grew up in a city at war; the Peloponnesian war began before he was born and lasted until he was 23 years old. He served in the military from the age of 18 until the end of the war. Plato's family was prominent in Athenian affairs and he was influenced by his uncles, Charmides and Critas, and their political views. The demoralization of Athens due to defeat during the war led to an oligarchy revolution, followed by a savage tyranny that finally gave way to the reestablishment of a democratic constitution. During this turmoil, Socrates was put to death on a charge of impiety and corrupting the youth. Some scholars maintain that Plato served as the "defense attorney" for Socrates during his trial. The fact that he lost the case, and his beloved mentor, had a profound effect on him, making him anxious to preserve the memory of Socrates.[2]

Plato was forced to leave Athens after the death of Socrates. Plato traveled to Asia Minor, Egypt, and Italy, studying the mathematical ideas of Euclid and of the Pythagoreans and the political ideas of Dionysis. He became a tutor for a royal household in Sicily.[3]

What do we know about the character and personality of Plato from his writings? He had a keen sense of humor and an impressive intellect, which allowed him to be single-minded and clever. Plato was courageous in the face of danger, which gave him a somewhat intimidating austerity and aloofness. However, he had nothing but sympathy and courtesy for his students. Plato enjoyed painting, poetry, good food, good drink, good society, and fine dress; he was a brilliant conversationalist. He never married.[4]

The Academy

When Plato returned to Athens, he founded the **Academy** in 387 B.C., the first institution of higher learning in Greece. It became the intellectual center in Greece and the equivalent of the first university in the history of Europe. It continued for over 900 years until it was dissolved by Justin in 529 A.D. along with other pagan institutions.[5] The ultimate object of all activities at the Academy was to achieve final philosophic truth. The method of teaching was by question and answer, argument, and discussion. Plato did give some lectures but his main method was oral discussion and dialogue (comparable to the modern day seminar class). The subjects taught at the academy included philosophy, mathematics, astronomy, and geometry.[6] It is interesting to note that two women students were members of the academy: the idea of collegiate co-education is apparently as old as the idea of a college itself. This, like other ideas proposed by the school, provoked criticism, as higher education for women went directly against the tradition of the times.[7] The Academy was a great success. (Aritostle came to Plato's Academy in 367 B.C. at the age of 17 and remained there until Plato died in 347 B.C.) Plato wrote the *Meno* and *Protagorus* around the same time as he founded the Academy; one can clearly see in the dialogues how much Plato was thinking about education and educational issues at the time.[8] (See the timeline for Plato's life in Figure 2.3.)

Plato, the Philosopher

Plato dedicated his life to the vindication of Socrates' memory and teachings. He wrote thirty-four dialogues; all the dialogues before *The Republic* were Socratic teachings, the later dialogues are Plato's teachings. Socrates was interested in making men lead better lives and asked such questions as: What is virtue? What is goodness? What is justice? and What is temperance? Plato went beyond these to question the conceptual meaning of things, asking: What is a tree or triangle? Why do we name things the way we do? It is the thing in our mind, not the word with which we are concerned. Plato wrote metaphorically; he engaged people in the process of philosophizing and discovering the truth (as Socrates did) rather than systematically expounding his own views.

Later Life

Plato made three trips to Sicily from 364–361 B.C. for philosophic and political purposes. Plato dreamed of founding an ideal state with such citizens as philosopher-kings, warriors, farmers, and artisans like those he had written about in *The Republic*. His disciples thought he would start this state in Sicily, but he returned to Athens when he saw the unfavorable political climate.[9]

Plato remained at the Academy teaching, writing, and living comfortably until he died in 347 B.C. at the age of 81. Aristotle eulogized his teacher by saying that Plato "clearly revealed by his own life and by the methods of his words that to be happy is to be good."[10]

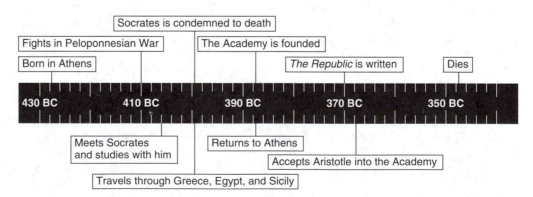

Figure 2.3   Plato's Life and Times

Plato's Contribution to Educational Thought

Plato was one of the first to propose equal education for men and women based on their ability to learn, not on their gender. He supported a type of vocational education, education to complete your role in life. For Plato, learning was more than having knowledge of the subject matter. It was the comprehensive process of the development of intellect, emotions, and will conducted according to the child's stages of development.[11] A good teacher helps students discover knowledge for themselves through dialogue.

The Republic

One of the astounding facts in the history of culture is that the first coherent treatise on government and education which we possess in Western civilization, Plato's *The Republic*, is the most profound. Plato's penetrating mind revealed the problems with which mankind has struggled, consciously or unconsciously, ever since it has had an organized society and education. Plato treats the subject of education in *The Republic* as an integral and vital part of a wider subject of the well-being of human society.

In *The Republic*, Plato tried to construct an ideal political system on the basis of education, showing how people can achieve justice through education. Plato outlined the nature of the just man and the ideal state in which man must develop virtues. The ultimate aim of education is to help people know the Idea of the Good, which is to be virtuous.[12] According to Plato, a just society always tries to give the best education to all of its members in accordance with their ability.

Plato's Philosophy of Education

In *The Republic*, Plato sets up a theory of what education means for both the individual and the state, focusing on the important role of those who must carefully choose the material to teach the future guardians of the state. The purpose of education is to help the students to grow and develop their character and ability to do good. Plato's curriculum is carefully chosen to include training for the spirit (music) and training for the body (gymnastics), with more difficult academic subjects added when the child is developmentally ready. Plato's educational theories have the practical aim of training for citizenship and leadership; his chief interest is education for character.[13] An important maxim proposed by Plato is, "The quality of the State depends on the kind of education that the members (groups) of the state receive."

Notes

1. Jane Day, *Plato's Meno in Focus* (London: Routledge, 1994), pp. 4–5.
2. T. M. Hare, *Plato* (Oxford: Oxford University Press, 1999), p. 113.
3. David Cooper, *Plato* (New York: Routledge, 2001), p. 10.
4. Hare, p. 105.
5. Day, p. 7.
6. Zhang Loshan, *Plato's Counsel on Education* (London: Routledge, 1998), pp. 37–38.
7. Rabbi Solomon Frank, *Education of Women According to Plato* (London: Routledge, 2000), pp. 302–3.
8. Day, p. 11
9. Ibid., p. 114–15; Losev, Alexei and Axa Takho-God, *Aristotle* (Moscow: Progress Publishers, 1990), p. 27.
10. L. Glenn Smith and Joan K. Smith, *Lives in Education: A Narrative of People and Ideas* (New York: St. Martin's Press, 1994), p. 25.
11. Myungjoon Lee, *Plato's Philosophy of Education: Its Implications for Current Education* (Milwaukee: Marquette University, 1994), p. 41.
12. Ibid., p. 52.
13. R. C. Lodge, *Plato's Theory of Education* (London: Routledge, 2000), pp. 12–14, 65.

Questions to Guide Your Reading

1. Write down the key subjects Plato includes in the curriculum of his schools in *The Republic*.
2. Is Plato in favor of the education of women? Why or why not? Do you agree with his argument?
3. As you read, do you think that Plato is an advocate of liberal education or vocational education?
4. Try to make a chart of the plan for education found in Book VII. List the ages of the students and what subjects they will be taught at those ages.

READING 2.3: THE REPUBLIC

by Plato

Persons of the Dialogue:
Socrates, who is the narrator;
Cephalus; Glacon; Thrasymachus;
Adeimantus; Cleitophon;
Polemarchus;
and others who are mute auditors.

The scene is laid in the house of Cephalus at the Piraeus; and the whole dialogue is narrated by Socrates, the day after it actually took place, to Timaeus, Hermocrates, Critias, and a nameless person, who are introduced in the Timaeus.

Book II   The Individual, The State, and Education
(Socrates, Glaucon)

Then he who is to be a really good and noble guardian of the State will require to unite in himself philosophy and spirit and swiftness and strength?

Undoubtedly.

Then we have found the desired natures; and now that we have found them, how are they to be reared and educated? Is not this an inquiry which may be expected to throw light on the greater inquiry which is our final end—How do justice and injustice grow up in States? for we do not want either to omit what is to the point or to draw out the argument to an inconvenient length.

••

Come then and let us pass a leisure hour in story telling, and our story shall be the education of our heroes.

By all means.

And what shall be their education? Can we find a better than the traditional sort?—And this has two divisions, gymnastics for the body, and music for the soul.

True.

Shall we begin education with music, and go on to gymnastics afterward?

By all means.

And when you speak of music, do you include literature or not?

Source: The Dialogues of Plato, translated by Benjamin Jowett, Macmillan and Co: New York Copyright 1892.

I do.

And literature may be either true or false?

Yes.

And the young should be trained in both kinds, and we begin with the false?

I do not understand your meaning, he said.

You know, I said, that we begin by telling children stories which, though not wholly destitute of truth, are in the main fictitious; and these stories are told them when they are not of an age to learn gymnastics.

Very true.

That was my meaning when I said that we must teach music before gymnastics.

Quite right, he said.

You know also that the beginning is the most important part of any work, especially in the case of a young and tender thing; for that is the time at which the character is being formed and the desired impression is more readily taken.

Quite true.

And shall we just carelessly allow children to hear any casual tales which may be devised by casual persons, and to receive into their minds ideas for the most part the very opposite of those which we should wish them to have when they are grown up?

We cannot.

Then the first thing will be to establish a censorship of the writers of fiction, and let the censors receive any tale of fiction which is good, and reject the bad; and we will desire mothers and nurses to tell their children the authorized ones only. Let them fashion the mind with such tales, even more fondly than they mould the body with their hands; but most of those which are now in use must be discarded.

But what stories do you mean, he said; and what fault do you find with them?

The narrative of Hephaestus binding Here his mother, or how on another occasion Zeus sent him flying for taking her part when she was being beaten, and all the battles of the gods in Homer—these tales must not be admitted into our State, whether they are supposed to have an allegorical meaning or not. For a young person cannot judge what is allegorical and what is literal; anything that he receives into his mind at that age is likely to become indelible and unalterable; and therefore it is most important that the tales which the young first hear should be models of virtuous thoughts.

Book V   On Matrimony and Philosophy (Socrates, Glaucon, Adeimantus)

Let us further suppose the birth and education of our women to be subject to similar or nearly similar regulations; then we shall see whether the result accords with our design.

Then, if women are to have the same duties as men, they must have the same nurture and education?

Yes.

The education, which was assigned to the men, was music and gymnastics.

Yes.

Then women must be taught music and gymnastics and also the art of war, which they must practice like the men?

Yes

And if, I said, the male and female sex appear to differ in their fitness for any art or pursuit, we should say that such pursuit or art ought to be assigned to one or the other of them; but if the difference consists only in women bearing and men begetting children, this does not amount to a proof that a woman differs from a man in respect of the sort of education she should receive; and we shall therefore continue to maintain that our guardians and their wives ought to have the same pursuits.

By all means.

One woman has a gift of healing, another not; one is a musician, and another has no music in her nature?

Very true.

And one woman has a turn for gymnastic and military exercises, and another is unwarlike and hates gymnastics?

Certainly.

And one woman is a philosopher, and another is an enemy of philosophy; one has spirit, and another is without spirit?

That is also true.

Then one woman will have the temper of a guardian, and another not. Was not the selection of the male guardians determined by differences of this sort?

Yes.

Men and women alike possess the qualities that make a guardian; they differ only in their comparative strength or weakness.

Obviously.

And those women who have such qualities are to be selected as the companions and colleagues of men who have similar qualities and whom they resemble in capacity and in character?

Very true.

And ought not the same natures to have the same pursuits?

They ought.

Then, as we were saying before, there is nothing unnatural in assigning music and gymnastics to the wives of the guardians—to that point we come round again.

Certainly not....

You will admit that the same education that makes a man a good guardian will make a woman a good guardian; for their original nature is the same?

Yes.

...And can there be anything better for the interests of the State than that the men and women of a State should be as good as possible?

There can be nothing better.

Book VII On Shadows and Realities in Education (Socrates, Glaucon)

And, for all these reasons, arithmetic is a kind of knowledge in which the best natures should be trained, and which must not be given up.

I agree.

Let this then be made one of our subjects of education. And next, shall we inquire whether the kindred science also concerns us?

You mean geometry?

Exactly so.

And surely you would not have the children of your ideal State, whom you are nurturing and educating—if the ideal ever becomes a reality—you would not allow the future rulers to be like posts, having no reason in them, and yet to be set in authority over the highest matters?

Certainly not.

Then you will make a law that they shall have such an education as will enable them to attain the greatest skill in asking and answering questions?

Yes, he said, you and I together will make it.

Dialectic, then, as you will agree, is the coping stone of the sciences, and is set over them; no other science can be placed higher—the nature of knowledge can no further go?

I agree, he said.

And, therefore, calculation and geometry and all the other elements of instruction, which are a preparation for dialectic, should be presented to the mind in childhood; not, however, under any notion of forcing our system of education...

Yes, I remember.

The same practice may be followed, I said, in all these things —labors, lessons, dangers—and he who is most at home in all of them ought to be enrolled in a select number.

At what age?

At the age when the necessary gymnastics are over: the period, whether of two or three years, which passes in this sort of training is useless for any other purpose; for sleep and exercise are unpropitious to learning; and the trial of who is first in gymnastic exercises is one of the most important tests to which our youth are subjected.

Certainly, he replied.

After that time those who are selected from the class of twenty year olds will be promoted to higher honor, and the sciences which they learned without any order in their early education will now be brought together, and they will be able to see the natural relationship of them to one another and to true being.

Yes, he said, that is the only kind of knowledge which takes lasting root ...

These, I said, are the points which you must consider; and those who have most of this comprehension, and who are most steadfast in their learning, and in their military and other appointed duties, when they have arrived at the age of thirty will have to be chosen by you out of the select class, and elevated to higher honor; and you will have to prove them by the help of dialectic, in order to learn which of them is able to give up the use of sight and the other senses, and in company with truth to attain absolute being: And here, my friend, great caution is required.

•••

Therefore, that your feelings may not be moved to pity about our citizens who are now thirty years of age, every care must be taken in introducing them to dialectic.

Certainly ...

Suppose, I said, the study of philosophy to take the place of gymnastics and to be continued diligently and earnestly and exclusively for twice the number of years which were passed in bodily exercise—will that be enough?

Would you say six or four years? he asked.

Say five years, I replied; at the end of the time they must be sent down again into the den and compelled to hold any military or other office which young men are qualified to hold: in this way they will get their experience of life, and there will be an opportunity of trying whether, when they are drawn all manner of ways by temptation, they will stand firm or flinch.

And how long is this stage of their lives to last?

Fifteen years, I answered; and when they have reached fifty years of age, then let those who still survive and have distinguished themselves in every action of their lives, and in every branch of knowledge, come at last to their consummation: the time has now arrived at which they must raise the eye of the soul to the universal light which lightens all things, and behold the absolute good; for that is the pattern according to which they are to order the State and the lives of individuals, and the remainder of their own lives also; making philosophy their chief pursuit, but, when their turn comes, toiling also at politics and ruling for the public good, not as though they were performing some heroic action, but simply as a matter of duty; and when they have brought up in each generation others like themselves and left them in their place to be governors of the State.

You are a sculptor, Socrates, and have made statues of our governors faultless in beauty.

Yes, I said, Glaucon, and of our governesses too; for you must not suppose that what I have been saying applies to men only and not to women as far as their natures can go.

There you are right, he said, since we have made them to share in all things like the men.

How will they proceed?

They will begin by sending out into the country all the inhabitants of the city who are more than ten years old, and will take possession of their children, who will be unaffected by the habits of their parents; these they will train in their own habits and laws, I mean in the laws which we have given them: and in this way the State and constitution of which we were speaking will soonest and most easily attain happiness, and the nation which has such a constitution will gain most.

There is no difficulty, he replied; and I agree with you in thinking that nothing more need be said.

Discussion Questions

1. Do you agree with Plato that "the young are not able to distinguish what is and what is not allegory but whatever opinions are taken into the mind at that age are wont to prove indelible and unalterable"? Do you think that books should be censored? Why or why not? What is the policy in the school district in which you hope to teach? Why is this important to know?

2. Plato is a strong advocate of the value of music in the curriculum. He mentions that it is education of the soul. What value do schools today place on music in the curriculum? Have you seen a change in your school district recently regarding the importance given to music instruction, bands, and choruses? What is research showing regarding the value of music as an area of study and students' enjoyment of school?

3. Gymnastics is also given an important place in the curriculum of *The Republic*. Some people think that American schools emphasize sports too much. How do you think Plato would reply to this criticism?

4. What is the role of education according to Plato's *The Republic*? Do you think that today's communities are accepting their responsibility for contributing to the education of the youth as outlined by Plato? What are some particular areas needing improvement?

5. Think about how much Socrates the teacher influenced his student Plato. Reflect on teachers in your past. Have any of them influenced you in a similar way? Explain.

6. Compare and contrast the Athens of Plato's time to contemporary United States. What are some similar economic, social, political, and educational issues in both societies, and in what way are the issues very different?

Plato Jigsaw Cooperative Problem-Solving Groups

    a. Form Home Groups of 4 to 6 persons.

    b. Each member of the Home Group discusses the Book of Plato's *The Republic* assigned to the group. Use the questions below to guide your discussion. See which aspect of Plato's philosophy of education is defined in the Book you read.

    c. At the signal, two people will stay Home to share their findings with other groups. Two students will go to each of the other Expert Groups on the different Books of *The Republic*. Record answers given in the other groups regarding Plato's philosophy of education.

    d. Return to your Home Group. Each person in the Home Group shares their findings from the other groups. See if you can construct a complete summary of Plato's philosophy of education.

        i. Who is the student according to Plato?

        ii. Who is the teacher and what is his/her role?

        iii. What is being taught, or should be taught?

        iv. How should it be taught?

        v. Why is it being taught?

For Further Research on the Internet

A brief biography of Plato with links to his life and works. http://www.philosophypages.com/ph/plat.htm

Home page on Plato with links to his dialogues. http://plato-dialogues.org/plato.htm

http://classics.mit.edu/Browse/browse-Plato.html

Suggestions for Further Reading

Cooper, David. "Plato." In *Fifty Major Thinkers on Education: From Confucius to Dewey*, edited by J. Palmer. New York: Routledge, 2001.

Day, Jane M. *Plato's Meno in Focus*. London: Routledge, 1994.

Frank, Rabbi Solomon. "Education of Women According to Plato." In *Plato's Theory of Education*, edited by R. C. Lodge. London: Routledge, 2001.

Hare, T. M. "Plato." In *Greek Philosophers*, edited by K. Thomas. Oxford: Oxford University Press, 1999.

Lee, Myungjoon. "Plato's Philosophy of Education: Its Implications for Current Education." Doctoral dissertation, Graduate School of Philosophy, Marquette University, Milwaukee, 1994.

Lodge, R. C. *Plato's Theory of Education*. Edited by The International Library of Philosophy. Vol VIII, *Ancient Philosophy*. First published in 1947. London: Routledge, 2000.

Losev, Alexei, and Axa Takho-God. *Aristotle*. Moscow: Progress Publishers, 1990.

Loshan, Zhang. "Plato's Counsel on Education." In *Philosophers on Education*, edited by A. O. Rorty. London: Routledge, 1998.

Smith, L. Glenn, and Joan K. Smith. *Lives in Education: A Narrative of People and Ideas*. 2nd ed. New York: St. Martin's Press, 1994.

Section 2.4: Aristotle (384–322 B.C.)

Did you know that we use Aristotle's terms all the time? If you are a secondary English major, you use Aristotle's literary ideas of the protagonist, climax, and denouement; biology secondary education majors use his genus, species classification often; all of us use the principles of his logic and ethics.

Aristotle's Life and Times

Aristotle was born in the summer of 384 B.C. in Stagira, a small town in Macedonia, Greece. His father, Nicomachus, a renowned physician, and his mother, Phaestis, had three children, two boys and a girl. Aristotle was introduced to medicine and biology at an early age and received a good education in natural science from his father. As a youth, he developed a great love for science, biology, and the study of the human person. Aristotle was a scrawny youth with skinny legs and tiny eyes who spoke with a lisp. He liked to wear expensive rings and style his hair. His father died when he was still young, so Aristotle was brought up by his older sister and her husband, Proxenus.

Aristotle Studies with Plato

Proxenus was a friend of Plato and some accounts say that he took Aristotle, then 17, to study with Plato at the Academy in Athens in 367 B.C.[1] Aristotle spent half of his active life in Athens, but never became an Athenian. Aristotle remained at the Academy for about twenty years. Plato was, by far, the most important formative influence on Aristotle's thought. Aristotle was a devoted pupil of Plato and his most brilliant student and he probably knew the author of *The Republic* best. At first, Aristotle adhered to the principles of Platonic Philosophy, but later departed from them. Plato recognized Aristotle as the Academy's brightest student, but also called him "a colt kicking his own mother" for foals kick their mother when they have had enough milk. Aristotle had a profound love for Plato and says in *The Ethics* that Plato was his friend but "piety requires us to honor truth above our friends."[2] Aristotle brought the work started by Socrates and Plato to a glorious completion. He gathered up all that was good in his predecessors and rejected what he deemed faulty. Aristotle significantly brought philosophy to completion, not that he finished it, but he formulated its broad outlines upon which many future generations of philosophers could build. Plato raised philosophy to unequaled heights. Aristotle anchored philosophy in reality.

Plato died in 347 B.C. and the question of who should succeed him as the head of the Academy arose. Plato's nephew, Speuisippus, was chosen over Aristotle. Aristotle left Athens at 37 years of age, a philosopher and scientist in his own right, and traveled through Macedonia and Asia Minor. He married Pythias, and the couple had a daughter whom Aristotle called Pythias. When Phthias died, Aristotle had a son named Nicomachus with Herphyllis, Pythias' young maid. The *Nicomachean Ethics* was written for his son's benefit.[3]

Aristotle, the Teacher

In 343 or 342 B.C., Philip II, king of Macedonia, invited Aristotle to become the tutor for his young son, Alexander. The education Alexander received from Aristotle was quite solid and contributed greatly to the personality of the future conqueror. However, a few years later, in 336 B.C., Philip was assassinated and Alexander became the head of the state.[4] (See the timeline of Aristotle's life in Figure 2.4.)

Around 334 B.C., Aristotle returned to Athens and, at the age of fifty, founded a school called the Lyceum in the northeast section of the city in a 200-year-old gymnasium. Since he was not an Athenian, Aristotle could not buy the land. Aristotle's followers, like those of Plato, were called *peripatetics* because they taught by walking around asking questions. Aristotle worked in the Lyceum for thirteen years, giving lectures in the morning and afternoon and leading scholarly discussions at night while dining with friends.[5] Aristotle lectured extensively on such subjects as physics, astronomy, zoology, botany, logic, ethics, and metaphysics. He wrote letters, poetry, and extensive literary works in the form of dialogues, like Plato, which were praised for their style and eloquence. Aristotle wrote nearly 150 different titles, but most of his writings were lost and we have less than one-fifth of his total writings. We have his lecture notes; although they are a little difficult to read, they are very logical, orderly, and rich in insight. They are mutilated and incomplete as the only edition found was hidden in a well for a century and a half.[6]

Aristotle's writings cover every branch of human knowledge known in his time. He thought that all things could be understood as unities of form and matter. He developed the four causes of nature: material, efficient, final, and formal. Science was to know things by their causes according to Aristotle, and philosophy was the study of the ultimate causes of all beings.

Aristotle was a good speaker, a lucid lecturer, and a persuasive conversationalist. He had to leave Athens after Alexander the Great died due to the political turmoil that developed; some were charging Aristotle with impiety as they had charged Socrates. Aristotle settled in the city of Chaleis on the island of Eubola.

Aristotle died in the autumn of 322 B.C., suffering from poor digestion. He was 62 years old and at the height of his influence.[7]

Aristotle's Contributions to Educational Theory

Aristotle's contributions to western intellectual thought include: his development of the science of biology, his development of the syllogism and the science of *Logic,* his explanation of virtue as the golden mean in his *Ethics,* the foundation of the study of literary crit-

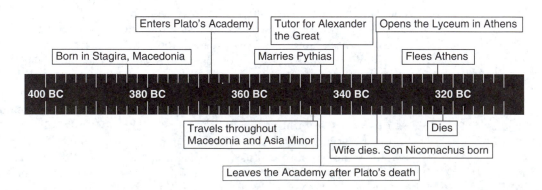

Figure 2.4   Aristotle's Life and Times

icism begun in his *Poetics,* and a the coherent philosophy of education he developed in *The Politics.*

Philosopher, educator, and scientist, Aristotle was one of the greatest and most influential thinkers in Western culture. In a number of his works, Aristotle dealt at length with the subject of education, examining education in relation to human and civic excellence in both the *Nicomachean Ethics* and *The Politics.* For Aristotle, ethics and politics both study practical knowledge, which is knowledge that enables people to act properly and live happily.

In *The Politics,* Aristotle's educational theory states that the good community is based on the cultivation of rationality. If education is neglected, the community suffers. Aristotle states that the highest aim of education is to produce virtuous men for the good of society.[8]

As education cultivated both the rational person and the rational society, Aristotle recommended compulsory public schools. Although his discussion of the ideal curriculum is incomplete because some pages of his manuscripts were never recovered, the plan he proposes shows how important he felt the education of youth was for the good of the community.

Aristotle's Philosophy of Education

Aristotle considered education to be an especially difficult art or skill that belonged by nature to the sphere of ethics and practical wisdom. A methodology had to be used that encouraged thinking and reflecting and then allowed for practice of the skills. The liberal education curriculum would train men to be good citizens and rulers, but also to make good use of leisure.[9]

The teacher is an expert who will take into consideration the successive stages in education which must be adjusted to the physical and psychological development of the individual student: the body, appetite, and reason must be taken successfully in hand as they develop.[10]

Aristotle saw the student as a human being, a "rational animal" whose function is to reason. Aristotle's ideal person practices behaving reasonably and properly until he or she can do so naturally and without effort. The result is a happy person, and happiness is the goal of all human beings. Aristotle believed that moral virtue is a matter of avoiding extremes in behavior and finding instead the mean that lies between the extremes. The aim of education is to help man shape himself as a human being, developing his intellectual knowledge and moral virtues, and at the same time conveying to him the spiritual heritage of the nation and civilization with which he is involved.

"We are the sum of our actions," Aristotle tells us, "and therefore our habits make all the difference."

Notes

1. Alexei Losev and Axa Takho-God, *Aristotle* (Moscow: Progress Publishers, 1990), p. 21.
2. Jonathan Barnes, *Aristotle* (Oxford: Oxford University Press, 1999), p. 219.
3. Losev and Takho-God, p. 64.
4. Ibid., p. 71.
5. Barnes, p. 200; Losev and Takho-God, 1990, p. 80.
6. Ibid, p. 196.
7. Losev and Takho-God, 1990, p. 134.
8. Andrea Wilson Nightingale, *Liberal Education in Plato's Republic and Aristotle's Politic* (Leiden, Netherlands: Koninklijke Brill, 2001), p. 155.
9. Ibid., p. 159.
10. C. D. Reeve, *Aristotelian Education* (London: Routledge, 1998), p. 54.

Questions to Guide Your Reading—*The Politics*

1. What evidence from *The Politics* would convince you that Aristotle was an advocate of liberal education or vocational education?
2. Try to outline Aristotle's system of education as you read the following selection. What are the age divisions and what is the subject matter taught at each age division? What does Aristotle think is the most important thing to be learned?
3. What kind of education does Aristotle recommend for women? What is the rationale for his policy? Do you agree or disagree with his position?
4. Would Aristotle approve of the emphasis on sports in today's schools? Why or why not?
5. After you read this selection, how you would summarize Aristotle's view of the role of the school?

READING 2.4: THE POLITICS

There are three things that make men good and virtuous: these are nature, habit, and reason. In the first place, everyone must be born a man and not some other animal; in the second place, he must have a certain character, both of body and soul. But some qualities there is no use having at birth, for they are altered by habit, and some gifts of nature may be turned by habit to good or bad.... We have already determined what natures are likely to be most easily molded by the hands of the legislator. All else is the work of education. We learn some things by habit and some by instruction.

...All these points the statesman should keep in view when he frames his laws; he should consider the parts of the soul and their functions, and above all the better and the end; he should also remember the diversities of human lives and actions.... In such principles children and persons of every age which requires education should be trained.

We have already determined that nature and habit and reason are required, and what should be the character of the citizens has also been defined by us. But we have still to consider whether the training of early life is to be that of reason or habit,

Source: *The Politics of Aristotle* by Chase, D. P. Publication: London: J. M. Dent & Sons; New York: E. P. Dutton & Co. 1928.

for these two must accord, and when in accord they will then form the best of harmonics. In the second place, as the soul and body are two, we see also that there are two parts of the soul, the rational and the irrational, and the corresponding state, reason and appetite. And as the body is prior in order of generation to the soul, so the irrational is prior to the rational. The proof is that anger and will and desire are implanted in children from their very birth, but reason and understanding are developed as they grow older. Wherefore, the care of the body ought to precede that of the soul, and the training of the appetitive part should follow: none the less our care of it must be for the sake of the reason, and our care of the body for the sake of the soul.

After the children have been born, the manner of rearing may be supposed to have a great effect on their bodily strength...Also, all the motions to which children can be subjected at their early age are very useful...Such care should attend them in the first stage of life.

The next period lasts to the age of five; during this no demand should be made upon the child for study or labor, lest its growth be impeded; and there should be sufficient motion to prevent the limbs from being inactive. This can be secured, among other ways, by amusement, but the amusement should not be vulgar or tiring or riotous. The Directors of Education, as they are termed, should be careful what tales or stories the children hear, for the sports of children are designed to prepare the way for the business of later life, and should be for the most part imitations of the occupations which they will hereafter pursue in earnest.... Besides other duties, the Directors of Education should have an eye to their bringing up, and should take care that they are left as little as possible with slaves. For until they are seven years old they must live at home; and therefore, even at this early age, all that is mean and low should be banished from their sight and hearing....

No one will doubt that the legislator should direct his attention above all to the education of youth, or that the neglect of education does harm to states. The citizen should be molded to suit the forum of government under which he lives. For each government has a peculiar character which is originally formed and which continues to preserve it.

Now for the exercise of any faculty or art a previous training and habituation are required; clearly, therefore, for the practice of virtue. And since the whole city has one end, it is manifest that education should be one and the same for all, and that it should be public, and not private—not as at present, when everyone looks after his own children separately, and gives them separate instruction of the sort which he thinks best; the training in things which are of common interest should be the same for all. Neither must we suppose that any one of the citizens belongs to himself, for they all belong to the state, and are each of them a part of the state, and the care of each part is inseparable from the care of the whole. In this particular the Lacedaemonians are to be praised, for they take the greatest pains about their children and make education the business of the state.

That education should be regulated by law and should be an affair of state is not to be denied, but what should be the character of this public education, and how young persons should be educated, are questions which remain to be considered. For mankind are by no means agreed about the things to be taught, whether we look to virtue or the best life.

Neither is it clear whether education is more concerned with intellectual or with moral virtue. The existing practice is perplexing; no one knows on what principle we should proceed—should the useful in life, or should virtue, or should the higher knowledge, be the aim of our training; all three opinions have been entertained. Again, about the means there is no agreement; for different persons, starting with different ideas about the nature of virtue, naturally disagree about the practice of it.

There can be no doubt that children should be taught those useful things which are really necessary, but not all things; for occupations are divided into liberal and illiberal; and to young children should be imparted only such kinds of knowledge as will be useful to them without vulgarizing them. And any occupation, art, or science, which makes the body or soul or mind of the freeman less fit for the practice or exercise of virtue, is vulgar; wherefore we call those arts vulgar which tend to deform the body, and likewise all paid employments, for they absorb and degrade the mind.

The customary branches of education are four in number: (1) reading and writing, (2) exercises, (3) music, to which is sometimes added (4) drawing. Of these, reading and writing and drawing are regarded as useful for the purposes of life in a variety of ways, and gymnastic exercises are thought to infuse courage. Concerning music a doubt may be raised. In our own days most men cultivate it for the sake of pleasure, but originally it was included in education because nature herself, as has often been said, requires that we should be able not only to work well but to use leisure well, for I must state once again that the first principle of all action is leisure. Both are necessary, but leisure is better than occupation and is its end ...

It is clear, then, that some branches of learning and education must be studied merely with a view to leisure spent in intellectual activity. These are to be valued for their own sake, whereas those kinds of knowledge which are useful in business are to be deemed necessary and exist for the sake of other things. That explains why our fathers accepted music as a part of education, not because of its necessity or its utility, since it is not necessary or useful in the same manner as reading and writing, which are useful in money-making, in running a household, in acquiring knowledge, and in politics ... There remains, then, the use of music for intellectual enjoyment in leisure, and this is evidently the reason for its introduction.

It is evident, then, that there is a sort of education in which parents should train their sons, not as being useful or necessary, but because it is liberal or noble. Whether this is of one kind only or of more than one, and if so, what they are and how they are to be imparted, must still be determined. This much we are now in a position to say, that the ancients witness to us, for their opinion may be inferred from the fact that music is one of the received and traditional branches of education.

Furthermore, it is clear that children should be instructed in some useful things—for example, in reading and writing—not only for their usefulness but also because many other sorts of knowledge are acquired through them. With a like view they may be taught drawing, not to prevent their making mistakes in their own purchases, or in order that they may not be imposed upon in the buying or selling of articles, but rather because it makes them judges of the beauty of the human form. To be seeking always after the useful does not become free and exalted souls. Now it is clear that in education habit must go before reason, and the body before the mind; and therefore boys should be handed over to the trainer, who creates in them the proper habit of body, and to the wrestling master, who teaches them their exercises.

Of these states which in our own day seem to take the greatest care of children, some aim at producing in them an athletic habit, but they only injure their forms and stunt their growth. But in truth, as we have often repeated, education should not be exclusively directed to this or to any other single end. And parents who devote their children to gymnastics while they neglect their necessary education, in reality vulgarize them; for they make them useful to the state in one quality only and even in this the argument proves them to be inferior to others. . . .

Discussion Questions—*The Politics*

1. Compare Aristotle's curriculum plan to that proposed by Plato in *The Republic*. Which seems to be closer to the actual curriculum plan we have today?
2. Do you agree with Aristotle that anger, will, and desire are implanted in children from their very birth? Does this mean that it is impossible to form a child's character for it is all a matter of heredity?
3. Why does Aristotle endorse a uniform public education for all? Would he support private schools? home schooling? In what way could Aristotle be considered the first advocate of equal educational opportunity for all?
4. Do you think children are "molded" by their environment or are their lives open to individual choices and experiences?
5. Aristotle says that we achieve our happiness when we fulfill our function. Is our function determined by what we learn in school, or are we born with a predetermined function? How do we figure out what our function in society will be according to Aristotle? Is this relevant to school children today?

Questions to Guide Your Reading—*Nicomachean Ethics*

1. What is the difference between moral and intellectual virtues according to Aristotle? How does this distinction help answer Meno's question, Can virtue be taught?
2. What is Aristotle's definition of virtue? Compare and contrast this to Socrates' definition of virtue in *Meno*.
3. What are the two parts of the soul according to Aristotle? Does modern science uphold this dual understanding of the person or how would it define the person?
4. Make a chart of the virtues Aristotle mentions with the virtue in the middle and the extreme on one side and the deficiency on the other. For example:

Deficiency	Virtue	Extreme
Cowardice	Courage	Foolhardiness

READING 2.5:
NICOMACHEAN ETHICS

Book II

Virtue, then, is of two kinds, intellectual and moral; intellectual virtue in the main owes both its birth and its growth to teaching (for which reason it requires experience and time), while moral virtue comes about as a result of habit whence also its name *ethike* is one that is formed by a slight variation from the word *ethos* (habit). From this it is also plain that none of the moral virtues arises in us by nature; for nothing that exists by nature can form a habit contrary to its nature.... Neither by nature, then, nor contrary to nature do the virtues arise in us; rather we are adapted by nature to receive them, and are made perfect by habit.

Again, of all the things that come to us by nature we first acquire the potentiality and later exhibit the activity (this is plain in the case of the senses; for it was not by often seeing or often hearing that we got these senses, but on the contrary we had them before we used them, and did not come to have them by using them); but the virtues we get by first exercising them, as also happens in the case of the arts as well. For the things we have to learn before we can do them, we learn by doing them, e.g. men become builders by building and lyre players by playing the lyre; so too we become just by doing just acts, temperate by doing temperate acts, brave by doing brave acts....

It makes no small difference, then, whether we form habits of one kind or of another from our very youth; it makes a very great difference, or rather all the difference.

Since, then, the present inquiry does not aim at theoretical knowledge like the others (for we are inquiring not in order to know what virtue is, but in order to become good, since otherwise our inquiry would have been of no use), we must examine the nature of actions; namely how we ought to do them; for these determine also the nature of the states of character that are produced, as we have said. Now, that we must act according to the right rule is a common principle and must be assumed—it will be discussed later, i.e. both what the right rule is and how it is related to the other virtues....

I mean moral virtue; for it is this that is concerned with passions and actions, and in these there is excess, defect, and the intermediate. For instance, both fear and confidence and appetite and anger and pity and in general pleasure and pain may be felt both too much and too little, and in both cases not well; but to feel them at the right times, with reference to the right objects, towards the right people, with the right motive, and in the right way, is what is both intermediate and best, and this is characteristic of virtue. Similarly with regard to actions also there is excess, defect, and the intermediate.... Therefore virtue is a kind of mean, since, as we have seen, it aims at what is intermediate.

For these reasons also, then, excess and defect are characteristic of vice, and the mean of virtue; For men are good in but one way, but bad in many. Virtue, then, is a state of character concerned with choice, lying in a mean, i.e. the mean relative to us, this being determined by a rational principle, and by that principle by which the man of practical wisdom would determine it. Now it is a mean between two vices, that which depends on excess and that which depends on defect; and again it is a mean because the vices respectively fall short of or exceed what is right in both passions and actions, while virtue both finds and chooses that which is intermediate. Hence, in respect to its substance and the definition which states its essence virtue is a mean, with regard to what is best and right and extreme.

But not every action nor every passion admits of a mean; for some have names that already imply badness, e.g. spite, shamelessness, envy, and in the case of actions adultery, theft, murder; for all of

Source: The *Nicomachean Ethics* of Aristotle, Chase, D. P. Publication: London: J. M. Dent & Sons; New York: E. P. Dutton & Co. 1928.

these and suchlike things imply by their names that they are themselves bad, and not the excesses or deficiencies of them. It is not possible, then, ever to be right with regard to them; one must always be wrong. . . .

With regard to feelings of fear and confidence, courage is the mean; of the people who exceed, he who exceeds in fearlessness has no name (many of the states have no name), while the man who exceeds in confidence is rash, and he who exceeds in fear and falls short in confidence is a coward. With regard to pleasures and pains—not all of them, and not so much with regard to the pains—the mean is temperance, the excess self-indulgence. . . .

That moral virtue is a mean, then, and in what sense it is so, that it is a mean between two vices, the one involving excess, the other deficiency, and that it is such because its character is to aim at the intermediate in passions and in actions, has been sufficiently stated. Hence also it is no easy task to be good. For in everything it is an easy task to find the middle, e.g. to find the middle of a circle is not for every one but for him who knows; so, too, any one can get it once—that is easy—but to do this to the right person, to the right extent, at the right time, with the right motive, and in the right way, *that is* not for every one, nor is it easy; wherefore goodness is both rare and laudable and noble.

Discussion Questions

1. Compare Aristotle's theory of virtue with that of Socrates and of Confucius. In what ways are they similar and in what ways do they differ? Do they support today's current understanding of virtues as character attributes?
2. Do you agree with Aristotle that there is a medium point for every virtue? Are there some virtues for which there is no excess or deficiency? Give some examples.
3. What does Aristotle have to offer to the character education movement in the schools today? Is it possible for the schools to help children develop character in the way that Aristotle suggests? i.e., how can students be given the opportunity to "become just by doing just acts"?

For Further Research on the Internet

Biographical information on Aristotle with links to his philosophical thought. **http:// www.philosophypages.com/ph/aris.htm**

The Internet Encyclopedia of Philosophy with links to his biography and works. **http:// www.utm.edu/research/iep/a/aristotl.htm**

A homepage developed by Lawrence Hinman emphasizing Aristotle's virtue ethics including conference lectures on real audio. **http://ethics.acusd.edu/aristotle.html**

Suggestions for Further Reading

Barnes, Jonathan. "Aristotle." In *Greek Philosophers,* edited by K. Thomas. Oxford: Oxford University Press, 1999.

Losev, Alexei, and Axa Takho-God. *Aristotle.* Moscow: Progress Publishers, 1990.

Nightingale, Andrea Wilson. "Liberal Education in Plato's *Republic* and Aristotle's *Politic.*" In *Education in Greek and Roman Antiquity,* edited by Y. L. Too. Leiden, Netherlands: Koninklijke Brill, 2001.

Reeve, C. D. C. "Aristotelian Education." In *Philosophers on Education,* edited by A. O. Rorty. London: Routledge, 1998.

CHAPTER ACTIVITIES

Linking the Past to the Present

1. Design a lesson plan on a current issue using the Socratic Method. Write the whole lesson as a series of questions getting the students to explore the different sides of the issue.

2. Choose one of the following to debate with a fellow student:

   a. Do you think books should be censored?
   b. Do you think students should be grouped according to ability?
   c. Do you think vocational education is more important so that students can 'get a job'?

Developing Your Philosophy of Education

What will be the role of character development in your philosophy of education? Will you teach it as a subject, model it as a teacher, or leave it to the realm of the home?

Connecting Theory to Practice

In your clinical experience find out how grouping is used in the classroom and in courses. What criteria is used for grouping students? Interview your teacher and ask him/her to explain their philosophy of grouping.

Educators' Philosophies and Contributions to Education

TABLE 2.1   Philosophy and Contributions of Greek Educators

Educator	Role of Teacher & Learner	View of Curriculum & Methodology	Purpose or Goal of Education	Major Contribution
Sappho	The teacher is a mentor for the girls who believes in the education of the whole person	Taught music, poetry, dancing, and reading by getting the girls involved and doing each activity	To prepare girls to be cultured, married women	First school for girls, first feminist who inspired many later women educators
Socrates	The teacher draws the knowledge out of the student	To ask questions in such a way that students discover the knowledge within and grow in virtue	To cultivate morally excellent people	Socratic Method
Plato	The teacher should carefully choose and censor the material the child is to learn	Training of the spirit (music), of the body (gymnastics), and of the mind (philosophy)	Help people know the Good and be virtuous members of the state	*The Republic.* The first to advocate teaching men and women basing their education on their ability, not on their gender
Aristotle	The teacher is the expert who teaches students how to think and act virtuously	Liberal education, intellectual and moral virtues taught through dialogue with the master teacher	To produce virtuous men for the good of society	Virtue ethics, also developed the sciences of biology, logic, and literary criticism

CHAPTER 3

Roman Educational Contributions

Historical Developments

The center of political and economic gravity shifted from Greece to Rome during the third and second centuries B.C. In 509 B.C. the Roman citizens rebelled against their king and Rome became a republic and developed a culture of its own. The Roman conquest of Greece in 200 B.C. brought thousands of Greek slaves to Rome. This brought Rome in contact with Greek educational theories, philosophy, literature, and culture. However, Rome must be seen as much more than a mere transmitter of Greek culture. Rome was, in her own way, a creator of culture. Her genius was practical, not contemplative. She was a builder of material marvels, realistic and pragmatic, not philosophical or idealized like the Greeks. The Romans selectively fashioned Greek educational principles into a uniquely Roman form of citizenship training.[1] In 27 B.C. Octavian Augustus seized royal power, "The Golden Age of Rome" began, and it continued until 284 A.D. (See Map 3.1 of Ancient Rome.)

Roman Life

Life in ancient Rome began and ended with the sun. The toga, a long tunic, was a Roman's uniform and a powerful symbol of citizenship. Breakfast was a glass of water and bread, dinner was in the middle of the day followed by a siesta and a visit to the public baths. At sunset the Senate meetings were adjourned and most people went home to bed.[2] The specific culture of the Roman republic was a way of life organized around one individual—the Roman citizen—who played many roles—soldier, voter, farmer, politician, or orator. Citizenship meant freedom but it also came with responsibilities to the city (civis, civitas, civilis). The Roman citizen had only one aim—to glorify his name in the eyes of the people by doing great deeds for his city, his community, his culture. Only that which was honorable—was considered good. So, from his youth, one had to prove his virtue, or his worth as a man, by doing good.

49

Map 3.1   Ancient Rome

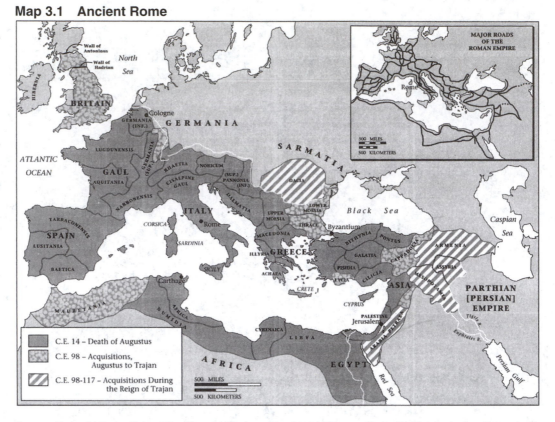

Source: From Anthony Esler, *The Human Venture, Combined Volume: From Prehistory to the Present,* 5th edition, 2004. Reprinted by permission of Pearson Education.

There were about one hundred or so families who were considered noblemen; they were high-born and wealthy families. Their sons had to reach positions that would allow them to become senators and orators. The senate was an assembly whose task was to advise the serving magistrate and make sure laws enacted conformed with the traditions of the city. The power of the senators was primarily of a moral nature.[3]

Roman Education

If education is understood as the shaping of young life in terms of a group ideal, this was very evident in early Rome. The Roman wanted his son to have strength of character and to be manly, courageous, honorable, loyal, and good. The goal of early education in Rome was the inculcation of these character traits.

The Romans had quite a different view from the Greeks of the family and its functions. The Roman family was a strong institution, and the Romans regarded the family circle as the proper place for the children to grow up and receive an education and to instill in them the family values. In early Rome the family was the major educational unit of society; every member of the household was subject to the father of the family and three generations could be included under one roof.[4] Nothing was more important than to make the Roman child what he/she was to be. In few places throughout history has the child been considered more important than here. For the Roman, the child was the bearer of tradition and the hope of the future.

Mother as Teacher

The mother was the child's first educational influence and principle teacher. Unlike her Athenian counterpart, the Roman mother held a respected position in her family. The mother raised and taught her own children, rather than passing on the duty to slaves or male tutors. Even the most aristocratic Roman women were said to feel honored to assume a place in the family as the guardian and teacher of the young. The first thing that every Roman child had to learn, whether boy or girl, was how to read and write.[5]

The mother served as a model of Roman womanhood to her daughters as she taught them the domestic skills that they would need as adults. Besides teaching them how to read and write, mothers taught the management skills necessary for operating a home. Girls had to be trained in domestic routine and the many practical duties required of a woman in a primarily agricultural community. The education of women seldom went beyond the confines of the household unless they were upper middle class women who might be more formally educated.[6]

Father as Teacher

As in Greece, however, the male child at age seven ceased to be under the exclusive guardianship of his mother. The father assumed the role of chief teacher. Essentially, it was the father, as the head of the household, to whom the state entrusted the process of inducting the young Roman boy into citizenship.[7] Roman aristocracy took great care in educating the young; the Romans believed in themselves as educators, as trainers of the next generation in a specific order of civilization. They developed a tough, aggressive education system that took little notice of individual talents and almost none of feelings or emotional development. Children were regimented and physical force was used to make them learn. Boys were turned over to tutors at the age of six or seven and forced to learn their letters.[8] The father was thought to be the male child's real teacher; even if he chose to send him to school, he still kept a close watch over this and expected these other male teachers to perform this function acting like fathers. At about age sixteen, the education of the aristocratic Roman boy moved outside the family. There was a ceremony to mark the beginning of the next stage: the boy took off his toga edged with purple and any other marks of childhood and put on the toga *virilis* instead. Now he was a citizen; but he had not finished his education. First, he had to spend a year preparing for public life and finish with the completion of military service.[9]

Though in matters of practical life there was a clear distinction between the education of the upper-class children and that of the lower classes, basically the family education of all Roman children was the same. A child in the lower class received a far more modest education. As the child was almost certainly destined to a life far less public than that of the upper-class youth, his education was focused more upon his place in society.

As devoted as the father was to his son's education, it was evident that, as society in Rome became more complex and moved from a city-state to a world empire, this would not be enough. As contacts between Greeks and Romans increased, the ruling elite group became conscious of their intellectual deficiencies and set out to capture Greek culture as they had captured Greek lands. As educational patterns became more formal, they needed to be entrusted to specialized institutions, or schools, which appeared in Rome sometime around 300 B.C.

The Roman School System

The Romans patterned their educational institutions on the Greek schools, curriculum, and teachers. However, the Romans achieved a pedantic mastery over subject matter. They forced their children to become little grammarians, since language and literature were the whole of their curriculum. Higher education was simply higher studies in language. In their aristocratic society they needed to communicate and they did marvelously well at this. They ignored science, studied almost no mathematics, and little history; there was no room for art or music, but they learned both written and oral Latin superbly well.[10]

The Romans mechanically organized a much better system of schools than that realized in Greece. Roman education in the late Republic evolved into a formal school system that included three distinct phases.

The Education of Women

The Roman elementary school, or *ludus litterarius,* was established for children ages seven through twelve. These schools were private and voluntary. Some girls as well as boys of the aristocratic class were taught to read and write Latin and to count using pebbles. The emphasis was on literacy—reading, writing, and arithmetic. A household slave, or *pedagogus,* would accompany the students to school, which was often held on an open porch protected from the noise of the street by a sheet of tent cloth stretched out front. Classes began at dawn and went into the afternoon. The Latin word for school *ludus* means "game" and refers to the way knowledge was drilled. Learning was a matter of imitation and repetition. Once the Roman child could recognize the letters of the alphabet, she or he would learn to read by repeating aloud and tracing against the text as his teacher was reading. The teacher, or *magister,* emphasized strenuous discipline and memorization; every time a mistake was made, the teacher would beat the child with a cane.[11] In comparison with Greek schools, instruction in music and gymnastics seem to have been lacking in Roman schools.

The Education of Men

A grammar school appeared as an institution of secondary education by the middle of the third century B.C. Under the direction of a grammar teacher, a *grammaticus,* Roman boys from the ages of ten to sixteen studied Greek and Latin grammar and composition. The Greek works of Homer and Euripides were studied. An educated Roman was expected to be thoroughly familiar with the works of Virgil and other Roman poets. The curriculum came to include all of the liberal arts and included grammar, rhetoric, dialectic, arithmetic, geometry, music, and astronomy. The arithmetic taught rarely went beyond addition and subtraction, for the Roman counting system did not use zeros; complicated summing was best done using an abacus. The Latin Twelve Tables, Rome's ancient and primary code of laws established in 450 B.C., were studied as the basis of their legal and civil system. In fact, younger children learned to write by copying the Twelve Tables. Lessons were also given in rhetoric or the art of public speaking, a key skill for any political career. Both rhetoric and literature also served as moral education, giving students an ethical ground and inculcating the virtues of fortitude, justice, and prudence.[12]

For higher studies, the Roman youth at ages sixteen to eighteen attended the rhetorical schools, similar to the university. Concerned with education of the orator, the rhetorical schools combined the Greek conception of liberal education with the Roman emphasis on practicality. In the Rhetorical School rhetoric, dialectic, philosophy, and law were studied. Throughout its existence, Roman civilization was devoted to law.[13]

The Orator

Rome's educational ideal was exemplified by the orator. The ideal Roman orator was broadly and liberally educated, and the educated man demonstrated an interest in the affairs of the republic, being himself a man of public life, i.e., a Senator, lawyer, teacher, civil servant, or politician. In the Roman view of education rhetoric was the main element of higher education and a Roman man was only properly educated if he could use his gifts of oratory in the service of his country. By examining the general Roman conception of the orator and the education that was designed to produce him, it is possible to achieve an understanding of Rome's educational ideal. There were two men of note in Roman education Cicero and Quintilian. Marcus Cicero, one of the leading Roman statesman, gave many speeches and wrote many documents, including one on the education of the Orator. Convinced that it was important to teach those who would teach the future orators how to teach, Marcus Quintilianus wrote *Institutio Oratoria*.

For Further Research on the Internet

The classics page has information about life, literature, art, and archeology in ancient Rome. http://www.classicspage.com/

Many links to aspects of life in ancient Rome, including one on their educational system. http://www.crystalinks.com/rome.html

Notes

1. Anthony Corbeill, *Education in the Roman Republic: Creating Traditions* (Leiden, Netherlands; Boston: Koln: Koninklijke Brill, 2001), p. 261.
2. Anthony Everitt, *Cicero: The Life and Times of Rome's Greatest Politician* (New York: Random House, 2001), pp. 72–73.
3. Florence Dupont, *Daily Life in Ancient Rome* (Oxford: Blackwell Publishers, 1992), pp. 8–13.
4. Ibid., pp. 103–105.
5. Joan Peterson, *The Education of Girls* (New York: Garland Publishing, Inc. 1999), p. 84.
6. Patricia Sexton, *Women in Education* (Bloomington, Indiana: Phi Delta Kappa Educational Foundation, 1976), pp. 25–26.
7. Dupont, p. 224.
8. Norman Cantor, *The Civilization of the Middle Ages* (New York: Harper Collins Publishers, 1993), p. 10.
9. H. I. Marrou, *A History of Education in Antiquity* (Madison: University of Wisconsin Press, 1982), p. 233.
10. Cantor, p. 10.
11. Dupont, p. 225.
12. Everitt, pp. 27–29.
13. Aubrey Gwynn, *Roman Education from Cicero to Quintillian* (New York: Russell & Russell, 1964).

Section 3.1: Marcus Tullius Cicero (106–43 B.C.)

A speech course or demonstrated competency in public speaking is required of all prospective teacher candidates today. We have Marcus Tullius Cicero to thank for this for, in a sense, Cicero was the first speech teacher to prepare future teachers. An accomplished orator himself, he was an excellent model of the skills he identified in his *De Oratore* as essential to the education of the orator.

Cicero's Life and Times

Rome in Cicero's day was a complex and sophisticated city with almost a million inhabitants and a very modern life style, including stores, theatres, and sports fields. Cicero wrote about how a state should best be organized and he was in favor of a mixed combination of monarchy, oligarchy, and democracy, a model later found in the original constitution of the United

States with the executive, judicial, and legislative branches.[1] Cicero is a fascinating man who lived through extraordinary times.

Cicero was born on January 3, 106 B.C. in Arpinum, a town some seventy miles south of Rome which had achieved Roman citizenship.[2] Cicero's family was part of the local aristocracy of landowners, farmers, and businessmen. Cicero's father, Marcus, was a scholar who loved to engage in philosophic debates and was very involved in his sons' education. We do not know much about his mother, Helvia, except that she was a sharp-eyed housewife from a wealthy family. Cicero had a younger brother named Quintus.[3]

Cicero's Education and Training

Cicero's father had high ambitions for his sons and made sure that they were given a good schooling. They may have been taught by a tutor in their home or sent to school, first the *ludus* and then the *grammaticus*. It seems that Cicero showed great academic ability and a sense of humor at an early age. When Cicero reached the age of sixteen, his secondary schooling ended and his father decided that his sons should complete their training in public speaking and study law in the capital of Rome. Marcus was placed under the tutelage of Quintus Mucius Scaevola, a great lawyer of Rome, thus beginning his study of law.[4] Later in his life, Cicero trained several young friends to be lawyers in the same way as he had been taught. Cicero also studied with Lucius Licinius Crassus, a celebrated orator, and Archias, a well-known Greek poet.

Cicero experienced both the old Roman and the Hellenic styles of education. He studied Greek grammar and literature and Latin literature and history, concentrating on rhetoric. He toured Greece and Asia Minor for two years, spending six months in Athens to study philosophy and rhetoric.

Cicero was determined from his boyhood to make a career in politics and become a leader, but first he had to make a name for himself. He was twenty-five years old when he made his debut as a lawyer and successfully won his first case.[5] In 79 B.C., at the age of twenty-seven, he married Terentia, a high-spirited young girl with a strong character and aristocratic parents who were able to present her to him with a handsome dowry. They had a daughter, Tullia, and a son, Marcus Tullius II. (See the timeline of Cicero's life in Figure 3.1.)

Cicero, the Politician

In 75 B.C. Cicero was elected to his first political office as a *quaestor,* assistant to the consuls, and continued to gain higher offices until he was elected *consul,* chief magistrate of the Senate, in 63 B.C. Cicero took office in difficult political and economic times and he stood for the rule of law and the maintenance of the constitution as he tried to preserve the old Roman values of honor, duty, and service.[6] Cicero handled several difficult cases admirably and gained popularity with the electorate while maintaining good standing with the nobility. Cicero convicted some of the leaders of a conspiracy to commit high treason and became a hero overnight.[7]

Cicero's many political speeches were actual models of rhetoric that young Romans could study and imitate. In addition, he contributed extensive treaties on every topic from technical material to rhetorical questions, educational ideas, aesthetics, and history.[8] He wrote *De Oratore,* his most important educational treatise, in 55 B.C. In the late Roman republic, oratory was a major form of literature and a critical tool of politics to sway the people and the Senate. Oratory was Cicero's primary genre and we have some fifty-eight of his speeches intact.

Cicero served in the Senate during the waning of the Roman republic, a time of civil war and much turmoil. He exposed different conspiracies against the government and had people removed from office, but Cicero himself was forced to leave the city in exile several times. At times Cicero enjoyed considerable prominence and influence in the Sen-

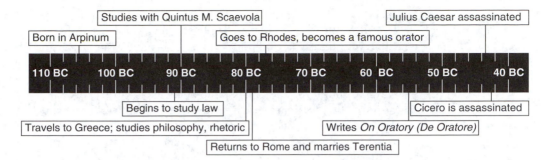

Figure 3.1   Cicero's Life and Times

ate. Cicero's life came to a tragic end on December 7, 43 B.C. when he was killed in retribution for his association with those who conspired to kill Julius Caesar.[9]

Cicero's Importance for Educational Thought

Marcus Tullius Cicero was a leading Roman senator, a distinguished orator, and an excellent example of the Roman ideal of *humanitas*—well-educated in Latin and Greek, grammar, literature, history, and rhetoric. Cicero wrote more than 800 letters that provide modern historians with valuable insights into late Roman republican politics. They also reveal Cicero's avid desire to prevent one-man rule in Rome and his belief in natural law governing the universe and applying to all mankind.[10]

De Oratore

Cicero is most significant in Western educational history for his writings on the preparation of the orator that appeared in *De Oratore* in 55 B.C. The dialogue contains the fullest statement of Cicero's educational theory and has had a permanent influence in the history of Greek, Roman, and European culture.[11]

When Cicero wrote *De Oratore,* he was concerned with the education of his son, Marcus, and his nephew, Quintus. *De Oratore* is a masterpiece of a dialogue in which Cicero proposes a major educational reform in the way the orator is educated.

Cicero attempts to synthesize the Roman view that oratory had practical consequences, such as the winning of debates in the Forum, with the Greek view that the orator be a person of broad culture or *humanitas*. He retains the best of both views and suggests that the orator should be broadly educated in the liberal arts so that his skill could be used for the public good and thereby promote the public interest.[12] The orator-statesman needed to study philosophy, law, and ethics so he would be a person of high ethics.

Cicero did not develop a systematic plan for education at the primary or secondary levels. He was concerned only with Roman higher education, or rhetoric. He did, however, comment on the work of the *grammaticus,* the secondary school teacher, insofar as it affected the preparation for rhetorical study. He wanted the *grammaticus* to provide instruction in Latin and Greek grammar, literature, poetry, and history.

Cicero's Philosophy of Education

After prospective students of rhetoric were adequately prepared in grammar, they embarked on higher studies, the liberal arts, needed for oratory. Although Cicero recommended that the orator acquire a general knowledge of ethics, psychology, military science, medicine, natural science, geography, and astronomy, the most important subjects were history, law, and philosophy. History provided the young Roman with a perspective into his tradition and the lives of his ancestors, through the study of the past deeds of Roman greatness. All Romans were devoted to the study of the Laws of the Twelve Tables, the basis for Roman jurisprudence. Jurisprudence, or practical ethics, is the Roman counterpart to Greek philosophy and abstract speculation. The orator was Cicero's ideal of the Roman man. Only one word gives full expression to his concept: *humanitas,* human excellence embodied in a cultured and articulate man.[13] Cicero summarized his educational theory when he said, "We must borrow our virtues from Rome and our culture from Greece."[14]

Notes

1. Anthony Everitt, *Cicero: The Life and Times of Rome's Greatest Politician* (New York: Random House, 2001), pp. vii, 1.
2. Christian Habicht, *Cicero the Politician* (Baltimore: The Johns Hopkins University Press, 1990), p. 16.
3. Everitt, pp. 25–26.
4. Habicht, p. 17.
5. Ibid, pp. 18–21.
6. Everitt, pp. 67, 95.
7. Habicht, pp. 31–33.
8. Alison Sharrock and Rhiannon Ash, "Cicero," in *Fifty Key Classical Authors,* edited by A. Sharrock and R. Ash (New York: Routledge., 2002), p. 205.
9. Plutarch, *Plutarch's Lives* (Cambridge, MA: Harvard University Press, 1967), p. 751.
10. Sharrock and Ash, p. 204.
11. Aubrey Gwynn, *Roman Education from Cicero to Quintillian* (New York: Russell & Russell, 1964), p. 81.
12. Gerald Gutek, *A History of the Western Educational Experience* (Prospect Heights, IL: Waveland Press, Inc., 1995), p. 66.
13. Gwynn, pp. 70, 119.
14. Marcus Cicero, *Cicero: On the Ideal Orator.* (Oxford: Oxford University Press, 2001).

Questions to Guide Your Reading

1. What areas of knowledge must every orator have according to Cicero?
2. Why did Cicero think that history was such an important subject to study?
3. What are some of the things one can do if they are able to speak well and persuasively?
4. List the three purposes of good oratory outlined by Cicero.

READING 3.1:
ORATORY AS THE AIM OF EDUCATION

13: In this city of our own assuredly no studies have ever had a more vigorous life than those having to do with the art of speaking.

14: For as soon as our world-empire had been established, and an enduring peace had assured us leisure, there was hardly a youth, a thirst to tame, who did not deem it his duty to strive with might and main after eloquence. At first indeed, in their complete ignorance of method, since they thought there was no definite course of training or any rules of art, they used to attain what skill they could by means of their natural ability and of reflection. But later, having heard the Greek orators, gained acquaintance with their literature and called in Greek teachers, our people were fired with a really incredible enthusiasm for eloquence.

15: The importance, variety, and frequency of current suits of all sorts aroused them so effectively, that, to the learning which each man had acquired by his own efforts, plenty of practice was added, as even better than the maxims of all the masters. In those days too, as present, the prizes open to this study were supreme, in the way of popularity, wealth, and reputation alike. As for ability, again there are many things to show that our fellow-countrymen have far excelled every other race.

16: And considering all this, who would not marvel that, in all the long record of ages, times, and states, so great a number of orators is to be found? But the truth is that this oratory is a greater thing, and has its sources in more arts and branches of study than people suppose. For, where the number of students is very great, the supply of masters of the very best, the quality of natural ability outstanding, the variety of issues unlimited, the prizes open to eloquence exceedingly splendid, what else could anyone think to be the cause, unless it be the really incredible vastness and difficulty of the subject?

17: To begin with, a knowledge of very many matters must be grasped, without which oratory is but an empty and ridiculous swirl of verbiage: and the distinctive style has to be formed, not only by the choice of words, but also by the arrangement of the same; and all the mental emotions, with which nature has endowed the human race, are to be intimately understood, because it is in calming or kindling the feelings of the audience that the full power and science of oratory are to be brought into play. To this there should be added a certain humor, flashes of wit, the culture befitting a gentleman, and readiness and terseness alike in repelling and in delivering the attack, the whole being combined with a delicate charm and urbanity.

18: Further, the complete history of the past and a store of precedents must be retained in the memory, nor may a knowledge of statute law and our national law in general be omitted. And why should I go on to describe the speaker's delivery? That needs to be controlled by bodily carriage, gesture, play of features and changing intonation of voice; and how important that is wholly by itself, the actor's trivial art and the stage proclaim; for there, although all are laboring to regulate the expression, the voice, and the movements of the body, everyone knows how few actors there are, or ever have been, whom we could bear to watch! What need to speak of that universal treasure-house the memory? Unless this faculty be placed in charge of the ideas and phrases which have been thought out and well weighed, even though as conceived by the orator they were of the highest excellence, we know that they will all be wasted.

19: Let us therefore cease to wonder what may be the cause of the rarity of orators, since oratory is the result of a whole number of things, in any one of which to succeed is a great achievement, and let us rather exhort our children, and the others whose fame and repute are dear to us, to form a true understanding of the greatness of their task, and not to believe that they can gain their coveted object by reliance on the rules, or teachers, or methods of practice employed by everybody, but to rest assured

---

Source: *Cicero on Oratory and Orators* edited by J. S. Watson, Philadelphia: David McKay Publisher, 1897.

that they can do this by the help of certain other means.

20: And indeed in my opinion, no man can be an orator complete in all points of merit, who has not attained a knowledge of all important subjects and arts. For it is from knowledge that oratory must derive its beauty and fullness, and unless there is such knowledge, well-grasped and comprehended by the speaker, there must be something empty and almost childish in the utterance. . . .

30: "Moreover," he continued, "there is to my mind no more excellent thing, than the power, by means of oratory, to get a hold on assemblies of men, win their good will, direct their inclinations wherever the speaker wishes, or divert them from whatever he wishes. In every free nation, and most of all communities that have attained the enjoyment of peace and tranquility, this one art has always flourished above the rest and ever reigned supreme.

31: For what is so marvelous as that, out of the innumerable company of mankind, a single being should arise, who either alone or with a few others can make effective a faculty bestowed by nature upon every man? Or what is so pleasing to the understanding and the ear as a speech adorned and polished with wise reflections and dignified language? Or what achievement so mighty and glorious as that the impulses of the crowd, the consciences of the judges, the austerity of the Senate, should suffer transformation through the eloquence of one man?

32: "Nay more (not to have you for ever contemplating public affairs, the bench, the platform, and the Senate-house), what in hours of ease can be a pleasanter thing or one more characteristic of culture, than discourse that is graceful and nowhere uninstructed? For the one point in which we have our very greatest advantage over the brute creation is that we hold converse one with another, and can reproduce our thought in word.

33: Who therefore would not rightly admire this faculty, and deem it his duty to exert himself to the utmost in this field, that by so doing he may surpass men themselves in that particular respect wherein chiefly men are superior to animals? To come, however, at length to the highest achievements of eloquence, what other power could have been strong enough either to gather scattered humanity into one place, or to lead it out of its brutish existence in the wilderness up to our present condition of civilization as men and citizens, or, after the abolishment of social communities, to give shape to laws, tribunals, and civic rights?

34: And not to pursue any further instance well-nigh countless as they are I will conclude the whole matter in a few words, for my assertion is this: that the wise control of the complete orator is that which chiefly upholds not only his own dignity, but the safety of countless individuals and of the entire State. Go forward therefore, my young friends, in your present course, and bend your energies to that study which engages you, that so it may be in your power to become a glory to yourselves, a source of service to your friends, and profitable members of the Republic."

Discussion Questions

1. Cicero says that one of the ways in which humankind differs from brute creation is our ability of converse with one another. Why is language considered a mark of human civilization? What does our current use of language indicate about our American society?
2. Americans often invoke the freedom of speech clause of the first amendment as their ability to say whatever they want whenever they want. How would Cicero interpret this first amendment freedom?
3. What do you think Cicero would say to teachers regarding the importance of their ability to speak well while teaching?

For Further Research on the Internet

The Cicero homepage with links to his biography by Plutarch, and links to his complete texts, with a timeline and a complete bibliography.
http://www.utexas.edu/depts/classics/documents/Cic.html

Plutarch's complete biography of Cicero. **http://classics.mit.edu/Plutarch/cicero.html**

The Internet Encyclopedia of Philosophy provides a chronological outline of his life, influence, thought, and achievements. **http://www.utm.edu/research/iep/c/cicero**

Suggestions for Further Reading

Cicero, Marcus Tullius. *Cicero: On the Ideal Orator.* Translated by James May and Jakob Wisse. Oxford: Oxford University Press, 2001.

Everitt, Anthony. *Cicero: The Life and Times of Rome's Greatest Politician.* New York: Random House, 2001.

Gutek, Gerald. *A History of the Western Educational Experience,* 2nd ed. Prospect Heights, IL: Waveland Press, Inc., 1995.

Gwynn, Aubrey. *Roman Education from Cicero to Quintillian.* New York: Russell & Russell, 1964.

Habicht, Christian. *Cicero the Politician.* Baltimore: The Johns Hopkins University Press, 1990.

Sharrock, Alison and Rhiannon Ash. "Cicero." In *Fifty Key Classical Authors,* edited by A. Sharrock and R. Ash. New York: Routledge, 2002.

Section 3.2: Marcus Fabius Quintilian (c. 35–95 A.D.)

Do you enjoy teaching writing to your students? A difficult skill to teach is now even more stressful due to the inclusion of a writing section on standardized tests. You probably use the "writing process" which has been in stages of development and practice in many classrooms for the past twenty years and creates student-centered, "real" writing situations where peers offer feedback to one another. This may seem like a new way to teach writing as it is vastly different from the teacher-assigned, traditional five-paragraph theme that dominated writing in the twentieth century. These are, however, the key ideas of the educational theories advocated 2,000 years ago by Marcus Fabius Quintilian in *Institutio Oratoria (The Education of the Orator).*[1]

Quintilian's Life and Family

Marcus Fabius Quintilian (Quintilianus) was born in 35 A.D. in Calagurris, Spain, to a well-educated Roman *rhetor.* His father taught him his own profession as a rhetorician. The family moved to Rome when Quintilian was sixteen years old, so he was able to receive a thorough education in the best secondary and rhetorical schools in Rome, studying with the colorful Remmius Palaemon and Domitius Afer, and soon becoming a distinguished rhetorician and lawyer.[2] In 58 A.D., once he completed his education, Quintilian returned to Spain and worked as a lawyer. Ten years later, he was brought to Rome with Galba, the governor of Spain and the new emperor of Rome.

Quintilian married and had two sons, both of whom died quite young. His wife died as well and Quintilian speaks in touching terms of the successive losses he sustained and the high hopes he had had for his little Quintilian.[3] (See the timeline of Quintilian's life in Figure 3.2.)

Quintilian, the Educator

Quintilian established a school of rhetoric in 68 A.D. Five years later, Vespasian, the new emperor of Rome and the patron of the "University of Rome," appointed Quintilian as the first State Professor of Rhetoric. The appointment marked Quintilian as a loyal Roman educator, the head of his profession, and gave him high social standing with the rank and dignity of a consul. Additionally, it made his school famous and prestigious. Although busy in the courts, Quintilian spent most of his time with the school: giving extensive lectures on rhetorical theory and declamations, listening to and critiquing the work of his students. He tried to develop a more classical literary style, emphasizing the style of Cicero and moral values.[4]

Quintilian was a man of broad cultural inclination. He knew Greek well and saw its value in providing the liberal basis needed for the education of the orator and all professional education. Quintilian's success as a teacher was mainly due to his reasonable nature and his devotion to the welfare of his students. He was a gentle man of extraordinary tenderness and urged teachers of orators to be gentle with their young charges. Quintilian retired from his official position as Professor of Rhetoric circa the year 90 A.D. and then began the writing of his great work, *Institutio Oratoria*. By the time Quintilian died in 95 A.D., he was well-known and his educational ideas were widely accepted.[5]

Quintilian's Importance for Educational Thought

Quintilian's most important work is *Institutio Oratoria*. (The most accurate translation in English is *The Education of an Orator.*) According to Kennedy, the Latin word *institutio* meant the "systematic training or education of the intellect," implying the implantation of knowledge in the mind. *Institutio Oratoria* is a spacious treatise composed of twelve books. According to the preface of the book, Quintilian was urged by his friends to write a treatise on the art of speaking upon his retirement. He wrote *Institutio Oratoria* as a textbook for the instruction of his sons, who died before the book was finished, and the son of Marcus Victorious. Quintilian's twenty years of experience as a teacher of rhetoric allowed him to reinstate basic principles of rhetoric which were slowly being lost during the century that divided him from Cicero. The outstanding qualities of the book reflect Quintilian's practical sagacity and good sense.

Quintilian's concern for a boy's education begins at the cradle, where the parents and the nurse have a role in helping the child learn to speak well and build his character. Pro-

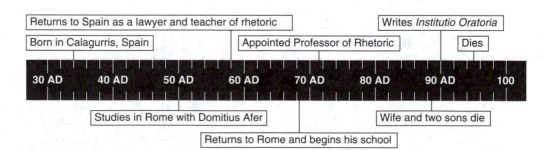

Figure 3.2   Quintilian's Life and Times

moting organized education in an elementary school, Quintilian emphasized a personal relationship between teacher and pupil similar to that between parent and child. He stressed the importance of students working at their own pace. He favored "public" or group education over tutorial and emphasized the importance of placing the best teachers with beginners (rather than with the advanced, as was frequently done at the time). Quintilian opposed corporal punishment; if the child was not learning, the teacher was to blame for not teaching correctly at the child's developmental level. He outlined clearly in *Institutio* a series of written and spoken exercises students were to master that are very similar to language arts activities today, emphasizing the interrelationship of reading, writing, speaking, and listening.[6]

The book includes information on rhetorical education (similar to Cicero's *De Oratore*) as well as a commentary on human nature emphasizing the importance of educating the whole person (cognition, volition, and emotions). Quintilian's comments on early childhood education in the home, the stages of development in a child's learning, and the value of general education are important parts of educational history.

In *Institutio Oratoria,* Quintilian puts forward his theory of a perfect man, stating the need for the orator to be educated to "be a good man" and a "perfect orator." Such an orator should possess not only "an eminence in the art of speaking" but also "all the moral virtues as well." He insisted upon the training of the will and the building of a character, which was just as important as the liberal training of the intellect. For Quintilian, only a good man can be an orator—perfect oratory implies a high moral standard as well as complete mastery over every form of speech.[7]

Quintilian's Philosophy of Education

Quintilian, like Cicero, synthesized Roman ideas with Greek culture into a coherent whole—in this case, a consistent educational philosophy. Quintilian supported the teaching of the liberal arts and moral education within the professional education of the orator. He presented the teacher's role as that of an expert who had to take into consideration the developmental level and needs of the students and teach with methods which motivated and stimulated students to learn. The goal of education was to form an orator, a public servant who could be employed in teaching, civil administration, or law. The purpose was to use the power of speech for high, ethical, noble purposes and serve the country. As Quintilian said, "It is the perfect orator that we are training and he cannot even exist unless he is a good man."

Notes

1. Janet Bloodgood, "Quintilian: A Classical Educator Speaks to the Writing Process," *Reading Research and Instruction* 42, no. 1 (2002), p. 31.
2. Alison Sharrock and Rhiannon Ash, *Quintilian* (New York: Routledge, 2002), p. 317.
3. Ibid, p. 318.
4. George Kennedy, *Quintilian* (New York: Twayne, 1969), p. 20.
5. Ibid, pp. 29–30.
6. Bloodgood, pp. 31–33.
7. Peter France, Quintilian and Rousseau: Oratory and Education, *Rhetorica,* The International Society for the History of Rhetoric (1995), p. 306; Aubrey Gwynn, *Roman Education from Cicero to Quintillian* (New York: Russell & Russell, 1964), p. 230.

Questions to Guide Your Reading

1. Where in Quintilian's *Institutio Oratoria* do you find a foreshadowing of the kindergarten?

2. From what Quintilian says about learning to read, would you say that he would be a supporter of phonics or of whole language?

3. Quintilian is significant in educational history because he is the first educational psychologist, i.e., the first to outline stages in the development of a child's learning which a teacher must accommodate by different teaching methods. Identify the different stages, or age groups, Quintilian outlines and the appropriate subject matter to be taught to each age group. Where applicable, also indicate the method Quintilian indicates is most appropriate for that age group.

READING 3.2:
ON EDUCATION

Book I, Introduction

6. This work I dedicate to you, Victorious Marcellus, a very dear friend, and a devoted lover of letters. I adjudge you in the highest degree worthy of this pledge of our mutual affection, it was also because it seemed likely that in the education of your son Geta, whose early years already reveal the clear light of genius, you would find a treatise useful in which my intention was to start from the very cradle, so to speak, of oratory, to deal successfully with all the studies which in any way contribute to the making of the orator, and to lead right up to the culmination of his art.

9. It is the perfect orator that we are training and he cannot even exist unless he is a good man. We therefore demand in him not only exceptional powers of eloquence but also every mental excellence.

18. Let us then define the orator as a man who can truly be called wise, perfect not only in character (for in my opinion, though some think differently, that is not enough) but also in knowledge and every sort of eloquence.

19. Such a man perhaps has never yet existed. But that is no reason why we should not strive towards the highest ideal, as was done by the ancients for the most part. For, although they considered that so far no wise man had been discovered, they none the less wrote down the precepts whereby wisdom might be attained.

25. I have therefore embodied in the small blocks not simply that small portion with which most authors have been content, but everything which I considered useful for the training of the orator. In all cases the treatment will be brief for, if I were to follow out all that could be said in detail, my work would never end.

Book I, Chapter 1

The Method of Primary Instruction

1. When his son is born, let the father first of all conceive the highest hopes concerning him, for so he will become more careful from the start.

4. Before all things else, let the speech of his nurses be correct. 'Cicero wished them, if it were possible, to be educated women,—at any rate he desired the best available to be selected. And of one first account must be taken of moral character; still let them also speak correctly.

5. Theirs are the voices the child will hear first, theirs the words he will try to reproduce. And further those very impressions which are less desirable are those the more enduring. Good things are easily changed for the worse but when will you turn vices into virtues? Do not then allow the boy, even in in-

Source: Selections from *Quintilian on Education Being a Translation of The Institutio Oratoria of Quintilian* with an English translation by H. E. Butler, M.A. London, William Heinemann, New York: G. P. Putnam's Sons, 1921.

fancy, to become familiar with a way of speaking which has afterwards to be unlearned.

6. In the parents I would fain have as much education as is possible. Nor do I refer to the fathers only. It is recorded that Cornelia, the mother of Gracchi, contributed in no small degree to the eloquence of her sons, and posterity may still enjoy her cultured way of speech and letters which have survived.

7. Those who have not themselves enjoyed the benefits of education must not devote less care to the proper instruction of their children, and their own deficiencies (in learning) should make them the more careful in all other particulars.

8. In the case of *pedagogues* (attendants) this further point should be insisted upon that they be either thoroughly educated—and this I should like to be the first consideration or else aware of their lack of education. Nothing is worse than those who have made some little progress beyond the first elements and on the strength of this are filled with a false idea of their own knowledge. . . .

12. I prefer that a boy should start with the Greek language: first because he will pick up Latin, which is in common use, whether we wish it or no, and second because he should be instructed first in Greek studies from which ours derive their origin. . . .

14. Latin therefore should follow at no great interval and before long the two languages should advance together. Thus it will come to pass that when we begin to give equal attention to both languages neither one will hurt the other.

15. Some have thought that children under seven years of age should not be taught letters because that is the earliest age at which such studies can be understood and such toil endured.

19. And this gain, carried forward through the years, and time thus saved in infancy is an acquisition to youth. Let the same rule be laid down for the years that follow so that the pupil may not be late in beginning to learn that which everyone has to learn. Let us not then lose the earliest years—the less so since rudiments of letters depend on memory alone: and memory not only exists in small children but is also most tenacious at that stage.

20. Let this first instruction be in the form of play; let the pupil be asked questions and praised for his answers, let him never rejoice in ignorance of anything; sometimes, when he will not learn, let another be taught of whom he may be jealous; let him compete sometimes with others and quite often

think himself victorious: let him also be excited by rewards, which at that age are eagerly sought after.

For example, I certainly do not approve of what I see to be common practice, viz. that children should learn the names and order of the letters before their forms.

25. This (practice) hinders the recognition of the letters since the child soon ceases to attend to their shapes and simply follows his memory which outstrips his observation. And so teachers even when they seem to have fixed the letters firmly enough in the minds of their pupils in the straightforward order in which they are at first usually written, hark back again and by varying the arrangement introduce confusion until their pupils know the letters by their appearance and not by their sequence. Thus, as in the case of persons, so in the case of letters they will best be taught appearance and name together.

26. But what is a hindrance in the case of letters will do no harm with syllables. Further, I approve of a practice devised to stimulate the child to learn, viz. that of giving him ivory letters to play with and anything else that can be proved to add to the child's pleasure, which it may be a delight to him to handle, look at, and name.

27. When the child begins to trace the outlines of the letters it will be useful to have them cut out on a board, in as beautiful a script as possible; so that his pen may be guided along them as if in furrows. Thus he will not go wrong as in writing on waxen tablets (for he will be confined within the edges on either side and will therefore be unable to deviate from his model), and by tracing definite outlines with greater speed and frequency he will develop the proper muscles and will not require the helping hand of a teacher placed upon his own.

28. Important, too, in this connection is a matter which is often apt to be neglected by educated people, I mean care in writing neatly and quickly. For since writing itself is the most essential thing in our studies and the one thing from which alone springs true and deeply rooted proficiency, a slow pen hinders thought and a badly formed and slovenly hand cannot be deciphered.

32. It is incredible how reading is retarded by undue haste. This gives rise to hesitation, stumbling, and repetition on the part of pupils who venture beyond their powers, and then when they go astray, lack confidence even in what they already know. . . .

Book I, Chapter 3

The Comparative Merits of Private and Public Education

1. But now let our young pupil begin gradually to grow and to leave his mother's lap and begin serious studies. The most important question now is whether it is better to keep the student in the privacy of his own home or to hand him over to a large school and to what may be termed public instructors.

2. The latter course, I observe, has won the approval not only of those who have molded the manners of most famous states but also by the most eminent authorities on education. It must, however, be admitted that some disagree with this well-nigh universal practice on grounds of private opinion. Two considerations in particular appear to weigh with these critics. The first is that it is safer on moral grounds: avoid a throng of youths whose age is peculiarly prone to vicious practices, whence it is claimed and I would the claim were false that evil consequences have frequently arisen. The second consideration is this, that no matter who the future teacher is, it seems likely that if he has but one pupil he will devote his time more freely to him than if he has to share that time amongst several.

3. The former plea is by far the more important. For if it were submitted that schools, whilst affording better instruction, do harm to morals, I should judge the principles of right living of more importance than those of the noblest oratory. But to my mind the two things are inseparably bound up together.

4. It is thought that in schools morals are corrupted. Now it is perfectly true that this does happen sometimes, but it happens in the home also: and of that we have countless instances, just as we have countless instances of the maintenance in both places and a spotless reputation. It is the natural disposition of the boy and the care taken of him which make all the difference. Given a mind inclined towards things evil, given carelessness in the molding and regarding of the boy's purity in early years, and it will be found that seclusion offers just as good an opportunity for evil practices. For a private tutor may be a scoundrel, and intercourse with wicked slaves no safer than intercourse with immoral youths of free birth.

5. But if the boy's natural disposition is good and if the parents are not sunk in blind and careless sloth, it is possible to choose the noblest instructors (and that is the foremost consideration).

6. Would that we did not ourselves corrupt the morals of our children! Even from earliest infancy we spoil them by our indulgence. The soft way in which we bring them up, calling it kindness, saps all strength of mind. . . .

Book I, Chapter 3

Discerning Ability in the Young and of Handling Them

1. The skilled teacher, when a pupil is entrusted to his care, will first discover his ability and natural disposition. A good memory is the chief indication of ability in a pupil and its excellence lies in two things, ease in acquiring knowledge and accuracy retaining it. Next comes the faculty of imitation, but that also is characteristic of a teachable nature, i.e. provided that the pupil reproduces what he is taught and not a person's appearance, for example.

14. As for corporal punishment, though it is a recognized practice and though Chrysippus does not object to it, I am altogether opposed to it, first because it is disgusting, fit only for slaves and undoubtedly an insult (as appears, if you change the age of the victim): in the next place, because a pupil whose mind so ill befits a free man's son as not to be corrected by reproof, will remain obdurate even in face of blows like the vilest of slaves: and finally because such chastisement will be quite unnecessary if there is some one ever present to supervise the boy's studies with diligence.

15. As things are, it seems usually to happen that the carelessness of *paedagogi* is amended by the pupils being punished for doing what is wrong instead of being compelled to do what is right. Then again, if you coerce the young child by means of blows, how would you deal with the grown youth who cannot thus be driven by fear and has more important things to learn?

16. Remember too that, when children are beaten, many unseemly cries, of which they will afterwards be ashamed, often escape them in their grief or fear, and the shame of this breaks and humil-

iates the spirit and makes them, sick at heart, shun the very light of day.

17. Now if, in choosing guardians and teachers, too little care has been taken to select those of sterling moral character, I am ashamed to mention the shameful practices for which men make this right of corporal punishment an excuse, and the opportunity sometimes afforded to others too by the terror of it in the wretched child's mind.

Book II, Chapter 2

The Character and Responsibilities of the Teacher

1. It is of especial importance that the moral character of these teachers should be considered.

2. I am led to emphasize this point here, not because I attach no importance to the matter in the case of other teachers, too (witness what I said in the preceding book), but because the very age of the pupils makes it more necessary to mention it.

5. He must have no vices himself and tolerate none in his pupils. Let him be stern but not melancholy, friendly but not familiar, lest in the one case he incur dislike, in the other contempt. He must constantly dwell upon the honorable and the good; for the more he admonishes his pupils the less he will require to punish them. He must never lose his temper, yet he will not pass over what deserves correction; he must be simple in his teaching, able to endure hard toil, persevering rather than exacting.

6. He must answer questions readily and put questions himself to those who do not ask them. In praising the recitations of his pupils he must not be either niggardly or extravagant, for in the former case he will arouse a distaste for toil, in the latter a spirit of self-complacency.

7. In correcting faults he will not be harsh and never abusive; for many are driven away from the studies they have entered upon by the fact that some teachers find fault as though they hated the offender.

Discussion Questions

1. Today there is an emphasis on the importance of parents reading to their pre-school children. Would Quintilian agree with this emphasis? What more might he add as important for ensuring their future success in schools?

2. Some people claim there is a second-grade burn-out in children because they are asked to learn too much too soon. How would Quintilian reply to this and what would he recommend?

3. In what ways is the method for teaching writing and reading that Quintilian proposes similar to or different from the methods used in schools today?

4. Is Quintilian in favor of public or private schools? In your opinion, substantiated from his document, would he be in favor of home schooling, charter schools, and/or magnet schools?

5. Quintilian emphasizes that in order to be a good speaker a person must also be of good character. Do you agree with him? Do you think that this is true of well-known public speakers today?

6. Quintilian is not in favor of corporal punishment. What is the policy in the school district in which you hope to teach? In what ways can you apply Quintilian's argument against corporal punishment to the assertive discipline system's use of putting a child's name on the board?

7. How can a school ensure that it only hires teachers with good moral character, as Quintilian suggests? In what ways is this even more important today than in the days of the Roman Empire?

For Further Research on the Internet

A Web page developed by the Molloy College Philosophy Department with many helpful links to Quintilian's work on rhetoric. **http://www.molloy.edu/academic/philosophy/ sophia/Quintilian/quintilian.htm**

A one-page summary of Quintilian's main educational contributions. **http://www.users .globalnet.co.uk/~loxias/quintilian.htm**

Suggestions for Further Reading

Bloodgood, Janet. "Quintilian: A Classical Educator Speaks to the Writing Process." *Reading Research and Instruction* 42 (1) (2002): 30–43.

France, Peter. "Quintilian and Rousseau: Oratory and Education." *Rhetorica, The International Society for the History of Rhetoric* XIII (3) (1995): 301–321.

Gwynn, Aubrey. *Roman Education from Cicero to Quintillian.* New York: Russell & Russell, 1964.

Kennedy, George. *Quintilian,* edited by S. Bowman, *Twayne's World Authors Series: A Survey of the Word's Literature: Latin Literature.* New York: Twayne, 1969.

Sharrock, Alison and Rhiannon Ash. "Quintilian." In *Fifty Key Classical Authors,* edited by A. Sharrock and R. Ash. New York: Routledge, 2002.

Smail, William. "Introduction." In *Quintilian on Education.* New York: Teacher's College Press, 1938.

CHAPTER ACTIVITIES

Linking the Past to the Present

1. Give a speech and have your classmates evaluate it according to a rubric developed according to Cicero's criteria. How does this compare with a Speech 101 rubric?

2. Choose one of the following to debate with a fellow student:

   a. Should home schooling be allowed by the state?   .
   b. Should corporal punishment be used in schools?
   c. Should the education majors have more general education classes or more specialized education classes?

Developing Your Philosophy of Education

The goal of Roman education was to develop the orator. What will be the goal of your teaching? What kind of people will you try to help your students become?

Connecting Theory to Practice

Try to get a scope and sequence chart for the subject you hope to teach in your clinical experience or in the curriculum room in the library. By studying the chart, or interviewing your clinical teacher, see how the subject matter is taught at different grades to accommodate the children's developmental levels.

Educators' Philosophies and Contributions to Education

TABLE 3.1 Philosophy and Contributions of Roman Educators

Educator	Role of Teacher & Learner	View of Curriculum & Methodology	Purpose or Goal of Education	Major Contribution
Cicero	An orator who would teach others rhetoric and how to speak well	Study philosophy, law, history, and jurisprudence or practical ethics	To develop the orator—a person of honor, duty, and high ethics	The first speech teacher—oration or good debates with moral content a basic for all teachers
Quintilian	Teacher is an expert who knows the development level of the child and does not use corporal punishment but respects the child	Rhetorical education, reading, writing, and speaking taught using appropriate methods for the child's age	To form an orator, a public servant, who was a good speaker and a good man	First teacher of teachers, and first to organize pedagogy around development levels of children

CHAPTER 4

Christian Education

The Rise of Christianity

Arising in the Jewish milieu of first-century Palestine, Christianity, the teaching of Christ's message, spread throughout the Roman Empire. The movement became a strong force with which the rest of the world had to reckon.

At the height of the Roman Empire, around the year 4 or 3 B.C., during the reign of the Roman emperor Augustus Caesar (27 B.C.–A.D. 14), Jesus Christ was born in Bethlehem. After living a hidden life working unobtrusively for thirty years, without following the normal educational studies to become a Jewish preacher, Jesus taught for three years a new interpretation of the Bible message emphasizing the love of God for all. Jewish religious leaders struggled with him and eventually had him put to death on a cross for saying he was the Son of God, but he rose from the dead and commissioned his disciples to "Go forth and teach all nations." Jesus, and his followers, will be the subject of this chapter.

His command to his disciples led them to spread his doctrines by traveling throughout the Roman empire. They relied heavily on Christ's pedagogical devices, imitating them so much so that they became characteristics of Christian preaching and Christian teaching. Since Christianity evolved out of Judaism, habits of reading and study in Christian assemblies continued on the trails blazed by Jews in the synagogues. Paul, the scribe, was an effective teacher and preacher who taught by doing textual teaching and writing in the style of the Jewish rabbis.[1] Paul taught that Christianity was for all, not just the Jewish people, and this included women. He became the "apostle to the gentiles," accommodating Christian tenets to Hellenistic thoughts.

In the beginning, Christians had no schools of their own. Christian education was accomplished in the home and the task of teaching was left to the parents and to the Church where, in communal worship through sermons, the dogmas were explained. Christians sent their children to the pagan schools with their classmates to study Greek and Roman literature and rhetoric. Their religious training was thus superimposed upon the classical education rather than being a substitute for it.[2]

Teaching Catechumens

The phrase "Christian education" first appears around 96 A.D. in the writings of Clement of Rome, but it does not indicate any well-developed institutional apparatus for the schooling of converts-to-Christianity. A two to three year period of instruction in the faith or "catechumenate" was common. The catechumens were both men and women, usually in their twenties and beyond, and the same educational process was applied to both sexes before they were admitted to the Church. The Bible was taught in great detail. Both Origen in Alexandria and Tertullian thought secular learning was indispensable to understanding Christianity so they had the students also study Greek literature.[3]

No separate educational system was worked out among the first few generations of believers because their efforts went to establishing the liturgy and ethics. Christian teachers were allowed to teach in classical (pagan) schools. By the fourth century A.D., Christians were employed at all levels of education from the elementary to higher education university chairs. They sought to translate Christian teachings into terms classical pagans could understand and accept.

The First Christian Teachers

The first well-defined institution for Christian education was the **Catechumen and Catechetical School.** The earliest is found in 160 A.D. under Justin Martyr. The teachers, or apologists, sought to teach the converts the difference between Christianity and other philosophies. The developing theory of education recommended that the context of instruction should be drawn mainly from scriptures and from some other Christian writings. The classics were to be included sparingly. The form of instruction followed the grammatical and rhetorical patterns of pagan schools with a few girls also studying with the boys. There was an attempt to build a Christian literature based on pagan sources and to develop a Christian system of schooling in which there was no conflict between faith and culture. Women converts of the wealthy Roman aristocracy as well as their male counterparts learned Greek and Hebrew and read both the scriptures and the homilies and studied the lives of the Church Fathers.[4]

A Christian School System

In 361 A.D. Emperor Julian forbade Christians to teach in pagan schools. He said that they could not teach Homer well if they did not believe in the Greek deities. This led the Christians to realize the importance of building up an extensive Christian school system geared directly to their religious mission with a curriculum that was derived almost exclusively from Christian sources. Clement of Alexandria (160–215 A.D.), Origen (185–254 A.D.) and Augustine (354–430 A.D.) sought a synthesis of pagan and Christian thought in order to develop a Christian culture. Catechetical schools produced theological literature and scholarly works in biblical and theological research (see Map 4.1, The Spread of Christianity). The schools enrolled pagans as well as Christians, laymen as well as clerics, women as well as men.[5] The Council of Constantinople (381 A.D.) decreed the establishment of gratuitous schools for children in every major population area. In 529 A.D. the decree of Justin closed pagan schools. This left Christian education without a rival. The

Map 4.1 The Spread of Christianity

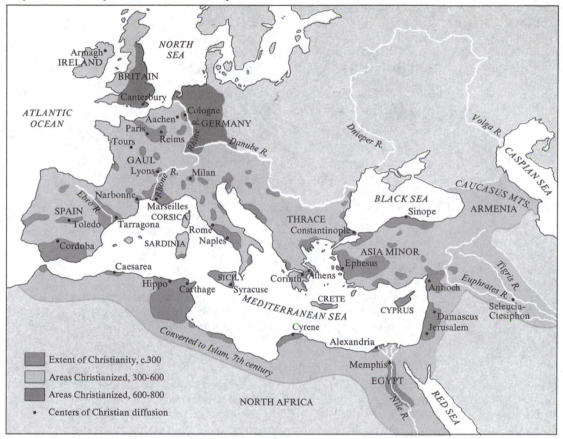

Source: Perry, et al. *Western Civilization: Ideas, Politics and Society,* 3rd online edition. 1989. Used with permission of Houghton Mifflin.

Church stood as the chief guide in determining how to assimilate the new Germanic culture with the Greco-Roman culture and Christian spirituality.

Classical education had promoted the ideal type—a model of the educated man—the orator. Augustine sought to craft a Christian version, which built a bridge between the high culture of classicism and the spirituality of Christian thought. The goal of Christian education was to create a person who realized their patrimony as a child of God and sought to live their life as one.

The age of Christian antiquity extends from the beginning of the Christian era (dated from the approximate time of Jesus' birth) through the fall of the western half of the Roman Empire in the fifth century. Why the Roman Empire fell is a question which scholars still debate today. From the point of view of education, we can note several factors: the family structure was weakened, citizenship and patriotism were no longer taught, and virtue was not stressed or sought as a way of life.[6] The schools were asked to fill in for what was lacking in the family and in society. Ultimately the Roman schools failed due to the barbarian invasions. With the fall of Rome, the age of Antiquity, i.e., the great Mediterranean civilizations of Greece and Rome, also fell. The decline of the Roman social political system saw the decay of pagan schools and the Greek and Roman influence in education. However, Christianity preserved western civilization, culture, and Roman law through the "dark ages" in their monasteries.

For Further Research on the Internet

Links and resources for study of the early church. **http://www.christianitytoday.com/history/features/pages/church.html**

The Ecole Initiative—a hypertext of early Church history on the World Wide Web. **http://www2.evansville.edu/ecoleweb/**

Notes

1. H. Gregory Snyder, "Teachers and Texts in the Ancient World: Philosophers, Jews and Christians," in *Religion in the First Christian Centuries*, edited by D. Sawyer and J. Sawyer (London: Routledge, Taylor & Francis Group, 2000), pp. 194, 202–205.
2. Gillian Clark, "The Fathers and the Children," in *Christianity and Society*, edited by E. Ferguson (New York: Garland Publishing, Inc., 1999), p. 255.
3. Paul McKechnie, "'Women's Religion' and Second-Century Christianity," in *Christianity and Society*, edited by E. Ferguson (New York: Garland Publishing, Inc., 1999), p. 42.
4. Joan Peterson, "The Education of Girls," in *Christianity and Society*, edited by E. Ferguson (New York: Garland Publishing, Inc., 1999), pp. 78–79.
5. Snyder, p. 189.
6. Hugh Trevor-Roper, *The Rise of Christian Europe* (London, New York: W.W. Norton, 1989), pp. 25–28.

Section 4.1: Jesus Christ (4 B.C.–29 A.D.)

Can you imagine teaching a group of people who could hardly read or write a very important body of knowledge that they had to master to such a degree that they could then teach it to others? This is what Jesus of Nazareth successfully did in the first century as a Jewish teacher in Palestine. He taught using stories, analogies, and allegories that touched the hearts of his listeners and were thus engraved in their minds. Jesus, like Socrates, did not personally write any books. He is known through the writings of his followers who wrote down what they heard him say. He was a very successful teacher who was able to convert people from all over the world to follow his message.

Jesus' Life and Times

Jesus Christ was born in Bethlehem in Roman-ruled Palestine in approximately 4 B.C. by today's calendar. Jesus' mother was Mary of Nazareth, daughter of Joachim and Anna. Mary was betrothed to a man named Joseph, a carpenter, who was a descendant of King

David, when she conceived a child. The virgin birth—a universal mythological theme, prefigured in the Old Testament—expresses the early Christian belief in Jesus' extraordinary conception and special identity.[1]

The historical fact of Jesus' existence is not subject to doubt. There are four accounts of Jesus' life found in the New Testament and, in addition, explicit reference is made to him in the *Annals* of the Roman historian Tacitus and in the *Jewish Antiquities* of Flavius Josephus.[2] Knowledge of Jesus as a historical person is provided mainly through the New Testament. However, many of the details of his life are unknown to us. His first thirty years were lived in obscurity.[3] The gospels give us only a few details about Jesus' life with Mary and Joseph. We know that after his birth in Bethlehem, his parents fled to Egypt to escape from Herod and spent several years there before they returned to Nazareth in Galilee, where Jesus grew up.

Jesus' Education

We can assume some facts about his early life from knowing about the education of middle- to lower-class Hebrews of that time; Jesus' education presumably followed the forms customary to a Jewish youth. His mother taught him behavior, tradition, and simple religion. At the synagogue school, he learned reading, writing, and the basic principles of religion as found in the Old Testament. He did not, however, study with any famous scribes as was customary for those training to be rabbis. Joseph taught Jesus his own professional skill as a carpenter. "Jesus must have resembled Joseph in his way of working, in the features of his character, in his way of speaking. Jesus' realism, his eye for detail ...his preference for using everyday situations ...all this reflects his childhood and the influence of Joseph."[4] Jesus spoke Aramaic, but he also understood Greek and Hebrew. He could read Hebrew aloud and showed himself well-versed in Jewish traditions and ritual, law, and scriptures.[5]

Jesus, the Teacher

At the age of thirty, Jesus began a more public life, gathering disciples around him, preaching in the synagogues, and allowing those who heard him to address him as Rabbi and Teacher.[6] (See the timeline of Jesus' life in Figure 4.1.) Jesus taught that all people should obey God's laws and love Him and love their fellow men. Jesus made a personal appeal to the hearts and emotions of his listeners, teaching that every human being is the child of a loving, heavenly Father who cares for his children.[7]

After preaching for three years, Jesus was arrested by the religious authorities and crucified by the Romans for "perverting the nation." The gospels report that Jesus rose from the dead on the third day and commissioned his followers to "go out into all the world and preach the good news." Jesus' teaching continues to provide light and guidance for moral conduct.

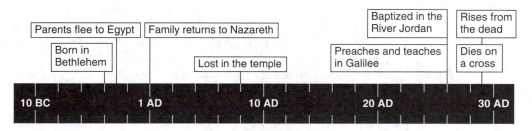

Figure 4.1   Jesus' Life and Times

Jesus' Importance for Education

Jesus was known as a teacher by his actions and words; he was depicted as such and called teacher in some forty texts in the gospels.[8] An analysis of Jesus as a teacher, and a study of his philosophy of education, can assist education students immensely.

Who Jesus taught was distinctive—people others would never accept as students, such as women, outcasts, tax collectors, and Romans. Especially in his dealings with women, Jesus professed a new cultural order. Jesus healed and showed compassion for women.[9]

Jesus taught in words as well as deeds. He was kind and caring towards everyone with whom he came in contact. Jesus shows masterly use of language to teach. Jesus did not write anything down because he took care to speak in a way that would be remembered.[10] Jesus knew that the majority of people were illiterate in his time so he taught orally and asked his followers to pass down his oral tradition. Jesus, who taught in his native Aramaic, mastered a style of speaking which had variety, originality, immediacy, and congruence. Jesus spoke with simplicity, using vivid imagery from everyday peasant life. Most of his neighbors were farmers or fishermen, so his parables are about fishermen fishing and farmers sowing seeds.[11] He used images that his audience could relate to directly.

Jesus' teachings can be linked to the wisdom tradition of Jerusalem as he used short sayings or proverbs to communicate familiar cultural and moral truths. An example is the familiar proverb, "No one puts a lamp under a lamp stand." This proverb is used to encourage his disciples to share the good news they have heard. Light is also used allegorically to refer to a person's understanding of the message preached by Jesus.[12]

A study of the sound of Jesus' teaching through sayings reveals his use of rhythm, rhyme, alliteration, assonance, and word-play suited in an impressively fine way to both the image and purpose of expression. According to the research of J. Dillon, there are five categories of form found in Jesus' language: his figures of speech, parables, illustrations, dialectic, and discourse. The figures of speech used by Jesus include similes, metaphors, aphorisms, allegories, and clever analogies. Jesus' parables are not merely characteristic but distinctive of his teaching.[13]

By using parables he kept the attention of his listeners, whether they were educated or not, and by means of the most ordinary parts of daily life, he shed light on the deepest supernatural mysteries. We can say without prejudice that he was an inspired speaker. The central concept in Jesus' preaching is the Reign of God, but other themes include justice and solidarity, wealth and riches, forgiveness, prayer, and love of one's enemies. Pheme Perkins states that "many people find the theme of love of one's enemies as the most unbelievable of all Jesus' teachings."[14]

Jesus' Philosophy of Education

Jesus' kind and caring personality as a teacher was a trait he wanted his disciples to share. He taught well and he wanted all of his students to learn well. "The multiplicity of Jesus' methods and principles shows his versatility as well as mastery of teaching. Furthermore, these methods seem to be modern. Not only did Jesus exhibit all the methods and principles of today, he also set the standard for the future, anticipating the whole of modern educational science and modern scientific pedagogy."[15] The didactic methods used by Jesus include: lecture, reading from texts (scripture), storytelling, illustration, parallel sayings (repetition), and silence (wait time). His interactive methods included: conversation, discussion forum, question-answer, and panel (answer-question). His activity methods were: object lesson, dramatics, demonstration, laboratory, and topical research.[16] Jesus' curriculum was scripture and the message of God's merciful love for all His creatures. Finally, the purpose of education was to reach one's supernatural end by following God's law and doing good while on earth. "You shall love the Lord your God with all your heart, with all your soul, and all your mind. And you shall love your neighbor as yourself. There is no other commandment greater than these."

Notes

1. Laurence Freeman, *Jesus the Teacher Within* (New York: Continuum International Publishing Co., 2000), p. 87.
2. Jose Maria Pujol Bertran, "God Made Man: Jesus Christ, the Incarnate and Redeeming Word," in *Faith Seeking Understanding; A Complete Course of Theology*, edited by C. Belmonte (Manila: Studium Theologiae Foundation, Inc., 1993), p. 259.
3. Freeman, p. 86.
4. Jose Maria Escriva de Balaguer, "In Joseph's Workshop," in *Christ Is Passing By* (Chicago: Scepter Press, 1973), p. 81.
5. J. T. Dillon, *Jesus as a Teacher: A Multidisciplinary Case Study* (Bethesda, MD: International Scholars Publications, 1995), p. 131.
6. Connie Leean Seraphine, "Jesus," in *Fifty Major Thinkers on Education*, edited by J. Palmer (London: Routledge, 2001), p. 21.
7. Marie Noel Keller, "Jesus the Teacher," *Journal of Research on Christian Education* 7 (1) (1998), p. 23.
8. Gregory John Riley, "Words and Deeds: Jesus as Teacher and Jesus as Pattern of Life," *Harvard Theological Review* 90 (Oct. 1997), p. 427.
9. Pheme Perkins, "Jesus as Teacher," in *Understanding Jesus Today*, edited by H. C. Kee (Cambridge: Cambridge University Press., 1990), p. 37.
10. Dillon, p. 124.
11. Keller, p. 23.
12. Perkins, pp. 42–43.
13. Dillon, p. 80.
14. Perkins, pp. 85–86.
15. Ibid., pp. 180–181.
16. Ibid.

Questions to Guide Your Reading

1. As you read Chapter 13 of St. Matthew, usually called the "parabolic discourse" list the different parables you encounter.
2. An analogy is a comparison of two things that agree with one another in some respect. Two figures of speech that express analogies are similes and metaphors. See how many analogies, similes, and metaphors you can find in Chapter 13.
3. An aphorism is a concise statement of a principle or maxim. It is a short, terse (polished, elegant, and to the point) formulation. See how many aphorisms you can find in Chapter 13.

READING 4.1:
MATTHEW CHAPTER 13
THE PARABLES OF THE KINGDOM

Parable of the Sower, the Meaning of the Parables

That same day Jesus went out of the house and sat beside the sea. And great crowds gathered about him, so that he got into a boat and sat there; and the whole crowd stood on the beach. And he told them many things in parables, saying: "A sower went out to sow. And as he sowed, some seeds fell along the path, and the birds came and devoured them. Other seeds fell on rocky ground, where they had not much soil, and immediately they sprang up, because they had no depth of soil, but when the sun rose they were scorched; and because they had no root, they withered away. Other seeds fell upon thorns, and the thorns grew up and choked them. Other seeds fell on good soil and brought forth grain, some a hundredfold, some sixty, some thirty. He who has ears, let him hear."

Then the disciples came and said to him, "Why do you speak to them in parables?" And he answered them, "To you it has been given to know the secrets of the kingdom of heaven, but to them it has not been given. For to him who has will more be given, and he will have abundance; but for him who has not, even what he has will be taken away. This is why I speak to them in parables, because seeing they do not see, and hearing they *do not hear,* nor do they understand. With them indeed is fulfilled the prophecy of Isaiah which says:

You shall indeed hear but never
understand, and you shall indeed see but
never perceive.
For this people's heart has grown dull,
and their ears are heavy of hearing,
and their eyes they have closed,

Source: From *The Navarre Bible: St. Matthew.* Revised Standard Version, Catholic Edition [RSVCE] copyrighted 1965, 1966 by The Division of Christian Education of The National Council of Churches of Christ in the U.S.A. and used by permission.

lest they should perceive with their
eyes, and hear with their ears,
and understand with their heart,
and turn to me to heal them.

And blessed are your eyes, for they see, and your ears, for they hear. Truly, I say to you, many prophets and religious men longed to see what you see, and did not see it, and to hear what you hear and did not hear it.

"Hear then the parable of the sower. When any one hears the word of the kingdom and does not understand it, the evil one comes and snatches away what is sown in his heart; this is what was sown along the path. As for what was sown on rocky ground, this is he who hears the word and immediately receives it with joy, yet he has no root in himself, but endures for a while, and when tribulation or persecution arises on account of the word, immediately he falls away. As for what was sown among thorns, this is he who hears the word, but the cares of the world and the delight in riches choke the word, and it proves unfruitful. As for what was sown on good soil, this is he who hears the word and understands it; he indeed bears fruit, and yields, in one case a hundredfold, in another sixty, and in another thirty."

The Parable of the Weeds

Another parable he put before them, saying, "The kingdom of heaven may be compared to a man who sowed his field, but while men were sleeping, his enemy came and sowed weeds among the wheat, and went away. So when the plants came up and bore grain, then the weeds appeared also. And the servants of the householder said to him, 'Sir, did you not sow good seed in your field? How then has it weeds?' He said to them, 'An enemy has done this.' The servants said to him, 'Then do you want us to go and gather them?' But he said, 'No; lest in gathering the weeds you root up the wheat along with them. Let both grow together until the harvest; and at harvest time I will tell the reapers, Gather the weeds first and bind them in bundles to be burned, but gather the wheat into my barn.'"

The Mustard Seed; the Leaven

Another parable he put before them saying, "The kingdom of heaven is like a grain of mustard seed which a man took and sowed in his field; it is the smallest of all seeds, but when it has grown it is the greatest of shrubs and becomes a tree, so that the birds of the air come and make nests in its branches."

He told them another parable. "The kingdom of heaven is like leaven which a woman took and hid in three measures of meal, till it was all leavened."

All this Jesus said to the crowds in parables; indeed he said nothing to them without a parable. This was to fulfill what was spoken by the Prophet:

I will open my mouth in parables.
I will utter what has been hidden
since the foundation of the world.

The Parable of the Weeds Explained

Then he left the crowds and went into the house. And his disciples came to him saying, "Explain to us the parable of the field." He answered, "He who sows the good seed is the Son of man; the field is the world, and the good seed means the sons of the kingdom; the weeds are the sons of the evil one, and the enemy who sowed them is the devil; the harvest is the close of the age, and the reapers are angels. Just as the weeds are gathered and burned with fire, so will it be at the close of the age. The Son of man will send his angels, and they will gather out of his kingdom all causes of sin and all evildoers, and throw them into the furnace of fire; there men will weep and gnash their teeth. Then the righteous will shine like the sun in the kingdom of their Father. He who has ears, let him hear."

The Hidden Treasure; the Pearl; the Net

"The kingdom of heaven is like a treasure hidden in a field, which a man found and covered up; then in his joy he goes and sells all that he has and buys that field.

"Again, the kingdom of heaven is like a merchant in search of fine pearls, who, on finding one pearl of great value, went and sold all that he had and bought it.

"Again, the kingdom of heaven is like a net which was thrown into the sea and gathered fish of every kind; when it was full, men drew it ashore and sat down and sorted the good into vessels but threw away the bad. So it will be at the close of the age. The angels will come out and separate the evil from the righteous, and throw them into the furnace of fire; there men will weep and gnash their teeth.

"Have you understood all this?" They said to him, "Yes." And he said to them, "Therefore every scribe who has been trained for the kingdom of heaven is like a householder who brings out of his treasure what is new and what is old."

No One Is a Prophet in His Own Country

And when Jesus had finished these parables he went away from there, and coming to his own country he taught them in their synagogue, so that they were astonished, and said, "Where did this man get this wisdom and these mighty works? Is not this the carpenter's son? Is not his mother called Mary? And are not his brethren James and Joseph and Simon and Judas? And are not all his sisters with us? Where then did this man get all this?" And they took offense at him. But Jesus said to them, "A prophet is not without honor except in his own country and in his own house." And he did not do many mighty works there, because of their unbelief.

Discussion Questions

1. Jesus' parables are a kind of puzzle used to gain the listeners' attention, excite their curiosity, and fix the parable in their memory. Jesus eventually explains the parable of the sower and the parable of the weeds to his listeners. Can you explain the symbolism of the parable of the mustard seed, the leaven, the hidden treasure, the pearl, and the net?
2. Jesus' students had to master what he was teaching them. In essence, he was the first to teach using "master learning" techniques. What are some other subjects which need to be mastered?
3. In the parable of the sower, Jesus speaks of the seed that falls on good ground and the seed that falls on stony ground. We can make an analogy using the student who learns what is needed to pass the test and forgets it and the student who actually learns the subject. What can we as teachers do so that we plant more seeds in students on good ground?

For Further Research on the Internet

A site with links to information on the life, history, and teachings of Jesus Christ.
http://www.lifeofchrist.com

An excellent and complete site on Jesus, his life and times, and the first Christians.
http://www.pbs.org/wgbh/pages/frontline/shows/religion/

Suggestions for Further Reading

Dillon, J. T. *Jesus as a Teacher: A Multidisciplinary Case Study*. Bethesda, MD.: International Scholars Publications, 1995.

Escriva de Balaguer, Jose Maria. "In Joseph's Workshop." In *Christ Is Passing By*. Chicago: Scepter Press, 1973.

Freeman, Laurence. *Jesus the Teacher Within*. New York: Continuum International Publishing Co., 2000.

Keller, Marie Noel. "Jesus the Teacher." *Journal of Research on Christian Education* 7 (1) (1998): 19–36.

Perkins, Pheme. "Jesus as Teacher." In *Understanding Jesus Today*, edited by H. C. Kee. Cambridge: Cambridge University Press, 1990.

Pujol Bertran, Jose Maria. "God Made Man: Jesus Christ, the Incarnate and Redeeming Word." In *Faith Seeking Understanding, A Complete Course of Theology*, edited by C. Belmonte. Manila: Studium Theologiae Foundation, Inc., 1993.

Riley, Gregory John. "Words and Deeds: Jesus as Teacher and Jesus as Pattern of Life." *Harvard Theological Review* 90 (Oct. 1997): 427–436.

Seraphine, Connie Leean. "Jesus." In *Fifty Major Thinkers on Education*, edited by J. Palmer. London: Routledge, 2001.

Section 4.2: St. Augustine (Aurelius Augustine) (354–430 A.D.)

Can you imagine teaching a class that has students who are young and old, rich and poor, men and women, boys and girls, literate and illiterate? This may seem to be an impossible task, but this mixed group can be found in citizenship classes, driver's education classes, G.E.D. classes, and religious instruction classes. Augustine wrote instructions that are still helpful to teachers today. He wrote them for his catechism teachers who had diverse classes.

Augustine's Life and Family

Aurelius Augustine was born on November 13, 354 A.D. in Thagaste, Africa. His father, Patricius, was a pagan citizen of slender means who struggled to give his son the best rhetorical education available at that time. His mother, Monica, was a devout Christian who instilled the truths of the faith in her son when he was very young and later prayed for her son's conversion back to the faith of his youth. The *Confessions* is Augustine's autobiography, and he was one of the first to write in this literary format.[1] It covers the first thirty-three years of his life. From Augustine's comments in this autobiography, we know that he had at least one brother, Navigius, and two sisters.

Augustine's Education

In *The Confessions,* Augustine gives details about his education. He loved words from his infancy and in school he learned spelling, grammar, vocabulary in Greek and Latin, and arithmetic by memorization. He developed an excellent memory and a love for Latin, but his slow learning of Greek and arithmetic led to many beatings, as corporal punishment was the accepted way to correct students' errors. Augustine, a sensitive, strong-tempered lad, later looked back on his school days as a miserable experience, valuable only as training for the conflicts, injustices, and disappointments of adult life.[2]

When Augustine was sixteen, he had to leave school due to his parents' lack of financial resources. It seems that Augustine's father died around this time and Monica took over responsibility for his education. The next year, he was able to go to Carthage to continue his education. He received a classical education in the best tradition of a fourth century Roman gentleman. In Africa, Roman education was highly esteemed and brought status to men fortunate enough to receive it. The aim of education was the same as envisioned by Cicero—to produce the orator, a man who could give pleasure through his argument, vivacity, and style.

Augustine the Orator, Philosopher, and Rhetorician

Augustine became a rhetorician (public orator) and teacher in Carthage and a renowned Latin scholar. He also became a well-known womanizer and took a concubine by whom he had a son, Adeodatus.[3]

Augustine began his philosophic journey at the age of nineteen. He was searching for wisdom when he read Cicero's *The Hortensius*. He experienced a profound change in his life, his first religious conversion, and although he fell into serious error, it was here that he began his lifelong search for truth.[4] He became enthralled with the Manichean philosophy, a philosophy that presents the universe as locked in a continual struggle between good and evil (similar to the later ideas of Marxism) and asserts that although reason is the human's highest ability, we cannot really know anything completely and are thus locked into skepticism.[5]

In 375, Augustine returned from Carthage to his hometown, Thagaste, to teach literature and propagate his Manichean "wisdom" among the educated Romans. Monica, an impressive woman who had dreams by which she foresaw her son's future life, prayed for her son's conversion.[6]

Augustine went to Rome in 382, and in 385 he was appointed professor of rhetoric in Milan, at the time a seat of imperial government, where he met Milan's bishop, Ambrose. He began to study Plato's philosophy and found an intellectual order and harmony not found in Manicheanism; this helped ready Augustine for his "intellectual" conversion to Christianity.[7] He was finally able to make his "moral" conversion when, on Easter night, April 24, 387, at the age of thirty-three, he received baptism from Ambrose. His son and friends were baptized, too. Due to ill health, he retired from his public position and soon returned to North Africa to begin writing.[8] His mother, Monica, died soon after his baptism—her life's work completed. A few years later Adeodatus died suddenly and Augustine gave himself completely to the Church. (See the timeline of Augustine's life in Figure 4.2.)

Augustine, the Bishop and Preacher

In 391, Augustine was ordained to the priesthood in Hippo Regius (modern Bone, Algeria); five years later he became bishop. Augustine was a powerful speaker and an excellent preacher. His classical education served him well and provided him with many examples and analogies to explain doctrines.[9] He used Greek philosophic content, especially Plato's ideas, to explain Christian theology. Augustine's extensive writings include 93 books, 300 letters, and 400 written sermons.[10] *The Confessions, The City of God, On Christian Doctrine,* and *De Magistro, a treatise on education,* had a profound influence on the subsequent development of Western thought, culture, and education. Augustine encouraged people to use the schools of the day to study classical culture along with the Christian doctrine, thus allowing the synthesis between the culture of antiquity and the developing Christian culture.

On August 24, 410, the inconceivable happened: a Gothic army entered Rome. By 429–430 A.D., the Vandals had invaded North Africa. Those who fought back were killed, those who accommodated the invaders lived to see the collapse of Roman society. Augustine reacted immediately to this disaster with long sermons and a series of letters. Augustine must be reckoned as one of the architects of the unified Christianity that survived the barbarian invasions of the fifth century and emerged as the religion of medieval Europe. Augustine died on August 28, 430 A.D., active in mind and body until the end.[11]

Augustine's Contribution to Educational Philosophy

Augustine sought to reconcile Christian faith with classical culture. Christians were not sure if they could send their children to pagan schools. Augustine helped to build a bridge between classicism and Christianity by explaining that the study of the Greek and Latin liberal arts (literature, rhetoric, grammar, logic, arithmetic, geometry, astronomy, and

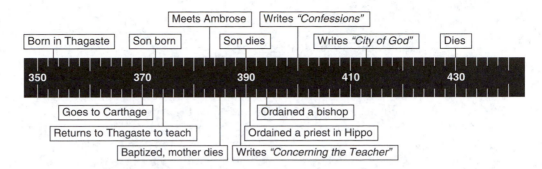

Figure 4.2   St. Augustine's Life and Times

music) would help students to develop intellectual skills. He felt that the liberal arts were fundamental disciplines because the principles on which they were founded are absolutely true and are the essential elements in understanding the truth. Such training could help the Christians to understand scriptures and doctrine.[12]

St. Augustine set the pattern and tone for Christian education in Western Europe for centuries to come by his synthesis of what today we call a "Christian classical liberal arts education" which was particularly influential in determining the content of the medieval curriculum in monastic schools.[13]

Only three of St. Augustine's works deal specifically with education. The first of these is *The Teacher (De Magistro)*, written in the form of a dialogue, and dealing with the problem of communication between teacher and pupil. In many ways, Augustine's study of words as signs makes him one of the first philosophic analysts, i.e., one who critically examines the language associated with teaching. The second is *On Christian Doctrine, De Doctrina Christiana*, which deals with the problem of Christian curriculum, setting out the Christian classical liberal arts education. Finally, in *The Instruction of the Uninstructed, De Catechizandis Rudibus*, Augustine speaks about the principles of teaching to be observed by the Christian teacher when he instructs those who come to seek an understanding of the faith.[14]

Augustine's Philosophy of Education

In these selections from *The Teacher* and *Concerning the Instruction of the Uninstructed*, St. Augustine's philosophy of language and philosophy of teaching are portrayed very clearly and one can see the important contributions he makes to the field. This work examines the encounter between teacher and student, explaining the relationship between the words we use as signs of the knowledge by which we know. In this work, Augustine expresses his definite and novel opinions on the role of the teacher, the methodology of instruction, and the importance of relating the curriculum to the needs of the students. He has practical advice of general value for teachers.

The teacher should teach like a father teaches his son, not striving to impart knowledge, but helping the child to understand words, signs, and the concepts they represent. Having a student memorize and recite someone else's text is not teaching, according to Augustine.[15] The teacher should take into consideration what his students already know and build on that, teaching using a dialogue format Augustine terms as "soliloquia"; two voices talking instead of one, interaction of teacher and student seeking the truth. Effective teaching means a teacher speaking with enthusiasm and motivating the students to want to learn. Augustine says that human beings can be teachers, but only in an analogical sense.[16] God is the true teacher within us that illuminates us and helps us understand things. Using visual metaphors, Augustine talks about the "flash of insight" we get when we understand. (Later we will see that Thomas Aquinas will also take up this issue.) Finally, he emphasizes that the teacher must be a role model, dealing fairly and compassionately with the students.

The curriculum includes the Bible and the teaching of the Fathers with a classical basis. Study is not just to memorize facts, but to discover the intelligibility of the material, to discover the truth in things. The educational environment should be pleasant, with students motivated to learn, and with the capacity to do so. The purpose of education is to help make us what we are to become, children of the heavenly city. Ultimately, education is for happiness.[17] "He teaches me who puts before my eyes, or any bodily sense, or even my mind itself, those things which I want to know."[18]

Notes

1.   Simon Harrison, "Augustine on What We Owe to Our Teachers," in *Philosophers on Education: New Historical Perspectives,* edited by A. O. Rorty. (London: Routledge, 1998), p. 66.
2.   Aurelius Augustine, *Confessions,* translated by H. Chadwick. (Oxford: Oxford University Press., 1991), pp. 14–15, 19–20.
3.   Peter Brown, *Augustine of Hippo: A Biography* (Berkeley: University of California Press, 1969), pp. 23–31, 36–37.
4.   Pope John Paul II, *Augustine of Hippo: Apostolic Letter* (Boston: Daughters of St. Paul, 1986).
5.   Gerald Gutek, *Historical and Philosophical Foundations of Education: A Biographical Introduction* (Upper Saddle River, NJ: Merrill/Prentice Hall, 2001), p. 58.
6.   Henry Chadwick, *Augustine* (Oxford: Oxford University Press, 1986), p. 7.
7.   Augustine, pp. 19–25, 28–30.
8.   Gary Wills, *Saint Augustine* (New York: Penguin Putnam Inc., 1999), p. 57.
9.   Harrison, p. 67.
10.   Wills, p. 121.
11.   Brown, pp. 109–110.
12.   Kim Paffenroth and Kevin Hughes, *Augustine and Liberal Education* (Aldershot, Hampshire, United Kingdom: Ashgate Publishing LTD, 2000).
13.   George Howie, *St. Augustine: On Education,* translated by George Howie (Chicago: Henry Regnery Company, 1969), pp. 18–19, 23–24; Donald Gallagher, "St. Augustine and Christian Humanism," in *Some Philosophers on Education,* edited by D. Gallagher (Milwaukee: Marquette University Press, 1956), p. 58.
14.   Fannie LeMoine, "Augustine on Education and the Liberal Arts," in *Saint Augustine the Bishop: A Book of Essays,* edited by F. LeMoine and C. Kleinhenz (New York & London: Garland Publishing, Inc., 1994), p. 181ff.
15.   Philip Quinn, "Augustinian Learning," in *Philosophers on Education: New Historical Perspectives,* edited by A. O. Rorty (London: Routledge, 1998), p. 81–82; Timothy Valentine, "Enlightened and Eloquent: Augustine on Education," *Philosophy of Education* (2001), p. 388.
16.   Timothy Valentine, "Enlightened and Eloquent: Augustine on Education," *Philosophy of Education* (2001), p. 388.
17.   Ibid., p. 390.
18.   Aurelius Augustine, "On the Teacher," in *Augustine,* edited by C. A. Kirwan (London: Routledge, 1989), p. 225.

Questions to Guide Your Reading

1. What are the two things St. Augustine says a teacher must do if he/she wants to be sure to present an effective lesson?

2. Before a teacher talks to a group, what must he/she find out about the people who are in the group? If a teacher is instructing only one person, is this also applicable or are there other things to find out about the person?

3. Above all, how must a teacher approach his/her task as a teacher?

READING 4.2:
THE TEACHER AND
CONCERNING THE INSTRUCTION
OF THE UNINSTRUCTED

The Teacher's Approach to His Task

I have a greater liking for learning than for teaching, for this is the advice given us by the Apostle James (1:19) "Let every man be quick to hear but slow to speak." Thus, the sweetness of truth should move us to learn, whereas teaching is imposed on us by the necessity of love. We should therefore hope that the need for one man to teach another will pass away and that we shall all lay ourselves open to the instruction of God.

There are many who learn peacefully but who teach in an agitated manner. Although they themselves have a patient teacher, they are harsh toward the learner. We all know how peacefully the scriptures teach us. A man comes and reads the precepts of God, drinking them in peacefully from a peaceful source; then, being approached by someone who wants to learn something from him, he storms and rages, accusing the learner of understanding too slowly and throwing him into confusion. The result is that the learner fails to get a sufficiently clear understanding of the lessons which the teacher himself has had the opportunity to hear in a more peaceful atmosphere.

Concerning the Instruction of the Uninstructed

Clearly there is one situation which we should not pass over. That is the case of a man coming to you to be instructed, who is well-educated in the liberal arts, has already made up his mind to be a Christian and has come with the express purpose of becoming one. It can almost be taken for granted that a man of this sort has already gained a considerable knowledge of our scriptures and literature. Furnished with

Source: *The Works of Aurelius Augustine.* Marcus Dods, ed. Edinburgh: Clark 1872–1888. Vol IX Christian Education and the Instruction of the Uninstructed.

this, he may now have come simply to become a partaker of the sacraments; for it is usual for such men to look carefully into things, not just at the moment when they become Christians but before that. At an early stage they enter into discussion with anyone they can find, and argue about the opinions they hold in their minds. Therefore, with such people we must adopt a briefer method, avoiding the boring repetition of what they already know and passing over it with a light and discreet touch. We would say that we understand they are already familiar with this and that, and then rapidly review all the facts which need to be impressed upon the minds of the uninstructed and uneducated. We should try to teach in such a way that, if our man of culture is already familiar with some part of our subject matter, he does not hear it coming as though from a teacher. At the same time, we should see to it that, if he is still ignorant of something, he will learn it while we are going over points with which we understand him to be already familiar. . . .

A sense of weariness is induced in a speaker when the person listening to him remains unmoved, either because in fact he feels nothing or because he does not indicate by any physical movement that he understands or is pleased with what is said. We feel like this, not because it is proper that we should be greedy for the praises of men, but because what we are offering belongs to God. The more we love those to whom we speak, the more we want them to like what is offered for their salvation. As a result, if we fail in this, we are pained, weakened, and lose heart in mid-career as if we were expending our efforts to no purpose. . . . We are forced to give instruction to someone either at the command of a person we are unwilling to offend or because of the persistence of people we cannot get rid of. In such circumstances we come with minds already perturbed to a task which requires great calmness; we bewail the fact that we are not allowed to maintain the orderly sequence we want to observe in our occupations and the fact that we cannot possibly be adequate for everything we are asked to do. Thus, our talk becomes less acceptable because of our distress, and flourishes less exuberantly because it is drawn from the arid soil of our sadness....

We often feel it wearisome to go over and over again matters which are thoroughly familiar to us and better suited to little children. If this is the case with us, then we should try to meet our pupils with a brother's, a father's and a mother's love. Once we are thus united to them in heart, all this subject matter will seem new to us exactly as it will to them. For so great is the power of a sympathetic disposition of mind that our hearers are affected while we are speaking and we are affected while they are learning. Thus, we take up our dwelling in each other, and in this way they are, as it were, speaking within us what they are hearing, and in some way we are learning within them what we are teaching. Is it not a common occurrence for us that, when we show to people who have never seen them certain extensive and beautiful vistas either in a city or in the country, scenes which we have been in the habit of passing by without any sense of pleasure simply because we have become accustomed to the sight of them, we find our own enjoyment renewed in their enjoyment of the novelty of the scene? We experience this more vividly in proportion to the intimacy of our friendship with the people concerned. Insofar as we are united to them by the bond of love, things which previously were old become new to us....

We should instill a sense of confidence so that he may give free expression to any objection which suggests itself to him; at the same time we should ask whether he has already heard the same things on a previous occasion and whether perhaps they are failing to move him now because they are well-known to him and commonplace. We should thus shape our course in accordance with his answers, either speaking in a simpler style with more detailed explanation, or refuting some antagonistic opinion. Instead of attempting a more prolonged exposition of matters which are well known to him, we might give a brief summary of them and pick out some of those events which are handled in a mystical manner in the scriptures, particularly in the narrative passages; by giving an exposition and explanation of these we may make our talk more attractive. But if our hearer is of a very sluggish disposition and deaf to all such sources of pleasure, then we must simply bear with him in a spirit of compassion. After briefly going over other points, we should then, in a man-

ner calculated to inspire him with awe, impress upon him the truths which are most indispensable on the unity of the Catholic Church, temptations, and the Christian manner of living in view of the judgment to come. In this way we ought to say much to God on his behalf rather than much to him about God.

It also happens frequently that a man who has at first been our attentive listener becomes exhausted, either by the effort of listening or by standing, and no longer opens his mouth to approve what is said but rather to yawn and gape—he even exhibits an involuntary desire to go away. When we observe this, it is our duty to refresh his mind by saying something seasoned with a decent cheerfulness and appropriate to the matter under discussion. Or we might say something wonderful and startling or perhaps even painful and distressing; whatever we say in this way will be all the better if it affects our hearer immediately so that a quick sense of self-concern may keep his attention on the alert. Nevertheless, it should not be of the sort which wounds his sense of shame by any harshness attached to it; rather it should be calculated to win him over by the friendliness it conveys....

There is a difference between the method of a person giving private instruction when there are no other people to hand to pass judgment, and the method of one teaching in public surrounded by an audience of people holding various opinions. Again, in the practice of teaching the effort will be of one sort when only one individual is being taught, while all the rest listen with the attitude of people judging and endorsing things well known to them. It will be different when all present are waiting for what we have to set before them. And again in this same instance one technique is necessary when all are seated in private with the intention of beginning a discussion and another is necessary when the people sit silently with their attention focused on a single speaker who is about to address them from a raised platform. Under these circumstances it will also make a big difference whether our audience is small or large, or whether it is composed of educated or uneducated people or of both. It will also matter whether they are city-bred, rustics, or a mixture of both, or whether it is an audience in which all sorts of people are mingled. For different people must necessarily have different effects on the man who has to speak to them and teach them. The address we deliver will bear certain features expressive of the feelings of the mind from which it proceeds, and it will affect the audience in various ways in accordance with the speaker's frame of mind; at the same time the listeners themselves will variously influence one another by their mere presence together. But since we are now talking about the instruction of uneducated people, I can tell you from my own experience that I find myself differently affected according as I see before me for the purpose of instruction a highly educated man or a dull fellow, a citizen or a foreigner, a rich man or a poor man, a private individual or a man of honors, a person occupying some position of authority, a civilian of this nation or that, of this or that age or sex, a member of one sect or another, or one associated with this or that popular error. My talk always takes its start, proceeds, and reaches its conclusion in accordance with the varying state of my feelings. Also, since the same medicine is not to be given to all, although to all the same love is due, so love labors hard with some people, becomes weak with others, is at pains to edify some, dreads being a cause of offense to others, stoops before some, lifts itself erect before others, is gentle to some, severe to others, an enemy to none, a mother to all.

Discussion Questions

1. Augustine states, "We bewail the fact that we are not allowed to maintain the orderly sequence we want to observe in our occupations which cannot possibly be adequate for everything we are asked to do." Explain how teachers in the twenty-first century would relate to this. What has and what has not remained the same?
2. Augustine indicates a briefer period of instruction for those who already know the basics. How could this be accomplished in a full classroom of students in today's school?
3. Augustine says that the teacher has to accommodate his instructions to fit all his students. How can a teacher alter instructions for the more educated students and also be able to suit the needs of the less capable students?
4. Augustine seems to say that a well-educated man is easier to bring into the faith. Does that mean Augustine felt that the educated made better Christians? Explain why you agree or disagree with him.

For Further Research on the Internet

An excellent site with links to his biography, images, and his works on the Internet, with commentaries. **http://ccat.sas.upenn.edu/jod/augustine.html**

A Britannica site on Augustine with links to his biography, *The City of God,* and *Confessions.* **http://www.geocities.com/Athens/1534/august.html**

Suggestions for Further Reading

Augustine, Aurelius. "On the Teacher." In *Augustine,* edited by C. A. Kirwan. London: Routledge, 1989.

Augustine, Aurelius. *Confessions.* Translated by H. Chadwick. Oxford: Oxford University Press, 1991.

Brown, Peter. *Augustine of Hippo: A Biography.* Berkeley: University of California Press, 1969.

Chadwick, Henry. *Augustine.* Oxford: Oxford University Press, 1986.

Gallagher, Donald. "St. Augustine and Christian Humanism." In *Some Philosophers on Education,* edited by D. Gallagher. Milwaukee: Marquette University Press, 1956.

Gutek, Gerald. *Historical and Philosophical Foundations of Education: A Biographical Introduction.* Upper Saddle River, NJ: Merrill/Prentice Hall, 2001.

Harrison, Simon. "Augustine on What We Owe to Our Teachers." In *Philosophers on Education: New Historical Perspectives,* edited by A. O. Rorty. London: Routledge, 1986.

Howie, George. *St. Augustine: On Education*. Translated by George Howie. Chicago: Henry Regnery Company, 1969.

John Paul II, Pope. *Augustine of Hippo: Apostolic Letter*. Boston: Daughters of St. Paul, 1986.

LeMoine, Fannie. "Augustine on Education and the Liberal Arts." In *Saint Augustine the Bishop: A Book of Essays,* edited by F. LeMoine and C. Kleinhenz. New York & London: Garland Publishing, Inc., 1994.

Paffenroth, Kim and Kevin Hughes. *Augustine and Liberal Education*. Aldershot, Hampshire, United Kingdom: Ashgate Publishing LTD, 2000.

Quinn, Philip. "Augustinian Learning." In *Philosophers on Education: New Historical Perspectives,* edited by A. O. Rorty. London: Routledge, 1998.

Wills, Gary. *Saint Augustine*. New York: Penguin Putnam Inc., 1999.

CHAPTER ACTIVITIES

Linking the Past to the Present

Develop a scavenger hunt that leads your students to solve a puzzle or a mystery. Each of the clues will be a hint (like an analogy) that is symbolic of the things that you want them to find. In this way your students can get hands-on practice with metaphors and similes.

Developing Your Philosophy of Education

Think of a metaphor to describe your philosophy of education and use it to introduce your paper. (For instance, "I see teaching as gardening, the teacher plants the seeds of knowledge and . . . ".)

Also in your philosophy of education paper be sure to include your view of yourself as the teacher. How will you approach your task as a teacher and accommodate your instruction to the needs of each of the students, some able to grasp things quickly, and others who will need a little more time to master everything?

Connecting Theory to Practice

Visit the church of your choice and interview the pastor. How is religious instruction organized at this church? At what age do children begin instruction? Who teaches them and what kind of training do the teachers receive? What is the curriculum? How is it determined that they have mastered the requirements? Do adults also receive classes or how do they learn about their religion?

Educators' Philosophies and Contributions to Education

TABLE 4.1   Philosophy and Contributions of Christian Educators

Educator	Role of Teacher & Learner	View of Curriculum & Methodology	Purpose or Goal of Education	Major Contribution
Jesus	A kind and caring teacher of all—men and women, young and old, poor and wealthy	Taught a new world order of peace using vivid imagery and storytelling so that all would master the new teaching	To reach one's supernatural end in heaven by learning that the goal of life is to love God and one's neighbors here on earth	Teaching through storytelling so that all, even the illiterate, can learn
Augustine	The teacher should love the students, assess their prior knowledge, and teach with enthusiasm, motivating the students to want to learn	The Bible and classical liberal arts education taught using a dialogue format or "solilloquia"	To make us what we are to become, happy here on earth and thus children of heaven	First philosophic analyst—studying words as expressions of our knowledge

CHAPTER 5

Medieval Educational Contributions

The Medieval Times as a Historical Period

As the Roman Empire collapsed after the invasion of the Germanic tribes, Europe entered a vast and varied period commonly referred to as the "Medieval Times" or the "Middle Ages." Modern historians generally date the Middle Ages from approximately 500 A.D. (because Rome fell in 476 A.D.) to 1500 (since the Reformation began in 1517). The Middle Ages is broken into three time blocks: Early (500–1000), High (1000–1300) and Late (1300–1500).[1]

By the sixth century what had been the Roman Empire was divided into several states or kingdoms, each ruled loosely by a Germanic tribal chieftain. The Franks became the most powerful and longest lasting of the Germanic kingdoms. Charlemagne expanded this kingdom until it rivaled the glory days of the Roman Empire, bringing about the "Carolingian Renaissance" in the "Early Middle Ages." Unfortunately Charlemagne's son Louis was not as skilled as his father and he divided the kingdom among his three sons. This lead to the disintegration of the empire and its vulnerability to invading tribes (see Map 5.1 of Charlemagne's Empire).

The High Middle Ages began after the breakdown of the Carolingian Empire, when the feudal system emerged as the dominant political system. Local lords took over parcels of land, called manors, and promised protection by their knights for the vassals and serfs who were allowed to live and work on the land. The High Middle Ages was a period of population and economic growth with several important institutions arising such as towns and universities. In the late Middle Ages, the feudal system gradually collapsed and national monarchies arose. When these grew to nation-states, the Middle Ages ended and the Modern Age began.[2]

Map 5.1   Charlemagne's Empire

Source: Anthony Esler, *The Human Venture, Combined Volume: From Prehistory to the Present,* 5th edition, 2004. Reprinted by permission of Pearson Education.

Educational Institutions During the Middle Ages

Most of the schools established by the Romans and the Christians were destroyed during the barbarian invasions. The Christian Church set about reestablishing a system of schools to illuminate faith with learning especially important for clerical training.

Three major lines of educational institutions developed in the medieval periods:

1. Those related directly to the Church—**church schools**
2. Those concerned with educating the feudal aristocracy with chivalric training of knights—**palace schools**
3. Those related to craft or vocational education—**guild training.**[3]

Schools related to the Church included the monastic and convent schools, parish schools, and the cathedral/episcopal schools.

Monasteries as Cultural Centers

Monasteries were the principal cultural and educational centers from the sixth through the eleventh centuries. The Rule of St. Benedict required the monks to spend time each day reading. Therefore books had to be available to be read. Libraries were collected in the monastery and manuscripts were copied. Each monastery had a *scriptorium* or writing room. The requirement of reading necessitated the organization of schools for monks in the monasteries. By the ninth century nearly all monastic houses had schools for the children of the neighborhood. These were called **monastic schools**. Literary education was emphasized but the methodology was rote memory. An eight- to ten-year course of study was developed. Children learned to read the Bible, calculate, and study the arts with an emphasis on grammar, rhetoric, dialectic, and mathematics. Between 600 A.D. and 1100 A.D., 90 percent of the literate men received their instruction in a monastic school.[4]

The Education of Women During the Middle Ages

Medieval civilization can be judged fairly well. Women enjoyed a greater degree of freedom in medieval Frankish society; at least within the nobility and freeman classes there was a more egalitarian and liberated view of women. They were more independent of their fathers and brothers, more capable of making decisions about their lives and allowed to hold landed property and play a role in political life. The education of the average lay woman compared very favorably with that of her husband, and some ladies were leaders of culture, like the royal patroness.

In Christianity there was a spiritual equality of men and women. Most of the learned women of the Middle Ages were nuns. Although the majority of the nuns were at best literate, most of the literary, artistic, scientific, and philosophical stars were found in the nunneries.[5] The nuns ran **convent schools** in which they taught young girls chants and choir-singing as well as reading and writing; and domestic arts such as cooking, weaving, and spinning wool.

Schools Run by the Church

Charlemagne promoted learning in his kingdom; he encouraged the clergy to reopen schools and the nobility to broaden their education. The **parish schools** were run by the priest in the rural areas in each parish and laid the basis for the village school system of later years. Boys and girls could attend to learn the rudiments of literacy. The **cathedral schools** were started to teach future clerics under the direction of the bishop. They were the equivalent of a high school. The **Episcopal schools**, attached to the cathedral, provided elementary level education for all, not just for priest candidates. By 700 A.D., parish schools were established in every area of the Roman Empire: Italy, Spain, Gaul, and Egypt.

Palace Schools

The most important secular school was the **palace school**. At the palace school the liberal arts of grammar, rhetoric, dialectic, arithmetic, astronomy, theology, and Latin were taught. Charlemagne invited Alcuin (735–804 A.D.) to come to direct his palace school and to be his minister of education in charge of educational affairs for the Frankish kingdom. As Charlemagne's chief educational advisor, Alcuin, a revered scholar and teacher, established that all schools should teach the following seven liberal arts: grammar, rhetoric, and logic (the trivium), and arithmetic, geometry, music, and astronomy (the quadrivium).

The sons of the nobility had to be educated into knighthood. The ideals of chivalric education can be summarized as service and obedience, religion, honor, and gallantry. There were three periods of training: (1) the young boy at home with his mother; (2) at 7 or 8 the child was placed with a secular lord or churchman as a page where he learned etiquette, chess, harp, pipe, and Latin; and (3) at 14 or 15 he became a squire. Finally, at age 21, he became a knight.[6]

Girls were also educated during the age of chivalry in the castle of some knight or lord. Their training consisted more of personal service, household duties, good manners, music, and conversation. They learned prayers and poetry, to play the harp, and some studied language and literature. Chivalric training had a beneficial effect on the society of the time.

Guild Schools

The most important vocational schools of the time were the **guild** and **burgher schools**. They represent the first secularization of education. They were controlled by the public authorities and represented the interests of the merchant and artisan classes. A young man who wished to learn a trade would first become an apprentice to a master, advance to become a journeyman, and finally he would be a master of that trade himself.[7]

Arabic Influence on Education

The Arabic world of the early Middle Ages was renowned for its intellectual achievements, its religious/philosophic contributions, and its commercial prosperity. The Islamic (or Moslem) religion spread as the followers of Mohammed traveled from the Middle East through North Africa and into Spain. These Arab scholars (called Moors) introduced Western educators to new ways of thinking about mathematics, natural science, medicine, and philosophy, for they had rediscovered Aristotle. Avicenna (980–1037 A.D.) translated Aristotle's texts of philosophy and had a profound impact on Western education, especially higher education. Averroes (1126–1198 A.D.) was a commentator on Aristotle. He believed that the teacher should seek truth and transmit it to students. Cordoba became known as an educational center for studying philosophy and mathematics.[8]

During the Crusades (1096–1204 A.D.), in the attempt to regain the Holy Land from the Moslems, the Europeans came in contact with Eastern philosophies and ideas as well as Muslim or Arab discoveries and culinary specialties (see Map 5.2, Medieval Expansion). This had a profound effect on helping to create a new world view.

Map 5.2 Medieval Expansion

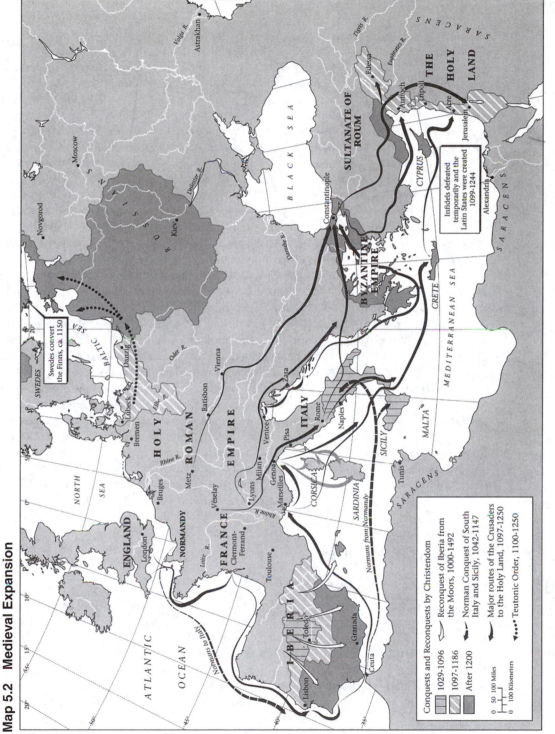

Source: Anthony Esler, *The Human Venture, Combined Volume: From Prehistory to the Present*, 5th edition, 2004. Reprinted by permission of Pearson Education.

The Rise of the University

Higher learning has existed in some form in each of the major groups studied thus far. The scribes and priests of ancient Egypt pursued advanced studies and preserved their research in libraries as early as 200 B.C. The ancient Greeks started the Lyceum and the Academy, models for future universities. However, with the downfall of the Roman Empire, many of these institutions were destroyed. One must look to the Byzantine in the East and to the Arab centers that developed with the spread of Islam for vestiges of institutions of higher learning during the Dark Ages. Important as each of these institutions were, they were not truly universities. "To be a university you need to have a permanent institution employing regular teaching staff and offering specific courses of higher learning, administering examinations, and granting certification of study."[9] This is the institution that emerged in the Middle Ages.

In most instances, universities evolved from the expanding *studium generale* or liberal arts curricula of the cathedral schools. It is impossible to assign an exact date to the rise of the university for the simple reason that it grew out of the existing schools over a considerable period of time. The original universities were societies or guilds of teachers who were paid individually by students. Both teachers and students would gather in a town, rent space (lofts or barns), and conduct classes.[10] Students began to flock in considerable numbers to certain towns that had a certain reputation for professors of a certain subject: theology, medicine, or law. The University of Salerno began in the tenth and eleventh centuries and specialized in medicine. The University of Bologna was chartered in 1158 A.D. and specialized in law. The University of Paris evolved from a cathedral school specializing in theology and was the first university to incorporate in 1208 A.D. Oxford began in 1214 A.D. and emphasized the liberal arts. Two general models of universities developed representing two differing philosophies: The University of Paris was in the hands of the Church, the teachers dominated in the institution, and the curriculum was set as the Ecclesiastical Studies and the seven liberal arts. The University of Bologna held a more secular view of learning and emphasized practical studies in law and medicine, and the institution was more student-centered and allowed for a student guild and union.[11] By 1500 A.D., the end of the Middle Ages, there were some eighty universities that had been founded in different parts of Europe.[12] (See Map 5.3 of the Growth of the Universities.)

The Life of a University Student

The medieval university had no permanent building at first. Classes were given by lecturing and to lecture meant to read at a lectern from the one copy of the book available. There were no books for the students to use; they had to take copious notes. After the Master read the passage, students debated it and had a disputation or discussion of the strong points and weaknesses in the argument presented. Students lived in *colleges* begun by privately endowed charitable foundations that served as hostels or residences.[13]

Oxford was the first to develop student halls and the college organization. In the beginning, there was no organization of the courses; professors would talk for unspecified amounts of times. Students did not know how long they would have to attend lectures in order to become qualified in the field. As more and more students came to study at the different sites, it was necessary to develop a curriculum and a schedule for class sessions. Charles Haskins gives us the typical daily schedule of the college student in his book, *The Rise of the Medieval Universities:*[14]

4:00 A.M.	Rise
5:00–6:00 A.M.	First lesson
6:00 A.M.	Breakfast
8:00–10:00 A.M.	Principal forenoon lesson
10:00–11:00 A.M.	Discussion and argument on the preceding lecture
11:00 A.M.	Dinner accompanied by reading the Bible
12–2:00 P.M.	Interrogation of the morning lessons
2:00–3:00 P.M.	Rest while someone read from a Latin poet or orator
3:00–5:00 P.M.	Principal afternoon lecture
5:00–6:00 P.M.	More discussion and argument on the theme
6:00 P.M.	Supper
6:30 P.M.	General discussion on all day's lectures
7:30 P.M.	Compline and Benediction
8:00 P.M.	In bed in winter (in summer at 9:00 P.M.)

Map 5.3   The Growth of the Universities

Source: Perry, et al. *Western Civilization: Ideas, Politics and Society,* 3rd edition, 1989. Used with permission of Houghton Mifflin.

Becoming a University Professor

The process of becoming a university professor was patterned on the guild system with the master/apprentice relationship. Students studied the seven liberal arts as the core preparation for any career. Students who studied as an Apprentice with a Master for five to seven years received the **Licentiate** (equivalent to our Bachelor's degree) and then could lecture under the direction of a master. They were thus formally introduced into the scholar's society and gave probationary lectures. The medieval lecture was literally the professor reading a passage from a text, and developing his interpretation by glossing the text. Since medieval textbooks were so expensive, three or four students would get together to buy a book and write down the professors' glosses on the text. There was little or no discussion between the professors and the students. The "new teaching method" of lecturing developed at this time is still, for better or worse, substantially in use today.

After two to three years of lecturing under supervision, professors could then apply for a license to teach. This is equivalent to today's **Master's.** Now they can begin to add their own interpretations of the issues. Once they were ready to present themselves for a formal oral examination in front of all the other professors, they were able to receive a gold ring and the doctor's hat and the **Doctorate.** We still have many of the medieval contributions to education currently in use today, i.e., the lecture; the academic gown and hood; the system of examinations, theses, and oral defense; and the administrative posts of Dean, Rector, and Chancellor.[15]

The Latin term for a teacher is a *magister scholar* or *scholasticus;* we use the term scholastic to refer to these medieval professors. The method they used to teach is now called the scholastic method; it was based on the *"disputio" or disputation.* The professor publicly defended the points of his teaching against challenges, presenting logical arguments similar to today's debate format with the "pros" and "cons." Students today are encouraged to write clear, logical essays using the scholastic style of presenting a thesis to be proven in the paper through supporting paragraphs that refute objections to the thesis.[16]

Women in Universities

There was little, if any provision for the university education of women in the Middle Ages. The University of Bologna was most progressive in this area. In the thirteenth century, Novella and Bettina Calderini, whose parents both held doctorates, were students at this university. They were known to substitute at the lectern for their father when he was unable to meet his class due to other commitments.[17]

A Medieval Philosophy of Education

The contributions of the medieval times to the philosophy of education include the preservation of knowledge and literacy in the monasteries and the later establishment of many of the educational institutions we still have today, especially the university. Convinced that spiritually men and women were equal, both were afforded education, although that of women was still inferior to that offered to men. The methodology of instruction developed in the monasteries was rote memorization; and the original lecturing in the university developed into the scholastic method, a form of which is still used in our schools today as the "debate." The curriculum developed by Alcuin was used for hundreds of years to organize the elementary and secondary educational program. The function of education was seen as twofold, intellectual and moral, and the purpose of the schools was to preserve and teach the traditional values and to teach men and women how to live rightly.

For Further Research on the Internet

Site with several excellent links to aspects of medieval life and education.
http://www.hwy66.com/~weid/education.htm

Information on medieval universities, their curriculum, and the education of women.
http://www.csupomona.edu/~plin/ls201/medieval2.html

Notes

1. John Butt, *Daily Life in the Age of Charlemagne* (Wesport, CT: Greenwood Press, 2002), p. viii.
2. Bruno Leone, ed., *The Middle Ages* (San Diego: Greenhaven Press, Inc., 2002), pp. 13–28.
3. Gerald Gutek, *A History of the Western Educational Experience,* 2nd ed (Prospect Heights, IL: Waveland Press, Inc., 1995), p. 79.
4. John Baldwin, *The Scholastic Culture of the Middle Ages 1000–1300* (Prospect Heights, IL: Waveland Press, Inc., 1997), pp. 35–37.
5. Norman Cantor, *The Civilization of the Middle Ages* (New York: Harper Collins Publishers; 1993), pp. 119–121, 153; Frances and Joseph Gies, *Women in the Middle Ages* (New York: Harper and Row, 1978), p. 64; Susan Groagbell, *Women: From the Greeks to the French Revolution* (New York: Wadsworth, 1973), pp. 98–99.
6. Frank Gravec, *A History of Education on During the Middle Ages* (Westport, CT: Greenwood Publishers, 1970), p. 65.
7. Jacques Le Goff, *Medieval Civilization* (Cambridge: Basil Blackwell, Ltd. 1990), pp. 65, 68, 97.
8. Cantor, pp. 138–140.
9. Willis Rudy, *Universities of Europe, 1100–1914 A.D.: A History* (Cranbury, NJ: Associated University Presses, 1984), pp. 13–16.
10. Leone, p. 195.
11. H. D. Ridder-Symoens, *A History of the University in Europe, Vol. 1: Universities in the Middle Ages* (Cambridge, Cambridge University Press, 1992), pp. 4–9.
12. Olaf Pederson, *The First Universities: Studium Generale and the Origins of University Education in Europe* (New York: Cambridge University Press, 1997), p. 29.
13. Ibid., p. 35.
14. Charles Homer Haskins, *The Rise of the Universities* (Ithaca, NY: Cornell University Press, 1957), p. 320.
15. Ridder-Symoens, pp. 139–147.
16. Sheila Dunn, *Philosophical Foundations of Education: Connecting Philosophy to Theory and Practice* (Upper Saddle River, NJ: Merrill/Prentice Hall, Inc., 2005), pp. 92, 105.
17. Rudy, p. 37.

Section 5.1: Charlemagne and Alcuin (742–814 A.D.)

As you look forward to teaching, you are preparing yourself for each of the subjects you will need to teach by taking the appropriate content and methods courses. What should be taught at the different levels of schooling is well known today. Can you imagine a time when it was not at all clear what should be taught and when? We have Charlemagne and Alcuin to thank for organizing the academic curriculum for the first schools in their empire.

Charlemagne's Life and Times

Charlemagne (Charles the Great) was the son of Pepin the Short, the king of the Franks whose grandfather was Charles Martel, who had halted the Moslem invasion of Western Europe at the Battle of Tours. Charlemagne established a common law marriage to Himitrude when he was around eighteen and had a son and a daughter with her. Charlemagne then entered a political marriage with the daughter of the King of Lombard but he repudiated her at the end of the year. Finally he married Hildegard, a woman of high birth, in a true religious ceremony. She was beautiful, mild, and charitable and this was his happiest marriage. She bore him nine children before she died at the age of twenty-five.[1] Charles had two other wives after Hildegard died, and seven more children.

Einhard, the private secretary for Charlemagne's son, Louis, wrote the earliest biography we have of Charlemagne. According to Einhard, Charlemagne was a strong, tall, and large man who especially enjoyed horseback riding and swimming. He had an alert mind and a forceful personality and could understand Greek and speak Latin, the language of educated people of his time, fluently; however, try as he did, he never learned to write.[2] Charlemagne was a religious man who attended Mass daily and bought sacred vessels for the Church and gave alms generously.

Charlemagne was a devoted family man who loved to be surrounded by his children. He had both his sons and daughters instructed in the liberal arts. Then the boys continued to learn horsemanship and the girls learned cloth-making, distaff, and spindle. He loved his daughters dearly, Einhard tells us, "but he was never willing to give them in marriage, either to men of his own nation or to foreigners."[3]

Although a poor reader himself, he expected something to be read during dinner and would have different members of the court read. Charlemagne's intellect was great and he recognized and understood the significance of learning so he surrounded himself with intellectuals.[4]

Emperor

Charlemagne and his brother, Carloman, shared the Frankish kingdom after their father died in 768 and Charlemagne became the sole ruler of the kingdom following his brother's death in 771. His kingdom covered what is now Belgium, France, Luxembourg, the Netherlands, and part of western Germany.

One of the first challenges Charlemagne faced was to subdue the Saxons, who had been fighting against the Franks for over thirty years. He also waged war in Spain and was returning from an expedition there in 778 when a mountain people called the Basques ambushed and wiped out his rear guard. This incident became the subject of the famous epic poem *The Song of Roland,* which takes poetic license and names the invaders as the Moors.[5]

By 800, Charlemagne's realm extended from central Italy north to Denmark and from eastern Germany west to the Atlantic Ocean. Throughout his reign, Charlemagne followed a policy of friendship and cooperation with the Christian church. He protected the church, continually extending its power, and was crowned emperor by Pope Leo III on Christmas Day, 800. (See the timeline of Charlemagne's life in Figure 5.1.)

Reformer

Charlemagne introduced a number of reforms to increase the supply of food by implementing more efficient methods of farming. He sought to establish a "continental state." He did this by dividing up the area; large estates were granted to loyal nobles, who, in return, provided military and political services to the king. The nobles also maintained the roads, bridges, and fortifications on their land. This was the forerunner of the system of feudalism that emerged upon his death.[6]

Although Charlemagne conquered much of Western Europe and united it under a great empire, his military conquests were of far less importance than his intellectual and spiritual reform of the same land. Charlemagne revived the political and cultural life of Europe, which had collapsed after the fall of the Roman Empire, by revitalizing the educational system.

Alcuin

Charlemagne actively recruited scholars and ecclesiastics from non-Frankish countries as they brought resources and abilities not found in Francia at that time.[7] He invited Alcuin (735–804 A.D.) to his court in 781 A.D. to be director of his palace school, later making him Minister of Education for the whole Frankish kingdom.

Alcuin was born in York, a Northumbrian of a noble family whose parents died when he was young. He thus was raised at the Cathedral School, the second seat of English Christendom, and a place of great intellectual importance. Alcuin studied with Bede and imitated his simple, clear, and classical Latin style and his allegorical exegesis method of explaining the scriptures.[8] Alcuin was a poet and a scholar; although not an original thinker, he was a man with a good ability to explain texts and ideas to his students. Alcuin arranged the curriculum for Charlemagne's palace school around the *trivium* and

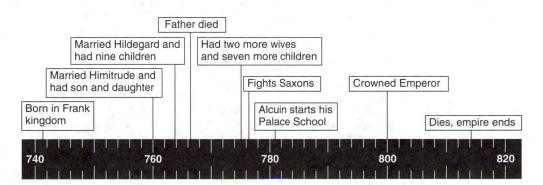

Figure 5.1   Charlemagne's Life and Times

quadrivium found in the writings of Boethius.[9] Alcuin thus made an indelible contribution to the education of every person in the West.

The Palace School

Charlemagne and Alcuin worked together well as they had a strong mutual respect and affection for one another. They had a formidable task ahead of them as literacy was woefully low, even in the monasteries. There were not enough schools or textbooks, and those that they had were faulty. Together they were able to transform the old palace school into a kind of Academy that taught students while also teaching them how to teach others.

Alcuin's first task was to obtain some books from England and write a few elementary grammar textbooks himself. Alcuin was able to attract the best teachers and students in Europe to Charlemagne's palace school. His students included the king himself, the king's sister, Gisela, his queen, the royal children, the chief personages of his court, clergymen, and boys of varying ages.

After Charlemagne died on January 28, 814, his empire fell apart and it ceased to exist by the late 800's. With the disintegration of central government, the system of feudalism rose as a way to promote safe living for all. This became the basic political and military system of Europe for the next 400 years as Europe was plunged into the political confusion of the "Dark Ages."[10] However, the cultural revival begun by Charlemagne had a lasting effect on European civilization. Charlemagne's empire also inspired later attempts to unite many European nations.

Charlemagne's Contribution to Education

Charlemagne was the most famous ruler of the Middle Ages and a key figure in European history as well as in educational history because of the work of Alcuin. Charlemagne pushed for the expansion and standardization of education and of language use, gathered within his realm scholars and artists who created a great stock of materials that bridged the ancient and medieval worlds, and laid the foundation of the educational system that arose during the later Middle Ages.[11]

Education of Women

No provisions were made officially for the education of women at this time. Nevertheless, Charlemagne supported women obtaining education and his own daughters and sister were among the many highly cultivated women of this time.

Education of Clergy

By educating the clergymen, Charlemagne strengthened the church, and Alcuin trained teachers for schools throughout the empire. Alcuin established and expanded schools, libraries, and *scriptoria* in all monasteries all over France. Because copyists in monasteries were taught how to accurately copy texts, the ancient Roman manuscripts were preserved; otherwise they would have been lost forever. The revival of learning and the improvement of education and culture under Charlemagne is called the Carolingian Renaissance. The impact of Alcuin's work can be seen in the great increase of literary and documentary materials surviving from the Carolingian period, which was decisive for the ninth and tenth century revivals.[12]

The Capitularies

One of the most valuable sources of information about Charlemagne's reign are the capitularies, or laws, he issued orally and in public that were then written down for distribution. In 787 Charlemagne issued his famous capitulary or proclamation, which is the first general Charter of Education for the Middle Ages. It is in the form of a letter to the abbots of the different monasteries reproaching their illiteracy. A capitulary is a distinctive document of the Frankish kingdom, an administrative mandate that derived its format from the ecclesiastical legislation of the time. Capitularies mean chapters, as they consist of a series of chapters of laws. They became blueprints for the new society Charlemagne was trying to bring into his kingdom.[13]

The Capitulary of 787 is the most important state paper from his reign. Through this document and other letters and proclamations on the subject of education, Charlemagne establishes his key policies.[14]

Charlemagne and Alcuin's Philosophy of Education

Charlemagne's importance in educational history lies in the fact that he was the first monarch in the history of Europe, and perhaps of the world, to attempt the establishment of universal, gratuitous primary education as well as of higher schools.

The establishment of the *trivium* and *quadrivium* as the curriculum of the school was an important contribution that influenced education for hundreds of years. The *trivium* was to be studied in the first years and included grammar, rhetoric, and dialectic. The *quadrivium* was comprised of arithmetic, geometry, astronomy, and music. Although arithmetic was limited to mostly Roman numerals, geometry included the entire natural world, from geography to the study of medicine.

The methodology of instruction emphasized accuracy. A new style of handwriting was also developed; it later became the model for printing. Alcuin's emphasis on spelling and orthography was important for the preservation of culture that became an important purpose of education for the next several centuries. As Charlemagne wrote, "Let there, therefore, be chosen for this work men who are both able and willing to learn, and also desirous of instructing others; and let them apply themselves to the work with a zeal equaling the earnestness with which we recommend it to them."

Notes

1. John Butt, *Daily Life in the Age of Charlemagne* (Westport, CT: Greenwood Press, 2002), p. 31.
2. Einhard, *The Life of Charlemagne,* translated by S. E. Turner (Ann Arbor: University of Michigan Press, 1960), pp. 50–55.
3. Ibid., pp. 45–48.
4. Butt, p. 50.
5. Russell Chamberlin, *Charlemagne: Emperor of the Western World* (London: Grafton Books: Collins Publishing Group, 1986), pp. 124–125.
6. John Baldwin, *The Scholastic Culture of the Middle Ages 1000–1300* (Prospect Heights, IL: Waveland Press, Inc., 1997), p. 3.
7. Roger Collins, *Charlemagne* (Toronto: University of Toronto Press, 1998), p. 102.
8. Gerald Ellard, *Master Alcuin, Liturgist* (Chicago: Loyola University Press, 1956), p. 143.
9. Chamberlin, pp. 34–35.
10. Norman Cantor, *The Civilization of the Middle Ages* (New York: Harper Collins Publishers, 1993), p. 196.
11. Butt, p. 7.
12. Cantor, p. 188.
13. Butt, p. 13.
14. Andrew Fleming West, *Alcuin and the Rise of Christian Schools,* in *The Great Educators,* edited by N. M. Butler (New York: Greenwood Press for Charles Scribner and Sons, 1969 (originally published in 1892), p. 53.

Questions to Guide Your Reading

1. List the key policies Charlemagne outlines in the Capitulary of 787 and compare them with policies you are aware of in today's educational system.

2. Why does Charlemagne think that the study of letters and of good speaking is important for the monks and priests? Do you think that it is also important for this group today or is there another group for which it is more important?

3. How, according to Charlemagne, does knowledge help one develop good morals? Is this still true today?

4. Why is it important for Church documents to be free of grammatical errors? Is his argument valid today?

READING 5.1: CHARLEMAGNE'S CAPITULARIES

Capitulary of 787

Charles, by the grace of God, King of the Franks and of the Lombards, and Patrician of the Romans, to Bangulfus, abbot, and to his whole congregation and the faithful committee to his charge:

Be it known to your devotion, pleasing to God, that in conjunction with our faithful we have judged it to be of utility that, in the bishoprics and monasteries committed by Christ's favor to our charge, care should be taken that there shall be not only a regular manner of life and one conformable to holy religion, but also the study of letters, each to teach and learn them according to his ability and the divine assistance. For even as due observance of the rule of the house tends to good morals, so zeal on the part of the teacher and the taught imparts order and grace to sentences; and those who seek to please God by living aright should also not neglect to please him by right speaking. It is written, "By thine own words shalt thou be justified or condemned;" and although right doing be preferable to right speaking, yet must the knowledge of what is right precede right action. Every one, therefore, should strive to understand what it is he would fain accomplish; and this right understanding will be the sooner gained according as the utterances of the tongue are free from error. And

if false speaking is to be shunned by all men, especially should it be shunned by those who have elected to be the servants of the truth.

During past years we have often received letters from different monasteries, informing us that at their sacred services the brethren offered up prayers on our behalf; and we have observed that the thoughts contained in these letters, though in themselves most just, were expressed in uncouth language, and while pious devotion dictated the sentiments, the unlettered tongue was unable to express them aright. Hence there has arisen in our minds the fear lest, if the skill to write rightly were thus lacking, so too would the power of rightly comprehending the sacred scriptures be far less than was fitting; and we all know that though verbal errors be dangerous, errors of the understanding are yet more so. We exhort you, therefore, not only not to neglect the study of letters, but also to apply yourselves thereto with perseverance and with that humility which is well pleasing to God; so that you may be able to penetrate with greater ease and certainty the mysteries of the Holy Scriptures. For as these contain images, tropes, and similar figures, it is impossible to doubt that the reader will arrive far more readily at the spiritual sense according as he is the better instructed in learning. Let there, therefore, be chosen for this work men who are both able and willing to learn, and also desirous of instructing others; and let them apply themselves to the work with a zeal equaling the earnestness with which we recommend it to them. It is our wish that you may be what it behooves the soldiers of the Church to be,

Source: F. V. N. Painter, *Great Pedagogical Essays from Plato to Spencer* (New York: American Book Company) 1905.

religious in heart, learned in discourse, pure in act, eloquent in speech; so that all who approach your house, in order to invoke the Divine Master or to behold the excellence of the religious life, may be edified in beholding you, and instructed in hearing you discourse or chant, and may return home rendering thanks to God most high. Fail not, as thou regardest our favor, to send a copy of this letter to all thy suffragans and to all the monasteries; and let no monk go beyond his monastery to administer justice, or to enter the assemblies and the voting-places. Adieu.

From Admonitio Generalis, 789

And we also demand of your holiness that the ministers of the altar of God shall adorn their ministry by good manners, and likewise the other orders who observe a rule and the congregations of monks. We implore them to lead a just and fitting life, just as God himself commanded in the Gospel [Matthew, v. 16]: "Let your light so shine before men that they may see your good works and glorify your Father which is in heaven" so that by their example many may be led to serve God; and let them join and associate to themselves not only children of servile condition, but also sons of free men. And let schools be established in which boys may learn to read. Correct carefully the Psalms, the signs in writing *(notas)*, the songs, the calendar, the grammar; in each monastery or bishopric, and the Catholic books: because often some desire to pray to God properly, but they pray badly because of the incorrect books. And do not permit your boys to corrupt them in reading or writing. If there is no need of writing the Gospel, Psalter and Missals let men of mature age do the writing with all diligence.

Discussion Questions

1. In what ways is education especially vital for the preservation of culture today as it was in the time of Charlemagne? Give examples.
2. A new form of spelling has been developed by those who use e-mail extensively. Do you think Alcuin would be in favor of this new orthography? Why or why not?
3. Why is it important to intellectually know one's religion according to Charlemagne? Is his argument valid today?
4. Why was the Church sermon so important in the days of Charlemagne for the people attending the services? Is it that important to people today? Why or why not?
5. Which, if any, of Charlemagne's educational policies are appropriate for contemporary educational practice today?

For Further Research on the Internet

A biography of Charlemagne taken from Will Durant's *History of Civilization Vol. III, The Age of Faith*. **http://www.chronique.com/Library/MedHistory/charlemagne.htm**

A page on Charlemagne with links to books and videos on him. **http://www.lucidcafe. com/library/96apr/charlemagne.html**

On-line version of Einhard's *Life of Charlemagne*. **http://www.fordham.edu/halsall/ basis/einhard.html**

Many medieval artistic representations of scenes from Charlemagne's life. **http://www.bnf.fr/enluminures/themes/t_1/st_1_04/a104_002.htm**

Suggestions for Further Reading

Baldwin, John. *The Scholastic Culture of the Middle Ages 1000–1300*. Prospect Heights, IL: Waveland Press, Inc., 1997.

Butt, John. *Daily Life in the Age of Charlemagne*. Westport, CT: Greenwood Press, 2002.

Cantor, Norman. *The Civilization of the Middle Ages.* (New York: Harper Collins Publishers, 1993.

Chamberlin, Russell. *Charlemagne: Emperor of the Western World.* London: Grafton Books: Collins Publishing Group, 1986.

Collins, Roger. *Charlemagne.* Toronto: University of Toronto Press, 1998.

Einhard. *The Life of Charlemagne,* translated by S. E. Turner. Ann Arbor: University of Michigan Press, 1960.

Ellard, Gerald. *Master Alcuin, Liturgist.* Chicago: Loyola University Press, 1956.

West, Andrew Fleming. *Alcuin and the Rise of Christian Schools* In *The Great Educators,* edited by N. M. Butler. New York: Greenwood Press for Charles Scribner and Sons, 1969 (originally published in 1892).

Section 5.2: Hildegard of Bingen (1098–1179 A.D.)

In your first year of teaching you will probably have a mentor to guide and coach you with your first classroom. This was not always the case. Hildegard of Bingen was the first woman to educate women in theology, philosophy, and the arts. She did this by working individually with each and mentoring them.

Hildegard's Life and Times

The woman known as Hildegard of Bingen was probably born in 1098 in Bermersheim, Germany, the tenth and last child of Mechthild and Hildebert, a knight of the Count of Sponheim. Hildegard spent the first eight years of her life with her brothers and sisters in the Court before her parents, who had promised her to the Church at her birth, gave her as an oblate to the nearby Benedictine monastery of Disibodenberg.[1]

Hildegard's Education

Hildegard was enclosed with Jutta of Sponheim and a few servants in a small cottage adjacent to the abbey Church of the Disibodenberg. Jutta taught Hildegard simple Latin, the basics of religion and moral life, and how to read the Psaltery, or the Songs of David, the "universal primer of the Middle Ages." She taught her the prayers and chants that were part of the monastic life, to play the ten-stringed psaltery, and to sew and embroider for the Church. Hildegard spoke very highly of Jutta, and as other young women came to her, their accommodations expanded and soon became a convent of nuns attached to the Benedictine monastery of monks. When Hildegard was fifteen, she took her vows as a Benedictine nun.[2]

Although she was considered "uneducated" by twelfth-century standards, lacking formal study of grammar, rhetoric, and dialectic, she was literate and familiar with part of the medieval canon through use of the monastery library. Scholars have identified in her writing a deep knowledge of the Scriptures, knowledge of the main Christian writers of the time, and some knowledge of classical authors.[3] Hildegard's use of expressions reveals her extensive reading.

Hildegard, the Infirmarian

Life in the convent was very structured, with eight hours of sleep, eight hours of work, four hours of prayer, four hours of study, recitation of the Divine Office, and two meals a day. It seems that Jutta served as infirmarian at the monastery of Disibodenberg in her earlier years and taught Hildegard, who worked as a nurse-physician for years. Hildegard diagnosed and cared for both female and male patients, and also grew and experimented with her own herbs.[4]

Abbess

Jutta died in 1136; and Hildegard, 38 years old, was appointed abbess of the nuns; this revolutionized her life, giving her a degree of independence and a voice for the first time. Breaking with custom, Hildegard allowed her nuns to adorn themselves as brides of Christ on holidays, wearing wedding gowns, and jewels. She also wrote uplifting music and songs for her nuns to sing.[5] Two years after Jutta's death, the number of nuns had risen from twelve to eighteen, all of them of noble lineage.

"Write What You See"

In her *Vita* (Saint's Life) written by Theodoric of Echternach, she says that she had visions and divine revelations since she was three years old. Sometimes they were so strong that she was left physically ill with a migraine after the experience. Soon after Jutta died, Hildegard, 43, was inspired to write her visions down. Her spiritual director and confessor, Volmar, a Benedictine monk, confirmed the authority of her spiritual insights and told her to obey the voice that told her to "write what you see and hear." He later became her secretary, spending forty years helping her write of what she saw.[6] (See the timeline of Hildegard's life in Figure 5.2.) Hildegard ultimately wrote six major works, nearly 400 letters, and 80 songs. The first book she wrote was *Scivias* (*Know the Ways of God*) which included all the knowledge needed by an individual soul to obtain salvation, written in a remarkable visionary format with attractive form, imagery, and myth-styled allegories. Although it took her ten years to finish the book, completing it in 1151, when Pope Eugenius read the first part, he gave it his full endorsement, making Hildegard a well-known and recognized prophet. Crowds of people began to seek her counsel and many new vocations joined the convent. She corresponded with many prominent people, including several popes and kings.[7]

Founding an Independent Community for Nuns

In a vision, Hildegard saw that she should move the convent from the cramped quarters of Disbodenberg and found a community with room for fifty nuns, independent of the men's monastery, at Rupertsberg. The monks were opposed to the idea because their monastery had received an enhanced reputation from their protégée and a steady income of dowries from the women postulates; however, they finally relented.[8]

First Woman Doctor

From 1152 to 1158, Hildegard was engaged in compiling two substantial scientific works, *Physica* and *Causae et Curae*. *Physica* is the first book in which a woman discusses plants, trees, and herbs in relation to their medicinal properties. Hildegard is the first woman to write about skin disease; in *Causae et Curae* she mentions leprosy, scabies, lice, burns, allergies, and other subjects and prescribes cures, some still in use today. These writings with their practical advice make her one of the first women doctors and scientists whose work survives.

Linguist and Musician

Hildegard had a secret language and alphabet, a code she said she invented by inspiration of God. Linguists argue that Hildegard's *Lingua Ignota* is the only imaginary language that exists intact from the Middle Ages.[9] Some musicologists have designated Hildegard of Bingen as the earliest named woman composer; others say that Sappho, the Greek lyric poet, was the first. Nevertheless, some 80 songs are attributed to Hildegard.

Hildegard's creative output is even more astounding when one realizes that she had a full-time job being abbess for some fifty nuns. She had to discipline, advise, and teach the nuns, administrate supplies of food, clothing, and fuel, receive visitors, attend to legal business, supervise work on the convent land and the cooking and cleaning of the convent. In Hildegard's work with the nuns we see that she foreshadowed the current trend of "mentoring" or teaching others as a coach or guide would do, and in this was furthering the work begun by her predecessor Sappho with her students.

Hildegard, the Preacher

Between 1158 and 1171, Hildegard went on four speaking tours because of a vision. She was 60 years old, of frail health, and forbidden by canon law to teach or preach because she was a woman, but she received the Pope's sanction to do so.[10] She traveled throughout Germany to different monasteries, denouncing the evil sweeping through the Church, speaking out against the heretical sects advancing through France and Italy. Hildegard preached during the era of the Papal Schism, a particularly difficult time in Church history when there were two popes, Victor IV and Alexander III.[11] In between preaching tours, she wrote her second vision book, *Book of Life's Merits,* a discourse between the virtues and the vices, and her final vision book, *Book of Divine Works.*

Life of Hildegard

In 1173, Volmar died, and Gottfried was appointed as his successor. He began the *Life of Hildegard,* but died in 1176, leaving the biography unfinished. Hildegard's brother Hugh took over the biography, but died a year later. Finally, the French monk Guilbert of Gembloux took over as her secretary for the last three years of her life.[12] Guilbert wrote about what he found in the convent to his friend.

> Hildegard was a mother to the nuns, exercising great affection and virtue with them. They honored and obeyed her. On Sundays they refrained from work and sit in composed silence in the cloister reading and learning chant. On ordinary days they are applying themselves in the workshops writing books, weaving robes, and other manual crafts. The holy reading gives them the light of divine knowledge. Hildegard pours herself out on all in charity, giving counsels required of her, solving the most difficult questions put to her, writing books, instructing her sisters, putting fresh heart into the sinners who approach her. She is wholly taken up by it all even though she is old and infirm.[13]

In 1178, at the age of eighty, Hildegard and her nuns were placed under an interdict forbidding them to hear Mass or receive sacraments because she had buried a local nobleman, who had been excommunicated but reconciled to the Church before he died, on the convent grounds. Hildegard accepted this, convinced that she was doing the will of God and finally, after a whole year the interdict was lifted, as the clergy were finally convinced that the man had died in the state of grace. Six months later Hildegard, 81, died on

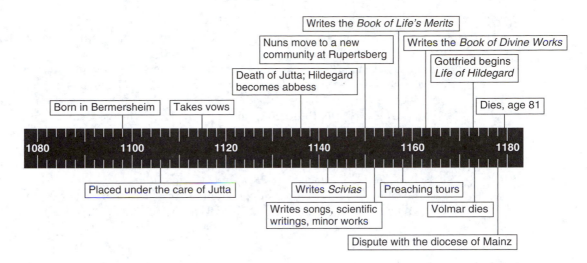

Figure 5.2   Hildegard's Life and Times

September 17, 1179. The process for her canonization was full of administrative delays, but today she is considered a German saint.[14] Her voice was silent for centuries, but renewed research on the occasion of the eight-hundredth anniversary of her death (1979) and the nine-hundredth anniversary of her birth (1998) has helped us to once again hear her powerful feminist voice in what was a man's world.

Hildegard's Importance for Education

Hildegard of Bingen is a complex, original, and important contributor to the religious, cultural, and intellectual life of the twelfth century. She is accessible today in a way that far exceeds any female philosopher who preceded her; all of her major works are available. According to Prudence Allen,

> No woman previous to Hildegard revealed such a wide range of knowledge and creative thought. The extraordinary breadth of her writing skills, which range from music to drama, from science to theology, from language games to the philosophy of psychology, reveal a genius unparalleled by women and matched by few men up to the twelfth century. Her original theory in support of the philosophy of sex complementarity makes her contribution to the history of the concept of woman in relation to man all the more significant.[15]

Hildegard transformed many of the traditions of the world in which she lived as the only woman in her time accepted as an authoritative voice on Christian doctrine, permitted by the Pope to write theological books and preach openly to clergy and laity. She wrote the first known morality play and was the first woman to write on natural science, medicine, and sexuality; the sheer volume of Hildegard's literary production is remarkable. She was an artist of great talent and a prolific composer of chant. She was the first philosopher to articulate a theory of sex complementarity; she saw men and women as equal yet different.

Education of Women in the Twelfth Century

Educational opportunities for women in the twelfth century were poor. They could receive elementary instruction from their mothers alongside their brothers. However, young men could go on to be tutored or educated in a monastery or school. Women could only attend such places disguised as men. Hildegard's importance for education lies in the way that she supported the intellectual growth of her sisters in her convent, working with them as their mentor, making the convent a place of higher learning for those women so disposed. The women in her monastery were engaged in all of the tasks in which the men were engaged in their monasteries: copying manuscripts, writing glosses, studying the classics and the Fathers of the Church. Hildegard proclaimed the equality of woman in the Church.[16]

In the century after Hildegard, learning shifted from the monasteries via the cathedral schools to the universities. From 1140, the master guilds began to form slowly in Paris, making it a cluster of philosophy and theology. Hildegard was aware of the gradual shift during her lifetime of the center of higher education from the Benedictine monasteries to the schools in Paris, which were to become the first universities.[17] The situation in Paris was radically different from the double monasteries where men and women learned and worked. By the time the master guilds evolved into the University of Paris, women were excluded from formal study and were to be so excluded for centuries.

Hildegard, the Teacher

Hildegard taught through her preaching tour. Her extensive travel and public speaking reveals that she believed women ought not be limited to the private sphere of activity or, inversely, that the public sphere ought not be limited to men. Hildegard claimed that women had been called to prophesize because men had become weak and/or immoral and were not doing it. One could say that Hildegard was the first woman preacher and public teacher.

Hildegard taught through her writings: she taught both the theology of the sacraments and doctrine and the "theology of the feminine." She wrote using allegorical symbolism, especially emphasizing feminine images. She presents images of a female "city-church," female virtues, and a female city and can be read and interpreted on many levels. She is regarded as one of the most important religious writers, as well as the leading feminist theorist, of the Middle Ages.

Hildegard's Philosophy of Education

Hildegard departed from the Neo-Platonic philosophy of her time that separated the body and the soul. She made unique contributions to the philosophy of the human person and saw the integration of body and soul as total but with a tension, which offered the greatest human potential—that of recognizing God. Her work abounds in metaphors that stress the complete integration of the human trinity: body and the two principal powers of the soul, intellect and will.[18]

Hildegard disagreed with the view of her time that the only function of education was to hand down everything from the past. She saw education as more active, as a forum for the human mind to discover and have new perceptions of art, divine truth, and culture.

Hildegard stands as an important transition figure of the Medieval Ages, a woman who gave other women the opportunity to pursue university studies.

> "Everyone who saw, heard, or understood these things, both great and humble judged favourably of them so that it was clearly God's will that all this should be legally fixed in writing."
>
> *Hildegard's Vita*

Notes

1. Sabina Flanagan, *Hildegard of Bingen: A Visionary Life,* 2nd ed. (New York: Routledge, 1998), pp. 22–24.
2. Fiona Maddocks, *Hildegard of Bingen: The Woman of Her Age* (New York: Doubleday/Random House, 2001), p. 38.

3. Maud Burnett McInerney, "Introduction, Hildegard of Bingen: A Book of Essays," in *Hildegard of Bingen: A Book of Essays,* edited by M. B. McInerney (New York: Garland Publishing, Inc., 1998), p. xxi.

4. Marcia Kathleen Chamberlain, "Hildegard of Bingen's Causes and Cures: A Radical Feminist Response to the Doctor-Cook Binary," in *Hildegard of Bingen: A Book of Essays,* edited by M. B. McInerney (New York: Garland Publishing, Inc., 1998), p. 61; Sister Prudence Allen, *The Concept of Women: The Aristotelian Revolution: 750 B.C.–1250 A.D.,* 2nd ed. (Grand Rapids, MI: William B. Eerdmans Publishing Co., 1997), pp. 294–295.

5. Norman Cantor, *Medieval Lives: Eight Charismatic Men and Women of the Middle Ages* (New York: Harper Collins Publishers, 1994), p. 95.

6. Maddocks, p. 60.

7. Andrea Hopkins, *Most Wise and Valiant Ladies: Remarkable Lives—Women of the Middle Ages* (London: Collins & Brown, Ltd., 1997), pp. 93–96.

8. Fiona Bowie, and Oliver Davies, "Introduction, Hildegard of Bingen: An Anthology," in *Hildegard of Bingen: An Anthology,* edited by F. Bowie and O. Davies (London: Courier International Ltd., 1990), p. 12; Flanagan, pp. 6–7.

9. Marcia Kathleen Chamberlain, "Hildegard of Bingen's Causes and Cures: A Radical Feminist Response to the Doctor-Cook Binary," in *Hildegard of Bingen: A Book of Essays,* edited by M. B. McInerney (New York: Garland Publishing, Inc., 1998), p. 53.

10. Beverly Sian Rapp, "A Woman Speaks: Language and Self-Representation in Hildegard's Letters," in *Hildegard of Bingen: A Book of Essays,* edited by M. B. McInerney (New York: Garland Publishing, Inc., 1998), p. 7.

11. Maddocks, pp. 215–219.

12. Flanagan, pp. 10–11.

13. Maddocks, p. 244.

14. Flanagan, p. 12.

15. Sister Prudence Allen, p. 295.

16. Cantor, p. 99.

17. Flanagan, p. 44.

18. Jan Emerson, "A Poetry of Science: Relating Body and Soul in Scivias," in *Hildegard of Bingen: A Book of Essays,* edited by M. B. McInerney (New York: Garland Publishing, Inc., 1998), pp. 77, 79.

Questions to Guide Your Reading

1. What are the capabilities of the soul at each of the three periods of life according to Hildegard? Is our system of education set up to capitalize on each of these capabilities? How would Hildegard want us to change it?

2. What are the three paths in the human being and how are they related to one another? Does a teacher teach to each path or to only one?

3. What does it mean to say that the will directs every action? We know motivation resides in the will. How then do you think Hildegard would advise a teacher to motivate students?

READING 5.2:
THE ACTION OF THE WILL

17. How the Soul Reveals Its Capabilities According to the Capabilities of the Body

The soul reveals her capabilities according to the capabilities of the body, so that in childhood she brings forth simplicity, in youth strength, and in the fullness of age, when all the veins of the human being are full, she brings forth her greatest strength in wisdom. In the same way a tree in its first growth brings forth tender shoots, goes on then to bear fruit, and finally ripens that fruit to the fullness of utility. But afterwards, in old age, when a human being's bones and veins incline to weakness, then the soul reveals gentler strengths, as though tired of human knowledge. In the same way, at the onset of wintertime, the sap of the tree withdraws from the leaves and branches as the tree begins to incline towards old age.

18. The Human Being Contains Three Paths

A human being contains three paths: namely, soul, body, and senses. On these three paths, human life runs its course. The soul fills the body with life and brings forth the senses; for its part the body attracts the soul to it and opens the senses; in turn the senses touch the body and draw the soul to them. The soul provides the body with life, like fire flooding the darkness with light; it has two major powers like two arms: the understanding and the will. Not that the soul has these limbs to move herself about; rather she reveals herself in these two powers like the sun manifesting itself in the splendour of its light. Therefore human being, you are not a bundle of veins; pay attention to the knowledge of the scriptures.

Source: *Scivias* I, 4 pages 6–8 in the book *Hildegard of Bingen: Selected Writings*, translated by Mark Anterton, 2001. Oxford: Penguin Classics, used with permission.

19. Human Understanding

Human understanding is connected to the soul like the arms to the body. For just as the arm is joined to the hand and the hand to the fingers, so also there is no doubt that understanding proceeds from the soul and activates the other powers of the soul, by which it knows and recognizes human actions. For over all the other powers of the soul it is understanding which distinguishes what is good from what is bad in human actions. Understanding is therefore a teacher through whom all things are known, for in this way he shakes out all things just as the wheat is separated from the stalks and husks; he examines what things are useful and what are useless, what things are lovable and what are hateful, what things belong to life and what to death.

Just as food without salt is bland, so also the other powers of the soul are weak and unknowing without it. Understanding is in the soul like the shoulders in the body, acting as the moving force behind the other powers of the soul, giving them strength like the shoulders give strength to the body. It is flexible, like the bend of the arm, discerning both the divine and the human in God. Thus human understanding works with true faith, for like the articulation of the fingers of the hand it can distinguish between many diverse actions. It therefore operates differently from the other forces of the soul. Why is this?

20. The Will

The will warms an action, the mind receives it, and thought brings it forth. The understanding, however, discerns an action by the process of knowing good and evil just as the angels also have an understanding that loves good and hates evil. And just as the body has a heart, so too the soul has understanding, which exercises its power in one part of the soul just as the will does in another.

How does this happen? The will in fact has great power in the soul. How does this come about? The soul stands, so to speak, in the corner of the house, that is, in the firm support of the heart, like a man standing in the corner of a house in order to survey the whole house and supervise its running. He raises his right arm to give a sign and points out things useful to the house as he turns towards the east. The soul does likewise on the roadways of the whole body when she looks towards the rising of the sun. The soul uses the will, as it were like her right arm, as a firm support for the veins and the bones and the movement of the whole body, for the will directs every action, whether for good or ill.

Discussion Questions

1. This reading outlines Hildegard's ideas on anthropology, or the study of human beings. Why is it important for a teacher to understand anthropology?

2. What does Hildegard mean when she says that understanding is a teacher through whom all things are known? Do you think she would be in favor of independent study or on-line classes? Why or why not?

3. Hildegard lived in a time when women were not afforded the same experiences, opportunities, or power as men. Although things have greatly changed in the eight hundred years since her death, in many ways women, and especially women of color and of ethnic diversity, still have not reached true equality with men. Can you mention specific instances, especially in the educational world, of this inequality?

4. Hildegard mentored her nuns in order to capitalize on their strengths and educate them to their full capacity. Why is mentoring a particularly important aspect of teaching especially if we are going to try to help under-represented groups obtain more equality of educational opportunity?

5. One could argue that Hildegard was one of the first feminists as she proposed the theory of sex complementarity, emphasizing the unique abilities and aptitudes of women that complement those of men. Compare and contrast Hildegard to some current feminist theorists' ideas on the relationship of the sexes. What do you think she would say about these issues?

6. Hildegard wrote using allegorical symbolism with religious and moral implications. How could her work be compared to current allegorical works such as *The Lord of the Rings* trilogy?

For Further Research on the Internet

A complete homepage regarding Hildegard. **http://www.hildegard.org/**

A professor's home page for Hildegard with many links. **http://www.fordham.edu/halsall/med/hildegarde.html**

Suggestions for Further Reading

Allen, Sister Prudence. *The Concept of Women: The Aristotelian Revolution: 750 B.C.–1250 A.D.*, 2nd ed. Grand Rapids, MI: William B. Eerdmans Publishing Co., 1997.

Bowie, Fiona, and Oliver Davies. "Introduction, Hildegard of Bingen: An Anthology." In *Hildegard of Bingen: An Anthology*, edited by F. Bowie and O. Davies. London: Courier International Ltd., 1990.

Cantor, Norman. *Medieval Lives: Eight Charismatic Men and Women of the Middle Ages.* New York: Harper Collins Publishers, 1994.

Chamberlain, Marcia Kathleen. "Hildegard of Bingen's Causes and Cures: A Radical Feminist Response to the Doctor-Cook Binary." In *Hildegard of Bingen: A Book of Essays,* edited by M. B. McInerney. New York: Garland Publishing, Inc., 1998.

Emerson, Jan. "A Poetry of Science: Relating Body and Soul in Scrivias." In *Hildegard of Bingen: A Book of Essays,* edited by M. B. McInerney. New York: Garland Publishing, Inc., 1998.

Flanagan, Sabina. *Hildegard of Bingen: A Visionary Life,* 2nd ed. New York: Routledge, 1998.

Hopkins, Andrea. *Most Wise and Valiant Ladies: Remarkable Lives—Women of the Middle Ages.* London: Collins & Brown, Ltd., 1997.

Maddocks, Fiona. *Hildegard of Bingen: The Woman of Her Age.* New York: Doubleday/Random House, 2001.

McInerney, Maud Burnett. "Introduction, Hildegard of Bingen: A Book of Essays." In *Hildegard of Bingen: A Book of Essays,* edited by M. B. McInerney. New York: Garland Publishing, Inc., 1998.

Rapp, Beverly Sian. "A Woman Speaks: Language and Self-Representation in Hildegard's Letters." In *Hildegard of Bingen: A Book of Essays,* edited by M. B. McInerney. New York: Garland Publishing, Inc., 1998.

Section 5.3: St. Thomas Aquinas (1125–1274 A.D.)

You have heard this goal before—"We need to develop students' thinking skills and help them to reason things out. If we can just help them to learn to think they will be able to learn on their own." We have Thomas Aquinas to thank for making deductive reasoning and logical argumentation so much a part of education today.

Thomas Aquinas' Life and Times

Thomas Aquinas was born around 1225 at the castle of Roccasecca near the small town of Aquino, which lies between Naples and Rome in Italy. His parents, Landulf and Theodora, were wealthy, well-educated members of a feudal noble class with eleven children. Thomas was the youngest son in this large family and as such, following the custom of the time, was dedicated to the Church by his parents.[1]

Thomas' Education

At the age of five Thomas went to the monastic school in the abbey of Monte Casino studying there for eight years, learning reading, writing, mathematics, grammar, harmony, Latin, and religion. He went to Naples in 1239 and enrolled in the *studium generale,* or the liberal arts courses, required as preparation for professional studies. During his years at Naples, Thomas grew from adolescence to maturity. He was a tall, quiet boy, silent, serious and given to prayer.[2]

Friar Thomas

While at Naples, Thomas became acquainted with the Dominican Friars who taught theology there and decided to enter the Dominican order. The Dominican order was a relatively new mendicant order that was academically rigorous. His parents had planned on him becoming a member of the Benedictines, a well-established, respected order, where he could become an abbot like his uncle. They even had his brothers kidnap Thomas and keep him in the family castle for a year trying to persuade him to change his mind. Thomas however spent the year reading the Bible and studying the letters of Peter Lombard, persevering in his vocation and determination to enter the Dominican order, which he finally did in 1245 (see the timeline of Aquinas' life in Figure 5.3). After earning his bachelor's degree at the Dominican monastery of the Holy Cross, he went, in 1252, to study, with Albert the Great as his teacher, in the *studium generale* at the University of Paris, the preeminent university in Europe for the study of theology.[3] Albert recognized the intellectual acumen of his student and gave him special assignments. The university was patterned on the guilds, and the master/apprentice relationship was geared toward admission to full standing in the profession.

University Professor

Thomas went with Albert to Cologne in 1248 and became a university lecturer (like today's graduate assistant) and for four years lectured on Peter Lombard's *Book of Sentences*. He was ordained to the priesthood in 1250 at the age of 25 (the youngest allowed). In 1256 (at the exceptionally early age of 31) he became a regular professor of theology at the Sorbonne in Paris and dedicated himself to teaching and research, writing an extensive number of treatises. In thirteenth century terms, his task was threefold: *legere, disputare, predicare*—to comment, to dispute, to preach.[4] Aquinas' writings emerged naturally out of his activities as a teacher. His most important works are *Summa Theologica,* a comprehensive theological work that used the philosophy of Aristotle and Plato and the interpretations of Augustine to explain the dogmas of Christianity; the *Summa Contra Gentiles* which became a manual for Christian teaching as it contained an explanation of the Christian doctrines, defending them from opposing views; and *de Magistro,* his main work about teaching and education.

Thomas Aquinas was truly brilliant but often so absorbed in his thoughts that he was absent-minded. He worked hard, was kind, devoted and pious, a humble and obedient friar. He had many mystical experiences; the last one on December 6, 1273, was so deep that he no longer wished to write about God—"all I have written seems to me like so much straw compared to what I have seen." God told Thomas that he had written well about him. "What would you like in return?", God asked him. "Only you," Thomas replied. God

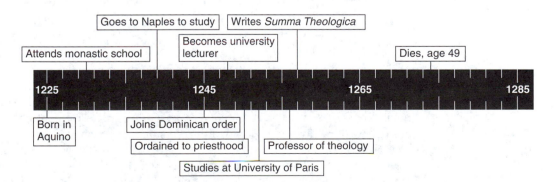

Figure 5.3   Thomas Aquinas' Life and Times

answered his prayer soon after that. Summoned by Pope Gregory X to the Council of Lyons in 1274, Aquinas became ill on the way and died on March 7 at the age of 49.

St. Thomas' Importance for Educational Thought

Thomas Aquinas sought to reconcile Greek reasoning and classical philosophy with the teachings of the faith. He completed the intellectual synthesis begun by Augustine. Christian faith and theology were challenged by the re-discovery of the philosophy of the Greeks by the Arabs. Aquinas synthesized the philosophy of Plato and Aristotle, the interpretations of Avicenna and Averroes, and the theology of St. Augustine into a coherent whole. His synthesis created a new world-view that was much more complete than the sum of its parts. His philosophical synthesis of faith and reason is one of the greatest achievements of medieval times.

Etienne Gilson and Jacques Maritain brought the ideas of St. Thomas to twentieth century American education, showing how faith and reason could be reconciled in contemporary issues. The parochial Catholic school system in America is, in many ways, a result of the work of Thomas in that it seeks to provide students with faith enlightened by reason. The Great Books movement started by Robert Hutchins and Mortimer Adler is a secular effort to promote Thomas' and the scholastics' emphasis on the classics and on deepening critical thinking skills in students.

The Scholastic Method

Thomas was very much a man of his age and environment. He made important contributions to university teaching which are a part of our intellectual heritage today. Scholasticism was the philosophic system of his time that emphasized the use of reason in exploring questions of philosophy and theology. The Scholastic Method, also called the Disputed Questions, was an extremely formal and sophisticated method used in teaching in the university. The teacher would lecture and dispute. *Lectio,* or lecturing, meant reading and commenting on a classical text. *Disputatio,* or disputation, was tied to the text and permitted the developed exposition of the main ideas.[5] The Disputed Question began with a problem stated by the teacher in the form of a question. The students listen to arguments for and against a certain solution to the question. The students, with the aid of the teacher, take a position on the problem. Then they deal, one by one, with arguments on all sides of the question. Using this method, the teacher helps the students reach a balanced solution. The entire Summa Teologica is written using the exposition of disputed questions. The Scholastic Method, a synthesis of the dialogue format of the ancient Greeks with the rhetorical arguments of the ancient Romans, can be seen as the forerunner of the debate of today.

Aquinas' Philosophy of Education

Aquinas had no "philosophy of education" per se, as he was a theologian who used philosophy to explain his theology as he taught; he would not be considered an educator. However, from his theological and philosophic writings on politics, ethics, and metaphysics we can extract what he says about human nature, learning and teaching, and the goal of human life and see important statements presenting an educational philosophy.[6] It contains a view of reality, a philosophy of the person, and a view on how we know and what is important to know.

According to Thomism, the world is created of a hierarchy of beings. God is the Supreme Being who has created all other beings. The student is a human being who is endowed by God with an intellect and free will. With our intellect we are able to know all created things; through our will we are able to choose how we will act. Reasoning is the human being's highest power. However, knowledge does not necessarily lead to morality. Education is a matter of helping students develop their intellectual abilities and form their character by using their power of choice well. The best one can hope to do is to accustom young people to acting virtuously so that they may develop good habits through the exercise of their own free action.[7] Aquinas' ideas are very relevant to today's emphasis on character development as they stress the importance of giving students opportunities to make good choices. Aquinas has a vision of the student with a potential for knowledge as well as with a potential for spiritual growth with the aid of grace.[8]

Teaching (*doctrina*) consists of communicating to others a truth mediated beforehand. It is assisting someone else to come to know or understand something that you know. The professor has to first discover the truth himself and then communicate his finding to others. Teaching is thus, for Thomas, the teacher helping students to discover, using the natural cognitive and reasoning powers illuminated by God, the truths that the teacher knows. The teacher helps the students to actualize their potentialities.[9] Thomas was one of the first to advocate that students learn through discovery; this discovery learning based in discovery truth was very different from that to be advocated by John Locke and the Enlightenment figures that based their discovery learning in man's thoughts alone.

What is to be taught is, first of all, a good understanding of language as expounded in the *trivium* and then a good basis in the liberal arts of the *quadrivium*. Aquinas saw value in studying the classics as they emphasized perennial truths about humans, the world, and their relationship with their creator.

The purpose of education is to obtain life's purpose, that is, to get to heaven. Education is thus a means to an end, helping people develop all their potential so they can learn to discover the good and the true in order to make good choices, live a good life, and thus gain heaven. A good education is one that teaches the art of inquiry that enables individuals to engage in activities that allow them to achieve their own good, happiness; and this kind of education only works when family, school, and the political community work together. Aquinas was influenced by Aristotle and the absurd view of his age regarding the capacities of women, and only refers to men in what he says about education. However he does see the important role of the family, i.e., mother and father, in the early education of children.[10]

Aquinas tells us "Just as one is inspired to virtue by another and by himself, so also he gets to know something by discovering for himself and by learning from another."[11]

For Further Research on the Internet

A comprehensive biography of Aquinas with many links. **http://plato.stanford.edu/entries/aquinas/**

A page of links leading to articles on Thomas Aquinas by current day scholars. **http://www.op.org/domcentral/study/TA.htm**

The Jacques Maritain Institute at Notre Dame shows the extent of Aquinas' influence in America today. **http://www.nd.edu/~maritain/**

Notes

1. Jan Emerson, "A Poetry of Science: Relating Body and Soul in Scrivias," in *Hildegard of Bingen: A Book of Essays,* edited by M. B. McInerney (New York: Garland Publishing, Inc., 1998) pp. 77, 79.
2. Jean-Pierre Torrell, *Saint Thomas Aquinas: The Person and His Work,* translated by Royal, Robert. 2 vols. Vol. 1. (Washington, DC: The Catholic University Press., 1996), pp. 1–4.

3. James Weisheipl, *Friar Thomas d'Aquino: His Life, Thought, and Work* (New York: Doubleday & Company, Inc., 1974), p. 17.
4. Torrell, p. 18ff.
5. Aidan Nichols, *Discovering Aquinas: An Introduction to His Life, Work and Influence* (Grand Rapids, MI: William B. Eerdmans Publishing Co., 2002), p. 7.
6. Ralph McInerny, *A First Glance at St. Thomas Aquinas* (South Bend, IN: University of Notre Dame Publishers, 1990), p. 17.
7. Alasdair MacIntyre, "Aquinas's Critique of Education: Against His Own Age, Against Ours," in *Philosophers on Education: New Historical Perspectives,* edited by A. O. Rorty (London: Routledge, 1998), p. 96.
8. John Donohue, *St. Thomas Aquinas and Education* (New York: Random House., 1968), pp. 60, 82ff.
9. Cristina Traina, "A Person in the Making: Thomas Aquinas on Children and Childhood," in *The Child in Christian Thought,* edited by M. Bunge (Grand Rapids, MI: William B. Eerdmans Publishing Company, 2001), p. 107.
10. MacIntyre, p. 102.
11. Ibid., pp. 99–100.

Questions to Guide Your Reading

The following selection is written using the Scholastic Method of the Disputed Questions. Think of it as a debate on paper. Identify the problem to be solved. Read the sections entitled "To the Contrary" and "Reply" first to get St. Thomas' answer to the problem. Then read number one of the "Difficulties" and number one of the "Answers to the Difficulties" as if they were two opinions expressed by debaters. Continue on, reading number two of the Difficulties and number two of the Answers to the Difficulties. Many times St. Thomas explains the applications of important philosophic concepts as he "answers the difficulties."

READING 5.3:
THE TEACHER
ON TRUTH, QUESTION XI ARTICLE II

In the Second Article We Ask: Can One be Called His Own Teacher?

Difficulties

It seems that he can, for

1. An activity should be ascribed more to the principal cause than to the instrumental cause. But in us the agent intellect is, as it were, the principal cause of the knowledge which is produced in us. But a man who teaches another is, as it were, an instrumental cause, furnishing the agent intellect with the instrument by means of which it causes knowledge. Therefore, the agent intellect is more than another man. If, then, because of what a speaker says we call him the teacher of the one who hears him, the hearer should in a much more fuller sense be called his own teacher because of the light of the agent intellect.

2. One learns something only insofar as he acquires certain knowledge. But such certitude is in us by reason of the principles which are naturally known in the light of the agent intellect. Therefore,

Source: *Philosophy of Teaching of St. Thomas Aquinas* by Mayer, Mary Hein. Copyright 1929 by Glencoe Publishing Co. Reproduced with permission of Glencoe Publishing Co. in the format textbook via Copyright Clearance Center.

the agent intellect is especially fitted to teach. We conclude as before.

3. To teach belongs more properly to God than to man. Hence, it is said in Matthew 23:8: "For one is your master." But God teaches us insofar as He gives us the light of reason, by means of which we can judge about everything. Therefore, we should attribute the activity of teaching especially to that light. The same conclusion follows as before.

4. It is more perfect to learn something through discovery than to learn it from another, as is clear in the Ethics. If, therefore, a man is called a teacher by virtue of that manner of acquiring knowledge by which one learns from another so that the one is called the teacher of the other, he should, with much greater reason, be called a teacher by virtue of the process of acquiring knowledge through discovery, and so be called his own teacher.

5. Just as one is inspired to virtue by another and by himself, so also he gets to know something by discovering for himself and by learning from another. But those who attain to works of virtue without having another as an instructor or a lawgiver are said to be a law unto themselves, according to Romans 2:14: "For when the Gentiles, who have not the law, do by nature those things that are of the law . . . they are a law to themselves." Therefore, the man who acquires knowledge by himself ought also to be called his own teacher.

6. The teacher is a cause of knowledge as the doctor is a cause of health, as has been said. But a doctor heals himself. Therefore, one can also teach oneself.

To the Contrary

1. The Philosopher says that it is impossible for one who is teaching to learn. For the teacher must have knowledge and the learner must not have it. Therefore, one cannot teach himself or be called his own teacher.

2. The office of teacher implies a relation of superiority, just as dominion does. But relationships of this sort cannot exist between a person and himself. For one is not his own father or master. Therefore, neither can one be called his own teacher.

Reply

Through the light of reason implanted in him and without the help of another's instruction, one can undoubtedly acquire knowledge of many things which he does not know. This is clear with all those who acquire knowledge through discovery. Thus, in some sense one can be a cause of his own knowledge, but he cannot be called his own teacher or be said to teach himself.

For in physical reality we find two types of active principles, as is clear from the Philosopher. Now, there is one type of agent which has within itself everything which it produces in the effect, and it has these perfections in the same way as the effect, as happens in univocal agents, or in a higher way than the effect, as in equivocal causes. Then, there is a certain type of agent in which there pre-exists only a part of the effect. An example of this type is a movement which causes health, or some warm medicine, in which warmth exists either actually or virtually. But warmth is not complete health, but a part of it. The first type of agent, therefore, possesses the complete nature of action. But those of the second type do not, for a thing acts insofar as it is in act. Hence, since it actually contains the effect to be produced only partially, it is not an agent in the perfect sense.

But teaching implies the perfect activity of knowledge in the teacher or master. Hence, the teacher or master must have the knowledge which he causes in another explicitly and perfectly, as it is to be received in the one who is learning through instruction. When, however, knowledge is acquired by someone through an internal principle, that which is the active cause of the knowledge has the knowledge to be acquired only partially, that is, in the seminal principles of knowledge, which are the general principles. Therefore, properly speaking, we cannot call a man teacher or master because of such causality.

Answers to Difficulties

1. Although to some extent the agent intellect is more the principal cause than another's teaching, the knowledge does not pre-exist in it completely, as it does in the teacher. Hence, the argument does not follow.

2. A like solution should be given to the second difficulty.

3. God knows explicitly everything which man is taught by Him. Hence, the character of teacher can suitably be applied to God. The case is not the same with the agent intellect, for the reason already given.

4. For the one learning a science, to learn it by discovery is the more perfect way of acquiring the knowledge because it shows that he is more skillful in the acquisition of knowledge. However, for the one causing the knowledge, it is more perfect to cause it by means of instruction. For a teacher who knows the whole science explicitly can teach it to a pupil more readily than the pupil himself could learn it from his own rather general knowledge of the principles of the science.

5. A law has the same relation to matters of action as a principle has to speculative matters, but not the same as a teacher. Consequently, if he is a law unto himself, it does not follow that he can be his own teacher.

6. A doctor heals insofar as he has health, not actually, but in the knowledge of his art. But the teacher teaches insofar as he has knowledge actually. Hence, he who does not have health actually can cause health in himself because he has health in the knowledge of his art. However, it is impossible for one actually to have knowledge and not to have it, in such a way that he could teach himself.

Discussion Questions

1. Aquinas says that the teacher has knowledge and the learner does not. If one who learns from discovery is his own teacher, then will there be a need for teachers if people are their own teachers? Why or why not?
2. What do you think a Thomistic-driven classroom would look like today? What would be the curriculum? What would be some of the methods used?
3. Aquinas saw "no conflict between research and teaching." Explain how Aquinas would envision today's university professor doing these two tasks.
4. Compare Aquinas' statement "God teaches us insofar as he gives us the light of reason, by means of which we can judge about everything" with Socrates' statement "Virtue is neither natural nor acquired but an instinct given by God to the virtuous." Do you think Aquinas and Socrates would agree with each other's statements and understandings of virtue? Would they be in favor of character education in the schools or not? Explain.

Suggestions for Further Reading

Bourke, Vernon. *Aquinas' Search for Wisdom*. Milwaukee: Bruce Publishing Co., 1965.

Copleston, Frederick. *Aquinas: An Introduction to the Life and Work of the Great Medieval Thinker*. New York: Penguin Books, 1986.

Donohue, John. *St. Thomas Aquinas and Education*. New York: Random House, 1968.

Gilson, Ettiene. *The Christian Philosophy of St. Thomas Aquinas*. New York: Random House, 1956.

MacIntyre, Alasdair. "Aquinas's Critique of Education: Against His Own Age, Against Ours." In *Philosophers on Education: New Historical Perspectives*, edited by A. O. Rorty. London: Routledge., 1998.

McInerny, Ralph. *A First Glance at St. Thomas Aquinas*. South Bend, IN: University of Notre Dame Publishers, 1990.

Nichols, Aidan. *Discovering Aquinas: An Introduction to His Life, Work and Influence*. Grand Rapids, MI: William B. Eerdmans Publishing Co., 2002.

Torrell, Jean-Pierre. *Saint Thomas Aquinas: The Person and His Work*. Translated by Robert Royal, 2 vols. Vol. 1. Washington, DC: The Catholic University Press, 1996.

Traina, Cristina. "A Person in the Making: Thomas Aquinas on Children and Childhood." In *The Child in Christian Thought*, edited by M. Bunge. Grand Rapids, MI: William B. Eerdmans Publishing Company, 2001.

Weisheipl, James. *Friar Thomas d'Aquino: His Life, Thought, and Work*. New York: Doubleday & Company, Inc., 1974.

CHAPTER ACTIVITIES

Linking the Past to the Present

1. Do a Google search on the Internet on "problem-based learning." Write a lesson plan in which you could teach PBL in a school. How is this similar to the way Aquinas taught through discovery learning?

2. Listen to a CD of Hildegard's music (also available on the Internet through a Google search). What aspects of her music make it still appealing one thousand years after it was composed?

Developing Your Philosophy of Education

In your philosophy of education, write what it is in the curriculum that you think is most important to teach. What subjects will make up your *trivium* and *quadrivium?*

How will you teach in order to promote higher level thinking? Will you use discovery learning methods, debates, and/or group discussions? What other methods will you use?

Connecting Theory to Practice

1. Interview an electrician or another tradesperson. Ask them to explain their training to become certified in their trade. Compare their training to that of the medieval guilds. In what ways is it the same, and how is it different?

2. Interview a Boy Scout or a Girl Scout. What character values are they taught in scouts? Are they similar to being "modern day" knights? Explain your answer.

Educators' Philosophies and Contributions to Education

TABLE 5.1   Philosophy and Contributions of Medieval Educators

Educator	Role of Teacher & Learner	View of Curriculum & Methodology	Purpose or Goal of Education	Major Contribution
Charlemagne and Alcuin	Teachers should teach all students—boys and girls—a standard curriculum in a standard way	The *trivium* (grammar, rhetoric, dialectic) and the *quadrivium* (arithmetic, geometry, astronomy, music) taught demanding accuracy in students	The preservation of culture, through a revival of learning including a new form of writing (printing)	The *trivium* and *quadrivium;* first to propose universal and free primary education of all

(continued)

Educator	Role of Teacher & Learner	View of Curriculum & Methodology	Purpose or Goal of Education	Major Contribution
Hildegard of Bingen	The teacher is a mentor supporting the total growth of her female students—their body body and soul, i.e, intellect and will	The classics and writings of the Fathers of the Church, music and songs, all aspects of higher learning: copying manuscripts and writing *glosses*	To help the human mind discover divine truth in aspects of culture, i.e., music, art, literature	Theory of sex complementarity, first woman to teach other women university-level intellectual topics
Thomas Aquinas	The teacher is a moral mentor who lectures and disputes, or debates, with the students in order to help them discover true knowledge on their own	The classics of Greek and Latin literature with the Fathers of the Church taught through the Scholastic Method	Goal is to help students develop their intellect and their will so that they live a life of virtue and make good moral choices that make them happy on earth and get them to heaven	Philosophic synthesis of faith and reason; the Scholastic Method

CHAPTER 6

Education in the Renaissance and the Reformation

The three hundred years from 1300 to 1600 was a general period of great progress and social change in Europe. Two significant events occurred that had a profound influence on civilization and education from then onward. They were the invention of the printing press in 1423 and the discovery by Christopher Columbus of America in 1492, which ushered in an Age of Exploration. The invention of the printing press made books more widely available and the Age of Exploration began a period of economic and intellectual leadership in Europe. At the beginning of this period, Spain and Italy were the most important countries; by the end of these three centuries, England, Holland, and France had risen to be the world leaders.

The Renaissance or "Re-birth"

The Renaissance is the historical period beginning in the fourteenth century that reached its height in the sixteenth century, basically 1300 to 1520 A.D. As medieval scholars had begun to use the classical authorities, especially Aristotle, as a basis for scholastic philosophy, the Renaissance ushered in a complete revival of interest not only in the Greek and Latin classics, but also in their art, literature, and architecture.[1] The commercial revival after the Crusades and the rise of urban life led to a "re-birth" of interest in the Greco-Roman culture and also led to a more secular set of values. This new philosophy of life was termed "humanism" as it glorified the individual and obtaining material goods. It is for this reason that many historians describe the Renaissance as the transitional period between the medieval and the modern age.

Life in the Renaissance

A unique set of social, political, and economic conditions eventually lead to the emergence of capitalism, commerce, cities, and nation states—much different from the feudal manors of medieval times. We see a move from craft guilds to merchants in towns. This society was based on individual property and private contracts and needed centralized bureaucracies to administer justice, collect taxes, and enforce national policies. The rise of the middle class had great importance for educational development. It also demanded the literacy, arithmetic, bookkeeping, and commercial skills necessary to sustain commercial and business enterprises. The scholastic educational patterns and content were inadequate to satisfy the needs of this class. It was most important that those who dealt in these vital commercial activities—lawyers, notaries, drafters, and recorders—be well educated. Although training in drafting legal documents was first given by apprenticeship, soon major centers of professional study grew. These centers of higher study allowed for the development of more sophisticated skills such as the mastery of Latin, basic law knowledge, and a literary base which allowed for the use of quotations from classical and Christian authors. This new learning grew up outside the colleges and universities, not in them. This new educated class, urban and mercantile, were really independent entrepreneurs who were free to follow this new philosophy of life.[2]

The new Renaissance state consisted of a great bureaucracy, with a high system of administrative centralization consisting of couriers and officers, cultivated patrons of the arts and letters, builders of palaces and colleges, and collectors of statues and books. So many "officers" or "princes" needed more and more staff for their councils and courts and to govern their territories. So the Renaissance princes founded schools and colleges, not to produce scholars but to staff vital offices.[3]

Renaissance Education

The history of Renaissance education is primarily that of individual humanist educators who developed distinctive pedagogical strategies designed to produce the well-rounded, liberally educated gentleman. The humanists objected to the narrow approach that dominated scholastic education. They made no attempt to embrace all of the traditional liberal arts (the *trivium* and *quadrivium*). (See Figure 6.1.)

Instead they emphasized the study of grammar, rhetoric, poetry, history, and moral philosophy. They attacked the Scholastic Method and its use of commentaries, or *sententia,* on authors and proposed in its place the return of broader knowledge and the actual reading and discussion of the original Latin and Greek texts. These educators generally believed that classical Greek and Latin literatures, by furnishing the basic elements of a liberal education, could produce this cultured gentleman. The style of writing of the classical authors, especially Cicero, would produce, it was believed, an elegance of style and expression. They emphasized the development of oratorical skills and social attitudes that would come from the study of grammar and rhetoric, history, and moral philosophy. Education implied an obligation for the educated person to be an involved citizen. Petrarch, the greatest representative of Renaissance humanism, was a great poet who conceived the humanistic program of education. Its success resulted from its being practical. Humanistic education developed skills—grammar led to clear and correct writing and speaking, rhetoric developed the ability to use persuasive argument and make practical decisions, and moral training led to the ability to participate in political life. The human-

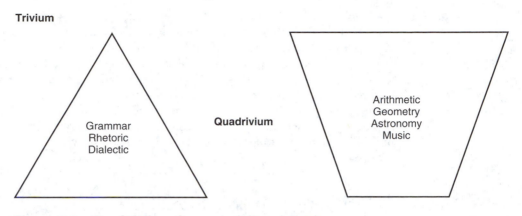

Figure 6.1   The Studium Generale (Liberal Arts)

ists criticized the traditional university education that concentrated on logic and Aristotelian science. The university existed to train experts and specialists. Humanist education would help to develop the effective judges, lawyers, and notaries so needed by the general society.

With the emphasis on a practical, occupation-related education for the commercial class came a renewed emphasis for higher and higher studies in the vernacular language. A two-tiered education system began to develop. Career and occupation-related education in the vernacular for the artisan and lower commercial classes and the classical education in Greek and Latin for the upper class. A concern for the vernacular developed and a battle began to win it a place next to Latin as a worthy vehicle for expression: in literature, in science, in philosophy, and in theology. This battle was won during the Reformation.[4]

The Education of Women During the Renaissance

Leonardo Bruni discussed the education of women in his treatise *On Studies and Letters*. He maintained that women should receive the same classical education as men, including grammar, rhetoric, poetry, history, and moral philosophy but with a special emphasis on virtue. Military training and exercise in oratory and disputation were omitted from their study. A handful of women from the upper classes did receive a genuine humanistic education, but they could not share their thoughts freely with male humanists nor could they participate in government or a profession. Many of their female contemporaries had only a rudimentary literacy in the vernacular with a little arithmetic.[5]

Little is known about the education of young girls before the Renaissance, but we do know that by the second part of the fourteenth century, more girls were literate than had been previously. In most families, it was the spiritual education that was of primary importance. Young girls learned to read from their Book of Hours based on stories from the Bible. The accepted educational goal was that they learned what they needed in order to, once they were married, manage their households and raise their children. Christine de Pizan spoke and wrote about the importance of women receiving a broad education so that they could have a profession. Soon we begin to see young noblewomen and the wives and daughters of Italian merchants being taught to read and write so that they could assist the men of the family with bookkeeping and correspondence.[6]

The growing prestige of the humanists led to the abandonment of the traditional Latin schools. Beginning in the 1420's, a number of humanists established schools on a new pattern, explicitly emphasizing the humanistic subjects taught through reading the classical texts instead of handbooks (the medieval textbooks). Little by little, the foundational "required" courses for a B.A. or M.A. degree changed from an emphasis on philosophy and logic to the study of classical literature and rhetoric.[7]

A Renaissance Philosophy of Education

A new philosophy of education developed during this time. The purpose of education was not the mastery of absolute truth, but the ability to make sound moral decisions during the process of daily living. The goal of life was not to know God, who is beyond limited reason, but to love God, which is something that depends on faith and emotion more than reason. This intellectual relativism is expressed by the humanistic methods of teaching using debate, discussion, and persuasion instead of lecture. The curriculum should consist of the more practical and useful studies.[8]

However, it was the influence of the Reformation that fostered an increase in the number of children attending schools and the consequent spread of literacy. During the Renaissance, the church's monopoly over parish, monastic, and cathedral schools was broken as princes, nobles, towns, and private teachers established their own schools.

Erasmus (1466–1536) was a scholar, classicist, critic, and author during the Renaissance. As a teacher he emphasized the humanistic content of the classics. He was a reformer who advocated a Christian and cosmopolitan humanism. An examination of the writings of Erasmus of Rotterdam will provide an example of many of the key Renaissance humanistic ideas.

The Reformation

The "Reformation" is the label historians use to describe the series of upheavals in the religious life of Europe during the sixteenth century. It was closely related to the Renaissance and the humanistic demand for freedom of scholarship but was more significant historically because it not only touched personal beliefs, but it also had a profound impact on the social, political, and economic spheres which had a far reaching effect on every area of life.[9]

The Reformation began in 1517 with Luther's attack on indulgences. Luther, an Augustian monk, embodied in his own person all the driving forces and reformation impulses of his time. The Reformation was born deep within a single individual, but emerged to become a public matter and a powerful historical force.[10] Martin Luther and John Calvin inaugurated their plans for reformation within the Catholic framework by protesting certain corrupt practices. Within a short time however, this developed into serious doctrinal differences. The Protestants became those who protested the authority and abuses of the Church. Soon, continental Europe was divided into three major contending creeds: Lutheran, Calvinist, and Roman Catholic. (See Map 6.1 of Europe after the Reformation.)

Map 6.1   Europe after the Reformation

Source: Anthony Esler, *The Human Venture, Combined Volume: From Prehistory to the Present,* 5th edition, 2004. Reprinted by permission of Pearson Education.

Daily Life in the Time of the Reformation

There were political, cultural, and religious "preconditions" of the Reformation which enabled this German push for religious reform to spread so rapidly. Politically weak emperors had led to the role of the Church as a political entity. The lack of coinage, legal system, and a semblance of order contributed to a lack of unity at a time when urban life was developing rapidly. Culturally, a large number of universities had been founded which contributed to a dissemination of humanist ideas and values in education, society, and religion. Religious preconditions included a poorly educated clergy and an intertwining of religion with social, economic, and political aspects of the person's material as well as spiritual life.[11] This led to several abuses including the sale of indulgences, which were writs given for the payment of money which was called a donation to the Church. These writs excused the recipient from deeds of satisfaction or suffering in purgatory upon repentance and confession of sins.[12]

TABLE 6.1   Literacy Rates

Year	Men	Women	Total
1500	10%	2%	12%
1600	28%	9%	37%
1700	40%	32%	72%

The number one cultural event was the invention of the printing press. Printing broadened literacy and contributed to both the improvement of the religious education of the clergy and a general rise in literacy in the laity. It encouraged the dissemination of works in the vernacular. The printing press met the need of the reform by supplying uniform liturgical books, prayer books, handbooks or confessors, manuals for priests, and collections of Biblical readings.[13]

Education During the Reformation

As far as education is concerned, the Reformation gave a new impetus to the reform of schooling. The Latin school was reorganized and the city council created a new German school for primary education. German schools were usually privately run institutions. From the 1530's onward, the catechism played a crucial role in the educational curriculum. The religious education given in the schools was considered essential in bringing the Reformation to the people. For the Lutheran, church and school were intimately connected; they represented supplemental avenues along which the Gospel could be spread. Literacy statistics show the success of the Protestant reform of schooling. By 1650, thirty to forty percent of the adult population was able to read.[14] (See Table 6.1 for the literacy rates.)

Municipal colleges were established and humanists had a disdain for the medieval "glosas" and the interpretation of texts. They emphasized reading the original primary classical sources. This led to the intellegentsia demanding an intellectually satisfying religion based on the primary text of Christianity—the Bible.[15]

The Counter-Reformation

Erasmus criticized the formalism, traditionalism, authoritarianism, and scholasticism of Roman Catholicism. He extolled the real, inner piety of the layman over the complacency of the indolent monks. With his satire, Erasmus sought to reform the abuses he saw.[16] Benedictines and Franciscans also urged that an internal reformation proceed within the context of a universal Christian synthesis. A counter-reformation was launched, fought in great part by Ignatius Loyola and his Jesuits. He developed the Jesuit system of education with the curriculum of the *ratio studiorum* taught in well designed lessons in order to produce many well-educated Catholics who could defend their religion. An effort was made to detach the Catholic Church from the Catholic princely state and correct the many abuses that had grown under this system. For thirty years (from 1618 to 1648), the Holy Roman Empire in Europe was besieged by a civil war and a series of religious wars between the Protestants and the Catholics.

A Reformation Philosophy of Education

The Protestant Reformation profoundly affected Western educational institutions, significantly shaping the development of a new educational philosophy. The various denominations developed their own theologies of education, established their own schools, and sought to commit the young members of the Church to "defend the faith" against rival creeds. They stimulated a desire to increase school attendance.

The general Protestant emphasis on individual biblical reading fostered a demand for universal literacy and promoted the development of **vernacular schools**—schools offering a basic curriculum of reading, writing, arithmetic, and religion in the language of the people. The literacy rate grew exponentially during these years.

For Further Research on the Internet

An outstanding site with information about the life of a child in Elizabethan Renaissance time. **http://www.twingroves.district96.k12.il.us/Renaissance/Town/Children.html**

The Center for Reformation and Renaissance Studies has resources and original documents from this time period. **http://www.crrs.ca/**

Notes

1. Hugh Trevor-Roper, *The Crisis of the Seventeenth Century: Religions, the Reformation and Social Change* (Indianapolis: Liberty Fund., 1999), p. 1.
2. Charles G. Nauert Jr., *Humanism and the Culture of Renaissance Europe, New Approaches to European History* (Cambridge: Cambridge University Press, 1995), pp. 1–5.
3. Trevor-Roper, p. 56.
4. Roy Porter, and Mikulas Teich, *The Renaissance in National Context* (Cambridge: University of Cambridge, 1992), pp. 37, 79.
5. Ibid., pp. 45–46.
6. Charity Cannon Willard, *Christine de Pizan, Her Life and Works* (New York.: Persea, 1984), p. 33.
7. Charles G. Nauert Jr., *Humanism and the Culture of Renaissance Europe, New Approaches to European History* (Cambridge: Cambridge University Press, 1995), pp. 132–133.
8. Nauert Jr., pp. 12–16.
9. Bob Scribner, Roy Porter, and Mikulas Teich, *The Reformation in National Context*, edited by B. Scribner (Cambridge: Cambridge University Press, 1994), pp. 1–5.
10. Lewis Spitz, *The Rise of Modern Europe* (New York: Harper & Row, Harper Torchbooks, 1987), p. 57.
11. Ibid., pp. 6–15.
12. Spitz, pp. 59–62.
13. Scribner, pp. 6–15; Spitz, p. 53.
14. Scribner, p. 42.
15. Ibid., p. 47.
16. Trevor-Roper, p. 22.

Section 6.1: Christine de Pizan (1364?–1430?)

In English class you probably learned about genres, or categories of literary composition: poetry, letters, essays, biographies, and autobiographies. You may have written an autobiography of "Why I want to be a teacher" for one of your education classes. As common as this is today, Christine de Pizan was the first woman to write an autobiography and the first to develop the genre of "essay," and was also one of the first advocates of liberal arts education for women.

Christine's Life and Times

Christine de Pizan was born in Venice, Italy around 1364. Her mother was from Venice and her father, Tommaso di Benvenuto da Pizzaro, was a lecturer in astrology at the University of Bologna.[1] Soon after Christine's birth, her father received an appointment to the court of the French King Charles V and left for Paris, leaving his family on his estate in Bologna. King Charles had fragile health and looked to Tommaso for his medical and astrological advice. Because the King thought highly of Tomasso and wanted to make the appointment permanent, he generously helped bring the family to France in 1368 and Tommaso and his wife shortened their last name to Pizan.[2] Christine became very familiar with life at court and later wrote that she and her two brothers had a happy childhood there.

Christine's Education

The King had one of the best libraries in France, with many of the famous Greek and Roman classics translated to French. Christine was an intelligent girl who showed an interest and aptitude for a more formal education and wanted to read more, which was unheard of for girls at this time. In her autobiography, Christine explained the poor system of education for girls and complained that she had not been able to spend her early years learning what would have been very useful to her later in life.

Christine's mother had the conventional view of her daughter's role in life, limited to learning how to spin, weave, cook, manage a household, and raise children.[3] Nevertheless, her enlightened father taught her to read French, Italian, and some Latin, and to write; much more than most girls of her time. She paid tribute to her father later in life in her allegorical poem *The Long Road to Learning* (1403).[4] Since Christine grew up in the court's book-filled environment, she became familiar with the many excellent books in the King's library, and these became an important source for her later writings.

Wife and Mother

When Christine was fifteen years old, her father chose a husband for her, Etienne de Castel, a twenty-five year old notary of good character and intelligence. Soon after he married Christine, he was made royal secretary, in charge of preparing the king's letters and accounts. The marriage was a happy one for ten years, and they had three children.

In 1380, King Charles V died and there were several uprisings in court between the king's brothers. Christine's father was retained by the king's household but at a greatly reduced salary; he died in 1385 leaving Etienne, 31, head of the Pizan household. Three years later, Etienne died in an epidemic. Christine was overwhelmed with grief by this loss. She was only 24 years old and was responsible for three children, her widowed mother, and a niece. Her brothers had left France for Bologna so she was all alone in Paris.[5] (See the timeline of Christine's life in Figure 6.2.)

Head of the Household

Christine had limited knowledge of her husband's financial affairs and when she tried to collect the money due his estate she was met by deception and dishonesty and burdened with lawsuits over her husband's property, which was rightfully hers. The extortion continued for more than fourteen years.[6] During this time, it seems that Christine continued copying court documents as Etienne had and copied manuscripts for others for a fee to maintain her household. She was just getting her financial affairs in order when she fell ill during the epidemic sweeping Europe in 1392.

Poet

Christine began, at the encouragement of her friends, to write poetry in middle French to relieve her heavy heart. Her poems were well-received and once recovered from her illness, she resolved to put her gift to use and complete her education.

Gilles Malet, the court librarian, helped her by giving her access to the royal library and helped her meet the Earl of Salisbury. He encouraged her poetry and took her son Jean into his household in England as a companion for his own son. Christine had no dowry money for her daughter's marriage so she helped her enter the royal Dominican convent at Poissy.

Christine launched herself on a program of self-education that would provide her with the material for her later work. Christine began writing poetry using fixed forms of verse (ballades, rondeau, and virelay), and had written enough to assemble a collection of 100 ballades by 1402. She turned her attention to more serious forms of writing, narrative

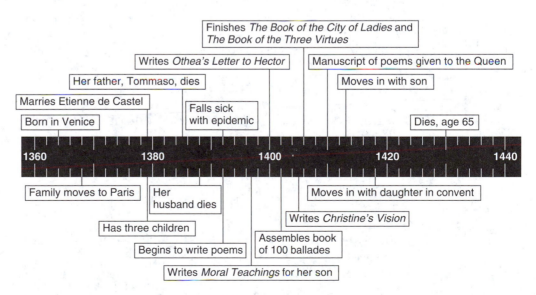

Figure 6.2   Christine de Pizan's Life and Times

poems, pastoral poems, and long allegorical dream-vision poems, producing prolifically. There is no record of there being any other women poets at this time.[7]

First Feminist

Christine's work became infamous when she wrote to criticize the literary merits of Jean de Meun's *Romance of the Rose,* which she thought promoted a deplorable attitude towards women. Christine became the first woman in the Middle Ages to defend her sex as one of the first true feminists.[8] She wrote letters, one to the Queen, protesting the poem's unjust slander of women, insisting on respect for women, and maintaining that the achievements of certain women rendered them as individuals, if not as a whole sex, equal or superior to men. These letters not only publicized Christine's ideas but also brought public attention to women and the roles they could play beyond the traditional domestic sphere. Long letters written by Christine were, in many ways, the forerunner of the modern essay.[9]

Moral Educator

In 1397, she wrote *Moral Teaching* and *Moral Proverbs* for her son Jean when he went to live in the household of the Earl of Salisbury. She wrote *Othea's Letter to Hector* around 1400, in which she developed a system of education for a young man of 15, the age of training for the knighthood. The book was well-accepted, printed in six editions, and translated into English. It took her three years to write the *Mutation of Fortune,* an autobiographical work that brought her to the attention of the Duke of Burgundy.

Biographer

He asked her to write the official biography of his brother, the late King Charles V. She patterned this "secular biography," one of the first of its kind in France, after Petrarch's Italian biography. It has historical value today as one of the first eye-witness accounts of the reign.

In 1405, she wrote her most important and individual work, full of autobiographical details, *Christine's Vision,* in three parts, becoming the first woman to leave an autobiography as a record of her evolution as a writer and as a person. According to biographer Charity Gannon Willard, "The last part of Christine's vision is best known to modern readers for the information it furnishes about Christine's life, her philosophy of life, and for the path of her progress from a retiring timid young woman to the independent woman who is not afraid to become the defender of her sex and ultimately of her adopted country."[10] The third part of this book shows her humanistic tendencies, including feelings, opinions, and experiences worth expressing, not just facts.

Famous Author of Women's Contributions

In 1406, Christine finished two of her most significant books, *The Book of the City of Ladies* and *The Book of the Three Virtues.* The first, with a title inspired by Augustine's *City of God,* is a summary of the important contributions made by women in the past. She shows, through these heroines, that women have the capacity to be warriors, teachers, orators, and artists, redressing the imbalance in the literary treatment of women so ingrained in medieval thought. This book of Christine's also complements Hildegard's *Scivias.* Both speak of constructing a city of the feminine; Hildegard's was heavenly and Christine's was secular; both use allegorical symbolism—the image of the light to show the splendor of the new city to be created.[11]

The Book of the Three Virtues attempts to teach women of all estates how to cultivate useful qualities in the city in which they live and explains how Christine would organize a school for all women who wished to attend.

Christine took up her pen in 1409 to write *The Book of the Feats of Arms and Chivalry*. In 1410, she wrote the *Lament on the Evils of the Civil War* and her lyrics were copied into a luxurious manuscript for the Queen. By 1413, Christine, now 50 years old, lived with her son, Jean, an established secretary in the Royal Chancery with a wife and three children. Her pen was idle as she helped raise her grandchildren. In 1418, her son had to flee into exile when the English occupied Paris, so Christine retired to live with her daughter in the abbey of Poissy, where she wrote *Hours of Meditation on the Lord*. Eleven years later, the extraordinary career of Joan of Arc brought her out of retirement to write her final poem, *The Tale of Joan of Arc,* the first poem to celebrate the Maid of Orleans and the only one written during Joan's lifetime.[12] It seems that Christine died sometime in 1430 around the age of 65. Her works continued to be read without interruption for more than one hundred years.

Christine's Importance for Education

Christine's writings cover many areas: morality, government, war, peace, history, and education. She wrote in many genres: poetry, letters, essays, biographies, and autobiographies. Christine deals with education specifically in several of her books: *Moral Teachings, Moral Proverbs, Othea's Letter to Hector, The Book of the Three Virtues,* and *The Book of the Body Politic* as well as indirectly in many of her other works written over some twenty years.[13] Christine's ideas on education were ahead of her time as she advocated a liberal education for women and stressed the importance of teaching young children through learning by doing and using rhyming verse to help them memorize.

Ideas on Moral Education

Moral Teachings and *Moral Proverbs* were written for the education of her son; she expresses the humanistic idea that education is concerned with the moral education of the young. Christine wrote *Moral Proverbs* in verse, as she understood children enough to know that verse helps the young memory to retain useful precepts, or maxims.[14]

In *Othea's Letter to Hector,* she outlines a suitable moral education for a young king. This was one of her more popular works, copied in French and English. One can conclude that her pedagogical ideas included therein had more impact than her political ideas expressed in other works.[15]

Advocate of Education for Women

In *The Book of the Three Virtues,* Christine presents something extraordinarily original: a school for all women who wished to attend. Nothing like this had ever been attempted for women. Christine's book is quite different from the other treatises written for women in the Middle Ages—she concerns herself with the problems of women of all social classes, not just a specific group of women. She is concerned not only with prescribing for them a domestic and spiritual life (which is the recognized lot of most women at that time), but encourages them to develop themselves and their talents to make some sort of contribution to society and dominate the conditions of their life instead of letting the conditions dominate them.[16]

Christine dedicated *The Book of the Three Virtues* to Marguerite, the future queen of France. It is apparent that the first part of the book was written with the princess in mind as it concerns itself with recommendations for the education of a young princess at her husband's court. She should be instructed by a wise and virtuous governess capable of guiding her toward virtue through kindness, good example, and stories used to engage her attention and then made use of to teach her expected behavior. Christine recommends kindness and making use of a child's natural curiosity, an innovative idea for her time period. The governess should play games with the princess to win her confidence and affection, so that she can be corrected later when necessary. Christine was advocating methods just at the time they were being incorporated into the first humanistic educational programs in Italy.[17] She had advanced educational ideas both of pedagogy and purpose, as she insisted on the importance of moral education for civic responsibility based on lessons of history, mythology, and famous people. Christine dedicated half of the book to the needs of queens and princesses, the most literate women in society. She devoted the other half to the wives of merchants and artisans, and also the poor and humble.

Christine turned to the education of the dauphin, Louis of Guyenne, when she wrote *The Book of the Body Politic*. Once again writing the book in three parts, she dealt with the education of princes in the first part, the education of nobles and knights in the second part, and the education of scholars, merchants, artisans, and laborers in the third part. Christine insists on virtue as the only basis for ruling a country and outlines the qualities a prince must cultivate in order to be ready for his future responsibilities.

The third part of this book is most interesting as she turns to the University of Paris and shows her devotion to learning and to those who give their lives to the pursuit of knowledge. Christine speaks of the contributions of early philosophers to human knowledge, including the poetry of Sappho, one of Christine's principal models as a poet. Christine insists that possession of knowledge is of little merit in itself if one makes no effort to make it available to others. More than prescribing an education that will turn a youngster into a philosopher-king, Christine is speaking in this book of the necessity of a society to confront its problems as a unified whole for the good of the political body.

Christine's Philosophy of Education

Christine insists that it is essential to provide the child with a tutor of excellent character who is capable of instructing with both kindness and firmness, teaching right from wrong, good from evil. The young student should be involved in hands-on participation in discussions in the royal courts so he can learn from his elders. Citing Cicero, Christine speaks of the importance of developing eloquence and oratorical skills in the future ruler for that will help him to convince his subjects to do his will.[18] She advocates physical education in the model of the Roman training for the young. The success of her books is due to her skill at putting sophisticated material in a relatively simple form, as good teachers do.[19]

Christine de Pizan did not have an opportunity for the classical education as advocated by the humanists of her time. She nevertheless wrote extensively about the value of such an education and its importance for developing civic responsibility and morality in the youth by exposing them to the lessons of history and the examples of famous people. She is only beginning to be appreciated today for the depth and originality of her ideas. She revered knowledge but maintained that it was to be shared with others. She continued to reach out to women through her writings, advising and instructing them to become more effective and to develop a strong moral character. We will see in the next chapter how Mary Wollstonecraft continues Christine's call for the educational and economic equality for women. Christine expresses her philosophy, saying, "Who makes the effort to acquire learning and good habits will find it pleasing in both this world and the next."[20]

Notes

1. Charity Cannon Willard, *Christine de Pizan, Her Life and Works* (New York: Persea Books, 1984), p. 17.
2. Sophia Okun Tracy, *A Woman Ahead of Her Time: Christine de Pizan, Defender of Womankind* (Greensboro N.C.: Avisson Press Inc., 2003), p. 14.

3. Norman Cantor, *Medieval Lives: Eight Charismatic Men and Women of the Middle Ages* (New York: Harper Collins Publishers, 1994), p. 111.
4. Tracy, p. 16; Sarah Lawson, "Introduction," *The Treasure of the City of Ladies* or *The Book of the Three Virtues* by Christine de Pizan (New York: Penguin Books, 1985), p. 17.
5. Rosalind Brown-Grant, "Introduction," *The Book of the City of Ladies* by Christine de Pizan (New York: Penguin Books, 1999), p. xxiv.
6. Christine de Pisan, "Christine's Vision," in *The Writings of Christine de Pizan*, edited by C. C. Willard (New York: Persea Books, 1994), part III, chapter 6.
7. Willard, p. 56.
8. Brown-Grant, p. xvii.
9. Willard, pp. 89–91.
10. Ibid., p. 161.
11. Christine McWebb, *Female City Builders: Hildegard von Bingen's Scivias and Christine de Pizan's Book of the City of Ladies*, p. 6; URL http://www.florin.ms/beth5a.html.
12. Cantor, p. 131.
13. Charity Cannon Willard, Christine de Pizan as Teacher, *RLA*, 1991, p. 1.
14. Willard, 1994, p. ix
15. Willard, 1991, p. 2.
16. Lawson, p. 22.
17. Willard, 1991, p. 2.
18. Lawson, p. 26; Willard, 1984, p. 179.
19. Willard, 1991, p. 4.
20. Willard, 1994, p. 47.

Questions to Guide Your Reading

1. How will a wise woman educate her children, according to Christine? Is this relevant to today's family?

2. What are the characteristics of a good governess for one's daughter? Is this still valid for girls in the twenty-first century?

3. What is the most important virtue Christine wants her son to acquire? Is this an important virtue for young men to develop today? Are there some virtues more for men and others that are more for women?

READING 6.1A:
THE THIRD TEACHING OF PRUDENCE, WHICH IS HOW THE WISE PRINCESS WILL CAREFULLY WATCH OVER THE WELFARE AND UPBRINGING OF HER CHILDREN

The third teaching of Prudence to the wise princess is that if she has children she should watch over them and their upbringing diligently, even the sons, although it is the father's responsibility to seek a teacher for them and take on such governors as are good and suitable. Although the lady perhaps does not care for so much responsibility, as it is the nature of a mother commonly to be more involved with the care of her children, she ought to consider carefully everything that pertains to them but more to that which touches discipline and teaching than to the training of the body.

Source: Christine de Pizan, *The Treasure of the City of Ladies*, translated by Sarah Lawson (London: Penguin Books [U.K.] Strand, 1985), pp. 66–68. Used with permission.

The wise princess will take care how they are disciplined and she will be very interested in those who have charge of them and how they carry out their duties. She will not wait for a report from someone else but she herself will often visit her children in their rooms. She will see them go to bed and get up and see how they are disciplined. It is no dishonour for a princess to do such things, for children are the greatest haven, security, and ornament that she can have. It often happens that someone would greatly like to harm the mother but would not dare to do it out of fear of the children: she ought to hold them very dear. It is great praise to say that she is careful about them for it is a sign that she is wise and good.

Therefore, the wise lady who loves her children dearly will be diligent about their education. She will ensure that they will learn first of all to serve God and to read and write and that the teacher will be careful to make them learn their prayers well. The wise lady will try to get the children's father to agree that they be introduced to Latin and that they understand something of the sciences. This instruction is very suitable for the children of princes and lords. When they grow older and have some understanding, she will also want them to be apprised of practical matters, government and everything princes should know about. She will want them to be told and shown all the precepts of virtue and taught the way to avoid vices. This lady will pay close attention to the behaviour and wisdom of the teacher and others who come in contact with her children. She will have them removed if they are not good and replace them with others.

She will want her children to be brought to her often. She will consider their appearance, actions and speech and she will correct them severely herself if they misbehave. She will make them respect her and she will want them to do her great honour.

She will converse with them in order to sense their understanding and their knowledge, and she will teach them wisely. Her daughters will be governed by good and wise ladies, and before she commits their upbringing to anyone, she will look into her attitudes, behaviour and life, for she must be very watchful about this matter. She must see that the lady or maiden to whom she entrusts the care of her daughter is of good reputation, devout and intelligent. She should be from a good family, and she should be wise and prudent so that she knows how to demonstrate the good manners and deportment fitting for the daughter of a prince. This governess ought to be mature so that she may be all the more wise in her habits and more esteemed and respected, even by the child whom she governs, and also by all those members of the court with more authority and power. A lady who has such a responsibility should take great care that there is no girl or woman around the prince's daughter of whom any reproach is known nor one who is of low rank, frivolous, silly or bad mannered, so that the child cannot follow any bad example. When the girl is old enough, the princess will wish her to learn to read. After she knows her religious offices and the Mass, she can be given books of devotion and contemplation or ones dealing with good behaviour. The princess will not tolerate books containing any vain things, follies or dissipation to be brought before her daughter, for the doctrine and teaching that the girl absorbs in her early childhood she usually remembers all her life. As the wise princess watches over the upbringing and education of her daughters, the older they get the more careful she will be. She will have them around her most of the time and keep them respectful. Her prudent behaviour and virtue will be an example to her daughters to govern themselves similarly.

READING 6.1B:
CHRISTINE'S TEACHINGS FOR HER SON, JEAN DU CASTEL

Son, I have no great treasure
To make you rich, but a measure
Of good advice which you may need;
I give it hoping you'll take heed.

From your youth pure and aglow
You must learn the world to know,
So that you can by following this
In any case mishaps to miss.

Study seriously to inquire
How Prudence you can acquire,
For, mother of all virtues, she
Can from ill Fortune make you free.

Whatever then may be your state,
By Fortune who controls your fate
Govern yourself in such a way
That good sense will there hold sway.

If you knowledge would pursue
A life of books is then for you
So make sure that by your hard work
You're not inferior to any clerk.

Never serve an evil master,
For you would only court disaster
By wickedness to gain his aid,
So avoid such service like the plague.

Would you long life and victory lure?
Teach your heart it must endure;
It's by endurance that one gains
Rewards and comfort for one's pains.

If Fortune gives you as reward
That over others you are lord
Among your subjects then be not
Dangerous nor too proud thought.

Always be truthful in your word;
Speak little, to the point be heard,
For too much talk in any guise
Makes others think one far from wise.

Another's wealth do not envy,
The envious in this life may see
The flames of Hell and feel its pains,
A burden heavier than chains.

Never believe all the false blame
Of women that some books proclaim,
For women can be good and sweet;
May it be your fortune such to meet.

Source: Christine de Pizan, *The Treasure of the City of Ladies*, translated by Sarah Lawson (London: Penguin Books [U.K.] Strand, 1985), pp. 66–68. Used with permission.

Discussion Questions

1. Christine feels that it is very important to have a good moral teacher for your children. What do you think she would say to mothers today who are concerned about the influences their children experience in the public schools?
2. Do you agree that a mother should be more concerned with that which pertains to the discipline of her children than that which pertains to the training of their body? Why or why not?
3. Compare and contrast Christine's admonitions of the proper education for women found in the first reading to the admonitions she gives in her poem to her son, Jean de Castel. Explain how they are the same or different.
4. Christine has much to say about moral education and the development of virtue. Compare what she says to the current debate about whether moral education or character education should be or can be taught in our public schools. On what side of the debate would she be?

5. In the *Book of Three Virtues* Christine proposes a school for all women who could attend. Do you think Christine would see value in having single-sex schools today in the twenty-first century? What are some of the advantages she might cite?

6. Christine is the first woman to write an autobiography. What is the important role of "autobiography" in the development of the history of thought? What are some other autobiographies of women that have had an important impact?

7. Christine tried to write over five hundred years ago about the many women who have made important contributions to civilization in the domains of law and governance, science, and philosophy and found them underrepresented. This book is meant to include women who have made important contributions to education in each important historical period, but information is hard to find on them and their writings. Why do you think that women's contributions are still so underrepresented even today?

For Further Research on the Internet

Home page for the Christine de Pizan Society which has a series of newsletters relating to current research on her. **http://www2.uni-wuppertal.de/FB4/romanistik/CdeP/**

A database with information on Christine's publications. **http://www.arts.ed.ac.uk/french/christine/cpstart.htm**

Home page on Christine. **http://home.infionline.net/~ddisse/christin.html**

Suggestions for Further Reading

Brown-Grant, Rosalind. "Introduction." In *The Book of the City of Ladies by Christine de Pizan*, edited by R. Brown-Grant. New York: Penguin Books, 1999.

Cantor, Norman. *Medieval Lives: Eight Charismatic Men and Women of the Middle Ages.* New York: Harper Collins Publishers, 1994.

de Pizan, Christine. "Christine's Vision." In *The Writings of Christine de Pizan*, edited by C. C. Willard. New York: Persea Books, 1994.

Lawson, Sarah. "Introduction." In *The Treasure of the City of Ladies* or *The Book of the Three Virtues by Christine de Pisan*, edited by S. Lawson. New York: Penguin Books, 1985.

McWebb, Christine. *Female City Builders: Hildegard von Bingen's Scivias and Christine de Pizan's Book of the City of Ladies.* http://www.florin.ms/beth5a.html., 2002.

Tracy, Sophia Okun. *A Woman Ahead of Her Time: Christine de Pizan, Defender of Womankind.* Greensboro, NC: Avisson Press, Inc., 2003.

Willard, Charity Cannon. *Christine de Pizan, Her Life and Works.* New York: Persea, 1984.

Willard, Charity Cannon. Christine de Pizan as Teacher. *RLA*. URL: http://tell.fll. purdue.edu/RLA-Archive/1991/French-html/Willard,Charitycannon.htm

Willard, Charity Cannon. "Introduction. In *The Writings of Christine de Pizan*, edited by C. C. Willard. New York: Persea Books, 1994.

Section 6.2: Erasmus (1466–1536)

"Read the original source, not a secondary source, and analyze the work yourself." You have heard this said before in most of your college classes. This is actually the premise of this book that provides you with the actual writings of famous educators. This was not the case during the medieval ages though, and we have Erasmus to thank for getting students back to original documents and not just summaries or "glosas" (Cliffnotes) of books.

Erasmus' Life and Times

Desiderius Erasmus Roterodamus was born on October 28, 1466 out of wedlock to Gerard and Margaret Rogerius, who were of Dutch lower middle class. His father was a skilled copyist of manuscripts in Italy, from whom he learned to love books.[1] He had an elder brother named Pieter. Erasmus was born in Rotterdam, a town more geared to commerce than literature, which he left when very young, never to return. He wanted to ignore the language of his parents and to forget his birthplace. He even tried to change his birth date to hide his illegitimacy.

Erasmus' Education

Erasmus began school when only four years old. At age nine he attended a school in Deventer operated by the Brethren of the Common Life, a Dutch religious association. At school Erasmus discovered a new world of studies, rooted in the medieval institutions of his time, which was to become the basis of his whole life. Some of Erasmus' teachers were humanists and they inspired him with an enthusiasm for Latin and Greek literature. He was a good student who read books continuously and spoke Latin fluently.

Erasmus' mother died of the plague when he was thirteen. He returned to live with his father, who died soon after. He wanted to go to the university but his tutors wanted him to become a monk.[2]

The Scholar-Priest

Erasmus entered the monastery and enjoyed the life of study in their library even if he did not enjoy their lifestyle. He was ordained a priest on April 25, 1492 and left the monastery at age twenty-four to become secretary for the bishop.[3]

Erasmus went to the Sorbonne in 1495 to study theology for a doctorate, but he only obtained his B.A. due to his poor health and lack of financial funding. While pursuing his theological studies, Erasmus was teaching Latin and tutoring. He went to England in May 1499 for six months and it was here that he became close friends with Thomas More and enrolled in Cambridge. Then he went to Turin, Italy and finally received his doctorate in theology there in 1506.

Erasmus, the Author

In 1500, Erasmus returned to France and wrote the *Adages or Familiar Quotations from the Classics*. This book established his reputation and became required reading for Renaissance schoolboys. This book affects us in modern life as we popularly use the word "adage" to indicate classical wisdom. Through his writing, Erasmus became the most admired person of his age among humanists and reformers. Many sought his correspondence and ideas, which led to his being appointed a professor at Cambridge University.

In 1509, Erasmus began writing *In Praise of Folly* while crossing the Alps on his way back to England. He finished it at More's house and dedicated the book to him. As he explains in his preface, the book's title is "In Praise of More" as "Moria" is the Greek word for Folly.[4] *In Praise of Folly* is a satire and is considered to be Erasmus' major work and one of the great books of the Renaissance. Folly is the only person in this composition and s/he is everywhere. Folly condemns the world for its errors and then attempts to bring about a genuine conversion to an authentic Christianity. *In Praise of Folly* earned Erasmus renown but no fortune. (See the timeline of Erasmus' life in Figure 6.3.)

The Humanist

Erasmus was a Christian humanist; he wanted to reconcile Christianity and antiquity without confusing them. He was a devoted and faithful priest all his life, writing extensively on theological matters, including commentaries on the Bible and prayers in the form of poems. He criticized the errors of popular devotion such as cults dedicated to suspect relics of saints, pilgrimages which were orchestrated tourism, and the selling of indulgences; however, he was always faithful to the teaching of the Church.

Erasmus spent his last years writing about and preparing for his own death. He died in Basel on July 11, 1536. Erasmus emerged on the eve of the Protestant Reformation as the leading representative of the humanist reform that challenged much of the academic, intellectual, and religious heritage of the Middle Ages and promoted a golden age of humanistic scholarship.[5]

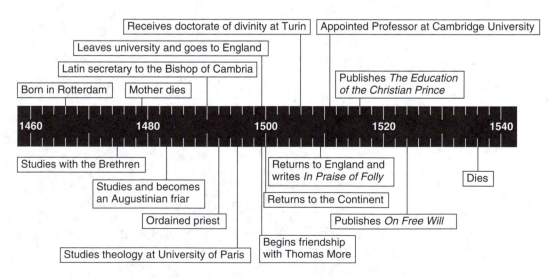

Figure 6.3   Erasmus' Life and Times

Erasmus' Educational Contributions

Erasmus was a scholar, classicist, critic, and author. He wrote *In Praise of Folly* (against education that just emphasized grammar). As a teacher he emphasized the humanistic content of the classics and the importance of early childhood, which needed gentle instruction; he felt children should be read fables and poems. Although he only worked as a tutor for a short time, Erasmus wrote several pedagogical works: *The Education of the Christian Prince* (1516) and *On the Method of Study, Foundations of Abundant Style,* and *On The Education of Children* (1529). Erasmus' great work on education and political philosophy is *The Education of the Christian Prince* (1516). It is similar to Plato's *Republic* in the sense that it develops Erasmus' theory of education by proposing the humanistic education proper for the ruler of the people.[6]

"Through his books, Erasmus became the teacher of teachers and the champion of precise language for the sake of elegant and effective discourse."[7] In *In Praise of Folly,* Erasmus attacked the teachers of grammar who emphasized trivial facts rather than substantial learnings. In *The Education of the Christian Prince* Erasmus expounds that an appropriate liberal education should include the study of history and geography, the humanities, and religion. In *The Education of Children* he explained that, in his opinion, nothing is superfluous, and nothing is without importance in the education of children. One should go beyond a concern for behavior and training to arrive at education. Erasmus believed in appealing to the child's reason and the use of repeated lessons.

Erasmus' Philosophy of Education

Erasmus developed a complete humanistic philosophy of education. He recognized the importance of parents teaching children virtues and learning began in early childhood. Erasmus preferred a curriculum with a broad general education in all the areas worthy of being known. This would include the study of the Greek and Latin languages and classical literature. His methodology for teaching emphasized understanding content more than style. Teachers should have a rich background and should gently instruct students using many examples to vividly explain the concepts. Erasmus proposed Christ as the teacher of all mankind as a model for teachers.[8] The purpose of education was to enlighten the youth and thus improve the civil state. Erasmus advocated a Christian and cosmopolitan education. He believed that education should promote a harmonious union of all persons under the fatherhood of God, and should engender understanding, tolerance, and gentleness between people.[9] In his words, "It is the height of folly that one should train the body to be comely, and wholly neglect that excellence of mind which alone can guide it aright."

Notes

1. Leon-E Halkin, *Erasmus: A Critical Biography,* translated by John Tonkini (Cambridge: Blackwell Publishing, 1994), p. 1.
2. Ibid., pp. 3–4.
3. Ibid., p. 10.
4. Ibid., pp. 74–75.
5. Charles G. Nauert Jr., *Humanism and the Culture of Renaissance Europe,* New Approaches to European History (Cambridge: Cambridge University Press, 1995), pp. 157–159.
6. A. G. Dickens, and Whitney R. D. Jones, *Erasmus the Reformer* (London: Methuen, 1994), p. 76.
7. Ibid., p. 40.
8. Dickens, p. 101.
9. Gerald Gutek, *A History of the Western Educational Experience,* 2nd ed. (Prospect Heights, IL: Waveland Press, Inc., 1995), p. 125.

Questions to Guide Your Reading

1. Erasmus says that "true knowledge includes what is best in both kinds of knowledge." What are the two kinds of knowledge he mentions? Is this division relevant to education today?

2. What are some of the things we learn best in our earliest years according to Erasmus? Are these things still taught to young children today or are other things more important?

3. What kind of tutor should a father get for his son, according to Erasmus? How does this compare to today's pre-school teacher?

4. What is the difference between men and animals according to Erasmus? Do you agree with his distinction? Can you add other points?

READING 6.2:
THE TREATISE OF ERASMUS, *DE RATIONE STUDII,*
THAT IS UPON THE RIGHT METHOD OF INSTRUCTION

The Argument of Erasmus of Rotterdam, That Children from Their Earliest Years be Trained in Virtue and Sound Learning

I desire to urge upon you, Illustrious Duke, to take into your early and serious consideration the future nurture and training of the son lately born to you. For, with Chrysippus, I contend that the young child must be led to sound learning whilst his wit is yet unwarped, his age tender, his mind flexible and tenacious. In manhood we remember nothing so well as the truths which we imbibed in our youth. Wherefore I beg you to put aside all idle chatter, which would persuade you that this early childhood is unmet for the discipline and the effort of studies.

The arguments, which I shall enlarge upon, are the following. First the beginnings of learning are the work of memory, which in young children is most tenacious. Next, as nature has implanted in us the instinct to seek for knowledge, can we be too early

in obeying her behest? Thirdly, there are not a few things, which it imports greatly that we should know well, and which we can learn far more readily in our tender years. I speak of the elements of Letters, Grammar, and the fables and stories found in the ancient Poets. Fourthly, since children, as all agree, are fit to acquire manners, why may they not acquire the rudiments of learning? And seeing that they must need be busy about something, what else can be better approved? For how much wiser to amuse their hours with Letters, than to see them frittered away in aimless trifling!

It is, however, objected, first, that such knowledge as can be thus early got is of slight value. But even so, why despise it, if so be it serve as the foundation for much greater things? For if in early childhood a boy acquires such useful elements he will be free to apply his youth to higher knowledge, to the saving of his time. Moreover, whilst he is thus occupied in sound learning he will perforce be kept from some of the temptations which befall youth, seeing that nothing engages the whole mind more than studies. And this I count a high gain in such times as ours.

Next, it is urged that by such application health may be somewhat endangered. Supposing this to be true, still the compensation is great, for by discipline,

Source: Selections from William Harrison Woodward, editor, *Desiderius Erasmus Concerning the Aim and Method of Education* (Cambridge: Cambridge University Press, 1904). Used with permission.

the mind gains far more in alertness and in vigor than the body is ever likely to lose. Watchfulness, however, will prevent any such risk as is imagined. Also, for this tender age you will employ a teacher who will win and not drive, just as you will choose such subjects as are pleasant and attractive, in which the young mind will recreation rather than toil.

Furthermore, I bid you remember that a man ignorant of Letters is no man at all, that human life is a fleeting thing, that youth is easily enticed into sin, that early manhood is absorbed by clashing interests, that old age is unproductive, and that few reach it. How then can you allow your child, in whom you yourself live again, to lose even one of those precious years in which he may begin to acquire those means whereby he may elevate his whole life and keep at arm's length temptation and evil?

The Importance of Skilled Control from the Outset

I urge you, therefore, to look even now for a scholar of high character and attainment to whom you may commit the charge of your boy's mind and disposition, leaving to wisely chosen nurses the care of his bodily welfare. By thus dividing control the child will be saved from the mischievous kindnesses and indulgence of foolish serving-women, and of weak relatives, who decry learning as so much poison, and babble about the unfitness of the growing boy for Letters. To such chatter you still turn a deaf ear. For, remembering that the welfare of your son demands not less circumspection from you than a man will gladly bestow upon his horse, his castle, his estate, you will take heed only to the wisest counsel which you can secure, and ponder that with yourself. . . . No, from the very day of his birth charge is taken lest mischief hap, and wisely, knowing that a weakly manhood may be thus avoided. Nay, even before the child be born, how diligent is the wise mother to see that no harm come to herself for her child's sake. . . .

The Supreme Importance of Education to Human Well-Being

To dumb creatures Mother Nature has given an innate power or instinct, whereby they may in great part attain to their right capacities. But Providence in granting to man alone the privilege of reason has thrown the burden of development of the human being upon training. Well, therefore, has it been said that the first means, the second, and the third means to happiness is right training or education. Sound education is the condition of real wisdom. And if an education which is soundly planned and carefully carried out is the very fount of all human excellence, so, on the other hand, careless and unworthy training is the true source of folly and vice. This capacity for training is, indeed, the chief aptitude which has been bestowed upon humanity. Unto the animals nature has given swiftness of foot or of wing, keenness of sight, strength or size of frame, and various weapons of defense. To Man, instead of physical powers, is given a mind apt for training; in this single gift all others are comprised, for him, at least, who turns it to due profit. We see that where native instinct is strong as in squirrels or bees, capacity for being taught is wanting. Man, lacking instinct, can do little or nothing of innate power; scarce can he eat, or walk, or speak, unless he be guided thereto. How then can we expect that he should become competent to the duties of life unless straightway and with much diligence he be brought under the discipline of a worthy education?

Reason, the True Mark of Man

Now it is the possession of Reason that constitutes a Man. If trees or wild beasts grow, men, believe me, are fashioned. Men in olden time who led their life in forests, driven by the mere needs and desires of their natures, guided by no laws, with no ordering in communities, are to be judged rather as savage beasts than as men. For Reason, the mark of humanity, has no place where all is determined by appetite. It is beyond dispute that a man not instructed through reason in philosophy and sound learning is a creature lower than a brute, seeing that there is no beast more wild or more harmful than a man who is driven hither and thither by ambition, or desire, anger or envy, or lawless temper.

Education of Their Children Is Duty Owed by Parents

Straightway from the child's birth it is meet that he should begin to learn the things which properly belong to his well being. Therefore, bestow especial pains upon his tenderest years, as Vergil teaches.

Handle the wax whilst it is soft, mold the clay whilst it is moist, dye the fleece before it gathers stains. It is no light task to educate our children aright. Yet think to lighten the burden how much comfort and honour parents derive from children well brought up: and reflect how much sorrow is engendered of them that grow up evilly. And further, no man is born to himself; no man is born to idleness. Your children are begotten not to yourself alone, but to your country: not to your country alone, but to God. Paul teaches that women are saved by reason that they bring up their children in the pursuit of virtue. God will straitly charge the parents with their children's faults; therefore, except they bring up their little ones from the very first to live aright, they themselves will share the penalty. For a child rightly educated is a comfort and a joy to his parents, but a foolish child brings upon them shame, it may be poverty and old age before their time.... They are called murderers who kill their newborn children: but such kill the mere body. How great, then, is their crime who destroys the soul? For what other thing is the death of the soul than to live in folly and sin? Such fathers do no less wrong to their country, to which, as far as in them lies, they give pestilent citizens. They do, equally, a wrong against God, at whose hands they receive their offspring to bring it up to His service.

Discussion Questions

1. Do you agree with Erasmus when he says, "a man ignorant of letters is no man at all?" What about those who, in today's society, are illiterate and cannot read?
2. What does Erasmus mean when he says, "the means to happiness is education?" Is that also true today?
3. Given the "back-to-basics movement," do you think that parents today would agree with Erasmus that "understanding content is more important than mastering style and grammar?" How does that relate to today's emphasis on meeting standards and testing well?
4. Erasmus quotes Lycurgus "Nature may be strong, yet Education is more powerful still." Do you agree? If so, why is there still a debate today as to whether a child's character and personality development is a matter of nature or nurture?

For Further Research on the Internet

On-line history of Erasmus with links to his writing and his place in history.
http://mithec.prohosting.com/history/content/erasmus.html

Home page of the Erasmus of Rotterdam Society dedicated to encouraging research and writing on Erasmus, with links to his works on line and papers on his thought.
http://www.sfu.ca/~pabel/ers.htm

Famous etching of Erasmus found in the Metropolitan Museum of Art.
http://www.metmuseum.org/toah/hd/refo/hod19.73.120.htm

Suggestions for Further Reading

Dickens, A. G. and Whitney R. D. Jones. *Erasmus the Reformer*. London: Methuen, 1994.

Gutek, Gerald. *A History of the Western Educational Experience*, 2nd ed. Prospect Heights, IL: Waveland Press, Inc., 1995.

Halkin, Leon-E. *Erasmus: A Critical Biography*. Translated by John Tonkini. Cambridge: Blackwell Publishers, 1994.

Nauert Jr., Charles G. *Humanism and the Culture of Renaissance Europe, New Approaches to European History*. Cambridge: Cambridge University Press, 1995.

Section 6.3: Martin Luther (1483–1546)

Have you ever studied a foreign language? Would you be able to study history and science if they were written in that language? Can you imagine having to learn another language (Latin) before you could study anything in school? No wonder very few people went to school. We have Martin Luther to thank for suggesting that we teach children (boys and girls) in their vernacular (or native) language.

Martin Luther's Life and Times

His Family

Martin Luther was born on November 10, 1483 in Eisleban, a small town in east-central Germany, 70 miles southwest of Wittenburg. Luther's father, Hans Luder, although from a peasant background, had attained a position of respect as a miner with a good income. His mother, Margarethe Lindemann, was from an established burgher (middle class) family who gave much importance to education. Martin learned to read from his mother and also learned piety from her. Martin's parents were strict disciplinarians who punished their son severely. Some biographers attribute psychological damage to Luther due to his early upbringing.[1]

Martin's Education

Six months after Martin was born the family moved to the larger town of Mansfield. Martin went to school there from six to fourteen years old and studied the fundamental medieval trivium of grammar, logic, and rhetoric, but learned little due to the poor teaching methods that tried to drum knowledge into children by means of strict and cruel discipline. This negative model later impelled him to reform education. Similar to educators who followed him, e.g., Comenius and Pestalozzi, Luther advocated a teaching system tailored to the child's needs, allowing pupils, both boys and girls, to learn joyfully and playfully at schools. They should be taught by both male and female teachers in half-day sessions so that they could also help their parents with the chores.[2]

When Luther was fourteen he was sent to Magdeburg and then to Eisehnach to study the last four pre-university years. He went to the University of Erfurt in 1501 (one of the most dynamic facilities in Europe) where he studied first the liberal arts and then law. Luther's education was permeated by the scholastic idea and his later ability for oral debate and written argumentation can be attributed to this training.

By the fall of 1502, Martin had passed his baccalaureate examination and could teach the trivium of liberal arts, and in 1505 he received his master's degree and then began to study law. That summer, while returning to Erfurt after visiting his parents, Martin was caught in a terrible thunderstorm. Terrified of a sudden death he vowed, "Help me, St. Anne. I will become a monk." (St. Anne was the patroness of miners and often had been invoked by his father.) Luther entered the Augustinian monastery two weeks later on July 17, 1505 and on April 4, 1507, he was ordained to the priesthood at 23 years of age. (See the timeline of Luther's life in Figure 6.4.)

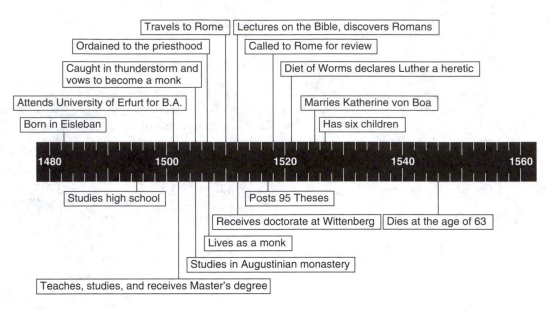

Figure 6.4 Luther's Life and Times

Luther, the Monk

From 1507 to 1517, Luther struggled to be a good monk, scrupulously trying to prove to himself that he was doing his best to please God. He feared death, sin, punishment, and the judgment of God, and worried about the certitude of salvation. Several biographers document that he suffered from periods of depression and acute anxiety.[3] Luther referred to these as melancholy and spiritual trials.

Luther went to Rome in 1510 with another monk on business and was appalled at the wickedness he saw there. He went to Wittenberg in 1512 to lecture on the Bible and he later received his doctorate there. He was systematically progressing through the Bible in his lectures, and began to lecture on the Romans in spring, 1515. Here he made his great discovery of the meaning of justification by faith alone while pondering Romans 1:17.

95 Theses

In order to build St. Peter's Church in Rome, alms were sought of Christians. For giving alms, one could receive indulgences, or remission of the guilt due to one's sins. Luther saw this as selling indulgences. On October 31, 1517, Luther nailed a copy of 95 Theses, or points of discussion, on the Church doors at Wittenberg to announce his intention to debate indulgences, purgatory, and other points of doctrine. The format of a public debate with the issues to be debated posted beforehand was common during this time. Due to the recent invention of the printing press, these Theses were quickly circulated all over Germany. Luther was summoned to Rome in August of 1518 to give an account of himself to determine if he was spreading heresies. Although Luther said he was only proposing these Theses for debate, he would not recant them. In 1521, the Diet at Worms declared Luther a heretic. Luther thought of himself as one who was reforming the wrongs he saw in the Church of his day. Erasmus and Luther were both displeased with the abuses that they saw in society and the Church of their time. Erasmus fought these with criticism and satire; Luther fought them by rebellion.

Luther's Reform

Luther now dedicated himself to the task of translating the Bible into German, believing that Christians everywhere should be nourished by the sacred text. To do this, they had to be able to read the Bible so Luther advocated the establishment of schools for boys and girls as the best investment in the future of the Church and society.

In June, 1525, Luther married Katherine von Boa and had six children with her. From 1527 on Luther's health began deteriorating quickly. His diet was poor, his heart was weak, and he drank too much. Nevertheless, he wrote prolifically and lived to the age of 63. Luther died in the town of his birth on February 18, 1546, leaving the world changed forever because he lived.[4]

Luther's Contribution to Educational History

Although it is generally not recognized, Luther brought about as important a reformation in education as in religion. In his 1524 treatise "To the Councilmen of all Cities in Germany that They Establish and Maintain Christian Schools," Luther contemptuously dismisses both the content and the methods of medieval pedagogy, recommending instead a liberal arts program including biblical languages, history, singing, and music, along with mathematics.[5] Like Erasmus, Luther undertook a humanistic reform of the curriculum of the university, drawing it away from scholasticism and more into the Renaissance mode of asking students to read the original sources rather than the glosas. More important, Luther promoted a system of public schooling in which the use of the German vernacular language enabled the general public to read the Bible, thus promoting mass literacy.[6]

Luther Encourages Mass Literacy

The very tenets of his "protest religion" (Protestantism) necessitated and encouraged popular education in several ways. Luther translated the Bible into German (he considered this to be his most important contribution) and thus placed the Bible into the hands of the laity and common folk. He preached that each must save themselves by reading and studying the Bible, therefore everyone—poor and rich, male and female—must learn to read.

Education was a primary interest of the State, as well as a necessity for the welfare of the Church, according to Luther. These two essential ideas come out in all that he wrote on education. His most significant writings are "Letter to the Mayors and Aldermen of All the Cities in Germany on Behalf of Christian Schools" and his sermon "Duty of Sending Children to School." His sermon serves as his most extensive educational treatise. In it he talks about both the spiritual and temporal benefits of education and the obligation of parents to educate their children to the level from which they are able to benefit.[7] Luther felt that education was of such vital importance that it should be compulsory and public, sustained by government supervision and support. He appeals to the authorities to act *in loco parentis* when the natural parents prevent able youngsters from pursuing an education.[8] He influenced the enactment of the first compulsory education laws in Germany. This later inspired the American colonists to enact the first law in the new land regarding the need for each town to establish a school where both boys and girls could learn to read the Bible.[9]

Luther's Philosophy of Education

Luther advocated compulsory primary schools for the common people (including girls) so that they could learn to read the Bible in German. He promoted Latin schools (both at the primary and secondary level) for those who would pursue professional careers in Church and State and universities in which some select would pursue true learning.

Luther highly esteemed the role of the teacher and sought to prepare enlightened and successful teachers at the University of Wittenberg. Teachers were to "speak kindly to each child in a low tone and show, in a friendly way, how each defect could be corrected."[10]

Luther's contributions in pedagogical method regarding catechetical instruction rank him with such educational reformers as Comenius and Pestalozzi. He was against the harsh, mechanical, and uninteresting methods of his day and suggested that the teacher motivate the children by using competitions and by taking into consideration the natural activity and inquisitiveness of the child. He felt that learning was a natural activity, and as long as appropriate instructional techniques were used, it should not be much of a burden to a normally endowed human being. He proposed three important components for effective learning; natural endowment, instruction, and practice.

The goal of education was that the entire population become literate so that they could read the scriptures. According to Luther's theology, there is a social and spiritual equality of all men in the sight of God. Since forgiveness and justification can come only through faith, scriptures must be read for man cannot save himself. And so Luther promoted the widespread teaching in the vernacular language and effected a rapid growth in literacy among all. In his words, "Is it not enough to teach the scriptures, which are necessary for salvation, in the mother tongue?"

Notes

1. Richard Marius, *Martin Luther: The Christian Between God and Death* (Cambridge, MA: Beknap Press of Harvard University, 1999), p. 27; Heiko Oberman, *Luther: Man Between God and the Devil,* translated by Eileen Wallieer-Schwarbart, (New Haven, CT: Yale University Press, 1989), p. 92; Erik Erickson, *Young Man Luther: A Study in Psychoanalysis and History* (New York: Norton, 1993).
2. Oberman, pp. 94–95.
3. Marius, p. 54; David Steinmetz, *Luther in Context,* originally published in 1986 by Indiana University Press, Bloomington, IN, (Grand Rapids, MI: Baker Books, 1995), p. 1; Roland Bainton, *Here I Stand: A Life of Martin Luther* (New York: Meridan Printing Penguin Group, 1995), p. 20.
4. Marius, p. 480.
5. Jane Strohl, "The Child in Luther's Theology," in *The Child in Christian Thought,* edited by M. Bunge (Grand Rapids, MI: William B. Eerdmans Publishing Company, 2001), p. 151.
6. Carmen Luke, "Luther and the Foundations of Literacy, Secular Schooling and Educational Administration," *The Journal of Educational Thought,* 23, No 2 (1989), pp. 120–140.
7. Strohl, p. 150.
8. Ibid., p. 152.
9. F. V. N. Painter, *Luther on Education* (St. Louis, MO: Concordia Publishing House, 1889), pp. 131–136.
10. Luke, p. 127.

Questions to Guide your Reading

1. Why did parents in Luther's time think that the only valid role of the school was to prepare their children to be priests and nuns? What do parents think is the main role of the schools today in preparing their children?

2. Why does Luther say the devil is interested in having people stay ignorant and uneducated? What is equivalent to Luther's "devil" in today's society?

3. Why should the mayors be interested in the education of the children in their town, according to Luther? Is this relevant to today's society?

4. What subjects does Luther think should be taught in the schools? Compare these subjects to those taught in school today.

READING 6.3:
LETTER TO THE MAYORS AND ALDERMEN OF ALL THE CITIES OF GERMANY ON BEHALF OF CHRISTIAN SCHOOLS (1524)

First of all, we see how the schools are deteriorating throughout Germany. The universities are becoming weak, and the monasteries are declining. For through the word of God the unchristian and sensual character of these institutions is becoming known. And because selfish parents see that they can no longer place their children upon the bounty of monasteries and cathedrals, they refuse to educate them. "Why should we educate our children," they say, "if they are not to become priests, monks, and thus earn a support?" . . .

It is no wonder that the devil meddles in the matter, and influences groveling hearts to neglect the children and the youth of the country. Who can blame him for it? He is the prince and god of this world. . . .

Yet no one thinks of this dreadful purpose of the devil, which is being worked out so quietly that it escapes observation; and soon the evil will be so far advanced that we can do nothing to prevent it. People fear the Turks, wars, and floods, for in such matters they can see what is injurious or beneficial; but what the devil has in mind no one sees or fears.

Therefore I beg you all, in the name of God and of your neglected youth, not to think of this subject lightly, as many do who do not see what the prince of this world intends. For the right instruction of youth is a matter in which Christ and all the world are concerned. . . .

Parents neglect this duty from various causes. In the first place, there are some who are so lacking in piety and uprightness that they would not do it if they could, but, like the ostrich, harden themselves against their own offspring, and do nothing for them. In the second place, the great majority of parents are unqualified for it, and do not understand how children should be brought up and taught. In the third place, even if parents were qualified and willing to do it themselves, yet on account of other employments and household duties, they have no time for it, so that necessity requires us to have teachers for public schools, unless each parent employ a private instructor.

Therefore it will be the duty of the mayors and councils to exercise the greatest care over the young. For since the happiness, honor, and life of the city are committed to their hands, they would be held recreant before God and the world, if they did not day and night, with all their power, seek its welfare and improvement. . . . The highest welfare, safety, and power of a city consists of able, learned, wise, upright, cultivated citizens, who can secure, preserve, and utilize every treasure and advantage.

But you say again, if we shall and must have schools, what is the use to teach Latin, Greek, Hebrew, and other liberal arts? Is it not enough to teach the scriptures, which are necessary to salvation, in the mother tongue? . . . Indeed, if the languages were of no practical benefit, we ought still to feel an interest in them as a wonderful gift of God. . . .

Even if there were no soul, as I have already said, and men did not need schools and the languages for the sake of Christianity and the scriptures, still, for the establishment of the best schools everywhere, both for boys and girls, this consideration is of itself sufficient, namely, that society, for the maintenance of civil order and the proper regulation of the household, needs accomplished and well-trained men and women. Now such men are to come from boys, and such women from girls; hence it is necessary that boys and girls be properly taught and brought up. Therefore, honored members of the city councils, this work must remain in your hands; you have more time and opportunity for it than princes and lords.

But were they instructed in schools or elsewhere, by thoroughly qualified male or female

Source: By Martin Luther as found in F. V. N. Painter, *Great Pedagogical Essays Plato to Spencer* (New York: American Book Company, Copyright 1905 by F. V. N. Painter).

teachers, who taught the languages, other arts, and history, then the pupils would hear the history and maxims of the world, and see how things went with each city, kingdom, prince, man, and woman; and thus, in a short time, they would be able to comprehend, as in a mirror, the character, life, counsels, undertakings, successes, and failures, of the whole world from the beginning. . . .

Now since the young must leap and jump, or have something to do, because they have a natural desire for it which should not be restrained (for it is not well to check them in everything), why should we not provide for them such schools, and lay before them such studies? By the gracious arrangement of God, children take delight in acquiring knowledge, whether languages, mathematics, or history. And our schools are no longer a hell or purgatory, in which children are tortured over cases and tenses, and in which with much flogging, trembling, anguish, and wretchedness they learn nothing.

As for myself, if I had children and were able, I would have them learn not only the languages and history, but also singing, instrumental music, and the whole course of mathematics. . . .

My idea is that boys should spend an hour or two a day in school, and the rest of the time work at home, learn some trade, and do whatever is desired, so that study and work may go on together, while the children are young and can attend to both. They now spend twofold as much time in shooting with crossbows, playing ball, running, and tumbling about.

In like manner, a girl has time to go to school an hour a day, and yet attend to her work at home; for she sleeps, dances, and plays away more than that. . . . But the brightest pupils, who give promise of becoming accomplished teachers, preachers, and workers, should be kept longer at school, or set apart wholly for study.

Everywhere we have had such teachers and masters, who have known nothing themselves, who have been able to teach nothing useful, and who have been ignorant even of the right methods of learning and teaching. How has it come about? No books have been accessible but the senseless trash of the monks and sophists. How could the pupils and teachers differ from the books they studied? That is the recompense of our ingratitude, in that we did not use diligence in the formation of libraries, but allowed good books to perish, and bad ones to survive.

In the first place, a library should contain the Holy Scriptures in Latin, Greek, Hebrew, German, and other languages. Then the best and most ancient commentators in Greek, Hebrew, and Latin.

Secondly, such books as are useful in acquiring the languages, as the poets and orators, without considering whether they are heathen or Christian, Greek or Latin. For it is from such works that grammar must be learned. Thirdly, books treating of all the arts and sciences.

Lastly, books on jurisprudence and medicine, though here discrimination is necessary. A prominent place should be given to chronicles and histories, in whatever languages they may be obtained; for they are wonderfully useful in understanding and regulating the course of the world, and in disclosing the marvelous works of God. . . .

Herewith I commend you all to the grace of God, to the praise and honor of God the Father, through Jesus Christ our Savior. Amen.

Wittenberg, 1524.

Discussion Questions

1. Do you agree with Luther that some parents are selfish and unqualified and do not have time or even know how to bring up their children? Is this true in today's society? What is the role of the school in the education of parents?
2. Should school libraries be limited to Holy Scripture, classical literature and books on science, history, law, and medicine as advocated by Luther? What about "popular culture" books? What do you think Luther would say about the freedom of speech which allows all sorts of material on the Internet?
3. Compare and contrast the curriculum Luther proposes to that in the schools today.
4. Do you think that contemporary public educational pedagogy carries a pan-Protestant tone? Why or why not?

5. Study the 95 Theses of Luther as found on the Web site http://www.luther.de/en/95thesen.html. Do you think any of these are still relevant issues today?

6. What relationship does Luther see between the good citizen and the good Christian? What do you think he would say about prayer in public schools and the posting of the Ten Commandments in public places? What do you think about the way Church and State is separated, especially in our schools today?

For Further Research on the Internet

Homepage dedicated to Luther with excellent links. **http://www.luther.de/en/**

Home page on Luther with excellent links for further research on many topics related to his theology and educational philosophy.
http://www.educ.msu.edu/homepages/laurence/reformation/Luther/Luther.htm

Project Wittenberg is an electronic library on Luther and Lutheranism.
http://www.iclnet.org/pub/resources/text/wittenberg/wittenberg-home.html

Suggestions for Further Reading

Bainton, Roland. *Here I Stand: A Life of Martin Luther.* New York: Meridan Printing Penguin Group, 1995.

Erickson, Erik. *Young Man Luther: A Study in Psychoanalysis and History.* New York: Norton, 1993.

Luke, Carmen. "Luther and the Foundations of Literacy, Secular Schooling and Educational Administration." *The Journal of Educational Thought,* 23, No. 2 (1989): 120–140.

Marius, Richard. *Martin Luther: The Christian Between God and Death.* Cambridge, MA: Beknap Press of Harvard University, 1999.

Oberman, Heiko. *Luther: Man Between God and the Devil.* Translated by Eileen Wallieer-Schwarbart. New Haven, CT: Yale University Press, 1989.

Painter, F. V. N. *Luther on Education.* St. Louis, MO: Concordia Publishing House, 1889.

Steinmetz, David. *Luther in Context.* Originally published in 1986 by Indiana University Press, Bloomington, IN. Grand Rapids, MI: Baker Books, 1995.

Strohl, Jane. "The Child in Luther's Theology." In *The Child in Christian Thought,* edited by M. Bunge. Grand Rapids, MI: William B. Eerdmans Publishing Company, 2001.

Section 6.4: Johann Amos Comenius (1592–1670)

You have heard the saying; "A picture is worth a thousand words." Don't you enjoy reading books that have pictures, especially textbooks? We have Comenius to thank for suggesting that pictures be included in books and be used to illustrate the abstract concept one is trying to teach. He also suggested using pictures of objects to teach the vocabulary of foreign languages.

Life and Times of Johann Comenius

Jan Amos Komensky—in Latin, Johann Amos Comenius—was born in the southeastern corner of the Czech state on March 28, 1592, the youngest of five children. His father, Martin, owned a mill and was a devout member of the Church of the United Brethren who lived a simple, peaceful life with a simple piety. When Jan Amos was ten years old, his parents and two of his sisters died of the plague. Jan and his two surviving sisters were entrusted to guardians, Jan going to live with his aunt.

Jan's Education

Jan attended an elementary school that was harsh and used rote learning, memorization, and excessive punishment of the students; he deplores this type of discipline in *The Great Didactic*. Jan attended a Latin secondary school in Prerov run by the Unity of Brethren when he was sixteen and was befriended by the headmaster who recognized his intellectual gifts and encouraged him to train for the ministry. Although Jan also critiqued the teaching methods used here, he did learn a lot and came to love Latin and scriptures and changed his name from Jan to the Latin Johann and added Amos, which means "loving," as his middle name.[1]

He went to the Naussau Academy in Hebron to take up studies to become an ordained minister. The scholars he studied influenced him in the formation of his educational principles: (1) the unity and integrity of all knowledge and (2) that a second language can most easily be learned by matching the new words to those in the mother tongue.[2]

The Teacher and Pastor

Going to the University of Heidelberg in 1613 to complete his theological studies, he left a year later to take up a teaching appointment at his old school in Prerov. He strove for "a more pleasant method of educating children" and began writing a Latin textbook. On April 16, 1616, at the age of twenty-four, Comenius was ordained a priest of the Brethren and appointed pastor of a parish at Fulnech, where he went with his wife, Marilyn Vizovska and where he also became the rector of the local school. Tragically, his wife and two children died due to the plague that spread in the aftermath of the Thirty Years War and Comenius himself had to go into exile, as all Protestants in Bohemia were banished. (See the timeline of Comenius' life in Figure 6.5.)

Comenius sought refuge in various estates and during this time wrote *The Labyrinth*, considered to be the greatest Czech work of literature of this period. He also tutored young children and formulated his pedagogical principles while doing so. In 1624, Comenius married his second wife and, after years of hiding from persecution, decided to leave the country, travelling to Leszno, Poland, where they spent the next 12 years. Comenius was appointed co-director of the Gymnasium where he began to implement his pedagogical ideas. It soon became known as the best high school of its kind in Poland.

Author, Educator, and Reformer

Comenius began writing *The Great Didactic* in which he presented a systematic exposition of his principles of pedagogy and his philosophy of education.[3] He also wrote a book on how to teach Latin—*The Gate of Tongues Unlocked*. This book was very well received. It became a "best seller" textbook and was translated into almost every European language. Comenius tried to extend his innovative and successful idea for the teaching of languages to the whole curriculum and wrote *The Gate of Things* and *A Reformation of Schools* during this time. Comenius proposed the idea of "pansophism" which entailed the concept of the organic unity or integrity of all knowledge. Other Western European educators, such as Jeremiah Benthaur, were to continue championing this idea of the "harmonization in all knowledge" into the next century.

On October 6, 1632, Comenius was ordained a Bishop of the Unity Church and he dedicated himself to trying to unite the Protestant Churches and to reconcile the worlds of science and religion, showing that there is a harmonization in all knowledge. Comenius was invited to England, Sweden, and Hungary to reform their educational systems and their schools. Between 1641 and 1655 he worked in these countries and wrote textbooks for the teaching of Latin. *The World in Pictures* was famous for its use of visual illustrations to teach Latin. This book was used for over 200 years and was even used in the United States up until 1810.[4] Not able to reform the schools to his satisfaction in any of these countries he returned to Leszno in 1655. There he found the Brethren were no longer welcome; his house was destroyed and he lost all of his possessions—his money, his library, and his unpublished manuscripts, over forty years of work.[5] Exiled once again, Comenius went to Amsterdam with his third wife, children, and son-in-law. Here he published all of his educational writing in four volumes—*Obera Didactica Omnia*. In 1665, his wife died and on November 4, 1670, Comenius himself died.

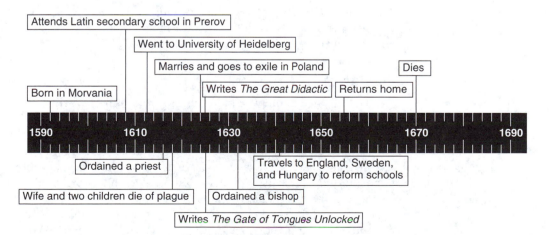

Figure 6.5 Comenius' Life and Times

Comenius' Contribution to Educational Thought

Comenius was considered to be the foremost educator of his time and is today ranked as one of the greatest educators, although his work was hidden until the last century. Piaget introduced Johann Amos Comenius to contemporary educators with his 1957 edition of Comenius' writings. Over two thousand scholars attended the 1992 International Conference in Prague celebrating the 400th anniversary of Comenius' birth. This event could only take place because the Communist regime had fallen just two years before, making libraries holding his original works open to scholars for the first time in almost a century.[6] Today we can see that Comenius' views on a child-centered education were truly progressive, and foreshadowed those of Rousseau by at least one hundred years.

In *The Great Didactic,* Comenius tells us that education should be modeled on the natural development of a child's ability to understand the principles of nature. All learning should be related directly to the everyday experiences of the pupil. Effective education can only be achieved when teachers work with children's natural inclinations, not against them.[7] Comenius proposed stages for the years of conventional learning, similar to the stages proposed by the ancient Roman educator Quintilian. He proposed that all learning proceeds through the senses so teachers should present students with objects they could hold, feel, smell, and sense, or at least provide them with pictures of objects. One could say that he was the first to propose that teachers take learning styles into consideration; that some things can best be learned visually, others auditorily, and some kinesthetically. His emphasis on the natural stages of the child's development and the importance of sensory education was to influence the pedagogical work of Johann Heinrich Pestalozzi and Friedrich Froebel, as we shall see in subsequent sections.

The teacher is like a gardener. The role of the educator is to nurture and cultivate this seed or kernel made in the image of God. He let the interests of the child drive the curriculum. The purpose of education was to get to know oneself so that one could direct oneself to God.[8]

Teaching should begin in the mother tongue, according to Comenius. The curriculum should thus be a systematic sequencing of content with order, depth, range, and coherence. Universal education implies a moral unity of all knowledge, so Comenius was opposed to specialization at all stages of education. Comenius put emphasis on the value of a child's play, and advocated the abandonment of the barbaric discipline he himself had experienced while in school. He encouraged instead the fostering of disciplined learning. All of this was the practical aim of education. His principles for teaching fit into what today is called "effective teaching."[9]

He really envisioned a true liberal education, i.e., the cultivation of the whole range of human potentiality—spiritual, religious, moral, emotional, aesthetic, intellectual, social, and physical.

Comenius' Philosophy of Education

Comenius developed a complete philosophy of education. He believed in universal education for all, no matter what their social background, religion, sex, or intellectual ability. He took it upon himself to create a truly universal education system that would be open to young women. He was one of the first to promote education for the deaf, the blind, and the retarded; all could be educated to some degree.[10] Universal education implied holistic development of the human; i.e., the integration of learning, virtues, and piety.

Comenius' famous picture book *Orbis Sensualium Pictus* (1658) was meant to be a textbook. It was framed didactically beginning with an *invitatio,* an invitation with a picture and a story in the text and ending with a *clausa,* a conclusion or moral with another picture and the end of the story.[11] The pictures were used in books to teach, presenting things as they are and at the same time, the way they are to be used rightly in the world.

The ultimate aim of education was, according to Comenius, the religious and moral formation of the child. He believed firmly in the role of parents as the primary educators and especially in their crucial role in character formation. The teacher is essential though and has to be a moral exemplar. Every teacher was to make the school a workshop for the virtues in order to help each student to develop themselves. Virtues should be promoted through three main methods: example, discipline, and instruction, and different virtues should be developed at each level, pre-primary, primary, high school, and college.[12] Teachers should encourage, be kind, give individual attention to students, and be open to all learners, creating a non-coercive atmosphere in which the subject matter is presented with variety and practicality. Teachers should be paid much more than they are, as their job is of such value and demands a high level of competence. The teacher has to combine moral integrity, enthusiasm, and diligence with pedagogic efficiency.[13]

In the words of Comenius, "School is the workshop where young souls are formed to virtue."[14]

Notes

1. Jennifer Wolfe, *Learning from the Past: Historical Voices in Early Childhood Education* (Mayerthrope, Alberta: Piney Branch Press, 2000), p. 18.
2. Daniel Murphy, *Comenius: A Critical Reassessment of his Life and Work* (Dublin: Irish Academic Press, 1995), pp. 8–12.
3. Jaroslave Panek, *Comenius: Teacher of Nations,* translated by Ivo Dvorak (Prague: Vychodoslovenske Vydavetelstov, 1991), pp. 25–33.
4. Wolfe, p. 22.
5. Murphy, p. 40.
6. Madonna Murphy, "Johann Amos Comenius: Moral Education Through Age Appropriate Virtue Formation," *Proceedings of the Midwest Philosophy of Education Annual Meeting,* Chicago, 2000, p. 384.
7. Glen Dixon, "Celebrating Comenius' 400th Birthday," *Childhood Education* 60 (4), p. 224.
8. Carol Ingall, "Reform and Redemption: The Maharal of Prague and John Amos Comenius," *Religious Education* 89 (3), pp. 258–276.
9. Bjorg Gundem, "Vivat Comenius": A Commemorative Essay on Johann Amos Comenius, 1592–1670, *Journal of Curriculum and Supervision* 8 (1) (1992), pp. 43–55.
10. Ibid., pp. 44–47.
11. Peter Menck, "The Formation of Conscience, a lost topic of Didaktik," *Journal of Curriculum Studies* 33 (3) (2001), pp. 261–275.
12. Murphy, M., p. 388.
13. Murphy, D., pp. 91–110.
14. Menck, p. 274.

Questions to Guide Your Reading

1. What does "didactic" mean according to Comenius? What aspects of his *The Great Didactic* are the same as our understanding of teaching today and which are different?

2. What is the golden rule for teachers according to Comenius? Why is this significantly different from the way that teaching had been done in the medieval ages?

3. If you cannot show students the actual object, what does Comenius suggest? What do you think he would suggest for teaching an abstract concept?

4. What are the four stages of schools Comenius proposes? Do you think he would be in favor of today's preschool?

5. List Comenius' nine principles of teaching. Can you condense his nine principles into a set that you would find relevant for you as a teacher in today's schools?

READING 6.4:
A UNIFIED APPROACH: SELECTIONS FROM *THE GREAT DIDACTIC OF JOHN AMOS COMENIUS*

The Great Didactic:

Setting forth The whole Art of Teaching all Things to all Men

Let the main object of this, our Didactic, be as follows: To seek and to find a method of instruction, by which teachers may teach less, but learners may learn more; by which schools may be the scene of less noise, aversion, and useless labour, but of more leisure, enjoyment, and solid progress; and through which the Christian community may have less darkness, perplexity, and dissension, but on the other hand more light, orderliness, peace, and rest.

God be merciful unto us and bless us, and cause his face to shine upon us;

Greeting to the Reader

DIDACTIC signifies the art of teaching. Several men of ability, taking pity on the serious labour of schools, have lately endeavored to find out some such art, but with unequal skill and unequal success. . . .

The venture to promise a GREAT DIDACTIC; that is to say, the whole art of teaching all things to all men, and indeed of teaching them with certainty, so that the result cannot fail to follow; further of teaching them pleasantness, that is to see, without annoyance or aversion on the part of teacher or pupil, but rather with the greatest enjoyment for both; further of teaching them thoroughly, not superficially—but in such a manner as to lead to true knowledge, to gentle morals, and to the deepest piety. Lastly, we wish to prove all this *a priori*, that is to say, from the unalterable nature of the matter itself drawing off, as from a living source constantly

Source: *A Unified Approach: Selections from The Great Diductic of John Amos Comenius.* Published with Introductions, Biographical and Historical, by M. W. Keatinge, B. A., Late Exhibitioneer of Exeter College, Oxford (London, Adam and Charles Black, 1896).

flowing runlets, and bringing them together again into one concentrated stream, that we may lay the foundations of the universal art of founding universal schools . . .

From this a golden rule for teachers may be derived. Everything should, as far as is possible, be placed before the senses. Everything visible should be brought before the organ of sight, everything audible before that of hearing. Odours should be placed before the sense of smell, and things that are testable and tangible before the sense of taste and of touch respectively. If an object can make an impression on several senses at once, it should be brought into contact with several. And although there might be parents with leisure to educate their own children, it is nevertheless better that the young should be taught together and in large classes, since better results and more pleasure are to be obtained when one pupil serves as an example and a stimulus for another.

Young children, especially, are always more easily led and ruled by example than by precept. If you give them a precept, it makes but little impression; if you point out that others are doing something, they imitate without being told to do so.

If the objects themselves cannot be procured, representations of them may be used. Copies or models may be constructed for teaching purposes, and the same principle may be adopted by botanists, geometricians, zoologists, and geographers, who should illustrate their descriptions by engravings of the objects described. The same thing should be done in books on physics and elsewhere. For example, the human body will be well explained by ocular demonstration if the following plan be adopted. A skeleton should be procured (either such a one as is usually kept in universities, or one made of wood), and on this framework should be placed the muscles, sinews, nerves, veins, arteries, as well as the intestines, the lungs, the heart, the diaphragm, and the liver. These should be made of leather and stuffed with wool, and should be of the right size and in the right place, while on each organ should be written its name and its function. For every branch of knowledge similar constructions (that is to say, images of things which cannot be procured in the original) should be made, and should be kept in the schools ready for use. It is true that expense and labor will be necessary to produce these models, but the result will amply reward the effort....

These points should be observed by those who teach the sciences, and may be expressed in nine very useful precepts.

(i) Whatever is to be known must be taught.

Unless that which is to be known be placed before a pupil, how is he to acquire a knowledge of it? The two things necessary are honesty and hard work.

(ii) Whatever is taught should be taught as being of practical application in every-day life and of some definite use.... In this way his energy and his accuracy will be increased.

(iii) Whatever is taught should be taught straightforwardly, and not in a complicated manner ....Objects should be placed before the eyes of the student in their true character, and not shrouded in words, metaphors, or hyperboles.

(iv) Whatever is taught must be taught with reference to its true nature and its origin; that is to say, through its causes. Therefore to explain the causes of anything is equivalent to making a true exposition of that thing's nature, in accordance with the principles: Objects can thus be best, easiest, and most certainly cognized through a knowledge of the processes that produced them.... If, however, the teacher reverse the order of nature, he is certain to confuse the student. Therefore, the method employed in teaching should be based on the method of nature. That which precedes should be taken first, and that which follows last.

(v) If anything is to be learned, its general principles must first be explained. Its details may then be considered, and not till then. We give a general notion of an object when we explain it by means of its essential nature and its accidental qualities. The essential nature is unfolded by the questions *what? Of what kind? And why?* Under the question *what* are included the name, the genus, the function, and the end. Under the question of *what kind* comes the form of the object, or the mode in which it is fitted to its end. Under the question *why* the efficient or causal force by which an object is made suitable to its end....

(vi) All the parts of an object, even the smallest, and without a single exception, must be learned with reference to their order, their position, and their connection with one another.

(vii) All things must be taught in due succession, and not more than one thing should be taught at one time ... the mind can only grasp one thing at a time. We should, therefore, make a distinct break in our progress from one thing to another, that we may not overburden the mind.

(viii) We should not leave any subject until it is thoroughly understood.... The pupil should therefore not pass on from any point in a science until he has thoroughly mastered it and is conscious that he has done so. The methods to be employed are emphatic teaching, examination, and iteration, until the desired result is attained.

(ix) Stress should be laid on the differences that exist between things, in order that what knowledge of them is acquired may be clear and distinct.

Much meaning lies concealed in that celebrated saying: "He who distinguishes well is a good teacher." For too many facts overwhelm a student, and too great a variety confuses him.

On the General Organization of the School System

A certain fixed time ought to be set apart for the complete education of youth, at the end of which they may go forth from school to the business of life, truly instructed, truly moral, truly religious. The time that is required for this is the whole period of youth, that is to say, from birth to manhood, which is fully attained in twenty-four years. Dividing the twenty-four years into periods of six years each, we ought to have a school suited to each period, viz., the school of:

1. Infancy: the mother's lap up to six years of age
2. Boyhood: *luaus literaries*, or vernacular public school
3. Adolescence: the Latin School or Gymnasium
4. Youth: the University *(Academia)*, and travel

The Infant School should be found in every house, the Vernacular School in every village and community, the Gymnasium in every province, and the University in every kingdom or large province.

Discussion Questions

1. Comenius believes that knowledge can only be gained if it is perceived through the senses. How does Comenius' *The Great Didactic* significantly move Medieval and Renaissance educational thought forward in the area of sensory education? How does that movement still impact teaching practices today? Give examples.
2. Comenius outlines a school structure where students should be divided according to age. What would Comenius think about today's middle school; its philosophy, and curriculum?
3. Comenius believed that whatever is taught should be taught as being of practical application in everyday life. To what extent can teachers today show the practical applicability of everything in the curriculum they must teach?
4. Do you think Comenius knew about teaching to learning styles? Give examples from the reading to support your answer.

For Further Research on the Internet

Home page on Comenius with links that show how his work is living on through "Comenius" projects—programs that teach foreign languages to others. http://www.comeniusfoundation.org/comenius.htm

Radio show transcripts and audio clips on Comenius and his importance in Czech history and education. http://www.radio.cz/en/article/25962

The Comenius Museum in the Netherlands with video and links on Comenius, in German. http://www.comeniusmuseum.nl/

Suggestions for Further Reading

Dixon, Glen. "Celebrating Comenius' 400th Birthday." *Childhood Education* 60 (4) (1992): 224.

Gundem, Bjorg. "Vivat Comenius: A Commemorative Essay on Johann Amos Comenius, 1592–1670." *Journal of Curriculum and Supervision* 8 (1) (1992): 43–55.

Ingall, Carol. "Reform and Redemption: The Maharal of Prague and John Amos Comenius." *Religious Education* 89 (3) (1994): 258–276.

Menck, Peter. "The Formation of Conscience, a Lost Topic of Didaktik." *Journal of Curriculum Studies* 33 (3) (2001): 261–275.

Murphy, Daniel. *Comenius: A Critical Reassessment of His Life and Work.* Dublin: Irish Academic Press, 1995.

Murphy, Madonna. Johann Amos Comenius: Moral Education through Age Appropriate Virtue Formation. *Proceedings of the Midwest Philosophy of Education Annual Meeting,* Chicago, 2000.

Panek, Jaroslave. *Comenius: Teacher of Nations.* Translated by Ivo Dvorak. Prague: Vychodoslovenske Vydavetelstov, 1991.

Wolfe, Jennifer. *Learning from the Past: Historical Voices in Early Childhood Education.* Mayerthrope, Alberta: Piney Branch Press, 2000.

CHAPTER ACTIVITIES

Linking the Past to the Present

Figure 6.2 Simulation of the Fifteenth Century–Role Play

The Situation

Europe, the 1500's. The humanistic ideas of Erasmus have come forward from the Renaissance (rebirth) of the ancient Greek and Latin classics. Christine de Pizan advocates that the education of youth is key to this re-flowering of humanity. Luther challenges these ideas and tries to reform society, recognizing that educational reform was key to religious reformation. Comenius tries to reconcile everyone's ideas.

Preparation

Form groups at your table; pair up by fours, each taking the part of one of the authors, Christine, Erasmus, Luther, or Comenius. Discuss the following current day trends in education that we are using to "reform" our schools from the perspective of your author.

Task

Taking the character of your author, give your opinion on the following matters by role-playing a public debate or a heated discussion in the "park."

1. The value of "head start" programs and early childhood education
2. Home schooling
3. Censorship of books
4. Private schools vs. parochial schools
5. Sports and extracurricular activities
6. The role of schools/the aim of education
7. Gender-fair schooling (education of women)
8. Bilingual education
9. Vocational education or liberal education
10. The main problem with education in the schools today

Developing Your Philosophy of Education

During the Renaissance and the Reformation, importance was placed on learning languages, whether it was Greek, Latin, or one's own vernacular. As you write your philosophy of education include your ideas on the importance of teaching foreign languages early to children and your opinion on bilingual education in the schools. If you teach in a racially diverse school, what will be your stance on teaching "black English"? How will knowing other languages help your students to understand other cultures?

Connecting Theory to Practice

Visit the library at your clinical school. Note the kinds of books they have. Are there many classical books or do they mainly have contemporary books? Are there books on famous women and are there books written by women? (Do you think Christine, Erasmus and Luther would be content reading in this library?) Interview the librarian to see how the books are chosen. How much is in the library budget? How much comes from federal Title II monies? What kind of restrictions do they have on the kinds of books that can be bought?

Educators' Philosophies and Contributions to Education

TABLE 6.2   Philosophy and Contributions of Renaissance and Reformation Educators

Educator	Role of Teacher & Learner	View of Curriculum & Methodology	Purpose or Goal of Education	Major Contribution
Christine de Pizan	A wise and virtuous teacher guides her students by exposing them to stories of famous moral models	A classical curriculum of history, mythology, poetry, oratory, and physical education taught to young children by doing and using rhyming verse for memorization	Moral education for civic responsibility	First to advocate liberal education for all women in a school for women
Erasmus	Teacher of teachers so the important not the trivial is taught. Parents gently teach virtues to young children using good fables and poems	A broad humanistic curriculum with the classics read from the original, not a glosa. Teaching content and reasoning is more important than rhetoric and style	To enlighten the youth and improve the civil state to promote understanding and tolerance among all peoples	Read the original works in order to develop critical thinking skills of analysis, synthesis, and evaluation
Martin Luther	Teachers are "in loco parentis" (take the place of the parents) and should speak kindly and correct gently	History, singing, Biblical languages, mathematics taught in a motivating way by using competition	Public schooling so that the entire population can learn to read the Bible	Promoted mass literacy by advocating education for all teaching in the vernacular. First compulsory education law in Germany
Comenius	Teach according to the developmental level of the child, taking learning styles into consideration, relating content to child's daily life	Curriculum should be a systematic sequencing of content, and as all knowledge proceeds through the senses objects should be used in instruction	Universal education of all, goal is education of the whole child: religious, moral, social, emotional, aesthetic, intellectual, and physical	Child-centered education, use of pictures in books. Pansophism—organic unity of knowledge. First to promote education for all, even children with special needs

CHAPTER 7

New Educational Ideas in the Enlightenment

The Enlightenment, also known as the Age of Reason, was an intellectual movement in Western Europe that also had repercussions in society, politics, religion, science, and education. In the eighteenth century this daring and dramatically new movement began with the work of John Locke and the scientist Isaac Newton but soon engaged thinkers on both sides of the English Channel. The term Enlightenment so appropriately used the metaphor of light as discovered by Isaac Newton when he put light through a prism and revealed its multicolored nature. The Enlightenment heralded new thinking about once unquestioned truths; truths no longer considered black or white, but now of many colors.[1]

John Locke's *Two Treatises of Government* is seen by many as the true opening of the Enlightenment with its questioning of the "divine right of Kings" theory and its proposal for a political order based on a contract between the people and the government. Newton inspired the scientific cause of the Enlightenment, as his experiments changed pre-existing beliefs and presented a new world view that said that mathematical principles and laws (not God and religious beliefs) ruled the universe.[2]

The French Revolution is generally considered to mark the end of the Enlightenment period and the beginning of the Age of Revolution. The question historians still debate is whether the Enlightenment caused the French Revolution or whether the French Revolution is a repudiation of the Enlightenment.[3]

Life During the Enlightenment

During the sixteenth, seventeenth, and eighteenth centuries in Europe people dared to imagine a different world; they desired to build new social and political structures that would serve all people.[4] The political roots of the European Enlightenment grew out of a profound revulsion against political abuses of the 1600s on both sides of the English

Channel. What had begun in the 1680s as a movement against religious intolerance had become by the 1780s an agenda for reform, threatening courts, princes, and lay and clerical oligarchies.[5]

The Enlightenment is best understood as the eclipse of the medieval world view and life style that had been a unified tapestry with a philosophy, anthropology, politic, and theology all interconnected, with God as the source of everything, and the gradual movement to a modern worldview and life style that had man, science, and intellect as the source of all truth.[6]

Enlightened people read books and journals. They were not timid followers of the clergy. Sometimes they did not even go to Church or believe in God. Science allowed alternatives to be imagined in everything from politics to religion. Some argued for a rational religion free of mysteries, miracles, and the Trinity. Gradually, highly educated Protestants and Catholics (mostly in France) thought more about God's works as revealed by science than by his Biblical word. Science captured their imagination. The religions of the educated began to be more private than public, more individualistic than collective; thought rather than ceremonies began to define the believer.[7]

Religious tolerance thus became a key Enlightenment idea. According to Alasdair MacIntyre, the "Enlightenment Project" became a search for an independent, rational justification of morality that would be based on a common view of nature, but a human nature, which no longer found its meaning or "telos" in God.[8]

A new group of Protestant journalists, theorists, scientists, clerics, publishers, and book sellers created the context wherein the new, enlightened ideas flourished. They questioned all forms of authority and turned their attention to concrete social and governmental reforms, e.g., representative government, the need to abolish the privileges of the clergy, and a more accepting approach to human nature, virtue and vice, sexuality and gender.[9]

By the late eighteenth century, new forms of civil society arose in almost every major town from London to Berlin. The cities of Europe grew, becoming centers of commerce and sites of many public gatherings. The Enlightenment created the modern democratic and representative government that now challenges people in every cultural setting to be open-minded.[10] (See Map 7.1, Europe in the 18th Century.)

Education in the Enlightenment Period

The Enlightenment gave a new purpose to schools—they were to cultivate the student's ability to reason. Schools were to be progressive institutions that encouraged students to enjoy learning, to learn through discovery using the empirical method of science, and to be open-minded, questioning everything.[11] A new kind of schooling should be created— one that was based on scientific reasoning. There was a great spread of literacy and a change in the nature of reading during the Enlightenment. All over Europe new institutions and organizations where ideas could be explored and discussed were established— academies and societies, public lectures, coffee houses, and lending libraries. More reading material was available and more reading was done by a broader reading public than before. Perhaps this is why the Enlightenment ideas spread so much and penetrated every level of society in many different countries.[12]

John Locke was a part of the first stirring of enlightened educational thought. In *Some Thoughts Concerning Education* he expresses an essentially Christian understanding of human beings that saw virtue and rationality as inseparably linked so that virtue could be learned and practiced, taught by parents and tutors.[13] Locke emphasized the role of sense impressions in the formation of abstract concepts; this is the philosophy of empiri-

Map 7.1   Europe in the 18th Century

Source: From Anthony Esler, *The Human Venture, Combined Volume: From Prehistory to the Present,* 5th edition, 2004. Reprinted by permission of Pearson Education.

cism that says that man can only know appearances, not the real essences of external things. Science became the study of nature and the only true source of knowledge. Locke's idea that each person possesses inalienable rights of life, liberty, and property influenced the American colonists and their revolution. They tried to construct a political order according to reason—the constitution.

Jean-Jacques Rousseau was another key theorist of the Enlightenment period whose ideas contributed to the transformation of education in Europe. Rousseau's beliefs regarding the individual child-centered approach to education, expressed in *Emile,* provoked a revolution in education that had a profound influence on subsequent educational thought in the nineteenth and twentieth centuries.[14]

Johann Heinrich Pestalozzi and Friedrich Froebel applied these new views of the student and dramatically changed educational philosophy and instructional methods to take into consideration the needs and abilities of the students. This philosophy became the forerunner of modern day progressive education. Johann Herbart built upon these ideas, discoveries, and the exaltation of science and developed a science of pedagogy.

Education of Women

The Enlightenment devoted great efforts to the definition of gender, attempting to determine the differences between the sexes, the meaning of femininity, and the important role of mothers. Many of the women of the Enlightenment used their talents as novelists or playwrights or they educated their children to be fair-minded, well-disposed toward science, and eager to learn. During the Enlightenment, women became more involved in public life through travel, conversation, reading, and writing. Indeed the Enlightenment put women's rights and their general education on the intellectual agenda as never before. As writers, a few women became public intellectuals, yet everywhere in the Western world women were still excluded from formal higher education in any institutional setting. The necessity for female education appeared in almost every tract written to advance women's status as the issue of women's education and status was raised again and again.[15]

Mary Wollstonecraft pointed out the contradictions implicit in the Enlightenment's ideas about gender and equated the denial of rights to slaves and the denial of rights to women. On the other hand, the eighteenth century saw the emergence, for the first time, of a sizable number of women who independently earned their living.[16]

Mary Astell championed the cause of women's education as the key to all progress. As a charity school teacher she wrote *A Serious Proposal to the Ladies*, declaring that women are as capable of learning as men. Astell believed in isolating women in their education.

Catherine Macauley, born in 1731 and rigorously trained by her father, wrote an eight volume history of England, and in 1790 *Letters on Education,* in which she endorsed serious education for women. Macauley believed that girls and boys learn better when together under the same roof.[17]

An Enlightenment Philosophy of Education

No educational philosophy can be completely understood unless linked to the human conditions that produced it. Transitional eras in scientific, ethical, political, and religious thought are also eras of corresponding changes in educational theory and practice. Educational theory is closely involved in the life of each civilization and, indeed, in the life of every people. The Enlightenment referred to a process of education for man, an education in the use of reason, for the foremost idea of this era was the supremacy of reason.[18]

The key contributions of the Enlightenment to educational philosophy include:

1. educational opportunities for a wider class of people based on the idea that the masses needed to be prepared to take their role as citizens
2. the adoption of new pedagogical techniques based on a new concept of the child as an innocent being
3. teaching of the scientific method throughout a curriculum which included science, social science, and math
4. a belief in the supremacy of reason led to a change in moral and religious instruction and a glorification of "progress" over heaven

For Further Research on the Internet

Professor Richard Hooker's page on the Enlightenment from his World Civilization course has many excellent links. **http://www.wsu.edu/~dee/ENLIGHT/ENLIGHT.HTM**

The Internet Modern History Sourcebook with references and links to Enlightenment philosophers and thinkers. **http://www.fordham.edu/halsall/mod/modsbook10.html**

Eighteenth century resources and links. **http://andromeda.rutgers.edu/~jlynch/18th/**

Topics two, three and four have philosophers and thinkers of the Enlightenment and their educational theories. **http://prenhall.com/foundations-cluster**

Notes

1. Margaret Jacobs, *The Enlightenment: A Brief History with Documents* (Boston/New York: Bedford/St. Martin's, 2001), pp. 1–2.
2. Ibid. p. 15.
3. Dornda Outram, *The Enlightenment* (Cambridge: Cambridge University Press, 1995), pp. 53, 115–121.
4. Rita Guare, "Reclaiming Thoughtfulness and Imagination in Educational Leadership: A Moral Commitment to Enlightened Reason," in *Moral Philosophy and Education in the Enlightenment,* edited by D. Jedan, C. Luth, C. Bulach, R. Kump and D. MacLeay (Bochum, Germany: Winkler, 2001), p. 46.
5. Jacobs, p. 3.
6. Guare, p. 45.
7. Jacobs, pp. 16–18.
8. Alasdair MacIntyre, *After Virtue,* 2nd ed. (South Bend, IN: Notre Dame Press, 1984), pp. 44–51.
9. Jacobs, pp. 13–14.
10. Ibid., p. 20.
11. Gerald Gutek, *A History of the Western Educational Experience,* 2nd ed. (Prospect Heights, IL: Waveland Press, Inc., 1995), pp. 159–161.
12. Robert Allan Houston, *Literacy in Early Modern Europe* (London: New York, 1988), p. 14; Outram, p. 20.
13. Jacobs, p. 8.
14. Guare, p. 45.
15. Jacobs, pp. 22–27.
16. Outram, pp. 41, 65, 80–89.
17. Diane Jacobs, *Her Own Woman: The Life of Mary Wollstonecraft* (New York: Simon & Schuster, 2001), p. 99; M. Jacobs, p. 26.
18. Outram, pp. 1–4.

Section 7.1: John Locke (1632–1704)

Do you remember the spelling bees and Jeopardy games you would play in order to review before a test? Well, we have John Locke to thank for telling us that education should be fun and educational games should be used to motivate students so that they want to learn.

John Locke's Life and Times

John Locke was born August 29, 1632 in the southwestern part of England, some 125 miles from London. His father, John Locke, Sr., was a lawyer, a small landowner, and a strong Calvinist Presbyterian and his mother, Agnes Keefe Locke, was ten years older than her husband. John grew up in a small cottage home in the village of Pensford.

John's Education

John received the early part of his elementary education at home from his parents. Later in his educational writings, Locke expressed a preference for tutorial education rather than public schools, reflecting his own early educational experience. In 1647 Locke went to the prestigious Westminster School in London and studied the elementary curriculum of the day, ancient and oriental languages taught through rote memorization, emphasizing grammar but with little interpretation. The discipline was notorious and the birch whip was used often on the students to force them to memorize their lessons. In his writings, Locke becomes a strong critic of corporal punishment, certainly responding to this negative childhood experience.

John's exceptional intellectual skills allowed him to excel at the competitive public orations (called elections) and earn a scholarship to Christ College in Oxford. He followed the traditional course of undergraduate study there—Aristotelian logic, metaphysics, and classics. In 1656, Locke earned his bachelor's degree; two years later he earned his Master's. While at Christ College, he had his first work published in an anthology printed by the Dean of Christ College. (See the timeline of Locke's life in Figure 7.1.)

University Lecturer

With the M.A. degree, Locke was granted a "studentship," or a permanent university position. This was under the condition that he did not marry and that he took holy orders once he reached a level of seniority in the college. Although Locke never married, he also never became a priest. Some attribute this to scruples he had about his own character and suitability for the priesthood, others feel he was more interested in science and medicine than the Anglican Church of England.[1]

Locke was appointed lecturer in Greek in 1660, Reader in Rhetoric in 1662 and Censor of Moral Philosophy in 1663. John's mother died in 1654 and his father died in 1661 leaving him an amount of money that would have secured him a nice life as a university don. However, Locke was interested in pursuing other avenues and accepted a diplomatic mission to the Netherlands with Sir Walker Vane that allowed him to see Calvinists, Lutherans, and Catholics living and working peacefully under one government. This inspired his liberal views on toleration.

Locke, the Medical Doctor

As this first venture into political life was not that rewarding, John returned to Oxford to pursue his true interest in science and medicine, earning a bachelor's degree in medicine (M.B.) in 1664.[2] In 1666, Locke joined Anthony Ashley Copper, the future Earl of Shaftsbury, as his medical doctor and political advisor. Locke successfully operated on Lord Ashley, curing him of a liver ailment, and lived in the Ashleys' home for nine years.

Some Thoughts Concerning Education

In 1675, Locke had to leave London due to his lung and respiration problems with the pollution there. He went to France for four years and then to Holland due to the political turmoil. He even assumed an alias, Dr. Van der Linden. During this time he wrote letters to Edward and Mary Clark regarding the education of their ten-year-old son, Edward, which were later published as *Some Thoughts Concerning Education* (1693).

Locke, the Political Philosopher

The political situation more stable, Locke returned to England in 1689, and in the next two years he published everything he had been working on for the past decade: *Letter Concerning Toleration, Two Treatises of Government,* and *Essay Concerning Human Understanding.*[3] Locke's *Second Treatise* is very important as it influenced the American colonists, especially Thomas Jefferson. In it Locke presents the idea of natural law, i.e.,

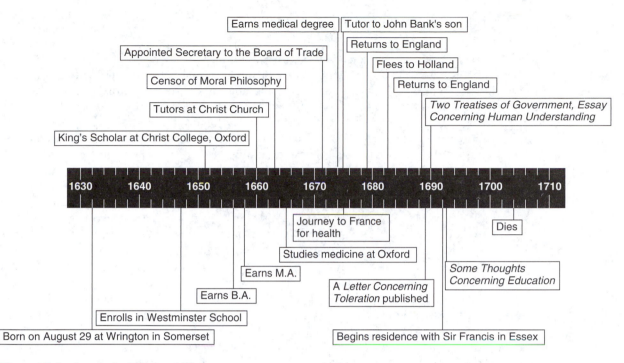

Figure 7.1   Locke's Life and Times

that all men are created free and equal, and government is the result of their common agreement to unite. Now at the height of his career, Locke maintained a full social, political, and ceremonial schedule, with important public duties. Locke left London and moved into the home of Sir Francis and Damaris Masham out in the country. Here he lived the final twelve years of his life, traveling into London when he had political engagements. On October 28, 1704 he died while his closest friend and companion, Damaris Masham, read to him from the Psalms.[4]

Locke's Contribution to Educational Thought

Some Thoughts Concerning Education is the richest source of Locke's educational theory and his philosophy of education; it is a public appeal for a general reformation of education. Through these commentaries (in the letters he wrote to the Clarks) Locke expresses his vision of human nature and moral virtue, a program of an appropriate curriculum and method of teaching, and he shows how important the family and education are for the political state.[5]

Locke did not support the Christian notion of Adam's fall that meant that children were born depraved because of the taint of original sin. He believed in the child's potential and his educational thoughts emphasize the heart as well as the mind, feeling as well as philosophy. The first goal of education is to get the child to recognize that learning is enjoyable and can even be a passion.[6]

Although *Some Thoughts Concerning Education* was aimed largely at male children, Locke's ideas were taken as a license to educate all children and even to allow women to teach. Locke can be seen as one who put the issue of women's education on the Western agenda along with other feminist precursors.[7]

Locke's Philosophic Principles of Liberalism and Empiricism

In *Two Treatises of Government,* Locke explains his political philosophy of liberalism, which states that man is endowed with natural rights such as life, liberty, and property. Thomas Jefferson was very influenced by these ideas and used them in the Declaration of Independence. Locke spoke about the importance of the social contract of government—to preserve the rights to life and liberty for all citizens, both those who possess property (the gentlemen) and those who do not (the workingmen). Although he proposed that the children of the propertied class be educated in a way quite different from children of the poor, he did propose that all, poor and wealthy of both sexes between the ages of three and fourteen, should be educated.

Locke's *Essay Concerning Human Understanding* is important in philosophy and education as it outlines his theory of empiricism. The mind is without ideas at birth, according to Locke; he supports the *tabula rasa* theory of Aristotle that suggests that the mind is like an empty slate waiting to be written upon by experiences, able to constantly learn things as it experiences sensations and impressions. We can only know what we can experience. Words are our expression of ideas gained from experiences. The meaning of a word is always the idea it signifies in the minds of those who use it.

Curiosity is the desire and appetite to know. It should be encouraged in children by always answering their questions and giving them truthful and complete explanations, and letting them experience things if possible. Locke advocates that instead of requiring children to do things under the threat of punishment or even as duties, it is better to allow them to do desired things freely or as a privilege. Locke vigorously opposed the use of corporal punishment. He recommends the use of praise and blame as proper rewards and punishment for particular acts.

Locke's Philosophy of Education

According to Locke's philosophy of education, children have a basic uniform rational nature and God-given potential, but it must be developed and brought out through the process of education and socialization. Locke recommends private education in the home rather than the one obtained in schools and stresses the importance of looking for a good and virtuous tutor. The ideal tutor must be a person of upright Christian character who can gently and without force guide the student toward virtue through example and the formation of habit, encouraging the student at the appropriate stage of intellectual and moral development. The tutor needs to recognize the innate character traits or natural dispositions and temperament of each child and work with them in the hope of forming a moral person responsible for his actions. Children should never be thought of as merely youngsters, but as adults in the making. You need to reason with them so they understand why they should act appropriately. Locke's contention that children should be treated as rational creatures is one of his greatest contributions to educational thought.[8]

Locke's educational plan is a whole program for intellectual and moral enrichment, with an emphasis on the importance of character formation over mastery of specific content or curriculum. Virtue is harder to obtain than knowledge of the world for it involves cultivating one's reason so that it will direct one's desires. The virtues are taught by appealing to the child's natural sensibilities—to pleasure and pain, and by carefully observing the child's individual nature and accommodating the teachings to it. The motivation for our moral behavior is, according to Locke, what we perceive as being in the interest of our happiness and pleasure, rather than what we know to be the good. This is very different from Aristotle's presentation of virtue in which virtue helps us to choose the good, thereby developing our true human potential so as to reach our end and realize true happiness.[9]

Locke criticized the medieval trivium and quadrivium, stating that subjects should instead be integrated. You could learn Latin and French while learning to write and read. Within the specific discipline, Locke recommended a definite order of learning based upon the natural connections of subject matter.[10] Locke is considered the Father of Modern Education in England because of how the curriculum and methodology was changed after his writing. Locke's ideas on the curriculum were also implemented by the American colonists who needed practical and utilitarian studies which would help them survive in the new world, rather than Greek and Latin. He also inspired the colonists with the importance of education for the new nation. In Locke's own words "We are born with faculties and powers, capable almost of anything; as it is in the body, so it is in the mind, practice makes it what it is."

Notes

1. Kevin L. Cope, *John Locke Revisited*, edited by J. Bartolomeo, *Twayne's English Author Series* (New York: Twayne Publishers, 1999), pp. 1–5; W. M. Spellman, *John Locke* (New York: St. Martin's Press, 1997), pp. 9–11.
2. Spellman, pp. 12–16.
3. Cope, pp. 7–15.
4. Spellman, pp. 26, 30.
5. Nathan Tarcov, *Locke's Education for Liberty*. (Lanham, MD: Lexington Books, 1999), pp. 2, 79.
6. Cope, pp. 28–29.
7. Margaret Jacobs, *The Enlightenment: A Brief History with Documents* (Boston/New York: Bedford/St. Martin's, 2001), p. 31.
8. John Yolton, *John Locke and Education* (New York: Random House, 1971), pp. 68–83.
9. Concepción Naval, *Educar Ciudadanos: La Polemica liberal-communitarista de educación* (Pamplona, España: Ediciones Universidad de Navarra, S.A., 1995), p. 290.
10. Yolton, p. 74.

Questions to Guide Your Reading

1. What does Locke think is the main mistake parents make in raising their children? Do parents today make this same mistake?
2. What does Locke say happens to a child who is beaten or punished too severely? Although corporal punishment is not allowed in schools today, what demeaning techniques are still used?
3. What are the most effective motivators according to Locke? Would they also be effective in schools today?
4. Why is it so important to develop good habits according to Locke?
5. What are the four things every man desires for his son according to Locke? Are they relevant for children in the twenty-first century? If not, can you name four other desires?

READING 7.1:
SOME THOUGHTS CONCERNING EDUCATION

1. A sound mind in a sound body, is a short but full description of a happy state in this world: he that has these two, has little more to wish for; and he that wants either of them, will be but little the better for anything else. Men's happiness or misery is, [for the] most part, of their own making. . . . And I think I may say, that, of all the men we meet with, nine parts of ten are what they are, good or evil, useful or not, by their education. It is that which makes the great difference in mankind. The little, or almost insensible, impressions on our tender infancies, have very important and lasting consequences. . .

32. . . . We have reason to conclude that great care is to be had of the forming of children's minds, and giving them that seasoning early, which shall influence their lives always after. . .

33. As the strength of the body lies chiefly in being able to endure hardships, so also does that of the mind. And the great principle and foundation of all virtue and worth is placed in this, that a man is able to deny himself his own desires, cross his own inclinations, and purely follow what reason directs as best, though the appetite lean the other way.

34. The great mistake I have observed in people's breeding their children has been that this has not been taken care enough of in its due season; that the mind has not been made obedient to discipline, and pliant to reason, when first it was most tender, most easy to be bowed.

38. It seems plain to me that the principle of all virtue and excellency lies in a power of denying ourselves the satisfaction of our own desires, where reason does not authorize them. This power is to be got and improved by custom, made easy and familiar by an early practice.

39. I say not this as if children were not to be indulged in anything, or that I expected they should, in hanging-sleeves, have the reason and conduct of counselors. I consider them as children, who must be tenderly used, who must play, and have play things. . . . I have seen children at a table, who, whatever was there, never asked for any thing, but contentedly took what was given them: and at another place I have seen others cry for everything they saw, must be served out of every dish, and that first too. What made this vast difference but this, that one was accustomed to have what they called or cried for, the other to go without it? The younger they are, the less, I think, are their unruly and disorderly appetites to be complied with. . .

40. Those, therefore, that intend ever to govern their children, should begin it whilst they are very little; and look that they perfectly comply with the will of their parents. . .

46. . . . [I]f the mind be curbed and humbled too much in children; if their spirits be abased and broken much, by too strict a hand over them; they lose all their vigour and industry, and are in a worse state than the former. . . .

47. The usual lazy and short way by chastisement and the rod, which is the only instrument of government that tutors generally know, or ever think of, is the most unfit of any to be used in education; because it tends to both those mischiefs.

49. This sort of correction naturally breeds an aversion to that which it is the tutor's business to create a liking to. How obvious is it to observe that children come to hate things which were at first acceptable to them, when they find themselves whipped, and teased about them?. . .

52. Beating then, and all other sorts of slavish and corporal punishments, are not the discipline fit to be used in the education of those who would have wise, good, and ingenuous men; and therefore very rarely to be applied, and that only on great occasions and cases of extremity . . .

54. But if you take away the rod . . . how then (will you say) shall children be governed? . . . I advise their parents and governors always to carry this in their minds that children are to be treated as rational creatures. . .

56. The rewards and punishments then whereby we should keep children in order are quite

Source: John Locke, "Some Thoughts Concerning Education," in *Works of John Locke* (London: Thomas Tegg, et al., Vol. IX, 1823).

of another kind; and of that force, that when we can get them once to work, the business, I think, is done, and the difficulty is over. Esteem and disgrace are, of all others, the most powerful incentives to the mind, when once it is brought to relish them. If you can once get into children a love of credit, and an apprehension of shame and disgrace, you have put into them the true principle, which will constantly work, and incline them to the right. But, it will be asked, how shall this be done?

63. But if a right course be taken with children there will not be so much need of the application of the common reward and punishments, as we imagined, and as the general practice has established. For all their innocent folly, playing, and childish actions, are to be left perfectly free and unrestrained, as far as they can consist with the respect due to those that are present; and that with the greatest allowance.

64. And here give me leave to take notice of one thing I think a fault in the ordinary method of education; and that is, the charging of children's memories, upon all occasions, with rules and precepts, which they often do not understand, and are constantly as soon as forgot as given.... But it is much easier for a tutor to command, than to teach. Having this way cured in your child any fault, it is cured forever; and thus, one by one, you may weed them all out, and plant habits you please.

65. I have seen parents so heap rules on their children that it was impossible for the poor little ones to remember a tenth part of them, much less to observe them. However, they were either by words or blows corrected for the breach of those multiplied and often very impertinent precepts. . . .

God has stamped certain characters upon men's minds, which, like their shapes, may perhaps be a little mended; but can hardly be totally altered and transformed into the contrary . . . . For, in many cases, all that we can do, or should aim at, is to make the best of what nature has given; to prevent the vices and faults to which a constitution is most inclined, and give it all the advantages it is capable of. Everyone's natural genius should be carried as far as it could; but to attempt the putting of another upon him will be but labour in vain; and what is so plastered on will at best be but untowardly, and have always hanging to it the ungracefulness of constraint and affectation. . .

81. It will perhaps be wondered that I mention reasoning with children: and yet I cannot but think that the true way of dealing with them. They understand it as early as they do language; and, if I misobserve not, they love to be treated as rational creatures sooner than is imagined. It is a pride that should be cherished in them, and, as much as can be, made the greatest instrument to turn them by. But when I talk of reasoning, I do not intend any other but such as is suited to the child's capacity and apprehension . . .

118. Curiosity in children . . . is but an appetite after knowledge, and therefore ought to be encouraged in them, not only as a good sign, but as the great instrument nature has provided, to remove that ignorance they were born with, and which without this busy inquisitiveness will make them dull and useless creatures . . . And I doubt not but one great reason, why many children abandon themselves wholly to silly sports, and trifle away all their time insipidly, is, because they have found their curiosity baulked, and their inquiries neglected. But had they been treated with more kindness and respect, and their questions answered, as they should, to their satisfaction, I doubt not but they would have taken more pleasure in learning, and improving their knowledge, wherein there would be still newness and variety, which is what they are delighted with, than in returning over and over to the same play and play things.

134. That which every gentleman (that takes any care of his education) desires for his son, besides the estate he leaves him, is contained (I suppose) in these four things, virtue, wisdom, breeding, and learning. . .

147. You will wonder, perhaps, that I put learning last, especially if I tell you I think it the least part. This may seem strange in the mouth of a bookish man. . . . Reading, and writing, and learning, I allow to be necessary, but yet not the chief business. I imagine you would think him a very foolish fellow that should not value a virtuous, or a wise man, infinitely before a great scholar. Not but that I think learning a great help to both, in well-disposed minds; but yet it must be confessed also, that in others not so disposed, it helps them only to be more foolish, or worse men. . . .

Discussion Questions

1. Locke believes that curiosity in children is a key part of their learning experience, provided they receive answers. How is this curiosity a reflection of different learning styles? Why, then, do you suppose that parents become tired of answering their children's questions?
2. Do you agree with Locke's contention that children are born with "blank slates"? What does educational psychology teach us about learning?
3. What kind of rules and discipline system do you think Locke would have in his classroom?
4. Do you agree with Locke "men are nine times out of ten what they are by their education"? Why or why not?

For Further Research on the Internet

A brief biography of Locke with good links to his work and times. **http://www.philosophypages.com/ph/lock.htm**

The Internet Encyclopedia of Philosophy has a lengthy biography of John Locke with many excellent links. **http://www.utm.edu/research/iep/l/locke.htm**

Stanford Encyclopedia with many additional links for Locke. **http://plato.stanford.edu/entries/locke/#Oth**

Suggestions for Further Reading

Cope, Kevin L. *John Locke Revisited*. Edited by J. Bartolomeo, *Twayne's English Author Series*. New York: Twayne Publishers, 1999.

Jacobs, Margaret. *The Enlightenment: A Brief History with Documents*. Boston/New York: Bedford/St. Martin's, 2001.

Naval, Concepción. *Educar Ciudadanos: La Polemica liberal-communitarista de educación*. Pamplona, España: Ediciones Universidad de Navarra, S.A., 1995.

Spellman, W. M. *John Locke*. New York: St. Martin's Press, 1997.

Tarcov, Nathan. *Locke's Education for Liberty*. Lanham, MD: Lexington Books, 1999.

Yolton, John. *John Locke and Education*. New York: Random House, 1971.

Section 7.2: Jean-Jacques Rousseau (1712–1778)

Do you remember the field trips you went on in your elementary and high school classes? Did you ever participate in an "outdoor living" experience where you went to a camp with your class and learned about botany and nature outdoors? We have Jean Jacques Rousseau to thank for encouraging us to go "back to nature" to learn.

Rousseau's Life and Times

Rousseau was born on June 28, 1712 in Geneva, Switzerland to Isaac Rousseau and Suzanne Bernard; both were from bourgeois families and in their thirties when they married. Jean-Jacques was baptized into the Calvinist faith on July 4 and two days later his mother died of a fever. Isaac would often tell his son about his gentle, beautiful, and virtuous mother. Their father, their aunt, and a nursemaid reared Jean-Jacques and his ten-year-old brother, Francois. His father was a watchman by trade who taught his sons to read by reading with them late into the night from an unusual collection of books, which ranged from romantic novels to classics such as Plutarch's *Lives of Famous Men*. These books, according to Rousseau, gave him a highly romanticized and sentimental vision of the world.[1]

Jean-Jacques' Education

In 1722, Rousseau's father fled Geneva in order to avoid imprisonment after an altercation with a French army captain. Francois was apprenticed to a watchmaker and later disappeared from Rousseau's life. Jean Jacques was placed under the care of his uncle, Gabriel Bernard, who also had a ten-year-old son, Abraham. Pastor Lambercier tutored the boys for three years, assisted by his sister, Mademoiselle Lambercier, who used the paddle often to discipline the students. This was all the formal education Jean Jacques had. He then began his professional training as an apprentice to an engraver, but left that to try being a notary, and then he unsuccessfully went through a series of apprenticeships.

Finally, Rousseau left Geneva in 1728 to find a place for himself in the world. He ended up in the pension house of Madame de Warens who took him under her tutelage. She enabled him to acquire a classical education, taught him about sexual intimacy, and encouraged him to learn about the Catholic faith, to which he converted.[2] However, he later abjured and became anti-Catholic and anti-religion.

Settling Down in Paris

In 1739, Rousseau took a position as a tutor for two sons in the Mably household and wrote his first treatise on education based on this experience. He left this position to travel and try a series of jobs (twelve in all), going from job to job because he had difficulty working with other people. Rousseau's biographers attribute this instability to his upbringing.[3] Finally, Rousseau settled, in 1745, in Paris, the intellectual seat of the Enlightenment, and lived in the Hotel Saint-Quentin where he met Therese Levasseur, a simple, gentle, and timid woman of twenty-four years. For years she was his mistress, then his housekeeper, and finally, in 1768, his wife. Therese bore Rousseau five children. Each was given to an orphanage at birth.[4] This is the man who later writes a great educational novel, *Emile,* which is all about children, their upbringing, and their intrinsic natural value. One can only conclude that Rousseau was psychologically unstable to abandon his own children.

The Author

The turning point for Rousseau's unsuccessful career attempts came in 1749. He won a contest for the best essay on "Has the Progress of the Arts and Sciences Contributed More to the Corruption or Purification of Morals?" Overnight, Rousseau and his essay became a sensation, for in it he argued that human beings are, by nature, good and it is society's institutions that have made them bad.[5] In 1758, the Duke and Dutchess of Luxembourg offered the Rousseaus a house on their estate. (See the timeline of Rousseau's life in Figure 7.2.) In the four years that he lived there, Rousseau produced three of his most famous works: *The New Heloise, Emile,* and *The Social Contract.*[6] In 1760, Rousseau began to write two books at once, *Emile* and *The Social Contract. Emile* embodies his ideas on education and *The Social Contract* is a political treatise that established the principles of the natural rights of the individual citizen, which ensure the integrity of the political community of the state. Rousseau planned that the political ideas in the last book of *Emile* would be a summary and preview of those he intended to elaborate on in *The Social Contract.* Both books were published in 1762. In *Emile,* Rousseau rejects the notion of original sin and proposes instead a notion of the human being as a "noble savage." "Man is naturally good," he wrote; "Our original, natural condition is not to blame for the ills we see in our world."[7] The ideas found in *Emile* came to be criticized and rejected by the established authorities from both Church and State; and Rousseau had to go into exile. In 1765, Rousseau started his *Confessions,* the source of most of the information we have about his life, in which he shows that he suffered from an unstable mental condition that resulted in an inability to function in a socially acceptable manner. In 1767, Rousseau returned to Paris under a false name and finished his *Confessions.* On July 2, 1778, Rousseau died suddenly at Ermenonville with Therese at his side, following a brief illness.[8]

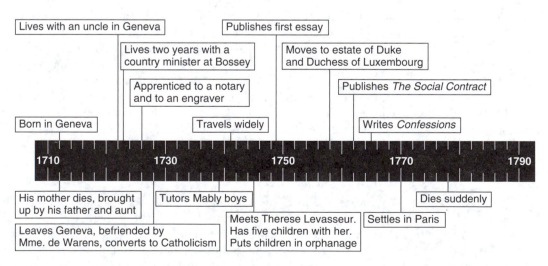

Figure 7.2   Rousseau's Life and Times

Rousseau's Importance for Educational Thought

Rousseau was one of the key theorists of the eighteenth century whose ideas contributed to the Romantic Movement, the French Revolution, and the transformation of education in Europe. Rousseau's ideas regarding the individual child-centered approach to education are expressed in *Emile,* his educational treatise in which he gave his "vision and dreams about education."[9] Rousseau's innovations provoked a revolution in education that had a profound influence on subsequent educational thought in the nineteenth and twentieth centuries. Educational philosophy and instructional methods were dramatically changed into what has become modern day progressive education.[10]

Emile

Emile is a novel about an imaginary boy named Emile whose education was to be completely given over to Rousseau, who was to make him into an autonomous man, morally and intellectually independent as was Plato's philosopher king.[11] Emile had a tutor who became a father, mother, educator, and moral mentor for him. It is possible Rousseau used Emile to replace, in some small way, the loss of his own children. There are many parallels in the book to Rousseau's own life. Emile is an orphan, like Rousseau was. Parents are warned not to begin reading books too early in a child's life, like Rousseau's father did. The comments given on religion and sex have direct similarity to Jean-Jacques' unusual experiences.

Emile is divided into five books, each dealing with a separate stage in the child's development: infancy, boyhood, early adolescence, adolescence, and manhood. In the first book, Rousseau explains his basic theory that children are born good and are fashioned by education from nature. In the second book, he states that, with young children, parents are to avoid trying to reason with the child, whose thought processes are not yet developed. Rousseau's discovery that the primary problem in education was the attempt to try to teach children to reason as if they were small adults is one of his great contributions to education. Rousseau had, without a professional background in psychology, an unusual grasp of the nature of the thought processes of children, presenting in general terms in *Emile* many of the ideas that were later to be developed more explicitly by Piaget.[12]

Rousseau states that children are amoral and unreasonable until age twelve. At that age they can begin to read their first book, *Robinson Crusoe.* The moral education of the young Emile in book three is limited to the effective establishment of the rule that he should harm no one. Rousseau attempts to convey the emotional quality which educational experiences should have for the young and, in this way, pre-figures today's discussion of "emotional intelligence."[13]

In book four, Emile learns about the world, sexuality, and religion. Finally, in book five, having completed his physical and moral education, the tutor now undertakes to find for Emile a wife who must have an education comparable to his. Having introduced Sophie, Rousseau discourses on the education of women, explaining that the primary aim of the education of the civilized man and woman is to prepare them for one another. Sophie is to be educated in order to tend to the welfare of others; she defines herself through her capacity to nourish and to nurture others.[14] In reality, Rousseau gives very little attention in *Emile* to the education of women, differing from Plato in this regard.

Rousseau's Philosophy of Education

Rousseau attempts to propose a better way of "teaching, instructing and educating" in his educational treatise *Emile,* and in the process proposes a revolutionary new philosophy of education, i.e., instead of education being centered on what is taught (the subject matter), he says that it should be centered on who is taught (the child). This was a radical shift of emphasis in the educational process—subject matter is no longer the basic element in the educational process nor is the teacher the basic authority figure. According to Rousseau, the right kind of education puts a child in direct contact with nature without the inter-mixture of opinions, i.e., it is education independent of society.[15] The *Emile* of Jean-Jacques Rousseau is thus one of the writings about education that has exercised a profound effect on the course of educational thought and practice as it introduces the in-dividual child-centered approach to education. Rousseau's concept of childhood sharply contrasted with the Calvinist doctrine of human depravity prevalent in his day that be-lieved that children were born prone to evil.

Emile created a moral revolution in Europe. By proposing "natural education" Rousseau suggests that education should interfere as little as possible with the free, nat-ural development of the child—both physically and psychologically. By proposing the natural goodness of the child that is corrupted by society, Rousseau says that the educa-tional system, which is merely a reflection of the superficiality of society, also corrupts children. *Emile* is an embodiment of the Enlightenment's ideas. Rousseau's work is one of the sources of the tradition that replaces virtue and vice as the cause of man's being good or bad, happy or miserable, with psychological concepts such as sincere/insincere, au-thentic/inauthentic, and the real self/alienated self. In doing so Rousseau begins the philo-sophic movement of naturalism and inspires the twentieth-century alternative education movement promoted by John Holt and Herbert Kohl.[16]

In his preface to *Emile*, Rousseau says "I will say little of the importance of a good ed-ucation nor will I stop to prove that the current one is bad. I will only note that for the longest time there has been nothing but a cry against the established practice without anyone taking it upon himself to propose a better way."

Notes

1. Jean-Jacques Rousseau, *The Confessions and Correspondence,* translated by Christopher Kelley, edited by C. Kelly, R. Masters and P. Stilman, 5 vols. Vol. 5, *The Collected Writings of Rousseau* (Hanover: University Press of New England, 1990), p. 15.
2. David Gauthier, "Making Jean-Jacques," in *Jean-Jacques Rousseau and the Sources of the Self,* edited by T. O'Hagan (Aldershot, Hants, England: Brookfield, VT: Avebury, 1997), pp. 6–9.
3. Jennifer Wolfe, *Learning from the Past: Historical Voices in Early Childhood Education* (Mayerthrope, Alberta: Piney Branch Press, 2000), p. 37.
4. Maurice Cranston, *Jean-Jacques: The Early Life and Work of Jean-Jacques Rousseau 1712–1754* (Chicago: The University of Chicago Press, 1991), pp. 208–209, 239, 244–245.
5. Ibid., pp. 234–236.
6. Timothy O'Hagan, *Rousseau* (New York: Routledge, 1999), p. 4.
7. J. J. Rousseau, *Emile or On Education* (New York: Basic Books, Inc., 1979).
8. Maurice Cranston, *The Solitary Self: Jean-Jacques Rousseau in Exile and Adversity,* 3 vols. Vol. 3 (London: Allen Lane, 1997), p. 297.
9. Rousseau, 1979, preface, p. 34.
10. Sally Scholoz, *On Rousseau, Wadsworth Philosophers Series* (Belmont, CA.: Wadsworth/Thomson Learning, Inc., 2001), p. 5.
11. O'Hagan, p. 71; Allan Bloom, "Introduction," *Emile or On Education* (New York: Basic Books, Inc., 1979), p. 6.
12. Eugene Iheoma, "Rousseau's views on teaching," *Journal of Educational Thought* 31 (April 1997), pp. 69–81, 70.
13. Mitchell Masters, and Mitchell Holifield, "Rousseau Revisited: Compassion as an Essential Element in De-mocratic Education," *Education* 116 (Summer 1996), p. 561.
14. Amelie Oksenberg Rorty, "Rousseau's Educational Experiments," in *Philosophers on Education: New Histori-cal Perspectives,* edited by A. O. Rorty (London: Routledge, 1998), p. 249.
15. Iheoma, p. 69; Bloom, p. 9.
16. Rita Guare, "Reclaiming Thoughtfulness and Imagination in Educational Leadership: A Moral Commit-ment to Enlightened Reason," in *Moral Philosophy and Education in the Enlightenment,* edited by D. Jedan, C. Luth, C. Bulach, R. Kump and D. MacLeay (Bochum, Germany: Winkler, 2001), p. 48; Bloom, p. 15.

Questions to Guide Your Reading

1. To what extent is modern-day educational practice shaped by each of Rousseau's "three teachers"? Which of these three teachers has been most important in your life and why?

2. What incontestable principle does Rousseau lay down? Do you agree with him? Why or why not?

3. Outline the steps of development for the child identified by Rousseau in books two and three. In what ways are these similar to Quintilian's stages and in what way are they different?

4. How does Rousseau define "self-esteem"? In what ways is this similar to and different from how it is defined today?

READING 7.2:
ON KEEPING EDUCATION NATURAL

Book I

Plants are fashioned by cultivation, men by education. We are born feeble and need strength; possessing nothing, we need assistance; beginning without intelligence, we need judgment. All that we lack at birth and need when grown up is given us by education. This education comes to us from nature, from men, or from things. The internal development of our faculties and organs is the education of nature. The use we learn to make of this development is the education of men. What comes to us from our experience of the things that affect us is the education of things. Each of us therefore is fashioned by three teachers. When their lessons are at variance the pupil is badly educated, and is never at peace with himself. When they coincide and lead to a common goal he goes straight to his mark and lives single-minded. Now, of these three educations the one due to nature is independent of us, and the one from things only depends on us to a limited extent. The education that comes to us from men is the only one within our control and even that is doubtful. Who can hope to have the entire direction of the words and deeds of all the people around a child?

There would be no difficulty if our three educations were merely different. But what is to be done when they are at cross-purposes? Consistency is plainly impossible when we seek to educate a man for others, instead of for himself. If we have to combat either nature or society, we must choose between making a man or a citizen. We cannot make both. There is an inevitable conflict of aims, from which come two opposing forms of education: the one communal and public, the other individual and domestic.

To get a good idea of communal education, read Plato's *Republic*. It is not a political treatise, as those who merely judge books by their titles think. It is the finest treatise on education ever written. Communal education in this sense, however, does not and can not now exist.

There remains then domestic education, the education of nature . . . A man of high rank once suggested that I should be his son's tutor. But having had experience already I knew myself unfit and I refused. Instead of the difficult task of educating a child, I now undertake the easier task of writing about it. To provide details and examples in illustration of my views and to avoid wandering off into airy speculations, I propose to set forth the education of Emile, an imaginary pupil, from birth to manhood . . .

Source: Jean-Jacques Rousseau, *The Emile of Jean Jacques Rousseau: Selections,* ed. William Boyd (New York: Teachers College Press, 1956). Reprinted by permission.

I assume that Emile is no genius, but a boy of ordinary ability: . . . that he is rich, . . . that he is to all intents and purposes an orphan, whose tutor having undertaken the parent's duties will also have their right to control all the circumstances of his upbringing; and, finally, that he is a vigorous, healthy, well-built child. . . .

Book II

The more children can do for themselves the less help they need from other people. Added strength brings with it the same sense needed for its direction. With the coming of self-consciousness at this second stage individual life really begins.

Memory extends the sense of identity over all the moments of the child's existence. He becomes one and the same person, capable of happiness or sorrow. From this point on it is essential to regard him as a moral being . . .

Your first duty is to be humane. Love childhood. Look with friendly eyes on its games, its pleasures, and its amiable dispositions. Which of you does not sometimes look back regretfully on the age when laughter was ever on the lips and the heart free of care? Why steal from the little innocents the enjoyment of a time that passes all too quickly? . . .

If we are to keep in touch with reality we must never forget what befits our condition. Humanity has its place in the scheme of things. Childhood has its place in the scheme of human life. We must view the man as a man and the child as a child. The best way to ensure human well being is to give each person his place in life and keep him there, regulating the passions in accordance with the individual constitution. The rest depends on external factors without our control . . .

"Reason with children" was Locke's chief maxim. It is the one most popular today, but it does not seem to me justified by success. For my part I do not see any children more stupid than those who have been much reasoned with. Of all the human faculties, reason which may be said to be compounded of all the rest develops most slowly and with greatest difficulty. Yet it is reason that people want to use in the development of the first faculties. A reasonable man is the masterwork of a good education: and we actually pretend to be educating children by means of reason! That is beginning at the end. If children appreciated reason they would not need to be educated. . . .

Nature wants children to be children before they are men. If we deliberately depart from this order we shall get premature fruits which are neither ripe nor well flavored and which soon decay. We shall have youthful sages and grown up children. Childhood has ways of seeing, thinking, and feeling peculiar to itself: nothing can be more foolish than to seek to substitute our ways for them. I should as soon expect a child of ten to be five feet in height as to be possessed of judgment.

Let us lay down as an incontestable principle that the first impulses of nature are always right. There is no original perversity in the human heart. Of every vice we can say how it entered and whence it came. The only passion natural to man is self-love, or self-esteem in a broad sense. This self-esteem has no necessary reference to other people. Insofar as it relates to ourselves it is good and useful. It only becomes good or bad in the social application we make of it. . . .

Here comes Emile, and at his approach I have a thrill of joy in which I see he shares. . . . Health glows in his face; his firm step gives him an air of vigor. His ideas are limited but precise. If he knows nothing by heart, he knows a great deal by experience. If he is not as good a reader of books as other children, he reads better in the book of nature. His mind is not in his tongue but in his head. He has less memory and more judgment. He only knows one language, but he understands what he says; and if he does not talk as well as other children he can do things better than they can. . . .

Work and play are all the same to him. His games are his occupations: he is not aware of any difference. He goes into everything he does with a pleasing interest and freedom. . . . Emile has lived a child's life and has arrived at the maturity of childhood, without any sacrifice of happiness in the achievement of his own perfection. He has acquired all the reason possible for his age, and in doing so has been as free and as happy as his nature allowed him to be. . . .

Book III

Here is our child, ready to cease being a child and to enter on an individual life. More than ever he feels the necessity which binds him to things. After training his body and his senses, we have trained his mind and his judgment. In short, we have combined the use of his limbs with that of his faculties. We have made him an efficient thinking being and nothing further remains for us in the production of a complete man but to make him a loving, sensitive being: in fact, to perfect reason through sentiment . . .

I will be told that in training the child to judge, I am departing from nature. I do not think so. Nature chooses her instruments, and makes use of them not according to opinion but according to necessity. There is a great deal of difference between natural man living in nature and natural man living in the social state. Emile is not a savage to be banished to the deserts: he is a savage made to live in a town. He must know how to get a living in towns, and how to get on with their inhabitants, and to live with them, if not to live like them. . . .

Emile, who has been compelled to learn for himself and use his reason, has a limited knowledge, but the knowledge he has is his own, none of it half-known. . . . He has a universal mind, not because of what he knows, but from his faculty for acquiring knowledge: a mind open, intelligent, responsive, and (as Montaigne says) if not instructed, capable of being instructed. I am content if he knows the "wherefore" of all he does, and the "why" of all he believes. . . .

Book IV

But man is not meant to be a child forever. At the time prescribed by nature he passes out of his childhood. As the fretting of the sea precedes the distant storm, this disturbing change is announced by the murmur of nascent passions. . . .

When I see young people confined to the speculative studies at the most active time of life and then cast suddenly into the world of affairs without the least experience, I find it as contrary to reason as to nature and am not at all surprised that so few people manage their lives well. By some strange perversity we are taught all sorts of useless things, but nothing is done about the art of conduct. We are supposed to be getting trained for society but are taught as if each one of us were going to live a life of contemplation in a solitary cell. You think you are preparing children for life when you teach them certain bodily contortions and meaningless strings of words. I also have been a teacher of the art of conduct. I have taught my Emile to live his own life, and more than that, to earn his own bread. But that is not enough. To live in a world one must get on with people and know how to get a hold on them. . . .

It is by doing good that we become good. I know of no surer way. Keep your pupil occupied with all the good deeds within his power. Let him help poor people with money and with service, and get justice for the oppressed. Active benevolence will lead him to reconcile the quarrels of his comrades and to be concerned about the sufferings of the afflicted. By putting his kindly feelings into action in this way and drawing his own conclusions from the outcome of his efforts, he will get a great deal of useful knowledge. In addition to college lore he will acquire the still more important ability of applying his knowledge to the purposes of life. . . .

Discussion Questions

1. What do you think Rousseau meant when he said "to be educated we must know our true selves?" Would Rousseau say that we spend too much time worrying about what others think of us instead of what we think of ourselves?

2. Do you agree with Rousseau that "the true, innate, and natural guide for us . . . is in our innate feelings" for "to exist is to feel"?

3. Rousseau would agree with the current maximum of "just let kids be kids." Do you think that teachers, society, and parents push children too hard and take their childhood away from them today?

4. Rousseau believes that we should learn from nature as our first educator. Is that the best way to learn? How do today's schools apply this principle?

5. Rousseau speaks about self-esteem. In what ways do teachers play an important role in developing students' self-esteem?

For Further Research on the Internet

A brief biography with many good links. http://www.philosophypages.com/ph/rous.htm

Specially dedicated to Rousseau's importance to education. http://www.infed.org/thinkers/et-rous.htm

The homepage of the Rousseau Association, a bilingual, international, and interdisciplinary society devoted to the study of Jean-Jacques Rousseau. http://www.wabash.edu/Rousseau/

Suggestions for Further Reading

Bloom, Allan "Introduction." In *Emile or On Education*. New York: Basic Books, Inc., 1979.

Cranston, Maurice. *Jean-Jacques: The Early Life and Work of Jean-Jacques Rousseau 1712–1754*. Chicago: The University of Chicago Press, 1991.

Cranston, Maurice. *The Solitary Self: Jean-Jacques Rousseau in Exile and Adversity*. 3 vols. Vol. 3. London: Allen Lane, 1997.

Gauthier, David. "Making Jean-Jacques." In *Jean-Jacques Rousseau and the Sources of the Self*, edited by T. O'Hagan. Brookfield, VT: Avebury, 1997.

Guare, Rita. "Reclaiming Thoughtfulness and Imagination in Educational Leadership: A Moral Commitment to Enlightened Reason." In *Moral Philosophy and Education in the Enlightenment*, edited by D. Jedan, C. Luth, C. Bulach, R. Kump and D. MacLeay. Bochum, Germany: Winkler, 2001.

Iheoma, Eugene. "Rousseau's Views on Teaching." *Journal of Educational Thought* 31 (April 1997): 69–81.

Masters, Mitchell, and Mitchell Holifield. "Rousseau Revisited: Compassion as an Essential Element in Democratic Education." *Education* 116 (Summer 1996): 559–64.

O'Hagan, Timothy. *Rousseau*. New York: Routledge, 1999.

Rorty, Amelie Oksenberg. "Rousseau's Educational Experiments." In *Philosophers on Education: New Historical Perspectives*, edited by A. O. Rorty. London: Routledge, 1998.

Rousseau, Jean-Jacques. *The Confessions and Correspondence*. Translated by Christopher Kelley. Edited by C. Kelly, R. Masters and P. Stilman. 5 vols. Vol. 5, *The Collected Writings of Rousseau*. Hanover: University Press of New England, 1990.

Rousseau, J.-J. *Emile or On Education*. New York: Basic Books, Inc., 1979.

Scholoz, Sally. *On Rousseau, Wadsworth Philosophers Series*. Belmont, CA: Wadsworth/Thomson Learning, Inc., 2001.

Wolfe, Jennifer. *Learning from the Past: Historical Voices in Early Childhood Education*. Mayerthrope, Alberta: Piney Branch Press, 2000.

Section 7.3: Johann Heinrich Pestalozzi (1746–1827)

Can you imagine being a teacher if your whole job consisted of listening to students read to you one-by-one? In the schools of the 1700s, students learned by rote memory and recited their lessons to the teacher, for this is what teaching was until Johann Heinrich Pestalozzi introduced "simultaneous group instruction" and used actual objects of things to teach words. Both of these techniques are very common to us now, but they were not found in the crowded schools of Enlightenment Europe.

Johann Heinrich Pestalozzi's Life and Times

Johann Heinrich Pestralatz (original last name) was born in Zurich on January 12, 1746. Heinrich's father, Johann Baptiste, was an eye surgeon who died when his son was only five years old, leaving his family in financial straits. Their mother, Susanna Hotz, a proud, resourceful, and honorable woman, and the household servant brought up Heinrich and his two older siblings. The education Heinrich (as he was called) received from his mother left ineffaceable memories in his heart and influenced his educational philosophy in which he designates mothers as the ideal educators.[1] Heinrich had a gentle, almost feminine disposition, with a cheerful temperament, a witty humor, and a benevolence and kindness that he learned from his mother and Babeli (the servant). However, the Pestalatz children were not allowed to play outside with the other children so their clothes would last longer; thus Heinrich grew up shy and socially incompetent, slow and lacking dexterity, given to daydreaming. Fortunately, he was allowed to spend the summers with his grandfather, Andreas Pestalozzi, a pastor, and the only father figure in his life. He learned from him to care for children and the poor and to be concerned about the welfare of others.

Heinrich's Education

Heinrich attended the primitive schools of his time and received a conventional education. First he attended a vernacular elementary school and then the grammar school. When he was eight years old he entered the preparatory school at Grossmunster—Schola Abbastisana—and three years later transferred to School Carolina, another classical Latin secondary school. He entered the two-year college preparatory program at Collegium Humanitatis and then, at seventeen years old, he entered the Collegium Carolinium where he studied the classical curriculum of his day: Latin, Greek, Hebrew, rhetoric, logic, philology, and philosophy.[2]

At first, Heinrich thought of following his grandfather and becoming a minister, then he began to study law but was blocked due to his political involvement with the Helvetic Society, an organization that had tried to overcome social injustices and reform society. Finally, he left college without obtaining a degree and turned to agriculture.

Educator and Headmaster

Johann Heinrich Pestalozzi married Anna Schulthess, a well-educated and cultured daughter of one of the wealthiest merchants in Venice in 1769. They had one son who they named Jacob, and Pestalozzi developed some of his educational principles by observing how his son developed.[3] Pestalozzi used his wife's dowry and the small patrimony his father's death had left him to purchase a rural farm which he called Neuhof or New Farm, and in 1774 he began to take children into his house to educate them. He tried to run Neuhof having the fifty paupers and orphans do the farming and handicrafts while also studying. Pestalozzi was not a good organizer and he did not succeed at being the manager, schoolmaster, farmer, and businessman all at once. The school was forced to close in 1779 and Pestalozzi spent his next ten years at Neuhof writing about his educational ideas, publishing *Leonard and Gertrude* in 1781, *Christopher and Eliza* in 1782, and continuing through the decade writing for journals.[4] (See the timeline of Pestalozzi's life in Figure 7.3.)

In September 1798, Pestalozzi was asked to be the headmaster for a war orphans school in Stans, but when this was closed at the end of the academic year due to the onset of another war (the Napoleonic Wars were raging across Europe), he went to Burgdorf to establish a government-funded school for war orphans.

Pestalozzi was small in stature, clumsy and awkward; not well dressed and rather careless in his appearance; absent-minded and given to long hours of study and writing. Nevertheless he was a man with a noble character and a big heart dedicated to relieving the misery of the many poor orphan children, convinced that education would relieve their misery.[5]

Yverdon

In 1805, Heinrich moved the school to Yverdon Castle and set up a boarding school for the wealthy and middle-class, a day school for the poor, and a teacher's seminary that used the school as its laboratory for training teachers. Here Pestalozzi was able to successfully implement his educational ideas that had been well tried in a variety of settings. He had perfected what he called his general method and his special method with object learning, simultaneous instruction, and hands-on learning. A typical day at Yverdon consisted of ten lessons spread throughout the day. Students rose at 5:30 a.m. for their first lesson at 6:00 a.m., followed by Morning Prayer and breakfast. Then they had lessons

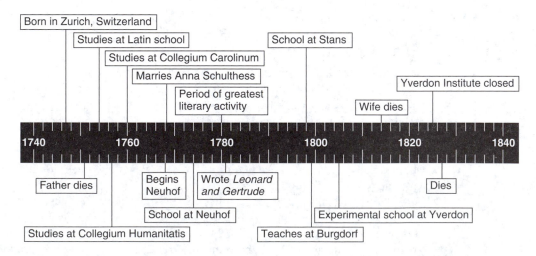

Figure 7.3 Pestalozzi's Life and Times

from 8:00 a.m. to noon with a recess break with a snack at 10:00 a.m. After an hour of recreation, students had dinner at 1:00 p.m. and then more lessons until 4:30 p.m. After another snack, recreation, and a final lesson, students had supper at 8:00 p.m., evening prayers, and then went to bed by 9:00 p.m. Of course there were breaks from this schedule that allowed the children to take longer walks or to go into town for Church services.[6] Educators from all over Europe and the United States came to visit his school and Pestalozzi became famous. Yverdon School operated for twenty years but closed in 1825, once again a victim of Pestalozzi's lack of administrative and economic abilities. Pestalozzi was overwhelmed by the death of his wife and the closing of his school. He died February 17, 1827 in Brugg.

Pestalozzi's Educational Contributions

Johann Heinrich Pestalozzi inspired what became the great educational reforms of the nineteenth and twentieth centuries. Pestalozzi incorporated Rousseau's ideas of the innate goodness of the child and natural education and Comenius' ideas of sensory education beginning from the concrete and proceeding to the abstract in his pedagogical theory. He sought to create an emotionally secure environment in his schools that was conducive to learning and made students feel like members of a loving family.[7]

Pestalozzi wrote *Leonard and Gertrude,* patterning it after Rousseau's *Emile* as a way of explaining his educational principles. This novel is about the fictional village of Bonnel, and Gertrude, the mother figure who regenerates her village by starting a school that functions as the moral, educational, and vocational heart of the village. In this book, Pestalozzi explains his belief that structure and discipline is needed along with an unwearying love and natural simplicity when educating children.[8]

Pestalozzi's theory involved two methods. The "general method" stressed an emotionally secure and loving relationship between the teacher and student in which the students' moral, intellectual, and physical abilities (mind, heart, and hands) were harmoniously and naturally developed. The "special method" was part of the general method and it identified the way things should be taught, emphasizing language, form, and number. He emphasized proceeding from the concrete to the abstract and from the general to the particular to fit instruction to the way that children develop naturally. His pedagogical principles were founded on a realism that based knowledge on direct concrete observation, sense perception, and sense impression of objects—"Anschauung."[9] It included an emphasis on involving the child in self-activity as a means of learning and the efficiency of simultaneous instruction (teaching to a whole group of students) instead of individual recitation.

Pestalozzi brought in the actual objects to teach vocabulary and concepts. Spelling and reading were taught with movable letters, arithmetic was taught with pebbles and fractions were taught by cutting fruits into parts.[10] A strong advocate of the vocational nature of education as a means to function in society, Pestalozzi emphasized learning agricultural skills, handicrafts, and industry. He emphasized the importance of moral development and criticized the home for not providing the essential initial instruction in value preferences and emotional dispositions due to the impact of industrialization on changing the family structure. His criticism of the home of his day can certainly be echoed today.

Pestalozzi had incredible success in teaching culturally diverse and economically impoverished children and his methods are of value for today's schools. He emphasized understanding each child, their culture, language, and learning style; and insisted that correct education should allow each child to grow inwardly and educationally. Pestalozzi maintained that society can be regenerated by education and that the education of the whole child can produce an ethical and humane as well as an economically viable society.[11]

Pestalozzi's pedagogy was introduced in the United States by William Maclure in the mid-1820s. Maclure visited Yverdon and convinced Pestalozzi's assistant, Joseph Neef, to emigrate to the United States and introduce the Pestalozzi method in Philadelphia and New Harmony, Indiana. Henry Barnard enthusiastically endorsed the Pestalozzian method and tried to have it introduced in teacher institutes and implemented in the common schools. Finally, Edward Sheldon, head of the Oswego Normal School, Oswego, New York (1850–1890s) made the Pestalozzi object lesson a part of every teacher's training. Pestalozzi's method was to influence John Dewey and the progressives and is seen today in child-centered curriculum and character education efforts.[12]

Pestalozzi's Philosophy of Education

Pestalozzi's educational philosophy made contributions that still impact education today. He believed that children were made up of head, heart, hand, body, feelings, and intellect, thus introducing the concept of educating the "whole child" long before the twentieth-century theorists advocated this. His deep commitment to providing disadvantaged and poor children an equal opportunity to receive a sound and caring education continues as an emphasis in today's schools.

Pestalozzi emphasized that learning had to be stimulated by the interests and motivation of the child, not by punishment and fear. Learning had to be completed at each stage before going on to the next stage. Pestalozzi believed in extending educational opportunity to girls and the poor based on a belief that education should not be denied to anyone.[13] The teacher was like a gardener helping the child to unfold; and it was important for teachers to take into consideration the child's emotional and social needs while attempting to educate them. He suggested that there be a loving, caring teacher-student relationship where the teacher respects the child and bases discipline on love. The school should be a good home and the teacher should be like a good parent.[14] Vocational skills were important, but the education of the fundamental capacities of the child had to have precedence. Finally, Pestalozzi's successful method of group instruction using object lessons transformed elementary education into the system we have today.

The purpose of education, according to Pestalozzi, was to bring human beings in harmony with themselves by developing inherent mental, moral, and physical powers given them at birth. One could say that Pestalozzi was a Christian humanist and a social reformer.[15] As Pestalozzi said in a letter to a friend on his work in the school, "For it is my opinion that if public education does not take into consideration the circumstances of family life, and everything else that bears on a man's general education, it can only lead to an artificial and methodical dwarfing of humanity."[16]

Notes

1. Roger De Guimps (Re-publishing of the 1892 book), *Pestalozzi: His Life and Work*, translated by J. Russell, *International Education Series* (Bristol, U.K.: Themmes Press, 1999), p. 5.
2. Gerald Gutek, *Pestalozzi and Education* (Prospect Heights, IL: Waveland Press, 1999), p. 23; Robert Downs, *Heinrich Pestalozzi: Father of Modern Pedagogy* (Boston: Twayne Publishers, 1975), p. 21.
3. De Guimps, p. 40.
4. George Eduard Biber, *Henry Pestalozzi and His Plan of Education*. Reprint of the 1831 edition. (Bristol, England: Themmes Press, 1994), p. 15; Gutek, p. 31.
5. De Guimps, p. 24.
6. Biber, p. 62.
7. Downs, p. 15.
8. Jennifer Wolfe, *Learning from the Past: Historical Voices in Early Childhood Education* (Mayerthrope, Alberta: Piney Branch Press, 2000), p. 55; Johanna Nel, and Donald Seckinger. "Johann Heinrich Pestalozzi in the 1990s," *Kappa Delta Pi: The Educational Journal* 57 (4) (1993), p. 397.

9. Silvia Schmid, "Pestalozzi's Idea of 'Innere Anschauung.'" *Proceedings of the Midwest Philosophy of Education Society,* 1996, p. 239; Barbara Ruth Peltzman, *Pioneers of Early Childhood Education: A Bio-bibliographical Guide* (Westport, CT: Greenwood Press, 1998), p. 91.

10. Gutek, pp. 38–43.

11. Nel, p. 396.

12. Gerald Gutek, *Historical and Philosophical Foundations of Education: A Biographical Introduction,* 3rd ed. (Upper Saddle River, NJ: Merrill/Prentice Hall, 2001), p. 171.

13. Peltzman, p. 91.

14. Kenneth Henson, "Foundations for Learner-Centered Education: A Knowledge Base," *Education* 124 (1) (2003), p. 9.

15. Nel, p. 396.

16. De Guimps, p. 152.

Questions to Guide Your Reading

1. Why does Pestalozzi want the teacher to bring the child out to nature? Do you think Pestalozzi would support today's "outdoor education" programs as meeting these objectives of his? Why or why not?

2. What is the main teaching method advocated by Pestalozzi? What are some modern-day manifestations of this method?

3. What is the foundation of human knowledge according to Pestalozzi? Is this true in the twenty-first century, or is there a different foundation to our human knowledge?

READING 7.3: PESTALOZZI'S IDEAS: SELECTIONS FROM HIS WRITINGS

Diary, 1774

No education would be worth a jot that resulted in a loss of manliness and lightness of heart. So long as there is joy in the child's face, ardor, and enthusiasm in all his games, so long as happiness accompanies most of his impressions, there is nothing to fear. Short moments of self-subjugation quickly followed by new interests and new joys do not dishearten. To see peace and happiness resulting from habits of order and obedience is the true preparation for social life.

Be in no hurry to get on, but make the first step sound before moving; in this way you will avoid confusion and waste. Order, exactness, completion alas, not thus was my character formed. And in the case of my own child in particular, I am in great danger of being blinded by his quickness and rapid progress, and, dazzled by the unusual extent of his knowledge, of forgetting how much ignorance lurks behind this apparent development, and how much has yet to be done before we can go farther. Completeness, orderliness, absence of confusion—what important points!

Lead your child out into Nature, teach him on the hilltops and in the valleys. There he will listen better, and the sense of freedom will give him more strength to overcome difficulties. But in these hours of freedom let him be taught by Nature rather than by you. Let him fully realize that she is the real teacher and that you, with your art, do nothing more than walk quietly at her side. Should a bird

Source: Selections translated by F. V. N. Painter in his *Great Pedagogical Essays Plato to Spencer* (New York: American Book Company, 1905), pp. 352–355.

sing or an insect hum on a leaf, at once stop your talk; bird and insect are teaching him; you may be silent.

I would say to the teacher, be thoroughly convinced of the immense value of liberty; do not let vanity make you anxious to see your efforts producing premature fruit; let your child be as free as possible, and seek diligently for every means of ensuring his liberty, peace of mind, and good humor. Teach him absolutely nothing by words that you can teach him by the things themselves; let him see for himself, hear, find out, fall, pick himself up.

How Gertrude Teaches Her Children, The Method: A Report by Pestalozzi

I am trying to psychologize the instruction of mankind; I am trying to bring it into harmony with the nature of my mind, with that of my circumstances and my relations to others. I start from no positive form of teaching, as such, but simply ask myself:—

"What would you do if you wished to give a single child all the knowledge and practical skill he needs, so that by wise care of his best opportunities, he might reach inner content?"

I think, to gain this end, the human race needs exactly the same thing as the single child.

I think, further, the poor man's child needs a greater refinement in the methods of instruction than the rich man's child does.

Nature, indeed, does much for the human race, but we have strayed away from her path. The poor man is thrust away from her bosom, and the rich destroy themselves both by rioting and by lounging on her overflowing breast.

The most essential point from which I start is this

Sense impression of Nature is the only true foundation of human instruction, because it is the only true foundation of human knowledge.

All that follows is the result of this sense impression, and the process of abstraction from it.

Source: Johann H. Pestalozzi, *How Gertrude Teaches Her Children*, trans. Lucy E. Holland and Francis C. Turner (London: Swan Sonnenschein and Co., 1907), pp. 199–211.

Hence in every case where this is imperfect, the results also will be neither certain, safe, nor positive; and in any case, where the sense impression is inaccurate, deception and error follow.

I start from this point and ask:—"What does Nature herself do in order to present the world truly to me, so far as it affects me? That is,—By what means does she bring the sense impressions of the most important things around me, to a perfection that contents me?" And I find,—She does this through my surroundings, my wants, and my relations to others.

Thus all the Art (of teaching) men is essentially a result of physico-mechanical laws, the most important of which are the following:

1. Bring all things essentially related to each other to that connection in your mind that they really have in Nature.

2. Subordinate all unessential things to essential, and especially subordinate the impression given by the Art to that given by Nature and reality.

3. Give to nothing a greater weight in your idea than it has in relation to your race in Nature.

4. Arrange all objects in the world according to their likeness.

5. Strengthen the impressions of important objects by allowing them to affect you through different senses.

6. In every subject try to arrange graduated steps of knowledge, in which every new idea shall be only a small, almost imperceptible addition to that earlier knowledge which has been deeply impressed and made unforgettable.

7. Learn to make the simple perfect before going on to the complex.

8. Recognize that as every physical ripening must be the result of the whole perfect fruit in all its parts, so every just judgment must be the result of a sense impression, perfect in all its parts, of the object to be judged. Distrust the appearance of precocious ripeness as the apparent ripeness of a worm-eaten apple.

9. All physical effects are absolutely necessary; and this necessity is the result of the art of Nature, with which she unites the apparently heterogeneous elements of her material into one whole for the achievement of her end. The Art, which imitates her, must try in the same way to raise the results at which it aims to a physical necessity, while it unites its elements into one whole for the achievement of its end.

10. The richness of its charm and the variety of its free play cause the results of physical necessity to bear the impress of freedom and independence. Here, too, the Art must imitate the course of Nature, and by the richness of its charm and the variety of its free play, try to make its results bear the impress of freedom and independence.

11. Above all, learn the first law of the physical mechanism, the powerful, universal connection between its results and the proportion of nearness or distance between the object and our senses. Never forget this physical nearness or distance of all objects around you has an immense effect in determining your positive sense impressions, practical ability, and even virtue. But even this law of your nature converges as a whole towards another. It conveys towards the centre of our whole being, and we ourselves are this centre. Man! never forget it! All that you are, all you wish, all you might be, comes out of yourself. All must have a centre in your physical sense impression, and this again is yourself. In all it does, the Art really only adds this to the simple course of Nature.— That which Nature puts before us, scattered and over a wide area, the Art puts together in narrower bounds and brings nearer to our five senses, by associations, which facilitate the power of memory, and strengthen the susceptibility of our senses, and make it easier for them, by daily practice, to present to us the objects around us in greater numbers, for a longer time and in a more precise way.

Burgdorf, June 27th, 1800.

Discussion Questions

1. Pestalozzi believed that emotional security was a precondition for skill learning. How would you apply Pestalozzi's principles in teaching today's "at–risk" students? How would you, as a teacher, create an emotionally secure learning environment for these children who may very well come from violent neighborhoods?

2. Compare Pestalozzi's general method and special method to modern-day theories of learning, such as that of Lev Vygotsky who believed that all learning involves tying new information to prior experiences.

3. Compare Pestalozzi's ideas on natural education to those of Rousseau. Which one do you think has more influence on today's child-centered classroom?

4. What do you think Pestalozzi would do today to make our schools free of bullying, teasing, and violence and more emotionally secure and character building?

5. Do you agree with Pestalozzi that the teacher–student relationship should be regulated by love? Can this be done in today's classroom where the teacher has to be overly cautious of his/her relations with students?

6. Debate the current emphasis on educational standards from Pestalozzi's point of view. Do you think standards-based instruction encourages active or passive learning styles? What do you think Pestalozzi would say?

For Further Research on the Internet

A homepage on Pestalozzi with pictures, a short biography, and bibliography.
http://www.infed.org/thinkers/et-pest.htm

Pestalozzi goes Internet has excellent pictures of Pestalozzi's home and his schools.
http://www.heinrich-pestalozzi.info/

A short biography on Pestalozzi sponsored by the Pestalozzi International Village, a school set up following Pestalozzi's philosophy of education and methodology.
http://www.pestalozzi.org.uk/

Suggestions for Further Reading

Biber, George Eduard. *Henry Pestalozzi and His Plan of Education.* Reprint of the 1831 edition. Bristol, England: Themmes Press, 1994.

De Guimps, Roger. (Re-publishing of the 1892 book.) *Pestalozzi: His Life and Work.* Translated by J. Russell, *International Education Series.* Bristol, U.K.: Themmes Press, 1999.

Downs, Robert. *Heinrich Pestalozzi: Father of Modern Pedagogy.* Boston: Twayne Publishers, 1975.

Gutek, Gerald. *Historical and Philosophical Foundations of Education: A Biographical Introduction,* 3rd ed. Upper Saddle River, NJ: Merrill/Prentice Hall, 2001.

Gutek, Gerald. *Pestalozzi and Education.* Prospect Heights, IL: Waveland Press, 1999.

Henson, Kenneth. "Foundations for Learner-Centered Education: A Knowledge Base." *Education* 124 (1) (2003): 5–17.

Nel, Johanna, and Donald Seckinger. "Johann Heinrich Pestalozzi in the 1990s." *Kappa Delta Pi: The Educational Journal* 57 (4) (1993): 394–401.

Peltzman, Barbara Ruth. *Pioneers of Early Childhood Education: A Bio-bibliographical Guide.* Westport, CT: Greenwood Press, 1998.

Schmid, Silvia. Pestalozzi's Idea of "Innere Anschauung." *Proceedings of the Midwest Philosophy of Education Society,* 1996, 239–245.

Wolfe, Jennifer. *Learning from the Past: Historical Voices in Early Childhood Education.* Mayerthrope, Alberta: Piney Branch Press, 2000.

Section 7.4: Mary Wollstonecraft (1759–1797)

Today women write books as often as men, but this was not always true. In fact, the first time Mary Wollstonecraft's now famous book *A Vindication of the Rights of Women* was published the author was anonymous, because the publisher felt it would be better received. An overnight sensation, the second edition proudly displayed her name.

Mary Wollstonecraft's Life and Times

Mary Wollstonecraft was born on April 27, 1759 in London to Edward John Wollstonecraft, an alcoholic, and an Irish mother, Elizabeth Dickson. Edward received his father's estate when he died, so the family moved out to a farm in Barking, then to Yorkshire and finally to the affluent community of Beverley. However, Edward was not a successful farmer and soon lost most of his inheritance due to his drinking and gambling.[1]

Mary's Education

Mary's brothers began to study Latin, literature, and mathematics at the Beverley Grammar School while Mary attended a day school in which she learned French, needlework, music, dancing, writing, and how to do accounts; tasks that would make her marriageable.[2] At home, Mary read books, magazines, and newspapers and was involved in learning about national and community social issues. Mary was encouraged to develop her reading and writing abilities by the intellectual parents of her friend, Jane Ardens.

In 1775, Edward moved his family to London to try his hand at business. Mary's schooling ended with the move and she began to complain of violent headaches, gloom, and nervous fevers, symptoms of depression and melancholy that she would have throughout her life.[3] Mary's neighbor, Mr. Clare, saw how intellectually gifted she was and invited her to study with him, introducing Mary to Fanny Blood, another girl he tutored. The two became intimate friends, walking, talking, and reading together.

Helping Others

In 1778, Mary accepted a job as a companion for a widow in Bath but returned home to help her younger sister, Eliza, care for their dying mother. Shortly after Elizabeth's death, Eliza married and Edward remarried, so Mary went to live with Fanny. Eliza gave birth to her first child and fell into a post-partum depression. She told Mary that she wanted to leave her husband so Mary helped her escape, but they had to leave the child behind because by British law the child belonged to the man. "For Mary, this incident with Eliza was crucial as it was the first time in her life that she took action and asserted her own will instead of doing the will of another. The idea for her great book, *The Vindication of the Rights of Women,* was born the day Eliza fled," according to biographer Diane Jacobs.[4]

A School for Girls

Mary, Eliza, their other sister Elverina, and Fanny opened a school for twenty girls in a house outside of London in an effort to become financially independent. Fanny soon left them to marry, but she died one week after giving birth to her first child. Mary was depressed at the loss of her bosom friend and the school closed soon after. Elverina and Eliza had to become teachers and older women's companions, as those were the only jobs open to women.

The First Self-Supporting Woman Author

At the suggestion of a friend, Mary wrote a forty-nine-page manual which encouraged women to educate and improve themselves called, *"Thoughts on the Education of Daughters,"* which was published by Joseph Johnson and excerpted in one of the nation's leading women's journals, the *Lady's Magazine.*[5] Mary received an offer to tutor girls for a family in Ireland, but was let go after one year, so she returned to England to be a writer. "I am going to be the first of a new genus," Mary wrote, "a self-supporting woman writer."[6]

Joseph Johnson generously offered her a room and a place at his table until she could establish herself. In the fall of 1787, Mary wrote *Original Stories for Children,* didactic stories teaching children to bear the sufferings of life well. The book was well received and Mary's financial situation vastly improved. She took over the family financial affairs from her brother Ned, sent her father his living stipend, moved Eliza to a school nearer to London, and sent Elverina to study in France.

Mary met Henry Fuseli at Johnson's and found him to be a stimulating intellectual companion. In July of 1789, Edmund Burke wrote *Reflections on the Revolution in France,* expressing his opinion against the revolution. Mary Wollstonecraft's *A Vindication of the Rights of Men* appeared twenty-eight days after Burke's *Reflections.* In this book she attacked the customs and laws that subordinated one part of humanity to another, and attacked aristocracy, privilege, power of rank, and wealth as used to limit human freedom.[7] Anticipating its timeliness, Johnson printed each page as she wrote it, leaving her no time to edit it. *The Rights of Men* was a great success. The first edition appeared anonymously and readers assumed male authorship. In the second edition, Johnson proudly put Mary's name on the title page. Mary became a philosopher and minor celebrity in her own right.[8] (See the timeline of Wollstonecraft's life in Figure 7.4.)

A Vindication of the Rights of Women

Mary moved into a larger house and began her great work—*A Vindication of the Rights of Women*—the first frankly feminist manifesto in the history of human rights. The work was a shocking confrontation to the ideas of Rousseau from the title to the last page of the 449-page volume. The main tenet of the book is that the minds of women are no different than the minds of men. Mary emphasized women's freedom and education, calling for co-educational, government-supported schools for all. As Mary finished each page of the *Rights of Women,* it was rushed to the printer, again leaving her no time for editing. Once published, the work was widely reviewed as "a sensible work on education." Applauded by many, others claimed that the *Rights of Women* was corrupting their young daughters; nevertheless it made Mary a well-known author.[9]

A Stay in Revolutionary France

Mary decided to go to France in October of 1792 to escape her infatuation with Fuseli, a married man, and to write about the political ferment. While in Paris, Mary found salons in which men and women could meet and converse on topics in an intellectual way; where she heard support for women's right to vote, inherit property, and have rights for child custody as divorcees. Mary was appointed to serve on Condorcet's Commission on Education as one of the foremost educational theorists of the late eighteenth century.

An Affair and a Child

Mary met Gilbert Imlay, an American, in the spring of 1793 at one of these gatherings and talked with him about intellectual and political matters. Soon she fell in love and had an affair with him. She became vivacious, playful, and cheerful and began to send install-

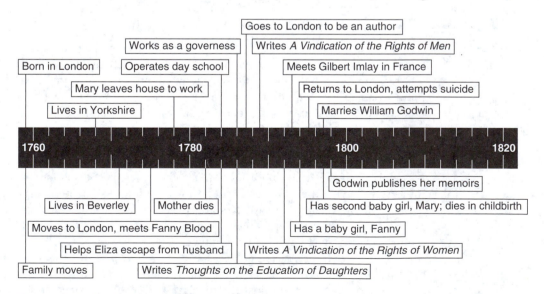

Figure 7.4 Wollstonecraft's Life and Times

ments of her new book, *An Historical and Moral View of the Origins and Progress of the French Revolution,* to Johnson to be published. Paris was no longer safe for foreigners so she moved out to a house in the country where Imlay visited her.[10] It became unsafe for British citizens to remain in France, so Imlay registered Mary as his wife in the American embassy and she took his last name; however, they never married as neither of them thought much of the social convention. She returned to live in Paris with Imlay, who was often away on business. Mary became pregnant at the age of 35 and on May 14, 1794, she gave birth to a baby girl who she named Fanny after her girlhood friend. Imlay said he was proud of his new family but was absent more often with his business. "Mary was a mother dependent both emotionally and financially on a capricious man."[11] Imlay went to England and though he kept saying he would return, he didn't, and in April 1795, Mary left Paris for England to join Imlay with her daughter and nursemaid. She saw him and knew that he no longer loved her. Although he provided his "family" with a furnished house, Mary was emotionally distraught and tried to commit suicide, but Imlay found her suicide note and arrived in time to save her. He asked her to help him with his business; but he did not meet her as promised when she returned from a business trip. Mary had to resign herself to the inevitable and pass herself off as a married woman to maintain her social status.

A Married Woman

In January of 1796, Mary Wollstonecraft was reintroduced to William Godwin, an unmarried, progressive Enlightenment thinker and author she had met in 1791 at Johnson's table. By the spring, the two were meeting constantly and in August they began to have an affair. Mary was afraid that he would eventually leave her as Imlay had, so when she became pregnant, she convinced Godwin to marry her, eager to embrace the institution that she had despised for so long. Mary began to write *Maria, or the Wrongs of Women,* an angry and radical work. She gave birth to a daughter, Mary, on August 31, 1797 but died herself ten days later from complications. In adulthood, Wollstonecraft's daughter, Mary Shelley, wrote *Frankenstein.* William Godwin wrote *Memoirs of Mary Wollstonecraft,* and Johnson published this work in 1798.[12]

Wollstonecraft's Importance for Education

Mary Wollstonecraft is called a Revolutionary feminist since she was an advocate of the rights of women in specific revolutionary situations, i.e., the French Revolution and the cultural revolution that founded the modern state of England. Both revolutions were struggles for power, and Mary sought to get power for women. She did so by advancing feminist arguments in writing, using the available sources of style, genre, and discourse to show that the limited education, experience, and opportunities assigned to women could lead to feminist consciousness and the emancipation of women instead of the subordination of women.[13] The ideas put forth in *A Vindication of the Rights of Women* are Mary's main contribution to educational history, but her other books also have important parts addressing education.

The Education of Women in the Eighteenth Century

There were two kinds of private schools in vogue in England at the time Mary wrote *Vindication:* boarding schools and day schools. Mary was against private schools and she spoke from experience, for she tried to conduct a day school and saw how the parents intervened and how competitive everyone in the school was. Mary was in favor of government-supported day schools for boys and girls in which the family and home can work with the school to form the children. Mary was ahead of her times in many of the educational ideas she advocated, e.g., a modern kindergarten, using the Socratic form of teaching, teaching religions, history, politics and home industrial training. Mary was very moderate in her demands for the higher education of women as she was treading on unknown territory, as women were not accepted at Oxford or Cambridge.[14] The book was seen as "a sensible work on education," but also an extensive criticism of the ideas of Jean-Jacques Rousseau as expressed in his *Emile*. Mary disagreed with Rousseau's main tenet that women were different from men, weaker and submissive, and therefore required a distinct education. Nor did she agree with him that women should have power over men, but said that women should "have but power over themselves." Mary maintained that Rousseau's main problem was his own sexual repression. Line-by-line Mary criticized the ideas put forth in *Emile,* and thus made Rousseau appear ignorant of his main subject—women. The "mocking" of the ideas of the cultural icon—Rousseau—was the most shocking aspect of her book.[15]

Wollstonecraft's Philosophy of Education

Thoughts on the Education of Daughters accepted the prevailing Lockean view of the mind as a blank slate that needed to be safeguarded from the passions of reason to function. The book was robustly censorious, disapproving of baby talk, cosmetics, theatre, frivolity, and artificial manners. Mary recommends physical exercise for the body as the foundation of mental exercise. She insists that women acquire critical thought capacity by reflecting on their experiences. Writing and reading are advocated strongly as they help the mind become independent of the senses.[16]

Wollstonecraft rebelled against the common, male-authored book morality that saw female education solely as preparation for marriage and dependence, and preached an education for women that would cultivate their minds. Education was in vogue during Mary's life as some saw it as the cure for the many ills of the individual and society. Female education fascinated the public who were trying to define the role of middle-class women whose economic, social, and moral importance was declining.[17]

In *A Vindication of the Rights of Women,* Wollstonecraft argues for women's liberation, starting with education, leading to full participation in the middle-class cultural revolution, resulting in social usefulness and legal and civic equality.[18] Education for girls should be on a par with boys, so that women could take their proper place in society, and that place was not solely to be a wife to a man. Mary had an insight into the needs of the human race beyond that of many educationalists of her time.[19] Mary emphasized the moral identity of men and women; they each had an immortal soul, called to the same religious end. Virtues were not sex-specific. Women could not be moral without independence, autonomy, and an escape from male dominance. They should develop sensibility, delicacy, modesty and chastity as good human virtues, not in relation to men. Women should be open and frank; truth and equality should exist between the sexes.[20]

Mary begins her great work, *The Vindication of the Rights of Women,* with the goal of her life—"The education of women has, of late, been more attended to than formerly; yet they are still reckoned a frivolous sex, and ridiculed or pitied by the writers who endeavour by satire or instruction to improve them."

Notes

1. Diane Jacobs, *Her Own Woman: The Life of Mary Wollstonecraft* (New York: Simon & Schuster, 2001), p. 20.
2. Janet Todd, *Mary Wollstonecraft: A Revolutionary Life* (New York: Columbia University Press, 2000), p. 12.

3.   Jacobs, p. 26.
4.   Ibid., p. 35.
5.   Todd, p. 77.
6.   Gary Kelly, *Revolutionary Feminism: The Mind and Career of Mary Wollstonecraft* (New York: St. Martin's Press, 1992), p. 55.
7.   Gerald Gutek, *Historical and Philosophical Foundations of Education: A Biographical Introduction.* 3rd ed. (Upper Saddle River, NJ: Merrill/Prentice Hall, Inc. Simon & Schuster, 2001), p. 202.
8.   Todd, p. 164.
9.   Jacobs, pp. 102–108.
10. Todd, p. 321ff.
11. Jacobs, p. 174.
12. Ibid., p. 256ff.
13. Kelly, p. 1.
14. Emma Rauschenbusch-Clough, "Mary Wollstonecraft's Demands for the Education of Woman," in *A Vindication of the Rights of Women: An Authoritative Text,* 2nd ed., edited by C. H. Poston (New York: W.W. Norton, 1988), pp. 282–283.
15. Todd, pp. 180–82.
16. Kelly, p. 30.
17. Todd, p. 77.
18. Kelly, p. 108.
19. Rauschenbusch-Clough, p. 284.
20. Todd, p. 183.

Questions to Guide Your Reading

1. What are some of the advantages of public education over private education, according to Mary Wollstonecraft? What do you think she would say to the many parents who send their children to same-sex parochial schools?

2. Why does Mary want all children to dress alike? Compare her reasons to those who advocate having uniforms in public schools. In what ways are they similar?

3. What subjects does Wollstonecraft think girls should study in school? Why were these subjects thought to be so revolutionary for her day?

READING 7.4:
CHAPTER XII–ON NATIONAL EDUCATION

The good effects resulting from attention to private education will ever be very confined, and the parent who really puts his own hand to the plow, will always, in some degree, be disappointed, till education becomes a grand national concern. A man cannot retire into a desert with his child, and if he did he could not bring himself back to childhood, and become the proper friend and play-fellow of an infant or youth. And when children are confined to the society of men and women, they very soon acquire that kind of premature manhood which stops the growth of every vigorous power of mind or body. In order to open their faculties they should be excited to think for themselves; and this can only be done by mixing a number of children together, and making them jointly pursue the same objects. . . .

I have already animadverted on the bad habits which females acquire when they are shut up

Source: Excerpts from *The Vindication of the Rights of Women,* Norton Critical Edition, Second Edition by Mary Wollstonecraft, edited by Carol H. Poston, copyright © 1988, 1975 by W.W. Norton & Company, Inc. New York, N.Y. Used with permission of W.W. Norton & Company, Inc.

together; and, I think, that the observation may fairly be extended to the other sex, till the natural inference is drawn which I have had in view throughout—that to improve both sexes they ought, not only in private families, but in public schools, to be educated together. If marriage be the cement of society, mankind should all be educated after the same model, or the intercourse of the sexes will never deserve the name of fellowship, nor will women ever fulfill the peculiar duties of their sex, till they become enlightened citizens, till they become free by being enabled to earn their own subsistence, independent of men; in the same manner, I mean, to prevent misconstruction, as one man is independent of another. Nay marriage will never be held sacred till women, by being brought up with men, are prepared to be their companions rather than their mistresses; for the mean doublings of cunning will ever render them contemptible whilst oppression renders them timid. So convinced am I of this truth, that I will venture to predict that virtue will never prevail in society till the virtues of both sexes are founded on reason; and, till the affections common to both are allowed to gain their due strength by the discharge of mutual duties.

To render this practicable, day schools, for particular ages, should be established by government, in which boys and girls might be educated together. The school for the younger children, from five to nine years of age, ought to be absolutely free and open to all.

But nothing of this kind could occur in an elementary day-school, where boys and girls, the rich and poor, should meet together. And to prevent any of the distinctions of vanity, they should be dressed alike, and all obliged to submit to the same discipline, or leave the school.

The school-room ought to be surrounded by a large piece of ground, in which the children might be usefully exercised, for at this age they should not be confined to any sedentary employment for more than an hour at a time. Reading, writing, arithmetic, natural history, and some simple experiments in natural philosophy, might fill up the day; but these pursuits should never encroach on gymnastic plays in the open air. The elements of religion, history, the history of man, and politics, might also be taught by conversations, in the Socratic form.

After the age of nine, girls and boys, intended for domestic employments, or mechanical trades, ought to be removed to other schools, and receive instruction, in some measure appropriated to the destination of each individual, the two sexes being still together in the morning; but in the afternoon, the girls should attend a school, where plain-work, mantua-making, millinery, &c. would be their employment.

The young people of superior abilities, or fortune, might now be taught, in another school, the dead and living languages, the elements of science, and continue the study of history and politics, on a more extensive scale, which would not exclude polite literature.

Girls and boys still together? I hear some readers ask: yes. And I should not fear any other consequence than that some early attachment might take place; which, whilst it had the best effect on the moral character of the young people, might not perfectly agree with the views of the parents, for it will be a long time, I fear, before the world will be so far enlightened that parents, only anxious to render their children virtuous, shall allow them to choose companions for life themselves. . . .

There would be schools of morality and the happiness of man, allowed to flow from the pure springs of duty and affection, what advances might not the human mind make? Society can only be happy and free in proportion as it is virtuous; but the present distinctions, established in society, corrode all private, and blast all public virtue.

I have already inveighed against the custom of confining girls to their needle, and shutting them out from all political and civil employments; for by thus narrowing their minds they are rendered unfit to fulfill the peculiar duties which nature has assigned them. Only employed about the little incidents of the day, they necessarily grow up cunning. . . .

Instead of pursuing this idle routine, sighing for tasteless shew, and heartless state, with what dignity would the youths of both sexes form attachments in the schools that I have cursorily pointed out; in which, as life advanced, dancing, music, and drawing, might be admitted as relaxations, for at these schools young people of fortune ought to remain, more or less, till they were of age. Those, who designed for particular professions, might attend, three or four mornings in the week, the schools appropriated for their immediate instruction. . . .

My observations on national education are obviously hints; but I principally wish to enforce the necessity of educating the sexes together to perfect both, and of making children sleep at home that they may learn to love home; yet to make private support, instead of smothering public affections, they should be sent to school to mix with a number of equals, for only by the jostling of equality can we form a just opinion of ourselves. To render mankind more virtuous and happier of course, both sexes must act from the same principles; but how can that be expected when only one is allowed to see the reasonableness of it? To render the social compact truly equitable, and in order to spread those enlightening principles, which alone can meliorate the fate of man, women must be allowed to found their virtue on knowledge, which is scarcely possible unless they be educated by the same pursuits as men. . . .

I speak of the improvement and emancipation of the whole sex.

In public schools women, to guard against the errors of ignorance, should be taught the elements of anatomy and medicine, not only to enable them to take proper care of their own health, but to make them rational nurses of their infants, parents, and husbands; for the bills of mortality are swelled by the blunders of self-willed old women, who give nostrums of their own without knowing any thing of the human frame. It is likewise proper only in a domestic view, to make women acquainted with the anatomy of the mind, by allowing the sexes to associate together in every pursuit; and by leading them to observe the progress of the human understanding in the improvement of the sciences and arts; never forgetting the science of morality, or the study of the political history of mankind.

Discussing the advantages which a public and private education combined, as I have sketched, might rationally be expected to produce, I have dwelt most on such as are particularly relative to the female world, because I think the female world oppressed; yet the gangrene, which the vices engendered by oppression have produced, is not confined to the morbid part, but pervades society at large: so that when I wish to see my sex become more like moral agents, my heart bounds with the anticipation of the general diffusion of that sublime contentment which only morality can diffuse.

Discussion Questions

1. Do you agree with Mary Wollstonecraft that co-educational school is more helpful to students' development than single-sex schools? Are there some ages at which single-sex schools are more helpful?

2. Mary Wollstonecraft emphasizes the equality of men and women. Hildegard of Bingen emphasizes the complementarity of men and women. What do you think the feminists of today would stress as more important for women?

3. Mary Wollstonecraft addresses women's rights and the right to an education for women. In what ways are these still issues today? Although there have been advances, can you give examples of inequalities in these areas?

4. Wollstonecraft speaks about the moral and social development of women and virtues that specifically fit women and their needs. This is a debatable issue even today. Do you think virtues are sex specific? Do you think that gender differences are something constructed by society or something with which we are born? What are some ways in which gender impacts schooling today?

5. Wollstonecraft is in favor of governmental-supported public schools for all. What do you think she would say about the current trends regarding charter schools, magnet schools, and home schooling?

6. Mary Wollstonecraft thinks that the subjection of one person to another or others is not good. What exactly does she mean by subjection? In answering this consider what sort of relationships will count as relations of subjection, and what are the ill effects of subjection on those who are subjected and on those who subject others.

7. Using Mary Wollstonecraft's own words, what recommendations of policy changes do you think that she would make to educators today to improve our schools?

For Further Research on the Internet

A history site with a biography of Mary and links to important people in her life and her books. http://www.spartacus.schoolnet.co.uk/Wwollstonecraft.htm

A brief discussion of the life and works of Mary Wollstonecraft, with links to electronic texts and additional information. http://www.philosophypages.com/ph/woll.htm

Suggestions for Further Reading

Gutek, Gerald. *Historical and Philosophical Foundations of Education: A Biographical Introduction;* 3rd ed. Upper Saddle River, NJ: Merrill/Prentice Hall, 2001.

Jacobs, Diane. *Her Own Woman: The Life of Mary Wollstonecraft.* New York: Simon & Schuster, 2001.

Kelly, Gary. *Revolutionary Feminism: The Mind and Career of Mary Wollstonecraft.* New York: St. Martin's Press, 1992.

Rauschenbusch-Clough, Emma. "Mary Wollstonecraft's Demands for the Education of Woman." In *A Vindication of the Rights of Women: An Authoritative Text,* 2nd ed., edited by C. H. Poston. New York: W.W. Norton, 1988.

Todd, Janet. *Mary Wollstonecraft: A Revolutionary Life.* New York: Columbia University Press, 2000.

Section 7.5: Johann Friedrich Herbart (1776–1841)

It is generally accepted today that teachers become so by studying in a college of education. Principles of educational psychology make up much of this study on instructional methodology and lesson planning. You have probably chosen to become a teacher because you want to help young people to develop both their intellectual and their social and moral capabilities. As common as these beliefs are today, they were not so before the time of Johann Friedrich Herbart.

Johann Friedrich Herbart's Life and Times

Johann Friedrich Herbart was born in Oldenburg, Germany on May 4, 1776. Two months after his birth a new nation was born across the Atlantic. Herbart's ideas were to inspire the educational system of this new nation years after Herbart died. It was an exciting time in which to live; Herbart's contemporaries were Goethe, Kant, Mozart, Beethoven, Hegel, and Napoleon. It was a period of political revolutions and the evolution of new systems of thought.

Johann was the only child of two unhappily married parents. His father was a lawyer who liked the quiet life and his mother was a high strung, energetic, active, and strong willed woman who dedicated herself exclusively to her son once he was born.

Johann's Education

Due to an early childhood accident, Johann was tutored at home as a young child. At the age of twelve, he went to the local Latin school in Oldenburg. Johann showed himself to be intelligent—actually precocious, diligent, a hard-working student, and an accomplished musician, but also a shy fellow who had difficulty making friends.[1] What was to be his life-long interest in morality was already apparent in a high school speech he gave in Oldenburg in 1793, entitled "Something about the Most Common Causes Which Effect the Rise and Fall of Morality in Nations" which was later published.[2]

In the summer of 1794, Johann set out for the University of Jena, where he studied philosophy, especially the recently published works of Immanuel Kant, under the guidance of Johann Fichte.

Tutor and Educator

Johann did not complete his studies at this time because, in 1797, he received a job offer to tutor the two older children of Karl Friedrich von Steiger in Switzerland. For the next three years, Herbart tried out many of the devices and procedures that were to become "his system." While in Switzerland, Herbart visited Johann Heinrich Pestalozzi's school in Burgdorf and was very impressed with his methods.[3] Herbart returned to Oldenburg in 1800 and wrote and lectured on Pestalozzi's ideas and two years later he finally received his degree from Gottingen. (See the timeline of Herbart's life in Figure 7.5.)

Author

In 1804, Herbart published the first work in which he presented his own ideas on education, *The Aesthetic Presentation of the World as the Chief Business of Education*, in which he proclaimed that morality was the main work of the educator. Two years later, when he was only thirty years old, he published what is considered his most important work, *General Pedagogy Deduced from the Aim of Education* which was translated into English as *The Science of Education*. The book contains nearly all of Herbart's main educational ideas

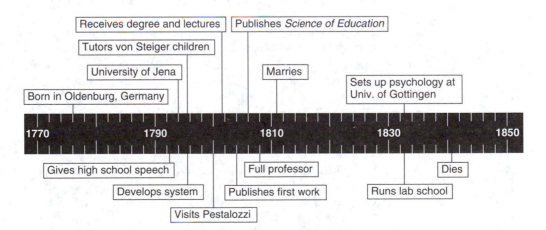

Figure 7.5   Herbart's Life and Times

and can be compared with *The Great Didactic* of Comenius.[4] His *Lehrbuch zur Psychologie*, first published in 1816, made a crucial contribution to making psychology a science in its own right. Herbart proposed that the metaphysical study of psychology (which had made it a branch of philosophy) be supplemented by the methods of natural sciences and mathematics thus launching the evolution of the science of psychology.[5]

Professor of Philosophy, Pedagogy, and Psychology

Herbart was offered Kant's chair as a full professor at the University of Konigsberg in 1808 and worked there for the next twenty-five years, setting up a practice teaching seminar, the forerunner of the modern-day student teaching experience. Herbart married Mary Drake, a young English girl half his age, in 1811. Although apparently a happy marriage, they had no children so Mary dedicated herself to helping as the housemother for the students in the teaching seminar.

Herbart was a professor at the University of Gottingen for the last eight years of his life, from 1833 to 1841, and here set up the discipline of psychology as a science in its own right. Herbart dedicated himself to giving public lectures on pedagogy and his "system." He demonstrated his theories in his practice seminar, the first "lab school." He continued writing all his life especially on his psychology. His health deteriorated and he died in Gottingen of a cerebral hemorrhage on August 14, 1841.[6]

Herbart was unknown in English-speaking countries until fifty years after his death, although his ideas continued to be expounded in Germany by the neo-Herbartian disciples. When Charles de Garmo from Illinois State went to Germany in 1890 to study the best ideas of pedagogy found in the German universities he came in contact with the pedagogical ideas of Johann Herbart, translated Herbart's work, and introduced him to American schools where memorization, drill, and recitation were the method of instruction. Herbart's new method of instruction was introduced and there was a flury of interest in him for two decades.[7] The Hebartian Society was formed and had among its members John Dewey. The Herbartian movement in the United States in the last two decades of the nineteenth century focused on "detailed planning of classroom practices" that still impact classrooms today.[8] Although over time Herbart's method of instruction was magnified to include five components instead of four and some of his other theories were distorted, his impact on teacher education was enduring.[9]

Herbart's Importance for Educational Thought

Although popular during his lifetime, Herbart has not received the recognition due him for his many contributions that have impacted the way we "do education" even today. Renewed interest in his work may be developing, as he was recently mentioned as one of the ten most influential educators that has made an enduring influence on American education because of his outline of the lesson plan.[10]

I will outline here the three major contributions from Herbart that I think still affect American education today:

1. He brought education into the university as a science and discipline in its own right. This made Herbart the "Father of the Modern Science of Education."[11]
2. He gave scientific precision to instructional methodology by founding it upon a system of psychology. Therefore he was also the "Father of the Lesson Plan."
3. He emphasized that the ultimate goal of education is the development of moral character, which must be based on a system of ethics.[12]

Herbart gave education status and independence by bringing it into the university as a science and discipline in its own right. For Herbart, man attained fullness only through becoming a citizen and he did this by means of education. Herbart's educational "system" was based on his psychology for its means, on his ethics for its ends, and on his metaphysics for its basic assumptions. He believed that each child is born with a unique potential, his "Individuality," but this potential remained unfulfilled until it was analyzed and transformed by education in the values of civilization. The product of this transformation, he termed "Character." "Thus the main purpose of education was the intelligent applications of pedagogy to the transformation of Individual into Character."[13]

Herbart's educational system was to be taught to prospective teachers. It was based on a psychology that explained ideas as developing from a process of apperception, in which new ideas are absorbed and reflected upon by those already present in the consciousness. Herbart was, in many ways, one of the founders of the field of psychology, independent of philosophy and based on science.[14] Herbart's psychological theory anticipated Piaget's ideas of assimilation and accommodation. The task of instruction was to help the student organize what he knew.

From this psychological base, Herbart developed his four-step method of instruction: clarity, association, system, and method. This method can be seen to be the forerunner of the modern day lesson plan.[15]

Herbart made three original contributions to educational philosophy: (1) he emphasized the aesthetic basis of morality, i.e., children recognize moral principles intuitively, (2) he presented five "practical ideas" or basic virtues that he thought all had to develop if they were to become good people and good citizens, and (3) he insisted that moral development must be itself grounded in intellectual education.[16]

Herbart gave virtually no attention to the differences between girls and boys in their respective cultures and spoke of girls in an unflattering way, typical of his time. Herbart's own teaching was almost entirely with boys; nevertheless, his principles and practical ideas could easily refer also to girls.

Herbart's Philosophy of Education

Herbart introduced the idea of "educational teaching." Education (from its Latin derivative of "educatio") means the shaping and development of character with a view to the improvement of the person. Teaching is the conveying of new knowledge, developing aptitudes, and imparting useful skills. Education should not just impart knowledge and shape aptitudes and skills, but it had to serve to develop a "moral insight" and to "strengthen character" which are aspects of the will.[17] The task of education then is to produce the good will and morality in the pupil. This can be accomplished in several ways.

Students can learn moral standards from their family and friends, and they can also learn them in school by means of the subject matter, especially history and literature. The goal is to help the students develop a moral code that will guide their life. Teaching should gain the interest of the students and thus motivate them to want to learn by developing many-sided interests.

Interdisciplinary instruction would help the student to develop these interests. Herbart chose the subjects of the curriculum for their moral potential. Scientific subjects appeal to the knowledge interests and include science and mathematics. Historical subjects appeal to the sympathy interests and include history, geography, languages, and literature.[18] Perhaps Herbart would ask us to examine our current day curriculum and ask ourselves "Are we teaching students a value-rich content that will help them to become morally good?"

For Herbart the goal of education was to help students become morally good. Like Socrates he thought that morality and virtue depended upon having the right knowledge.

Herbart's five moral principles are summarized in his *Outlines of Educational Doctrine*. Herbart said, "the one and the whole task of education can be summed up in the concept—morality."

Notes

1. Harold B. Dunkel, *Herbart and Education* (New York: Random House, 1969), pp. 4–6.
2. Ursula Stendel Hendon, "Herbart's Concept of Morality" in *Education and Its Role in America*. Dissertation, Department of Secondary Education in the Graduate School, University of Alabama (1980), p. 14.
3. H. M. Knox, "The Progressive Development of J. F. Herbart's Educational Thought." *British Journal of Educational Studies* XXIII (3) (1975), p. 265.
4. Ibid., p. 267.
5. Robert Epstein, "A Convenient Model for the Evolution of Early Psychology as a Scientific Discipline," *Teaching of Psychology* 8 (1) (1981), pp. 42–43.
6. Charles de Garmo, *Herbart and the Herbartians*, reprint from 1895 edition (Honolulu: University Press of Pacific, 2001), p. 16.
7. Madonna Murphy, "J. F. Herbart and Moral Education," paper presented at the *Midwest Philosophy of Education Annual Meeting* (November, 1999), p. 94.
8. Joel Spring, *The American School* (New York: McGraw Hill, 2005), p. 272.
9. Stefan Hopmann, and Kurt Rigquarts, "Start a Dialogue: Issues in a Beginning Conversation Between "Didaktik" and the Curriculum Traditions." *Journal of Curriculum Studies* 27 (1) (1995), p. 5.
10. Marlow Ediger, "Influence of Ten Leading Educators on American Education," *Education* 118 (2) (1997), p. 269.
11. Erwin Johanningmeier, "Dunkel's Herbart Revisited: The Milieu in Which He Worked," *Midwest History of Education Society Journal* 17 (1989), p. 155.
12. de Garmo, p. 10.
13. Alan Blyth, "From Individuality to Character: The Herbartian Sociology Applied to Education," *British Journal of Educational Studies* XXIX (1) (1981), p. 70.
14. Epstein, p. 42.
15. de Garmo, p. 74.
16. Blyth, p. 72.
17. Norbert Hilgenbeger, Johann Friedrich Herbart, *Prospects in Education* 23 (3 & 4) (1994), pp. 653–665.
18. Hendon, p. 124.

Questions to Guide Your Reading

1. See if you find Herbart's five moral principles as summarized in his *Outlines*. Which two are essentially individual in their orientation and which three involve interaction with others? What are five modern terms/virtues for these principles?

2. How does Herbart define "interest"? Is it the same or different from today's concept of motivation?

3. What are some examples of many-sided interests according to Herbart? Can you give modern terms for these interests?

READING 7.5:
THE EDUCATION OF MORAL CHARACTER
THE ETHICAL BASIS OF INSTRUCTION

8. The term virtue expresses the whole purpose of education. Virtue is the idea of inner freedom which has developed into an abiding actuality in an individual. Whence, as inner freedom is a relation between insight and volition, a double task is at once set before the teacher. It becomes his business to make actual each of these factors separately, in order that later a permanent relationship may result.

9. But even here at the outset we need to bear in mind the identity of morality with the effort put forth to realize the permanent actuality of the harmony between insight and volition. To induce the pupil to make this effort is a difficult achievement; at all events, it becomes possible only when the twofold training mentioned above is well under way. It is easy enough, by a study of the example of others, to cultivate theoretical acumen; the moral application to the pupil himself however, can be made, with the hope of success, only in so far as his inclinations and habits have taken a direction in keeping with his insight. If such is not the case, there is danger lest the pupil, after all, knowingly subordinate his correct theoretical judgment to mere prudence. It is thus that evil in the strict sense originates.

10. Of the remaining practical or ethical concepts, the idea of perfection points to health of body and mind; it implies a high regard for both, and their systematic cultivation.

11. The idea of good will counsels the educator to ward off temptation to ill will as long as such temptation might prove dangerous. It is essential, on the other hand, to imbue the pupil with a feeling of respect for good will.

12. The idea of justice demands that the pupil abstain from contention. It demands, furthermore, reflection on strife, so that respect for justice may strike deep root.

13. The idea of equity is especially involved in cases where the pupil has merited punishment as requital for the intentional infliction of pain. Here the degree of punishment must be carefully ascertained and acknowledged as just.

14. Where a number of pupils are assembled there arises, naturally, on a small scale, a system of laws and rewards. This system, and the demands which in the world at large spring from the same ideas, must be brought into accord.

15. The concept of an administrative system has great significance for pedagogics, since every pupil, whatever his rank or social status, must be trained for cooperation in the social whole to fit him for usefulness. This requirement may assume very many different forms.

16. Of the system of civilization only the aspect of general culture, not that of special training, must be emphasized at this point.

17. For the business of education, the idea of perfection, while it does not rise into excessive prominence, stands out above all others on account of its uninterrupted application. The teacher discovers in the as yet undeveloped human being a force which requires his incessant attention to intensify, to direct, and to concentrate.

18. The constant presence of the idea of perfection easily introduces a false feature into moral education in the strict sense. The pupil may get an erroneous impression as to the relative importance of the lessons, practice, and performance demanded of him, and so be betrayed into the belief that he is essentially perfect when these demands are satisfied.

19. For this reason alone, if others were wanting, it is necessary to combine moral education proper, which in everyday life lays stress continually on correct self-determination, with religious training. The notion that something really worthy has been achieved needs to be tempered by humility. Conversely, religious education has need of the moral also to forestall cant and hypocrisy, which are

Source: Johann Friederich Herbart, *Outlines of Educational Doctrine*, trans. Alexis F. Lenge (New York: The Macmillan Company, 1901).

only too apt to appear where morality has not already secured a firm foothold through earnest self-questioning and self-criticism with a view to improvement. Finally, inasmuch as moral training must be put off until after insight and right habits have been acquired, religious education, too, should not be begun too early; nor should it be needlessly delayed.

The Aim of Instruction

62. The ultimate purpose of instruction is contained in the notion, virtue. But in order to realize the final aim, another and nearer one must be set up. We may term it, *many-sidedness of interest*. The word *interest* stands in general for that kind of mental activity which it is the business of instruction to incite. Mere information does not suffice; for this we think of as a supply or store of facts, which a person might possess or lack, and still remain the same being. But he who lays hold of his information and reaches out for more, takes an interest in it. Since, however, this mental activity is varied, we need to add the further determination supplied by the term *many-sidedness*.

63. We may speak also of indirect as distinguished from direct interest. But a predominance of indirect interest tends to one sidedness, if not to selfishness. The interest of the selfish man in anything extends only so far as he can see advantages or disadvantages to himself. In this respect the one-sided man approximates the selfish man, although the fact may escape his own observation; since he relates everything to the narrow sphere for which he lives and thinks. Here lies his intellectual power, and whatever does not interest him as means to his limited ends, becomes an impediment.

64. As regards the bearings of interest on virtue, we need to remember that many-sidedness of interest alone, even of direct interest such as instruction is to engender, is yet far from being identical with virtue itself; also that, conversely, the weaker the original mental activity, the less likelihood that virtue will be realized at all, not to speak of the variety of manifestation possible in action. Imbeciles cannot be virtuous. Virtue involves an awakening of mind.

65. Scattering no less than one-sidedness forms an antithesis to many-sidedness. Many-sidedness is to be the basis of virtue; but the latter is an attribute of personality, hence it is evident that the unity of self-consciousness must be impaired. The business of instruction is to form the person on many sides, and accordingly to avoid a distracting or dissipating effect. And instruction has successfully avoided this in the case of one who with ease surveys his well-arranged knowledge in all of its unifying relations and holds it together as his very own.

Discussion Questions

1. Can you relate each of the components of Herbart's four-step instruction system to the current lesson plan you learn in your methods classes?
2. Given that Herbart says "The idea of equity is especially involved in cases where the pupil has merited punishment ... the degree of punishment must be carefully ascertained," what kind of classroom management and discipline plan do you think Herbart would want teachers to use?
3. What do you think Herbart would say are key components of moral character? How can these be conveyed to students?

For Further Research on the Internet

Some Herbart links. http://elvers.stjoe.udayton.edu/history/people/Herbart.html

Simple homepage on Herbart by Donald Clark. http://www.nwlink.com/~donclark/hrd/history/herbart.html

Herbart as a pioneer of psychology. http://educ.southern.edu/tour/who/pioneers/herbart.html

Suggestions for Further Reading

Blyth, Alan. "From Individuality to Character: The Herbartian Sociology Applied to Education." *British Journal of Educational Studies* XXIX (1) (1981): 69–79.

de Garmo, Charles. *Herbart and the Herbartians,* reprint from 1895 edition. Honolulu: University Press of Pacific, 2001.

Dunkel, Harold B. *Herbart and Education.* New York: Random House, 1969.

Ediger, Marlow. "Influence of Ten Leading Educators on American Education." *Education* 118 (2) (1997): 267–276.

Epstein, Robert. "A Convenient Model for the Evolution of Early Psychology as a Scientific Discipline." *Teaching of Psychology* 8 (1) (1981): 42–44.

Hendon, Ursula Stendel. *Herbart's Concept of Morality in Education and Its Role in America.* Dissertation, Department of Secondary Education in the Graduate School, University of Alabama, 1980.

Hilgenbeger, Norbert. "Johann Friedrich Herbart." *Prospects in Education* 23 (3 & 4) (1994): 649–664.

Hopmann, Stefan, and Kurt Rigquarts. "Start a Dialogue: Issues in a Beginning Conversation Between "Didaktik" and the Curriculum Traditions." *Journal of Curriculum Studies* 27 (1) (1995): 3–12.

Johanningmeier, Erwin. "Dunkel's Herbart Revisited: The Milieu in Which He Worked." *Midwest History of Education Society Journal* 17 (1989): 150–163.

Knox, H. M. "The Progressive Development of J. F. Herbart's Educational Thought." *British Journal of Educational Studies* XXIII (3) (1975): 265–275.

Murphy, Madonna. *J. F. Herbart and Moral Education.* Paper presented at the Midwest Philosophy of Education Annual Meeting, November 1999.

Spring, Joel. *The American School.* New York: McGraw Hill, 2005.

Section 7.6: Friedrich Froebel (1782–1852)

Have you seen the poster "All I Really Need to Know I Learned in Kindergarten" from Robert Fulghum's book? You can probably still remember your kindergarten days—singing songs, playing games, having circle time, doing finger plays, and eating snacks. We have Friedrich Froebel to thank for promoting this wonderful preschool experience.

Friedrich Froebel's Life and Times

Friedrich Wilhelm August Froebel was born on April 21, 1782 at Oberweissbach, a village in the Thuringian Forest in Germany, the sixth child of the village parson, Jakob Froebel, whose wife died when Friedrich was only nine months old. As principal pastor for several villages, his father was away from home often so Friedrich's care fell principally on his older brothers. Many of Froebel's biographers feel that it was this yearning for motherly love that was the significant motivating factor in his invention of the kindergarten, his dedication to bringing happiness to children, and his efforts to extol motherhood and women teachers.[1]

Friedrich's Education

Unsuccessful in his efforts to teach his son to read, Friedrich's father sent him to the village school. But Friedrich continued having difficulty and so his older brother Christopher tried to tutor him, thus becoming his closest friend.

When Friedrich was ten he went to live with his uncle, Herr Hoffman, and spent five of the happiest and most carefree years of his life with him. As he states in his autobiography: "My uncle's house had gardens attached into which I could go if I liked, but I was also at liberty to roam the whole region."[2] Froebel went to the town school and finally learned to read and write because it was well taught there.

Finishing elementary school, Friedrich returned home to serve a two-year apprenticeship with a forester and a surveyor living in Neuhaus, and continued learning about nature from books and actual experience. This later inspired his educational theory based on hands-on experience.

In 1799, Froebel entered the University of Jena to study botany, mathematics, and mineralogy and he enjoyed learning but criticized the curriculum, which was a group of courses that failed to show the interconnectedness between subjects—another important idea of his future educational philosophy. After two years, his college studies were abruptly ended due to the poor management of his funds, and he returned home discouraged and frustrated. For a while he went from job to job but when his father fell seriously ill in 1801, Friedrich began to help him with his parish, getting to know him in a special way before he died a year later.[3]

When Friedrich's uncle died in 1805 and left him an inheritance, he decided to return to college and went to Frankfort to study architecture.

Teacher

Before he finished his studies however, he met Dr. Anton Gruener, who invited him to teach at the Frankfurt Model School, developed on Pestalozzi's principles. Froebel accepted the position, going first to Yverdon to meet Johann Heinrich Pestalozzi and to observe his school methodology.[4] Friedrich was 24 years old when he taught his first class of forty boys ages nine to eleven years old and from the first day he knew that he had finally discovered his vocation. He taught for two years in the school and then became the private tutor for three young brothers aged six to eleven, teaching the boys in a small house on the estate using a patch of the property as a garden in order to give the boys opportunities for direct observations of nature and hands-on experiences.[5] Wishing to supplement their education, Froebel took the three boys to study in Yverdon where he could further study Pestalozzi's methods. Two years later, Froebel ended his tutoring assignment and went to study first at the University of Gottinger and then at the University of Berlin. Serving a short term of service in the military during the Napoleonic Wars, Froebel received a post at the Royal Museum of Mineralogy and while working here he developed the idea of his "gifts."[6]

Schoolmaster and Educator

Friedrich left the Royal Museum to teach his nephews in the family home at Griesheim when his brother died, but after a year he started a school in Keilhau, basing it on Pestalozzi's ideas and the number of students grew from twelve in 1820 to fifty-six in 1825.

Classes at the Keilhau School were as inspiring to the students as play. They often went for long walks to learn from nature. It was at Keilhau that Froebel began using his system of geometric blocks to teach children.[7] The school was an educational success, although it was constantly plagued by financial problems. Froebel wrote the book *The Education of Man* in 1826, basing it on his experiences at Keilhau.

In September 1818 he married Henrietta Wilhelmine Hoffmeister who he had met at the University of Berlin and, although she was unable to have children herself, Henrietta mothered all of Froebel's students for the next thirty years.[8]

The Kindergarten

In 1831, at the request of the Duke of Meiningen, Froebel drew up a plan for a new school in the Manor of Helba in which he outlined his ideas for educating children from early childhood to adulthood according to their gifts and abilities. Froebel went to Switzerland to begin this new school. (See the timeline of Froebel's life in Figure 7.6.)

Froebel was invited to Burgdorf to run an orphanage, with a day school and a boarding school attached, and a training class of sixty students preparing to be teachers. For the first time, Froebel was able to work with preschool children, for at this time in Germany, children under the age of seven did not attend school as it was believed that they did not have the ability to focus or develop cognitive and emotional skills until this age.[9]

In 1836 Froebel opened his first kindergarten as an institution of early childhood education in Blankenburg, a village near Keilhau.[10] Wilhelmine died two years later but her memory continued to support and inspire Froebel; the last fifteen years of his life were his most productive and creative period.

On June 28, 1840, Froebel renamed his school to be the Universal German Kindergarten or the "children's garden." This fits so well with his philosophy of education in which a child's nature needs to be tended and cultivated like a good gardener tends a young plant. According to Froebelian philosophy, a "thirsty plant" is a metaphor for the natural curiosity of the young children who are aroused to activity by having the seeds of their interests awakened, cultivated, unfolded, and ripened.[11]

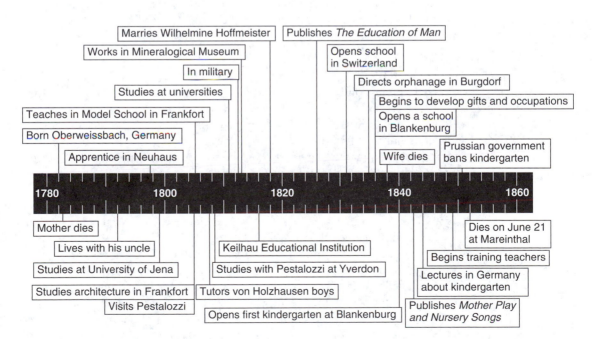

Figure 7.6   Froebel's Life and Times

Training Women to Be Kindergarten Teachers

Between 1840 and 1844 Froebel wrote his most influential book, *Mother Play and Nursery Songs*. He crisscrossed Germany for the next five years, gaining support for the kindergartens and setting them up in different cities. In 1849, Froebel started the first normal school for the training of kindergarten teachers, encouraging women to consider this career. He was convinced that women, because of their strong maternal instincts, made the best teachers of young children; he emphasized the important role of women as no one had before.[12]

By 1851, the sixty-nine-year-old Froebel had successfully started 51 kindergartens in Germany.[13] It was a year of highs and lows: Froebel married Luise Levin, one of his protegées, but that same year the Prussian court issued a decree forbidding the teaching of kindergarten. Although this edict was abrogated eight years later, this was the final blow for Friedrich. He died June 21, 1852 at the age of seventy.[14] Luise and Froebel's followers continued to spread his teachings; many of them went to England and the United States after the failed Prussian revolutions. Margarethe Meyer Schurz started the first kindergarten in the United States in 1856 in Watertown, Wisconsin.[15]

Froebel's Educational Contributions

Contributions to education made by Froebel include a belief that learning should be an active process, play is an actual educational method, and the understanding that childhood is a unique time. Froebel's school, or children's garden, promoted a cooperative environment in which each child's natural abilities could unfold.[16]

It was Froebel's conviction that the child's intellectual development begins on the day he is born that led him to start the kindergarten. The mother is the child's first teacher, and the family is the child's first school. As the earliest years are the most important learning period in the child's life, it is important that the kindergarten become an extended family with a teacher who is like a mother, a facilitator, and a guide helping the child develop physically, emotionally, and intellectually. Froebel viewed his kindergarten as a means of taking the child from a state of self-centeredness to a "society of children."[17]

Froebel's Philosophy of Education

Froebel's philosophy of education was closely linked to his philosophy of the human person. He believed that children are naturally good and that any evil is due to negative influences. Children should be free from inappropriate teaching that was not geared to their age and ability. Froebel used Pestalozzi's ideas as the basis for his theories, but he rejected Comenius' notion that the child could be shaped and bent, as well as Locke's belief that the child's mind was a blank slate.[18] Froebel believed that, given freedom, children would play, participate, observe, and learn new knowledge through self-activity at their own speed of learning. Froebel's child-centered curriculum included self-activity, physical activity, music, outdoor activities, and a series of manipulative materials called "Gifts and Occupations."[19]

Froebel developed the gifts, occupations, movement games, and mother songs that were key to his educational theory. The gifts are six mathematically structured materials from which and with which the child could learn about number, size, weight, texture, color, and shape in an interesting way. The occupations are the equipment—scissors and paper, sticks and clay, sand and stones—from which children are encouraged to build, construct, model, weave and sew, cut out and paste in order to make things. The movement games are games that encourage spontaneous behavior and provide experiences that demand speech. Finally the mother songs introduce physical play between mother and child involving the limbs and senses, knowledge of the world around the child, and the meaning of life.[20]

There had been educational circles for small children before the time of Froebel. Even the ancient Romans spoke of the importance of early childhood education. These infant schools, or créches, were still more like day care centers. It is to Friedrich Froebel that we are indebted for the age-appropriate enriching play environment of the kindergarten that has had such a strong influence in the United States extending the educational ladder downward.[21] For in his words, "In play a child reveals his own original power."

Notes

1. Norman Brosterman, *Inventing Kindergarten* (New York: Harry N. Abrams, Inc., 1997), pp. 14–15; Joachim Liebschner, *A Child's Work: Freedom and Play in Froebel's Educational Theory and Practice* (Cambridge: The Lutterworth Press, 1992), pp. 1–2; Robert Downs, *Friedrich Froebel* (Boston: C. K. Hall & Co., Twayne Publishers, 1978), pp. 11–12.
2. Friedrich Froebel, *Autobiography,* translated by Emilie Michaelis and H. Keatley (Syracuse, NY: C. W. Bardeen Publishers, 1889), p. 18.
3. Liebschner, pp. 3–4.
4. Clem Adelman, "Over Two Years, What Did Froebel Say to Pestalozzi?" *History of Education* 29 (2) (2000), p. 108.
5. Scholastic, "Friedrich Froebel: Founder, First Kindergarten," *Early Childhood Today* 15 (1) (2000), p. 63.
6. Jennifer Wolfe, *Learning from the Past: Historical Voices in Early Childhood Education* (Mayerthrope, Alberta: Piney Branch Press, 2000), p. 407.
7. Mary Ruth Moore, "An American's Journey to Kindergarten's Birthplace," *Childhood Education* 79 (1) (2002), p. 17.
8. Liebschner, p. 11.
9. Scholastic, p. 63.
10. Downs, pp. 35–42.
11. Elizabeth Cole, "An Experience in Froebel's Garden," *Childhood Education* (Fall, 1990), p. 18.
12. Moore, p. 17.
13. Ibid., p. 20.
14. Brosterman, pp. 26–28.
15. Adelman, p. 103.
16. Barbara Ruth Peltzman, *Pioneers of Early Childhood Education: A Bio-bibliographical Guide* (Westport, CT: Greenwood Press, 1998), p. 25.
17. Joel Spring, *The American School* (New York: McGraw Hill, 1997), p. 200.
18. Moore, p. 18.
19. Peltzman, p. 25.
20. Liebschner, pp. 55ff–116, 132.
21. Marlow Ediger, "Influence of Ten Leading Educators on American Education," *Education* 118 (2) (1997), p. 271.

Questions to Guide Your Reading

1. What, according to Froebel, is the purpose of education? Do you think this is a valid purpose for today's schools?
2. Why are the gifts and the occupations important in the kindergarten?
3. What is the value of play, according to Froebel?
4. Why is it important for each child to have his own garden? Do you think we should have gardens in schools today?

READING 7.6:
FROEBEL, *THE EDUCATION OF MAN*

Education, in instruction, should lead man to see and know the divine, spiritual, and eternal principle which animates surrounding nature, constitutes the essence of nature, and is permanently manifested in nature; and, in living reciprocity and united with braining, it should express and demonstrate the fact that the same law rules both (the divine principle and nature), as it does nature and man. If man is to attain fully his destiny, so far as earthly development will permit this, if he is to become truly an unbroken living unit, he must feel and know himself to be one, not only with God and humanity, but also with nature.... The Christian religion entirely completes the mutual relation between God and man; all education which is not founded on the Christian religion is one-sided, defective, and fruitless ... I would educate human beings who with their feet stand rooted in God's earth, whose heads reach even into heaven and there behold truth, in whose hearts are united both earth and heaven...

The destiny of nations lies far more in the hands of women, the mothers, than in the possessors of power, or those of innovators who for the most part do not understand themselves. We must cultivate women, who are the educators of the human race; else the new generation cannot accomplish its task. The union of family and school life is the indispensable requisite of education ... if indeed men are ever to free themselves from the oppressive burden and emptiness of merely extraneously communicated knowledge heaped up in memory. Only the quiet, secluded sanctuary of the family can give back to us the welfare of mankind.

Froebel's Kindergarten

Would you, O parents and educators, see in miniature, in a picture, as it were, what I have here indicated, look into this education-room of eight boys, seven to eight years old. The mind grows by self-revelation. In play the child ascertains what he can

do, discovers his possibilities of will and thought by exerting his power spontaneously. In work he follows a task prescribed for him by another, and doesn't reveal his own proclivities and inclinations; but another's. In play he reveals his own original power.

This unifying and, at the same time, self-reliant spirit unites all things that come near and seem adapted to its nature, its wants, and inner status—unites stones and human beings in a common purpose, a common endeavor. And thus each one soon forms for himself his own world; for the feeling of his *own power* implies and soon demands also the possession of his *own space* and his *own material* belongings exclusively to him.

Be his realm his province, his land, as it were, a corner of the courtyard, of the house, or of the room: be it the space of a box of a chest, or of a closet: be it a grotto, a hut, or a garden—the human being, the boy at this age, needs an external point, if possible, chosen and prepared by himself to which he refers all his activity.

When the room to be filled is extensive, when the realm to be controlled is large, when the whole to be represented or produced is complex, then brotherly union of similar-minded persons is in place. And when similar-minded persons meet in similar endeavor and their hearts find each other, then either the work already begun is extended or the work begun by one becomes a common work...

The gifts are intended to give the child from time to time new universal aspects of the external world, suited to a child's development. The occupations, on the other hand, furnish material for practice in certain phases of the skill. Nothing but the first gift can so effectively arouse in the child's mind the feeling and consciousness of a world of individual things; but there are numberless occupations that will enable the child to become skillful in the manipulation of surfaces. The gift leads to discovery; the occupation to invention. The gift gives insight; the occupation, power. The occupations are one-sided; the gifts, many-sided, universal. The occupations touch only certain phases of being; the gifts enlist the whole being of the child. Each gift should aid the child to make the external internal,

---

Source: Friedrich W. Froebel, *The Education of Man*, trans. W. N. Hailmann (New York: D. Appleton and Company, 1887).

the internal external, and to find the unity between the two.

On the large table of the much-used room there stands a chest of building blocks, in the form of bricks, each side about one sixth of the size of actual bricks, the finest and most variable material that can be offered a boy for purposes of representation. The material for building in the beginning should consist of a number of wooden blocks whose base is always one inch square and whose length varies from one to twelve inches. If, then, we take twelve pieces of each length, two sets—e.g., the pieces one and eleven, the pieces two and ten inches long, etc.—will always make up a layer an inch thick and covering one foot of square surface; so that all the pieces, together with a few larger pieces, occupy a space of somewhat more than half a cubic foot. It is best to keep these in a box that has exactly these dimensions; such a box may be used in many ways in instruction, as will appear in the progress of a child's development.

It is intermission, and each one has begun his own work. There in a corner stands a chapel quite concealed, a cross and an altar indicate the meaning of the structure: it is the creation of a small, quiet boy. There on a chair two boys have united to undertake a considerably greater piece of work: it is a building of several stories, and probably represents a castle, which looks down from the chair as from a mountain into a valley. But what has quietly grown under the hands of that boy at the table? It is a green hill crowned by an old, ruined castle. The others in the meanwhile, have erected a village in the plain below.

Now, each one has finished his work; each one examines it and that of the others. In each one rises the thought and the wish to unite all in a connected whole; and scarcely has this wish been recognized as a common one, when they establish common roads from the village to the ruin, from this to the castle, and from the castle to the chapel, and between them lie brooks and meadows.

At another time some had fashioned a landscape from clay, another had constructed from pasteboard a house with doors and windows, and a third had made miniature ships from nutshells. Each one examines his work: it is good, but it stands alone. He sees his neighbor's work: it would gain so much by being united. And immediately the house, as a castle crowns the hills, and the tiny ship floats on the small artificial lake and to the delight of all, the youngest brings his shepherd and sheep to graze between the mountain and the lake. Now they all

stand and behold with pleasure and satisfaction the work of their own hands.

Again, what busy tumult among those older boys at the brook down yonder! They have built canals and sluices, bridges and seaports, dams and mills, each one intent only on his own work. Now the water is to be used to carry vessels from the higher to the lower level: but at each step of progress one trespasses on the limits of another realm, and each one equally claims his right as lord and maker, while he recognizes the claims of the other. What can serve here to mediate? Only treaties, and like states, they bind themselves by strict treaties. Who can point out the varied significance, the varied results of these plays of boys? Two things, indeed, are clearly established. They proceed from one and the same spirit of boyhood and the playing boys made good pupils, intelligent, and quick to learn, quick to see and to do, diligent and full of zeal, reliable in thought and feeling, efficient and vigorous. Those who played thus are efficient men, or will become so. A child who plays and works thoroughly, with perseverance, until physical fatigue forbids will surely be a thorough, determined person, capable of self-sacrifice.

Children are like tiny flowers; they are varied and need care, but each is beautiful alone and glorious when seen in the community of peers. In answering the question 'What is the purpose of education?' I started at that time from the observation that man lives in a world of objects which influence him and which he wishes to influence, and so he must know these objects in their characteristics, their essence, and their relation to one another and to mankind.

Play is the highest expression of human development in childhood for it alone is the free expression of what is in a child's soul. The character and purpose of these plays may be described as follows: They are a coherent system, starting at each stage from the simplest activity and progressing to the most diverse and complex manifestations of it. The purpose of each one of them is to instruct human beings so that they may progress as individuals and members of humanity in all its various relationships. Collectively they form a complete whole, like a many-branched tree, whose parts explain and advance each other. Each is a self-contained whole, a seed from which manifold new developments may spring to cohere in further unity. They cover the whole field of intuitive and sensory instruction and lay the basis for all further teaching. They begin to establish spatial relationships and proceed to sensory and language training so that eventually man comes to see himself as a sentient, intelligent, and rational being and as such strives to live.

Particularly helpful at this period of life is the cultivation of gardens owned by the boys, and their cultivation for the sake of the produce. For here man for the first time sees his work bearing fruit in an organic way, determined by logical necessity and law—fruit which, although subject to the inner laws of natural development, depends in many ways upon his work and upon the character of his work! This work fully completes, in many ways, the boy's life with nature, and satisfies his curiosity concerning her workings, his desire to know her—a desire that urges him again and again to give thoughtful and continuous attention and observation to plants and flowers. Nature, too, seems to favor these promptings and occupations, and to reward them with abundant success; for a glance upon these gardens of children reveals at once the fact that, if a boy has given his plants only moderate care and attention, they thrive remarkably well; and that the plants and flowers of the boys who attend to them with special care live in sympathy with these boys, as it were, and are particularly healthy and luxuriant.

If the boy cannot have the care of a little garden of his own, he should have at least a few plants in boxes or pots, filled not with rare and delicate or double plants, but with common plants that have an abundance of leaves and blossoms, and thrive easily.

The child, or boy, who has guarded and cared for another living thing, although it be of a lower order, will be led more easily to guard and foster his own life. At the same time the care of plants will gratify his desire to observe other living things, such as beetles, butterflies, and birds, for these seek the vicinity of plants. . . .

Discussion Questions

1. Froebel used the scenario of boys creating individual works and then collectively assembling them. How would this compare to today's cooperative learning?
2. Can you give examples from today's kindergarten that are similar to Froebel's gifts, occupations, Mother songs, and movement games?
3. Do you think that if he were living today, Froebel would require kindergarten attendance for all children? Why or why not?
4. What do you think Froebel would say about today's home schooling movement?
5. Why are children getting "burned out in second grade"? Do you think today's kindergarten is faithful to Froebel's original idea?

For Further Research on the Internet

Home page on Froebel with links to his gifts and blocks. **http://www.geocities.com/Athens/Forum/7905/frobel.html**

Homepage on Froebel with bibliography. **http://www.infed.org/thinkers/et-froeb.htm**

A school built on Froebel's principles. **http://www.froebel.com/**

Froebel gifts for sale. **http://www.froebelgifts.com/**

The story of how Margarethe Meyer Schurz started the kindergarten movement in the United States. **http://www.jsonline.com/news/state/wis150/stories/0208sesq.stm**

Suggestions for Further Reading

Adelman, Clem. "Over Two Years, What Did Froebel Say to Pestalozzi?" *History of Education* 29 (2) (2000): 103–114.

Brosterman, Norman. *Inventing Kindergarten*. New York: Harry N. Abrams, Inc., 1997.

Cole, Elizabeth. "An Experience in Froebel's Garden." *Childhood Education* (Fall, 1990): 18–21.

Downs, Robert. *Friedrich Froebel.* Boston: C. K. Hall & Co., Twayne Publishers, 1978.

Ediger, Marlow. "Influence of Ten Leading Educators on American Education." *Education* 118 (2) (1997): 267–276.

Froebel, Friedrich. *Autobiography.* Translated by Emilie Michaelis and H. Keatley. Syracuse, New York: C. W. Bardeen Publishers, 1889.

Liebschner, Joachim. *A Child's Work: Freedom and Play in Froebel's Educational Theory and Practice.* Cambridge: The Lutterworth Press, 1992.

Moore, Mary Ruth. "An American's Journey to Kindergarten's Birthplace." *Childhood Education* 79 (1) (2002): 15–20.

Peltzman, Barbara Ruth. *Pioneers of Early Childhood Education: A Bio-bibliographical Guide.* Westport, CT: Greenwood Press, 1998.

Scholastic. "Friedrich Froebel: Founder, First Kindergarten." *Early Childhood Today* 15 (1) (2000): 63.

Spring, Joel. *The American School.* New York: McGraw Hill, 1997.

Wolfe, Jennifer. *Learning from the Past: Historical Voices in Early Childhood Education.* Mayerthrope, Alberta: Piney Branch Press, 2000.

CHAPTER ACTIVITIES

Linking the Past to the Present

1. Write a lesson plan using Herbart's components. Then compare it to the lesson plan your school uses. Try teaching the lesson.
2. Look in your college catalog for courses in women's studies or feminist philosophy. Is Mary Wollstonecraft included in these courses or some other course at your school? What do you think she would say about the role of women today in the United States?
3. Does your school have a support group for "Adult Children," i.e., those who grew up in dysfunctional families with a parent who was an alcoholic or drug user? Why is it important to have these support groups in schools?

Developing Your Philosophy of Education

The educators in this chapter present a new view of the child. As you write your philosophy of education, include a section on your understanding of the role of children in their education and learning.

In your philosophy of education also think about your classroom management plan. How will you create a safe and emotionally secure classroom for your students in which no bullying occurs? How will you show your students that you are a warm and caring person while still ensuring that they learn their lessons?

Connecting Theory to Practice

1. Visit a kindergarten and observe and note activities similar to those in Froebel's kindergarten. What are modern versions of his gifts?
2. Visit a primary school classroom. Observe the classroom teaching and see if you can find examples of Pestalozzi's object lesson and the general and special methods.
3. Go on a field trip with your clinical class. Note the things that the students learn from going from the class to nature, or the site visited, that are best learned through experience.

Educators' Philosophies and Contributions to Education

TABLE 7.1   Philosophy and Contributions of Enlightenment Educators

Educator	Role of Teacher & Learner	View of Curriculum & Methodology	Purpose or Goal of Education	Major Contribution
Locke	Private education in the home with a tutor who makes learning enjoyable; recognizing the child's unique potential as a rational creature	Integration of curriculum for practical and utilitarian purposes; the mind is an empty slate that learns through experiences	All children of both sexes between the ages of three and fourteen should be educated so they are capable of self-government	Father of Modern Education, promoting instruction with the empirical method, i.e., through sense experiences
Rousseau	Tutor who is a moral mentor; children are born good and learn best from nature, uncorrupted by schools and society	A curriculum centered on the child's needs not on the subject matter; learning freely from nature	To allow children's natural goodness to flourish as they develop themselves	Father of the field trip and permissive education; romantic view of the child, opposed to the child-depravity view; forerunner of progressivism
Pestalozzi	General method—The teacher creates an emotionally secure environment in which the "whole child" is taught—head, heart, hand, body, and feelings	Special method—teach from the concrete to the abstract using the actual objects; teaching a whole group with simultaneous instruction	To develop the child's moral, intellectual, and physical abilities harmoniously so that they can work in peace in society	Transformed schooling with simultaneous instruction and the "object lesson"
Wollstonecraft	Teachers could be men or women teaching in government-supported day schools for boys and girls in which the school and family work together	Education for women on a par with that for men; writing and reading, teaching religions, history, politics, and home industrial training, using the Socratic method	Education for women that would cultivate their mind so that women could take a place in society, and not solely be only the wife of a man	One of the first feminist educators arguing for women's liberation; women and men are philosophically identical, i.e., each has an intellect and an immortal soul called to a religious end so each should have an identical education.
Herbart	Educational teaching to convey knowledge and morality; each child is born with a unique potential to develop many-sided interests	An interdisciplinary curriculum of subjects with moral potential, taught with a method of teaching based on psychology	The ultimate goal of education is the development of moral character; man attains fullness through becoming a citizen and this he does through education	Developed the lesson plan; brought education into the university as a science in its own right
Froebel	The teacher is like a mother; women are excellent teachers for the youngest children; the child is naturally good	A child-centered curriculum taught by play, self-activity, physical activity, music, and the "gifts and occupations"	Help children grow physically, emotionally, and intellectually so they go from a state of self-centeredness to a society of children	Founder of the kindergarten and early childhood education

CHAPTER 8

Education in the New World

Native American Civilization and Education

This anthology began with Confucius and education in prehistoric times. This section on education in America commences with ancestors of Confucius. Archeological discoveries support the theory that the first inhabitants of the North American continent were of Asiatic origin. They crossed what is today the Bering Strait (at that time it was one big glacier) around 15000 B.C.

These first Americans spread across the North American continent and southward into present day Central and South America, settling in various areas and setting up indigenous societies. Some of these societies were simple hunting and gathering communities, but others evolved into large and complex agrarian societies.[1]

Mayan Indians

The Mayans in Central America were the only Indian culture to develop an advanced form of writing, similar to the hieroglyphic writing of the Egyptians. In addition they achieved outstanding success in astronomy, arithmetic, architecture, and art; and they used this to build great cities. Most Mayan children learned, from their parents at home, customs, religious beliefs, and necessary survival skills. However, sons of chiefs and priests went to schools where they studied history, hieroglyphic writing, astronomy, and medicine.[2] As the Mayan civilization waned and they abandoned their cities, other civilizations grew.

The Incas and Aztecs

The Incas developed an empire in South America from 1200 to 1532. The Incas never developed true writing but they worked out a system of recording numbers using knotted strings. Most children did not attend school, but learned at home by helping their parents. Some sons of the noblemen went to the capital of Cusco to study warfare, history, religion, and language; and a few select girls attended a school in Cusco where they were trained to serve in the emperor's palace (see Map 8.1 of the New World).

During the 1400s, the Aztecs, who were skilled in medicine, music, and poetry, built an empire that extended throughout what is now Mexico. Parents taught children until they were twelve, then both boys and girls attended formal schooling in the "cuicacalli" to learn the tribal songs, dances, and music of the society. The purpose of Aztec education was to promote socially appropriate behavior in conformity with tribal expectations.[3]

The Cherokees

The Cherokee Indians settled along the Tennessee River in the Appalachian Mountains and thrived in the area all the way to Virginia. They also built villages, with the houses made of wood and stone; they gathered nuts and berries, planted fields of tobacco, and knew how to cure the game they caught so it would last for the winter. They made dugout canoes to travel the rivers and built roads in order to trade with other Indians. They were a people of high ethical standards; today they are the largest Native American tribe in the United States today.

Native American Informal Education

One sees similarities in that each of these different Native American peoples passed on to their children survival skills, a common language, culture, customs, and a spiritual outlook. Similar in many ways to the children of Sparta, Greece, Native American boys and girls had to master certain knowledge and skills in order to be mature members of their tribe. Boys mastered the survival skills necessary to be hunters, farmers, warriors, and builders. Girls learned to prepare the various foods, whether meat, grains, fish, or other edible foods, and to make clothing and prepare shelter from the available materials.

Native American children learned from an early age the shared wisdom and knowledge of the tribe. The family was the most important teacher, but the extended family and, in fact, all the elders of the tribe took part in their education. Spiritual and cultural lessons were given through storytelling, thus passing their traditions and outlook on life down from one generation to the next. Education was, therefore, an integral part of life itself, not something apart and separate.[4]

The onset of puberty, and the attendant coming of age rituals, sharply divided childhood from adulthood. "Praise and rewards for good deeds were used effectively as a means of character development to acknowledge the young person's great feats."[5] Shame was employed to expose a youth's misdeeds, but corporal punishment was usually avoided.

The Explorers and the "Indians"

Christopher Columbus discovered this "New World" in 1492; thinking he had arrived in India, he called the natives he met "Indians." (In Europe at this time, Luther was advocating education in the vernacular to read the Bible and Erasmus was promoting the Renaissance revival of reading the classics in their original language of Greek or Latin.) Columbus, and the European explorers that followed, insisted that the Native Americans be "civilized and Christianized." They did not realize that these people already had a very high level of civilization, culture, and their own spirituality. Columbus, and those who followed him, sought to dominate and acculturate the natives, and this meant they made them learn a new language, undergo a new and different kind of education, adopt new customs and manners, and embrace new spiritual doctrines and practices. Those who would not adapt were killed. In addition to bringing these new cultural patterns and ways

Map 8.1 New World

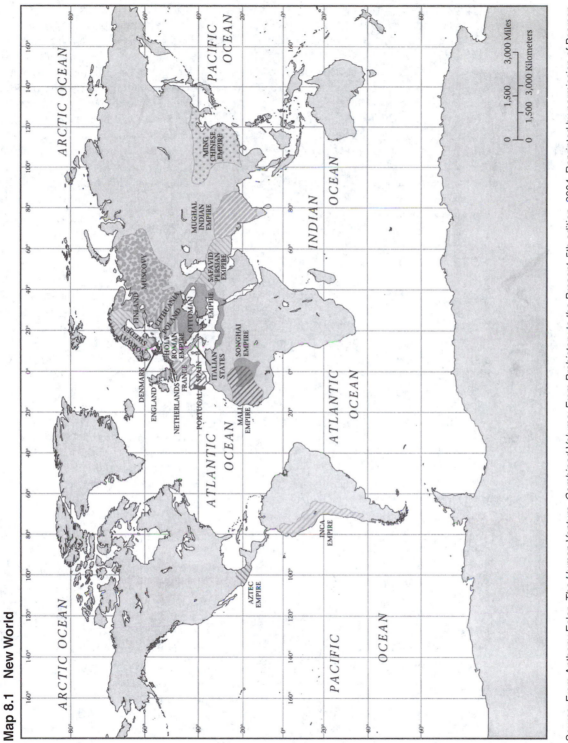

Source: From Anthony Esler, *The Human Venture, Combined Volume: From Prehistory to the Present*, 5th edition, 2004. Reprinted by permission of Pearson Education.

of thinking, the Europeans brought new diseases, alcohol, and weapons of war. These elements contributed to the rapid reduction of the Native American population by as much as eighty percent in many areas within just a few years of the arrival of the European explorers.[6]

The Cherokee Indians first came in contact with Hernando de Soto in 1540 while he was looking for gold in their land. The Cherokees were hospitable, offering the travelers much needed food—wild turkey and corn. At first the Cherokee allowed the Spanish to live with them; the Spanish taught them how to mine and smelt; they also gave them firearms as well as their diseases. The first contact of the Cherokees with the English colonists was in 1654; they traded with them at first, but then they fought, and finally signed a treaty in 1684.

Sequoya (George Guess) was born in 1770 in the Cherokee Village of Taskigi in Tennessee. He was the son of a Dutch/English peddler, George Gist, and a Cherokee Indian. Crippled with rheumatism, Sequoya worked as the tribe's scribe using the typical Indian hieroglyphics. Impressed by the way the white men wrote things down on "talking leaves" (pieces of paper), Sequoya sought to develop a way to also write down the Cherokee language. He worked from 1809 to 1821 and developed a Cherokee alphabet with eighty-five symbols. He taught this system of writing to the Cherokees; thousands of them learned to read and write and they began to publish newspapers and books in their own language. The Bible was translated into Cherokee and many of the tribe became Christians. This made the Cherokees the most benevolent, moral, and intellectual of all the Indian tribes in the eyes of the Europeans.[7] Sequoya was a soldier in the War of 1812 and moved to Arkansas in 1817 with the great migration (when the Indians were moved by the government to reservations). He received a medal of honor in 1832 for his service to the nation, but was shot and killed by soldiers in Texas on June 9, 1831. The contact with the Europeans changed the Cherokee people, as it changed the other Native American tribes, from a peace-loving group to a warring nation that had to fight to maintain their land and way of living.[8]

Colonial Education in America

The first permanent European settlement in the territory that eventually became the United States of America was in St. Augustine, Florida, in 1565. With the intent of establishing a colony of Spain here, a complete population arrived: the five ships that landed had 600 men including 250 soldiers, 125 experienced farmers, and 26 families. They included groups of skilled laborers such as stonecutters, blacksmiths, carpenters, smelters, weavers, tanners, coopers, bakers, barbers, priests, and even a notary. A classical school for the children of the Spanish colonists was in existence in St. Augustine at least as early as 1606.[9] Franciscan friars began establishing missions along the coast and into the interior. Each mission became a school of instruction for the natives in the cultural and religious doctrines and moral values of the colonists. Gradually missions spread into the areas that would later become New Mexico, Texas, Arizona, and California. "These mission communities laid the foundation for the extension of the Spanish religious and cultural influence through the western region of the country."[10] Some of the missionaries tried to immerse themselves in tribal societies and learn their languages, cultures, and skills in order to better convert them to their religion. In the process, they themselves learned from their hosts important survival skills that proved essential for their continued prosperity. The mission influence was twofold. The Spanish received labor and corn from the Indians; but they gave back by introducing them to wheat, cattle, and plows and by teaching them carpentry and irrigation.[11]

Education in the Southern Colonies

The first permanent English settlement in North America was in Jamestown, Virginia in 1607. Although not successful at first due to famine and disease, in 1611, Thomas Dale arrived with 300 more men and began a system of giving land to settlers who had come as indentured servants but had completed the terms of their contract. One of these men was John Rolfe, who married the Native American maiden Pocahontas in 1613 and began cultivating a variety of tobaccos that came to be in great demand in England. As tobacco became the staple crop of Virginia, all aspects of life began to change. In 1619, a Dutch ship unloaded the first Africans; although originally coming as indentured servants, they were eventually enslaved.[12] In addition, ninety women arrived, ready to marry. Families and commerce thus began in this expanding colony.

Education in the Southern colonies was influenced by the social and economic developments that defined life in the area. The dispersed agrarian population deterred the development of anything like a "system of schools." Most Southern colonists accepted the prevailing European precept that education was essentially a family concern. "Home schooling" by a parent became common, although they usually taught them only basic reading and some writing. Some of the more wealthy sent their children "back home" for a proper English education. Other plantation owners brought English and Scottish trained tutors to teach both their sons and daughters English grammar, reading, Latin, ciphering, music, and dance. As few parents could afford live-in tutors, some ministers established "parson schools" in order to supplement their income. George Washington, James Madison, James Monroe, and Thomas Jefferson each studied at Rev. James Maury's Parson Boarding School in Fredericksburg Parish in Virginia. The Church was not officially involved in either supporting or maintaining these schools. However in the South, the Anglican Church dominated and their Society for the Propagation of the Gospel (SPG) raised funds and books for the education of orphans, Indians, and paupers in Charity Schools.[13] In some rural areas of sufficient population density, groups of citizens erected "old field" schoolhouses on worn out land parcels. Parents paid a fee for their children to attend that helped pay the salary of the teacher. In some areas, benefactors endowed "free schools" that were open to all children in the vicinity, regardless of their ability to pay. About a dozen of these schools provided instruction up to the secondary level. The College of William and Mary began in 1693 as an Anglican institution to prepare young men for positions of leadership in the Church and the state.

The colonists encouraged the tribes to trade their Native American prisoners of war that they then put into slavery on their plantations. They and the African-American slaves were trained to be agricultural workers, field hands, craftspeople, or domestic servants. The African-Americans were generally forbidden to learn reading or writing. They tried to educate the Indian children in English homes, hoping both to civilize and convert them. In general, the Indian response was negative, as they were satisfied with their culture and saw little need to emulate the English institutions, customs, or beliefs.[14]

For the poor white children of subsistence farmers, formal education was nonexistent. Educational opportunity was determined almost exclusively by one's social class. This discrepancy in educational opportunity in the South remained until the reconstruction period following the Civil War. Nevertheless, many of the most learned and able leaders in the revolutionary period were educated in the South. We will see how Thomas Jefferson's ideas on education for the new country were influenced by his own educational experience.

Education in the Middle Colonies

In 1625, Peter Minuit, of the West India Company, bought an island at the mouth of the Hudson River from the Native Americans and began a settlement called New Amsterdam on the island of Manhattan. This was the first truly multicultural society in North America.

Almost half of the population in 1600 was Dutch, but Germans, French, and Scandinavians joined them. Religions represented included Quakers, Dutch Reformed, Baptists, Lutherans, Catholics, Jews, and Muslims; languages included eighteen different European and African dialects. Primarily a trading camp, the settlement at first did not include churches, schools, or other permanent institutions, just taverns and eating-houses.[15]

In 1638, the Dutch West India Company established and financed a town school in New Amsterdam and encouraged the establishment of other schools in the outlying areas. By 1659, a classical secondary school was also operating in New Amsterdam. In 1664, the British took over New Amsterdam and renamed it New York. However, the localized settlements of Dutch, Germans, English, Scots, Swedes, French, Norwegians, and Irish tended to isolate themselves from the other groups thus establishing their own school to preserve their linguistic, religious, and cultural distinctiveness.[16] These schools were either parochial schools supported by the dominant church in the area, or private schools in which all those who attended paid tuition, each student paying a "rate" that his parents could afford.

The Spanish were the first to explore Maryland and the Chesapeake Bay area in the 1500's. Lord Baltimore of England, a Roman Catholic, established St. Mary's City near the southern tip of the Potomac River in 1634. He named the region Maryland. He wanted it to be an area in which his faith and other faiths were free to worship and, in 1649, passed a religious toleration law. The Jesuits soon started establishing schools in Maryland.

The Dutch in New Amsterdam started private schools in which reading, writing, and the Dutch reformed religion were taught. Once the English came, a number of Charity Schools were started by the SPG. Since New Amsterdam, now New York, was a commercial colony, secondary level private schools were established that taught specific trades and skills such as navigation, surveying, bookkeeping, geography, and mechanics.[17] Some of the schools later became known as "academies" after Benjamin Franklin founded the Philadelphia Academy in 1751. According to John Pulliam "The seeds of the American comprehensive high school, which offered vocational subjects, were planted in the private and parochial schools of the Middle colonies."[18]

The apprenticeship method of education was common in all three areas, but especially in the Middle Atlantic colonies. Apprenticeships emerged, as we saw in previous chapters, from the guild system common throughout medieval Europe. A master craftsman would only allow others to enter the trade after a proper period of training. The apprentice worked with the master for a period of years at a very low salary. Benjamin Franklin worked as an apprentice to his brother and then became a printer in his own right.

In 1681, William Penn received the area that was to become Pennsylvania from King Charles II as payment of a debt. Penn had converted to the Society of Friends, known as the Quakers, a religious sect that rejects violence. Penn's colony was soon to become a haven for Quakers, who established schools that were open to all children, including blacks and Native Americans. Quaker teachers respected the individual dignity of the child and rejected corporal punishment. Like the other primary schools in the area, the Quaker schools taught reading, writing, arithmetic, and religion. In addition, they included vocational training in the form of handicrafts, domestic science, and agriculture.[19]

Education in the New England Colonies

On November 22, 1620, one hundred and two people, consisting of twenty women and thirty-two children, arrived from Plymouth, England to a new land that they were to call "Plymouth" in what is now Massachusetts.[20] The majority of these Pilgrims were of the Puritan religion. They were dissatisfied with the Anglican religion of England and had unsuccessfully tried to "purify" it. Believing that they and their families would be corrupted if they stayed in England, they decided to come to the New World. Although only about half of this first group survived the first winter, new arrivals continued to come. They were determined to begin a new colony—the Massachusetts Bay Colony—where they could freely practice their religion. Whole families came, including all the necessary professions—shoemakers, coopers, joiners, weavers, carpenters, tradesmen, farmers, and ministers. The Puritans were a literate people and they quickly sought to establish schools.[21] In 1635, the Boston town officials agreed to hire a schoolmaster "for teaching the children." The Boston Latin Grammar School opened in 1636. It is recognized as the first formal "public" school in the colonies. It was public in the sense that it was supported by public funds, under public control, and was accessible to children in the local community. Schools were soon established in some twenty-two different towns in Massachusetts.[22]

In 1642, the Massachusetts General Court enacted legislation that affirmed the primary responsibility of parents to educate their children and compelled them to ensure that their children learned "to read and write and understand the principles of religion and of the capital laws of the country." Children, especially those whose own parents were not literate, went to "dame schools" which were not really schools at all, but literate women who would teach them basic reading, counting, prayers, and the catechism using only a hornbook and perhaps the Bible. The women usually carried out their household duties while they drilled the students in their alphabet and they usually charged a modest fee for teaching other children along with their own children.[23]

Going a step further, in 1647, the General Court enacted what was to become known as the "Old Deluder Satan Act." The Act of 1647 required every town of fifty or more families to appoint a reading and writing teacher. Towns of one hundred or more were to establish a school and hire a teacher. The teacher's wages were to be paid by the students' parents or shared by all in the community. Students were to be taught to read and write so that Satan, the "Old Deluder," could not keep them from reading the scriptures so that they would be saved.[24]

The Town School thus became established in the New England colonies. Boys and girls aged anywhere from six to thirteen or fourteen attended. Attendance was only for a few short months a year—when the children were not needed at home to work on the farm. The school curriculum included reading, writing, arithmetic, catechism, and singing religious hymns. Students began formal training in the use of pen, ink, and paper, items not customarily found in early colonial homes.[25] Arithmetic was primarily a matter of counting, adding, and subtracting. The children learned the alphabet, syllables, words, and sentences by memorizing the hornbook. The hornbook was a wood paddle to which a single page of parchment was attached; the parchment was covered with a transparent material made by flattening the horns of cattle (thus the name) to preserve it. The parchment had the alphabet, a few syllables containing vowels and consonants (the "syllabarium") and the Lord's Prayer or a Biblical verse. Students were to memorize the entire contents of the hornbook and recite it to the schoolmaster. The hornbook was a common feature in all the colonies. Older children used the *New England Primer.* The Primer began with the alphabet, followed by the standard syllabarium ab, eb, ib, ob, ub, etc. Then words of one syllable were followed by those of two, three, up to six syllable words. The most famous feature of the Primer was the twenty-four wood cut illustrations of the alphabetic rhymes beginning with "In Adam's sin, we sinned all." An Alphabet of Lessons for youth consisted of a series of instructive lessons taken from the Bible.[26]

In 1684, a writing school opened in Boston. Penmanship was considered a craft and writing was taught as a specialized skill requiring years of practice for mastery. Men taught writing to other young men whose parents wanted them to acquire this skill which was important for them as future ministers, lawyers, clerks and businessmen. More and more women learned to write in the closing decades of the colonial period as it became necessary from both an economic and instrumental point of view.[27]

Boys who aspired to a profession requiring a collegiate education went to the Latin grammar school (the equivalent of a secondary school) after the town school. These Latin schools were, according to historian Samuel Morrison, "one of colonial America's closest links to the European educational experience, resembling the classical humanist schools of the Renaissance." Instruction was offered in Latin, Greek, and Hebrew. Students read the classical authors such as Cicero, Virgil, and Homer. Geography, history, mathematics, and writing completed the course offerings. The complete curriculum took about seven years to master.

In 1636, the Massachusetts General Court agreed to establish a college—which was named Harvard in 1638 after John Harvard who died and left his entire library of 400 books to the college. The college was established to "advance learning and perpetuate it to posterity" providing those called to the ministry and other positions of leadership with a sound classical education. At Harvard, students read, wrote, and spoke in Latin, studying the "trivium" of grammar, logic, and rhetoric thus learning how to think and express their thoughts clearly and persuasively.[28] In 1701, Yale College began in Connecticut and Dartmouth began in 1769. All had similar curricula. They were originally theological seminaries; later they developed curricula to train men in other professions such as law, medicine, and science.

Summary of Colonial Education

Despite the regional variations noted above, there were several common elements in all the colonies. All three eventually were dominated by British rule and were heir to Western European educational traditions and the white Anglo-Saxon Protestant values. Despite linguistic and religious differences, similar basic ideas and values governed individuals and groups. Religion held a high priority in the value structure and the family played a strong formative role in shaping ideas, values, and skills.[29] In all three regions, sex and socioeconomic class limited educational opportunities. Both boys and girls attended the Town School; Latin grammar schools and colleges were restricted to males. In the beginning, colonial schools followed the European dual track system of schooling in which the lower socioeconomic class attended only the primary school in which education was in the vernacular. Only the sons of the upper classes attended the Latin grammar school and college. Once the new nation began, the dual track system disbanded and an American system of schooling developed.

For Further Research on the Internet

Has great links to the Mayan, Aztec, and Native American Indian sites. **http://www. crystalinks.com/ancient.html**

The History of American Education Web Project. An excellent resource with links to many important educators in America. **http://www .nd.edu/~rbarger/www7/**

The Blackwell History of Education Research Museum has information on hornbooks and early textbooks. **http://www.niu.edu/acad/leps/blackw1.html**

Notes

1. Ted Morgan, *Wilderness at Dawn: The Settling of the North American Continent* (New York: Simon & Schuster, 1993), pp. 19, 23, 33.
2. Robert Shaver, *The Ancient Mayan* (Palo Alto, CA.: Stanford University Press, 1994).
3. Richard Townsend, *The Aztecs* (London: Thames & Hudson, 1992); Timothy Reagan, *Non-Western Educational Traditions* (Mahwah, NJ: Lawrence Erlbaum Associates, Publisher, 1996), p. 49.
4. Reagan, pp. 63–64.
5. Wayne Urban and Jennings Wagoner, *American Education: A History,* 2nd ed. (Burr Ridge, IL: McGraw Hill, 2000), p. 3.

6. Ibid., pp. 6, 11.

7. Stan Hoig, *Sequoyah, the Cherokee Genius* (Oklahoma City: Univ. of Oklahoma Press, 1995), URLS: http://www.thehawksnest.com/html/sequoya.html and http://www.daltonstate.edu/sequoya2.htm

8. URL: http://cherokeehistory.com.

9. Lawrence Cremin, *American Education: The Colonial Experience 1607–1783*, 2nd ed. (New York: Harper & Row, Publishers, 1972), pp. 21–23.

10. Urban and Wagoner, p. 8.

11. Morgan, p. 211.

12. Ibid., p. 226.

13. Margaret Connell Szasz, *Indian Education in the American Colonies, 1607–1783* (Albuquerque: University of New Mexico Press, 1988), p. 43.

14. Ibid., p. 55.

15. Cremin, pp. 18–21.

16. Urban and Wagoner, p. 52.

17. Jurgen Herbst, *The Once and Future School: Three Hundred and Fifty Years of American Secondary Education* (New York: Routledge, 1996), p. 18.

18. John Pulliam and James Van Patten, *History of Education in America,* 8th ed. (Upper Saddle River, NJ: Merrill/Prentice Hall, 2003), p. 61.

19. Allan Ornstein and Daniel Levine, *Foundations of Education,* 7th ed. (Boston: Houghton Mifflin Company, 2000), p. 139.

20. Urban and Wagoner, p. 31.

21. Ibid., p. 33.

22. Ibid., pp. 42, 47.

23. Pulliam and Van Patten, p. 58; Urban and Wagoner, p. 43.

24. Herbst, p. 12.

25. Gloria Main, "An Inquiry into When and Why Women Learned to Write in Colonial New England," *Journal of Social History* 24 (3) (1991), p. 579.

26. Urban and Wagoner, p. 45.

27. Main, p. 583.

28. Herbst, p. 15.

29. Ornstein and Levine, p. 140.

Section 8.1: Charles Eastman (Hakadah) (1858–1939) and Elaine Goodale Eastman (1863–1953)

Can you remember the stories your grandparents told you about when they were growing up—perhaps "during the war"? Didn't you find it interesting listening to them? Can you imagine having your whole schooling from you grandparents and their stories? That is how the Native American children learned.

Their Lives and Times

Charles Eastman, or Hakadah (which means pitiful last), was the fifth child born in Mankato, Minnesota in 1858 to Santee Sioux parents. His mother, a handsome woman with black luxurious hair and deep eyes with Caucasian features, was dangerously ill when she gave birth to Hakadah. She gave her child to her mother-in-law (Uncheedah) on her deathbed. Hakadah's grandmother was wise and endowed with ingenuity and a wonderful memory. Hakadah learned from her the cultural attributes and skills that he would need to survive as an adult Sioux.[1]

Informal Education: Learning the Indian's Ways

When Hakadah was four years old, there was an uprising in Minnesota in which many were massacred, and the family fled to British Columbia. Hakadah's father and two brothers were betrayed to the authorities and were imprisoned for ten years. Thinking his father was dead, Hakadah's uncle, his father's younger brother, known as one of the best hunters and bravest warriors of the Sioux, became his advisor and teacher. From 1858 to 1874 Hakadah's grandmother and uncle taught him the ways, language, culture, and oral history of the Woodland Sioux.

Hakadah grew up with his brother, Chatanna, who was three years older, his cousin, Oesedah, the only girl in her family, and a little white boy of ten who had been taken captive. Hakadah's uncle traded Chatanna to a Canadian who had six daughters and no sons and Hakadah never saw his brother again.[2]

Formal Education: Learning the White Man's Ways

At the age of fifteen, Hakadah was reunited with his father, who had been imprisoned in Davenport, Iowa for his alleged role in the uprising in Minnesota. His father had been taught in the prison and had been converted by the pioneer missionaries. Although under sentence of death, he was finally pardoned by President Lincoln when no direct evidence was found. Believing life on a reservation was degrading, he tried the white man's way of gaining a livelihood on a homestead. He then sought his lost sons.[3]

His father took Hakadah to Flandreau, South Dakota where Hakadah had to wear "civilized" clothes, learn about the Bible, and begin his "formal" education in schools. His father insisted that he receive the white man's education. Hakadah attended the Santee Normal School where he adopted the name Charles. He then went to Beloit preparatory college in Wisconsin and then moved on to Knox College. He transferred to Dartmouth College where he had to take two years of academic work before he could enroll in the pre-medicine classes. Finally, he enrolled in the Boston University School of Medicine, earning his M.D. in 1890.[4] In his first job as physician for the Pine Ridge, South Dakota Indian agency he met and later married Elaine Goodale. (See the timeline of Hakadah's [Charles Eastman's] life in Figure 8.1A.)

Elaine Goodale's Life

Elaine Goodale was born in 1863 on a farm in New England. Her childhood was plain but close to nature and wildlife and full of the classics. She read Shakespeare, Dickens, Hawthorne, and Longfellow from her family library. She and her sister Dora published their first book of poetry, *Apple Blossoms: Verses of Two Children* when she was just fifteen years old. When she was twenty, her family sold the farm and Elaine needed a job. General Samuel Chapman Armstrong, founder of Hampton Institute, offered her a position as a teacher for one hundred Sioux Indians who had been added to the enrollment of the school in an attempt to "civilize" them and teach them the ways of white society. Elaine later said that, after her parents, General Armstrong had the strongest influence on her life. "I caught fire from the irresistible enthusiasm, making bold almost at once to spread the new gospel of opportunity for the red man through impassioned articles in … leading journals."[5]

Elaine Learns About the Indian Culture

Not content to teach the Indians without understanding their culture, she persuaded Armstrong to send her to the Dakota Territory in 1885. The trip influenced her so much that the following year she moved to Dakota to work as a teacher at the Indian Day School on a Sioux reservation. She wanted her school to serve as a model for educating Indian children. In 1891, she was appointed Supervisor of Indian Education for the Two Dakotas. In this role, she visited day schools on every reservation, initiated teacher's institutes, and tried to get better materials for the schools. She worked against the system that removed Native American children from their families and sent them to distant boarding schools. Here they had to cut their hair, wear western dress, adopt western customs (they were forbidden to speak their own language), and become Christians. Elaine put her faith in the reservation day schools to "lift up" the Indians and help them assimilate, convinced that if they failed to assimilate, they would be annihilated. Elaine loved the Sioux and their culture but she always believed in the superiority of her own Anglo culture. She knew what would be lost if the Indians entirely adopted the ways of the white people: their culture and identity, the very qualities that she most loved in them.

Mr. and Mrs. Eastman

Elaine Goodale wrote her *Sister to the Sioux* in which she described the summer she spent traveling hundreds of miles and living off the land outside the Pine Ridge Agency. Here in 1890 she met a young, handsome, educated Santee Sioux, Charles Alexander Eastman, or Hakadah. In him she saw her soul mate, the man she hoped would help her bridge the two worlds in which she lived. In the course of six weeks the two fell in love and had no sooner announced their engagement when they were thrown together in the Wounded Knee Massacre. Both were horrified by the brutality of the army's response to Big Foot's pitiful protests—many women and children were killed in that massacre. Elaine helped nurse the wounded that Dr. Eastman cared for and the comradeship in the face of disaster sealed their relationship. Within six months, they married in New York in a highly publicized wedding. Elaine spoke of her marriage as "my gift of myself to a Sioux." From that point onward she used her literary talents to support her husband's career. (See the timeline of Elaine Goodale Eastman's life in Figure 8.1B.)

Charles lost his job because he had treated the injuries of the survivors of Wounded Knee, so in 1892, he and his family (now they had one child) settled in St. Paul, Minnesota where he tried to practice medicine but was met with much racism. Charles took a job with the YMCA organizing programs on Indian reservations. He was a strong advocate for Native American causes and worked as a physician to set up YMCA units for Indians across the country but lost this job because he became embroiled with the government's Bureau of Indian Affairs. The family constantly needed money. Charles would give the shirt off his back to whoever needed it, but Elaine had to keep food on the table for the growing family.[6]

Indian Boyhood

With Elaine's encouragement, Charles started to write about his Indian childhood, thus beginning a literary career. Elaine "carefully edited" Charles' stories and sent them to *St. Nicholas Magazine,* a publication that had published her poetry fifteen years earlier. The stories appeared in the magazine in 1893 and 1894 and were later collected into Charles Eastman's first book, *Indian Boyhood,* published in 1902. Charles never forgot his cultural roots and within the next two decades wrote a total of ten books, some for children, some for adults. Elaine edited all of these books and was co-author of two of them *Wigwam Evenings* (1909) and *Smokey Day's Wigwam Evenings* (1910). Charles publicly acknowledged his wife's assistance saying, "We have worked together, she in the little leisure remaining to the mother of six children, and I in the intervals of lecturing and other employment."[7] Additionally, he dedicated *The Soul of the Indian* (1911) to her saying, "in grateful recognition of her ever-inspiring companionship in thought and work and in love of her most Indian-like virtues."

Charles' books made him famous as the leading Indian of the times, a sought-after lecturer. He spent much of his life trying to reconcile the opposing values and beliefs of white society and Sioux culture. He worked as a lobbyist for the restoration of Santee Sioux treaty rights. From 1900 to 1903 he worked as a physician at the Crow Creek Agency in South Dakota. The family moved from Crow Creek to Bald Eagle Lake, Minnesota, and finally settled in Amherst, Massachusetts in 1903 at Elaine's request.

Here Charles continued his literary pursuits, making many public presentations. Elaine took over the management and publicity of his speaking tours. Ever loving the outdoors, Charles became active in the Boy Scout movement and in 1915, he and his wife started a girls' summer camp in southern New Hampshire that was to be in harmony with Native American philosophy. The camp ran until 1924, but was so exhausting to run that it proved to be a real trial to their marriage. In 1923, Charles accepted a three-year appointment as a U.S. Indian Inspector. He was considered one of the foremost-educated Indians at that time. He served as an advisor to the Coolidge administration on Indian policy and was a national spokesman for Indian concerns. From that point until his death in 1939, Eastman lived in Detroit, advising lobbyist groups and telling his stories to interested audiences.[8] Elaine lived her later years with her daughters in Amherst and Northampton, Massachusetts and died in 1953.

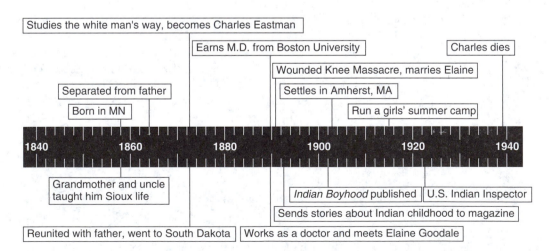

Figure 8.1A   Hakadah's (Charles Eastman's) Life and Times

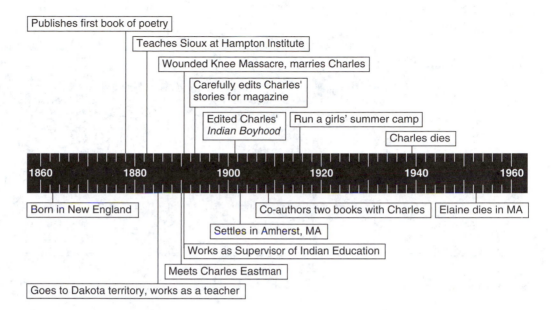

Figure 8.1B   Elaine Goodale Eastman's Life and Times

Their Importance for Educational History

Charles Eastman is recognized as the first Indian writer of real fame among white readers. His classic work, *Indian Boyhood*, describes his traditional Santee Sioux education and the role that his grandmother and uncles played in it, giving us a firsthand account of the Native American method of informal education. Other books written by Charles Eastman include *The Madness of Bald Eagle, Old Indian Days*, and *Indian Child Life*. In each he tries to pass on the Indian culture he grew up in to his own children who grew up in the white man's culture. These books have been translated and reprinted and are read today as classic Indian works. Eastman's life was remarkable because of the transformation he was able to make from one way of life to another.

Elaine Goodale Eastman is also important in educational history in her own right as a writer, a poet, an editor, a teacher, and an activist. She had considerable influence on the U.S. government's policies toward the education of Native American children. She lived at a time when few women spoke out publicly, but she was the voice for Native American rights, and perhaps was listened to more because she was herself of the dominant white culture.[9]

Native American Philosophy of Education

As the Eastmans explain, Indian children were taught how things behave so that they could analyze other similar behavior. The child's relationship with the natural world was fostered by his parents and elders with ever-increasing sophistication; knowledge and understanding came not by intuition but by training.

Education was by imitation and direct application. It provided the child with the essential qualities needed to exist within the tribal social structure. The home provided a forum in which to practice his newly learned skills; relatives provided discipline, morals, manners, and generosity. Religion was the center of all Indian educational undertakings.[10] As Hakadah explains, "Very early the Indian boy assumes the task of preserving and transmitting the legends of his ancestors and his race."

Notes

1. Charles Eastman, *Indian Boyhood* (Garden City, NY: Doubleday, Page & Company, 1910), pp. 4–5.
2. Ibid., p. 85.
3. Ibid., p. 286.
4. David DeJong, *Promises of the Past: A History of Indian Education in the United States* (Golden, CO.: North American Press, 1993), p. 6. URL: http://www.kstrom.net/isk/stories/authors/estman.html.
5. Ruth Ann Alexander, "Elaine Goodale Eastman and the Failure of the Feminist Protestant Ethic," *Great Plains Quarterly*, Spring, 1988. URL: http://www.gp-chautauqua.org/html/alexander_on_eastman.html, p. 3.
6. Ibid., p. 7.
7. Charles Eastman, *From the Deep Woods to Civilization* (Boston: Little, Brown & Co., 1916).
8. URL: http://users.multipro.com/whitedove/encyclopedia/eastman-charles-alexander-ohiyesa-the%20winner-hakadah-pitiful-last-child-1858–1939.html, p. 2.
9. URL: http://www.pbs.org/onlyateacher/elaine.html
10. DeJong, pp. 4–5.

Questions to Guide Your Reading

1. Who were Hakadah's main teachers?
2. What was the main method used in his instruction?
3. Was the content of instruction exclusively life skills?

READING 8.1:
AN INDIAN BOY'S TRAINING

It is commonly supposed that there is no systematic education of the children among the aborigines of this country. Nothing could be farther from the truth. All the customs of this primitive people were held to be divinely instituted, and those in connection with the training of children were scrupulously adhered to and transmitted from one generation to another.

The expectant parents conjointly bent all their efforts to the task of giving the new-comer the best they could gather from a long line of ancestors. A pregnant Indian woman would often choose one of the greatest characters of her family and tribe as a role model for her child. This hero was daily called to mind. She would gather from tradition all of his noted deeds and daring exploits, rehearsing them to herself when alone. In order that the impression might be more distinct, she avoided company. She

isolated herself as much as possible, and wandered in solitude, not thoughtlessly, but with an eye to the impress given by grand and beautiful scenery.

Scarcely was the embryo warrior ushered into the world when he was met by lullabies that speak of wonderful exploits in hunting and war. Those ideas that so fully occupied his mother's mind before his birth are now put into words by all about the child, who is as yet quite unresponsive to their appeals to his honor and ambition. He is called the future defender of his people, whose lives may depend upon his courage and skill. If the child is a girl, she is at once addressed as the future mother of a noble race.

Very early, the Indian boy assumed the task of preserving and transmitting the legends of his ancestors and his race. Almost every evening a myth, or a true story of some deed done in the past was narrated by one of the parents or grandparents while the boy listened with parted lips and glistening eyes. On the following evening, he was required to repeat

Source: From *Indian Boyhood,* by Charles Eastman. New York: McClure, Phillips and Co., 1902.

it. The household became his audience by which he was alternately criticized and applauded. This sort of teaching at once enlightens the boy's mind and stimulates his ambition. His conception of his future careers comes as a vivid and irresistible force. Whatever there is for him to learn must be learned; whatever qualifications are necessary to a truly great man he must seek at any expense of danger and hardship. Such was the feeling of the imaginative and brave young Indian. It became apparent to him early in life that he must accustom himself to rove alone and not to fear or dislike the impression of solitude.

It seems to be a popular idea that all the characteristic skill of the Indian is instinctive and hereditary. This is a mistake. All the stoicism and patience of the Indian are acquired traits, and continual practice alone made him master of the art of woodcraft. Physical training and dieting were not neglected. I remember that I was not allowed to have beef soup or any warm drink. The soup was for the old men. General rules for the young were never too take their food very hot, nor to drink much water.

My uncle, who educated me up to the age of fifteen years, was a strict disciplinarian and a good teacher. When I left the teepee in the morning, he would say. "Hakadah, look closely to everything you see;" and at evening, on my return, he used often to catechize me for an hour or so.

"On which side of the trees is the lighter-colored bark? On which side do they have most irregular branches?"

It was his custom to let me name all the near birds that I had seen during the day. I would name them according to its color or the shape of the bill or their song or the appearance and locality of the nest—in fact, anything about the bird that impressed me as characteristic. I made ridiculous errors, I must admit. He then usually informed me of the correct name. Occasionally I made a hit and this he would warmly commend.

He went much deeper into this science when I was a little older, that is, about the age of eight or nine years. He would say, for instance: "How do you know that there are fish in yonder lake?" "Because they jump out of the water for flies at midday." He would smile at my prompt but superficial reply.

"What do you think of the little pebbles grouped together under the shallow water? And what made the pretty curved marks in the sandy bottom and the little sandbanks? Where do you find the fish-eating birds? Have the inlet and the outlet of a lake anything to do with the question?" He did not expect a correct reply at once to all the voluminous questions that he put to me on these occasions, but he meant to make me observant and a good student of nature.

"Hakadah," he would say to me, "you ought to follow the example of the shunktokocha (wolf). Even when he is surprised and runs for his life, he will pause to take one more look at you before he enters his final retreat. So you must take a second look at everything, you see.

"It is better to view animals unobserved. I have been a witness to their courtships and their quarrels and have learned many of their secrets in this way. I was once the unseen spectator of a thrilling battle between a pair of grizzly bears and three buffaloes—a rash act for the bears, for it was in the moon of the strawberries, when buffaloes sharpen and polish their horns for bloody contests among themselves.

"I advise you, my boy, never to approach a grizzly's den from the front, but to steal up behind and throw your blanket or a stone in front of the hole. He does not usually rush for it, but first puts his head out and listens and then comes out very indifferently and sits on his haunches on the mound in front of the hole before he makes any attack. While he is exposing himself in this fashion, aim at his heart. Always be as cool a the animal himself." Thus he armed me against the cunning of savage beasts by teaching me how to outwit them.

Of this nature were the instructions of my uncle, who was widely known at that time as among the greatest hunters of his tribe. All boys were expected to endure hardship without complaint. In savage warfare, a young man must, of course, be an athlete and used to undergoing all sorts of privations. He must be able to go without food and water for two or three days without displaying any weakness, or to run for a day and a night without any rest. He must be able to traverse a pathless and wild country without losing his way either in the day or nighttime. He cannot refuse to do any of these things if he aspires to be a warrior.

Sometimes my uncle would waken me very early in the morning and challenge me to fast with him all day. I had to accept the challenge. We blackened our faces with charcoal, so that every boy in the village would know that I was fasting for the day.

Then the little tempters would make my life a misery until the merciful sun hid behind the western hills.

When Indians went upon the warpath, it was their custom to try the new warriors thoroughly before coming to an engagement. For instance, when they were near a hostile camp, they would send the novices to go after water and make them do all sorts of things to prove their courage. In accordance with this idea, my uncle used to send me off after water when camped after dark in a strange place. Perhaps the country was full of wild beasts, and, for aught I knew, there might be scouts from hostile bands of Indians in that very neighborhood.

Yet I never objected, for that would show cowardice. I picked my way through the woods, dipped my pail in the water, and hurried back, always careful to make as little noise as a cat. Being only a boy, my heart would leap at every crackling of a dry twig or distant hoot of an owl, until at last, I reached our teepee. Then my uncle would perhaps say: "Ah, Hakadah, you are a thorough warrior, empty out the precious contents of the pail, and order one to go a second time."

Imagine how I felt! But I wished to be a brave man as much as a white boy desires to be a great lawyer or perhaps even President of the United States. Silently I would take the pail and endeavor to retrace my footsteps in the dark.

With all this, our manners and morals were not neglected. I was made to respect the adults and especially the aged. I was not allowed to join in their discussions, nor even to speak in their presence, unless requested to do so. Indian etiquette was very strict, and among the requirements was that of avoiding the direct address. A term of relationship or some title of courtesy was commonly used instead of the personal name by those who wished to show respect. We were taught generosity to the poor and reverence for the "Great Mystery." Religion was the basis of all Indian training.

I recall to the present day some kind of warnings and reproofs that my good grandmother was wont to give me. "Be strong of heart—be patient!" she used to say. She told me of a young chief who was noted for his uncontrollable temper. While in one of his rages he attempted to kill a woman, for which he was slain by his own band and left unburied as a mark of disgrace—his body was simply covered with green grass. If ever I lost my temper, she would say: "Hakadah, control yourself, or you will be like that young man I told you of, and lie under a blanket!"

In the old days, no young man was allowed to use tobacco in any form until he had become an acknowledged warrior and had achieved a record. If a youth should seek a wife before he had reached the age of twenty-two or twenty-three, and been recognized as a brave man, he was sneered at and considered an ill-bred Indian. He must also be a skillful hunter. An Indian cannot be a good husband unless he brings home plenty of game.

Discussion Questions

1. Are there any aspects of Native American educational methods that could work well in today's schools?
2. Motivation is so important for learning. How does Hakadah's uncle motivate him? Could this work in today's schools?
3. Character formation was a part of Native American education. What did Native Americans value? Are these values relevant to today's schools?

For Further Research on the Internet

The National Indian Education Association homepage; a national organization advocating Indian education to support traditional native cultures and values. http://www .niea.org

A site with links to K–12 schools and colleges specializing in Native American education or with Native American educational programs. http://wwww.hanksville.org/naresources/indices/NASchools

A biography of Charles Eastman. **http://www.bigchalk.com/cgibin/WebObjects/ WOPortal.woa/wa/HWCDA/file?fileid=19797&flt=cab**

A biography of Charles Eastman with a bibliography of his writings. **http://www.indigenouspeople.org/natlit/ohiyesa.htm**

Biography of Elaine Goodale Eastman. **http://www.pbs.org/onlyateacher/elaine.html**

Suggestions for Further Reading

Alexander, Ruth Ann. "Elaine Goodale Eastman and the Failure of the Feminist Protestant Ethic." *Great Plains Quarterly* (Spring, 1988).

DeJong, David. *Promises of the Past: A History of Indian Education in the United States.* Golden, CO.: North American Press, 1993.

Eastman, Charles. *From the Deep Woods to Civilization.* Boston: Little, Brown & Co., 1916.

Eastman, Charles. *Indian Boyhood.* Garden City, NY: Doubleday, Page & Company, 1910.

Section 8.2: Benjamin Franklin (1706–1790)

Do you remember taking some "practical and fun" classes in middle school or high school such as computers, woodwork, home economics, or graphic design? We have Benjamin Franklin to thank for proposing that secondary education offer a practical curriculum with vocational importance. Franklin invented many things we take for granted today such as the Franklin stove, bifocal glasses, the harmonica, odometers, and lightning rods. In addition, he proposed many institutions that are now a part of everyday life such as lending libraries, fire companies, hospitals, police forces, insurance companies, and the University of Pennsylvania. All of this was accomplished by a man who had only one year of formal education!

His Life and Family

Benjamin Franklin was born in Boston, Massachusetts on January 17, 1706. His father, Josiah, left England for New England with his wife and three children in 1683.[1] After his first wife, Ann Child, died giving birth to their seventh child, Josiah married Abiah Folger. They had ten children, the eighth of whom was Benjamin. His parents were deeply religious and Ben was baptized on the day of his birth.[2]

Franklin's Education

Franklin outlines his early education in his autobiography: He explains that all of his elder brothers were apprentices in different trades, but his father put him in grammar school when he was eight years of age, intending to devote him to the service of the church. He went to grammar school for less than a year and then entered Mr. George Brownell's school for writing and arithmetic. Ben learned to write well but was unable to learn arithmetic well in this short time. When he was ten years old, his father took him out of school because he could not afford the college education necessary for a minister. He wanted Ben to help him in his business as a tallow chandler and soap boiler, but Ben disliked the trade. Since his father knew how fond he was of reading, he indentured him to his son James to become a printer. Ben was to serve as his apprentice from twelve years to twenty-one years of age. He made great progress in the business and became a useful hand to his brother.[3]

Ben loved to read and did so both before and after work, during lunch and dinner breaks, and on Sundays. He read the classics, studied grammar, logic, mathematics, the sciences, and foreign languages on his own and he became one of the best self-educated men of his time.

Franklin, the Printer

Ben worked for his brother for nine years. When James found out that the articles he had been printing in his newspaper, *The New England Courant,* written under the pseudonym Silence Dogood, were actually written by his younger brother Ben, he refused to print any more of them. Ben then decided to leave his brother and venture out on his own. He went to New York and then Philadelphia to work for Keimer, one of the two printers in the city. Ben saved up his money and was able to open his own printing house at the age of 24. (See the timeline of Franklin's life in Figure 8.2.)

Franklin's Philosophy of Life

The next decade was central for Franklin in the formation of his philosophy of life. He realized that he had made a series of mistakes and needed to change his behavior. Influenced by the Puritans in Boston and the Quakers in Philadelphia, Ben embraced the Protestant work ethic, enthusiastically valuing industry, frugality, prudence, and econ-

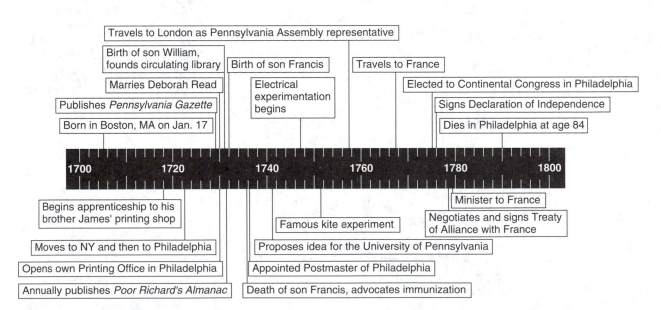

Figure 8.2 Franklin's Life and Times

omy.[4] Franklin "conceived the bold and arduous project of arriving at moral perfection."[5] He drew up his program of the thirteen virtues and proposed a project for personal character development (see Reading 8.2). A consequence of his more responsible attitude was the decision to marry Deborah Read, the daughter of his first Philadelphia landlady. "She proved a good and faithful helpmate, assisted me much by attending the shop; we throve together and ever mutually endeavored to make one another happy."[6] They had three children together, two boys and a girl; one of his sons, William, became governor of New Jersey.

Franklin's Publications

Franklin's printing business prospered from the start because of two successful publications: *The Pennsylvania Gazette,* one of the most successful newspapers in the colonies, and *Poor Richard's Almanac*, published under the pseudonym of Richard Saunders.[7] Franklin used the *Gazette* to propose his civic reform projects to the general public. In this way, his ideas for starting a library, a hospital, a fire company, a police force, and to improve the postal service gained popular support. *Poor Richard's Almanac* was a calendar and weather forecaster, scattered through with wise and witty sayings of Franklin's, for which he has become famous, regarding the best way to live and extolling the virtues of life such as "Early to bed and early to rise, makes a man healthy, wealthy, and wise." Franklin was not a church-attending man, but he believed in God, asserting that the best way to serve God was by doing good to men.[8]

Franklin published *Proposals Relating to the Education of Youth in Pennsylvania* in 1749. Here he outlines his plan for an English grammar school and an Academy in which English instruction would be provided regarding subjects of use in the trades.

Franklin, the Statesman

In 1757, the Pennsylvania legislature sent Franklin to London as a delegate from the colonies; he returned on May 5, 1775, two weeks after the Revolutionary War had begun. Franklin helped draft the Declaration of Independence; he was one of its signers. Then in 1776, when he was 70, Congress asked Franklin to go to France to garner support for the American Revolutionary War effort. Franklin, with his plain knee-length coat and gray hair under a fur cap, was well received in France as "the humble philosopher from the New World, the American Socrates."[9] He succeeded in getting them to sign a Treaty of Alliance. Finally, in 1783, he drafted and co-signed the Treaty of Paris, which ended the Revolutionary War. Returning to Philadelphia in 1785, Franklin helped to draft the Constitution of the United States, mediating many compromises. Franklin died in 1790 at the age of 84, serving his country up until the end.

Franklin's Contributions to Educational Thought

Although he had only one year of formal education himself, Franklin's interest in youth and in establishing educational institutions makes him one of the foremost names in American education. Franklin saw education as centrally important for preparing citizens of the New Republic for their role; he used his business as a printer to publish things to further education in the new country. Franklin saw the mission of his *Autobiography* as helping with the education of the new nation. He proposed a moral ideal and a method for developing virtue to help develop good citizens who would be happy to serve their fellow man. According to Steven Forde, Franklin's autobiography is a deliberate attempt to construct a new, model American.[10]

Franklin's Academy

Perhaps no other man of America's founding period contributed as much to education as Franklin.[11] Franklin's plan for an English grammar school was first sketched in 1743 in his autobiography as "A Proposal for Promoting Useful Knowledge," which he finally published in 1749 as *Proposals Relating to the Education of Youth in Pennsylvania*. In this proposal, Franklin envisioned a secondary school with a complete and practical curriculum in English, instead of the then popular Greek and Latin, to prepare youth for the professions of ministry, law, and medicine. The curriculum would include mathematics, history, physical and natural sciences, philosophy, and English grammar, spelling, speaking, and writing. "Useful studies" to be included consisted of modern foreign languages, penmanship, accounting, drawing, commercial studies, gardening, agriculture, and physical exercise.[12] Franklin's hope was that with this sort of education, "youth would come out of this school ready for learning any business, calling, or profession." The more advanced segment of Franklin's proposal, the College of Philadelphia, prospered and eventually became the University of Pennsylvania.[13]

Franklin's Philosophy of Education

Education must concern itself, Franklin believed, with both knowledge and character. Franklin envisioned his academy as laying the foundation for healthy habits of mind and body and cultivating a spirit of service, which he regarded as "the great aim and end of all learning." Franklin's philosophy assumes that morality can be taught, there is a common good, and virtue can be attained. "Many people," he writes, "lead bad lives but would gladly lead good ones but do not know how to make the change." Franklin suggested a "mechanical" approach to morality, reducing it to a series of ready aphorisms—which leave a strong and lasting impression. He placed his thirteen virtues in a natural order of progression and suggested a daily self-examination. Franklin felt that virtue is present in the life of a person who lives in accordance with the knowledge of how to attain happiness.[14]

Benjamin Franklin helped to begin what would become the "American philosophy of education." Education in the new nation should be American, not European; it should be useful, not classical; and it should meet the needs of a self-governing republic in which every voting citizen participates. As Franklin begins his *Proposal*, "the good Education of Youth has been esteemed by wise Men in all Ages, as the surest Foundation of the Happiness both of private Families and of Commonwealths."

Notes

1. H. W. Brands, *The First American: The Life and Times of Benjamin Franklin* (New York: Doubleday, division of Random House Publishing, 2000), p. 13.
2. James Campbell, *Recovering Benjamin Franklin* (Peru, IL: Open Court Publishing Co., 1999), p. 10.
3. Benjamin Franklin, *Benjamin Franklin: The Autobiography and Selections from His Other Writings*, edited by S. Schiff (New York: The Modern Library Edition, Random House, 2001), pp. 13–14, 17.
4. Nian-Sheng Huang, *Benjamin Franklin in American Thought and Culture 1790–1990* (Philadelphia: American Philosophical Society, 1994), pp. 9–12.
5. Franklin, p. 90.
6. Ibid., p. 77.
7. Brands, p. 121.
8. Huang, p. 57.
9. Franklin, p. 273; Brands, pp. 4, 139.
10. Steven Forde, "Ben Franklin's Autobiography and the Education of America," *American Political Science Review* 86 (2) (1992), p. 366.
11. George L. Rogers, ed. *Benjamin Franklin's The Art of Virtue: His Formula for Successful Living* (Eden Prairie, MN: Acorn Publishing, 1986), p. 10.

12. Brands, p. 196.
13. Campbell, p. 210; Jurgen Herbst, *The Once and Future School: Three Hundred and Fifty Years of American Secondary Education* (New York: Routledge, 1996), p. 20.
14. Forde, p. 366.

Questions to Guide Your Reading

1. Why did Franklin decide to start this program of moral perfection?
2. Which virtue did he find most difficult to live? Why?
3. List the subjects Franklin thinks should be taught in the Academy. Compare these subjects to those Plato proposed in *The Republic*. In what ways are they similar? And how are they different?

READING 8.2:
CHAPTER VIII
FROM *THE AUTOBIOGRAPHY OF BENJAMIN FRANKLIN*

It was about this time I conceiv'd the bold and arduous project of arriving at moral perfection. I wish'd to live without committing any fault at any time; I would conquer all that either natural inclination, custom, or company might lead me into. As I knew, or thought I knew, what was right and wrong, I did not see why I might not always do the one and avoid the other. But I soon found I had undertaken a task of more difficulty than I had imagined. While my care was employ'd in guarding against one fault, I was often surprised by another; habit took the advantage of inattention; inclination was sometimes too strong for reason. I concluded, at length, that the mere speculative conviction that it was in our interest to be completely virtuous, was not sufficient to prevent our slipping; and that the contrary habits must be broken, and good ones acquired and established, before we can have any dependence on a steady, uniform rectitude of conduct. For this purpose I therefore contrived the following method.

In the various enumerations of the moral virtues I had met with in my reading, I found the catalogue more or less numerous, as different writers included more or fewer ideas under the same name.... I propos'd to myself, for the sake of clearness, to use rather more names, with fewer ideas annex'd to each, than a few names with more ideas; and I included under thirteen names of virtues all that at that time occurr'd to me as necessary or desirable, and annexed to each a short precept, which fully express'd the extent I gave to its meaning.

These names of virtues, with their precepts, were

1. TEMPERANCE. Eat not to dullness; drink not to elevation.
2. SILENCE. Speak not but what may benefit others or yourself; avoid trifling conversation.
3. ORDER. Let all your things have their places; let each part of your business have its time.
4. RESOLUTION. Resolve to perform what you ought; perform without fail what you resolve.
5. FRUGALITY. Make no expense but to do good to others or yourself; i.e., waste nothing.
6. INDUSTRY. Lose no time; be always employ'd in something useful; cut off all unnecessary actions.
7. SINCERITY. Use no hurtful deceit; think innocently and justly, and, if you speak, speak accordingly.

Source: Franklin, Benjamin. *Autobiography and Selections from His Other Writings.* 1936 New York: Random House Inc. Modern Library Editions, edited by S. Schiff.

8. JUSTICE. Wrong none by doing injuries, or omitting the benefits that are your duty.
9. MODERATION. Avoid extremes; forbear resenting injuries so much as you think they deserve.
10. CLEANLINESS. Tolerate no uncleanliness in body, clothes, or habitation.
11. TRANQUILLITY. Be not disturbed at trifles, or at accidents common or unavoidable.
12. CHASTITY. Rarely use venery but for health or offspring, never to dullness, weakness, or the injury of your own or another's peace or reputation.
13. HUMILITY. Imitate Jesus and Socrates.

Conceiving then, that, agreeably to the advice of Pythagoras in his Golden Verses, daily examination would be necessary, I contrived the following method for conducting that examination. I made a little book, in which I allotted a page for each of the virtues. I rul'd each page with red ink, so as to have seven columns, one for each day of the week, marking each column with a letter for the day. I cross'd these columns with thirteen red lines, marking the beginning of each line with the first letter of one of the virtues, on which line, and in its proper column, I might mark, by a little black spot, every fault I found upon examination to have been committed respecting that virtue upon that day. I enter'd upon the execution of this plan for self-examination, and continu'd it with occasional intermissions for some time. I was surpris'd to find myself so much fuller of faults than I had imagined; but I had the satisfaction of seeing them diminish... I always carried my little book with me...

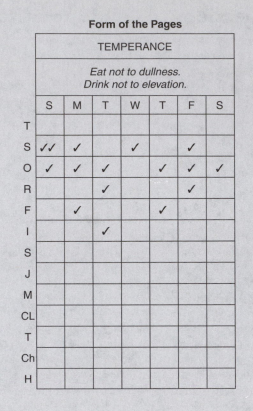

Form of the Pages

TEMPERANCE						
Eat not to dullness. Drink not to elevation.						
S	M	T	W	T	F	S

	S	M	T	W	T	F	S
T							
S	✓✓	✓		✓		✓	
O	✓	✓	✓		✓	✓	✓
R			✓			✓	
F		✓			✓		
I			✓				
S							
J							
M							
CL							
T							
Ch							
H							

PROPOSALS RELATING TO THE EDUCATION OF YOUTH IN PENNSILVANIA-PHILADELPHIA PRINTED IN THE YEAR, MDCCXLIX

Proposals

The good Education of Youth has been esteemed by wise Men in all Ages, as the surest Foundation of the Happiness both of private Families and of Commonwealths. Almost all Governments have therefore made it a principal Object of their Attention, to establish and endow with proper Revenues, such Seminaries of Learning, as might supply the succeeding Age with Men qualified to serve the Public with Honor to themselves, and to their Country.

Many of the first Settlers of these Provinces were Men who had received a good Education in *Europe,* and to their Wisdom and good Management we owe much of our present Prosperity. But their Hands were full, and they could not do all Things. The present Race are not thought to be generally of equal Ability: For though the *American* Youth are allow'd not to want Capacity; yet the best Capacities require Cultivation, it being truly with them, as with the best Ground, which unless well tilled and sowed with profitable Seed, produces only ranker Weeds.

That we may obtain the Advantages arising from an Increase of Knowledge, and prevent as much as may be the mischievous Consequences that would attend a general Ignorance among us, the following Hints are offered towards forming a Plan for the Education of the Youth of *Pennsylvania*, *viz.* It is propos'd,

That some Persons of Leisure and public Spirit apply for a CHARTER, by which they may lie incorporated, with Power to erect an ACADEMY for the Education of Youth, to govern the same, provide Masters, make Rules, receive Donations, Purchase Lands, etc., and to add to their Number, from Time to Time such other Persons as they shall judge suitable.

That the Members of the Corporation make it their Pleasure, and in some Degree their Business, to visit the Academy often, encourage and countenance the Youth, countenance and assist the Masters and by all Means in their Power advance the usefulness and reputation of the Design; that they look on the students and in some sort their Children, treat them with Familiarity and Affection, and, where they have behav'd well, and gone through their Studies, and are to enter the World, zealously unite, and make all the Interest that can be made to establish them, whether in Business, Offices, Marriages, or any other Thing for their Advantage, preferably to all other Persons whatsoever even of equal Merit.

That a House be provided for the ACADEMY if not in the Town, not many Miles from it; the Situation high and dry, and if it may be, not far from a River, having a Garden, Orchard, Meadow, and a Field or two.

That the House be furnished with a Library (if in the Country, if in the Town, the Town Libraries may serve) with Maps of all Countries, Globes, some mathematical Instruments, an Apparatus for Experiments in Natural Philosophy, and for Mechanics; Prints, of all Kinds, Prospects, Buildings, Mechanics, &c.

That the Rector be a Man of good Understanding, good Morals, diligent and patient, learn'd in the Languages and Sciences, and a correct pure Speaker and Writer of the *English* Tongue; to have such Tutors under him as shall be necessary.

That the boarding Scholars diet together, plainly, temperately, and frugally. That, to keep them in Health, and to strengthen and render active their Bodies, they be frequently exercis'd in Running, Leaping, Wrestling, and Swimming, &c.

That they have peculiar Habits to distinguish them from other Youth, if the Academy be in or near the Town, for this, among other Reasons, that their Behaviour may be the better observed.

As to their STUDIES, it would be well if they could be taught *every Thing* that is useful, and *every Thing* that is ornamental: But Art is long, and their Time is short. It is therefore propos'd that they learn those Things that are likely to be *most useful and most ornamental*, Regard being had to the several Professions for which they are intended.

All should be taught to write a *fair hand*, and swift, as that is useful to All. And with it may be learned something of *Drawing*, by Imitation of Prints, and some of the first Principles of Perspective. *Arithmetick*, *Accounts*, and some of the first Principles of *Geometry* and *Astronomy*. The *English* Language might be taught by Grammar; in which some of our best Writers, as *Tillotson, Addison, Pope, Aigernoon Sidney, Cato's Letters, etc.*, should be Classicks: the *Stiles* principally to be cultivated, being the *clear*, and the *concise*. Reading should also be taught, and pronouncing properly, distinctly, emphatically; not with an even Tone, which *under-does*, nor a theatrical, which *over-does* Nature.

To form their Stile they should be put on Writing Letters to each other, making Abstracts of what they read; or writing the same Things in their own Words; telling or writing Stories lately read, in their own Expressions. All to be revis'd and corrected by the Tutor, who should give his Reasons, And explain the Force and Import of Words, &c.

To form their pronunciations, they may be put on making Declamations, repeating Speeches, delivering Orations, &c., the Tutor assisting at the Rehearsals, teaching: advising, correcting their Accent, &c,

But if History be made a constant Part of their Reading, such as the Translations of the *Greek* and *Roman* Historians, and the modern Histories of ancient *Greece* and *Rome*, &c. may not almost all Kinds of useful Knowledge be that way introduc'd to Advantage, and with Pleasure to the Student?

GEOGRAPHY, by reading with Maps, and being required to point out the Places *where* the greatest Action were done, to give their old and new Nations, with the Bounds, Situation, Extent of the Countries concern'd, &c. . . .

MORALITY, by descanting and making continual Observations on the Causes of the Rise or Fall of any Man's Character, Fortune, Power &c. mention'd in History; the Advantages of Temperance, Order, Frugality, Industry, Perseverance &c. Indeed the general natural Tendency of Reading good History must be, to fix in the Minds of Youth deep Impressions of the Beauty and Usefulness of Virtue of all Kinds, Public Spirit, Fortitude, &c. . . .

The Idea of what is true Merit should also be often present to Youth, explain'd and impress'd on their Minds, as consisting in an Inclination join'd with an Ability to serve Mankind, one's Country, Friends and Family; (which Ability is with the blessing of God) to be acquir'd or greatly encreas'd by true Learning and should indeed be the great Aim and End of all Learning.

Discussion Questions

1. If all of Benjamin Franklin's thirteen virtues are mastered, is a person considered completely virtuous? Are there any other virtues that you think are important and necessary?
2. Compare Franklin's idea of virtue to that of Aristotle. Are they similar or different? In what ways?
3. Do you agree that virtues can be acquired in such a systematic manner? Compare Franklin's plan to today's self-improvement plans. Is character development a matter of developing human virtues or is it more involved?
4. Compare the curriculum in Franklin's Academy to that in the comprehensive high school. In what ways are they similar and different?
5. Do you agree with Franklin that only those subjects that are useful for future jobs should be studied in school? Why or why not?

For Further Research on the Internet

The Franklin Institute on-line with an excellent multimedia presentation of Ben's life. **http://sln.fi.edu/franklin/**

A documentary and chronological history of Benjamin Franklin's life with great pictures of Franklin at the different periods of his life. **http://www.english.udel.edu/lemay/franklin**

Suggestions for Further Reading

Brands, H. W. *The First American: The Life and Times of Benjamin Franklin*. New York: Doubleday, division of Random House Publishing, 2000.

Campbell, James. *Recovering Benjamin Franklin*. Peru, IL: Open Court Publishing Co., 1999.

Forde, Steven. "Ben Franklin's Autobiography and the Education of America." *American Political Science Review* 86 (2) (1992): 357–368.

Franklin, Benjamin. *Benjamin Franklin: The Autobiography and Selections from His Other Writings*. Edited by S. Schiff. New York: The Modern Library Edition, Random House, 2001.

Herbst, Jurgen. *The Once and Future School: Three Hundred and Fifty Years of American Secondary Education*. New York: Routledge, 1996.

Huang, Nian-Sheng. *Benjamin Franklin in American Thought and Culture 1790–1990*. Philadelphia: American Philosophical Society, 1994.

Rogers, George L., ed. *Benjamin Franklin's The Art of Virtue: His Formula for Successful Living*. Eden Prairie, MN: Acorn Publishing, 1986.

Section 8.3: Thomas Jefferson (1743–1826)

Did you ever wonder who first proposed that our schools be organized on a statewide basis but with local control by agencies responsible to the public? Who actually started the public school system with its concern for fostering not religion, but democracy? In many ways, Thomas Jefferson was responsible for the origin of these basic features that are now such a part of our educational system today.

Jefferson's Life and Family

Thomas Jefferson was born in Shadwell, Virginia on April 13, 1743. He was the third child, and first son, of Peter Jefferson and Mary Randolph Jefferson. When Mary's father died, the Jefferson family moved to the Randolph estate to care for the family. Tom and his two older sisters were tutored with the Randolph children, learning to read, write, and pray; his father taught him penmanship and mathematics. When Tom was nine, his father sent him to Rev. William Douglas' school, where he studied French, Latin, and Greek for the next five years.

Thomas believed that the most powerful influence on his young life was his father who died in 1757, leaving his wife and eight children with a large estate and a small fortune.[1] Now as the head of the family, Tom attached himself to several older men as he grew up and sought their advice. Later, Tom acted as a father figure to several young men as they were growing up.

Tom's Education

When Tom was fourteen, he went to study at Rev. James Maury's classical academy. For two years, he learned literature, language, prose, and philosophy; reading the classics in Latin and Greek and preparing himself for entry into the College of William and Mary in 1760. Tom at this time was a "youth with . . . shy manners, a precocious mind and earnest habits of reading and writing."[2] One of Tom's teachers was William Small, who introduced him to the Enlightenment philosophers. Jefferson regarded Small as a father and looked to him for help as he struggled to form his character.[3] In college, Tom studied natural philosophy and moral philosophy: logic, ethics, rhetoric, and "bella letres".

After graduating, Tom began legal studies with George Wythe, the first law professor in America, who became a mentor and another father figure in his life. After five years of reading law, Tom became a practicing lawyer in 1767. In seven years he took over 1,000 cases, but the courts closed once the Revolution began in 1774, and Jefferson never returned to law.[4]

Jefferson, the Statesman

His public life began in 1769 when he took a seat in the House of Burgesses in Williamsburg, Virginia and worked on a bill for the separation of the church from state affairs. He also worked on a bill to free the slaves, but it was not passed.

In 1770, a fire at Shadwell destroyed Jefferson's books, notes of law cases, and ledgers so he began to build Monticello, a house to match his classical tastes. On January 1, 1772,

Jefferson married Martha Wayles Skelton. In September of that year, their first child, Patsy, was born. His wife was weak and ill after each of her six childbirths.[5] (See the time-line of Jefferson's life in Figure 8.3.)

Jefferson attended the First and Second Continental Congresses in Philadelphia and was asked by a committee to write the first draft of the Declaration of Independence, which he did from June 11 to June 28. Congress debated and edited the document line by line from July 2 to July 4 and finally, all the members signed it. It embodies the essentials of American philosophy, basing government on the unalienable rights of life, liberty, and the pursuit of happiness.[6]

Jefferson took a seat in the Virginia legislature in 1776 to help write the Virginia State Constitution. This constitution, with three branches of government, became a model for the other states and the Federal republic of the United States. Jefferson, in short, invented the governmental form of the United States of America.[7] He wrote many bills during this time, but he regarded the bill for general education, which was not passed until 1796, one of his key bills.[8]

On June 1, 1779, Jefferson was elected governor of Virginia under a constitution he did not like so he did not seek reelection. On September 6, 1782, his wife Martha died after giving birth to their sixth child. After two years of mourning, Jefferson was reelected to his old seat in the Virginia delegation to Congress. Jefferson was a better legislator than an administrator; he wrote documents to help strengthen the American Confederacy; one was the Ordinance of 1784 that lay the foundation for the gradual and orderly expansion west.[9]

Jefferson went to France in July 1784 as a diplomat, eventually taking Benjamin Franklin's place as the American Ambassador to France. Jefferson was well accepted in France as an author and a statesman and admired because of his interest in art, music, and philosophy. He corresponded with those writing the Constitution and insisted that a Bill of Rights be included with the Constitution to clearly define the limits of the national government and the rights of individual citizens.[10]

President Jefferson

Jefferson returned to the United States in 1789 to become the first Secretary of State under George Washington. When Washington announced that he would not seek a third term, John Adams (a Federalist) received the highest number of votes and Jefferson (a Republican)

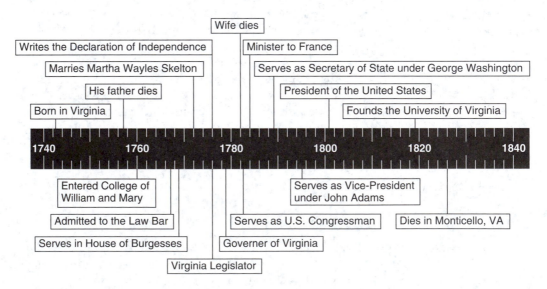

Figure 8.3   Jefferson's Life and Times

the second highest, so Jefferson became the vice-president. The two friends who had written the Declaration of Independence could not see eye-to-eye on many issues affecting the new nation, so they ran against each other for presidency in 1800. Although the Electoral College votes were tied, Jefferson eventually won through the House vote. Jefferson invented "the modern American Presidency" by writing a State of the Union message, writing Congress' agenda, slashing away at federal spending, and writing bills to be approved by Congress.[11] The greatest diplomatic achievement of his career was the acquisition of the vast Louisiana Territory. He did not seek a third term, but supported the candidacy of James Madison.

The University of Virginia

Back at his beloved Monticello, surrounded by his grandchildren, Jefferson drew up plans for what would become the University of Virginia. It took seven years to get the bill passed, but he considered this one of the most important accomplishments of his life.[12] To meet debt obligations that he had inherited, Jefferson sold his 10,000-volume library to the national government and started what is today the Library of Congress.[13] He and John Adams died on July 4, 1826.

Jefferson's Contribution to Education

Jefferson considered his *Bill for the More General Diffusion of Knowledge* as his most important piece of legislation, which he continued to promote even though it failed to pass in the revolutionary era. Jefferson saw the function of education in a democratic society as threefold: (1) to furnish all citizens with the knowledge and training that will enable them to pursue happiness as private persons, (2) to prepare all citizens to exercise their rights of self-government, and (3) to provide the knowledge and training that would enable extraordinarily gifted citizens to use their intellectual and moral powers in leadership.[14] Jefferson, like Plato, proposed the education of students according to their ability. Education was meant to teach a method of analysis to learn about the range of human experiences in order to effectively participate in government.[15]

At a time when there was no public education at all in the South, Jefferson's proposal to recruit an aristocracy of virtue and talent from all classes was truly revolutionary. According to biographer Dumas Malone, Jefferson was "the chief prophet of public education in the first half-century of the Union."[16] Education became Jefferson's most enduring crusade, in his words, "a crusade against ignorance, to establish and improve the law for educating the common people." After his study of Plato, Cicero, Erasmus, Bacon, Locke and Montesquieu, Jefferson echoed their idea that those who govern need a good and appropriate education and that since just government is derived from the consent of the governed, such a government needs citizens who can think and reason.[17]

Fear of a strong centralized government was a large part of Jefferson's Republican philosophy. Jefferson argued that no public educational institution should impose religious beliefs or practices contrary to students' individual beliefs. Therefore, he initiated a movement to remove religious instruction and practice from the public schools. Jefferson was a deeply religious man; however, he wanted the separation of Church and State in schools as stated in the U.S. Constitution. In essence, Jefferson became the first in Western educational history to specify a virtually secular system of public education for a society.[18] He was strongly in favor of moral development, which he saw as an essential responsibility of the schools as well as the parents, who were to use every opportunity to help the young develop virtuous habits. An avid reader, Jefferson wrote about how good books could aid in developing moral reasoning by presenting the reader with real life situations in which the main characters have to make moral choices. He also thought that reading about acts of charity could stimulate a strong desire in the student also to do charitable acts.[19]

Jefferson designed the University of Virginia's physical campus and curricular focus. The campus he designed was an academic village with lawns, the forerunner of many college campuses around the country today. He drew up the plans for the great domed library building. He specified the classical books that were to be part of the learning of each student and included among them the Federalist Papers, Washington's Farewell Address, and his Virginia Resolution of 1799.

Jefferson's Philosophy of Education

Jefferson believed in the equality of men, no matter their race, religion, or habitat. He had a belief in man's inherent goodness and perfectibility and he looked to education to assist in this formation. He had great confidence in the ability of higher education to bring the lower class up to a higher class. As he grew older, Jefferson believed more in education as the only hope to teach not only useful skills but to change attitudes, to improve morality, and to spread civilization. As he said, "Above all things I hope the education of the common people will be attended to, convinced that on their good sense we may rely with the most security for the preservation of a due degree of liberty."

Notes

1. Willard Sterne Randall, *Thomas Jefferson: A Life* (New York: Henry Holt & Company, Inc., 1993), p. 13.
2. Max Lerner, *Thomas Jefferson—America's Philosopher-King* (New Brunswick, NY: Transaction Publishers, Inc., 1996), p. 13.
3. Mark Wenger, "Thomas Jefferson, the College of William and Mary, and the University of Virginia," *The Virginia Magazine of History and Biography* 103 (3) (1995), p. 348.
4. Robert D. Heslep, "Thomas Jefferson & Education," edited by P. Nashm, *Studies in the Western Educational Tradition* (New York: Random House, 1969), pp. 19–20.
5. Randall, p. 59ff.
6. Lerner, p. 20; Randall, p. 274.
7. Randall, p. 306.
8. Heslep, p. 48.
9. Lerner, pp. 22–24.
10. Randall, pp. 367, 488.
11. Ibid., p. 509.
12. Wenger, p. 339.
13. Lerner, p. 115.
14. Heslep, p. 50.
15. Holly Brewer, "Beyond Education: Thomas Jefferson's 'Republican Revision of the Laws Regarding Children,'" in *Thomas Jefferson and the Education of a Citizen*, edited by J. Gilreath (Washington, DC: Library of Congress, 1999), pp. 52–54.
16. Randall, p. 303.
17. Joseph Ketcham, "The Education of Those Who Govern," in *Thomas Jefferson and the Education of a Citizen*, edited by J. Gilreath (Washington, DC: Library of Congress, 1999), p. 294.
18. Heslep, p. 122.
19. Jennings L. Wagoner, "'That Knowledge Most Useful to Us'—Thomas Jefferson's Concept of Utility in the Education of a Republican Citizen," in *Thomas Jefferson and the Education of a Citizen*, edited by J. Gilreath (Washington, DC: Library of Congress, 1999), p. 122.

Questions to Guide Your Reading

1. What does Jefferson say, in the Preamble of his Bill, is the purpose of his proposed legislation?

2. According to Jefferson, who should attend these elementary schools and for how many years?
3. What curriculum does Jefferson think should be taught to all children?
4. How does Jefferson propose to select the boys who will go on to the grammar school?
5. What does Jefferson say about religion in this bill?

READING 8.3:
A BILL FOR THE MORE GENERAL DIFFUSION OF KNOWLEDGE, 1779

SECTION I. Whereas it appeareth that however certain forms of government are better calculated than others to protect individuals in the free exercise of their natural rights, and are at the same time themselves better guarded against degeneracy, yet experience hath shown, that even under the best forms, those entrusted with power have, in time, and by slow operations, perverted it into tyranny; and it is believed that the most effectual means of preventing this would be, to illuminate, as far as practicable, the minds of the people at large, and more especially to give them knowledge of those facts, which history exhibiteth, that, possessed thereby of the experience of other ages and countries, they may be enabled to know ambition under all its shapes, and prompt to exert their natural powers to defeat its purposes; And whereas it is generally true that people will be happiest whose laws are best, and are best administered, and that laws will be wisely formed, and honestly administered, in proportion as those who form and administer them are wise and honest; whence it becomes expedient for promoting the public happiness that those persons, whom nature hath endowed with genius and virtue, should be rendered by liberal education worthy to receive, and able to guard the sacred deposit of the rights and liberties of their fellow citizens, and that they should be called to that charge without regard to wealth, birth or other accidental condition or circumstance; but the indigence of the greater number disabling them from so educating, at their own expense, those of their children whom nature hath fitly formed and disposed to become useful instruments for the public, it is better that such should be sought for and educated at the common expense of all, than that the happiness of all should be confined to the weak or wicked . . .

SECTION IV. The said Aldermen on the first Monday in October, if it be fair, and if not, then on the next fair day, excluding Sunday, shall meet at the court-house of their county, and proceed to divide their said county into hundreds, bounding the same by water courses, mountains or limits, to be run and marked, if they think necessary, by the county surveyor, and at the county expense, regulating the size of the sad hundreds, according to the best of their discretion, so as that they may contain a convenient number of children to make up a school, and be of such convenient size that all the children within each hundred may daily attend the school to be established therein, and distinguishing each hundred lay a particular name; which division, with the names of the several hundreds, shall be returned to the court the county and be entered of record, and shall remain unaltered until the increase or decrease of inhabitants shall render an alteration necessary, if the opinion of any succeeding Alderman, and also in the opinion of the court of the county.

SECTION V. . . . The electors being so assembled shall choose the most convenient place within their hundred for building a school-house. If two or more places, having a greater number of votes than any others, shall yet be equal between themselves, the Aldermen, or such of them as are not of the same hundred, on information thereof shall decide

Source: From *The Writings of Thomas Jefferson*, Lipscomb, Andrew; Bergh, Albert. Washington, D.C., Thomas Jefferson Memorial Assn., 1903–04. Willey Book Company, New York, 1943.

between them. The said Aldermen shall forthwith proceed to have a school-house built at the said place, and shall see that the same shall be kept in repair, and, when necessary, that it be rebuilt . . .

SECTION VI. At every of those schools shall be taught reading, writing, and common arithmetick, and the books which shall be used therein for instructing the children to read shall be such as will at the same time make them acquainted with Grecian, Roman, English, and American history. At these schools all the free children, male and female, resident within the respective hundred, shall be entitled to receive tuition gratis, for the term of three years, and as much longer, at their private expense, as their parents, guardians, or friends shall think proper.

SECTION VIII. Every teacher shall receive a salary of _____ by the year, which, with the expenses of building and repairing the school-houses, shall be provided in such manner as other county expenses are by law directed to be provided and shall also have his diet, lodging, and washing found him, to be levied in like manner, save only that such levy shall be on the inhabitants of each hundred for the board of their own teacher only.

SECTION IX. And in order that grammar schools may be rendered convenient to the youth in every part of the commonwealth, be it therefore enacted, . . . that they shall fix on such place in some one of the counties, in their district as shall be most proper for situating a grammar school-house, endeavoring that the situation be as central as may be to the inhabitants of the said counties, that it be furnished with good water, convenient to plentiful supplies of provision and fuel and more than all things that it be healthy. . . .

SECTION XI. The said overseers shall forthwith proceed to have a house of brick or stone, for the said grammer school, with necessary offices, built on the said lands, which grammer school-house shall contain a room for the school, a hall to dine in, four rooms for a master and usher, and ten or twelve lodging rooms for the scholars.

SECTION XIII. In either of these grammar schools shall be taught the Latin and Greek languages, English Grammer, geography, and the higher part of numerical arithmetick, to wit, vulgar and decimal fractions, and the extrication of the square and cube roots.

SECTION XIV. . . . They shall have power to choose their own Rector, who shall call and preside at future meetings, to employ from time to time a master, and if necessary, an usher, for the said school, to remove them at their will, and to settle the price of tuition to be paid by the scholars. They shall also visit the school twice in every year at the least, either together or separately at their discretion, examine the scholars, and see that any general plan of instruction recommended by the visitors of William and Mary College shall be observed.

SECTION XVI. Every overseer of the hundred schools shall, in the month of September annually, after the most diligent and impartial examination and inquiry, appoint from among the boys which shall have been two years at the least at some one of the schools under his superintendence, and whose parents are too poor to give them farther education, some one of the best and most promising genius and disposition, to proceed to the grammer school of his district; which appointment shall be made in the court-house of the county . . . the said overseer being previously sworn by them to make such appointment, without favor or affection, according to the best of his skill and judgment, and being interrogated by the said Aldermen, either can on their own motion, or on suggestions from the parents, guardians, friends, or teachers of the children, be competitors for such appointment . . .

SECTION XVII. Every boy so appointed shall be authorized to proceed to the grammar school of his district, there to be educated and boarded during such time as is hereafter limited; and his quota of the expenses of the house together with a compensation to the master or usher for his tuition, at the rate of twenty dollars by the year, shall be paid by the Treasurer quarterly on warrant from the Auditors.

SECTION XVIII. A visitation shall be held, for the purpose of probation, annually at the said grammer school on the last Monday in September, if fair, and if not, then on the next fair day, excluding Sunday, at which one third of the boys sent thither by appointment of the said overseers, and who shall have been there one year only, shall be discontinued as public foundationers, being those who, on the most diligent examination and enquiry, shall be thought to be the least promising genius and disposition, and of those who shall have been there two years, all shall be discontinued save one only the best in genius and disposition, who shall be at liberty to continue there four years longer on the public foundation, and shall thence forward be deemed a senior.

SECTION XIX. The visitors for the districts … in every other year, to wit, at the probation meetings held in the years distinguished in the Christian computation by odd numbers, and the visitor for all the other districts at their said meetings to be held in those years distinguished by even numbers, after diligent examination and enquiry as before directed shall chose one among the said seniors, of the best learning and most hopeful genius and disposition, who shall be authorized by them to proceed to William and Mary College; there to be educated, boarded, and clothed, three years; the expense of which annually shall be paid by the Treasurer on warrant from the Auditors.

Discussion Questions

1. Jefferson in his "Bill for the More General Diffusion of Knowledge," tried to have equal educational opportunity for all at the primary level of education. Why do you think the bill was defeated three times before it was finally passed years later?
2. Jefferson proposed that those more capable of leadership go on to higher education. Similar to Plato's system in *The Republic,* everyone is educated for the job they will have. Do you agree with this system?
3. Compare Jefferson's arguments for the separation of Church and State with current issues such as prayer in public schools, vouchers for private schools and teaching about evolution versus creation. What do you think Jefferson would say about these current issues?

For Further Research on the Internet

An excellent digital archive of Jefferson's life and works. **http://etext.lib.virginia.edu/jefferson/**

An excellent exhibit of Thomas Jefferson maintained by the Library of Congress. **http://www.lcweb.loc.gov/exhibits/jefferson**

The website for Jefferson's home Monticello, a national museum. **http://www.monticello.org/**

Suggestions for Further Reading

Gilreath, J., editor. *Thomas Jefferson and the Education of a Citizen.* Washington, DC: Library of Congress, 1999.

Lerner, Max. *Thomas Jefferson—America's Philosopher-King.* New Brunswick, NY: Transaction Publishers, Inc., 1996.

Nasham, P., editor. *Thomas Jefferson & Education: Studies in the Western Educational Tradition.* New York: Random House, 1969.

Randall, Willard Sterne. *Thomas Jefferson: A Life.* New York: Henry Holt & Company, Inc., 1993.

Wenger, Mark. "Thomas Jefferson, the College of William and Mary, and the University of Virginia," *The Virginia Magazine of History and Biography* 103 (3) (1995) : 339–364.

Section 8.4: Noah Webster (1758–1843)

Have you noticed how people in one section of our country use one word for something and people in another use a different word? Perhaps they pronounce words with a slightly different accent. Nevertheless, the majority of the time we use the same words, expressions, and pronunciations. We can easily watch news or movies made in New York or California and understand one another perfectly. This may not have been the case if Noah Webster had not worked so diligently all his life to create the "American Language" now found in the dictionary that bears his name.

Webster's Life and Times

Noah Webster was born on October 16, 1758, in West Hartford, Connecticut, the fourth of five children of Noah, Sr. and Mercy Steele.[1] He was born into a colonial world at war but had a typical childhood doing chores and watching his siblings.

His Education

Before he went to school, his well-educated mother taught him the alphabet, the Lord's Prayer and Decalogue, and his numbers. Noah went to the town school and, with his parents' encouragement, became a skilled reader, strong writer, and gifted flutist. His father decided that Noah should go to college and put him under the tutelage of Rev. Nathan Perkins, a graduate of Yale College. Noah completed his pre-collegiate studies in two years, working half the time to help his father with the farm.[2]

Admitted to Yale at sixteen years of age in 1774, Noah joined the class of forty students that became one of Yale's most distinguished classes. Webster read Locke and rejected the Puritan concept of original sin, preferring the Lockean idea of a kind teacher working with the "tabula rasa." Webster developed his life convictions at Yale and concluded that universal public education was essential to the preservation of liberty in a self-governing politic, and extended this concept to include women. Although the school session was interrupted several times due to the war, Noah stayed at Yale and graduated in July of 1778.[3]

Noah, the Teacher

Because of finances, Webster decided to teach at the common school while studying law. He enjoyed teaching, but was frustrated with the low pay, poor facilities, and lack of textbooks.[4] In 1781 there was little work for lawyers, so Webster opened his own academy in Sharon, Connecticut and it became an immediate success. Webster began to write down his theories on education and presented his thesis on the general diffusion of knowledge to Yale University, earning his Master's degree. Noah wanted to create a complete system of universal public education that would give all classes of Americans the intellectual skills they needed to govern themselves as well as the practical skills they needed to sustain themselves and their families. When the war ended, Noah went to Goshen to reopen Farmer Hall Academy and his school was filled to capacity due to the fame of his excellent school in Sharon.[4]

Webster's American Speller

There were few textbooks available and English authors wrote those that existed. So Noah wrote a new spelling book that included wartime writings of American patriots. Having experienced the different languages of the patriots, he became convinced that only a uniform method of speaking a common language would ensure the new American nation's unity and peaceful self-government. "Only four years out of college and a mere 24 years of age, Noah Webster believed he could unite the American people by creating a new, common language."[5]

Webster's American speller became a key component of American cultural history. Webster included American cities, names, words, and examples instead of the English ones in his speller. He also grouped words according to pronunciation instead of spelling and taught teachers how to teach reading and spelling. In addition, he included in the book the secular teaching of morality as an end in itself, not as related to a particular religion. In 1782, none of the American states had a copyright law.[6] Wanting to protect his work, he began to speak out about the necessity of forming a new, stronger central government; he is now considered the father of the American copyright law. The year the speller was published was the year the Revolutionary War ended, which was no accident; the speller was an educational Declaration of Independence.[7]

Webster then worked on grammar, which would also be different from the English grammar in use. He based the rules of American English on the rules of Latin. Webster helped to establish a system of education appropriate for the new American republic with his grammar book.[8] He also wrote a reader that included short stories, history of the Revolutionary War, and American geography to teach moral principles along with patriotic themes.[9]

Webster married Rebecca Greenleaf on October 19, 1789. He then set up a law practice in Hartford, Connecticut and became involved in the community as a councilman

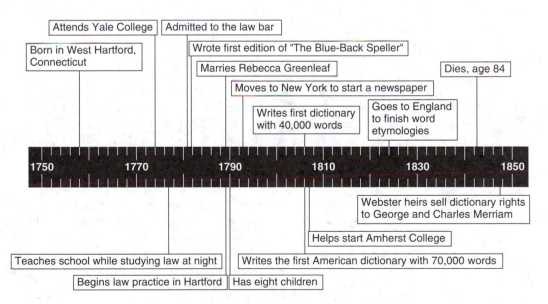

Figure 8.4   Webster's Life and Times

while assisting his aging father and relatives.[10] In 1793, Webster quit his law practice and moved, with his wife and two young daughters, to New York, where he started a pro-American newspaper, which eventually became the greatest circulating paper in New York.[11] (See the timeline of Webster's life in Figure 8.4.)

The family moved to New Haven, Connecticut and had three more children. Webster's speller sold more than 1.5 million copies, but as the fourteen-year copyright was ending, he wrote a vastly improved new edition that included stories about his children. He also wrote four new textbooks on history and geography and produced a small dictionary to go with the speller.

The Webster Dictionary

Published in 1806, Webster's first dictionary had 40,000 words, with 5,000 new American words and sold for $1.50. "To the surprise of his critics, it was the most innovative and comprehensive dictionary ever produced up to that time."[12] Soon after, Webster sold his home and moved to Amherst, Massachusetts where he helped found Amherst College.

Becoming enraptured with etymology, orthography, and lexicography, Webster envisioned the largest and most complete dictionary of the English language ever compiled. He began what was to become a twenty-year project. He went to England in 1824 to consult books that would allow him to finish some of the etymologies he needed. In 1825, he finally finished his dictionary and held the first published copy of the book in his hands a few weeks after his 70th birthday.[13]

Webster heard unconditional praise from across the country for his literary work. In 1830 in Washington, D.C. he was received as the "Father of the American Language." Webster was finally able to get a federal copyright law passed and his dictionary was the first to apply for a copyright to be honored in all the states.

Webster wrote a new spelling book, two more school dictionaries, and then began to transcribe the Bible into American English. He died on May 28, 1843, at the age of 84. "I am ready to go, my work is done," he told his daughter before he passed.[14] In 1847, the Webster heirs sold exclusive rights to the dictionary to George and Charles Merriam, who are still the official publishers of the Webster Dictionary.

Noah Webster's Importance for Educational Thought

Although well known for his dictionary, it was Webster's speller that impacted the spread of literacy and grants Webster an eminent place in the history of education. According to Webster biographer Harlow Unger, "It not only changed the course of education in the United States, it eventually changed the English language as no other book had or ever would. It gained a virtual monopoly in American classrooms for over a century. It created a new language for a new nation and ensured that all Americans would speak alike. Webster's speller was a declaration of American cultural independence conceived to unite the Americans in peace just as the Declaration of Independence had united them in war."[15]

Noah's reader was also a significant pioneering work in the history of American education and of school texts; it was the first literary anthology for children ever published and the first anthology of its kind to contain significant amounts and varieties of literature by American authors.[16] Although the McGuffey Readers displaced Webster's reader in American classrooms in 1836, they nevertheless reaffirmed the importance of continued use of his speller, as McGuffey spelled words in his readers according to Webster's preferred spellings.

Webster's Philosophy of Education

In the fourteen essays Webster wrote for the *The American Magazine,* we see his philosophy of education emerge from his main ideas. Webster, along with Washington, Jefferson, Madison, and Rush, favored a provision in the Constitution for universal public education. Colleges and academies should not be only for the sons of the rich, he said, but for the good of the republic there should be schools for all, including girls. A former teacher himself, he knew our country depended upon good teachers that knew how to teach well. He believed in the importance of a curriculum that taught a common language that would unite all Americans. Webster's articles on education were reprinted for decades and his ideas influenced Horace Mann and others in their quest for the common school.[17]

Notes

1. From his father he was a direct descendant of John Webster, governor of Connecticut from 1656 to 1657, and his mother was a great granddaughter of William Bradford, governor of Plymouth Colony from 1621 to 1651; D. Micklethwait, *Noah Webster and the American Dictionary* (Jefferson, NC: McFarland & Company, Inc., 2000), p. 12.
2. H. G. Unger, *Noah Webster: The Life and Times of an American Patriot* (New York: John Wiley & Sons, Inc., 1998), pp. 8–12.
3. K. A. Snyder, *Defining Noah Webster: Mind and Morals in the Early Republic* (Lanham, MD: University Press of America, 1990), p. 32.
4. Micklethwait, pp. 19–22.
5. Unger, p. 45.
6. Micklethwait, p. 54.
7. Ibid., p. 10.
8. Unger, p. 71.
9. Snyder, pp. 74–77.
10. Micklethwait, p. 127.
11. Snyder, pp. 151–155, 173; Unger, p. 209.
12. Unger, p. 251.
13. Snyder, p. 294.
14. Unger, p. 326.
15. Ibid., p. 54.
16. Ibid., p. 80.
17. Ibid., pp. 142–43.

Questions to Guide Your Reading

1. Why does Webster think it is important to have an American dictionary of the English language?
2. What are some of the important functions of language?
3. What are some of the benefits Webster hopes this dictionary will give to his fellow citizens?

READING 8.4:
"THE CHIEF GLORY TO THE NATION . . ."

In the year 1783, just at the close of the revolution, I published an elementary book for facilitating the acquisition of our vernacular tongue and for correcting a vicious pronunciation which prevailed extensively among the common people of this country. Soon after the publication of that work, I believe in the following year, that learned and respectable scholar the Rev. Dr. Goodrich of Durham, one of the trustees of Yale College, suggested to me the propriety and expediency of my compiling a dictionary which should complete a system for the instruction of the citizens of this country in the language. At that time I could not indulge the thought, much less the hope, of undertaking such a work, as I was neither qualified by research, nor had I the means of support during the execution of the work, had I been disposed to undertake it. For many years, therefore, though I considered such a work as very desirable, yet it appeared to me impracticable, as I was under the necessity devoting my time to other occupations for obtaining subsistence.

About twenty-seven years ago, I began to think of attempting the compilation of a dictionary. I was induced to this undertaking not more by the suggestion of friends than by my own experience of the want of such a work while reading modern books of science. In this pursuit I found almost insuperable difficulties from the want of a dictionary for explaining many new words, which recent discoveries in the physical sciences had introduced into use. To remedy this defect in part, I published my *Compendious Dictionary* in 1806, and soon after made preparations for undertaking a larger work.

My original design did not extend to an investigation of the origin and progress of language, much less of other languages. I limited my views to the correcting of certain errors in the best English dictionaries, and to the supplying of words in which they are deficient. But after writing through two

Source: Noah Webster Reading from *On Being American: Selected Writings 1783–1828*, edited and with an introduction by Homer Babbidge Jr. Frederick A. Praeger Publications. 1967. Used with permission.

letters of the alphabet, I determined to change my plan... Then, laying aside my manuscripts and all books treating of language except lexicons and dictionaries, I endeavored, by a diligent comparison of words having the same or cognate radical letters in about twenty languages, to obtain a more correct knowledge of the primary sense of original words, of the affinities between the English and many other languages, and thus to enable myself to trace words to their source . . .

I spent ten years in this comparison of radical words and in forming a synopsis of the principal words in twenty languages, arranged in classes under their primary elements or letters. The result has been to open what are to me new views of language and to unfold what appear to be the genuine principles on which these languages are constructed.

After completing this synopsis, I proceeded to correct what I had written of the dictionary and to complete the remaining part of the work. But before I had finished it, I determined on a voyage to Europe, with the view of obtaining some books and some assistance which I wanted, of learning the real state of the pronunciation of our language in England as well as the general state of philology in that country, and of attempting to bring about some agreement of coincidence of opinions in regard to unsettled points in pronunciation and grammatical construction. In some of these objects I failed; in others my designs were answered.

It is not only important, but in a degree necessary, that the people of this country should have an *American Dictionary* of the English language; for, although the body of the language is the same as in England and it is desirable to perpetuate that sameness, yet some differences must exist. Language is the expression of ideas, and if the people of one country cannot preserve an identity of ideas, they cannot retain an identity of language. Now an identity of ideas depends materially upon a sameness of things or objects with which the people of the two countries are conversant. But in no two portions of the earth remote from each other can such identity be found. Even physical objects must be different. But the principal differences between the people of this country and of all others arise from different forms of government, different laws, institutions, and customs. Thus the practice of hawking and hunting, the institution of heraldry, and the feudal system of England originated terms which formed, and some of which now form, a necessary part of the language of that country; but in the United States many of these terms are no part of our present language—and they cannot be, for those things which they express do not exist in this country ... On the other hand, the institutions in this country which are new and peculiar give rise to new terms or to new applications of old terms unknown to the people of England, which cannot be explained by them and which will not be inserted in their dictionaries unless copied from ours ... No person in this country will be satisfied with the English definitions of the words *congress, senate,* and *assembly, court,* &c., for although these are words used in England, yet they are applied in this country to express ideas which they do not express in that country ...

But this is not all. In many cases the nature of our government and of our civil institutions requires an appropriate language in the definition of words, even when the words express the same thing as in England. Thus the English dictionaries inform us that a *Justice* is one deputed by the King to do right by way of judgment—he is a *Lord* by his office, Justices of the Peace are appointed by the *King's commission—language* which is inaccurate in respect to this officer in the United States. So, *constitutionally* is defined by Todd or Chalmers *legally,* but in this country the distinction between *constitution* and law requires a different definition. In the United States a *plantation is* a very different thing from what it is in England. The word *marshal* in this country has one important application unknown in England or in Europe.

A great number of words in our language require to be defined in a phraseology accommodated to the condition and institutions of the people in these states and the people of England must look to an American dictionary for a correct understating of such terms.

The necessity, therefore, of a dictionary suited to the people of the United States is obvious; and I should suppose that, this fact being admitted, there could be no difference of opinion as to the *time* when such a work ought to be substituted for English dictionaries ...

A life devoted to reading, and to an investigation of the origin and principles of our vernacular language and especially a particular examination of the best English writers with a view to a comparison of their style and phraseology with those of the best American writers and with our colloquial usage, enables me to affirm with confidence that the genuine English idiom is as well preserved by the unmixed English of this country as it is by the best *English* writers. Examples to prove this fact will be found in the introduction to this work. It is true that many of our writers have neglected to cultivate taste and the embellishments of style, but even these have written the language in its genuine *idiom.* In this respect Franklin and Washington, whose language is their hereditary mother tongue unsophisticated by modern grammar, present as pure models of genuine English as Addison or Swift. But I may go farther and affirm with truth that our country has produced some of the best models of composition ...

The United States commenced their existence under circumstances wholly novel and unexampled in the history of nations. They commenced with civilization, with learning, with science, with constitutions of free government, and with that best gift of God to man, the Christian religion. Their population is now equal to that of England; in arts and sciences our citizens are very little behind the most enlightened people on earth—in some respects they have no superiors—and our language, within two centuries, will be spoken by more people in this country than any other language on earth except the Chinese in Asia, and even that may not be an exception.

It has been my aim in this work, now offered to my fellow citizens, to ascertain the true principles of the language in its orthography and structure, to purify it from some palpable errors, and reduce the number of its anomalies, thus giving it more regularity and consistency in its forms, both of words and sentences, and in this manner to furnish a standard of our vernacular tongue which we shall not be ashamed to bequeath to *three hundred millions of people* who are destined to occupy and, I hope, to adorn the vast territory within our jurisdiction ...

This dictionary, like all others of the kind, must be left in some degree imperfect; for what individual is competent to trace to their source and define in all their various applications—popular, scientific, and technical—sixty or *seventy thousand* words! It satisfies my mind that I have done all that my health, my talents, and my pecuniary means would enable me to accomplish. I present it to my fellow citizens, not with frigid indifference, but with my ardent wishes for their improvement and their happiness and for the continued increase of the wealth, the learning, the moral and religious elevation of character, and the glory of my country.

To that great and benevolent Being who during the preparations of this work has sustained a feeble constitution amidst obstacles and toils, disappointments, infirmities, and depression, who has twice borne me and my manuscripts in safety across the Atlantic and given me strength and resolution to bring the work to a close, I would present the tribute of my most grateful acknowledgments. And if the talent which he entrusted to my care has not been put to the most profitable use in his service, I hope it has not been "kept laid up in a napkin" and that any misapplication of it may be graciously forgiven.

Discussion Questions

1. What do you think Noah Webster would say about the current emphasis on bilingual education in our schools? Do you think he would favor giving instruction in the child's native tongue or emphasizing English as a Second Language programs? Support your response.
2. Given the cultural diversity of our country, how can public schools prepare students to read and speak English well while still valuing their unique cultural backgrounds that may include different native languages?
3. If the Native Americans had a common language would this have allowed them to avoid European domination?
4. What values would Webster want the schools to foster in order to help students become good citizens and members of a truly democratic society?

For Further Research on the Internet

A site about Webster and the dictionary company that has continued his work.
http://www.m-w.com/about/noah.htm

A virtual tour of Webster's house and the museum now in his home.
http://www.ctstateu.edu/noahweb/index.html

Suggestions for Further Reading

Micklethwait, D. *Noah Webster and the American Dictionary.* Jefferson, NC: McFarland & Company, Inc., 2000.

Snyder, K. A. *Defining Noah Webster: Mind and Morals in the Early Republic.* Lanham, MD: University Press of America, 1990.

Unger, H. G. *Noah Webster: The Life and Times of an American Patriot.* New York: John Wiley & Sons, Inc., 1998.

CHAPTER ACTIVITIES

Linking the Past to the Present

Get the latest edition of the Webster's Dictionary. What are some of the new words included in this edition? How are these words a reflection of our changing society?

Developing Your Philosophy of Education

In your philosophy of education write about what you think the goal or purpose of education is in relationship to the family and the country. Do you think the goal is to teach students to get a good job so they can support their family? To carry on one's family traditions and name? To be good citizens?

Connecting Theory to Practice

Get the yearly report card for your clinical school that summarizes its state scores and school demographics. How many of the students are from a lower socioeconomic status (SES) family? Interview the principal to see what extra services are provided to those of lower SES. Do you think financial aid in schools should be based solely on need or should academic merit also be considered?

Figure 8.1   Worksheet Relating Franklin's 13 Virtues to Today's World

Read the situation given. Using Benjamin Franklin's list of virtues, write down the name of the virtue that is being described, using each virtue only once. Afterwards, try writing your own virtue cases.

1. _____ Faith is humble and considers all people equal to her.
2. _____ Even though Misty loves cookies, she only ate two because she is watching her diet.
3. _____ Mike takes great care of his teeth.
4. _____ Sheila and Rob will wait until marriage before having sex.
5. _____ Freida was hurt by her brother's remark but she soon forgave him.
6. _____ Phillip knows not to work too hard or to play too hard; he has a good balance.
7. _____ Even though Brenda deserved to have her good vase broken, Jackie held her tongue.
8. _____ Mr. Proctor is a very organized teacher.
9. _____ Whenever Nathaniel says he'll be at practice, he is always there.
10. _____ Milton has an impressive savings account balance.
11. _____ Tito keeps busy 24 hours a day with his art projects.
12. _____ Zelda told her friends she would wait for them to come before she played the game.
13. _____ Renata tries to keep her thoughts free of hurtful ideas.

Educators' Philosophies and Contributions to Education

TABLE 8.1 Philosophy and Contributions of Early American Educators

Educator	Role of Teacher & Learner	View of Curriculum & Methodology	Purpose or Goal of Education	Major Contribution
Hakadah	Parents and extended family informally teach children to learn from nature	Life skills and values learned by imitation and training	Reservation schools wanted Native Americans to assimilate, to adopt the Anglo culture	First Indian writer; tried to preserve Sioux values and beliefs by writing them down
Franklin	Education of knowledge and character cultivating a spirit of service; goal to teach morality and virtues	Useful studies in English along with mathematics, history, sciences, philosophy, and English grammar and penmanship	Education is important for preparing citizens for their role in the republic	First to propose an American philosophy of education; useful vocational studies in the English language
Jefferson	Believed in the equality of men and wanted all (male) students to be educated according to their ability	Use good books to promote moral reasoning using real life situations; teach a method of analysis	Educate the common people in order to prepare citizens to exercise self-government	First to propose a secular system of public education with the separation of church and state
Webster	Good teachers that know how to teach well; universal public education for all including girls; for a uniform way of speaking would ensure unity	A curriculum that taught a common language; taught reading, grammar, spelling; reader was first American literary anthology	Education in a common language for the good of the Republic	First to promote an American language through publication of his speller and dictionary

CHAPTER 9

Developing an American Educational System

Education in the New Nation

The Declaration of Independence was signed on July 4, 1776 and officially began the American Revolutionary War that ran until 1781. Fear of a strong centralized government was central to the new nation's philosophy; therefore, the Articles of Confederation reserved to each state its sovereignty, freedom, and independence and established a form of government in which Americans were citizens of their own states first and of the United States second.[1] As George Washington, Thomas Jefferson, Benjamin Rush, Noah Webster, and others soon saw, these articles did not permit any kind of legislation for all of the states, and impeded their economic development. A constitutional convention was called in 1787 and the Constitution of the United States resulted. How much power was to be reserved to the states and how much power was to be given to the central government was of continuous debate throughout the convention. Although Washington, Jefferson, Madison, and Monroe were in favor of a Federal system overseeing education, this was not written into the Constitution as one of the powers of the new government; according to the Tenth Amendment, it was a responsibility of the state. (The Tenth Amendment states that "any powers not specifically delegated to the federal government or prohibited to the state by the Constitution are 'reserved' to the power of the states.") Everyone agreed about the importance of education but some wanted it to continue as private and sectarian schools, as begun in the colonies, and others were in favor of the state governments now starting public, tax-supported schools.

Education as a State Responsibility

As each state wrote its constitution, it addressed the importance of education for the state, and set up a system for local school districts that eventually included a school in each town. Invoking the Preamble to the Constitution that states that its purpose is to "promote the general welfare," Congress felt that they had the power to enact federal legislation regarding education, as this was for the general welfare. As new areas of the country petitioned to become new states of the United States, the Northwest Land Ordinances of 1785 and 1787 were passed. The Land Ordinance of 1785 specified that "the sixteenth section of each thirty-six square mile township be set aside for the funding of public schools" in the new territories to the north and west of the Ohio River. This was the first Federal education legislation enacted by the new country and was the first use of land grants to finance education. See Map 9.1 regarding the American Expansion.

The Northwest Ordinance of 1787 had three historic guarantees: (1) it provided that the new states would eventually enter the union on an equal footing with the original states; (2) it promised that "Religion, morality, and knowledge, being necessary to good government and the happiness of mankind, schools and the means of education shall forever be encouraged"; and (3) it permitted neither slavery nor involuntary servitude in the said territory.[2]

Importance of Schools for the National Welfare

George Washington, in his Farewell Address of 1796, cited the importance of schools for the national welfare. Noah Webster was convinced that what would really unite the states was a common American, not English, language and so he wrote his *Elementary Spelling Book* that replaced the *New England Primer* in all the schools. In this "Blue-Back Speller" as it was called, he stressed moral virtue, middle class values, and the value of hard work.

The importance of education for the new country was agreed upon by all, but the question remained: Should education be public and tax-supported or private and sectarian? In colonial America, as we have seen, education had historically been considered an individual or private matter, a concern of family or church, a local affair.[3] Those of like class, religion, ethnicity, or gender went to the same school. Many church-related institutions continued to offer charity education as they had in the colonial times until the government began to support a system of education.

Two systems found in England were tried in the new country in order to instill "proper morals" in the youth: the Sunday schools and the monitorial schools. The Sunday schools provided poor children who worked during the week with rudimentary reading and writing instruction on Sundays, along with instruction on the Bible, sin, and salvation. Monitorial schools, started in England by Joseph Lancaster and Andrew Bell, instructed hundreds of children using one teacher. The first monitorial school in America started in New York City in 1806. In this school, one teacher instructed monitors or student teachers that then taught the lessons they learned to small groups of students. The "factory-manner" of these schools led to their demise by 1830, as they left much to be desired in their excessive uniformity and poor discipline.[4]

The Common School

Horace Mann was the most influential and important advocate of the common school. Mann, "The Father of American Education," promoted the notion of a common school, open to the rich and poor, girls and boys, and eventually children of different races and nationalities. Through his influence, the "common school movement" grew immensely from 1820 to 1850, gaining popular support for publicly financed elementary schools that would have a common basic curriculum of reading, writing, and arithmetic. A common consensus was formed that tax support for education was an investment in prosperity. Citizens needed to be prepared well in civic education, so school became a birthright of

Map 9.1   American Expansion

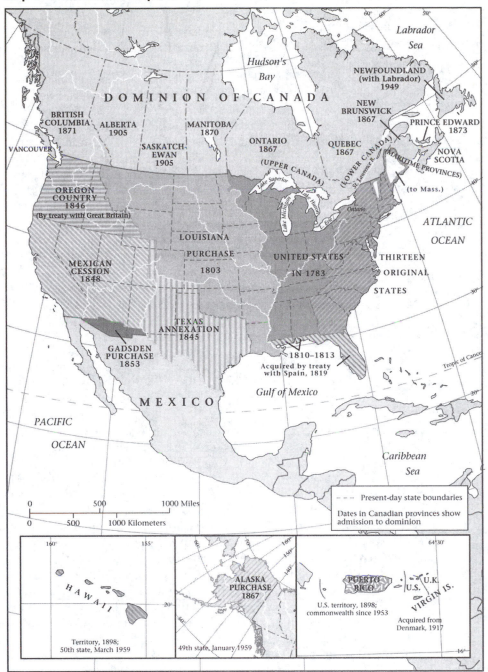

Source: From Anthony Esler, *The Human Venture, Combined Volume: From Prehistory to the Present*, 5th edition, 2004. Reprinted by permission of Pearson Education.

each citizen. The creation of the common school with its grassroots governance and common curriculum was one of the triumphs of the nineteenth century.

From the beginning, education in America served a political function, serving to acculturate all into the dominant culture of the country. The public schools would be purely secular, but with a common set of values based on a core of Christian beliefs that could be taught to all. A nonsectarian reading of the Bible would be a part of every school. (*Note:* These were the white, Anglo-Saxon, Protestant values that we will see in the next chapter were not shared by all and were protested against by several groups, especially the Catholics.)[5] Finally, teachers needed to be prepared to teach in these schools so Horace Mann also promoted Normal Schools.

In 1819, the Office of Indian Affairs was established and the "Civilization Fund Act" was passed for the purpose of introducing the Indian tribes to "the habits and arts of civilization" by "employing capable persons of good moral character to instruct them in the mode of agriculture suited to their situation for teaching their children in reading, writing and arithmetic." Government grants supported various kinds of schools for the Native Americans but the majority of them were vocational training schools that sought to mainstream the Native Americans into the dominant social, political, and economic life. As we saw in the past chapter, these schools did little to meet the cultural needs of education for the Native Americans, as they did not respect their values and character.[6]

The One-Room School

The One-Room School became the most predominant type of common school in the new nation. Modeled after the Town School of the New England colonies, it typically had a cast iron stove, a coat closet, several long benches (desks were not introduced until much later), a raised desk for the teacher, and a slate board in the front of the room. The students learned the basics of reading, writing, arithmetic, spelling, geography, and history with moral development stressing the virtues of punctuality, honesty, and hard work. In the rural areas, students of all ages would travel many miles to attend school for a few months each year—after planting season and before harvesting season. This one-room schoolhouse was often painted red, so for many the term is synonymous with the "little red schoolhouse." Although in the city the one-room schoolhouse began to give way to graded classrooms as early as 1840, the rural one-room schoolhouse was still in use until the 1970s. As it was built in each town using the taxpayers' monies, the school building was also used as a cultural center for the community. Not only did the citizens attend the students' spelling bees, patriotic celebrations, and graduations but they also used the building for school board meetings, civic meetings, and for speakers passing through town. The teachers were typically men until the 1830s, when female teachers began to replace men in some of the eastern states. Due to the work of Emma Willard and Catharine Beecher, public opinion changed and teaching began to be accepted as a woman's profession for both economic and pedagogical reasons. Between 1840 and 1880, the number of male teachers actually declined as the percentage of females in the teaching force bolted to 77.8 percent, and in cities women constituted 90 percent of the teaching force.[7] Many women teachers enjoyed the autonomy of teaching in the one-room schoolhouse and lamented the loss of authority that the transition to the graded school involved.[8]

One of Horace Mann's goals was to standardize the curriculum in the common schools. Noah Webster's speller and reader were used for over fifty years as common textbooks. Then, in 1836, William Holmes McGuffey (1800–1873) wrote a series of readers that were graded kindergarten to sixth grade. McGuffey, a Presbyterian minister, stressed the basic moral outlook of white, Anglo-Saxon, Protestant America. These readers featured wholesome American stories that stressed good character traits and patriotism but stayed clear of sectarian matter. It is estimated that over 120 million copies of McGuffey's readers were sold between 1836 and 1920.[9] In the next chapter we will see how the Irish and Italian immigrants later protested against the anti-Catholic statements and values found in some of these readers.

Origins of the High School

As we have seen, the Latin Grammar School was the first form of a secondary school. It taught a classical curriculum and prepared students for college. The Academy proposed by Benjamin Franklin in the 1700s was the forerunner of the modern high school that has both academic and vocational courses. Both of these institutions were private, run by a religious denomination, or endowed with a Board and therefore were attended by the sons and daughters of the middle to upper class (however, schools were usually restricted to one sex until after the Civil War). The curriculum included college preparatory, classical subjects, and vocational and technical courses. Phillips Exeter Academy was incorporated in 1781 in New Hampshire and taught "English, Latin, Greek, writing, arithmetic, music, the art of speaking, geometry, logic, geography and other liberal arts and science or languages as opportunity presents itself."[10]

In the 1800s, there was a popular move, especially in the urban areas, for free high schools like the common elementary schools; in 1821, the first public high school opened in Boston: the Boston High School. In 1824, the first public high school for girls only was opened in Worcester, Massachusetts and in 1826, the Boston Girl's High School opened. In 1827, Massachusetts passed a law to have tax-supported high schools.

Coeducational primary schools had become common, and since separate schools for each sex were more expensive, Bridgewater, Connecticut opened the first coeducational public high school in 1826 and, shortly thereafter, high schools became generally coeducational, and were firmly established as such by the mid-nineteenth century.[11] When the 1860s witnessed a marked increase in the rate of high school openings, some taxpayers began to question the authority of local school boards to burden all taxpayers with the expense of the high school when only a very small segment of the youth attended. In Kalamazoo, Michigan the taxpayers brought a suit to court that maintained that "if high schools were to continue, they should be paid for by those who seek them and not by general tax."[12] In 1874, the Michigan Supreme Court ruled in favor of the legislature saying that they had full powers to provide the schools deemed necessary for the welfare of the state. This firmly established the legal basis for the high school, as the "connecting link" between the common school and the university. Before the Kalamazoo case, there were about 300 high schools in the entire United States; by 1890, there were 2,500 high schools; by the turn of the century, there were 6,000 high schools. What was to be the function and subsequently the curriculum of the high school, that is, was it to be exclusively preparation for college or was it to be preparation for a job was a question that was in continuous debate. Finally, in 1892, the National Education Association appointed a Committee of Ten to study the question and make recommendations to them.

Education of Women

Historically, women have not been afforded equal educational opportunities in the United States. Colonial schools did not provide education for girls in any significant way. Dame schools set up in the homes of local women offered girls a year or two of basic instruction, usually limited to the rudiments of reading and writing, very little arithmetic, catechism, and the Lord's Prayer.[13] The Quakers were the pioneers in women's education, already seeing the importance during the colonial times of educating mothers for religious reasons. Other religious groups also started schools for girls, e.g., the Ursuline Sisters in New Orleans who established a school for girls in 1727.[14] Political needs led to dramatic improvements in female education following the American Revolution, as women were now assigned a political role in the education of their sons who would become citizens.

After the Revolution, town schools throughout New England were generally opened to girls, and a novel type of secondary school arose, the academy or female seminary for girls. Probably the first genuine academy or seminary for girls was the "Young Ladies Academy of Philadelphia" which opened around 1780. Sarah Pierce's Litchfield Academy opened in 1792 and was attended by many leading women. These private day or boarding schools taught girls from well-to-do families such subjects as reading, grammar, penmanship, mathematics, geography, music, dancing, painting, drawing, needlework, and French—rather impractical studies for provincial, frontier women. According to Averil McClelland, the term "female academy" is the term used in the eighteenth century and the term "female seminaries" was more frequently used in the nineteenth century, though both were in many ways like "finishing schools."[15] The development of female academies was a major advance for women because, within the space of two decades, it made higher education available to young American women. Although the all-girl academies founded by women differed significantly from those led by male reformers, they began to "close the gap" by stressing academic subjects and encouraging women to take up a leadership role by preparing for professions such as teachering or nursing.[16]

There was a remarkable increase in female schooling between 1790 and 1830. This profound shift developed from a convergence of social, religious, political, and economic conditions which educators of women exploited resourcefully. According to Barbara Miller Solomon, educational reform for women was one of the most dramatic and complex developments of the nineteenth century, and many of the most important curricular innovations of the nineteenth century were the products of women educators who were free to "experiment" in their schools for girls.[17]

In the readings in this chapter we will see how Emma Willard founded the Troy Female Seminary in New York in 1821, generally considered to be the first institution of higher education for girls with a liberal arts curriculum on a par with the contemporary men's colleges. Catharine Beecher founded the Hartford Female Seminary and encouraged women to choose teaching as the proper career for a woman. In 1837, Catharine left the schools she had founded to become a full-time advocate of normal schools for women (to train them for teaching) and public schools for both sexes. The first normal school for women only was opened in 1839 in Lexington, Massachusetts.[18]

Emma Willard, Catharine Beecher, and Mary Lyon are credited with being the chief proponents of formal advanced schooling for girls.[19] Mary Lyon's Mount Holyoke Female Seminary began in 1837. It was eventually endowed and in 1861 expanded its program to four years, and changed its name in 1886 to Mount Holyoke Seminary and College. Oberlin College in Ohio was the first to admit women in 1837, having already admitted African-Americans at its founding. Antioch College in Ohio admitted women at its opening as did the University of Iowa, the first public institution to do so. Matthew Vassar in 1861 established Vassar College, in Poughkeepsie, New York, a college entirely for women.[20]

The growth of academies reached a climax in the 1850s, when other relatively new institutions such as the normal/teacher training school and the public high school emerged as educational alternatives.[21] These female seminaries became the first normal schools to train teachers. At the beginning, it was thought that two years of study in academic courses and educational principles, and a model school to practice in, was sufficient to be trained as a teacher. However, as the high schools became more prevalent, the normal school training moved first to three and then to four years as Normal Colleges. Later these colleges were fully recognized as degree granting institutions and integrated into universities as Colleges of Education.

Origins of the College and University

As mentioned earlier, Harvard, the first college in the New World, was established in Cambridge, Massachusetts in 1636. Similar institutions grew in each of the colonies; each was private, sectarian, and attended by well-to-do young men: College of William and Mary (1693) in Virginia, Yale College (1701) in New Haven, Columbia (1754) in New York, University of Pennsylvania (1779), Brown (1764) in Rhode Island, and Rutgers (1766) in New Jersey. Dartmouth College (1769) was unique in that Eleazar Wheelock founded it as the extension of a school he had started in Lebanon for Native-American women. It was originally chartered as a private college for Native-Americans, both men and women, but as they did not find the studies there useful or relevant to their culture, the school soon filled with Anglo-Saxons.[22] Dartmouth had the same curricula as the other colleges, patterned after the Oxford and Cambridge models. Students studied Latin, Greek, and Hebrew, they studied the "trivium" of grammar, logic, and rhetoric, and the new "quadrivium" of logic, mathematics, natural philosophy, and metaphysics. The University of Virginia, begun through Thomas Jefferson's efforts in 1819, was one of the first institutions to deviate from this pattern by emphasizing public, not private, control and a scientific and vocational curriculum, instead of a classical one.[23] Other states followed this lead and began their own public universities—University of Indiana (1820), University of Michigan (1837), and University of Wisconsin (1848). They developed curricula to train men in professions such as law, medicine, and science. The establishment of state universities was encouraged by the federal land grant policy as stated in the Northwest Ordinance—as new states entered the Union they were granted part of each township for education. Although this was usually used for elementary schools, some used it for their university.

Morrill Act

Between 1800 and 1825, some fifty new colleges started; most of them were denominational colleges. Oftentimes, an academy would also develop a higher education curriculum. Then, in 1862, President Abraham Lincoln signed the Morrill Act that granted land for the establishment of higher education instruction in agricultural and industrial studies (which of course also included the usual scientific and classical studies). The second Morrill Act of 1890 provided land-grant colleges in agricultural and mechanical studies for blacks. Perhaps no other bills have aided the establishment of higher education in the United States more than these two acts. Although their growth was slow at first, because they did not have the prestige of the liberal arts colleges, the largest universities in many states today began as "land-grant colleges."[24]

In 1836, some Americans went to visit German colleges, models in which research was emphasized, and classes were given as seminars; there were graduate departments, and students working with mentors completing dissertations. Johns Hopkins was founded in 1876 in Maryland, and was the first to emulate the German research model. The University of Chicago, founded in 1892, also followed this model. Charles Eliot was President of Harvard from 1869 to 1909 and led the transformation of Harvard College to Harvard University, making it, and higher education in general, more responsive to the needs of a modernizing, technological nation. Yale, Columbia, and Princeton followed Harvard's lead, seeking to also transform their colleges into "universities."

Junior Colleges

In the process of developing the research emphasis of their institutions in the late nineteenth century, college presidents, lead by William Rainey Harper of Chicago, sought to divide the college undergraduate curriculum into two years of liberal learning followed by two years of research in a field of specialization. The terms *junior college* and *senior college* were coined, eventually leading to the establishment of a separate institution with the first two years of study. Joliet Junior College was the first to be established in the country in 1901 in Joliet, Illinois. Other junior colleges slowly grew at other sites, getting some impetus from the 1917 Smith-Hughes Act, which provided federal aid for vocational education. California was the first to establish a statewide system of junior colleges in 1921, followed by Florida, New York, Texas, and Illinois. The post–World War II era saw the renaming of the college to the "community college," which offered both the first two years of collegiate studies for transfer to a four-year institution and terminal two-year professional and technical degrees. By the year 2000, there were more than 1,240 two-year colleges in the nation.[25]

After World War II, American higher education experienced its greatest growth due to the Servicemen's Readjustment Act, popularly known as the GI Bill. From 1950 to 1965, college enrollments doubled from 2.4 million to 4.9 million students, doubling again by 1975. By the year 2000, college attendance figures reached 13.4 million.[26]

For Further Research on the Internet

Connections are provided for links to many of the important events mentioned in this chapter. http://www.nd.edu/%7Erbarger/www7/common.html

Rural education in the late 1800s.
http://www.emints.org/ethemes/resources/s00001565.5htm/school.htm

Notes

1. Wayne Urban and Jennings Wagoner, *American Education: A History,* 2nd ed. (Burr Ridge, IL: McGraw Hill, 2000), p. 69.
2. URL: *http://odur.let.rug.nl/'usa/D/1776–1800/ohio/norwes.htm;* Ibid., p. 79.
3. John Pulliam and James Van Patten, *History of Education in America,* 8th ed. (Upper Saddle River, NJ: Merrill/Prentice Hall, 2003), p. 51f.
4. Ibid., p. 115.
5. Sarah Mondale, and Sarah Patton, eds. *School: The Story of American Public Education* (Boston: Beacon Press, 2001), p. 5.
6. Ibid., p. 173.
7. Kathryn Kish Sklar, *Catharine Beecher: A Study in American Domesticity* (New York: Norton & Co., 1976), pp. 97, 180.
8. Sally Schwager, "Educating Women in America," *Signs: Journal of Women in Culture and Society* 12, no. 21 (1987), p. 359.
9. Pulliam and Van Patten, p. 99.
10. Jurgen Herbst, *The Once and Future School: Three Hundred and Fifty Years of American Secondary Education* (New York: Routledge, 1996), p. 20.
11. Patricia Sexton, *Women in Education, Perspectives in American Education* (Bloomington, IN: Phi Delta Kappa Educational Foundation, 1976), p. 43.
12. Herbst, p. 63.
13. Sexton, p. 43; Willystine Goodsell, ed., *Pioneers in Women's Education in the United States* (New York: McGraw-Hill, 1931), pp. 6–7.
14. Averil Evans McClelland, *The Education of Women in the United States: A Guide to Theory, Teaching and Research* (New York: Garland Publishing, 1992), p. 24.
15. Ibid., p. 23.

16. Schwager, pp. 336, 340.
17. Barbara Miller Solomon, *In the Company of Educated Women* (New Haven, CT: Yale University Press, 1985), p. 14.
18. Sexton, p. 46.
19. McClelland, p. 24.
20. L. Glenn Smith and Joan K. Smith, *Lives in Education: A Narrative of People and Ideas,* 2nd ed. (New York: St. Martin's Press, 1994), p. 322.
21. Solomon, p. 23.
22. Margaret Connell Szasz, *Indian Education in the American Colonies, 1607–1783* (Albuquerque: University of New Mexico Press, 1988), p. 219.
23. Gerald L. Gutek, *An Historical Introduction to American Education* (Prospect Heights, IL: Waveland Press, Inc., 1991), pp. 139, 141.
24. Ibid., p. 147.
25. Ibid., pp. 155–158.
26. Allan Ornstein and Daniel Levine, *Foundations of Education,* 7th ed. (Boston: Houghton Mifflin Company, 2000).

Section 9.1: Horace Mann (1796–1859)

Did you go to one elementary school? Or were you like fifty percent of all students who transfer at least once during their elementary school years? Maybe you even transferred in the middle of the academic year. As traumatic as this is for young children, having to say goodbye to your teacher and friends, at least as you transfer from third grade in one school to third grade in another, the curriculum is relatively the same. We have Horace Mann to thank for this. Known as the "Father of the Common School,"[1] he did much to standardize the curricula of the public common schools. He also improved the training of teachers so that teaching would be more interactive between student and teacher.

Mann's Life and Times

Horace Mann was born on a farm in Franklin, Massachusetts on May 4, 1796, the fourth of five children of Thomas and Rebecca Mann. (The town was named after Benjamin Franklin, who founded the oldest public library in America there.)[2] The Mann family was tightly knit and largely self-sufficient on their farm.

Horace's Education

Horace remembered his childhood as one of hard work and constant church attendance with only about ten weeks a year dedicated to schooling in a cold, run-down schoolhouse. Horace tried to read all of the books in the town library. When he was thirteen years old his father died, and one year later, his older brother died. Horace found no consolation in the preacher's sermons at their funerals and turned away from the Calvinist religion to a more benevolent religion that included the joy of heaven and the happiness of a virtuous life.[3] Horace saw Franklin changing from a farming town to an industrial town and as he had no desire to dedicate his life to the family farm, he decided to go to college. At the age of twenty, he scored so high on the exams that he was admitted into the sophomore class at Brown University. Although the teaching in most of his classes was mediocre, relying extensively on recitation and emphasizing form more than content, Mann excelled in his studies and was chosen as valedictorian when he graduated in 1819. He was offered a job as a tutor at Brown, where he worked for two years.

The Lawyer and Legislator

Mann went to study law in Litchfield at the first law school in America. (At that time, you could practice law without a college degree as long as you were admitted to the bar.)[4] After giving a eulogy for Thomas Jefferson and John Adams, his fame as an able orator spread. Mann was elected to the State House of Representatives in 1827. He worked for legislation to improve the care of the insane and those in prison.[5]

On September 29, 1830, Horace married Charlotte Messer, the daughter of the Brown University President. Weak of constitution, she died two years later and Mann spent years in mourning. Excessive dedication to work was the only way he could ease the pain, but this also contributed to recurring personal illnesses.

In January 1835, Mann was elected to the Massachusetts Senate. In 1837, the legislators passed "An Act Relating to Common Schools" that established a Massachusetts State Board of Education charged with "collecting information on the conditions and efficiency of the common schools and diffusing widely information regarding the most successful methods of education."[6]

Secretary of the Board of Education

Mann was elected the Secretary of the Board of Education (see the timeline of Mann's life in Figure 9.1). He gave up his lucrative law practice and promising political career to accept this low-paying position because he saw this as his opportunity to serve humanity by shaping the destiny of American education.

Mann read extensively on education, collected statistics and information on school conditions, and rode throughout the state on horseback to visit schools. He found the schoolhouses to be run down, with poor attendance, poor teaching, and poorly written textbooks. Private academies attracted the children of the well-to-do who could pay the tuition. On December 31, 1837, Mann presented his First Annual Report to the Board on the State of the Schools in which he proposed the need for improved school buildings and books as well as teacher seminaries to improve teaching methodology. Mann stressed the need for competent teachers. "Teaching," he states, "is the most difficult of all arts and the profoundest of all sciences."[7]

The report was well received by the Board of Education and Mann had their encouragement to seek appropriate legislation. As a lobbyist he had, in one year, as much educational legislation passed as had been passed in the previous twenty years.[8] Mann was also able to procure financial donations, such as a $10,000 grant from a wealthy Boston businessman, which was matched by state monies, leading to the establishment of four teacher normal schools throughout the state. The normal school curriculum included three basic elements: subject matter preparation, methodology of teaching, and practice teaching.[9]

Each year Mann proposed educational changes needed in his annual report and then worked to enact those changes. His reports covered such issues as teachers' salaries, the supply of qualified teachers, teacher preparation in the content area, and the methodology of teaching. He drew up plans for the construction of new school buildings that were well-ventilated, well-lit, and used standardized textbooks; he also began school libraries. Mann was opposed to sectarian teaching in the public and normal schools, but he was supportive of the general teaching of Christianity, the Ten Commandments, and the Bible. He felt that

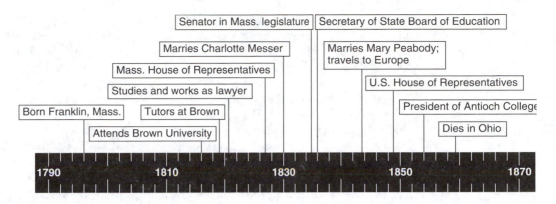

Figure 9.1   Mann's Life and Times

the principal aim of education was the development of the child's moral and religious character and that character formation was a direct responsibility of the common school.[10]

On May 1, 1843, he married Mary Peabody and eventually they had three sons. Horace and Mary went to Europe for their honeymoon and while there, toured schools and prisons in eight different countries. Mann was very impressed with the activity in the Scottish classrooms, the German methodology of teaching, and the organization of Prussian schools. Mann gained international acclaim and requests for advice came to him from different countries and states.

Subsequent reports sought to implement the ideas he had seen in Europe: graded classrooms, lesson plans, abolition of corporal punishment, and a demanding education for all children ages four to sixteen years. Mann began the *Common School Journal* as a means to promote these ideas.

John Quincy Adams died on February 21, 1848 and Mann was asked to run for his House of Representatives seat, which he did in order to promote the cause of education on a national level. He wrote his twelfth and last Report to the Board of Education, an eloquent and compelling justification of the existence of public education.[11] Mann found that most of his efforts in the House were dedicated to the slavery issue. In 1852, he accepted the presidency of the newly forming Antioch College in Yellow Springs, Ohio to return to educational work. In June 1859, Mann gave his last speech at commencement. Having won many victories for humanity and education, Horace Mann died on August 2, 1859, at the age of 63.

Mann's Contribution to Educational Thought

Mann's professions as lawyer, politician, and educator all helped him make contributions to education. He raised issues in the 1840s regarding education that are still relevant today. Mann believed that education proceeded according to scientific laws, which, once learned, would promote real learning. Mann was not an educational theorist, but an administrator and leader. He would pick and choose the ideas of others that he felt would contribute to improving teaching in America; he had the ability to actualize these ideas.

Mann's Philosophy of Education

Through his twelve annual reports and many speeches, a clear philosophy of education emerged. Mann was convinced of the Protestant work ethic of industriousness, diligence, productivity, and punctuality, which he included in the ethos of his schools. Like Jefferson,

Mann believed that the common school was necessary to develop contributing citizens and responsible members of society; it was also necessary for providing literate, moral workers, necessary for economic welfare.[12] Mann believed in the fundamental uniformity of human nature in all nations and ages, and thus was convinced that there could be a common, universal system of intellectual and moral education for all people. These values were essential to citizenship in a democracy, and although not identified with any particular religious sect, were compatible to all with a common Christian basis.[13] Mann viewed the purpose of education as a broad process bringing about the harmonious education of body, intellect, and spirit and so he supported physical and artistic education in addition to academic preparation. Mann promoted a common elementary school curriculum, similar to today's system. The common school was to be financed by the taxes of the local citizens with help from the state and the business community. Public education, open to all, would be the "great equalizer" that would give children upward social and economic mobility. Mann realized that the common school would only be effective with well-trained and professional teachers. Mann is best known for founding the first state-funded institutions in the country for training teachers.[14] Through the normal schools and teacher academies, he helped make teaching a "professional" career. Mann's life can be summarized in the pronouncement he made at his last commencement speech at Antioch College: "Be ashamed to die until you have won some victory for humanity."

Notes

1. Wayne Urban, and Jennings Wagoner, *American Education: A History,* 2nd ed. (Burr Ridge, IL: McGraw Hill, 2000), p. 101.
2. Robert B. Downs, *Horace Mann: Champion of Public Schools,* edited by S. Smith, *Twayne Great Educator's Series* (New York: Twayne Publishers, 1974), p. 11.
3. Jonathan Messerli, *Horace Mann: A Biography* (New York: Alfred A. Knopf, 1972), p. 22.
4. Messerli, p. 74.
5. Downs, p. 23.
6. Ibid., p. 27.
7. Ibid., p. 37.
8. Messerli, p. 292.
9. Downs, p. 53.
10. Neil G. McCluskey, *Public Schools and Moral Education* (Westport, CT: Greenwood Press Publishers, 1975), p. 94.
11. Urban, p. 106.
12. Lawrence Cremin, *American Education: The National Experience 1783–1876* (New York: Harper & Row, Publishers, 1980), p. 137.
13. Sybil Eakin, "Giants of American Education: Horace Mann," *Technos: Quarterly for Education and Technology* 9 (2)(2000), p. 7.
14. Eakin, p. 9.

Questions to Guide Your Reading

1. How does Horace Mann define the common school in this report? Who will go to this common school? Is the common school the same as today's public school? In what ways are they the same or different?

2. What is the great experiment that has never been tried?

3. For what ages or grades does Mann propose children go to school?

4. Is Mann in favor of teaching religion in the schools? If so, what kind of religion?

READING 9.1:
REPORT NO. 12 TO THE MASSACHUSETTS SCHOOL BOARD (1848), HORACE MANN

Under the Providence of God, our means of education are the grand machinery by which the "raw material" of human nature can be worked up into inventors and discoverers, into skilled artisans and scientific farmers, into scholars and jurists, into the founders of benevolent institutions, and the great expounders of ethical and theological science. By means of early education, these embryos of talent may be quickened, which will solve the difficult problems of political and economical law; and by them, too, the genius may be kindled which will blaze forth in the Poets of Humanity. Our schools, far more than they have done, may supply the Presidents and Professors of Colleges, and Superintendents of Public Instruction, all over the land; and send, not only into our sister states, but across the Atlantic, the men of practical science, to superintend the construction of the great works of art. Here, too, may those judicial powers be developed and invigorated, which will make legal principles so clear and convincing as to prevent appeals to force; and, should the clouds of war ever lower over our country, some hero may be found,—the nursling of our schools, and ready to become the leader of our armies,—that best of all heroes, who will secure the glories of a peace, unstained by the magnificent murders of the battle-field. . . .

Without undervaluing any other human agency, it may be safely affirmed that the Common School, improved and energized, as it can easily be, may become the most effective and benignant of all the forces of civilization. Two reasons sustain this position. In the first place, there is universality in its operation, which can be affirmed of no other institution whatever. If administered in the spirit of justice and conciliation, all the rising generation may be brought within the circle of its reformatory and elevating influences. And, in the second place, the

materials upon which it operates are so pliant and ductile as to be susceptible of assuming a greater variety of forms than any other earthly work of the Creator. The inflexibility and ruggedness of the oak, when compared with the lithe sapling or the tender germ, are but feeble emblems to typify the docility of childhood, when contrasted with the obduracy and intractableness of man. It is these inherent advantages of the Common School, which, in our own State, have produced results so striking, from a system so imperfect, and an administration so feeble. In teaching the blind, and the deaf and dumb, in kindling the latent spark of intelligence that lurks in an idiot's mind, and in the more holy work of reforming abandoned and outcast children, education has proved what it can do, by glorious experiments.

Now I proceed, then, in endeavoring to show how the true business of the schoolroom connects itself, and becomes identical, with the great interests of society. The former is the infant, immature state of those interests; the latter, their developed, adult state. As "the child is father to the man," so may the training of the schoolroom expand into the institutions and fortunes of the State. . . .

Intellectual Education, as a Means of Removing Poverty, and Securing Abundance

. . . According to the European theory, men are divided into classes,—some to toil and earn, and others to seize and enjoy. According to the Massachusetts theory, all are to have an equal chance for earning, and equal security in the enjoyment of what they earn. The latter tends to equality of condition; the former to the grossest inequalities. Tried by any Christian standard of morals, or even by any of the better sort of heathen standards, can any one hesitate, for a moment, in declaring which of the two will produce the greater amount of human welfare; and which, therefore, is the more conformable

Source: Lawrence A. Cremin, ed., *The Republic and the School: Horace Mann on the Education of Free Men* (1957), NY, Teachers College Press. Used with permission.

to the Divine will? The European theory is blind to what constitutes the highest glory, as well as the highest duty, of a State....

Now, surely, nothing but Universal Education can counter-work this tendency to the domination of capital and the servility of labor. If one class possesses all the wealth and the education, while the residue of society is ignorant and poor, it matters not by what name the relation between them may be called; the latter, in fact and in truth, will be the servile dependents and subjects of the former. But if education be equably diffused, it will draw property after it, by the strongest of all attractions; for such a thing never did happen, and never can happen, as that an intelligent and practical body of men should be permanently poor. Property and labor, in different classes, are essentially antagonistic; but property and labor, in the same class, are essentially fraternal....

Education, then, beyond all other devices of human origin, is the great equalizer of the conditions of men—the balance wheel of the social machinery. I do not here mean that it so elevates the moral nature as to make men disdain and abhor the oppression of their fellow men. This idea pertains to another of its attributes. But I mean that it gives each man the independence and the means by which he can resist the selfishness of other men... The spread of education, by enlarging the cultivated class or caste, will open a wider area over which the social feelings will expand; and, if this education should be universal and complete, it would do more than all things else to obliterate factitious distinctions in society.

Political Education

However elevated the moral character of a constituency may be; however well informed in matters of general science or history, yet they must, if citizens of a Republic, understand something of the true nature and functions of the government under which they live. That any one who is to participate in the government of a country, when he becomes a man, should receive no instruction respecting the nature and functions of the government he is afterwards to administer, is a political solecism. In all nations, hardly excepting the most rude and barbarous, the future sovereign receives some training that is supposed to fit him for the exercise of the powers and duties of his anticipated station.... Hence, the constitution of the United States, and of our own State, should be made a study in our Public Schools. The partition of the powers of government into the three co-ordinate branches,—legislative, judicial, and executive,—with the duties appropriately devolving upon each; the mode of electing or of appointing all officers, with the reason on which it was founded; and, especially, the duty of every citizen, in a government of laws, to appeal to the courts for redress, in all cases of alleged wrong, instead of undertaking to vindicate his own rights by his own arm; and, in a government where the people are the acknowledged sources of power, the duty of changing laws and rulers by an appeal to the ballot, and not by rebellion, should be taught to all the children until they are fully understood.

But to all doubters, disbelievers, or despairers in human progress, it may still be said, there is one experiment that has never yet been tried. It is an experiment, which, even before its inception, offers the highest authority for its ultimate success. Its formula is intelligible to all; and it is as legible as though written in starry letters on an azure sky. It is expressed in these few and simple words: "Train up a child in the way he should go; and when he is old, he will not depart from it." This declaration is positive. If the conditions are complied with, it makes no provision for a failure. Though pertaining to morals, yet, if the terms of the direction are observed, there is no more reason to doubt the result than there would be in an optical chemical experiment.

But this experiment has never yet been tried. Education has never yet been brought to bear with one-hundredth part of its potential force upon the natures of children, and through them, upon the character of man and of the race.

Indeed, so decisive is the effect of early training upon adult habits and character, that numbers of the most able and experienced teachers—those who have had the best opportunities to become acquainted with the errors and the excellencies of children, their waywardness, and their docility—have unanimously declared it to be their belief, that if all the children in the community, from the age of four years to that of sixteen, could be brought within the reformatory and elevating influences of good schools, the dark host of private vices and public crimes which now embitter domestic peace and stain the civilization of the age, might, in ninety-nine cases in every hundred be banished from the world....

I believed then, as now, that religious instruction in our schools, to the extent to which the constitution and laws of the state allowed and prescribed, was indispensable to their highest welfare, and essential to the vitality of moral education. That as now, also, I believe that sectarian books and sectarian instruction, if their encroachments were not resisted, would prove the overthrow of the schools. . . .

For our system earnestly inculcates all Christian morals; it founds its morals on the basis of religion, it welcomes the religion of the Bible, and in receiving the Bible, it allows it to do what it is allowed to do in no other system, to speak for itself. But here it stops, not because it claims to have compassed all truth, but because it disclaims to act as an umpire between hostile religious opinions.

Discussion Questions

1. Horace Mann says that education is the "great equalizer." Is this true in the schools today for students of lower socioeconomic status?
2. Do you think Mann would approve of mainstreaming and inclusion? Why or why not?
3. Mann established the first normal schools to give better preparation to teachers. What do you think Mann would say about teacher education institutions today, the emphasis on standards, and the status of the teaching profession?
4. Mann gives great importance to education to develop responsible citizens. Do schools today still see this as an important role?
5. Do you agree with Mann's statement that teachers have a responsibility for morally educating their students? Is this true today? Is it possible to find common values in our pluralistic society?
6. Compare and contrast Mann's views on the inclusion of religious instruction and the teaching of morals in the public schools with Jefferson's ideas on these issues. Whose views are we following more in our schools today?

For Further Research on the Internet

A short biography of Mann's life. http://www.famousamericans.net/horacemann/

A biography of Mann, emphasizing his contributions to education.
http://www.pbs.org/onlyateacher/horace.html

Shows all the educators (including Mann) involved in the Common School Movement.
http://www.nd.edu/%7Erbarger/www7/common.html

Suggestions for Further Reading

Cremin, Lawrence. *American Education: The National Experience 1783–1876*. New York: Harper & Row, Publishers, 1980.

Downs, Robert B. *Horace Mann: Champion of Public Schools*. Edited by S. Smith, *Twayne Great Educator's Series*. New York: Twayne Publishers, 1974.

Eakin, Sybil. "Giants of American Education: Horace Mann." *Technos: Quarterly for Education and Technology* 9 (2)(2000): 4–14.

McCluskey, Neil G. *Public Schools and Moral Education*. Westport, CT: Greenwood Press Publishers, 1975.

Messerli, Jonathan. *Horace Mann: A Biography*. New York: Alfred A. Knopf, 1972.

Urban, Wayne, and Jennings Wagoner. *American Education: A History*, 2nd ed. Burr Ridge, IL: McGraw Hill, 2000.

Section 9.2: Emma Willard (1787–1870)

Many of you reading this book are women attending a college. What seems so commonplace today was not always so. Until the time of Emma Willard, men thought that higher studies were not only impossible for women, but also would make them ill. Emma, while striving to be "politically correct," convinced the new country and many people in Europe that educating women was good for the strength of the republic.

Emma Willard's Life and Times

Emma Hart was born on February 23, 1787, in Berlin, Connecticut, the sixteenth child of Samuel Hart, a self-taught farmer, and his second wife Lydia Hinsdale. The family worked hard producing wool on the farm, but also enjoyed the family gatherings at night. Although books were hard to come by in those days, the family was able to get these treasures and spend nights reading them aloud. They also enjoyed hearing the stories their father told about the Revolutionary War days.

Emma's Education

Before the war, public schools had been open to boys only. Now, for the success of the new nation, it was generally felt that greater knowledge was needed; and women were encouraged to attend the primary schools. Emma attended the district school, learning reading, writing, and spelling with a little arithmetic, catechism, and geography.

When Emma was 15, she enrolled in an Academy, the closest to secondary education in existence at that time, studying science, geography, and writing.

Emma, the Teacher

At 17, she began teaching, revealing the natural gift as an educator that distinguished her throughout her career.[1] Instead of teaching rote repetition, Emma began to form classes with higher studies, something she would do all her life. She continued her own studies at the Patten School and then the Royse School when her school was not in session. The Royse School was one of the best at that time, allowing students to study reading, writing, arithmetic, geography, French, dancing, painting, and needlework when educational opportunities for women were very limited and no college or high school would admit them. Poor girls had no education beyond the district school, and even the boarding schools for well-to-do girls stressed such "accomplishments" as sewing, music, and art, more than academic subjects. Society did not expect women to think for themselves, discuss religion or politics, or earn money.[2]

In 1806, Emma took a position at the very school in Berlin where she had so recently been a student. Her great success as a teacher brought her various offers for teaching positions, and she took charge, in Middlebury, VT, of one of the first academies for women in the country.

Emma, Wife, Mother, and Teacher

At the academy she met Dr. John Willard, a man twice widowed with four children, and married him on August 10, 1809. Emma left teaching to enthusiastically begin the life of a married woman. One year later, Emma had her own child, John Hart Willard. When her husband's nephew came to live with them as he studied at Middlebury College, Emma followed along with his studies, seeing clearly the poor level of education received by women in comparison to what was available for men.[3]

During the War of 1812, Emma opened a boarding school for girls in her home. To her students, the daughters of some of the best families in town, Emma first taught the typical "accomplishment" curriculum, but gradually began to introduce them to the higher studies of mathematics, history, and language, trying to "introduce a grade of schools for women higher than any heretofore known."[4] (See the timeline of Emma Willard's life in Figure 9.2.)

She arranged a schedule of studies, recreation, and time together as "a family" and "believed heartily in training both the mind and the hands, feeling that the woman's sphere demanded skill in handiwork."[5] Emma Willard's school was a success in every way; the girls learned the higher studies with ease and the parents were pleased with their daughters' accomplishments.

Emma worked toward a better system of education for girls, convinced that married life would be happier if the wife could also be an intellectual companion to the husband. Refused permission for her students to attend classes at Middlebury College, Emma taught the same subjects to her students as soon as she herself could learn them. Emma developed her own unique method of instruction. First, she taught the subject to the students, helping them understand the material; second, she had them recite what they had learned to aid their memories; finally, she had them communicate the information to one another, convinced that this would show if they really understood the material.[6] She invited the professors of Middlebury College and the prominent citizens of Hartford to the end-of-the-year examinations so that they could see that girls were capable of comprehending collegiate studies.

Once Emma proved to herself the ability of her students to master these higher subjects, she had found her life's mission. Using the term "Female Seminary" as a name for a higher institution of learning for women, Emma worked on her "Plan for Improving Fe-

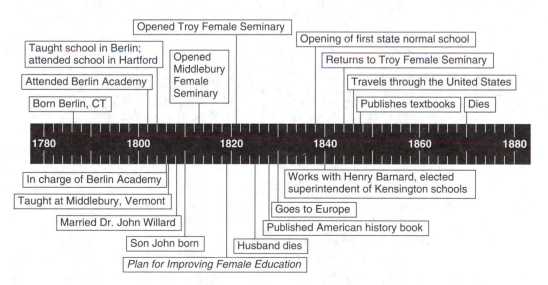

Figure 9.2   Willard's Life and Times

male Education"; her arguments cogent and persuasive.[7] Written like a law brief, it aimed to convince the public that reform, with the aid of the legislature, was necessary regarding female education.

Emma Willard published her plan and sent it to the prominent men of her time, i.e., Monroe, Adams, Jefferson, and Governor De Witt Clinton of New York, who received it favorably. In 1818, Governor Clinton passed a charter for the Waterford Academy for Young Ladies, the first legislative act recognizing a woman's right to higher education.[8] Emma eventually moved her school to Troy, New York.

Troy Female Academy

In 1821, the Troy Female Seminary began with ninety students. Emma enlarged the curriculum, making higher mathematics a permanent part of the studies there. Emma regarded religious training as the basis of all education and while giving instruction in a non-sectarian manner, she tried to instill in the girls a love of God. No girls' school in the country offered such a complete course of studies.[9] Wanting all qualified students to be able to attend her school, Emma loaned, over the years, approximately $75,000 to various girls for their education. She was probably the first woman to offer scholarships for women.

From the Seminary's first year, Emma took a special interest in teacher training, both those teaching at her seminary and her graduates. Believing that moral improvement is the true end of the intellectual, she urged her teachers to make more reflections on the events of history when appropriate. Encouraging graduates of her seminary to enter the profession, Emma was one of the first educators to take definite steps to train women teachers. A forerunner of the normal school, the Seminary did much to change public opinion regarding the education of women.[10] In 1826, the first public schools for girls were established in both Boston and New York.

Emma wrote several textbooks, becoming a rich woman on the royalties. Her Seminary now had an unrivaled reputation, with 300 students and an imposing curriculum not equaled in any girls' school in the country.[11] She also began to help Henry Barnard in his mission to promote the common school in Connecticut. There were seventy-nine incorporated colleges and universities for men in the United States and not one endowed female seminary. Barnard and Willard tried to found a school exclusively for teachers in Connecticut, but could only found a six-week Teacher's Institute. Emma was elected to head the schools of Kensington, Connecticut and became the first woman superintendent in the nation. Retiring to Troy, she traveled, spoke, and conducted teacher institutes herself. At all the seminaries she visited, students and teachers looked up to her as a pioneer educator, as the woman of all women to whom they owed their existence.[12]

She received a gold medal at the World's Fair of 1851 in London for her educational work. She spoke there about women's special ability to care for schools for young children and beyond the primary school. When she returned to a country in turmoil, she was taken prisoner by Confederates during the Civil War. As soon as the war was over, she was busy bringing her history textbooks up to date. On April 15, 1870 she died, still a pioneer in the cause of woman's education.

Willard's Influence on Educational Thought

When Emma Willard opened Troy Female Academy, she was the first woman to embark on such a venture. Troy was the first school to provide higher education for women, offering primarily high school courses at a time when no high schools were open to females.

The school also offered some college level courses such as physiology and advanced algebra and geometry. Public sentiment at that time was that women's minds were not acute enough to handle mathematics or the natural sciences. Emma Willard advanced the cause of women's education dramatically by eroding the conventional belief that there were differences in mental capacity between men and women.[13] The Willard Plan was the first public claim that education should be available for all women. It called for a liberal arts curriculum that would incorporate some essentials from men's colleges, but would be taught exclusively by women.[14] According to Willard biographer, Alma Lutz, "In this movement for the higher education of women, Emma Willard must be given first place. No other woman had made such definite experiments in education, no other woman had so daringly stepped into the limelight to wage her fight for education."[15]

One of her great achievements was the obtaining of public grants for the first time for the education of women.[16] Emma Willard's emphasis on training women to become teachers, her organization of an alumnae network, and her curricular and organizational innovations were unprecedented.[17]

Although the explicit purpose of Troy, according to its founder, was "to educate women for responsible motherhood and train some of them to be teachers," the school also became a generator of a new style of female personality. Emma Willard was a woman rooted in the social conventions of her time, but she was also a woman of the future, able to integrate new values with the traditional notions of women's proper role.[18] Troy gave attention to the intellectual development of women, cloaking it in the rhetoric of preparing them for the role of Republican Motherhood. By encouraging graduates to become teachers, it radically reformed womanhood to include professional work in society. Troy graduates went on to become geologists, missionaries, translators, and midwives.[19]

Troy Seminary became one of the first schools to incorporate a systematic study of pedagogy. For most of the nineteenth century, it sent its graduates to all parts of the country to teach and found schools of their own based on the Troy model.[20] One of Emma Willard's many contributions to the history of education was her development of teacher preparation.[21]

Emma Willard's Philosophy of Education

In 1819, when Emma Willard published her *Plan for Improving Female Education* and established her school under state patronage at Waterford, she laid the foundation upon which every women's college now rests. Echoing Plato and Jefferson, Willard said, "for the sake of the Republic, women must be educated. Women of education and character would bear nobler sons and train them for useful citizenship."[22] In her work at Troy, Willard developed a curriculum that was far more innovative in its pedagogy and introduced such courses as science and geography, not found in the male academies or colleges.[23] Far ahead of her time, preceding modern educational psychologists, Emma recommended that the studies undertaken should lead women to understand the operations of the human mind—since mothers exert such an influence over the impressionable minds of their children, they need to be taught to mold them correctly.

Emma Willard also made valuable contributions to teaching methodology. With a limited knowledge of psychology and abundant intelligence and zeal for the improvement of teaching, she hit upon objective methods of imparting knowledge still used, in modified form, in teaching today. She was an intelligent student of the effects of her methods on developing students' minds. She was particularly successful in teaching geography by appealing to the eye through charts and maps.[24]

Emma Willard's definition of education still stands today; "Education should seek to bring its subjects to the perfection of their moral, intellectual, and physical nature in order that they may be the greatest possible use to themselves and others."[25]

Notes

1. Willystine Goodsell, ed., *Pioneers in Women's Education in the United States* (New York, McGraw-Hill, 1931), p. 17.
2. Alma Lutz, *Emma Willard, Daughter of Democracy* (Washington, DC, Zenger Publishing, 1975), p. 30.
3. Ibid., p. 45.
4. Goodsell, p. 20.
5. Lutz, p. 52.
6. Ibid., pp. 56–57.
7. Goodsell, pp. 21–22.
8. Lutz, pp. 60–68.
9. Ibid., p. 83.
10. Ibid., p. 98.
11. The students studied Bible, composition, elocution, drawing, singing, gymnastics, dancing, modern languages (French, Spanish, Italian, German), Latin, algebra, geometry, trigonometry, moral and natural philosophy, logic, botany, chemistry, geology, astronomy, zoology, rhetoric, literature, and history.
12. Lutz, p. 275.
13. Maxine Green, "The Impacts of Irrelevance: Women in the History of American Education," in *Woman and Education; Equity or Equality?*, by E. Fennema and M. J. Ayer (Berkeley, CA: McCutchan Publishing Corp., 1984), p. 26.
14. Barbara M. Solomon, *In the Company of Educated Women* (New Haven, CT: Yale University Press, 1985), p. 18.
15. Lutz, p. 75.
16. Shirley Nelson Kersey, *Classics in the Education of Girls and Women* (Metuchen, NJ: Scarecrow Press, 1981), p. 268.
17. Sally Schwager, "Educating Women in America," *Signs: Journal of Women in Culture and Society* 12 (21) (1987), pp. 344–345.
18. Schwager, p. 343.
19. Ibid., pp. 343–344.
20. Averil Evans McClelland, *The Education of Women in the United States: A Guide to Theory, Teaching and Research* (New York: Garland Publishing), 1992, p. 124.
21. Kersey, p. 268.
22. Lutz, p. 72.
23. Schwager, p. 345.
24. Goodsell, p. 29.
25. Lutz, p. 70.

Questions to Guide Your Reading

1. What are the four areas of instruction Emma thinks every woman should study? Are these important for women to study today?

2. How would female seminaries benefit the common schools?

3. What are some special abilities of women that make them especially suited for teaching?

READING 9.2:
SKETCH OF A FEMALE SEMINARY

From considering the deficiencies in boarding schools, much may be learned with regard to what would be needed for the prosperity and usefulness of a public seminary for females.

I. There would be needed a building with commodious rooms for lodging and recitation, apartments for the reception of apparatus, and for the accommodation of the domestic department.

II. A library, containing books on the various subjects in which the pupils were to receive instruction; musical instruments, some good paintings, to form the taste and serve as models for the execution of those who were to be instructed in that Art; maps, globes, and a small collection of philosophical apparatus.

III. A judicious board of trust, competent and desirous to promote its interests, would in a female, as in a male literary institution, be the cornerstone of its prosperity. On this board it would depend to provide,

IV. Suitable instruction. This article may be subdivided under four heads.

1. Religious and Moral
2. Literary
3. Domestic
4. Ornamental

1. **Religious and Moral.** A regular attention to religious duties would, of course, be required of the pupils by the laws of the institution. The trustees would be careful to appoint no instructors who would not teach religion and morality, both by their example, and by leading the minds of the pupils to perceive that these constitute the true end of all education....

2. **Literary Instruction.** To make an exact enumeration of the branches of literature which might be taught would be impossible unless the time of the pupils' continuance at the seminar, and the requisites for entrance, were previously fixed.

It is highly important that females should be conversant with those studies which will lead them to understand the operations of the human mind. The chief use to which the philosophy of the mind can be applied is to regulate education by its rules. The ductile mind of the child is entrusted to the mother: and she ought to have every possible assistance in acquiring a knowledge of this noble material, on which it is her business to operate, that she may best understand how to mould it to its most excellent form.

3. **Domestic instruction** should be considered important in a female seminary. It is the duty of our sex to regulate the internal concerns of every family; and unless they be properly qualified to discharge this duty, whatever may be their literary or ornamental attainments, they cannot be expected to make either good wives, good mothers, or good mistresses of families: and if they are none of these, they must be bad members of society; for it is by promoting or destroying the comfort and prosperity of their own families, that females serve or injure the community. To superintend the domestic department, there should be a respectable lady, experienced in the best methods of house-wifery, and acquainted with propriety of dress and manners. Under her tuition the pupils ought to be placed for a certain length of time every morning. A spirit of neatness and order should here be treated as a virtue, and the contrary, if excessive and incorrigible, be punished with expulsion.

4. **The Ornamental branches,** which I should recommend for a female seminary, are drawing and painting, elegant penmanship, music, and the grace of motion. Needle-work is not here mentioned. The best style of useful needle-work should either be taught in the domestic department, or made a qualification for entrance; and I consider that useful which may contribute to the decoration of a lady's person or the convenience and neatness of her family. But the use of the needle for other purposes than these, as it affords little to assist in the formation of the character, I should regard as a waste of time.

Source: Willard, Emma. "A Plan for Improving Female Education." 1819. Reprinted in Goodsell, Willystine (ed.). *Pioneers of Education in the United States* (1931), New York: AMS Press.

Exercise is needful to the health, and recreation to the cheerfulness and contentment.

It has been doubted whether painting and music should be taught to young ladies because much time is requisite to bring them to any considerable degree of perfection, and they are not immediately useful. Though these objections have weight, yet they are founded on too limited a view of the objects of education. They leave out the important consideration of forming the character. The harmony of sound has a tendency to produce a correspondent harmony of soul; and that art, which obliges us to study nature in order to imitate her, often enkindles the latent spark of tastes—of sensibility for her beauties, till it glows to adoration for their author, and a refined love of all his works.

5. There would be needed, for a female as well as for a male seminary, a system of laws and regulations, so arranged that both the instructors and pupils would know their duty; and thus the whole business move with regularity and uniformity.

The laws of the institution would be chiefly directed to regulate the pupil's qualifications for entrance, the kind and order of their studies, their behavior while at the institution, the term allotted for the completion of their studies, the punishments to be inflicted on offenders, and the rewards or honors to be bestowed on the virtuous and diligent.

The direct rewards or honors used to stimulate the ambition of students in colleges are first, the certificate or diploma, which each receives who passes successfully through the term allotted to his collegiate studies: and secondly, the appointments to perform certain parts in public exhibition, which are bestowed by the faculty as rewards for superior scholarship.

Perhaps the term allotted for the routine of study at the seminary might be three years. The pupils, probably, would not be fitted to enter till about the age of fourteen. Whether they attended to all or any of the ornamental branches should be left optional with the parents or guardians. Those who were to be instructed in them should be entered for a nicer term, but if this were a subject of previous calculation, no confusion would arise from it.

The writer has now given a sketch of her plan. She has by no means expressed all the ideas which occurred to her concerning it. She wished to be as concise as possible, and yet afford conviction that it is practicable to organize a system of female education which shall possess the permanency, uniformity of operation, and respectability of our male institutions; and yet differ from them so as to be adapted to that difference of character and duties to which early instruction should form the softer sex.

It now remains to enquire more particularly what would be the benefits resulting from such a system.

Benefits of Female Seminaries

In inquiring concerning the benefits of the plan proposed, I shall proceed upon the supposition that female seminaries will be patronized throughout our country.... Let us now inquire; what benefits would result from the establishment of female seminaries.

They would constitute a grade of public education superior to any yet known in the history of our sex; and through them, the lower grades of female instruction might be controlled. The influence of public seminaries over these would operate in two ways; first, by requiring certain qualifications for entrance; and secondly, by furnishing instructresses initiated in their modes of teaching and imbued with their maxims.

Female seminaries might be expected to have important and happy effects on common schools in general; and in the manner of operating on these, would probably place the business of teaching children in hands now nearly useless to society; and take it from those whose services the state wants in many other ways.

That nature designed for our sex the care of children, she has made manifest by mental as well as physical indications. She has given us, in a greater degree than men, the gentle arts of insinuation, to soften their minds and fit them to receive impressions; a greater quickness of invention to vary modes of teaching to different dispositions; and more patience to make repeated efforts. There are many females of ability to whom the business of instructing children is highly acceptable and who would devote all their faculties to their occupation.

The inquiry to which these remarks have conducted us is this—What is offered by the plan of female education here proposed, which may teach or preserve among females of wealthy families that purity of manners which is allowed to be so essential to national prosperity, and so necessary to the existence of a republican government.

Thus, laudable objects and employments would be furnished for the great body of females who are not kept by poverty from excesses.... Such aspiring minds we will regulate by education, we will remove obstructions to the course of literature which has heretofore been their only honorable way to distinction; and we offer them a new object worthy of their ambition, to govern and improve the seminaries for their sex.

Discussion Questions

1. Do you agree with Emma Willard that women possess special abilities that make them especially suited for teaching? Does the fact that the majority of elementary school teachers today are women support Emma's proposal or demonstrate that there is still a discrimination against women?
2. Do you think Emma Willard would be pleased with the current state of education for women today? Why or why not? If you were to rewrite her "Sketch for a Female Seminary" for schools in the twenty-first century, what would you add?
3. What do you think Emma Willard would say about the current trend to no longer offer home economics in schools?
4. Do you think we should offer the "ornamental branches" of study in our schools today? Why or why not?

For Further Research on the Internet

An excellent historical piece about Emma Willard and a list of the works she authored. http://www.emmawillard.org/about/history

Leads you to the Emma Willard School homepage. http://www.emma.troy.ny.us

Suggestions for Further Reading

Goodsell, Willystine. ed. *Pioneers in Women's Education in the United States*. New York: McGraw-Hill, 1931.

Green, Maxine. The Impacts of Irrelevance: Women in the History of American Education. In *Woman and Education; Equity or Equality?* by E. Fennema and M. J. Ayer. Berkeley, CA: McCutchan Publishing Corp., 1984.

Kersey, Shirley Nelson. *Classics in the Education of Girls and Women*. Metuchen, NJ: Scarecrow Press, 1981.

Lutz, Alma. *Emma Willard: Daughter of Democracy*. Washington, DC: Zenger Publishing, 1975.

McClelland, Averil Evans. *The Education of Women in the United States: A Guide to Theory, Teaching, and Research*. New York: Garland Publishing, 1992.

Schwager, Sally. "Educating Women in America." *Signs: Journal of Women in Culture and Society* 12 (21) (1987): 333–372.

Solomon, Barbara M. *In the Company of Educated Women*. New Haven, CT: Yale University Press, 1985.

Section 9.3: Catharine Beecher (1800–1878)

How many of you are women studying for an education degree in a College of Education? In the beginning, only men were permitted to teach in the common schools, and they did so without studying how to become teachers. Catharine Beecher popularized education as a career for women and standardized education training to be at least two years long.

Beecher's Life and Times

Catharine Beecher was born on September 6, 1800 in East Hampton, Long Island (later Connecticut), the first of eight children of Lyman and Roxana Beecher. Lyman was a Calvinist minister with a dominating personality that exerted a strong influence on all of his children.

Her Education

At first home-schooled, Catharine entered Miss Pierce's school for young ladies when her family moved to Litchfield in 1809. Here she learned "lady-like manners and cultivated and refined conversation."[1] Catharine's character was formed during these years, learning from her mother to be cheerful, optimistic, and neat, with a strong sense of justice.[2] In 1816 when her mother died, Catharine withdrew from school and helped at home until her father remarried one year later. In 1818, she began to teach at Miss Pierce's school and then went to teach needlework, drawing, and painting at a school for girls in New London, Connecticut.[3]

In 1821, Catharine met Alexander Fisher, a young professor of natural philosophy at Yale and was engaged to him a year later. In April, 1822, he went to Europe to visit the universities, but died when his ship sank. Catharine was devastated but, as she read Fisher's papers, became intellectually stimulated. She tutored one of his siblings and began to think about having a school of her own, helping other women to pursue more rewarding studies than those at the finishing schools.

The Hartford Female Seminary

With the assistance of their father and brother, Catharine and her sister Mary opened the Hartford Female Seminary in Hartford, Connecticut in 1823. (See the timeline of Beecher's life in Figure 9.3.) Her career began in earnest. She decided that she did not have to marry to find fulfillment as she was seriously engaged in the life of a professional, intellectual woman teacher. She became active in the town's social life, using her home for meetings and discussions on current issues.

The Hartford Female Seminary was an enormous success and within five years had its own building, eight teachers, and students from the leading families of Hartford. Catharine's competence as an educator was steadily growing and she began to innovate new pedagogical materials, publish articles, develop curriculum, and write textbooks. Beecher saw the goal of her school as twofold: (1) to better instruct women in intellectual

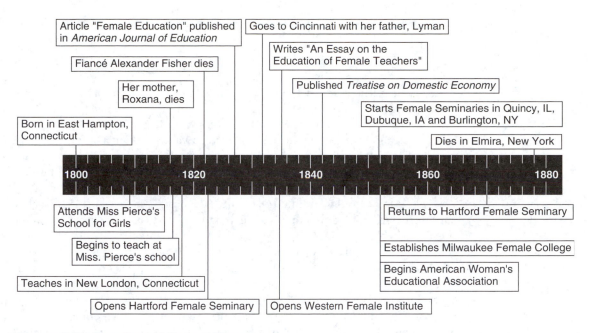

Figure 9.3   Beecher's Life and Times

development, and (2) to form moral character, good habits, and a refined feminine character.[4]

The *American Journal of Education* published her article entitled "Female Education" in 1827. Her chief point in this essay was that the education of women should be taken seriously and the community should want "refined and well-educated women because they would confer a beneficial influence on society."[5] This was to become Catharine's main message as an educational reformer.

Teacher of Teachers

In 1830, Catharine turned her attention to the great need for teachers as the nation moved west and immigrants flocked to the new world. She decided to turn her seminary into a training school for women to learn social, religious, and moral principles and then establish their own schools elsewhere on the same principles. She sought out a new group of teachers who agreed to devote three years of their lives to this project. Teaching was important to Catharine because it provided women with a respectable alternative to marriage. Catharine tried to get the Hartford community to support an endowment fund campaign but she was unsuccessful. Strong-willed, Catharine was exhausted and did not like her plans to be contradicted, so she decided to leave Hartford for Cincinnati with her father in 1832.

At thirty-five, she again established a place for herself among the city's social elite and began the Western Female Institute, patterned after the Hartford Female Seminary.[6] In 1835, she gave an address in New York that was subsequently published, "An Essay on the Education of Female Teachers." In it she called for "permanent female institutions with regular systematic courses of instruction fitting woman for her peculiar duties—the physical, intellectual, and moral education of children."[7] She called for the creation of a corps of women to civilize the immigrants and the lower class by creating a national system of teacher seminaries where women would be trained and then go on to train others. She wanted to establish the first model seminary for this national system in Cincinnati. However, once again, she was unable to raise enough funds. Catharine left the school and spent several years writing and encouraging her sister, Harriet Beecher Stowe, to finish *Uncle Tom's Cabin.*

Authority on Home Economics

In 1841, Catharine published her *Treatise on Domestic Economy.* This book was a success, reprinted annually from 1841 to 1856, establishing Catharine as a national authority on the American home. Catharine saw the home as an integral part of the national system, reflecting and promoting mainstream American values. Women were essential to the nation in their role at home promoting the character formation of the young. According to her biographer, Kathryn Kish Sklar, by the end of the 1840s, Catharine Beecher was one of the most widely known women in America.[8]

She began traveling around the country, advocating a special role for her sex, that of educator. Her own life was the living embodiment of that role. Catharine proposed a national benevolent movement to raise money for teachers and schoolrooms. Her efforts gained the endorsement of the most prominent American educators like Horace Mann and Henry Barnard. In 1852, Catharine began the American Woman's Educational Association as an "agency that would prepare women with a liberal education and preparation as teachers to go out west."[9] More than 400 women from the East were placed in teaching positions in schools in the West.[10] Catharine started Female Seminaries in Quincy, Illinois; Dubuque, Iowa; and Burlington, New York. Finally, she started the Milwaukee Female College in the fall of 1852. It was to be the model for other women's colleges started later: (1) founded in large towns or cities, (2) have faculty organized on the college plan, and (3) have the purpose to prepare women for their true profession as educators and homemakers.[11] Catharine worked here until 1856, and then, as she had done all her life, left the project for others to carry on to fruition. Catharine spent the next years writing on moral philosophy. She came out of retirement in 1870 to work as principal of the Hartford Female Seminary. She lived for some time with her sister's and brother's families before she died in 1878 at the age of 78.

Catharine Beecher's Importance for Educational History

Catharine Beecher's importance for the history of education in America can be summarized as comprising three interrelated aspects: the promotion of a demanding and complete liberal education for women, the subsequent conception of a rigorous and complete curriculum to prepare women to be teachers, and the consequent popularization of teaching as a profession for women.

The Hartford Female Academy became one of the most celebrated academies in New England. According to Sklar, "her contemporaries believed and historians have since held that Catharine Beecher's school constituted one of the most significant advances made in early nineteenth century education for women."[12] The curriculum at Hartford was rigorous and complete, including grammar, geography, rhetoric, philosophy, chemistry, history, arithmetic, algebra, geometry, moral philosophy, natural theology, and Latin.[13] The premise followed that advocated by Emma Willard—women could and should learn all the subjects that men studied—but Catharine completed this idea with the addition of a teacher-training curriculum as an essential part of the seminary. Education, according to Catharine Beecher, did not stop with the communication of knowledge. She taught her teachers that character formation was the end of education and they should stress punctuality, order, neatness, and other virtues.[14]

Beecher's Philosophy of Education

These women's colleges, planned for key locations in major western cities, had the express purpose of preparing female teachers for the common schools. Their curriculum was to be equal in character and quality to that found in the colleges for men, with a special emphasis on moral and nondenominational religious instruction. Each teacher's college had a model primary school attached for practice teaching.[15] In the 1830s, teaching was not a woman's profession. Although Emma Willard had, for a decade, linked her curriculum at Troy with preparation for a teaching career, Catharine Beecher was the first to envision teaching as a profession dominated by women, indeed exclusively belonging to them. According to Lawrence Cremin, Catharine Beecher was the most influential reformer of women's education, altering the general course of popular education.[16] Demographic and economic development in the United States during the 1840s and 50s supported Catharine Beecher's vision. A rapidly expanding economy demanded more teachers, but swiftly developing industrialization left fewer males available for nonindustrial jobs. Added to this was Mann's success at instituting tax-supported schools and the expansion of the population in the west. According to Beecher's speeches, there were then a million and a half children in need of ninety thousand teachers.[17] Although female teachers began to replace men in some eastern states in the 1830s, the economic and fiscal utility and the pedagogic benefits of this shift were discovered by state and local boards of education from 1840 to 1880. By 1888, sixty-three percent of American teachers were women and in cities women constituted ninety percent of the teaching force.[18]

Catharine Beecher advocated college level education for women at the same level as that given to men. Unlike her contemporaries, Emma Willard and Mary Lyon, Catharine did not confine her efforts to a single institution, but sought to influence the education in the whole country. In her words, "The cultivation of the immortal mind shall be presented to woman as her special and delightful duty."[19]

Notes

1. Kathryn Kish Sklar, *Catharine Beecher: A Study in American Domesticity* (New York: Norton & Co., 1976), p. 16.
2. Mae Elizabeth Harveson, *Catharine Ester Beecher (Pioneer Educator)* (New York: Arno Press, Inc., 1969), p. 18.
3. Ibid., p. 28.
4. Sklar, p. 90.
5. Margaret Thorp, *Female Persuasion: Six Strong-Minded Women* (New York: Archon Books, 1971), p. 23.
6. Valerie Gill, "Catharine Beecher and Charlotte Perkins Gilman: Architects of Female Power," *Journal of American Culture* 21 (2) (1998), p. 17.
7. Harveson, p. 179.
8. Sklar, p. 164.
9. Harveson, p. 120.
10. Patricia Sexton, *Women in Education* (Bloomington, IN: Phi Delta Kappa Educational Foundation, 1976), p. 46.
11. Sklar, p. 200.
12. Ibid., p. 59.
13. Lawrence Cremin, *American Education: The National Experience 1783–1876* (New York: Harper & Row, Publishers, 1980), p. 144.
14. Harveson, p. 53.
15. Cremin, p. 145.
16. Ibid., p. 144.
17. Harveson, p. 180.
18. Sklar, pp. 97, 180.
19. Sklar, p. 95.

Questions to Guide Your Reading

1. What are some of the difficulties Catharine perceives in the current set-up of schools for women?
2. Why does Catharine think it is important for women's colleges to have a uniform curriculum?
3. What does Catharine think is the most important duty of the female sex?
4. What is one of the most important deficiencies of the schools of the day, according to Catharine?
5. How many teachers does Catharine say the nation needs?

READING 9.3:
ESSAY ON THE EDUCATION OF FEMALE TEACHERS

The topic proposed for consideration in this essay cannot properly be presented without previously adverting to certain difficulties in regard to female education; and, in the same connection, suggesting the most practicable methods of securing their remedy.

One of the first objects that need to be attempted in regard to female education, is to secure some method of rendering female institutions permanent in their existence, and efficient in perpetuating a regular and systematic course of education. This is secured for the other sex, by institutions so endowed that the death or removal of an individual does not hazard their existence or character. They continue year after year, and sometimes for ages, maintaining the same system of laws, government, and course of study. But in regard to female institutions, every thing is ephemeral; because, in most cases, every thing depends upon the character and enterprise of a single individual. A school may be at the height of prosperity one week, and the next week entirely extinct.

Another object to be aimed at in regard to female education is a remedy for the desultory, irregu-

lar, and very superficial course of education now so common in all parts of our country. When young men are sent to obtain a good education, there is some standard for judging of their attainments; there are some data for determining what has been accomplished. But, in regard to females, they are sent first to one school, and then to another; they attend a short time to one set of studies, and then to another; while everything is desultory, unsystematic, and superficial...

The remedy for this evil (in addition to what is suggested in previous remarks) is to be sought in cooperating efforts among leading female schools in the country, to establish a uniform course of education, adapted to the character and circumstances of females, to correspond with what is done in colleges for young gentlemen....

Another object to be aimed at in regard to female education is, to introduce into schools such a course of intellectual and moral discipline, and such attention to mental and personal habits, as shall have a decided influence in fitting woman for her peculiar duties. What is the most important and peculiar duty of the female sex? It is the physical, intellectual, and moral education of children. It is the care of health, and the formation of the character, of the future citizen of this great nation.

Woman, whatever are her relations in life, is necessarily the guardian of the nursery, the compan-

Source: Beecher, Catharine. Paper read at the annual meeting of the American Lyceum, 1835. Reprinted in Goodsell, Willystine (ed.) *Pioneers of Women's Education in the United States*, New York: AMS Press, 1931.

ion of childhood, and the constant model of imitation. It is her hand that first stamps impressions on the immortal spirit, that must remain forever. And what demands such discretion, such energy, such patience, such tenderness, love, and wisdom, such perspicacity to discern, such versatility to modify, such efficiency to execute, such firmness to persevere, as the government and education of all the various characters and the tempers that meet in the nursery and schoolroom? Woman also is the presiding genius who must regulate all those thousand minutiae of domestic business, that demand habits of industry, order, neatness, punctuality and constant care. And it is for varied duties that woman is to be trained. For this her warm sympathies, her lively imagination, her ready invention, her quick perceptions, all need to be cherished and improved; while at the same time those more foreign habits of patient attention, calm judgment, steady efficiency, and habitual self-control, must be induced and sustained. . . .

None will deny the importance of having females properly fitted for their peculiar duties; and yet few are aware how much influence a teacher may exert in accomplishing this object. School is generally considered as a place where children are sent, not to form their habits, opinions, and character, but simply to learn from books. And yet, whatever may be the opinion of teachers and parents, children do, to a very great extent, form their character under influences bearing upon them at schools. They are proverbially creatures of imitation, and accessible to powerful influences. Six hours every day are spent with teachers, whom they usually love and respect, and whose sentiments and opinions, in one way or another, they constantly discover. They are at the same time associated with companions of all varieties of temper, character, and habit. Is it possible that this can exist without solving constant and powerful influences, either good or bad?

The simple fact that a teacher succeeds in making a child habitually accurate and thorough in all the lessons of school may induce mental habits that will have a controlling influence through life. If the government of schools be so administered as to induce habits of cheerful and implicit obedience, if punctuality, neatness, and order in all school employments are preserved for a course of years, it must have some influence in forming useful habits. . . .

Nor is the course of study and mental discipline of inferior consequence. The mere committing to memory of the facts contained in books is but a small portion of education. Certain portions of time should be devoted to fitting a woman for her practical duties: such, for example, as needlework. Other pursuits are designed for the cultivation of certain mental faculties, such as *attention, perseverance,* and *accuracy.* This, for example, is the influence of the study of mathematics; while the conversation and efforts of a teacher, directed to this end, may induce habits of investigation and correct reasoning, not to be secured by any other method. Other pursuits are designed to cultivate the taste and imagination: such as rhetoric, poetry, and other branches of polite literature. Some studies are fitted to form correct moral principles, and strengthen religious obligation: such as mental and moral philosophy, the study of the evidences of Christianity, the study of the Bible, and of collateral subjects. Other studies are designed to store the mind with useful knowledge: such, for example, as geography, history, and the natural sciences. The proper selection and due proportion of these various pursuits, will have a decided influence in forming the mental habits and general character of the pupils . . .

But the most important deficiency, and one which is equally felt by both sexes, is the want of a system of moral and religious education at school, which shall have a decided influence in forming the character, and regulating the principles and conduct of future life.

When it is asserted that it is of more consequence that women be educated to be virtuous, useful, and pious, than that they become learned and accomplished, every one assents to the truth of the position. When it is said that it is the most important and most difficult duty of parents and teachers to form the moral character, the principles, and habits of children, no one will dissent. All allow it to be a labor demanding great watchfulness, great wisdom, and constant perseverance and care. For what comfort would parents find in the assurance that their children are intelligent, learned, and accomplished, if all is to be perverted by indolence, vice, and irreligion? And what is the benefit to society in increasing the power of intellect and learning if they only add to the evils of contaminating example and ruinous vice? The necessity of virtuous intelligence in the mass of the community is peculiarly felt in a form of government like ours, where the people are not held in restraint by physical force, as in despotic governments, but where, if they do not voluntarily submit to the restraints of virtue and religion, they must inevitably run loose to wild misrule, anarchy, and crime. For a nation to be virtuous and religious, the females of that nation must be deeply imbued with these principles: for just as the wives and mothers sink or rise in the scale of virtue, intelligence, and piety, the husbands and the sons will rise or fall. These positions scarce any intelligent person will deny: so that it may be set down as one of the current truisms of society, that the formation of the moral and religious principles and habits is the most important part of education, even in reference to this life alone. To this is added the profession of all who reverence Christianity, that the interests of an immortal state of being are equally suspended on the same results. . . .

We find that in one of our smallest middle states, thirty thousand adults and children are entirely without education and without schools. In one of the largest middle states, four hundred thousand adults and children are thus destitute. In one of the best educated western states, one-third of the children are without schools; while it appears that, in the whole nation, there are a million and a half of children, and nearly as many adults, in the same deplorable ignorance, and without any means of instruction. At the same time, thousands and thousands of degraded foreigners, and their ignorant families, are pouring into this nation at every avenue . . . That terrific crisis is now before us; and a few years will witness its consummation, unless such energetic and persevering efforts are made as time never saw.

Public sentiment must be aroused to a sense of danger; so the wealthy and intelligent must pour out their treasures to endow seminaries for teachers; moral and religious education, and the best methods of governing and regulating the human mind, must become a science; those who have had most experience, and are best qualified in this department, must be called upon to contribute their experience and combined efforts, to qualify others for these duties; men of talent and piety must enter this as the noblest and most important missionary field; females who have time and talents, must be called to aid in the effort; seminaries for teachers, with their model schools, must be established in every state; agents must be employed to arouse and enlighten the people; and, when the people are sufficiently awake to the subject, legislative and national aid must be sought.

At this rate, *ninety thousand* teachers are this moment wanted to supply the destitute; and to these must be added every year twelve thousand, simply to meet the increase of population. But if we allow thirty pupils as the average number for every teacher, then we need thirty thousand teachers for the present wants, and an annual addition of four thousand for increase of population.

It is woman, fitted by disposition and habits, and circumstances, for such duties, who, to a very wide extent, must aid in educating the childhood and youth of this nation; and therefore it is that females must be trained and educated for this employment. And, most happily, it is true, that the education necessary to fit a woman to be a teacher, is exactly the one that best fits her for that domestic relation she is primarily designed to fill. . . .

"Whom shall we send, and who will go for us?" and from amid the green hills and white villages of New England, hundreds of voices, through the whole length of the land, would echo the reply.

Discussion Questions

1. Compare and contrast the curriculum of the Willard Seminary School with that of the Beecher Seminary. Is either more like the teachers' colleges curricula of today?
2. Compare and contrast the special abilities of the women Beecher mentions that prepare them especially for teaching. In what ways are they the same and how are they also different from what Willard mentioned?
3. Beecher includes religious instruction in her schools. Given the growing cultural diversity of the expanding population at this time, is it possible to find nondenominational religious values upon which all will agree?
4. Catharine puts a major emphasis on the role of the schools to promote character and moral development and believes that it can be done. Do you agree with her that you can evaluate the character development of students?

For Further Research on the Internet

PBS series on famous educators includes a biography with a picture. http://www.pbs.org/onlyateacher/beecher.html

The complete social, political, and educational writings of Beecher on-line. http://www.thoemmes.com/american/beecher.htm

Suggestions for Further Reading

Cremin, Lawrence. *American Education: The National Experience 1783–1876.* New York: Harper & Row, Publishers, 1980.

Gill, Valerie. "Catharine Beecher and Charlotte Perkins Gilman: Architects of Female Power." *Journal of American Culture* 21 (2)(1998): 17–25.

Harveson, Mae Elizabeth. *Catharine Ester Beecher (Pioneer Educator).* New York: Arno Press, Inc., 1969.

Sexton, Patricia. *Women in Education.* Bloomington, IN: Phi Delta Kappa Educational Foundation, 1976.

Sklar, Kathryn Kish. *Catharine Beecher: A Study in American Domesticity.* New York: Norton & Co., 1976.

Thorp, Margaret. *Female Persuasion: Six Strong-Minded Women.* New York: Archon Books, 1971.

CHAPTER ACTIVITIES

Linking the Past to the Present

1. Look in your college catalog at several different academic majors including education. How many course credits are required for a degree in that major? How many courses are prescribed and how many electives are allowed? How are electives chosen? Evaluate the current system. Role play Emma Willard. What do you think she would propose for colleges in the twenty-first century?

2. Have a debate in which one person takes the role of Horace Mann and one takes the role of Catharine Beecher. Debate the following topics:

   a. What does the first amendment really say about religion in schools?

   b. Should the Christmas holiday be changed to winter holiday? Can religious songs be sung in a Christmas concert?

   c. Should non-denominational prayer and/or a moment of silence be allowed in public schools? What about allowing students to pray at certain times?

   d. Should students be allowed to wear religious garb and/or medals or signs in school?

Developing Your Philosophy of Education

Identify the values that you think can and should be taught today in the public schools in your philosophy of education. Consider what values can be taught given our pluralistic and multicultural student body. Identify the curricular areas in which you can most easily incorporate instruction in these values.

Connecting Theory to Practice

Interview your clinical teacher. Ask him/her to evaluate their own teacher training program. In what ways do they think they were well trained? What things do they wish they had been taught? How have they continued to learn things to help them be better teachers? What is their opinion about teaching values in the public schools? If taught, how did their school arrive at a consensus regarding which values should be taught?

Educators' Philosophies and Contributions to Education

TABLE 9.1   Philosophy and Contributions of American Educators

Educator	Role of Teacher & Learner	View of Curriculum & Methodology	Purpose or Goal of Education	Major Contribution
Mann	Teachers need to be competent so they need to be taught how to teach; develop student's body, intellect, and spirit; child's moral character and religious formation	Common elementary school curriculum; no sectarian teaching of religion, only general teaching of Christianity	To develop contributing citizens and responsible members of society	The Common School idea with graded classrooms, lesson plans, education for all financed by local taxes; first teacher training schools
Willard	Higher education for women taught by women	Liberal arts curriculum, a systematic study of pedagogy; teaching history and geography using charts and maps	To educate women for responsible motherhood, useful citizenship, and to train some to be teachers	First higher education for women—Troy Female Seminary; first scholarships for women's education
Beecher	Women are particularly suited for teaching; schools are needed for all children in the country, including immigrants and farmers	Liberal education for women; teach social, moral, and religious principles; rigorous teacher preparation program	Refined and well-educated women would be beneficial for society; end of education was character formation	National system of teacher seminaries; collegiate level studies for women

CHAPTER 10

Education for All?

Public Support for Religion in the Schools

As noted in Chapter 8, missionaries in Florida, Texas, and California (which were not part of the original colonies that formed the United States) started schools in the early 1600s. The first state constitutions expressly endorsed public support for denominational schools emphasizing the "free exercise" clause of the First Amendment over the "establishment" clause. (Today we emphasize the principle of Church-State separation over the freedom of religion guarantee.) Where Church and State were united, there was no hard and fast distinctions made between public and sectarian schools. The main purpose of public education was to develop good character; and as moral education comes from religious teachings as found in the Bible, religious teaching and reading the Bible in publicly supported schools was a common practice.[1] The major shift from private to public education occurred in the nineteenth century, for prior to 1800 there was no such thing as a state system of public education anywhere in the United States.

The Establishment of Parochial School Systems

The first Roman Catholic School in New York was established in 1801, and at that time it received funding from the city's state school subsidy. When the common Council voted to restrict allocations from the state to nondenominational institutions, the Roman Catholics in the city objected strenuously saying the "so-called nondenominational schools of the public school society were Protestant, not nondenominational. They taught from the Protestant Bible and were very hostile to Catholic history and culture."[2] Bishop John

Hughes led the campaign to allow state funds to once again be used for the Catholic schools as it was for the Protestant common school. Governor William Seward of New York was supportive and recommended that immigrant groups be permitted to have public schools presided over by teachers of their own language and faith but the recommendation was not acted upon. The new law passed in 1842 stated that public tax monies were not to be used in any school that taught a sectarian religion.

With the large influx of Irish immigrants in the first half of the nineteenth century, the American parochial school system expanded greatly. By 1840, Catholics had created seventy-five elementary parochial schools, twenty-five high schools, and six colleges.[3] After the Catholic bishops met in a Plenary Council in Baltimore in 1884, they required all parishes to provide schools for Catholic youngsters following the model established by Elizabeth Seton in 1808 in Maryland. As a result there were, within the decade, three thousand Catholic schools in the country. Today in the United States there are over 1,700 Catholic high schools with more than 300,000 students and more than 8,500 Catholic elementary schools with over 2,000,000 students.[4]

As early as 1820, there were 240 Lutheran parochial schools in Pennsylvania. Henry Muhlenberg and the Missouri Synod Lutheran Church continued to establish and maintain a well-developed parochial school system in all the states. Currently there are approximately 1,700 Lutheran elementary and secondary schools that enroll about 200,000 pupils in the United States.[5] There were also schools created by Quakers, Jews, and other religious sects. In addition to religious schools, private schools and academies continued to operate as either military schools or as elite college preparatory schools.

Bitter opposition to parochial schools existed in some parts of the United States. Efforts were made to close parochial schools—the most famous case occurred in Oregon where, in 1922, the legislature passed a law requiring all children to attend public schools through eighth grade. The Society of Sisters of the Holy Name of Jesus and Mary brought a case against Governor Pierce to keep their schools open. Finally going all the way to the U.S. Supreme Court (*Pierce vs. The Society of the Holy Name of Jesus and Mary,* 1925), it was decided that the state law was unconstitutional; the state had a right to regulate and inspect private schools, but the state did not have a monopoly on education.[6] Parents had the right and liberty to choose the education they desired for their children. More recent court decisions have upheld this right, also asserting that the principle of Church/State separation did not prohibit indirect aid to sectarian schools for such needs as bus transportation, school lunches, and textbooks. The Lemon case established criteria for supporting aid to nonpublic schools as long as it was for a secular purpose, did not advance religion, and did not involve an excessive entanglement of religion.[7] Today we still see this issue debated with the idea of vouchers. In the late twentieth century, the more fundamentalist Protestant sects became just as dissatisfied with the "Godless" character of public schools as were nineteenth-century Catholics. They have begun to establish Christian schools in reaction to the failures of public schools to respect their position.[8]

Education of Students with Special Needs

There have always been students with special needs, but there have not always been special educational services to address their needs. In the pre-Revolutionary era, the most society had to offer children with disabilities was protection—asylum from a cruel world into which they did not fit and in which they could not live with dignity, if they could survive at all. After the revolutionary wars in America and in France, the ideas of democracy, individual freedom, and egalitarianism swept through these countries and people began to champion the cause of children and adults with disabilities. Political reformers and leaders in medicine and education began to urge that these "idiots," as they were called, be taught skills that would allow them to become independent, productive citizens. Early in the nineteenth century, beginning in France with the work of Jean-Marc-Gaspard Itard and Edouard Sequin, special methods and techniques were developed to teach these children. Many of these methods are still used today to educate these children who are now labeled as mentally challenged, emotionally or behaviorally disordered, or visually or hearing impaired.[9]

Teaching the Deaf

In the United States, Thomas Hopkins Gallaudet successfully taught his neighbor, Alice Cogswell, who was deaf. He went to Europe to study the latest methods for teaching the deaf, and returned to the United States to start, in 1817, the American Asylum for the Education and Instruction of the Deaf (now known as the American School for the Deaf) in Hartford, Connecticut. His son started the first liberal arts college for the deaf, now known as Gallaudet University.

Teaching the Blind

Samuel Gridley Howe, an 1824 graduate of Harvard Medical School, became a champion of the education of students with special needs. Howe was a physician, educator, and a political and social reformer. He successfully taught Laura Bridgman, who was deaf and blind, thus greatly influencing the future education of Helen Keller. Howe was instrumental in founding the New England Asylum for the Blind, now known as the Perkins School for the Blind, in Watertown, Massachusetts, and organized an experimental school for children with mental retardation.

Nineteenth-century reformers such as Horace Mann and Dorothea Dix worked with Gallaudet and Howe, giving impetus to the establishment of residential schools for these children. From 1817 to the beginning of the Civil War, a span of more than forty years, many states established residential schools for children who were deaf and blind. Providence, Rhode Island opened the first school for "backward" or mentally retarded children in 1896. Students with special needs were provided with schooling throughout the twentieth century, but segregated in their own schools and/or rooms until the 1970s.[10]

Special Education Laws

As late as 1950, seventy-two percent of disabled school-age children were still not enrolled in schools.[11] The Rehabilitation Act of 1973 was enacted to protect the handicapped from job discrimination and required organizations receiving federal funds to provide sign interpreters for the deaf. In 1975, the landmark Education for All Handicapped Children Act (Public Law 94–142) was passed, establishing the right of all handicapped children to a free and appropriate education from the ages of three to twenty-one years and granting economic aid for all handicapped children who need education in specialized facilities. (At that time there were some 3.7 million students with documented special needs.)[12] The Individuals with Disabilities Education Act of 1990 and 1997 stated that education should be provided in the least restrictive environment.

Education of African Americans

African Americans have contributed to the nation in significant ways since colonial times, but have rarely received equal education. The Boston School for Blacks opened in 1798, the first of its kind in the country. Frederick Douglas, a runaway slave, spoke eloquently in favor of black rights in 1817, advocating vocational education for all. John Adams was the first black teacher in a school in Washington, D.C. in 1824.

Prudence Crandwell, a Quaker in Connecticut, opened a boarding school for girls. When one black girl applied, Prudence accepted the girl, but the other students left. Prudence then recruited other black girls for her school. The whites passed a law against educating blacks, but Prudence went to jail rather than close her school.

Education for Blacks After the Civil War

When the Emancipation Proclamation in 1863 liberated four million slaves, only five percent of all the blacks in the country were literate; those who were lived in the north. After the Civil War, the schools lay in ruins both in the north and in the south. Many teachers from both sides had been killed in the war. The North viewed education as the social cement that could bring the nation together. Some reduced the Civil War to ignorance on the part of the Southerners about basic political science. (See Map 10.1, the United States before the Civil War.) Congress established the Freedmen's Bureau in 1865 to provide relief to the war-torn South, and especially to the black population. It issued food rations, established hospitals, and most significantly, it coordinated the establishment of educational programs and activities. By 1870, when the education activity of the bureau came to an end, 4,329 schools had been established with some 9,500 teachers working with more than 247,000 pupils.[13]

In 1867, two years before he died, George Peabody established an Education Fund to be used for the "intellectual, moral or industrial education" of the young southerners. This fund helped to rebuild schools in the south for blacks. In 1882, John F. Slater established a fund of one million dollars to be used to "assist in the education of the Negro people of the South."[14]

Vocational Education or Professional Education?

Booker T. Washington, born in 1856, lived through the transition from slave to freeman experienced by all Negroes living in this time period. Washington founded the Tuskegee Institute in Alabama, with a mission of providing blacks with a practical, vocational education. Washington believed that the blacks would find their place in society by obtaining a skill that would give them an occupation and provide them with economic security. He stressed his philosophy of the value of hard work and the dignity of labor.

Is "Separate But Equal" Ever Really Equal?

W. E. B. DuBois was born in 1868, after the Civil War ended. He was the first African American to earn a doctorate from Harvard University. Coming from a completely different background than Booker T. Washington (although only a few years apart in age)

Map 10.1   The United States Before the Civil War

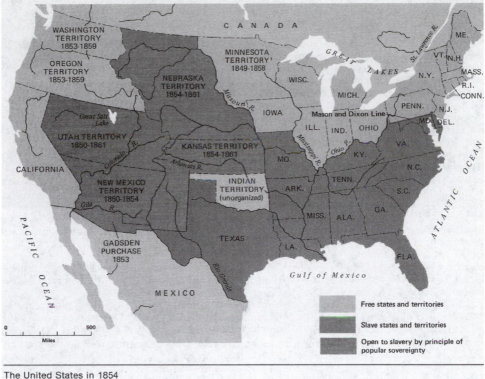

The United States in 1854

Source: Aaron, Daniel; Hofstadter, Beatrice; Miller, William; Litwack, Leon; *United States, Volume I, Conquering a Continent,* 5th edition, © 1982. Reprinted by permission of Pearson Education, Inc., Upper Saddle River, NJ, p. 328.

DuBois advocated education in the professions for blacks. He worked for social change and helped found the National Association for the Advancement of Colored People (NAACP) in 1909. The NAACP became the leading organization seeking to reverse the "separate but equal" doctrine of the *Plessy vs. Ferguson* case of 1896 in which the United States Supreme Court rejected the claim that state segregation laws violated the rights of equal citizenship guaranteed to blacks and all Americans. The Court upheld the constitutionality of a Louisiana law that allowed railroads to provide separate but equal accommodations in different train cars for African Americans and whites. Separate was **not** equal. There was a great lack of equality between schools for white children and schools for black children in America; one taught higher level thinking skills and the other barely taught the basics. The NAACP reached its goal of overthrowing this landmark case in 1954 with the *Brown vs. Topeka* case, a class-action suit involving thirteen black families in Topeka, Kansas.[15]

On May 17, 1954, Chief Justice Earl Warren announced the court's unanimous decision: "It is doubtful that any child may reasonably be expected to succeed in life if he is denied the opportunity of an education. Such opportunity ... is a right which must be made available to all on equal terms. Separate educational facilities are inherently unequal."[16]

TABLE 10.1   Population Growth in America

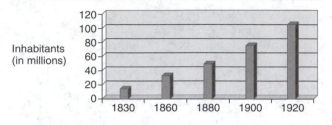

Inhabitants (in millions)

Growth in Number of Schools

When Horace Mann was promoting the common school in the 1830s there were some 13 million Americans; by the Civil War this number had tripled to 32 million, in part due to the Mexican-American War that resulted in the annexation of the southwestern states from California to Texas. Due to a staggering influx of some four million immigrants from Ireland, Germany, Poland, Italy, Russia, China and Japan in the 1880s, the population rose to 76 million by the turn of the century and 106 million by 1920 (see Table 10.1 showing the population growth).

The implications for education were great because not only the school-age population grew, but the percentage of students attending school grew as the nation moved from an agricultural to an industrial nation and more people lived in cities than in rural areas. The end of the nineteenth century saw explosive growth in America's public schools. Public school enrollments increased from 7.6 million in 1870 to 12.7 million in 1880 and school expenditures rose from $69 million in 1880 to $147 million in 1890. The United States was providing more schooling to more children than any other nation on earth thanks to the nineteenth century school reform movement.[17] Between 1890 and 1920 the school-age population increased by forty-nine percent but school enrollments grew by seventy percent.

Education for Immigrants

By 1900, the United States was becoming increasingly urban. Cities were crowed with immigrants arriving from every part of the globe. Between 1890 and 1930, nearly 22 million people came to the United States, bringing with them over 3 million children. "For them school was the place where the American dream was nurtured and the future itself took shape."[18] The school now took on a very important role of socialization and cultural patrimony. The working class wanted upward social and economic mobility and they looked to the schools to provide them with this American dream.

Yet as school enrollments multiplied, questions continually arose about what to teach, whether to give the same kind of education to all children, and how to allocate educational opportunities among different groups of children. The debates of this period centered on differing ideas about what sort of education a democratic society should offer its children.[19] According to Joel Spring, in the latter half of the nineteenth century the educational treatment of Hispanics, Asians, Native Americans, and African Americans ran counter to the common school ideal of uniting all children in the same school house.[20]

Native Americans were sent to special government schools where they were forced to abandon their tribal languages, customs, and dress for they could only become American citizens if the adopted the European culture. As early as 1870 a law was passed in Texas mandating English-only instruction in the public schools. Spanish speaking children could only receive bilingual instruction in the Catholic schools. Asian Americans immigrated as early as 1850 to join the Gold Rush, but they were also met with much hostility. In the years before World War I, schools in many cities taught courses in the language of the major immigrant group, such as German. But by 1917 the United States was at war and an English-only curriculum was proposed.

It was 1968 before the Bilingual Education Act (Title VII) was passed and teaching was allowed in the Native American, Spanish, and Chinese language. Soon afterwards it was mandated by the 1974 Supreme Court decision of *Lau vs. Nichols* and the federal government published teaching materials in nearly seventy languages and allocated $68 million for bilingual programs. However, the purpose of bilingual education is still debated today. Is it to bring a non-English speaker into the mainstream? Or is it to preserve diverse languages and cultures?[21]

For Further Research on the Internet

Homesite of the National Catholic Education Association with information and statistics on Catholic Schools in the United States. **http://www.ncea.org/**

Homesite of the Lutheran Schools. **http://www.elca.org/schools/**

Council on the Education of the Deaf. **http://www.deafed.net**

Milestones in Education of African Americans with many excellent links. **http://www. africanamericans.com/EducationMilestones.htm**

National Association for Bilingual Education. **http://www.nabe.org/**

Notes

1. Sarah Mondale, and Sarah Patton, eds., *School: The Story of American Public Education* (Boston: Beacon Press, 2001), p. 4.
2. Lawrence Cremin, *American Education: The National Experience 1783–1876* (New York: Harper & Row, Publishers, 1980), p. 166.
3. John Pulliam, and James Van Patten, *History of Education in America* (Upper Saddle River, NJ: Merrill/Prentice Hall, 2003), p. 131.
4. Leonard Feeney, *Mother Seton: Saint Elizabeth of New York (1774–1821)* (Still River, MA: The Ravengate Press, 1991), p. 3.
5. James Johnson, Victor L. Dupuis, et al., *Introduction to the Foundations of American Education,* 11th ed. (Boston: Allyn and Bacon, 1999), p. 322.
6. Pulliam and Van Patten, p. 132.
7. Ibid., p. 237.
8. Wayne Urban and Jennings Wagoner, *American Education: A History* (Burr Ridge, IL: McGraw Hill, 2000), p. 115.
9. Daniel Hallahan and James Kauffman, *Exceptional Learners: Introduction to Special Education* (Boston; Allyn and Bacon, 2000), pp. 25–26.
10. Ibid., p. 27; Samuel Kirk, James Gallagher, et al., *Educating Exceptional Children* (Boston: Houghton Mifflin, 2000), p. 43.
11. Mondale and Patton, p. 133.
12. Ibid., p. 162.
13. Urban and Wagoner, p. 143.
14. Ibid., p. 149.
15. Mondale and Patton, p. 38.
16. Ibid, p. 138.
17. Ibid, p. 58.
18. Ibid., p. 72.
19. Ibid., p. 64.
20. Joel Spring, *The American School: 1642–2000* (New York: McGraw Hill, 2001), p. 168.
21. Mondale and Patton, p. 58.

Section 10.1: Elizabeth Ann Seton (1774–1821)

Did you go to a private or public elementary school? Some private schools are very exclusive and expensive; others are much more affordable because they are connected with a local parish. We have Elizabeth Seton to thank for promoting parochial education for all those so interested. The parochial educational system in the United States is one of the largest in the world.

Elizabeth Seton's Life and Times

Elizabeth Ann Bayley was born in New York City on August 28, 1774, the second of three girls to Dr. Richard Bayley, New York's first public health officer. Elizabeth's mother died in childbirth when Elizabeth was three, and the infant died two years later, which made a deep impression on young Elizabeth, who thought about her mother and little sister in heaven.[1] Her father remarried and had seven more children, so Elizabeth was often sent to stay with her grandparents or her uncle, with whom she found love and attention. Eager for a parent's love, she turned to her heavenly Father for consolation, reading the Bible. Elizabeth studied music, drawing, French, literature, sewing, dancing, and housekeeping.

Wife and Mother

Elizabeth's life in high society began when she attended George Washington's Inaugural Ball. She was beautiful and was courted profusely in her youth.[2] On January 25, 1794, Elizabeth Ann Bayley married William Magee Seton, a New York businessman. He was a kind and thoughtful husband and Elizabeth was enthusiastically accepted into his large family. In eight years, Elizabeth had five children. In addition to caring for her children, she organized a charity that provided aid to poor widows and orphans. Her father died ministering to Irish immigrants with the plague, quarantined on Staten Island, and Elizabeth found his death very difficult.[3] When her father-in-law died, her husband took in his younger sisters, Rebecca and Cecelia. They became close to Elizabeth as she home schooled the young girls. School began at ten o'clock in the parlor studying grammar, reading, writing, spelling, sewing, figures, and religion.[4]

The Seton shipping business sank after the father's death as privateers attacked ships and storms capsized vessels. With legal suits for lost cargo, William's financial situation suffered dramatic reverses—the house and furniture were repossessed.[5] Elizabeth was as equal to poverty as to wealth but her husband became depressed and sick with tuberculosis.

Elizabeth sought spiritual direction at this difficult time and began a plan of prayer and Bible reading that was to continue all of her life.[6] On August 15, 1802, she received the sacrament of the Lord's Supper. Following the advice of her husband's doctors, they sailed for Italy with their oldest daughter to visit William's business friends, the Filicchi brothers, Filippo and Antonio. Arriving in Italy, they were quarantined due to a yellow fever outbreak in New York. They spent a month in a hospice for those with infectious diseases and Elizabeth cared for her husband as well as she could, praying and reading the

Bible to him, and telling stories to her daughter. They finally entered Italy, but William died on December 27, 1803.[7] (See the timeline of Seton's life in Figure 10.1.)

Converted to Catholicism

Elizabeth and Anna stayed with the Filicchi family in Leghorn until they could make the return voyage to America. The high point of her stay in Italy was a trip she made to Florence where she visited her first Catholic Church—the Church of the Annunciation. Elizabeth was impressed and moved by the rich ornaments and by the piety of the people in the Church.[8] Elizabeth loved the Filicchi family life with daily Mass and prayers throughout the day. Antonio and his wife Amabalia answered all her questions about the Catholic faith. By the time Elizabeth and her daughter returned to the United States, Elizabeth was seriously thinking about converting.

Elizabeth was thirty, a widowed mother of five, and a pauper, because her husband's business had completely collapsed while they were in Italy. Elizabeth went through the greatest spiritual crisis of her life—the tug of war between Protestant or Catholic left her confused and exhausted. Finally, she was received into the Church and was instructed for her confirmation by Bishop John Carroll. All of New York City high society was buzzing about Elizabeth's conversion. She was ostracized, criticized, in poor health, with five children, a disgraced name, and no money.[9]

Teacher and School Foundress

Elizabeth began to teach in a Protestant school and was doing well until Cecelia Seton, her sixteen-year-old sister-in-law, decided to become a Catholic. Her family greatly opposed this and tried to get Elizabeth expelled from the city. On June 9, 1808, at the age of 35, Elizabeth left New York City, invited by Father DuBourg, President of St. Mary's Seminary, and Bishop Carroll to start a school in the large Catholic city of Baltimore.[10] Elizabeth started a school for girls in a small mansion on Paca Street, teaching them reading, writing, arithmetic, French, and needlework. Fr. Babade from St. Mary's Seminary taught the religion and catechism classes.[11] Catholic parents from the town asked that their children be given religious instruction at the school and Elizabeth admitted these girls to prepare for their first Holy Communion. It was this idea of accepting girls from the parish, free of charge, that earned Elizabeth Seton the title of "Founder of the Catholic parochial school system."[12]

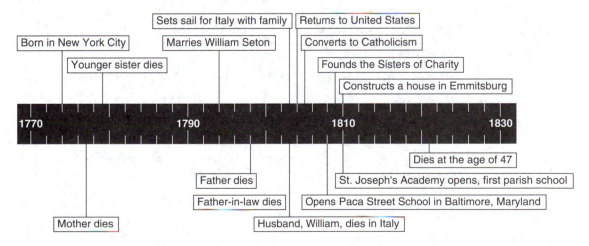

Figure 10.1 Seton's Life and Times

Mother Seton

Elizabeth felt the call to dedicate her life to God. Young girls who felt they had a religious vocation came to assist Elizabeth with teaching. With the help of Bishop Carroll and Father DuBong, on March 25, 1809, Elizabeth and the others took vows of poverty, chastity, and obedience, appointing Elizabeth as their directress. Cecelia Seton came from New York to join Elizabeth, or "Mother Seton" as she was now called.[13]

Mr. Samuel Sutherland Cooper donated money as well as property at Emmitsburg in order to "establish an institution for the advancement of Catholic female children in habits of religion." The Emmitsburg plan, entrusted to Elizabeth, was "to construct a house which would serve the threefold purpose of a boarding house for girls whose tuition would be the principal revenue of the sisters, a school for poor children, and a home for the aged."[14] In February of 1810, they were able to move into their new house and opened St. Joseph's Academy with five boarders and three children from the village in the day school, who were the first pupils of a parish school in America. This became the primary cell of the modern Catholic parochial school system. The school was a great success and by the end of the year, there were thirty boarding children and forty day students.

Mother Seton was the guiding spirit of the literary and religious department and visited classrooms daily, manifesting the interest she felt in the improvement of the students. As supervisor of the school, she encouraged the students and the teachers in the performance of their respective duties.[15] The teachers kept a daily record on the behavior and progress of each girl. Medals and certificates were awarded for excellence.

Mother Seton contracted a fever and tuberculosis. On January 4, 1821, she died, at only forty-seven years of age. The order she founded, The Sisters of Charity, grew and spread, starting schools, hospitals, colleges, nursing homes, and convents throughout the world. In his homily at her canonization, Pope Paul VI gave her as an example to the modern world, "She was like so many women today, a single working mother" who dedicated herself to doing God's will on earth.[16]

Her Contribution to Education

The schools started by Elizabeth Seton were not the first Catholic schools in the United States. As we have seen, missionaries founded schools in the early 1600s in Florida, Texas, and California (which were not part of the United States when Elizabeth started her schools). The first Roman Catholic school in New York was established in 1801, but at that time it received funding from the city's state school subsidy. Elizabeth's school at Emmitsburg is considered the first Catholic parochial school because it was free for the Catholic children from the parish who helped to subsidize it. As Seton biographer Annabelle Melville explains, "The American Catholic Parochial School System may be defined as a system of schools by which free education in a religious atmosphere under religious auspices and with religious teachers is provided for the children of the parish."[17]

The educational aims of Mother Seton and her community were to establish free common schools for the poorer class, not academies for the well-to-do. Elizabeth was the mother of the parish school, and, as America's first parochial school teacher, can be considered the pioneer of Catholic school teachers.[18]

Seton's Philosophy of Education

Elizabeth Seton's philosophy of education placed an entire educational program under the guidance and inspiration of religion. She believed in religious and moral training in a religious atmosphere with good discipline and respect for authority, the distinctive characteristics of parochial schools today. Founded on solid principles of piety and culture, the most absorbing objective of the school, for Elizabeth, was the education of students, while forming their hearts to virtue and inspiring them with a proper aversion to sin. She impressed on her pupils sound principles of morality and good conduct. She was kind yet firm when correcting them, only desiring their good. Her amiable manner led to an extra-ordinary influence over all her pupils.[19]

Elizabeth possessed the intellectual, moral, and spiritual qualities requisite in an edu-cator and she had a natural talent and affinity for teaching. Elizabeth regarded the girls of her school as a sacred trust committed to her by divine Providence to be cultivated with solicitude similar to that which God has for his creatures. She told her sisters that they should consider themselves the guardian angels of their students. Her concept of human nature made her see each child entrusted to her as a creature of God, endowed with knowing, feeling, and spiritual faculties. She had a holistic view of education and was concerned about the girls' physical and spiritual well-being. She saw to it that they had a wholesome diet, healthy amusements, and interesting recreation along with hours of in-tense study. She kept the parents informed of their girls' progress and enlisted their aid.[20]

Today in the United States, the Catholic parochial system is the largest in the world, as it evolved from Elizabeth Seton's initiative.[21] Elizabeth Seton lived the gospel message she preached, "When so rich a harvest is before us, why do we not gather it? All is in our hands if we will but use it."

Notes

1. Joseph Dirvin, *The Soul of Elizabeth Seton: A Spiritual Portrait* (San Francisco: Ignatius Press, 1990), p. 21.
2. Elaine Murray Stone, *Elizabeth Bayley Seton: An American Saint* (Mahwah, NJ: Paulist Press, 1993), pp. 5–6.
3. Leonard Feeney, *Mother Seton: Saint Elizabeth of New York (1774–1821)* (Still River, MA: The Ravengate Press, 1991), pp. 7–12.
4. Dirvin, p. 133.
5. Stone, p. 11.
6. Feeney, p. 51.
7. Ibid., pp. 69, 90.
8. Stone, pp. 25–26.
9. Feeney, p. 139.
10. Ibid., pp. 150–51.
11. Stone, p. 47.
12. Ellin, Kelly and Annabelle Melville, eds. *Elizabeth Seton: Selected Writings* (New York: Paulist Press, 1987), p. 19.
13. Feeney, p. 169.
14. Seton, "Letter of February 8th, 1809," in Ellen Kelly, and Annabelle Melville, eds. *Elizabeth Seton: Selected Writings* (New York: Paulist Press, 1987), p. 245.
15. John Agnes La Mantia, "Life and Work of Mother Seton with Particular Emphasis on Her Educational Prin-ciples," Masters thesis, Department of Education (Chicago: DePaul University, 1958), p. 28.
16. Stone, pp. 84–85.
17. Annabelle Melville, *Elizabeth Bayley Seton 1774–1821* (New York: Charles Scribner & Son., 1960), p. 224.
18. La Mantia, pp. 28–29.
19. Ibid., pp. 28, 35.
20. Ibid., pp. 25, 34.
21. Feeney, p. 3.

Questions to Guide Your Reading

1. What are the three purposes that Samuel Cooper had for the fortune he was donating to Reverend DuBourg?
2. How will the two separate houses be divided? Why?

READING 10.1:
LETTER TO ANTONIO FILICCHI

Baltimore February 8th, 1809

My dear Filicchi,

You will think I fear that the poor little woman's brain is turned who writes you so often on the same subject, but it is not a matter of choice on my part, as it is my indispensable duty to let you know every particular of a circumstance which has occurred since I wrote you last week relative to the suggestions so strongly indicated in the letters I have written both yourself and our Antonio since my arrival in Baltimore—some time ago I mentioned to you the conversion of a man of family and fortune in Philadelphia—this conversion is as solid as it was extraordinary, and as *the person* is soon to receive the Tonsure in our seminary, ill making the disposition of his fortune he has consulted our Rev. Mr. Dubourg the President of the College on the plan of establishing an institution for the advancement of Catholick female children in habits of religion and giving them an education suited to that purpose—he also desires extremely to extend the plan to the reception of the aged and also uneducated persons who may be employed in spinning, knitting, etc., etc. so as to found a manufactory on a small scale which may be very beneficial to the poor—

[Y]ou see I am bound to let you know this disposition of Providence that you may yourself judge how far you may concern with it—Dr. Matignon of Boston, to whom [along] Mr. Chevrus, the Bishop-elect, Antonio referred me on every occasion, had suggested this plan for me before the gentleman in question even thought of it—I have invariably kept in the background and avoided even reflecting voluntarily on any thing of the kind knowing that Almighty God alone could effect it if indeed it will be realized. My *Father*, Mr. Dubourg, has always said the same, be quiet, God will in his own time discover his intentions, nor will I allow one word of entreaty from my pen—His blessed Will be done.

[I]n my former letter I asked you if you could not secure your own property and build something for this purpose on the lot (which is an extensive one) given by Mr. Dubourg—if you should resolve to do so the gentleman interested will furnish the necessary expenditures for setting us off, and supporting those persons or children who will not be able to support themselves—Dr. Matignon will appoint a director for the establishment which if you knew how many good and excellent Souls are sighing for would soon obtain an interest in your breast, so ardently desiring the glory of God, but all is in his hands.

If I had a choice and my will should decide in a moment, I would remain silent in his hands. Oh how sweet it is there to rest in perfect confidence, yet in every daily Mass and at communion I beg him to prepare your heart and our dear Antonio's to dispose of me and mine in any way which may please him—You are our Father in him, thro' your hands we received that new and precious being which is indeed true life, and may you in your turn be rewarded with the fullness of the divine benediction. Amen a thousand times. MEA Seton

Also I must tell you that the idea of the building calculated extends to a division into two separate houses, one for the rich children who may be educated in a general manner, the other for the poor and such persons as may be employed in the manufactory as the infirm etc. [I]t is unnecessary to tell you how backward I feel, my dear Filicchi, in saying all this—but you know the motive and that is enough—

Source: From *Elizabeth Seton: Selected Writings*. Edited by Ellin Kelly and Annabelle Melville. Paulist Press, NY 1987, pp. 245–246. Used with permission.

Discussion Questions

1. What do you think the educational system would be like today if we continued exclusively with parochial schools like those found in the middle colonies?
2. Are the purposes of a parochial school any different than those of a secular school that teaches Christianity and morality as envisioned by Horace Mann?
3. A current issue in American education today is the use of vouchers. Parents could receive a yearly voucher for the education of their children and could use it to send them to the school of their choice, public or private. Are you in favor of vouchers? Why or why not?

For Further Research on the Internet

Home page for the National Shrine to Elizabeth Seton at Emmitsburg, Maryland. **http://emmitsburg.net/setonshrine/**

Home site of the Elizabeth Seton museum. **http://www.setonmuseum.org/index.html**

A comprehensive biography of Elizabeth Seton. **http://www.catholicism.org/pages/ seton.htm**

Suggestions for Further Reading

Dirvin, Joseph. *The Soul of Elizabeth Seton: A Spiritual Portrait*. San Francisco: Ignatius Press, 1990.

Feeney, Leonard. *Mother Seton: Saint Elizabeth of New York (1774–1821)*. Still River, MA: The Ravengate Press, 1991.

Kelly, Ellin and Annabelle Melville, eds. *Elizabeth Seton: Selected Writings*. New York: Paulist Press, 1987.

La Mantia, John Agnes. "Life and Work of Mother Seton with Particular Emphasis on Her Educational Principles." Master's thesis, Department of Education. Chicago: De-Paul University, 1958.

Melville, Annabelle. *Elizabeth Bayley Seton 1774–1821*. New York: Charles Scribner & Sons, 1960.

Stone, Elaine Murray. *Elizabeth Bayley Seton: An American Saint*. Mahwah, NJ: Paulist Press, 1993.

Section 10.2: Thomas Hopkins Gallaudet (1787–1851)

Although well accepted today, we owe the founding of the first school for the deaf in the United States, The American School for the Deaf in Hartford, Connecticut, to Thomas Gallaudet. His son helped carry out his dream, helping him to establish secondary-level and college-level education for the deaf. Gallaudet College is the only college in the world devoted exclusively to hearing-impaired students. All of this was founded by a humble man with very poor health.

Thomas Gallaudet's Life and Times

Thomas Hopkins Gallaudet was born on December 10, 1787, in Philadelphia, the first of twelve children of Peter Wallace Gallaudet and Jane Hopkins.[1] From his youth, Tom was small and frail due to a condition in his lungs that often left him breathless.[2]

His Education

Thomas attended the Hartford Grammar School. In 1802, Thomas applied to Yale and was accepted into the sophomore class. There he studied the typical liberal arts curriculum of the day that included history, Greek, Latin, English, chemistry, astronomy, logic, and philosophy. Thomas joined the debating team and was well known for his cheerful temperament and sound reasoning skills. Thomas was the Latin salutatorian and graduated from Yale in 1805 at 19 years of age, the youngest of his class.[3] He entered a firm to study law but had to resign due to health problems—an inability to breathe among the pipe smoke of the lawyers. Thomas returned to Hartford and wrote essays and editorials for the *Hartford Courant* and the *Children's Magazine*.[4]

Thomas, the Tutor

In 1808, he began a position at Yale as a tutor and was well received as the "tutor that knew all the answers." Thomas later on saw this as an experience that prepared him for his life work, as it introduced him to the subject of education as a science and its practical duties as an art.[5] Thomas worked as a tutor for two years and earned his master's degree but had to return home due to his health. In 1814, he graduated from his studies of divinity, but had to decline the many full-time job offers he received because of his poor health.[6]

Teaching a Deaf Child

In the summer, he went home and met Alice Cogswell, a nine-year-old deaf and dumb neighbor. Thomas spent some time with her on his first day home and was able to teach her the word for "hat." Alice's father, Dr. Mason Cogswell, was astonished with the progress his daughter had made in one afternoon. He had researched deafness and deaf education completely, finding that, although there were 84 deaf in Connecticut, 400 in

New England and 1,000 in America, there were no schools for them in the United States. Schools had begun in England, Scotland, France, and Spain, but he did not want to send his daughter so far away. Dr. Cogswell asked Thomas Gallaudet to continue teaching his daughter, giving Tom a French manual of finger spelling, signs, and the manual alphabet.[7] Tom's success with Alice encouraged local parents of deaf children to send Thomas to Europe to learn methods of teaching the deaf and then start a school in Hartford.

On May 25, 1815, Thomas sailed for England, where he found that the oral instruction of the deaf had been controlled since the mid 1700s by the Braidwood family. Monopolizing the method they had developed, they charged highly for the instruction of deaf students; they would train teachers in their method only if they pledged a bond of $1,000 against divulging the methods to others. Thomas could only learn the method if he agreed to a three-to-five-year indenture, working eleven hours a day.[8] Fortunately, while in England, Thomas met Abbe Sicard, who invited him to France to observe the French system of signs. He went to France to the Royal Institution for the Deaf and Dumb to study with the Abbe. In two busy months, he became proficient in every aspect of training offered by the institution. Laurent Clerc, a highly educated deaf mute and one of the best teachers at the Paris Royal Institute, was aware of Thomas' mission and suggested that he come to America as his assistant and to help establish the school.[9]

A School for the Deaf

When they arrived in America, they began seven months of traveling and fund-raising for the new school. On April 15, 1817, the American Asylum at Hartford for the Deaf and Dumb opened its doors to seven students; by the end of the school year, there were thirty-three students. Thomas hoped to teach both the sign method and his own improvised oral method. Classes were organized in alphabet, writing, reading, and sign. Later Thomas introduced classes in grammar, history, arithmetic, geography, speech, and practical trades such as furniture making, shoemaking, and sewing. In class, Thomas counted a word learned when it could be signed, finger-spelled, written, and read by the student. Thomas taught six hours each day and always led the evening prayers. His mission was to tell the

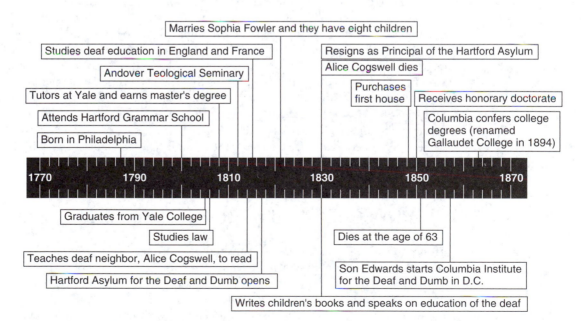

Figure 10.2 Gallaudet's Life and Times

students with sign language and speech about God, their Father in Heaven. The school was an immediate success, and was visited by many people, including President James Monroe. On May 22, 1821, a new three-story school building was dedicated on seven acres of land with a workshop for cabinet making and shoemaking; the school had 128 students and 5 teachers.[10] (See the timeline of Gallaudet's life in Figure 10.2)

Later that summer, on August 29, 1821, Thomas married Sophia Fowler, one of the older students in the first class of the school. They had eight children, two of whom would follow in his footsteps working with the deaf.[11]

Observing the results of the Hartford School, other states became interested in starting schools and they looked to the American School for teachers and teacher training. In 1830, Thomas decided to resign as principal of the American School, citing his health issues and a desire to promote deaf education at the high school and college levels. The Board of Directors accepted his resignation with the condition that he remain on the board as a general director and advisor for the school, which he gladly did. Thomas received dozens of offers for jobs, but he preferred to stay in Hartford, close to the American School. He began to write children's books and his first book, *The Child's Book on the Soul,* sold over a million copies and was translated into many languages. He wrote a series of biographies on Bible characters and helped to organize the first teachers' convention presided over by Noah Webster. He wrote and spoke promoting female education, secondary education for the deaf, and college for women and the deaf.[12]

On September 26, 1850, students from the first graduating class of the American School hosted a reunion for all past alumni (with their former principal and teacher). They presented Thomas Gallaudet and Laurent Clerc with commemorative silver pitchers etched with engravings showing the history of the American School. Thomas was very proud of the graduates, now successfully employed as photographers, carpenters, farmers, and industrial workers.

Thomas received an honorary degree of a Doctor of Laws from the Case Western Reserve College in 1851, in "recognition for his work as a promoter of education in many forms" and died later that year on September 10, at the age of 63.

Thomas's work was carried on by his sons. In 1837, his oldest son, Thomas, Jr., began teaching the deaf in New York. His youngest son, Edward, served as a superintendent of a new elementary school in the nation's capital. Committed to his father's goal of higher education for the deaf, Edward began the Columbia Institute for the Deaf and Dumb, which, in 1864, received legislative approval from President Abraham Lincoln to confer college degrees.[13] Edward retraced his father's steps, going to Europe to learn more about oral instruction. The first college in the world for the deaf used the "Combined System" so each student could learn in the method most helpful to them. On the centennial of his father's birth in 1887, Edward wrote a biography of his father *Life of Thomas Hopkins Gallaudet.* A statue of Thomas Gallaudet and Alice Cogswell was unveiled at the National Deaf-Mute College, renamed Gallaudet College in 1894 and then Gallaudet University in deference to the memory of the pioneer of education for the deaf.

Gallaudet's Contributions to Educational Thought

Thomas Gallaudet made general contributions to American education, especially to deaf education. He promoted female education from secondary school to college and joined those of his day who saw teaching as a profession well done by women. Thomas Gallaudet opened the Hartford School for the Deaf in 1817, and the Perkins School for the Blind soon followed, opening its doors in 1832. Thirteen other schools for the deaf developed rapidly in each state and more schools were started for students with other disabilities.

Ponce de Leon and Juan Pablo Bonet were the first to teach the deaf sons of the wealthy to read and write in the sixteenth century. They developed the signing method of instruction. A mere handful of schools existed in Europe for the deaf, and none existed in America before Gallaudet's time.[14]

In 1880, the National Association of the Deaf formed in Cincinnati, Ohio, promoting job opportunities for the deaf. In the 1970s, mainstreaming became popular and the combined system first urged by Thomas was renamed Total Communication.

In 1977, the first deaf-born lawyer graduated from the Massachusetts Institute of Technology. Today the National Technical Institute for the Deaf in Rochester, New York, confers Ph.D.s on the deaf in technical subjects. Deaf men and women are currently active as teachers, authors, lawyers, dancers, artists, actors, chemists, veterinarians, computer programmers, mechanical engineers, accountants, system analysts, and medical technicians. In 1981, *Children of a Lesser God,* an award-winning play later made into a movie, brought the subject of deafness to public acclaim.

Gallaudet's Philosophy of Education

In proposing that deaf children could and should be educated, Gallaudet promoted the general education of all children with disabilities. A child might be deaf, dumb, and/or blind, but that did not mean that he or she would be incapable of understanding and learning. Children with disabilities were not "freaks" that should be institutionalized. The intelligence within them needed to be awakened using special methods.

Two methods of instruction existed for teaching the deaf during Gallaudet's time: (1) the oral method, which is learning to read lips and parrot some words (popular in England and Scotland), and (2) the signing method which involved signing for words and spelling others using a manual alphabet (popular in Spain and France). Thomas' philosophy led him to propose the "Combined System," using both oral and signing methods so that each student could learn in the method most helpful to them. Even though the International Conference of Teachers of the Deaf in 1880 passed a resolution favoring the Pure Oral Method, the signing method continued strongly in the United States.

Thomas Gallaudet's dream is continually realized in the progress that deaf children are making in the United States today. In his words, "Aside from the leading and more important uses of giving instruction to the deaf and dumb, their education might be made to subserve the general cause of humanity."

Notes

1. Henry Barnard, *Tribute to Gallaudet: A Discourse in Commemoration of the Life, Character, and Services of the Rev. Thomas H. Gallaudet, LL.D.* (New York: F. C. Brownell, 1852), p. 9.
2. Anna E. Neimark, *A Deaf Child Listened: Thomas Gallaudet; Pioneer in American Education* (New York: William Morrow & Co., 1983), pp. 2–3.
3. Etta DeGering, *Gallaudet: Friend of the Deaf* (Washington, DC: Gallaudet University Press, 1987) (originally published by David McKay Co., Inc., in 1964), pp. 18, 25.
4. Neimark, p. 13; DeGering, pp. 26–27.
5. Barnard, p. 11.
6. Neimark, p. 17.
7. DeGering, pp. 45–46; Neimark, p. 20.
8. Neimark, pp. 34–37.
9. Barnard, p. 18.
10. Neimark, pp. 54–55, 64; DeGering, p. 101.
11. DeGering, p. 110.
12. Ibid., p. 118.
13. Ibid., pp. 156–59.
14. Neimark, p. 23.

Questions to Guide Your Reading

1. What are some of the advantages Gallaudet mentions that will come from the establishment of this Asylum?
2. What are the five ways the instructions of the deaf and dumb will aid the research of the philanthropist and the philosopher, according to Gallaudet?
3. What is worse than sickness for the body or chains in a dungeon according to Gallaudet?
4. In order to empathize with a deaf child, try watching a television show with your eyes closed and then continue watching the same show with the voice muted. Is it easier to understand what is going on while blind or deaf?

READING 10.2:
A SERMON

Just two years have elapsed since the first steps were taken toward the establishment, in this city, of an Asylum for the instruction of the deaf and dumb. It has met indeed with difficulties, and still labors under embarrassments, which are incident to almost all the untried efforts of benevolence. Yet, in its gradual progress, it has been encouraged by the smiles of a kind providence, and is at length enabled to commence its practical operation.

At such a season, the directors of its concerns have thought that a remembrance of past favors, and a conviction of future dependence on God, rendered it proper again to unite in solemn acts of religious worship. . . . It is at their request that the speaker rises to address this respectable assembly. May the spirit of grace impress these truths upon our hearts, while we take as the guide of our thoughts that portion of scripture which is contained in the 35th chapter of Isaiah, and the 5th and 6th verses.

"Then the eyes of the blind shall be opened, and the ears of the deaf shall be unstopped. Then shall the lame man leap as a hart, and the tongue of the dumb sing; For in the wilderness shall waters break out, and streams in the desert."

These words depict a part of the visions of futurity which gladdened the eye of Isaiah, and irradiate his writings with so cheering a luster, that he has been called "the evangelical prophet." His predilections are assuming in our day, some of their most glorious forms of fulfillment. For although they had a more direct reference to the time of our Saviour, by whose miraculous energy the ears of the deaf were opened, and the tongue of the dumb loosened, yet, without doubt, as might be proved from the general scope and tenor of the prophetic writings, they equally allude to the universal diffusion of the gospel in these latter ages of the church, and to its happy influence upon the hearts of all mankind. The same Saviour, who went about doing good, is also the Lord of this lower creation. It should be matter, therefore, of encouragement to us, that the establishment, which is now ready to receive within its walls the sons and daughters of misfortune, however humble may be its sphere of exertion, is not overlooked in the economy of the Redeemer's kingdom; that its probable influence is even shadowed forth in the sayings of prophecy; and that it forms one link in that golden chain of universally good-will, which will eventually embrace and bind together the

Source: Delivered at the Opening of the Connecticut Asylum for the Education and Instruction of Deaf and Dumb Persons, April 20th, 1817, by Rev. Thomas H. Gallaudet. from Henry Barnard "Tribute to Gallaudet" NY F. C. Brownwell, 1852.

whole family of man. Let it awaken our gratitude to think that our feeble efforts are not disregarded by the great Head of the church, and that we are permitted thus to cast our mite into his treasury. . . .

The whole plan of my discourse, then, will be to state several advantages which will arise from the establishment of this Asylum, and to propose several motives which should inspire those who are interested in its welfare, with renewed zeal, and the hopes of ultimate success.

The instruction of the deaf and dumb, if properly conducted, has a tendency to five important aids to many researches of the philanthropist, the philosopher, and the divine. The philanthropist and the philosopher are deeply interested in the business of education. The cultivation of the human mind is paramount to all other pursuits; inasmuch as spirit is superior to matter, and eternity to time. Youth is the season in which the powers of the mind begin to develop themselves, and language, the grand instrument by which this development is to take place. Now it is beyond all doubt, that great improvement has been made in the mode of instructing children in the use and power of language. To what extent these improvements may yet be carried, time alone can determine. The very singular condition in which the minds of the deaf and dumb are placed, and the peculiar means which are necessarily employed in their instruction, may furnish opportunities for observation and experiment, and the establishment of principles, with regard to the education of youth, which will not be without essential service in their general application. How much light also, may in this way be thrown upon what are supposed to be the original truths, felt and recognized to be such by the mind, without any reasoning process. Many speculations to which now are obscure and unsettled, respecting the faculties of the human mind, may be rendered more clear and satisfactory. How many questions, also, may be solved, concerning the capability of man to originate of himself, the notion of a God and of a future state, or, admitting his capacity to do this, whether, as a matter of fact, he ever would do it. What discoveries may be made respecting the original notions of right and wrong, the obligations of conscience, and, indeed, most of the similar topics connected with the moral sense. These hints are sufficient to show that aside from the leading and more important uses of giving instruction to the deaf and dumb, their education might be made to subserve the general cause of humanity, and of correct philosophy and theology.

But I pass to considerations of more immediate advantage; and one is, that of affording consolation to the relatives and friends of these unfortunate parents! Make the case your own! Fathers and mothers! Think what would be your feelings, were the son of your expectations, or the daughter of your hopes, to be found in this unhappy condition. The lamp of reason already lights its infant eye; the smile of intelligence plays upon its countenance; its little hand is stretched forth in significant expression of its wants; the delight. . . .

Ah! My hearers, I could spread before you scenes of a mother's anguish, I could read to you letters of a fathers anxiety, which would not fail to move your hearts to pity, and your eyes to tears, and to satisfy you that the prospect, which the instruction of their deaf and dumb children opens to parents, is a balm for one of the keenest of sorrows, inasmuch as it is a relief for what has been hitherto considered an irremediable misfortune.

The most important advantages, however, in the education of the deaf and dumb, accrue to those who are the subjects of it, and these are advantages which it is extremely difficult for those of us who are in possession of all our faculties duly to appreciate. He, whose pulse has always beat high with health, little understands the rapture of recovery from sickness. He, [whose] shoe has always trod the soil, and [who has] breathed the air of freedom, cannot sympathize with the feelings of ecstasy which glow in the breast of him, who, having long been the tenant of some dreary dungeon, is brought forth to the cheering influence of light and liberty.

But there is a sickness more dreadful than that of the body; there are chains more galling than those of the dungeon—the immortal mind preying upon itself, and so imprisoned as not to be able to unfold its intellectual and moral powers, and to attain to the comprehension and enjoyment of those objects which the Creator has designed as the sources of its highest expectations and hopes. Such must often be the condition of the uninstructed deaf and dumb! What mysterious darkness must sadden their souls! How imperfectly can they count for the wonders that surround them. Must not each one of them, in the language of thought, sometimes say, "What is it that makes me differ from my fellow men? Why are they so much my superiors? What is that strange mode of communication, by which they understand each other with the rapidity of lightning, and which enlivens their faces with the brightest expressions of joy? Why do I not possess it, or why can it not be communicated to me? What are those mysterious characters, over which they pore with such incessant delight, and which seem to gladden the hours that pass by me so sad and cheerless....

Behold these immortal minds! Some of them are before you; the pledges, we trust, of multitudes who will be rescued from the thralldom of ignorance: pursue, in imagination, their future progress in time and in eternity, and say, my hearers, whether I appreciate too highly, the blessings which we wish to be made the instruments of conferring upon the deaf and dumb?

For the means of anticipating these blessings, the deaf and dumb owe much to the liberality of generous individuals in our sister states; whose benevolence is only equaled by the expanded view which they take of the importance of concentrating, at present, the resources of the country in one establishment, that, by the extent of its means, the number of its pupils, and the qualifications of its instructors, it may enjoy the opportunity of maturing a uniform system of education for the deaf and dumb, and of training up teachers for such remoter places, as may need similar establishments.

This state, too, has we trust, given a pledge that it will not abandon an Asylum, which its own citizens have had the honor of founding; and which claims a connection, (a humble one indeed) with its other humane and literary institutions.

In this city, however, have the principal efforts been made in favor of this undertaking? Here, in the wise dispensations of his providence, God saw fit to afflict an interesting child with this affliction calamity, that her misfortune might move the feelings, and rouse the efforts, of her parents and friends in behalf of her fellow-sufferers. Here was excited, in consequence, that spirit of research which led to the melancholy discovery that our own small state probably contains one hundred of these unfortunates. Here were raised up the original benefactors of the deaf and dumb, whose benevolence has enabled the Asylum to open its doors for the reception of pupils much sooner than was at first contemplated. Here the hearts of many have been moved to offices of kindness, and labors of love, which the objects of their regard will have reason ever to remember with affectionate gratitude; and here is witnessed, for the first time in this western world, the affecting sight of a little group of fellow-sufferers assembling for instruction, whom neither sex, nor age, nor distance, could prevent from hastening to embrace the first opportunity of aspiring to the privileges that we enjoy, as rational, social, and immortal beings. They know the value of the gift that is offered them, and are not reluctant to quit the delights of their native home, (delights doubly dear to those whose circle of enjoyment is so contracted) nor to forsake the endearments of the parental roof, that they may find, in a land of strangers, and through toils of indefatigable perseverance, the treasures of wisdom and knowledge!

Discussion Questions

1. Gallaudet sees language as important for developing reasoning skills. How can children learn abstract concepts such as God, free will, and eternity if they cannot hear?

2. What are other ways that humans communicate besides speaking? Are they as effective as speech? Why or why not?

3. It is said that deaf persons feel more isolated from others than blind persons do because of their inability to hear communication. What are some ways you can help a deaf person feel that he or she belongs to the group?

4. How has our understanding and education of children with disabilities, including those who are blind and deaf, changed since the time of Gallaudet?

5. Gallaudet, in his speech, presents a religious view of the state of deafness. How would you challenge some of the things he says? What is the current legal understanding of deaf children and those with other disabilities?

For Further Research on the Internet

The Gallaudet University Visitor's Center contains biographies of its founders.
http://pr.gallaudet.edu/VisitorsCenter/GallaudetHistory/

A biography of Thomas Gallaudet. http://clerccenter.gallaudet.edu/infotogo/751.html

Suggestions for Further Reading

Barnard, Henry. *Tribute to Gallaudet: A Discourse in Commemoration of the Life, Character and Services, of the Rev. Thomas H. Gallaudet, LL.D.* New York: F. C. Brownell, 1852.

DeGering, Etta. *Gallaudet: Friend of the Deaf.* Washington, DC: Gallaudet University Press, 1987. (Originally published by David McKay Co., Inc., in 1964).

Neimark, Anna. E. *A Deaf Child Listened: Thomas Gallaudet; Pioneer in American Education.* New York: William Morrow & Co., 1983.

Section 10.3: Booker T. Washington (1856–1915)

Booker T. Washington is among the most celebrated African American men in American history. He was the first black man to dine with the President of the United States, and the first to have tea with the Queen of England. He was the first of the Negro race to receive honorary doctoral degrees and the first black American honored on a postage stamp and on a coin. All of this happened because this leading educator, school administrator, and spokesman for his race promoted the value of industrial education and the dignity of work well done.

Booker T. Washington's Life and Times

Booker was born on a plantation in Franklin County, Virginia on April 5, 1856.[1] He lived in a log cabin with his mother, Jane, his older brother, John, and his sister, Amanda. His mother was the plantation cook, with little time to rear her children. From the moment they were able, the children were occupied in work on the plantation carrying water, bringing corn to the mill, and fanning flies in the master's house. In his autobiography, Booker remembered the momentous day on which the Emancipation Proclamation was read to all the slaves on the plantation, proclaiming all of them free.[2] Then Jane took her family to join her husband, Washington Ferguson, in Malden, West Virginia, where she could give her total attention to her children.

His Education

Although Booker wanted to go to school, he and his brother joined their father working in the salt furnace and coal mine. His mother got him a copy of Webster's Blue-Back speller so he could teach himself the alphabet. Booker went to night school and for a short time he attended day school, where he needed a complete name, so he named himself Booker Taliaferro Washington.[3] Returning to full-time work to help the family, he got a job in the home of General Lewis and Viola Ruffner. After work, he was allowed to read from Mrs. Ruffner's library and attend night school.

Booker was determined to go to the Hampton Normal and Agricultural Institute in Virginia, which he entered in the fall of 1872, working as the janitor to pay for his room and board. At Hampton, Booker learned about personal hygiene, the value of work well done, and academics. He mastered his agricultural studies, worked hard to become an effective teacher, and acquired a love of Scripture. The principal, General Samuel Chapman Armstrong, an advocate of black freedom and leadership through educational advancements, influenced him. Washington's mother, his constant source of encouragement, died shortly after he had returned home during a summer break. In his autobiography, Washington says, "If I have done anything in life worth attention, I feel sure that I inherited the disposition from my mother."[4] Booker graduated from Hampton in June, 1875, having learned "what education was expected to do for an individual, to love labor for its own sake, and that the happiest individuals are those who do the most to make others useful and happy."[5]

Founding Tuskegee Institute

Booker returned to Malden to teach at the local school for Negroes before continuing his studies at the Wayland Seminary in Washington, D.C. He was not impressed with the program there because it taught students Latin and Greek but failed to teach them about life.[6] General Armstrong invited Booker back to Hampton to teach, and, in May 1881, he was recommended to a committee to start a normal college for Negroes in Tuskegee, Alabama. On July 4, 1881, Booker opened the Tuskegee Institute in an old shanty for thirty students aged fifteen or over. Booker implemented the Hampton Institute philosophy at Tuskegee, teaching the students personal hygiene, culture, academics, and a vocational trade.[7]

Olivia A. Davidson, a graduate of Hampton, came to help Booker as a co-teacher and fundraiser. They were able to buy an old plantation for use as the site of the central school building, which was built by the students just as future buildings were. Booker worked hard overseeing the daily operations, teaching, leading Sunday chapel exercises, and continuously fundraising. Success was crucial, as this was the first time in the nation's history that an educational institution was begun, run, and controlled by a Negro. Tuskegee functioned like a preparatory school in a model black community, acquainting students with the middle class way of life and teaching them the skills needed to participate in America's commercial life.

In the summer of 1882, Booker T. Washington married Fannie N. Smith, another graduate of Hampton Institute. They had one child before Fannie passed away in May 1884. In 1885, Booker married Olivia Davidson, who bore him two children before she died in 1889. In 1893, he married Margaret James Murray, a graduate of Fisk University. Margaret assisted Booker in his work, serving as Lady Principal at Tuskegee.[8] George Washington Carver joined Tuskegee's faculty in 1897 and headed the State Agricultural Experiment Station, discovering hundreds of uses for the peanut and sweet potato before his death in 1943.[9]

Public Speaker

In 1884, General Armstrong invited Booker to accompany him on a fund-raising tour in the northern states to raise money for Tuskegee. Armstrong introduced Booker to Andrew Carnegie and representatives from the John Slater Fund and the Peabody Fund. The tour procured thousands of dollars and Washington received his first public speaking request from the President of the National Educational Association. All 4000 people present were pleased with Washington's ideas that the future of the race rested upon whether education could help make the Negro of undeniable value to the community, through his skill, intelligence, and character.[10] On September 18, 1895, Washington was selected to represent Negro achievements in a speech to a vast audience of whites and blacks at the Atlanta Cotton States International Exposition. Washington presented a win-win option for both races: he urged whites to encourage black economic advancement, which would rebound in help for the white community, and he urged blacks to strive for educational and economic advancement rather than agitation for civil and political rights (see reading selection). After the speech, Washington became a national public figure and received more requests for speaking engagements than he could accept.[11] (See the timeline of Washington's life in Figure 10.3.)

In 1899, worn out from spending so much time on the road giving speeches, Booker and Margaret were given funds for a tour of Europe by a benevolent group of ladies from Boston. Upon returning to America, he was invited by Charles Eliot to receive an honorary degree from Harvard University, the first of his race to receive an honorary degree from a New England university.[12] On December 16, 1899, President William McKinley visited Tuskegee Institute on his way to a conference in Atlanta. On October 16, 1901, Booker dined with President Theodore Roosevelt in the White House, becoming his chief advisor regarding race relations and southern politics.[13]

Up from Slavery

In 1901, Booker published his autobiography, *Up from Slavery,* an immediate success that gave Washington international acclaim. After reading it, Andrew Carnegie gave him a $600,000 endowment for Tuskegee.[14]

Washington continued to raise funds and make improvements at Tuskegee Institute until it had sixty-six buildings on 2300 acres of land with 1400 students coming from various states, territories, and countries. The Institute continues to give its students thorough academic, religious, and industrial training. The industrial training enables students to

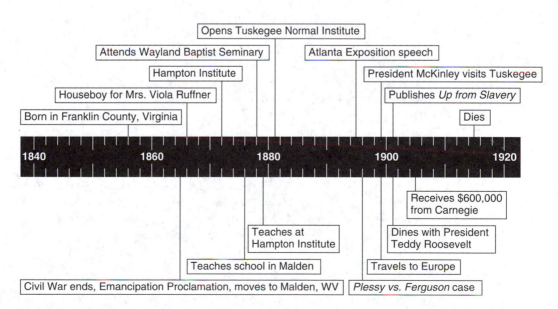

Figure 10.3   Washington's Life and Times

gain immediate employment upon graduation. Their intelligence and moral character enables them to make a living for themselves, knowing that labor is dignified and beautiful.[15]

W. E. B. DuBois was one of the most vocal critics of Washington's educational philosophy. Although DuBois had supported Washington's work initially and had been offered a job teaching at Tuskegee, he criticized Washington, claiming that overemphasis on industrial education led to the neglect of higher education that would condemn blacks to political, social, and economic subordination.[16] Tuskegee was not a college and it provided only a secondary school education, which Washington had no intentions of changing. After the 1896 *Plessy v. Ferguson* case, blacks were forced further into segregation and political subordination; Washington was criticized for not speaking out more against segregation and for the civil rights of African Americans.

Booker T. Washington kept on working until the end; he collapsed while giving a speech in New York City and died on November 14, 1915 in Tuskegee.[17]

Washington's Contribution to Educational Thought

Booker T. Washington was an outstanding educator who grappled with the challenges of his time to create a vision for the future. Washington transformed Tuskegee into the best-known black institution in the South with its philosophy of industrial education.[18] His ideas still impact educational thought, although we use different terms such as school-to-work education, cooperative education, and career education.

Washington maintained that economic self-reliance was the key to salvation for the black masses in America; the useful person is an irresistible socioeconomic commodity who would contribute to the common good in society. Washington has been criticized for articulating a brand of industrial education that was outmoded at the time. He was a man of his times and his times were rapidly changing because of the Industrial Revolution.[19]

In another way, it could be said that Booker T. Washington was an exceedingly perceptive and sensitive leader and his convictions are still compelling in the twenty-first century. Today, there is still a real need for strong black businesses and a revalorization of a common labor work ethic. People need to be self-reliant, for welfare has enslaved the recipients. Our generation is struggling with the very issues Washington addressed with such insight: racial hatred and division, the problems of corruption and vice, and the need for trained industrial and service industry workers.[20]

Today, about one-third of black Americans live in poverty and are still struggling within the enslaving system of welfare, perpetuated by a lack of education and training for jobs. However, two-thirds of black Americans earn a middle class income or higher, demonstrating that Washington's dream of character, education, and work really did come true.[21]

Washington's Philosophy of Education

For Washington, the central question of his public career was "How can free blacks make steady progress toward full citizenship and economic independence in view of the realities of their slave past and white racism?"[22] Washington had a holistic vision of individual development that he said would come through a systematic development of industrial education for the hands, intellectual education for the head, and moral education for the heart: thus his educational motto, "hand, head, and heart." He sought to guide the character formation and economic progress of black individuals and of the race. To become a moral person, one needed to develop physically, intellectually, and spiritually—and education was the means to achieve this. "I have always advised my race to acquire property, intelligence and character as the necessary bases of good citizenship,"[23] he explained.

Notes

1. Although in his autobiography, Booker T. says he never knew the date or year of his birth, his birthday was recorded in the Burroughs family Bible. Louis R. Harlan, *Booker T. Washington: The Making of a Black Leader, 1856–1901* (New York: Oxford University Press, 1972).

2. Booker T. Washington, *Up from Slavery: An Autobiography of Booker T. Washington* (New York: Bantam Books, 1963), p. 14.

3. Stephen Mansfield, *The Darkness Fled: The Liberating Wisdom of Booker T. Washington* (Nashville: Highland Books, 1999), p. 57; Washington, pp. 25–26.

4. Ibid., p. 19; Mansfield, p. 131.

5. Washington, p. 51.

6. Mansfield, p. 74; Robert Michael Franklin, *Liberating Visions: Human Fulfillment and Social Justice in African-American Thought* (Minneapolis: Fortress Press, 1990), p. 14.

7. Franklin, p. 16.

8. Mansfield, pp. 94–101.

9. Ibid., p. 112.

10. Washington, p. 142.

11. Kevern Verney, *The Art of the Possible: Booker T. Washington and Black Leadership in the United States, 1881–1925* (New York: Routledge, 2001), p. 9.

12. Mansfield, p. 251.

13. Harlan, p. 304; Mansfield, pp. 115–16.

14. Mansfield, pp. 106–107.

15. Washington, p. 221.

16. Verney, p. 10.

17. Mansfield, p. 123.

18. Verney, pp. 8–9.

19. Franklin, pp. 22–24.

20. Mansfield, p. 24.

21. Ibid., p. 256.

22. Franklin, p. 7.

23. Ibid., pp. 11, 18, 24.

Questions to Guide Your Reading

1. What does Booker T. Washington mean by the phrase "cast down your bucket where you are"?

2. What is the greatest danger facing his people at this time?

3. How large is the nation's African American population at this time?

READING 10.3:
ON ACHIEVING SOCIAL EQUALITY

Mr. President and Gentlemen of the Board of Directors and Citizens.

One-third of the population of the South is of the Negro race. No enterprise seeking the material, civil, or moral welfare of this section can disregard this element of our population and reach the highest success. I convey to you, Mr. President and Directors, the sentiment of the masses of my race when I say that in no way have the value and manhood of the American Negro been more fittingly and generously recognized than by the managers of this magnificent Exposition at every stage of its progress. It

Source: Booker T. Washington, "Atlanta Exposition Address," from his *Up from Slavery*. Garden City, NY (Doubleday, Page and Co., 1901, 1933).

is a recognition that will do more to cement the friendship of the two races than any occurrence since the dawn of our freedom.

Not only this, but the opportunity here afforded will awaken among us a new era of industrial progress. Ignorant and inexperienced, it is not strange that in the first years of our new life we began at the top instead of at the bottom; that a seat in Congress or the state legislature was more sought than real estate or industrial skill; that the political convention of stump speaking had more attractions than starting a dairy farm or truck farm.

A ship lost at sea for many days suddenly sighted a friendly vessel. From the mast of the unfortunate vessel was seen a signal, "Water, water; we die of thirst!" The answer from the friendly vessel at once came back, "Cast down your bucket where you are." A second time the signal, "Water, water; send us water!" ran up from the distressed vessel, and was answered, "Cast down your bucket where you are." And a third and fourth signal for water was answered, "Cast down your bucket where you are." The captain of the distressed vessel, at last heeding the injunction, cast down his bucket, and it came up full of fresh, sparkling water from the mouth of the Amazon River. To those of my race who depend on bettering their condition in a foreign land or who underestimate the importance of cultivating friendly relations with the Southern white man, who is their next-door neighbor, I would say: "Cast down your bucket where you are"—cast it down in making friends in every manly way of the people of all races by whom we are surrounded.

Cast it down in agriculture, mechanics, in commerce, in domestic service, and in the professions. And in this connection it is well to bear in mind that whatever other sins the South may be called to bear, when it comes to business, pure and simple, it is in the South that the Negro is given a man's chance in the commercial world, and in nothing is this Exposition more eloquent than in emphasizing this chance. Our greatest danger is that in the great leap from slavery to freedom we may overlook the fact that the masses of us are to live by the productions of our hands, and fail to keep in mind that we shall prosper in proportion as we learn to dignify and glorify common labour and put brains and skill into the common occupations of life; shall prosper in proportion as we learn to draw the line between the superficial and the substantial, the ornamental gewgaws of life and the useful. No race can prosper till it learns that there is as much dignity in tilling a field as in writing a poem. It is at the bottom of life we must begin, and not at the top. Nor should we permit our grievances to overshadow our opportunities.

To those of the white race who look to the incoming of those of foreign birth and strange tongue and habits for the prosperity of the South, were I permitted I would repeat what I say to my own race, "Cast down your bucket where you are. Cast it down among the eight millions of Negroes whose habits you know, whose fidelity and love you have tested in days when to have proved treacherous meant the ruin of your firesides. Cast down your bucket among these people who have, without strikes and labour wars, tilled your fields, cleared your forests, built your railroads and cities, and helped make possible this magnificent representation of the people, helping and encouraging them as you are doing on these grounds, and to education of head, hand, and heart, you will find that they will buy your surplus land, make blossom the waste places in your fields, and run your factories. While doing this, you can be sure in the future, as in the past, that you and your families will be surrounded by the most patient, faithful, law-abiding, and unresentful people that the world has seen. As we have proved our loyalty to you in the past, in nursing your children, watching by the sick-bed of your mothers and fathers, and often following them with tear dimmed eyes to their graves, so in the future, humble way, we shall stand by you with a devotion that no foreigner can approach, ready to lay down our lives, if need be, in defense of yours, interlacing our industrial, commercial, civil, and religious life with yours in a way that shall make the interests of both races one. In all things that are purely social we can be as separate as the fingers, yet one as the hand in all things essential to mutual progress."

There is no defense or security for any of us except in the highest intelligence and development of all. If anywhere these efforts tended to curtail the fullest growth of the Negro, let these efforts be turned into stimulating, encouraging, and making him the most useful and intelligent citizen. Effort or means so invested will pay a thousand percent interest. These efforts will be twice blessed—"blessing him that gives and him that takes."

There is no escape through law of man or God from the inevitable:

*The laws of changeless justice bind
Oppressor with oppressed;
And close as sin and suffering joined
We march to fate abreast.*

Nearly sixteen millions of hands will aid you in pulling the load upward, or they will pull against you the load downward. We shall constitute one-third and more of the ignorance and crime of the South, or one-third its intelligence and progress; we shall contribute one-third to business and industrial prosperity of the South, or we shall prove a veritable body of death, stagnating, depressing, retarding every effort to advance the body politic.

Gentlemen of the Exposition, as we present to you our humble effort at an exhibition of our progress, you must not expect overmuch. Starting thirty years ago with ownership here and there in a few quilts and pumpkins and chickens (gathered from miscellaneous sources), remember the path that has led from these to the inventions and production of agricultural implements, buggies, steam-engines, newspapers, books, statuary, carving, paintings, the management of drugstores and banks, has not been trodden without contact with thorns and thistles. While we take pride in what we exhibit as a result of our independent efforts, we do not for a moment forget that our part in this exhibition would fall far short of your expectations but for the constant help that has come to our educational life, not only the Southern states, but especially from Northern philanthropists, who have made their gifts a constant stream of blessing and encouragement.

The wisest among my race understand that the agitation of questions of social equality is the ex-tremest folly, and that progress in the enjoyment of all the privileges that will come to use must be the result of severe and constant struggle rather than of artificial forcing. No race that has anything to contribute to the markets of the world is long in any degree ostracized. It is important and right that all privileges of the law be ours, but it is vastly more important that we be prepared for the exercise of these privileges. The opportunity to earn a dollar is worth infinitely more than the opportunity to spend a dollar in an opera house.

In conclusion, may I repeat that nothing in thirty year has given us more hope and encouragement, and drawn us so near to you of the white race, as this opportunity offered by the Exposition; and here bending, as it were, over the altar that represents the results of the struggles of your race and mine both starting practically empty-handed three decades ago, I pledge that in your effort to work out the great and intricate problem which God has laid at the doors of the South, you shall have at all times the patient, sympathetic help of my race, only let this be constantly in mind, that while from representations in these buildings of the product of field, of forest, of mine, of factory, letters, and art, much good will come, yet far above and beyond material benefits will be that higher good that, let us pray God, will come, in a blotting out of sectional differences and racial animosities and suspicions, in a determination to administer absolute justice, in a willing obedience among all classes to the mandates of law. This, coupled with our material prosperity, will bring into our beloved South a new heaven and a new earth.

Discussion Questions

1. How did Booker T. Washington's life model his educational ideology?
2. What were the key factors of Washington's success as an educational leader?
3. What does Booker T. Washington mean when he says, "there is as much dignity in tilling a field as in writing a poem?" Do you think today's society would agree with him?
4. Do you oppose or support the educational philosophy of Booker T. Washington? Defend your opinion. Would you feel differently if you were living in 1895?
5. What current educational initiatives are also trying to help African American youth develop a strong character and good citizenship qualities in order to succeed in society? In what way are they similar to the Tuskegee idea and in what way are they different?

For Further Research on the Internet

The Booker T. Washington papers. http://www.historycooperative.org/btw/

Up from Slavery and other Washington articles. http://xroads.virginia.edu/~HYPER/WASHINGTON/cover.html

Home page for the Tuskegee Institute. http://www.nps.gov/tuin/

Suggestions for Further Reading

Franklin, Robert Michael. *Liberating Visions: Human Fulfillment and Social Justice in African-American Thought*. Minneapolis: Fortress Press, 1990.

Harlan, Louis R. *Booker T. Washington: The Making of a Black Leader, 1856–1901*. New York: Oxford University Press, 1972.

Mansfield, Stephen. *The Darkness Fled: The Liberating Wisdom of Booker T. Washington*. Nashville: Highland Books, 1999.

Verney, Kevern. *The Art of the Possible: Booker T. Washington and Black Leadership in the United States, 1881–1925*. New York: Routledge, 2001.

Washington, Booker T. *Up from Slavery: An Autobiography of Booker T. Washington*. New York: Bantam Books, 1963.

Section 10.4: W. E. B. DuBois (1868–1964)

Imagine living for 96 years as did W. E. B. DuBois! Born five years after the Emancipation Proclamation and dying seven years after the Brown decision and the day before the historic civil rights demonstration in Washington, DC, he lived through some of the most significant years for African Americans and played a key role in helping to shape the direction of the fight for civil rights freedom during this period.

Life and Times of William Edward Burghardt DuBois

William Edward Burghardt DuBois was born in freedom on February 23, 1868 in Great Barrington, Massachusetts, the only child of Alfred DuBois and Mary Silvina Burghardt. Alfred was not accepted by the Burghardt family and left town when they fired at him one night. Although DuBois describes his childhood as happy and carefree, his mother suffered from depression after her husband left. Nevertheless, she did her best to raise her son with sound morals.[1]

DuBois' Education

Willie, as he was called, attended the local elementary school for ten years, worshipped at the First Congregational Church with his mother, and became the first Burghardt to attend high school. He was seldom absent or tardy and learned the curriculum of reading, writing, spelling, arithmetic, geography and grammar.[2] Frank Hosmer, the principal, had an important influence on Willie as he grew into adolescence, encouraging him to take the college preparatory courses (instead of the vocational courses). Willie loved to read, especially history, and devoured Macaulay's five-volume *History of England*. Willie helped supplement his mother's income by mowing lawns, working at the grocery store, and delivering newspapers.[3] He began to write articles on Church and local events for the town newspaper, which he delivered, and in his senior year, submitted articles to the *Springfield Republican*.[4] In 1884, W. E. B. DuBois became the first African American to graduate from Great Barrington High School.[5]

DuBois dreamed of going to Harvard, but his mother died suddenly in March 1885, leaving him short of funds. Through the help of three men in his community, he received enough money to go to Fisk University in Nashville, Tennessee, a Congregational school for blacks committed to producing cultured African American "ladies" and "gentlemen." He entered the sophomore class due to his superior northern secondary education and studied Greek, Latin, French, German, theology, natural sciences, music, moral philosophy, history, chemistry, and physics.[6] DuBois wrote for the Fisk *Herald*, becoming editor in his senior year. Instead of going home, he spent his summers teaching fifteen students aged six to twenty in a one-room schoolhouse.[7] W. E. B. DuBois graduated from Fisk University in 1888 and, armed with several excellent letters of recommendation, was admitted to Harvard University. DuBois was the sixth African American to enroll in the college and eventually the first to earn a doctoral degree.[8] He entered the undergraduate program as a junior because Harvard would not honor his southern college degree so he graduated Cum Laude on June 25, 1890 with a bachelor's degree from Harvard and then received a fellowship to enter the graduate school to study history, economics, and political science. Receiving his M.A. degree in 1892, he obtained a scholarship study at the University of Berlin with the famous sociologist, Max Weber. While in Europe, DuBois also studied the theories of Karl Marx and Hegel, which he later applied in his writings depicting blacks as victims of an exploitative capitalism.[9]

Professor

DuBois returned to the United States in 1894 to work as a professor of languages at the Wilberforce University, an African Methodist Episcopal college, the oldest college for Negroes in the United States. He completed his doctorate at Harvard a year later and defended his dissertation on "The Suppression of the African American Slave Trade to the United States of America 1658–1870."[10] At Wilberforce, DuBois met and married Nina Gomez and took her with him to his new position at the University of Pennsylvania as a research director.

The Philadelphia Negro Study

DuBois conducted a comprehensive historical and sociological study of Philadelphia's African American population using the sociological survey method he had learned in Germany. He visited some 2500 households and published his findings in the 1899 book, *The Philadelphia Negro*. DuBois maintained that his research showed that racial discrimination limited the African American economic and education opportunities and in essences still enslaved them at the economic bottom. He also identified an evolving elite, a moderate sized middle-class of blacks that he predicted would lead the African American advance. This study made him a recognized scholar and DuBois became known as the "best educated Negro in America," receiving a professorship at Atlanta University, where he taught economics and history for the next 13 years.[11] Nina and DuBois had two children, only one surviving to adulthood. Booker T. Washington offered DuBois a position at Tuskegee Institute but DuBois and his wife wanted to leave the segregated and prejudiced South so

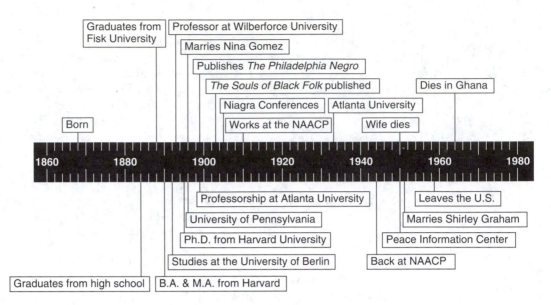

Figure 10.4   DuBois's Life and Times

he tried unsuccessfully to obtain employment at a school in Washington, DC.[12] (See the timeline of DuBois' life in Figure 10.4.)

The Souls of Black Folk

The Souls of Black Folk was published in 1903; its impact was "greater upon and within the Negro race than any other single book published in the country since *Uncle Tom's Cabin.*" We still consider the book of essays indispensable to understanding the history of race and democracy in America. This book presented two of DuBois' critical ideas: (1) The problem of the twentieth century is the problem of the color-line; and (2) the talented tenth of the elite African-Americans who went to college would be the leaders of their race.[13]

W. E. B. DuBois began to challenge Booker T. Washington and his theories of accommodation and vocational education for economic security, stating that African Americans should seek higher education and strive to become leaders, businessmen, doctors, and lawyers. In 1905, DuBois and a group of twenty-nine black and white educators, lawyers, publishers, and physicians met in Erie, Ontario to start an organized action of promoting Negro freedom and growth; by 1910 this became the National Association for the Advancement of Colored People (NAACP), which worked for the civil, social, and educational progress of all people of color.[14] DuBois resigned from Atlanta University in 1910 to accept the position of Director of Publicity and Research in the NAACP and became the founding editor of *The Crisis,* the NAACP's national monthly magazine. By 1915, the NAACP had branches set up across the county and once Booker T. Washington died, DuBois became the spokesman for African Americans through his editorials in *The Crisis.* DuBois was an intellectual, born free in the urban, industrial north, who could talk about a new black elite who went to college, became leaders, and defended their country through the service.

Civil Rights Advocate

In 1919, in France DuBois attended the first of a series of international congresses, the Pan-African Congress, and began a movement that would assume worldwide significance for the political and economic potential of people of color around the world. Whenever

DuBois traveled outside of America he felt liberated, free of American racism and Negro-sniping.

He returned home to the "Red Summer of 1919" of race riots and the lynchings of over seventy-five black men and women. Momentous changes were taking place among the African Americans. DuBois, *The Crisis,* and the NAACP became advocates of civil rights.

DuBois gave the commencement address for his alma mater at Fisk University in which he spoke on "The Negro College." "There can be no college for Negroes which is not a Negro college ... It has to begin with Negroes, use a variety of the English idiom which they understand and above all, (be) founded on a knowledge of the history of their people in Africa and in the United States, and their present condition."[15]

In 1933, the NAACP arranged for DuBois to be invited to Atlanta University as a visiting professor, allowing him to make a distinguished exit from the NAACP, immersing himself once again in his work as a scholar, researcher, historian, sociologist, and writer. For the next ten years, DuBois worked on his book, *Black Reconstruction,* and traveled around the world visiting many countries. In 1939, he published *Black Folk Then and Now* and started work on *The Encyclopedia of the Negro.* When the Atlanta University Board of Trustees voted for him to retire in 1944, DuBois went back to the NAACP as Director of Special Research. During the Red Scare, the NAACP was accused of being a communist front; DuBois was considered a liability to the organization with his verbal support of socialism and communism, so his contract was not renewed in 1948. He traveled to France and Russia and then headed the Peace Information Center. Nina, his wife of more than fifty years, died on July 1, 1950.

DuBois sailed to East Europe, the Soviet Union, China, and London with his new wife, Shirley Graham. On his ninety-fifth birthday, DuBois became a citizen of Ghana because the United States would not renew his passport. He died on August 27, 1963, the day of the historic March on Washington.

DuBois' Contribution to Education

William E. Burghardt DuBois was involved in education throughout his life, both as a professor and as an author of many books that sought to change the knowledge base about African Americans. Perhaps his major contributions to education over a half-century were his articles in *The Crisis* magazine. Through his editorials, DuBois worked to reverse appalling racial discrimination at Harvard, where colored men were barred from living in the freshman dormitories and at white colleges, where Negroes were not admitted due to race, regardless of ability. Eugene Provenzo, Jr. (2003) has edited a book, *DuBois on Education,* in which is compiled for the first time all of DuBois' writing on education. Education was essential in DuBois' mind because he saw it as the principal means toward black empowerment; without education, the black man was still enslaved.[16]

DuBois' Philosophy of Education

DuBois made higher education a key element in his philosophy of education for colleges, universities, and professional schools. He claimed it would produce the African American intellectual elite, "the Talented Tenth," that would lead their people to a new social and economic reality. The Negro race would be saved by its exceptional men, so education must first develop the Talented Tenth, who would then be able to guide the other members of their race. Every community, black or white, needed to have its contingent of college-educated individuals who could provide the foundation for the culture and have the perspective and insight necessary to advance it.[17]

DuBois wanted black colleges and universities that would be centers for cultural formation, promoting Black and African American and Africana studies and pursuing answers for black problems and issues. However, he did not promote segregated schools as better than mixed schools for the Negro, saying "The Negro needs neither segregated schools nor mixed schools. What he needs is education." DuBois encouraged the black community to respect teachers in black schools and see to it that they were paid decent salaries.[18]

Although pushing collegiate education for African Americans, DuBois was also concerned about improving the elementary and secondary education for blacks. In 1921, he started *The Brownie Book,* a magazine for children designed to stimulate young black children's early learning through its stories, legends, and poems. However, it did not get enough subscriptions to continue. It was, in many ways, ahead of its time, anticipating the modern ideas of multicultural education.[19] DuBois argued that it was the whole system of human training from family, community, and schools that had to be committed to the education of the young people. DuBois did not think there should be one single model of education for the Negro and contrary to what most critics say, he saw Washington's model of industrial education as fulfilling an important role.[20]

Through DuBois' use of his extensive survey method research throughout his life, he was able to document the growing educational disparities between the schooling of black and white children. DuBois defined education as the process of drawing out of human powers, one's own and others'.[21] He felt that blacks had been systematically "mis-educated," only taught about the European culture and history. He proposed that an Afro-centric curriculum be introduced in the schools to teach a world and cultural history, including the history of the Negro in America and in Africa as an integral part of critical inquiry.

Derrick Alridge recognizes W. E. B. DuBois as "one of the significant educational thinkers of the twentieth century," stating that his educational views have relevance to contemporary African American social, economic, and political life. He thinks that it is not correct to assert that DuBois was diametrically opposed to Booker T. Washington's vocational/industrial education. It would be more accurate to say that DuBois favored classical education as a means of social uplift, but saw the importance of Hampton and Tuskegee Institutes for training students in morality, Christianity, the ethics of hard work, and the dignity of labor.[22] Although never clearly articulated as such, he says that a careful reading of DuBois' works on education reveal a comprehensive Afro-centric educational philosophy that integrated race and class issues and the structure of capitalism and exploitation. DuBois challenged America to live up to its claims of democracy and attempted to use education as a means of providing for a more democratic society.

Barry McSwine says that DuBois saw education as inextricably bound up with life, and to the extent that it failed to teach people how to live (morals/ethics/character), it was to that extent a failure for him. Applying this to today's society, he believes that DuBois would say that education is too committed to economic success and not committed enough to character development and moral/ethical and spiritual life.[23]

"Education and work are the levers to uplift a people. Work alone will not do it unless inspired by the right ideals and guided by intelligence. Education must not simply teach work—it must teach Life."[24]

Notes

1. W. E. B. DuBois, *The Autobiography of W. E. B. DuBois: A Soliloquy on Viewing My Life from the Last Decade of Its First Century* (New York: International Publishers, 1997), pp. 73–74, 81.
2. Ibid., p. 77.
3. Ibid., pp. 87–88, 95, 101.
4. David Levering Lewis, *W. E. B. DuBois: Biography of a Race 1868–1919* (New York: Henry Holt & Co., 1993), p. 47.
5. DuBois, 1997, p. 99.

6. Ibid., pp. 107, 112.

7. Ibid., p. 117.

8. Lewis, 1993, p. 84.

9. Gerald Gutek, *Historical and Philosophical Foundations of Education: A Biographical Introduction,* 3rd ed. (Upper Saddle River, NJ: Merrill/Prentice Hall, Inc., 2001), p. 368.

10. Lewis, 1993, p. 155.

11. DuBois, 1997, p. 205; Lewis, 1993, p. 209.

12. Lewis, 1993, pp. 245–251.

13. David Levering Lewis, "W.E.B. DuBois' Souls of Black Folk: One Century Hence," *Crisis,* 2003, pp. 17–20.

14. Gutek, *A History of the Western Educational Experience* (Prospect Heights, IL: Waveland Press, Inc., 1995), p. 509.

15. Lewis, *W.E.B. DuBois: The Fight for Equality and the American Century 1901–1963* (NY: Henry Holt & Company, 2000.), pp. 312–313.

16. Ibid. p. 495.

17. Eugene F., Provenzo Jr., ed. *DuBois on Education* (Walnut Creek, CA: AltaMira Press/Rowman & Littlefield Publishers, Inc., 2002.), p. 6.

18. Reiland Rabaka, "W. E. B. DuBois's Evolving Africana Philosophy of Education," *Journal of Black Studies,* March, 2003, 33 (4), p. 417.

19. Provenzo Jr., pp. 12–15, 134.

20. Lewis, 2000, p. 32; Provenzo Jr., p. 15.

21. Provenzo Jr., p. 5.

22. Rabaka, p. 400.

23. Derrick Alridge, "Conceptualizing a DuBoisian Philosophy of Education: Towards a Model of African-American Education," *Educational Theory,* 1999, Vol. 49, No 3, pp. 362–363.

24. Bartley L. McSwine, "The Educational Philosophy of W. E. B. DuBois," *Midwest Philosophy of Education Society Conference Proceedings,* Chicago 1998.

Questions to Guide Your Reading

1. What are some of the ways education will help society according to DuBois? Are these still goals of education in our society today?

2. What are the four periods of Southern education since the Civil War as outlined by DuBois? How will historians characterize the period from the death of DuBois to the current day? In what ways has education of black people in the South improved and in what ways has it stayed the same? Give examples.

3. What is the function of the Negro College according to DuBois? Do you think we should still have all-black colleges?

READING 10.4:
OF THE TRAINING OF BLACK MEN

Training for life teaches living; but what training for the profitable living together of black men and white?

In rough approximation we may point out four varying decades of work in Southern education since the Civil War. From the close of the war until 1876 was the period of uncertain groping and temporary relief. There were army schools, mission schools, and schools of the Freedmen's Bureau in chaotic disarrangement, seeking system and cooperation. Then followed ten years of constructive definite effort toward the building of complete school systems in the South. Normal schools and colleges were founded for the freedmen, and teachers trained there to man the public schools. Mean-

Source: W. E. Burghardt DuBois, from *The Souls of Black Folk,* Everyman's Library, New York: Knopf. Distributed by Random House, 1993.

time, starting in this decade yet especially developing from 1885 to 1895, began the industrial revolution of the South. The land saw glimpses of a new destiny and the stirring of new ideals. The educational system, striving to complete itself, saw new obstacles and a field of work ever broader and deeper. The Negro colleges, hurriedly founded, were inadequately equipped, illogically distributed, and of varying efficiency and grade; the normal and high schools were doing little more than common school work, and the common schools were training but a third of the children who ought to be in them, and training these too often poorly. . . . In the midst, then, of the larger problem of Negro education sprang up the more practical question of work, the inevitable economic quandary that faces a people in the transition from slavery to freedom, and especially those who make that change amid hate and prejudice, lawlessness and ruthless competition.

The industrial school springing to notice in this decade, but coming to full recognition in the decade beginning with 1895, was the proffered answer to this combined educational and economic crisis, and an answer of singular wisdom and timeliness.

Especially has criticism been directed against the former educational efforts to aid the Negro. In the four periods I have mentioned, we find first boundless, planless enthusiasm and sacrifice; then the preparation of teachers for a vast public school system; then the launching and expansion of that school system amid increasing difficulties; and finally the training of workmen for the new and growing industries. The white teachers who flocked South went to establish a common school system. They had no idea of founding colleges; they themselves at first would have laughed at the idea. But they faced, as all men since them have faced, that central paradox of the South, the social separation of the races. Then it was the sudden volcanic rupture of nearly all relations between black and white, in work and government and family life. Thus, then and now, there stand in the South two separate worlds; and separate not simply in the higher realms of social intercourse, but also in church and school, on railway and street car, in hotels and theatres, in streets and city sections, in books and newspapers, in asylums and jails, in hospitals and graveyards.

This the missionaries of '68 soon saw; and if effective industrial and trade schools were impractical before the establishment of a common school system, just as certainly no adequate common schools could be founded until there were teachers to teach them. Southern whites would not teach them; Northern whites in sufficient numbers could not be had. If the Negro was to learn, he must teach himself, and the most effective help that could be given him was the establishment of schools to train Negro teachers. Above the sneers of critics at the obvious defects of this procedure must ever stand its one crushing rejoinder: in a single generation they put thirty thousand black teachers in the South; they wiped out the illiteracy of the majority of the black people of the land, and they made Tuskegee possible.

Such higher training schools tended naturally to deepen broader development: at first they were common and grammar schools, then some became high schools. And finally, by 1900, some thirty-four had one year or more of studies of college grade. This development was reached with different degrees of speed in different institutions: Hampton is still a high school, while Fisk University started her college in 1871, and Spelman Seminary about 1896. In all cases the aim was identical: to maintain the standards of the lower training by giving teachers and leaders the best practicable training; and above all to furnish the black world with adequate standards of human culture and lofty ideals of life. It was not enough that the teachers of teachers should be trained in technical normal methods; they must also, so far as possible, be broad-minded, cultured men and women, to scatter civilization among a people whose ignorance was not simply of letters, but of life itself. . . .

From such schools about two thousand Negroes have gone forth with the bachelor's degree. The number in itself is enough to put at rest the argument that too large a proportion of Negroes are receiving higher training. If the ratio to population of all Negro students throughout the land, in both college and secondary training, be counted, Commissioner Harris assures us "it must be increased to five times its present average" to equal the average of the land.

Fifty years ago the ability of Negro students in any appreciable numbers to master a modern college course would have been difficult to prove. Today it is proved by the fact that four hundred Negroes, many of whom have been reported as brilliant students, have received the bachelor's degree from Harvard, Yale, Oberlin, and seventy other leading colleges. Here we have, then, nearly twenty-five hundred Negro graduates, of whom the crucial query must be made. How far did their training fit them for life? In 1900, the Conference at Atlanta University undertook to study these graduates, and published the results. First they sought to know what these graduates were doing, and succeeded in getting answers from nearly two thirds of the living. The direct testimony was in almost all cases corroborated by the reports of the colleges where they graduated, so that in the main the reports were worthy of credence. Fifty-three per cent of these graduates were teachers,—presidents of institutions, heads of normal schools, principals of city school systems, and the like. Seventeen per cent were clergymen; another seventeen per cent were in the professions, chiefly as physicians. Over six per cent were merchants, farmers, and artisans, and four per cent were in the government civil service. Granting even that a considerable proportion of the third unheard from are unsuccessful, this is a record of usefulness. Comparing them as a class with my fellow students in New England and in Europe, I cannot hesitate in saying that nowhere have I met men and women with a broader spirit of helpfulness, with deeper devotion to their life-work, or with more consecrated determination to succeed in the face of bitter difficulties than among Negro college-bred men.

With all their larger vision and deeper sensibility, these men have usually been conservative, careful leaders. They have seldom been agitators, have withstood the temptation to head the mob, and have worked steadily and faithfully in a thousand communities in the South. As teachers they have given the South a commendable system of city schools and large numbers of private normal schools and academies. Colored college-bred men have worked side by side with white college graduates at Hampton; almost from the beginning the backbone of Tuskegee's teaching force has been formed of graduates from Fisk and Atlanta. And today the institute is filled with college graduates, from the energetic wife of the principal down to the teacher of agriculture, including nearly half of the executive council and a majority of the heads of departments.

In the professions, college men are slowly but surely leavening the Negro church, are healing and preventing the devastations of disease, and beginning to furnish legal protection for the liberty and property of the toiling masses. All this is needful work. Who would do it if Negroes did not? How could Negroes do it if they were not trained carefully for it? If white people need colleges to furnish teachers, ministers, lawyers, and doctors, do black people need nothing of the sort?

We ought not to forget that despite the pressure of poverty, and despite the active discouragement and even ridicule of friends, the demand for higher training steadily increases among Negro youth: there were, in the years from 1875 to 1880, twenty-two Negro graduates from Northern colleges; from 1885 to 1895 there were forty-three, and from 1895 to 1900, nearly 100 graduates. From Southern Negro colleges there were, in the same three periods, 143, 413, and over 500 graduates. Here, then, is the plain thirst for training; by refusing to give this Talented Tenth the key to knowledge can any sane man imagine that they will lightly lay aside their yearning and contentedly become hewers of wood and drawers of water?

The function of the Negro college then is clear: it must maintain the standards of popular education, it must seek the social regeneration of the Negro, and it must help in the solution of problems of race contact and cooperation. And finally, beyond all this, it must develop men.

I sit with Shakespeare and he winces not. Across the color line I move arm in arm with Balzac and Dumas, where smiling men and welcoming women glide in gilded halls I summon Aristotle and Aurelius and what soul I will, and they come all graciously with no scorn nor condescension. So, wed with Truth, I dwell above the Veil. Is this the life you grudge us, O knightly America? Is this the life you long to change into the dull red hideousness of Georgia? Are you so afraid lest peering from this high Pisgah, between Philistine and Amalekite, we sight the Promised Land?

Discussion Questions

1. DuBois' idea of the "talented tenth" echoes Plato's ideas in *The Republic*, that is, that there are only a select few men, not the majority, that are capable of "higher" training. Do you think that DuBois and Plato support honors and advanced placement classes as applications of their premises? Why or why not?

2. Do you think it is important for everyone to study an Afro-centric curriculum or is this only important for those of African American descent? Defend your position with examples.

3. Do you think DuBois would find the emphasis on multicultural education today an adequate expression of his curricular ideas? What would he want added or changed?

4. Compare DuBois' ideas of the talented tenth, the hundredth, and the talented third to the reality of African Americans in the twenty-first century. Are any of these accurate descriptions of their social, economic, political, and educational situation today?

5. DuBois would say that education is over-committed to economic success and under-committed to moral/ethical and spiritual life. What do you think DuBois would say about today's movement to integrate "values" or character education into modern public schools to resolve this issue?

6. Contrast Martin Luther King's pacifism with W. E. B. DuBois' and the NAACP's activism with the equal rights movement of the 60s and 70s that resulted in changes in America's treatment of blacks.

7. Work in groups. One group will outline Booker T. Washington's contributions to education and the other group will outline W. E. B. DuBois' contribution. Present your findings to the class.

For Further Research on the Internet

The W. E. B. DuBois Learning Center. The site includes a biography of DuBois and tutorial programs to help students improve their reading, math, science and computer skills. **http://www.duboislc.org/index.html**

The W. E. B. DuBois Institute for African-American research at Harvard University. **http://web-dubois.fas.harvard.edu**

Suggestions for Further Reading

Alridge, Derrick. "Conceptualizing a DuBoisian Philosophy of Education: Towards a Model of African-American Education." *Educational Theory* 49 (3) (1999): 359–379.

Butts, Sandra. "DuBois on Education." In *The Educational Theory of William Edward Burghardt DuBois*. http://www.newfoundations.com/GALLERY/DuBois.html Accessed 6/10/04: New Foundations.

DuBois, W. E. B. *The Autobiography of W. E. B. DuBois: A Soliloquy on Viewing My Life from the Last Decade of Its First Century.* New York: International Publishers, 1997.

Gutek, Gerald. *A History of the Western Educational Experience*, 2nd ed. Prospect Heights, IL: Waveland Press, Inc., 1995.

Gutek, Gerald. *Historical and Philosophical Foundations of Education: A Biographical Introduction*, 3rd ed. Upper Saddle River, NJ: Merrill/Prentice Hall, 2001.

Lewis, David Levering. *W. E. B. DuBois: Biography of a Race 1868–1919.* New York: Henry Holt & Co., 1993.

Lewis, David Levering. *W. E. B. DuBois: The Fight for Equality and the American Century 1919–1963.* New York: Henry Holt & Company, 2000.

Lewis, David Levering. "W. E. B. DuBois' *Souls of Black Folk:* One Century Hence." *Crisis,* Vol. 93 (March/April, 2003).

McSwine, Bartley L. The Educational Philosophy of W. E. B. DuBois. *Midwest Philosophy of Education Society Conference Proceedings,* Chicago, 1998.

Provenzo Jr., Eugene F., ed. *DuBois on Education.* Walnut Creek, CA: AltaMira Press/Rowman & Littlefield Publishers, Inc., 2002.

Rabaka, Reiland. "W. E. B. DuBois's Evolving Africana Philosophy of Education." *Journal of Black Studies,* 33 (4): (2003) 399–449.

CHAPTER ACTIVITIES

Linking the Past to the Present

1. Investigate the high school graduation rates for the last five years in your community along the lines of race, class, and gender. Compare your local results with another school district noted for its generous funding base. Discuss the similarities and differences. What do you think DuBois would say about this continued lack of equality of educational opportunity?

2. It is now fifty years since the *Brown vs. Topeka* case overturned segregation in schools. Using the Internet, review some of the newspaper articles printed on the fiftieth anniversary, May 17, 2004. Write your own newspaper article. Are schools today integrated and providing equal educational opportunity?

3. Have a panel discussion about the following topics regarding the reform of schools, both private and public:

   a. vouchers
   b. charter schools
   c. uniforms in public schools
   d. inclusion of children with disabilities in the least restrictive environment

Developing Your Philosophy of Education

As you write your philosophy of education paper, think about how you will accommodate your instruction to meet the needs of all of the children in your classroom. How will you differentiate your instruction, teach to different learning styles, and incorporate multiculturalism into your curriculum, capitalizing on the diverse backgrounds of your students?

Connecting Theory to Practice

For your clinical school, get the school yearly report card that summarizes their state scores and school demographics. What is the racial make-up of the student body? What percentage of the students have documented special needs? Observe in the cafeteria and on the playground. Do students of different races play together? Are students with special needs accepted by others? Interview the counselor at the school. What programs are offered at the school to help students learn to respect and get along with students of other races and backgrounds?

Educators' Philosophies and Contributions to Education

TABLE 10.2   Philosophy and Contributions of American Educators

Educator	Role of Teacher & Learner	View of Curriculum & Methodology	Purpose or Goal of Education	Major Contribution
Elizabeth Seton	A kind but firm teacher guards over her students as children of God; educate hearts to virtue and minds to study	Wholesome diet, healthy recreation, in an atmosphere of good discipline and respect	Holistic view of education—purpose is the religious and moral training of children	Founded the first American parochial school
Gallaudet	Taught deaf children to their fullest ability using "total communication"; women are especially suited to teaching	Taught reading, writing, and sign language with history, arithmetic, geography, speech, and practical trades, using both sign language and oral method	The education of all children no matter what their disability is for the good of humanity and to teach them about God	Opened the Hartford School for the Deaf, the first school for the deaf in the United States
Booker T. Washington	Teach the head, heart, and hands; helping the black students to develop physically, intellectually, and spiritually	Taught personal hygiene, academics, and a vocational trade by hands-on involvement of the students in the running of the school	Education would lead to economic self-reliance for the good of the black people and of society	Founded Tuskegee Institute, best known black institution in the South, with a philosophy of industrial education
W. E. B. DuBois	Advocated professional academic training for the African American intellectual elite, talented tenth of blacks who would then guide the others	Classical and vocational studies in a curriculum including black and African American studies	Education was the principal means to empowerment; family, community, and schools had to work together	Founded NAACP; encouraged blacks to become professionals and leaders: doctors, lawyers, businessmen

CHAPTER 11

Education
for Democracy

The Twentieth Century

The twentieth century experienced significant changes in the social, economic, and political life of America, which spurred great educational changes. As documented in the last chapter, the country experienced a great growth in population at the end of the nineteenth century due to the large tide of immigration that began in the late 1880s and continued until about 1920. See Map 11.1, Sources of Immigrants 1900–1920.

Map 11.1   Sources of Immigrants 1900–1920

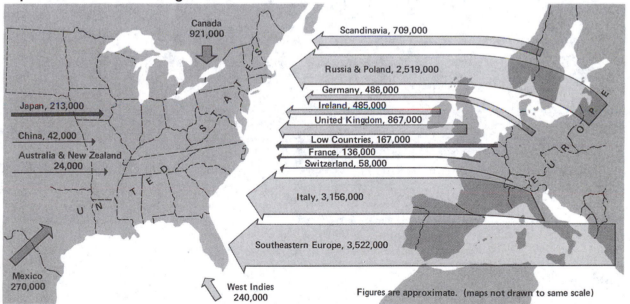

Canada 921,000

Scandinavia, 709,000

Russia & Poland, 2,519,000

Germany, 486,000

Japan, 213,000

Ireland, 485,000

United Kingdom, 867,000

China, 42,000

Low Countries, 167,000

Australia & New Zealand 24,000

France, 136,000

Switzerland, 58,000

Italy, 3,156,000

Southeastern Europe, 3,522,000

Mexico 270,000

West Indies 240,000

Figures are approximate.   (maps not drawn to same scale)

Source: Miller, William; Litwack, Leon; Aaron, Daniel; Hofstadter, Beatrice K. *United States, Volume II: Becoming a World Power*, 5th edition, © 1982. Reprinted by permission of Pearson Education, Inc., Upper Saddle River, NJ.

The annexation of Texas, California, and the southwest added 1,234,506 square miles of territory to the United States. The gold rush brought exploration of all the lands from the Mississippi River to the Pacific Ocean and by 1890 the frontier was closed. Due to the granting of extended suffrage, first to the blacks after the Civil War, and then to women in 1920, there were a great number of eager students who needed to be able to read and write in order to vote. By the turn of the century, there were some 130,000 school districts in the United States. Each state took control for the certification of teachers, the curriculum of the schools, and the standards of school facilities with the consequent responsibility for financial support. The growth in the student population was accompanied by an eighty percent growth in the number of teachers and staff. See Map 11.2, Twentieth-Century U.S. Women's Suffrage.

According to historians L. Dean Webb, Arlene Metha, and K. Forbis Jordan, the economic growth during this period was even more pronounced than the population growth.[1] From after the Civil War to right before World War I there was a tenfold increase in economic production. The expansion of the railroads and shipping, the invention of the telephone and other means of communication, and the growth of factories and big business made the United States the manufacturing king by 1920. Perhaps the invention

Map 11.2   Twentieth-Century U.S. Women's Suffrage

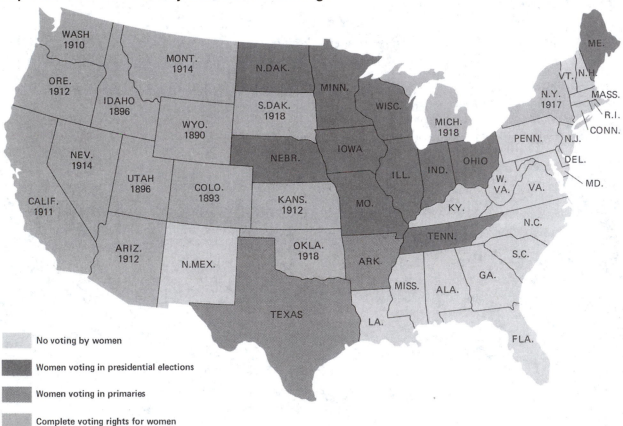

Source: Miller, William; Litwack, Leon; Aaron, Daniel; Hofstadter, Beatrice K. *United States, Volume II: Becoming a World Power,* 5th edition, © 1982. Reprinted by permission of Pearson Education, Inc. Upper Saddle River, NJ.

of the automobile made the most impact on education, for now children could commute to larger schools in the city.

The large increase in industry also brought abuses with it as workers (including children) worked in unsafe and unsanitary factories for long hours. Antitrust legislation was enacted to control monopolies and their unfair business practices. The progressive movement that emerged at the turn of the century addressed the labor of women and children, wages and hours, health and safety.

The Progressive Movement

The progressive movement impacted not only the political, social, and economic life of Americans, but also changed education. Before 1900 it was difficult to provide even the rudiments of education to the whole population. Now, due to the large increase of immigrants and the need for trained workers for industry, it was important to define educational goals and to develop an American philosophy of education. Following the child-centered ideas of Rousseau, Pestalozzi, and Froebel, educators suggested that learning should emanate from the interests and needs of the child and the curriculum should integrate subjects and provide hands-on instruction through project learning and field trips. John Dewey was one of the first to speak out against the rigid and formal, subject-centered schools of the day. Dewey suggested that education emphasize learning through experience. Problem solving, not rote memorization, would be the method of instruction; and the goal of education was to promote individual growth and to prepare the child for full participation in the democratic society.[2] Dewey looked at the child as a total organism with intellectual, social, emotional, and physical needs.

Education During the Depression

The crash of the stock markets in October, 1929 and the ensuing depression had a serious impact on the operation of schools. Until the depression, the federal government exerted little influence on education as it was constitutionally a function of the states. However, with people out of work, the federal government stepped in to train people in skills they could use. Under the "New Deal" the federal government created the Civilian Conservation Corps (CCC), the National Youth Administration (NYA), and the Public Works Administration (PWA), each of which provided work relief and training to the unemployed.

The experience of the depression had a significant impact on the progressive educators who began to believe that the school had a role to play in redressing social injustices. George S. Counts spoke at the Progressive Education Association in 1932 and in his speech entitled "Dare the Schools Build a New Social Order?" challenged the child-centered doctrine and urged educators to focus more on society. Counts asked the schools to take a lead in an intelligent reconstruction of society.

The Progressive Education Association also began a significant longitudinal study that was to be known as "The Eight Year Study," as it ran from 1932 to 1940. Ralph Tyler was asked to work as the chief evaluator of the study that involved thirty high schools that experimented with their curriculum, trying innovative subject content and different methodologies. The results, published in 1942, found that students from progressive high schools achieved higher than students from traditional high schools, and were better adjusted socially.[3]

World War II and After

December 7, 1941 once again dramatically altered the philosophy of education in America. The land-grant universities were asked to "research for federal defense needs." During the war the high school enrollments declined dramatically as young men left to join the military or to get a job to support the family. Large numbers of teachers also left the classroom to join the war effort. College enrollments were cut in half between 1941 and 1945. The Army and the Navy used the colleges as sites for specialized training for their enlisted men.

Toward the end of the war, the Servicemen's Readjustment Act of 1944 (known as the GI Bill) was passed to provide benefits to the veterans of the War, allowing them to further their education. A large number of men and women from varying social, economic, and racial groups now could attend college, thus popularizing higher education with the highest enrollments ever. In addition, the returning servicemen and women began families and within a decade after the war, a "baby boom" hit the public schools, increasing school enrollments by thirty-seven percent between 1946 and 1956.[4]

Back to Basics

In the postwar years, progressive education came under major criticism as it was held responsible for the decline in educational standards in the country. James Conant led a move for a "Back to Basics" curriculum. In 1959 he published his findings in *The American High School Today* and recommended increased rigor and a return to the academic basics of English, mathematics, science, and social studies.

Another event which had a great impact on education occurred in October of 1957 when the Russians launched *Sputnik*. The federal government reacted quickly by passing the National Defense Education Act (NDEA) in 1958 that directed significant amounts of federal funds for mathematics, science, and foreign language instruction. This was the first time the federal government attempted to directly influence the schools' curriculum.

Mary McLeod Bethune, one of the most important African American women in educational history, was a transitional figure with one foot in the nineteenth century and one foot in the twentieth.[5] She founded a school that would empower black women, for she felt that women needed a "distinctive education" different from that of men in order to transform society. She taught her girls the classical subjects—science, mathematics, literature, and foreign languages—that would enable them to become intelligent, self-confident women leaders. She combined these with vocational training that would help them become professional teachers, nurses, and librarians who could, with their economic independence and service, uplift their race.[6]

Civil Rights Movement

Efforts to integrate the Negro into American society had been sharply curtailed by the *Plessy vs. Ferguson* case in which the courts maintained that separate but equal accommodations were constitutional for African Americans and whites. Even though this case was overthrown in 1954 by the landmark *Brown vs. Board of Education of Topeka* court decision and the courts mandated an end to segregation in the schools, it would take further legislation and court orders in order to desegregate the schools. Ten years after this case, ninety-eight percent of black students were still in all-black schools and almost no white child in the South was in a black school.[7] Not much was done to integrate the schools until the Civil Rights Act of 1964. This Act authorized the federal government to withhold federal funds from programs that discriminated by race, color, or national origin.

According to the PBS documentary *School, The Story of American Public Education,* America in 1950 was fundamentally a different nation from that of present-day America. Public schooling was not equally available for ethnic minorities and white students. For example, whereas fifty-four percent of southern white children of high school age were enrolled in public high schools at this time, less than twenty percent of African American children of high school age were enrolled in secondary schools. Of those enrolled, ninety-eight percent of the black students in the South were still in all-black schools. The average schooling of Mexican Americans was only 4.7 years.[8]

In the fifty years since the Brown decision, efforts have been made by the federal government, school districts, and communities to integrate the schools, but many communities are still themselves segregated. Some historians argue that instead of bringing about better race relations and improved academic performance, the historic Brown decision has heightened racial tensions and fostered white flight from urban areas. Nevertheless, by 1972, ninety-one percent of southern black children attended integrated schools.[9]

War on Poverty

In the early 1960s, the federal government launched its "War on Poverty," stating that education was a major force in the elimination of poverty. Although from 1963 to 1969 two dozen educational acts were passed, the major educational legislation enacted was the Elementary & Secondary Education Act (ESEA) of 1965. Directed at specific programs, populations, and purposes (expressed in its different titles), this has been the most far-reaching federal legislation ever, providing over $1 billion in federal funds to education.[10] Title I was dedicated to providing funds for schools with large numbers of low income children, continuing the progress made by the Head Start early childhood program. Other titles provided funds for libraries, textbooks, research, and Native American and bilingual students. Congress also passed the Higher Education Act that provided financial assistance to institutes of higher education as well as loans and scholarships to college students. These acts dramatically increased federal involvement in education, providing vast sums of money for elementary and secondary schools, vocational schools and colleges. From 1963 to 1969, federal funds for education increased from $900 million dollars to $3 billion, and the federal government's share of financing education rose from 4.4 percent to 8.8 percent. In 1979, the federal government's share peaked at 9.8 percent, the highest percentage in our nation's history.[11]

Federal Involvement in Education

Beginning with the Civil Rights Act of 1964 that sought to desegregate the schools, the federal government began a definite involvement in the schools: It would withhold funds if schools did not follow its legislative acts. Funds were withheld from school districts if they did not desegregate their schools, if they discriminated against students by race, color, or national origin (Title VI), or if they discriminated by race, religion, origin, or sex in their employment of individuals (Title IX).

Funding for education fluctuated as the administration changed from Democratic to Republican and back again. Republican presidents reduced federal support for social and educational initiatives following their philosophy that the responsibility for domestic programs belongs to state and local governments, not the federal government. Democrats increased the funding. During Jimmy Carter's (1977–1981) tenure the federal budget for education increased to the highest percentage that it has ever been—9.8 percent. In addition, Carter established the Department of Education, making it a cabinet seat in its own right, and appointed Shirley Hufstadler as the first Secretary of Education.

A Nation at Risk

In 1983, the federal report *A Nation at Risk* was published, identifying the declining academic achievement of students. The report began by stating that "Our nation is at risk" because "the educational foundations of our society are presently being eroded by a rising tide of mediocrity that threatens our very future as a nation and as a people." Other reports followed and the "Educational Reform Movement of the 1980s" began. States enacted higher graduation requirements, standardized curriculum mandates, required teacher certification testing and increased testing of students.

In the early 1990s, for the first time in our nation's history, state and national leaders from both parties joined together in setting goals for the schools and issued America 2000—six goals for the schools to be met by the year 2000. Although not funded until 1992 under the name of Goals 2000: Educate America Act, it is significant because it formalized the nation's education goals and established a "new federal partnership to reform the nation's educational system." It established a National Education Standards and Improvement Council to develop standards for all major academic areas.[12] Perhaps the most important accomplishment of Goals 2000 was the Improving America's Schools Act that re-authorized the Elementary and Secondary Education Act and encouraged comprehensive reform at the state and local levels to meet the national goals. In the tradition of Horace Mann, the legislation promoted a national moral consensus and advocated the integration of character education into classroom instruction.[13] Various innovations have been developed which include establishing charter schools, using vouchers, giving parents choice, and privatizing education. In 2001 the "No Child Left Behind Act" mandated standardized tests to ensure that every child, no matter what their ethnic, racial, or economic background, would meet the standards of learning in the state curriculum.

The study of the history of American education demonstrates that schools reflect the society that supports them. A series of gun-related assaults on students by their classmates, especially at Columbine High School in Littleton, Colorado, called attention to increasing violence in schools and the importance of having "no bullying" and character education programs in schools. In the year 2000, "The 32nd Annual Phi Delta Kappa/Gallup Poll of the Public's Attitudes Toward the Public Schools" found violence, fighting, gangs, drugs, and dope as the five top problems faced by schools.[14] The terrorist attacks of September 11, 2001 changed, once again, how Americans viewed their world. Americans became more patriotic, more spiritual, and began to reassess the importance of family and friends. The value of education about different cultures, religions, and languages is once again very apparent if our country is to promote a respect for democratic values on our globe.

For Further Research on the Internet

This site provides information and links to various school choice proposals. **http://www. schoolchoices.org**

Go to Chapter 16 for links to current trends and issues in education. **http://www. prenhall.com/foundations-cluster**

Selected moments in the twentieth century with links for each decade. **http://fcis. oise.utoronto.ca/~daniel_schugurensky/assignment1/index.html**

Notes

1. L. Dean Webb, Arlene Metha and K. Forbis Jordan, *Foundations of Education,* 3rd ed. (Upper Saddle River, NJ: Merrill/Prentice Hall, 2000), p. 206.

2. John Pulliam and James Van Patten, *History of Education in America* (Upper Saddle River, NJ: Merrill/Prentice Hall, 2003), p. 193.

3. Wayne Urban, and Jennings Wagoner, *American Education: A History,* 2nd ed. (Burr Ridge, IL: McGraw Hill, 2000), pp. 267, 211.

4. L. Dean Webb, Arlene Metha and K. Forbis Jordan, *Foundations of Education,* 3rd ed. (Upper Saddle River, NJ: Merrill/Prentice Hall, 2000), p. 218.

5. Joyce Hanson, *Mary McLeod Bethune: Black Women's Political Activism* (Columbia, MO: University of Missouri Press, 2003), p. 3.

6. Ibid., p. 64.

7. Sarah Mondale and Sarah Patton, eds., *School: The Story of American Public Education* (Boston: Beacon Press, 2001), p. 144.

8. Ibid., p. 126.

9. Ibid., pp. 128, 144, 149.

10. Webb, p. 222.

11. U.S. Department of Education, p. 169.

12. Gerald Gutek, *American Education 1945–2000: A History and Commentary* (Prospect Heights, IL: Waveland Press, 2000), p. 293.

13. Joel Spring, *The American School 1642–2000* (New York: McGraw-Hill, 2001), p. 463.

14. Lowell Rose, and Alex Gallup. The 32nd Annual Phi Delta Kappa/Gallup Poll of the Public's Attitudes Toward the Public Schools, *Phi Delta Kappan* 46 (September, 2000).

Section 11.1: John Dewey (1859–1952)

Do you remember how the chairs were bolted to the floor in the one-room schoolhouse? This was the norm in all schools until John Dewey suggested children work in groups and do hands-on experiential learning. You can only do this if you have tables and chairs that can be moved in different ways. Thank goodness John Dewey suggested this.

John Dewey's Life and Times

John Dewey was born in Burlington, Vermont, on October 20, 1859 to Archibald Dewey, a grocer in his forties and Lucina Rich, in her twenties. They had four sons: John Archibald, Davis Rich, John and Charles. John was born nine months after his eldest brother John Archibald died in an accident at home, and was named after him.[1] Born two years before the Civil War, John's father was away in the army for three years during his childhood. John's mother was very religious and concerned about her children's spiritual and moral welfare. John's formal schooling was delayed due to the war.

His Education

John began his grade-school studies in the fall of 1867, at age eight, studying in an ungraded, overcrowded school with fifty-four pupils, ages seven to nineteen. Dewey did well with his studies in reading, writing, rhetoric, geography, and spelling and was able to catch up with his age group; he even passed into the next group, graduating from grade school at the age of twelve. John, or Johnny as his teachers called him, was quiet and reserved, shy with strangers, but courteous, well mannered and likeable.[2] He enrolled in the college preparatory course in high school in September 1872, studying a classical curriculum of Latin, Greek, and French in addition to mathematics and English language and literature, finishing the four-year program in three years. The teaching was as poor and rote as it had been in elementary school; John's later interest in education was a reaction to these early negative experiences.

John went with his brother Davis to the University of Vermont for undergraduate training following the prescribed curriculum until his senior year, when he could choose electives. John was introduced to Immanuael Kant, T. H. Huxley, and Auguste Comte. This marked a real turning point in his life as he decided to pursue philosophy as a career, even though almost all academic philosophers at that time were clergymen. John graduated from college at the age of 19, second in his class.[3]

Not sure of how he should proceed, Dewey taught Latin, algebra, and the natural sciences for three years in high schools, first in Pennsylvania and then back in Vermont. He continued his study of philosophy, encouraged by his ability to have articles published in the philosophical review. In 1882, he entered the newly established Johns Hopkins University—modeled after the European university system—to study philosophy at the graduate level. Here he was introduced to George Wilhelm Hegel's ideas, and tried to reconcile Hegelianism with Christianity. He wrote his dissertation on Kant's psychology and graduated in two years.[4]

College Professor

John was offered a position to teach philosophy at the University of Michigan, one of the few co-educational colleges in the United States at that time, for a salary of $900. Here he met and married Harriet Alice Chipman in 1886. John began to share her interest in education, applying psychology to the study of how we learn, focus attention, and think. (With the growth of America's population in the 1880s, public education had become a national topic as industry was looking to the schools to produce an educated citizenry.) John published his first book, *Psychology*, which was the first book on modern psychology published in America. Dewey's fame began to grow and he was invited to attend conferences, submit articles, and collaborate with others.[5]

His Family

As both Alice and John were fond of children, they had a large family, six children in all, two of whom died. Their first child, Frederick, was born in 1887. Dewey's temperament allowed him to assume the responsibilities of parenthood with relative ease, even though his work often took him on travels away from home. His son, Morris, died on his first trip to Europe in 1894 and his son, Gordon, died ten years later during another family trip overseas. While in Italy in 1904, the Deweys adopted Sabino, a boy who was the same age as Gordon would have been. Several of Dewey's children followed in his footsteps as college professors and authors of books.[6]

As the father of a growing family, Dewey was always looking to augment his salary. He went to the University of Minnesota in 1888 since they offered him a full professorship, but returned to the University of Michigan the following year when they offered him the chair of the philosophy department, with a salary of $2,200. He continued to write books and publish, teach large classes and give extra talks and lectures, both at his church and at conferences.

The University of Chicago

In 1894, William Rainey Harper, of the newly founded University of Chicago, offered Dewey a position as chair of the philosophy, psychology, and pedagogy (education) department at a salary of $4,000. Dewey built up the philosophy department and established pedagogy as a department of its own. In the fall of 1895, the University Elementary School (the Lab School) opened. Here Dewey developed insights about children while doing his greatest educational experiments; he attracted the attention of educators from around the country. Dewey wrote all this up in his book *The School and Society* (1899), which became his most widely read book. Dewey was not able to write as much as he wanted due to all his administrative duties; he took on many of the extra projects at the encouragement of President Harper, but also because of his personal interest in them and his desire for the extra stipends.[7] However, when he appointed his wife to be the principal of the lab school, Harper would only approve this appointment provisionally for one year. Due to this misunderstanding, both Deweys resigned their posts in 1904. John Dewey was deeply hurt all of his life by this dispute and would not return to the University of Chicago, even when invited to receive an award. Dewey fell away from organized religion while at the University of Chicago.

Flourishing at Columbia University

John Dewey accepted a position in the department of philosophy at Columbia University and began in 1905, after a year of travel in Europe. Given academic freedom at Columbia, without administrative responsibilities, Dewey's writing flourished. He wrote most of the articles and books on philosophy and on education for which he is most famous.[8] Now a world-famous philosopher of education, from 1919 to 1934 Dewey traveled abroad, visiting

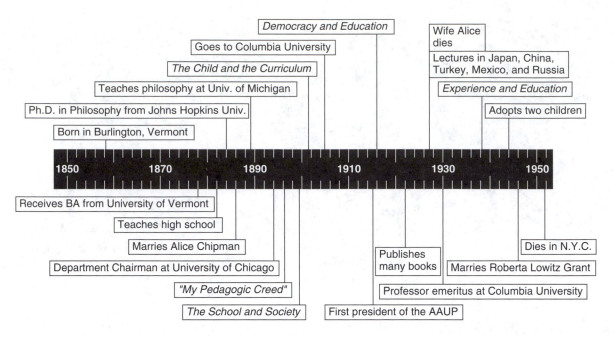

Figure 11.1 Dewey's Life and Times

Japan, China, Turkey, Mexico, the Soviet Union, and South Africa, working with government officials regarding educational issues.[9] (See the timeline of Dewey's life in Figure 11.1.)

Dewey experienced a great personal loss when his wife, Alice, died in July of 1927 due to a heart condition. Alice had shared his intellectual interests in education and social affairs for forty-one years. Two years later, his friends put on a conference for Dewey to help him celebrate his seventieth birthday. This helped him to begin writing again, and he completed some of his most important works in subsequent years: *The Quest for Certainty; Philosophy and Civilization; Art as Experience;* and *Logic: The Theory of Inquiry.*

In 1946, at eighty-seven years of age, Dewey married Roberta Lowitz Grant, who was forty-two years old. They adopted two children from Halifax, a brother and sister orphaned by the war. Spending as much time as possible in his last years on the family-owned farm in Pennsylvania, Dewey is remembered as a truly happy and loving father and husband. Dewey died on June 1, 1952 in New York City continuing to write until the very end. In all, Dewey had written some forty books and over nine hundred articles, essays, reviews, and works.[10]

Dewey's Contributions to Educational Thought

John Dewey was one of the most important philosophers of education of the twentieth century and few educational theorists have equaled his widespread influence that was not limited to the United States, but felt throughout the world. John Dewey wrote on philosophy and on education. Education was applied philosophy according to Dewey.

His Philosophic Ideas

In the area of philosophy, his ideas are categorized as pragmatism, experimentalism, and instrumentalism. His most important books for his philosophic thought include *Human Nature and Conduct* (1922), *Experience and Nature (1925),* and *The Quest for Certainty*

(1929). Dewey's pragmatism insisted on the practicality of knowledge, i.e., theory in practice. Pragmatism defines truth as a tentative assertion derived from human experience; it rejects metaphysical absolutes. If something works, it is true and useful; if it no longer works, it is no longer true.[11] Experimentalism sees experience as the basis for all knowledge; the human is in continuous interaction with its environment. Instrumentalism is a moral relativism that defines values as arising from the human response to various environmental situations.[12]

Truth, according to Dewey, is that opinion which is fated for acceptance by all investigators. There are no eternal, unchanging truths for Dewey and the truth is always changing. This is similar to the "constructionist" theory of learning and has important implications for the field of moral education. The moral agent is the one who proposes to himself an end to be achieved by action. The validity of moral principles however, for Dewey, will be found in their utility upon application.

Dewey stated that society was the most influential educator of character (more than family), and he gave prime importance to fostering character through a democratic school atmosphere and proposed that the school be a natural source of moral education in all that it does.[13] Nevertheless, he based his theory of moral education on a system that lacks any absolute values; Dewey's ideas inspired the values clarification education movement. There is great agreement with Dewey's contention that "the greatest defect of instruction today is that children leave school with a mental perspective which lacks faith in the existence of moral principles which are capable of effective application."[14]

Dewey's Philosophy of Education

Dewey outlined the educational implications based on his philosophy. The books most often read by educators are considered his seminal works: *The School and Society* (1899), *The Child and the Curriculum* (1902), *Moral Principles in Education* (1909), *How We Think* (1910), *Democracy and Education* (1916), and *Experience and Education* (1938).

The School and Society is Dewey's first expression of his philosophy of education—the three primary elements are the school, the evolving society, and the children. The idea of growth, or the reconstruction of experience, is central to Dewey's educational theory. One should not regard education as a preparation for life, but rather as a process of living in itself. The "activity method" or "hands-on" education and authentic educational experiences are outgrowths of these ideas, basing themselves on problem solving.[15]

Dewey's *The Child and the Curriculum* is not a discussion of curriculum as much as it is a plea to stop separating out methods of teaching, and work on teaching the process of thinking instead.[16] Dewey tells us "there is no line of demarcation within facts themselves which classifies them as belonging to science, history, or geography, respectively"... students should be helped to see the relations of studies to one another and to the intellectual whole to which all belong."[17] Thus he laid the basis of the "Whole Language" and "Thematic/Interdisciplinary Units" movements in the United States.

How We Think was designed as a guide for teachers on how to train young minds to think about problems and ethical issues. It encouraged teachers to go beyond the recitations of the day, and draw up lessons plans similar to those advocated by Johann Herbart in which Dewey's five steps of problem solving are followed.[18]

Democracy and Education was, according to him, his most important work and his fullest expression of his philosophic position. According to Dewey, in order to make students intelligent citizens, education must be democratic, providing students with free and intelligent choice between alternates and engaging them in meaningful interactions with their environment—the subject matter, the teachers, and peers.[19] Dewey's world was a very multicultural world with a flood of immigrants coming in the 1880s and 1890s. He saw the role of education as nationalizing, but also as fostering mutual respect among the diverse cultures. Dewey believed that there should be "methods of school activity which afford opportunity for reciprocity, cooperation, and positive personal achievement" and in so stating began what is today called cooperative learning. He also advocated service learning.[20]

Although credited with promoting "progressive education," child-centered education that emphasized the importance of teaching what interested the child, Dewey denied this explanation, saying that he advocated society-centered education, and the teacher was crucial in the learning process.[21] Dewey saw the child as a "bundle of intellectual, emotional, and moral potential" that needed to be guided by a teacher. Education was the supreme art as it was "the art of giving shape to human powers and adapting them to social service."[22]

The following essay, "My Pedagogic Creed," written in 1896, was Dewey's statement of his educational convictions. In this creed, Dewey tells us that "every teacher should recognize the dignity of his calling."

Notes

1. Robert Westbrook, *John Dewey and American Democracy* (Ithaca, NY: Cornell University Press, 1991), p. 1.
2. Jay Martin, *The Education of John Dewey: A Biography* (New York: Columbia University Press, 2002), p. 34.
3. Martin, p. 53.
4. Ibid., p. 85.
5. George Dykhuizen, *The Life and Mind of John Dewey* (Carbondale, IL: Southern Illinois University Press, 1973), p. 110.
6. Westbrook, p. 150.
7. Martin, pp. 199–201.
8. Westbrook, p. 130ff.
9. Martin, p. 243.
10. Ibid., p. 478.
11. Alan Ryan, "Deweyan Pragmatism and American Education," in *Philosophers on Education,* edited by A. Rorty (London: Routledge, 1998), p. 399.
12. Gerald Gutek, *Philosophical and Ideological Perspectives on Education* (Boston: Allyn and Bacon, 1988), pp. 87–97; H. M. Campbell, *John Dewey* (New York: Twayne Publishers, Inc., 1971), p. 21ff.
13. Holly Salls, "John Dewey and Character Education: Is He the Answer?", Midwest Philosophy of Education Conference Proceedings, Chicago, 1997, p. 36.
14. John Dewey, *Moral Principles in Education* (Carbondale, IL: Southern Illinois University Press, 1909), p. 100.
15. Ryan, p. 400; Martin, p. 199.
16. Ryan, p. 402.
17. John Dewey, *Moral Principles in Education* (Carbondale, IL: Southern Illinois University Press, 1909), p. 135.
18. Martin, p. 253; Ryan, p. 404.
19. Wei Rose Zhang, "John Dewey and Traditional Education," Proceedings of the Midwest Philosophy of Education Conference, at Chicago, IL, 1999, p. 185.
20. David Halliburton, "John Dewey: A Voice That Still Speaks to Us," *Change* 29 (1) (1997), p. 28.
21. Zhang, p. 190; Ryan, p. 397.
22. Ryan, p. 397.

Questions to Guide Your Reading

1. What is education, according to Dewey?
2. What is the starting point for all education?
3. What role does the home play, according to Dewey?
4. What is the role of the teacher, according to Dewey?

READING 11.1:
MY PEDAGOGIC CREED

Article I—What Education is

I Believe that:

—all education proceeds by the participation of the individual in the social consciousness of the race. This process begins unconsciously almost at birth, and is continually shaping the individual's powers, saturating his consciousness, forming his habits, training his ideas, and arousing his feelings and emotions. Through this unconscious education the individual gradually comes to share in the intellectual and moral resources which humanity has succeeded in getting together. He becomes an inheritor of the funded capital of civilization. The most formal and technical education in the world safely departs from this general process. It can only organize it or differentiate it in some particular direction.

—the only true education comes through the stimulation of the child's powers by the demands of the social situations in which he finds himself. Through these demands he is stimulated to act as a member of a unity, to emerge from his original narrowness of action and feeling, and to conceive of himself from the standpoint of the welfare of the group to which he belongs. Through the responses which others make to his own activities he comes to know what these mean in social terms.... For instance, through the response that is made to the child's instinctive babblings, the child comes to know what those babblings mean; they are transformed into articulate language.

—this educational process has two sides—one psychological and one sociological—and that neither can be subordinated to the other, or neglected, without evil results following. Of these two sides, the psychological is the basis. The child's own instincts and powers furnish the material and give the starting-point for all education. Save as the efforts of the educator connect with some activity that the child is carrying on of his own initiative independent of the educator, education becomes reduced to a pressure from without. It may, indeed, give certain external results, but cannot be called truly educative....If it chances to coincide with the child's activity it will get a leverage; if it does not, it will result in friction, or disintegration, or arrest of the child's nature.

—knowledge of social conditions, of the present state of civilization, is necessary in order properly to interpret the child's powers.

—the psychological and social sides are organically related, and that education cannot be regarded as a compromise between the two, or a superimposition of one upon the other. . . .

—with the advent of democracy and modern industrial conditions, it is impossible to foretell definitely just what civilization will be twenty years from now. Hence it is impossible to prepare the child for any precise set of conditions. To prepare him for the future life means to give him command of himself; it means so to train him that he will have the full and ready use of all his capacities. . . .

In sum, I believe that the individual who is to be educated is a social individual, and that society is an organic union of individuals. If we eliminate the social factor from the child we are left only with an abstraction; if we eliminate the individual factor from society, we are left with an inert and lifeless mass.

Article II—What the School is

I Believe that:

—the school is primarily a social institution. Education being a social process, the school is simply that form of community life in which all those agencies are concentrated that will be most effective in bringing the child to share in the inherited resources of the race, and to use his own powers for social ends.

—education, therefore, is a process of living and not a preparation for future living.

—the school must represent present life—life as real and vital to the child as that which he carries on

Source: From *The School Journal*. A Weekly Journal of Education, LIV (E. L. Kellogg & Co., January, 1897).

in the home, in the neighborhood, or on the playground...

—the school, as an institution, should simplify existing social life; should reduce it, as it were, to an embryonic form. Existing life is so complex that the child cannot be brought into contact with it without either confusion or distraction.

—as such simplified social life, the school life should grow gradually out of the home life; that it should take up and continue the activities with which the child is already familiar in the home...

—it is also a necessity because the home is the form of social life in which the child has been nurtured and in connection with which the child has had his moral training. It is the business of the school to deepen and extend his sense of values bound up in his home life.

—much of present education fails because it neglects this fundamental principle of the school as a form of community life. It conceives the school as a place where certain information is to be given, where certain lessons are to be learned, or where certain habits are to be formed. The value of these is conceived as lying largely in the remote future; the child must do these things for the sake of something else he is to do; they are mere preparations. As a result they do not become a part of the life experience of the child and so are not truly educative.

—the moral education centers upon this conception of the school as a mode of social life, that the best and deepest moral training is precisely that which one gets through having to enter into proper relations with others in a unity of work and thought. The present educational systems, so far as they destroy or neglect this unity, render it difficult or impossible to get any genuine, regular moral training.

—the teacher is not in the school to impose certain ideas or to form certain habits in the child, but is there as a member of the community to select the influences which shall affect the child and assist him in properly responding to these influences.

—the discipline of the school should proceed from the life of the school as a whole and not directly from the teacher.

—the teacher's business is simply to determine, on the basis of larger experience and riper wisdom, how the discipline of life shall come to the child.

—all questions of grading of the child and his promotion should be determined by reference to the same standard. Examinations are of use only so far as they test the child's fitness for social life and reveal the place in which he can be of the most service and where he can receive the most help.

Article III—The Subject-Matter of Education

I Believe that:

—the subject-matter of the school curriculum should mark a gradual differentiation out of the primitive unconscious unity of social life.

—we violate the child's nature and render difficult the best ethical results by introducing the child too abruptly to a number of special studies, of reading, writing, geography, etc. out of relation to this social life.

—the true center of correlation on the school subjects is not science, nor literature, nor history, nor geography}, but the child's own social activities.

— there is, therefore, no succession of studies in the ideal school curriculum. If education is life, all life has, from the outset, a scientific aspect, an aspect of art and culture, and an aspect of communication. It cannot, therefore, be true that the proper studies for one grade are mere reading and writing and that at a later grade, reading, or literature, or science be introduced. The progress is not in the succession of studies, but in the development of new attitudes towards, and new interests in, experience.

—education must be conceived as a continuing reconstruction of experience; that the process and the goal of education are one and the same thing. . . .

Article IV—The Nature of Method

I Believe that:

—the question of method is ultimately reducible to the question of the order of development of the child's powers and interests. The law for presenting and treating material is the law implicit within the child's own nature. Because this is so, I believe the following statements are of supreme importance as determining the spirit in which education is carried on:

—the active side precedes the passive in the development of the child-nature; that expression comes before conscious impression; that the muscular development precedes the sensory, that movements come before conscious sensations; I believe that consciousness is essentially motor or impulsive; that conscious states tend to project themselves in action.

—the neglect of this principle is the cause of a large part of the waste of time and strength in schoolwork. The child is thrown into a passive, receptive, or absorbing attitude. The conditions are such that he is not permitted to follow the law of his nature; the result is friction and waste . . .

—only through the continual and sympathetic observation of childhood's interests can the adult enter into the child's life and see what it is ready for, and upon what materials it could work most readily and fruitfully . . .

Article V—The School and Social Progress

I Believe that:

—education is the fundamental method of social progress and reform.

—the community's duty to education is, therefore, its paramount moral duty.

—when society once recognizes the possibilities in this direction, and the obligations that these possibilities impose, it is impossible to conceive of the resources of time, attention, and money which will be put at the disposal of the educator.

—it is the business of every one interested in education to insist upon the school as the primary and most effective interest of social progress and reform in order that society may be awakened to realize what the school stands for, and aroused to the necessity of endowing the educator with sufficient equipment properly to perform his task.

—education thus conceived marks the most perfect and intimate union of science and art conceivable in human experience.

—the teacher is engaged, not simply in the training of individuals, but in the formation of the proper social life.

—every teacher should realize the dignity of his calling; that he is a social servant set apart for the maintenance of proper social order and the securing of the right social growth.

—in this way the teacher is always the prophet of the true God and the usherer in of the true kingdom of God.

Discussion Questions

1. Do you agree with Dewey's idea of pragmatism that something is only of value if it works and is useful?
2. Are Dewey's criticisms of "subject-matter centered" education valid? Discuss why or why not.
3. Is Dewey's support for a "child-centered" form of education workable? Do you agree with some of the criticisms leveled against it? Explain.
4. Do you support Dewey's idea that the student and teacher are "learners together"? Explain why or why not.
5. How could Dewey's ideas be reflected in the classroom? What are some creative ways his thinking could be utilized? Remember, for Dewey, the classroom is a laboratory—do not be afraid to experiment!
6. Dewey placed a strong emphasis on moral training in schools that should extend into the home. What if a student comes from a home in which alcohol or drugs are abused? How would Dewey deal with this value discordance?
7. Dewey says that with the advent of democracy and modern industrial conditions, it is impossible to foretell what civilization will be like twenty years from now. How can education prepare a student for an unknown future?

For Further Research on the Internet

The Center for Dewey Studies sponsored by Southern Illinois University. **http://www.siu.edu/~deweyctr/**

The John Dewey Society home page. **http://cuip.uchicago.edu/jds/**

Suggestions for Further Reading

Campbell, Harry M. *John Dewey*. New York: Twayne Publishers, Inc., 1971.

Dewey, John. *Moral Principles in Education*. Carbondale, IL: Southern Illinois University Press, 1909.

Dykhuizen, George. *The Life and Mind of John Dewey*. Carbondale, IL: Southern Illinois University Press, 1993.

Gutek, Gerald. *Philosophical and Ideological Perspectives on Education*. Boston: Allyn and Bacon, 1988.

Halliburton, David. "John Dewey: A Voice That Still Speaks to Us." *Change* 29 (1) (1997): 24–29.

Martin, Jay. *The Education of John Dewey: A Biography*. New York: Columbia University Press, 2002.

Ryan, Alan. "Deweyan Pragmatism and American Education." In *Philosophers on Education*, edited by A. Rorty. London: Routledge, 1998.

Salls, Holly. John Dewey and Character Education: Is He the Answer? *Proceedings of the Midwest Philosophy of Education Society Annual Conference*, Chicago, 1997.

Westbrook, Robert. *John Dewey and American Democracy*. Ithaca, NY: Cornell University Press, 1991.

Zhang, Wei Rose. John Dewey and Traditional Education. *Proceedings of the Midwest Philosophy of Education Society Annual Conference*, Chicago, 1999.

Section 11.2: Mary McLeod Bethune (1875–1955)

If you are a woman reading this book, today you can aspire to any position in education you desire and reach your dream. This was not always so. Women in America, and especially women of color, have Mary McLeod Bethune to thank for promoting the large entry of women in higher education in the 1900s who completed college degree programs and entered the professions of education, law, and government.

Mary McLeod Bethune's Life and Times

Mary Jane McLeod Bethune was born on July 10, 1875 near Mayesville, South Carolina to former slaves Patsy and Samuel McLeod. She was the fifteenth of their seventeen children, the first born in freedom. Mary worked in her family fields although she dreamed of books and learning to read.

Mary's Education

There were no schools for blacks in Mayesville until a one-room mission school opened when Mary was eleven, so she walked five miles a day to this school and completed the elementary curriculum, learning to read, write, and do arithmetic, as well as studying history, geography, and the Bible. She then returned to the fields, as there was no high school for blacks in her area.[1]

One year later, Mary was granted a scholarship from Mary Chrissman, a Quaker dressmaker, to attend the Scotia Seminary in Concord, North Carolina where she studied for six years both academic and vocational courses while also learning etiquette and social skills. She was very involved in extracurricular activities such as chorus, debate, laundry, and baking. The faculty and student body were mixed at Scotia, giving Mary the opportunity to interact with whites for the first time and to see both races working together as equals.[2] She graduated from Scotia at the age of twenty and studied at the Moody Bible Institute in Chicago with Dwight Moody, the only African American student among the 1000 students.[3] Mary was an openly religious person who began each day with meditation and scripture reading and spoke of a personal relationship with God through dreams.[4]

Teacher and School Founder

After graduation, she returned south to teach at various schools in Georgia from 1896 to 1903.[5] In 1898, Mary McLeod married Albertus Bethune and had a son the following year. Mary was invited to be the director of a school in Palatka, Florida, where she worked for five years before moving to Daytona, Florida on October 3, 1904, to open the Daytona Educational and Industrial School for Negro Girls with her savings of $1.50. The first day she had five girls attending her school sitting on boxes in a rented house.[6] The catalogue stated that the aim of the school was "to uplift Negro girls spiritually, morally, intellectually, and industrially." The curriculum of the school included academic subjects such as reading, writing, spelling, arithmetic, and religion, as well as industrial arts courses such as homemaking, cooking, cleaning, and sewing."[7] According to Mary, "They will be trained in head, hand, and heart. Their heads to think, their hands to work, and their hearts to have faith.... I am teaching girls crafts and homemaking as well as reading and writing. I am teaching them to earn a living."[8]

Albertus helped with the school and was one of the Board of Trustees until 1908 when he returned to South Carolina for a better job, remaining there until he died ten years later. Mary had to do extensive fund-raising for the school and had her students sing in hotels to raise funds; she received support from philanthropists such as James M. Gamble of Procter and Gamble. By 1910 the school had 102 students enrolled; two years later it expanded to high school, and by 1920 it had 351 students and fourteen faculty members.

When a student in the school became ill and the local hospital would not care for her within the hospital because she was black, Mary began the McLeod Hospital, named after her father who had recently died; later this grew also to include a training program for nurses.[9] "Go as far as your aspirations and talents can take you," was Bethune's message.[10]

College President

The growth of the Daytona school led to a merger in 1923 with the Cookman Institute for Men and the new institution became the four-year, co-educational Bethune-Cookman College. It was the first fully accredited four-year college for blacks in Florida. Mary served as its president until 1942, by which time the institution had a faculty of 100 with a student population of more than 1000.[11] (See the timeline of Bethune's life in Figure 11.2.)

National Leader

Mary became a highly visible leader in black education and the black women's club movement. She presented a model of decorum, femininity, and studied propriety, with an impeccable appearance and good manners. She served as the president of the National Association of Teachers in Colored Schools in 1923 and of the National Association of Colored Women from 1924–28, using her natural leadership talents to move these groups toward a united consensus.[12]

Presidents Calvin Coolidge and Herbert Hoover each invited Mary to attend White House conferences in Washington, DC. Soon afterwards, she was given an appointment to a planning commission of the Federal Office of Education of Negroes charged with studying methods to improve black education.[13] In these federal positions Bethune worked with both Democrats and Republicans, leading her to be recognized by members of both parties as an expert in educational issues facing African Americans.

Bethune was invited to a luncheon hosted by Eleanor Roosevelt in 1927, the only black present. When it came time to sit down at the table, a tension filled the air until Sara Roosevelt, Franklin's mother, asked Mary to sit next to her, beginning a friendship and alliance between Sara, Eleanor, and Mary Bethune.[14]

International Leader

Mary toured nine European countries in 1927, was well received everywhere, and had an audience with Pope Pius XI, who blessed her for the work she was doing. Bethune received the Joel E. Spingarn Medal from the National Association for the Advancement of Colored People in 1935 for "the highest and noblest achievement of an American Negro."[15]

Franklin D. Roosevelt asked her to become a member of the National Youth Administration advisory board Division of Negro Affairs and the director of the Office of Minority

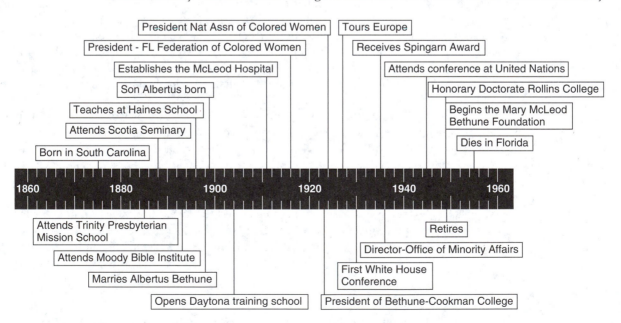

Figure 11.2   Bethune's Life and Times

Affairs of the NYA, making her the highest paid black in the U.S. government as well as making her a national black leader. According to Paula Giddings, it was Bethune's deft maneuvering in the FDR administration that helped her put her four major "passions"—race, women, education, and youth—on the national agenda for the first time in the history of black Americans.[16] In 1945, President Harry Truman appointed Bethune to his Civil Rights Commission and she was asked to go with W. E. B. DuBois and Walter White to the San Francisco Conference to draw up the charter for the United Nations; she was the only African American woman there in an official capacity. Mary McLeod Bethune became well known across the nation, and was sought out for speaking engagements with her repertoire of race-deprecating humor and homespun homilies that got her point across. During her lifetime, Bethune received numerous awards and eight honorary degrees.[17]

Mary Bethune retired to her campus home in Daytona in 1949 and, with the help of Eleanor Roosevelt, she began the Mary McLeod Bethune Foundation to promote her ideas of black educational advancement, interracial cooperation, and service to young people. Bethune worked internationally trying to end segregation and discrimination and to strengthen and sustain the United Nations for world peace. She welcomed Madame Vijaya Lakshmi Pandit, the first woman ambassador of India to the United States, to Bethune-Cookman College in 1951.

Mary lived almost eighty years; before she died, she saw the landmark *Brown vs. Topeka* case overthrow the "separate but equal" policy of *Plessy vs. Ferguson*. In many ways she was the female counterpart of W. E. B. DuBois and can rightly be considered one of the instigators of the civil rights movement. Mary died on May 18, 1955, leaving a legacy of interracial cooperation and increased educational opportunity for blacks.

Mary McLeod Bethune's Contribution to Education

One of the interesting facts about Mary McLeod Bethune is that although she had very little formal education and only two years at the collegiate level, she became a teacher, a college president, founder of an elementary school that became a high school and then a college, a government official on education committees, and a great orator. She was the first black woman to have a national monument dedicated to her in Washington DC, and the first on a postage stamp. She has several schools, streets, and public places named after her throughout the United States. She is known as one of the fifty greatest women in America.

Mary McLeod Bethune was one of the most important African American women in American political history; she made significant contributions to the Roosevelt era. Her unflagging concern for black women achieved the goal of having women, especially black women, counted among the new groups with legitimate demands that had to be taken into account on the national agenda.[18]

The statistics document her success. While she was at the NYA, she implemented a special fund for black youth going to college, and during her tenure helped 4,118 students receive $609,930 in aid. She involved the black universities in various training programs offered by the NYA. One project promoted the certification of black librarians to help black universities become accredited, another trained black high school teachers for the southern rural schools, and still another trained black pilots for military and civilian work. Bethune became a role model for black women, and by 1940 more black women received B.A. degrees from black colleges than black men. Also, more and more black women were receiving degrees beyond the baccalaureate, entering professions that had been exclusively male in the past.[19]

Bethune's vision of black empowerment was based on education, public life, and an unwavering, optimistic belief that American principles of democracy and equality would ultimately triumph over discriminatory practices based on color, race, and gender. She believed in the black women's moral superiority and unique responsibility for racial uplift, emphasizing the importance of women getting involved in decision-making positions in society and politics.[20] Mary preached black pride and the study and teaching of black history. She helped to define the role the black woman would play in achieving a racially integrated America.

Bethune's Philosophy of Education

Mary McLeod Bethune is one of the most important African American women in educational history because of her philosophy of education. Bethune believed that education, and especially higher education, was the key to advancement and the fulfillment of American democracy for black Americans. Her whole life she was committed to the improvement of education and the socioeconomic status of African American women. "I cannot rest while there is a single Negro boy or girl lacking a chance to prove his worth."[21]

Bethune founded a school that would train black women as community leaders, empower them, and instill an intense commitment to racial advancement and social service in them. In order to obtain this goal, she felt women needed a "distinctive education" different from that of men so they could take their place in transforming society. She provided her girls with a classical education in science, mathematics, literature, and foreign languages that would enable them to become intelligent, self-confident women leaders. She combined this with vocational training that would help them become professional teachers, nurses, librarians, and social workers who could, with their economic independence and service, uplift their race.[22]

Mary was a great team player, a persuasive consensus builder, and an energetic person who could build bridges between the races. Her ability can be seen in the ways that she used both Booker T. Washington's and W. E. B. DuBois' ideas in her program of education for black women. Like Booker T., she emphasized the importance of academic, vocational, and religious education for women in order for them to have economic independence. She also emphasized working within the system in order to change it. She became the representative voice of African American women in the 1900s. In many ways, she went much farther than Booker T. had gone as a representative voice. She imitated W. E. B. DuBois' advocacy of liberal arts and professional higher education for all capable blacks. She promoted a more activist civil rights stance and sought political change to advance the cause of African American women. Bethune believed her duty to her race was to prepare young black women to use their "heads, hearts, and hands" to shape opportunities for African American men and women. She taught the young black women in her charge to become a force that would take on administrative, managerial, and professional positions and help their race progress.[23]

In her words, "There is no such thing as Negro education—only education. I want my people to prepare themselves bravely for life, not because they are Negroes, but because they are human beings."[24]

Notes

1. Lerone Benner Jr., "Chronicles of Black Courage: Mary McLeod Bethune started a college with "$1.50 and faith," *Ebony* 57 (11) (2002), p. 97; Bernice Anderson Poole, *Mary McLeod Bethune: Educator, Black American Series* (Los Angeles: Melrose Square Publishing Company, 1994), p. 78.

2. Charles S. Johnson, "Interview with Bethune—1940," in *Mary McLeod Bethune: Building a Better World,* edited by A. T. McCluskey and E. Smith (Bloomington: Indiana University Press, 1999); Joyce Hanson,

Mary McLeod Bethune: *Black Women's Political Activism* (Columbia, MO: University of Missouri Press. 2003), pp. 37–38, 43.

3. Poole, p. 124.
4. Audrey Thomas McCluskey, "Introduction" in *Mary McLeod Bethune: Building a Better World; Essays and Selected Documents* (Bloomington: Indiana University Press, 1999), p. 13.
5. Paula Giddings, *When and Where I Enter: The Impact of Black Women on Race and Sex in America* (New York: Perennial: Harper Collins Publisher, 1996), p. 199.
6. Hanson, p. 45.
7. Mary McLeod Bethune, *Sixth Annual Catalogue of the Daytona Educational and Industrial Training School for Negro Girls* (Tallahassee: Florida State Archives, 1910–11); Giddings, p. 101; Hanson, p. 56.
8. M. F. de Tal, "Mary McLeod Bethune on Education," in *The Educational Theory of Mary McLeod Bethune*, http://www.newfoundations.com/GALLERY/Bethune.html, accessed 6/10/04: New Foundations.
9. Joyce Hanson, "Mary McLeod Bethune: Race Woman," *The New Crisis,* 110 (2) (2003), p. 35; Elaine Smith, Introduction, in *Mary McLeod Bethune Papers: The Bethune-Cookman College Collections 1922–1955*, edited by John H. Bracey and A. Meier (Bethesda, MD: University Publications of America, 1995), p. viii.
10. A. T. McCluskey, "Mary McLeod Bethune and the Education of Black Girls," *Roles* 21 (1/2) (1989).
11. Benner Jr., p. 100.
12. Giddings, p. 200.
13. McCluskey, p. 6.
14. Giddings, p. 202.
15. Poole, p. 15.
16. Giddings, p. 215.
17. Poole, p. 9; Hanson, *Mary McLeod Bethune: Black Women's Political Activism*, p. 5.
18. Giddings, p. 230.
19. Ibid., pp. 224, 244–245.
20. McCluskey, p. 10; Hanson, *Mary McLeod Bethune: Black Women's Political Activism*, p. 90.
21. M. W. Davis, ed., *Contributions of Black Women to America, Vol. II*, (Columbia, SC: Kenday Press, Inc., 1982).
22. Hanson, *Mary McLeod Bethune: Black Women's Political Activism*, p. 64.
23. Ibid., p. 75.
24. Poole, p. 198.

Questions to Guide Your Reading

1. What does Bethune see as the contribution that women can make to their race, if they are given the correct educational training? Do you think that this is still true today?

2. What are the unique responsibilities of the Negro women according to Bethune? Are these responsibilities important today or are other responsibilities more important?

3. What does Bethune see as important in a Negro girl's education? She says that this will help to remove the walls of interracial prejudice. Have the walls of interracial prejudice been removed or are barriers still up?

4. Taking words and phrases from the article see if you can outline's Bethune's philosophy of education. That is, what is her view of the student, of the teacher, the classroom environment, and the purpose of the schools?

READING 11.2:
A PHILOSOPHY OF EDUCATION
FOR NEGRO GIRLS (1926)

For the past seventy years the Negro has experienced various degrees of freedom. That which was given him in the early years of emancipation was more genuine and perhaps more benign than that which, today, he must take. For today he must free himself by reason of his ability and by merit, and by whatever trust and confidence may be found in himself.

A great deal of this new freedom rests upon the type of education which the Negro women will receive. Early emancipation did not concern itself with giving advantages to Negro girls. The domestic realm was her field and no one sought to remove her. Even here, she was not given special training for her tasks. Only those with extraordinary talents were able to break the shackles of bondage. Phyllis Wheatley is to be remembered as an outstanding example of this ability—for through her talents she was able to free herself from household cares that devolved upon Negro women and make a contribution in literary art which is never to be forgotten. The years still re-echo her words.

> "Remember, Christians, Negroes, black as Cain
> May be refined, and join the Angelic train."

Very early in my life, I saw the vision of what our women might contribute to the growth and development of the race—if they were given a certain type of intellectual training. I longed to see Negro women hold in their hands diplomas which bespoke achievement; I longed to see them trained to be inspirational wives and mothers; I longed to see their accomplishments recognized side by side with any woman, anywhere. With this vision before me, my life has been spent.

Has the Negro girl proved herself worthy of the intellectual advantages which have been given her? What is your answer when I tell you that Negro women stand at the helm of outstanding enterprises; such are Nannie Burroughs, Charlotte Hawkins Brown; they are proprietors of business. We recall Madame Walker and Annie Malone; they are doing excellent work in the field of Medicine, Literary Art, Painting and Music. Of that large group let us mention Mary Church Terrell and Jessie Fauset; Hazel Harrison, Caterina Jarboro and Marian Anderson as beacon lights. One very outstanding woman is a banker. Others are leaders in Politics.

In the rank of average training we witness strivings of Negro women in the schoolrooms of counties and cities pouring out their own ambitions to see them achieved in the lives of the next generation. The educated Negro girl has lifted the standard of the Negro home so that the present generation is better born and therefore has the promise of a better future.

If there is to be any distinctive difference between the education of the Negro girl and the Negro boy, it should be that of consideration for the unique responsibility of this girl in the world today. The challenge to the Negro home is one which dares the Negro to develop initiative to solve his own problems, to work out his own problems, to work out his difficulties in a superior fashion, and to finally come into his right as an American Citizen, because he is tolerated. This is the moral responsibility of the education of the Negro girl. It must become a part of her thinking; her activities must lead her into such endeavors early in her educational life, this training must be inculcated into the school curricula so that the result may be a natural expression born into her children. Such is the natural endowment which her education must make it possible for her to bequeath to the future of the Negro race.

The education of the Negro girl must embrace a larger appreciation for good citizenship in the home. Our girls must be taught cleanliness, beauty, and thoughtfulness, and their application in making home life possible. For proper home life provides the proper atmosphere for life everywhere else. The ideals of home must not forever be talked about; they must be living factors built into the everyday educational experiences of our girls.

Source: Mary McLeod Bethune Papers, Amistad Research Center, Tulane University, New Orleans, LA. Used with permission.

Negro girls must receive also a peculiar appreciation for the expression of the creative self. They must be taught to realize their responsibility and find ways whereby the home and the schoolroom may encourage our youth to be creative; to develop to the fullest extent the inner urges that make them distinctive and that will lead them to be worthy contributors to the life of the little worlds in which they will live. This in itself will do more to remove the walls of inter-racial prejudice and build up inter-racial confidence and pride than many of our educational tools and devices. This is the Gibraltar that we need. Lest it be sunken in the sea of carelessness and improper emphasis, let us, quickly, set it upon the table and let us stress this standard of conduct and individual creative nurturing in the education of our girls. The spiritual reactions are sure to harmonize when we safeguard this phase of our education.

Negro women have always known struggle. This heritage is just as much to be desired as any other. Our girls should be taught to appreciate it and welcome it.

"Let mine be a hearty soul that wins
By mettle and fairness and pluck
A heart with the freedom of soaring winds
That never depends on luck!"

This characteristic should he sought in an ardent way. Every Negro girl should pray for that pioneering spirit. Let her Arithmetic, History, Economics and what not, be taught with the zeal of struggle; the determination to win by mettle and fairness and pluck. For such she needs the school life and enters the Life's school.

"God give us girls-the time demands
Strong girls, good girls, true girls with willing hands:
Girls whom the world's gold cannot buy,
Girls who possess opinions and a will;
Girls who honor and will not lie
Girls who can stand before the motley crowd
And down its treacherous flatteries without winking
Tall girls, sun-crowned Girls whose voices cry aloud
And give us a challenge to the whole world's thinking."

Discussion Questions

1. Consider how Bethune, who herself had a limited education, could contribute so much to reform and improve education in her day. What other factors do you think impacted her and allowed her to realize this success? Can you mention any contemporary educators who have a similar background and still have made significant contributions?

2. Bethune mentions the large annual investment of money in education made by the government. Simulate a speech by her. What do you think would be her opinion about the No Child Left Behind legislation, its lack of funding, and its potential to discriminate against low-achieving African American students?

3. Do you agree with Bethune that there should be a different kind of education for Negro girls and for Negro boys; or is this just another form of segregation and discrimination?

4. In a group, discuss how education has changed since the times of Mary McLeod Bethune. What are some of her accomplishments that still impact education today?

5. Compare and contrast the responsibilities of black women in Bethune's time with your own pre-existing perceptions of the era.

6. Compare and contrast the lives of black women as detailed in the text with black males of the time, and then with contemporary black men and women. What commonalities exist? What differences? What are the consequences and/or origins of these differences?

For Further Research on the Internet

The Bethune-Cookman College home site founded by Mary McLeod Bethune includes links to her biography as the founder of the college, and also describes the history and mission of the school. http://www.bethune.cookman.edu/

The Mary McLeod Bethune Foundation started to identify, collect, develop, interpret, and preserve the legacy of Mary McLeod Bethune, including her unique focus on the individual and collective history of African American women. **http://www.nps. gov/mamc/bethune/archives/main.htm**

A short biography of Mary McLeod Bethune as a notable woman in history with links to other pages on her. **http://www.lkwdpl.org/wihohio/beth-mar.htm**

On-line classroom with resources for teaching your class about Bethune. **http://www. floridamemory.com/OnlineClassroom/MaryBethune/**

Suggestions for Further Reading

Benner Jr., Lerone. "Chronicles of Black Courage: Mary McLeod Bethune started a college with $1.50 and faith." *Ebony* 57 (11) (2002): 96–100.

Bethune, Mary McLeod. Sixth Annual Catalogue of the Daytona Educational and Industrial Training School for Negro Girls. In *Mary McLeod Bethune Papers*. Tallahassee: Florida State Archives, 1910–11.

Davis, M. W., ed. *Contributions of Black Women to America, Vol. II*, Columbia, SC: Kenday Press, Inc., 1982.

de Tal, M. F. Mary McLeod Bethune on Education. In *The Educational Theory of Mary McLeod Bethune*, 2000. http://www.newfoundations.com/GALLERY/Bethune.html, accessed 6/10/04: New Foundations.

Giddings, Paula. *When and Where I Enter: The Impact of Black Women on Race and Sex in America*. New York: Perennial, Harper Collins Publisher, 1996.

Hanson, Joyce. *Mary McLeod Bethune: Black Women's Political Activism*. Columbia, MO: University of Missouri Press, 2003.

Hanson, Joyce A. "Mary McLeod Bethune: Race Woman." *The New Crisis* 110 (2)(2003):34–37.

Johnson, Charles S. "Interview with Bethune—1940." In *Mary McLeod Bethune: Building a Better World*, edited by A. T. McCluskey and E. Smith. Bloomington: Indiana University Press, 1999.

McCluskey, Audrey Thomas. Introduction. In *Mary McLeod Bethune: Building a Better World; Essays and Selected Documents*, edited by A. T. McCluskey and E. M. Smith. Bloomington: Indiana University Press, 1999.

McCluskey, Audrey Thomas. "Mary McLeod Bethune and the Education of Black Girls." *Roles* 21 (1989) (1/2).

Poole, Bernice Anderson. *Mary McLeod Bethune: Educator, Black American Series*. Los Angeles: Melrose Square Publishing Company, 1994.

Smith, Elaine. Introduction. In *Mary McLeod Bethune papers: The Bethune-Cookman College Collections, 1922–1955*, edited by John H. Bracey, Jr. and August Meier. Bethesda, MD: University Publications of America, 1995.

Section 11.3: George S. Counts (1889–1974)

The terrorist attacks of September 11, 2001, impacted the lives of all Americans. Things will never be the same. The bombing of Pearl Harbor on December 7, 1941, had a similar effect on a previous generation. For George Counts, the crash of the stock market in 1929 changed everything. What is the role of the school when major events such as these dramatically change the attitudes, values, and beliefs of the American people? This is a question we still debate today.

George Counts' Life and Times

George Sylvester Counts was born on December 9, 1889, on a farm near Baldwin, Kansas, the third of six children of James and Mertie Gamble Counts. Although neither of his parents graduated from high school, they taught their children a system of values and ethics, the value of all human beings, and the Methodist religion.[1] At the age of five, George was already doing chores on the farm.

His Education

George began his formal education in a one-room school. He completed four years of study in two years, and then attended the public school, walking one and a half miles from his home, in the town of Baldwin. In high school, Counts was active in student affairs and was a member of varsity sports teams.[2] George attended Baker College (now Baker University), specializing in the classics—Latin and Greek—with courses in history, philosophy, and natural sciences. He graduated at the head of his class, receiving a Bachelor of Arts degree in 1911. George met Louise Hazel Bailey while a junior in college and married her on September 24, 1913; they later had two girls.[3]

Teacher, Principal, and then College Professor

George began his teaching career after graduating from college by teaching science and mathematics at Sumner County High School in Wellington, Kansas for the monthly salary of $85. The following year, he received an offer to be the principal of the public high school in Peabody, Kansas were he taught and coached for $100 a month.

In 1913, George went to the University of Chicago for graduate study in sociology, studying under Charles Hubbard Judd, who was working on developing a science of education.[4] Counts took all of the courses available in sociology, anthropology, education, economics, political science, and law at the University of Chicago and graduated magna cum laude in 1916, receiving a doctor of philosophy degree with a specialization in education and the social sciences.[5]

After graduation, as Counts explains in his autobiography, he became a college professor "for the rest of my life." In 1920, he went to Yale to be in the newly established Department of Education, where he stayed for six years, traveling to the Philippines, China, and Japan conducting research.

In 1927, Counts went to the Teacher's College of Columbia University, and he worked with John Dewey and other famous educational researchers; he stayed until he retired in 1955. Then Counts was a visiting professor at various universities, staying at Southern Illinois University the longest, from 1961 to 1971.[6] (See the timeline of Counts' life in Figure 11.3.)

Counts felt that it was his experience in the East with non-western cultures that led to the invitation from Teacher's College to be the associate director of the International Institute there.

Studying the Soviet Union

Counts' early research assignment at Yale was in the emerging field of international education, studying Russian education and society using the historical-cultural analysis method that became his major contribution to the field of educational research. In the summer of 1927, he made his first trip to various cities in the Soviet Union; he returned in 1929, with his Model A Ford so he could drive around the country. In 1931, he wrote his first book on Russia, *The Soviet Challenge to America,* which received the American Library Association's Most Distinguished Book Award. He made his last trip in 1936, for once he became a critic of the Soviet Union he was no longer permitted to enter the country.[7] He also visited countries across Europe in the 20s and 30s, Japan in 1946, and Brazil, Venezuela, and Puerto Rico in the 50s and 60s; altogether visiting seventeen countries, and lecturing in eleven of them.[8]

Dare the Schools Build a New Social Order?

When Counts returned to the United States after his second trip to Russia, he returned to a country turned upside down due to the Great Depression. Counts began to criticize the ineffectiveness of American schools and the weakness of the nation's teaching profession that had failed to produce the leaders the country needed. In 1932, he addressed the Progressive Education Association Meeting in Baltimore, asking, "Dare Progressive Education be Progressive?" According to one of the participants, "this great speech left his audience stunned."[9] The speech was so provocative that the group suspended the remaining agenda in order to devote itself exclusively to discussing the challenge Counts made in his speech. Counts included this speech with two others in a short pamphlet entitled; *Dare the Schools Build a New Social Order?* (reading selection following) which was widely read and discussed.[10]

Counts was a member of the Commission on the American Historical Association on the Teaching of Social Studies in the Schools, working to develop civic education, becoming the editor of their journal *Social Frontier.*[11] Counts was a member of the Education Policies Committee of the National Education Association and the American Federation of Teachers, and served as its president, a position that gave him the opportunity to give speeches around the country. "Counts was now a national figure: he was leader of the teacher's union, an authority on Russia, a perceptive education thinker, and a social commentator."[12]

During World War II, Counts served as a member of the nationwide Committee on Education and National Defense. In his own words, "sensing from early manhood the great danger threatening American democracy due to the rise of our urbanized and industrialized society, I have ever sought to make organized education serve the purpose of democracy."[13]

In 1952, Counts published *Education and American Civilization* and two years later, he received a medal for distinguished service at Columbia College. He continued to travel, lecture, write, and teach until his death on November 10, 1974. He had lived in a

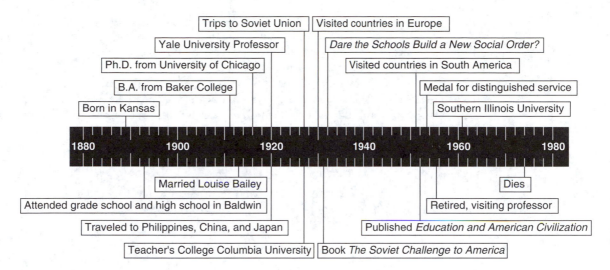

Figure 11.3   Counts' Life and Times

time of unprecedented changes in the country and the world, but throughout it all he reiterated his main theme that the teacher and the school can make a real difference in shaping the course of the future.

Counts' Contribution to Educational Thought and History

Counts will best be remembered in educational history for his provocative speech and pamphlet, *Dare the Schools Create a New Social Order?* Perhaps Counts' greatest contribution to educational thought is his assertion that schools essentially reflect the society of which they are a part. He admonished schools in a democratic society that they had an opportunity and responsibility to impact the society to which they belonged, stating that "education is always an expression of a particular society and culture at a particular time in history." The change of the United States from an agricultural nation to an industrial nation struck Counts as enormously important, for the industrial age heralded a new social order. Counts saw the introduction of the telephone, radio, television, and the automobile, all of which brought people together into a national community.[14] In addition, the change overnight from a prosperous country to one deep in a depression was an economic problem that should have been avoided and needed to be solved. Counts said that since education and other social institutions had developed in an age of agrarian individualism and had not changed with the times, they were unable to cope with economic interdependence.[15] Counts saw individualism as the principal cause of the Great Depression and called for the teaching of collectivism in the schools, so that a group ownership of society's productive resources would be fostered.

Counts' background in the disciplines of sociology, anthropology, and history gave him a special interdisciplinary lens through which to view education and allowed him to develop what Gutek coined as his "civilization philosophy of education" based on the premise that to understand the schools one must first understand the culture of which they are a part.[16] Counts formulated this philosophy as a response to the social and political events of his lifetime; in fact, he often said that education is the expression of a conception of life and civilization and a function of a particular society, in a particular time and place.[17] For this new interdisciplinary methodology, he has earned the title of "Father of Comparative Education."[18]

George Counts sought to inspire and encourage educators as he criticized current education. He served as a conscience for American educators; he was always analyzing American society and American education, concerned with the implications of his knowledge and of his research, and pointed out where reality fell short of the ideal.[19]

Counts continuously stressed that while educators in the twentieth century had problems to face which were unprecedented in human history, they also had unprecedented means at their disposal to create a great and noble educational system, and through this a great and noble society. He urged educators to become educational statesmen who would deliberately lead and bring about necessary social reconstruction instead of blindly following the ineffective patterns of the past.[20]

Comparing Counts' ideas in the 30s to today's educational challenges, one finds that many of the recommendations he made are still relevant to teaching today. He saw the importance of teacher preparation, foreign language instruction, global awareness, and multicultural/international education. In the 30s, Counts saw that separate was not equal, anticipating the Brown decision of 1954. Counts' challenge to education is being repeated today by concerned politicians, educators, and parents. Many commissions in the 80s and 90s repeated the main points of Counts' message: Foreign language instruction is essential; technology must be balanced by values; educators hold the key to positive change; there is a need for better training for effective educators; and we need citizens trained for our global society.

Counts' Philosophy of Education

Issues Counts raised are still pertinent to education in the twenty-first century. He developed a complete philosophy of education with implications for the teacher, the student, the curriculum, the methodology, and the role of the school.

According to Counts, the child enters the world with numerous potentialities that are or are not developed within the culture of the group. The school has an important role to play: It needs to educate for democracy and create a generation eager to serve its communities, nations, and world in times of peace. The schools have an obligation to educate for worldwide citizenship. He said that an understanding of other cultures was an imperative obligation of educators.[21]

Counts suggested that all youth needed to study science, the great cultural ingredient of the modern technological world. Not doing so was the reason so many Americans did not understand the world in which they lived. Students needed to study foreign languages and cultures, particularly European and Eastern, and their studies should commence in the middle years of elementary school to allow true mastery of the topics.

Counts wanted group activities to be introduced into the elementary school so that children would be given the opportunity to acquire the habits, dispositions, and attitudes necessary for adaptation to life in expanded society.

For Counts, the teacher held the key to the achievement of educational and social reform. He repeatedly called for selection, training, and economic remuneration of teachers like that found in the practice of medicine. He said that America should reward their teachers the way the Russians did and use the same percentage of the total national income on education as Russia did. Counts called for a broadening and deepening of the training of teachers, especially in the area of civilization studies that included knowledge of the great ethical, aesthetic, philosophical, and religious traditions of mankind.[22] According to Counts, teacher preparation programs should follow a liberal arts curriculum that develops knowledge of the democratic ideal and world cultures. The professional education courses and experiences should come later, perhaps in a fifth year. (Counts was a prophet of the Holmes report fifty years later.)

In his own words: "After 55 years of experiences as a teacher in secondary and higher schools, I am convinced that teaching is the greatest profession in terms of service to our people and to all mankind. Also I think it is the most interesting and challenging of all occupations and ways of life."[23]

Notes

1. George S. Counts, "Part I: A Humble Autobiography," *Leaders in Education: 70th Yearbook of the National Society for the Study of Education.* R. Havighurst, ed. (Chicago: National Society for the Study of Education, Vol. 70, Part 2, (1971), pp. 155–56.
2. Gerald Gutek, *George S. Counts and American Civilization* (Macon, GA: Mercer University Press, 1984), p. 6.
3. Counts, p. 168.
4. Lawrence J. Dennis, and Willma Eaton, eds., *George S. Counts: Educator for a New Age* (Carbondale, IL: Southern Illinois Press, 1980), p. 1.
5. Counts, p. 159; Gutek, p. 6.
6. Dennis and Eaton, p. 14. Raymond Callahan, "George S. Counts: Educational Statesman," *Leaders in Education: 70th Yearbook of the National Society for the Study of Education.* R. Havighurst, ed. Chicago: National Society for the Study of Education, Vol. 70, Part 2, (1971), p. 185; Carole Ann Ryan, "George S. Counts: Dare Educators Inspire World Vision?" *Educational Administration and Higher Education* (Carbondale, IL: Southern Illinois University, 1988), p. 171; Counts, p. 160; Dennis and Eaton, p. 2.
7. Ryan, p. 51; Gutek, p. 9.
8. Counts, p. 162.
9. Callahan, p. 178.
10. Wayne Urban and Jennings Wagoner, *American Education: A History* (Burr Ridge, IL: McGraw Hill, 2000), p. 263.
11. Lawrence A. Cremin, *American Education: The Metropolitan Experience, 1876–1980* (New York: Harper and Row, Inc., 1980), p. 188.
12. Dennis and Eaton, p. 12.
13. Counts, p. 164.
14. Dennis and Eaton, pp. 5–6.
15. Gutek, p. 25.
16. G. Gutek, *The Educational Theory of George S. Counts* (Columbus: Ohio State University Press, 1970), p. 202.
17. Ryan, p. 64.
18. Dennis and Eaton, p. 16.
19. Callahan, p. 178.
20. Ibid., p. 179; Gutek, (1984), p. 108.
21. Ryan, pp. 39–41.
22. Ibid., pp. 95–98.
23. Counts, pp. 173–74.

Questions to Guide Your Reading

1. What are the major tasks of education, according to Counts?
2. What is the goal of education, according to Counts?
3. What are some of the components of the civilization rising up in Counts' time?
4. List some of the contradictions he notes in the present condition of the nation.

READING 11.3:
DARE THE SCHOOLS BUILD A NEW SOCIAL ORDER?

Like all simple and unsophisticated peoples we Americans have a sublime faith, in education. Faced with any difficult problem of life we set our minds at rest sooner or later by the appeal to the schools. We are convinced that education is the one unfailing remedy for every ill to which man is subject, whether it be vice, crime, war, poverty, riches, injustice, racketeering, political corruption, race hatred, class conflict, or just plain original sin. We even speak glibly and often about the general reconstruction of society through the school. We cling to this faith in spite of the fact that the very period in which our troubles have multiplied so rapidly has witnessed an unprecedented expansion of organized education. This would seem to suggest that our schools, instead of directing the course of change, are themselves driven by the very forces that are transforming the rest of the social order.

The bare fact, however, that simple and unsophisticated peoples have unbounded faith in education does not mean that the faith is untenable. History shows that the intuitions of such folk may be nearer the truth than the weighty and carefully reasoned judgments of the learned and the wise. Under certain conditions education may be as beneficent and as powerful as we are wont to think. But if it is to be so, teachers must abandon much of their easy optimism, subject the concept of education to the most rigorous scrutiny, and be prepared to deal much more fundamentally, realistically, and positively with the American social situation than has been their habit in the past....

With regard to the past we always recognize the truth of this principle, but when we think of our own times we profess the belief that the ancient roles have been reversed and that now prophets of a new age receive their rewards among the living.

That the existing school is leading the way to a better social order is a thesis, which few informed persons would care to defend. Except as it is forced to fight for its own life during times of depression, its course is too serene and untroubled. Only in the rarest of instances does it wage war on behalf of principle or ideal. Almost everywhere it is in the grip of conservative forces and is serving the cause of perpetuating ideas and institutions suited to an age that is gone. But there is one movement above the educational horizon that would seem to show promise of genuine and creative leadership. I refer to the Progressive Education movement. Surely in this union of two of the great faiths of the American people, the faith in progress and the faith in education, we have reason to hope for light and guidance. Here is a movement, which would seem to be completely devoted to the promotion of social welfare through education...

If an educational movement, or any other movement, calls itself progressive, it must have orientation; it must possess direction. The word itself implies moving forward, and moving forward can have little meaning in the absence of clearly defined purposes.... Here, I think, we find the fundamental weakness, not only of Progressive Education, but also of American education generally. Like a baby shaking a rattle, we seem to be utterly content with action, provided it is sufficiently vigorous and noisy. And the last analysis, a very large part of American educational thought, inquiry, and experimentation is much ado about nothing....

There is the fallacy that the school should be impartial in its emphases, that no bias should be given instruction. We have already observed how the individual is inevitable molded by the culture into which he is born. In the case of the school a similar process operates and presumably is subject to a degree of conscious direction. My thesis is that complete impartiality is utterly impossible, that the school must shape attitudes, develop tastes, and even impose ideas. It is obvious that the whole of creation cannot be brought into the school. This means that some selection must be made of teachers, curricula, architecture, and methods of teaching. And in the making of the selection the dice must always be weighted in favor of this or that. Here is a fundamental truth that cannot be brushed aside as

Source: Counts, George, *Dare the Schools Build a New Social Order?* New York: The John Day Company, 1932.

irrelevant or unimportant; it constitutes the very essence of the matter under discussion. Nor can the reality be concealed beneath agreeable phrases...

If we may now assume that the child will be imposed upon in some fashion by the various elements in his environment, the real question is not whether imposition will take place, but rather from what source it will come. If we were to answer this question in terms of the past, there could, I think, be but one answer: on all genuinely crucial matters the school follows the wishes of the groups or classes that actually rule society; on minor matters that school is sometimes allowed a certain measure of freedom. But the future may be unlike the past. Or perhaps I should say that teachers, if they could increase sufficiently their stock of courage, intelligence, and vision, might become a social force of some magnitude.... That the teachers should deliberately reach for power and then make the most of their conquest is my firm conviction. To the extent that they are permitted to fashion the curriculum and the procedures of the school they will definitely and positively influence the social attitudes, ideals, and behavior of the coming generation...

We live in troublous times: we live in an age of profound change; we live in an age of revolution. Indeed it is highly doubtful whether man ever lived in a more eventful period than the present. On order to match our epoch we would probably have to go back to the fall of the ancient empires or even to that unrecorded age when men first abandoned the natural arts of hunting and fishing and trapping and began to experiment with agriculture and the settled life. Today we are witnessing the rise of a civilization quite without precedent in human history—a civilization founded on science, technology, and machinery, possessing the most extraordinary power, and rapidly making of the entire world a single great society. Because of forces already released, whether in the field of economics, politics, morals, religion, or art, the old molds are being broken. And the peoples of the earth are everywhere seething with strange ideas and passions. If life were peaceful and quiet and undisturbed by great issues, we might with some show of wisdom center our attention on the nature of the child. But with the world as it is, we cannot afford for a single instant to remove our eyes from the social scene or shift our attention from the peculiar needs of the age...

The age is pregnant with possibilities. There lies within our grasp the most humane, the most beautiful, the most majestic civilization ever fashioned by any people. This much at least we know today. We shall probably know more tomorrow.... The limits to achievement set by nature have been so extended that we are today bound merely by our ideals, by our power of self-discipline, by our ability to devise social arrangements suited to an industrial age. If we are to place and credence whatsoever in the word of our engineers, the full utilization of modern technology at its present level of development should enable us to produce at the very peak of prosperity, and with the working day, the working year, and the working life reduced by half. We hold within our hands the power to usher in an age of plenty, to make secure the lives of all, and to vanish poverty forever from the land. Our generation has the good or the ill fortune to live in an age when great decisions must be made.

Discussion Questions

1. What do you think: Is the role of the schools to create a new social order or is it the role of the schools to prepare students to live in the current society?
2. What is the role of society towards the schools? Is our society today living up to its responsibility? Why are teachers underpaid and schools underfunded?
3. What does Counts mean when he discusses the moral challenges facing teachers and schools?

For Further Research on the Internet

A brief biography of George Counts. http://www.uxl.eiu.edu/~cfrnb/gcounts.html

Inventory of the George S. Counts papers at Southern Illinois University. http://www.lib.siu.edu/spcol/inventory/SC134.html

A description of Counts' philosophy of social reconstructionsm. **http:// fcis.oise.utoronto.ca/~daniel_schugurensky/assignment1/sigevents30.html**

Suggestions for Further Reading

Callahan, Raymond. "George S. Counts: Educational Statesman." *Leaders in Education: 70th Yearbook of the National Society for the Study of Education.* R. Havighurst, ed. Chicago: National Society for the Study of Education. Vol. 70, Part 2 (1971): pp. 177–187.

Counts, George S. "Part I: A Humble Autobiography." *Leaders in Education: 70th Yearbook of the National Society for the Study of Education.* R. Havighurst, ed. Chicago: National Society for the Study of Education. Vol. 70, Part 2: (1971) 151–174.

Cremin, Lawrence A. *American Education: The Metropolitan Experience, 1876–1980.* New York; Harper and Row, Inc., 1980.

Dennis, Lawrence J. and Willma Eaton, eds. *George S. Counts: Educator for a New Age.* Carbondale, IL: Southern Illinois Press, 1980.

Gutek, Gerald. *The Educational Theory of George S. Counts.* Columbus: Ohio State University Press, 1970.

Gutek, Gerald. *George S. Counts and American Civilization.* Macon, GA: Mercer University Press, 1984.

Ryan, Carole Ann. "George S. Counts: Dare Educators Inspire World Vision?" *Educational Administration and Higher Education.* Carbondale, IL: Southern Illinois University, 1988.

Urban, Wayne and Jennings Wagoner. *American Education: A History.* Burr Ridge, IL: McGraw Hill, 2000.

Section 11.4: Ralph W. Tyler (1902–1994)

One of the important issues in education today is assessment: How do we know that the students are learning the material we are teaching them? We have Ralph Tyler to thank for setting up a clear system for evaluating learning, now used around the world.

Ralph Tyler's Life and Times

Ralph Winfred Tyler was born in Chicago on April 22, 1902, the sixth of eight children. Although never wealthy, his parents, William and Ella, provided their children a good education and a cultured and religious upbringing. The family moved to Table Rock, Nebraska, when William received a Church appointment as a Congregational minister.

Ralph's Education

Ralph attended kindergarten and elementary school in the demonstration school at the Peru Normal School, thus beginning his lifetime dedication to teacher education.[1] His father moved twice while Ralph was in grade school; Ralph skipped a grade upon entering each new school. He finished high school in just three years.

In 1921, Ralph graduated from Doane College in Nebraska magna cum laude with three majors at the age of 19.[2] After graduation, Ralph married Flora Olivia Volz, whom he had met through the school glee club, and they later had three children.

Science Teacher and Teacher of Teachers

On July 4, 1921, while visiting his family in Lincoln, Nebraska, an old family friend, the principal at the Pierre High School in South Dakota, invited Ralph to teach science at the school. Since teachers were in high demand in South Dakota, Ralph was easily able to get a temporary teaching license. Ralph's students were diverse, ranging from Indian children to the children of government officials, and he discovered that in order to teach children, you had to understand each of them individually. In Ralph's words, "it was such a demanding and challenging job that when I finished that year I wanted to stay on another year."[3] He went to the University of Nebraska that summer to take courses on science teaching, and stayed on teaching science. Ralph finished his master's degree in 1923 taking evening courses, working during the day at the University High School supervising student teachers. He wrote his thesis on the development of a standardized high school science test for the State of Nebraska. He was then employed by the university to help train science teachers.

In 1926, with advice and a loan from an old teacher and mentor, Ralph went to the University of Chicago to study science education and the psychology of learning with Charles Judd, George S. Counts, and W. W. Charters.[4] He worked with Judd on the concept of basing curriculum on educational psychology and studying how learning and the transfer of training takes place. He worked as a research assistant for W. W. Charters; the method he developed to analyze the large amount of data generated in this study later became his dissertation. Tyler earned his doctorate in educational psychology after just one year at the University of Chicago.

Evaluator

W. W. Charters asked Ralph to join him at Ohio State University working in the Bureau of Educational Research. In 1931, Ralph published his groundbreaking work on evaluation based on instructional objectives defined by the teacher. According to Schubert, "The essays Ralph wrote while at Ohio State University, when he was only thirty years old, revolutionized the study of grading, tests, and measurements, setting forth a more comprehensive, student-oriented conception of educational evaluation."[5] At Ohio State, through Tyler's work, the field of *educational evaluation* came into being.

Ralph's work attracted notice and he was asked to join the Eight-Year Study as the Director of Evaluation in its second year. The Eight-Year Study encouraged thirty high schools to develop new curricula for their students, with freedom to innovate in science, mathematics, social studies, and general education. Colleges agreed to accept students that graduated from the thirty "innovative" high schools, and then compare them to high school students who had studied the more traditional "college preparatory curriculum." The research showed that students who came from schools with the new curricula did as well or better than students who came from traditional programs; this spearheaded high school curricular innovation and led to more innovative college admissions policies.[6]

At the University of Chicago

In 1938, President Robert Hutchins invited Tyler to the University of Chicago, where two doctoral students, Benjamin Bloom and Lee Cronbach, joined him to complete the Eight-Year Study.[7] Tyler developed the course EDU 305: Basic Principles of Curriculum and Instruction, using the rationale he had developed during the Eight-Year Study. The course syllabus and notes became the textbook *The Basic Principles of Curriculum and Instruction* (1949), now a classic used internationally.

Tyler, a highly effective administrator, was appointed Dean of the Division of Social Studies at the University of Chicago in 1946. According to George Lackey, "During his 15 years at the University of Chicago, Tyler became the best known educator in the United States."[8] (See the timeline of Tyler's life in Figure 11.4.)

Center for Advanced Study in the Behavioral Sciences

In 1953, Tyler became the Director of the Center for Advanced Study in the Behavioral Sciences in California, which brought outstanding scholars in the behavioral studies to the center for a year to work on a research project of their choice with other outstanding scholars in their areas. Around this time, Tyler married his third wife, Mary Catherine McCord, who helped him at the center. Tyler gained international visibility and began to serve as an educational consultant for many countries.

Tyler served as advisor to six U.S. Presidents, research advisor to the U.S. Office of Education, Vice-Chairman of the 1965 White House Conference on Education, and was a member of many national education boards. He helped develop the Elementary and Secondary Education Act of 1965 and the National Assessment of Educational Progress, and proposed the foundation of the Regional Educational Laboratories.[9]

Tyler retired in 1967 but continued working in educational endeavors as a consultant and as a visiting professor and/or distinguished scholar at twenty different universities. (I was able to attend his lectures while Dr. Tyler taught at Loyola University in 1983, the last of his visiting professor positions.) Ralph Tyler died in March of 1994, one month short of his ninety-second birthday.

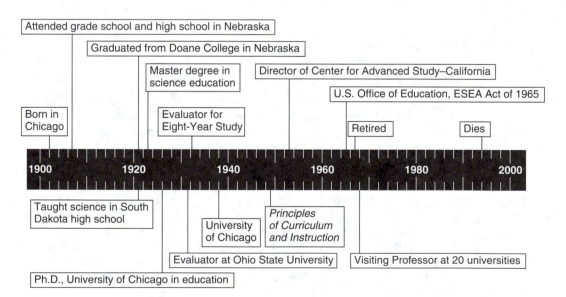

Figure 11.4   Tyler's Life and Times

Tyler's Contribution to Educational Thought

Ralph Tyler was fundamentally concerned with the practical utility of education and the quality of experience students had in education. He proposed a new paradigm that would relate curriculum, instruction, and evaluation. A prolific writer on curriculum and evaluation topics, spanning the whole range of elementary, secondary, and higher education, Tyler's record includes approximately 700 published works and his contributions to educational thought are innumerable.[10] However, for the purposes of this anthology, they can be summarized as including three main areas: curriculum evaluation, teacher training, and educational policymaking.

One of Tyler's most important contributions to education is the syllabus/book that he wrote for his course on curriculum, in which he introduced the idea of the instructional objective, a mainstay of course/lesson planning today. Although Tyler developed many effective tests over the years, doing pioneering work in the assessment of attitudes, ideals, and values, his major contribution was changing the emphasis from "testing" to "evaluation" in the education field. Tyler is considered by many to be the Father of the Evaluation Movement. He invented formative evaluation as a means whereby one could continually renew the educator's experience. Tyler introduced trans-curriculum objectives—the objectives with which the school or the community as a whole should be concerned. He viewed evaluation as a vehicle for encouraging teachers to think about how they might do their job differently, and to think about why they were teaching what they were teaching. In addition, he introduced the idea of authentic assessments and argued that testing was to be used not to measure students against one another, but to improve the curriculum.[11]

In an effort to enact new policies that would lead to systemic educational change, Tyler began many associations and organizations still in operation today. In 1929, he and his colleagues at Ohio State formed a society for curriculum study that grew into the Association for Supervision and Curriculum Development, a national organization. In 1965, Tyler helped write the Elementary and Secondary Education Act that was to result in the largest source of federal funding for schools in the history of American education. Today, in the twenty-first century, schools are still receiving funding through this act and are evaluating their programs according to the Tyler rationale.

Tyler's Philosophy of Education

Ralph Tyler believed that the purpose of life was learning and that the purpose of the school was to help children learn and develop the problem-solving skills that would help them to be citizens actively engaged in the work of a democratic society.[12]

In all of his work, Tyler saw the teacher as playing the key role in helping the student to learn. Education was, for Tyler, the process of changing the student's behavior, or ways in which the student thinks, feels, and acts.[13] During the Eight-Year Study, Tyler began summer in-service workshops for teachers, a mode of professional development commonly accepted today. He encouraged teachers to introduce new experiences to their students and later gained widespread acceptance of his progressive educational philosophy that schools should develop educational programs that would interest the students, meet their needs, and prepare them for colleges.

Tyler made significant contributions to the development and growth in use of cooperative learning methods and interdisciplinary study. Teachers and graduate students who worked with Tyler were encouraged by him in ways that helped them to excel. For example, Benjamin Bloom took Tyler's idea of the educational objective and did his seminal work defining them in the cognitive, affective, and psychomotor domains. Tyler was interested in the close relation between teaching and learning, and ways in which either could be helped or improved by the evaluation process. Today, there is consensus throughout the world on the importance of relating educational evaluation to the educational purposes of the classroom and the educational system.[14]

Throughout his life as a teacher, scholar, administrator, evaluator, creator of institutions, policymaker, speaker, traveler, advisor to Presidents, counselor, and friend, Tyler was always a student learning from others and learning from life. In his own words, as he followed the mission of his life to the very end: "Before I go to sleep I always ask myself three things: one, what did I learn; two, what did it mean; and three, how can I use it?"[15]

Notes

1. Ralph Tyler, William Schubert, and Ann Schubert, "A Dialogue with Ralph Tyler," *Journal of Thought* 21 (1) (1986), p. 92; George H. Lackey Jr. and Michael Rowls, *Wisdom in Education: The Views of Ralph Tyler* (Columbia: University of South Carolina, 1989), p. 4.
2. Miriam Rumjahn, *A Chronicle of the Professional Activities of Ralph W. Tyler: An Oral History* (Malibu, CA: Pepperdine University, 1984), p. 9; Claremont University Center archives—University of Chicago, Ralph Tyler papers.
3. Tyler, Schubert, and Schubert, p. 91.
4. Lackey Jr. and Rowls, p. 10.
5. William Schubert and Ann Lynn Schubert, "Ralph W. Tyler: An Interview and Antecedent Reflections;" *Journal of Thought* 21(1) (1986), p. 8; Lee Cronbach, "Tyler's Contribution to Measurement and Evaluation;" *Journal of Thought* 21 (1)(1986), p. 48.
6. Ralph Tyler, "Reflecting on the Eight-Year Study," *Journal of Thought* 21(1986), p. 19; Rumjahn, p. 28.
7. Lackey Jr., and Rowls, p. 16.
8. Ibid., p. 19.
9. Schubert and Schubert, p. 9.
10. Ibid., p. 10.
11. Benamin Bloom, "Ralph Tyler's Impact on Evaluation Theory and Practice;" *Journal of Thought* 21 (1986): pp. 36–37. Elliot Eisner, "Ralph Winfred Tyler," in *Fifty Modern Thinkers on Education: From Piaget to the Present,* edited by J. Palmer (London: Routledge, 2001), pp. 56–57; Cronbach, pp. 59–60.
12. Diana Buell Hiatt, "No limit to the possibilities-Ralph Tyler Interview, *Phi Delta Kappan* 75 (10), 785–790, p. 785.
13. Bloom, p. 38.
14. Ibid., pp. 39, 41.
15. Louis Rubin, "Ralph W. Tyler: A Remembrance," *Phi Delta Kappan* 75 (10) (1994), p. 784.

Questions to Guide Your Reading

1. What are the four fundamental questions for developing a curriculum?
2. What are some of the variables that impact the effectiveness of teaching?
3. How does Tyler define evaluation?
4. What are some of the methods Tyler suggests for evaluating student learning?

READING 11.4:
THE BASIC PRINCIPLES OF CURRICULUM AND INSTRUCTION

Introduction

This small book attempts to explain a rationale for viewing, analyzing and interpreting the curriculum and instructional program of an educational institution. It is not a textbook, for it does not provide comprehensive guidance and readings for a course. It is not a manual for curriculum construction, since it does not describe and outline in detail the steps to be taken by a given school or college that seeks to build a curriculum. This book outlines one way of viewing an instructional program as a functioning instrument of education. The student is encouraged to examine other rationales and to develop his own conception of the elements and relationships involved in an effective curriculum.

The rationale developed here begins with identifying four fundamental questions that must be answered in developing any curriculum and plan of instruction. These are:

1. What educational purposes should the school seek to attain?
2. What educational experiences can be provided that are likely to attain these purposes?
3. How can these educational experiences be effectively organized?
4. How can we determine whether these purposes are being attained?

This book suggests methods for studying these questions. No attempt is made to answer these questions since the answers will vary to some extent from one level of education to another and from one school to another. Instead of answering the questions, an explanation is given of procedures by which these questions can be answered. This constitutes a rationale by which to examine problems of curriculum and instruction....

Source: Ralph Tyler, 1949, *The Basic Principles of Curriculum and Instruction*, University of Chicago Press, Chicago, IL. Used with permission.

Chapter 4: How Can the Effectiveness of Learning Experiences be Evaluated?

Since we have considered the operations involved in choosing and formulating educational objectives and in selecting and organizing learning experiences, it may appear that we have completed our analysis of curriculum development. Although the steps previously discussed provide the plans for the day-by-day work of the school, they do not complete the planning cycle. Evaluation is also an important operation in curriculum development.

The Need for Evaluation

The steps thus far outlined have provided us with learning experiences that have been checked against various criteria derived from educational psychology and from practical experience. We have also utilized criteria regarding the organization of these learning experiences. In a sense, then, certain preliminary evaluations have already been made of the learning experiences. We may refer to these as intermediate or preliminary stages of evaluation. The learning experiences have been checked to see that they are related to the objectives set up and to see that they provide for other important psychological principles, so far as these principles are known. However, this is not an adequate appraisal of the learning experiences planned for curriculum and instruction. The generalizations used as criteria against which to check the learning experiences are general principles applying to generalized characteristics of the learning experiences and they are not highly precise statements of the exact conditions to be met in providing for the learning desired. Furthermore, any set of learning experiences involves a number of criteria, each of which can only be approximated so that we can only predict in general or with a certain degree of accuracy the likelihood that these experiences will actually produce the effects desired.

Finally, the actual teaching procedures involve a considerable number of variables including variations in individual students, the environmental conditions in which the learning goes on, the skill of the teacher in setting the conditions as they are planned, the personality characteristics of the teacher and the like. These many variables make it impossible to guarantee that the actual learning experiences provided are precisely those that are outlined in the learning units. Hence, it is important to make a more inclusive check as to whether these plans for learning experiences actually function to guide the teacher in producing the sort of outcomes desired. This is the purpose for evaluation and the reason why a process of evaluation is necessary after the plans themselves are developed.

It should be clear that evaluation, then, becomes a process for finding out how far the learning experiences, as developed and organized, are actually producing the desired results and the process of evaluation will involve identifying the strengths and weaknesses of the plans. This helps to check the validity of the basic hypotheses upon which the instructional program has been organized and developed, and it also checks the effectiveness of the particular instruments, that is, the teachers and other conditions that are being used to carry forward the instructional program. As a result of evaluation it is possible to note in what respects the curriculum is effective and in what respects it needs improvement.

Basic Notions Regarding Evaluation

The process of evaluation is essentially the process of determining to what extent the educational objectives are actually being realized by the program of curriculum and instruction. However, since educational objectives are essentially changes in human beings, that is, the objectives aimed at are to produce certain desirable changes in the behavior patterns of the student, then evaluation is the process for determining the degree to which these changes in behavior are actually taking place.

This conception of evaluation has two important aspects. In the first place, it implies that evaluation must appraise the behavior of students since it is change in these behaviors that is sought in education. In the second place, it implies that evaluation must involve more than a single appraisal at any one time

since, to see whether change has taken place, it is necessary to make an appraisal at an early point and other appraisals at later points to identify changes that may be occurring. On this basis, one is not able to evaluate an instructional program by testing students only at the end of the program. Without knowing where the students were at the beginning, it is not possible to tell how far changes have taken place. In some cases, it is possible that the students had made a good deal of progress on the objectives before they began the instructional program. In other cases, it may very well be that the students have very little achievement before they begin instruction and almost all of that noted at the end took place during the time the instruction went on. Hence, it is clear that an educational evaluation involves at least two appraisals—one taking place in the early part of the educational program and the other at some later point so that the change may be measured.

However, it is not enough to have only two appraisals in making an educational evaluation because some of the objectives aimed at may be acquired during an educational program and then be rapidly dissipated or forgotten. In order to have some estimate of the permanence of the learning, it is necessary to have still another point of evaluation that is made sometime after the instruction has been completed. Hence, schools and colleges are making follow-up studies of their graduates in order to get further evidence as to the permanence or impermanence of the learnings which may have been acquired during the time these young people were in school. This is a desirable part of the evaluation program. In fact, so far as frequency of evaluation is concerned, much can be said for at least an annual appraisal carried on year after year as the children move through the school so that a continuing record of progress can be obtained and evidence accumulated to indicate whether desirable objectives are being realized and to indicate places where these changes are not actually taking place.

Since evaluation involves getting evidence about behavior changes in the students, any valid evidence about behaviors that are desired as educational objectives provides an appropriate method of evaluation. This is important to recognize because many people think of evaluation as synonymous with the giving of paper and pencil tests. It is true that paper and pencil tests provide a practicable procedure for getting evidences about several kinds of student behavior. For example, if one wishes to find out what knowledge students have, it may be easily gotten from paper and pencil tests if the students are able to express their ideas in writing, or can read and check off various items in a multiple response test or other similar tests. As another illustration, paper and pencil tests are useful devices to get at the ability of students to analyze and deal effectively with various types of verbal problems, with vocabulary, with reading, and a number of other types of skills and abilities easily expressed in verbal form. However, there are a great many other kinds of desired behaviors that represent educational objectives that are not easily appraised by paper and pencil devices. For example, such an objective as personal–social adjustment is more easily and validly appraised through observations of children under conditions in which social relations are involved. Observations are also useful devices to get at habits and certain kinds of operational skills. Another method which is useful in evaluation is the interview which may throw light upon changes taking place in attitudes, in interests, in appreciations, and the like. Questionnaires sometimes serve to give evidence about interests, about attitudes, and about other types of behavior. The collection of actual products made by students is sometimes a useful way of getting evidence of behavior. For example, the collection of themes students have written many serve to give some evidence of the writing ability of students, or the paintings students have made in an art class may serve to give evidence of skill and possibly interest in this area. Objects made in the shop or in the clothing construction course are additional illustrations of the collection of samples of products as an evaluation device. Even records made for other purposes sometimes provide evidence of types of behavior or interest in terms of educational objectives. For example, books withdrawn from the library may provide some indication of reading interests. Menus checked in the cafeterias may provide some evidence of the eating habits of students. Health records may throw some light on health practices. These are all illustrations of the fact that there are many ways of getting evidence about behavior changes and that when we think of evaluation we are not talking about any single or even any two or three particular appraisal methods. Any way of getting valid evidence about the kinds of behavior represented by the educational objectives of the school or college is an appropriate evaluation procedure.

Discussion Questions

1. Tyler suggests an annual appraisal of student progress. However, many complain about the amount of testing done in our schools. How do you think these two forces can be reconciled?

2. Is it possible to evaluate *all* student learning? Are there some areas that are impossible to evaluate? Give examples to support your position.

3. Tyler suggests a pre-test and a post-test to show what students have learned through a particular course. However, other factors may also impact student learning. What are some of these other factors?

4. Can you validly evaluate a student's attitude, a student's values, or character development? How would you measure these more abstract concepts?

For Further Research on the Internet

An oral interview of Ralph Tyler conducted by Jeri Nowakowski, Ed. D. **http://www.wmich.edu/evalctr/pubs/ops/ops13.html**

Home page of the Center for the Advanced Study in the Behavioral Sciences in California. **http://casbs.stanford.edu/**

Suggestions for Further Reading

Bloom, Benjamin. "Ralph Tyler's Impact on Evaluation Theory and Practice." *Journal of Thought* 21 (l)(1986): 46.

Cronbach, Lee. "Tyler's Contribution to Measurement and Evaluation." *Journal of Thought* 21 (1)(1986): 47–52.

Eisner, Elliot. "Ralph Winfred Tyler." In *Fifty Modern Thinkers on Education: From Piaget to the Present,* edited by J. Palmer. London: Routledge, 2001.

Hiatt, Diana Buell. "No Limit to the Possibilities: Ralph Tyler Interview." *Phi Delta Kappan* 75 (10)(1994): 785–790.

Lackey, Jr. George H. and Michael D. Rowls. *Wisdom in Education: The Views of Ralph Tyler.* Columbia: University of South Carolina, 1989.

Rubin, Louis J. "Ralph W. Tyler: A Remembrance." *Phi Delta Kappan* 75 (10)(1994): 784–787.

Rumjahn, Miriam Cassandra. "A Chronicle of the Professional Activities of Ralph W. Tyler: An Oral History." Doctoral dissertation, Graduate School of Education and Psychology, Pepperdine University, 1984.

Schubert, William, and Ann Lynn Schubert. "Ralph W. Tyler: An Interview and Antecedent Reflections." *Journal of Thought* 21 (1)(1986): 7–14.

Tyler, Ralph. "Reflecting on the Eight-Year Study." *Journal of Thought* 21 (1)(1986): 15–23.

Tyler, Ralph, William Schubert, and Lynn Lopez Schubert. "A Dialogue with Ralph Tyler." *Journal of Thought* 21 (1)(1986): 91–118.

CHAPTER ACTIVITIES

Linking the Past to the Present

1. Role play Ralph Tyler giving a speech to Congress regarding the No Child Left Behind Act. What do you think he would say regarding the way this Act uses testing? What modifications to the Act do you think he would propose?

2. Give your own "Dare the Schools Create a New Social Order?" speech for the twenty-first century. What do you think the role of the school is in America today? To preserve democratic culture/society? To change and reform culture/society? Or to prepare students for a new culture/society?

Developing Your Philosophy of Education

In your philosophy of education include the methods you will use to teach the students and to evaluate their learning. Will you use cooperative learning, interdisciplinary/thematic instruction, and/or project/activity based learning? How will you assess their learning? Will you use authentic assessments and performance assessments in addition to traditional tests?

Connecting Theory to Practice

1. In your clinical school, ask to see standardized test scores for the students. Ask your supervising teacher if these scores are accurate reflections of the students' ability. What other methods does your teacher use to assess student learning and to evaluate the effectiveness of his/her teaching?

2. Go to the National Center for Educational Statistics website at http://nces.ed.gov/ and search for degree conferred by sex and race. How many African American women received degree in the most recent year? What level of degree? Do you think May McLeod Bethune would be pleased with these statistics? What could you suggest to improve these numbers?

Educators' Philosophies and Contributions to Education

TABLE 11.1 Philosophy and Contributions of Twentieth-Century American Educators

Educator	Role of Teacher & Learner	View of Curriculum & Methodology	Purpose or Goal of Education	Major Contribution
Dewey	Teacher creates a learning environment in which students can have meaningful interactions learning with peers	Making and doing history and science using the scientific problem-solving method using interdisciplinary studies	To make intelligent citizens, education must be the democratic process of living itself	Problem solving, activity-based education in a community of learners; the Five-Step Process of Problem Solving
Bethune	Black college teachers should help prepare other black women to use their head, heart, and hands to shape the future for their race	Classical studies of literature, foreign language, mathematics and science, black studies, and professional vocational training	Education is the key to advancement and fulfillment of American democracy, especially for blacks	Founded a college for black women with a distinctive education to prepare leaders
Counts	Teachers, well trained in the liberal arts, need to prepare students to be leaders and problem solvers for an unknown future	Science, foreign languages, and civilization studies taught through group activities	Have organized education serve the purpose of democracy; schools as a reflection of their society and culture	*Dare the Schools Build a New Social Order?;* started reconstructionism; Father of Comparative Education
Tyler	Teachers need to be trained to evaluate their teaching so that students learn better	Instructional objectives guide curriculum implementation; cooperative learning methods and interdisciplinary study; formative and summative authentic assessments	Purpose of school is to help children learn and develop problem-solving skills that would help them be citizens engaged in democratic society	Father of Educational Evaluation; developed instructional objectives

CHAPTER 12

Education for a Global World

Now, in the twenty-first century, we can only continue tracking the history of educational development if we once again look out from the United States to Europe and to the world. Since World War II ended in 1945, the United States has been an important player in global issues. The goal of education in America is no longer just to help one become an American citizen as it was in the time of Jefferson, Mann, and Dewey; the purpose is now to help one become a citizen of the world. Global education emphasizes education that helps develop citizens of the world society.[1]

International Historical Events

The past sixty years have seen the Cold War come and go; the threat of nuclear annihilation; civil wars and violence in Korea, Vietnam, Lebanon, Afghanistan, Nicaragua, Iraq, Ethiopia, Bosnia, in the Gulf, and in the Middle East; the 1960s protests of students, women, and African-Americans; as well as the cultural revolution of the 1970s.

With today's media and technology, there can be no cultural isolation as in the past. The massacre of students in Tiananmen Square, the shooting in Columbine High School, and the terrorist destruction of the World Trade Center were all carried immediately to an international audience.

The past twenty-five years have seen events that truly have changed history as whole countries were transformed. In 1989, the Berlin Wall fell and overnight East and West Germany became one. In 1990, Poland became free of the Communist government. In 1991, the Soviet Union dissolved and fifteen free republics took its place. Overnight whole curricula became obsolete. World views were completely changed; values were reversed.

Global environmental issues have become an important issue for the world as seen in the explosion of the Soviet nuclear reactor at Chernobyl in the Ukraine that had devastating consequences to human and environmental health. An important, and seemingly obvious principle of global international education is that events in other places in the world can have a dramatic effect on life in the United States.[2] (See Map 12.1 of the Global World of Developing Nations.)

The Need for International Education

Many of the educators that we have studied have endorsed international education, either as a philosophy or as an actual methodology. Erasmus believed that the liberally educated person would study the liberal arts of philosophy, theology, and literature using the classics of Greece and Rome and not just the Dutch or French works. Comenius' philosophy of pansophism sought organic unity or integrity in all knowledge as he proposed that there be a "universal" language that all would learn. He himself traveled through many countries trying to promote his educational ideas and peaceful coexistence.

Other educators practiced international education by visiting foreign countries to learn from them. Horace Mann traveled to eight different European countries to bring back ideas for American schools. Gallaudet went to England and France to learn how to teach the deaf; Margarethe Schurz brought Froebel's kindergarten from Germany to the United States; George Counts visited the Soviet Union and then began the field of comparative education.

International education helps us to develop a global outlook or perspective that allows us to see the world in which we live as a social, political, and economic unity. It is based on the ethical principle that recognizes that although human beings have different cultural backgrounds, speak different languages, and have different skin pigmentation, they all share a common humanity.[3] Maria Montessori saw this common humanity in the child.

International Studies of the Young Child

Maria Montessori, an Italian medical doctor, established a school for the poor and impoverished children of Rome. Although these children were considered to be mentally handicapped and psychologically impaired, by providing them with a specially prepared environment rich in sensorial materials, and developing a special method of self-directed activities, she enabled them to learn on their own. Maria later developed her ideas into a complete philosophy of education for early childhood. Montessori traveled and taught her method in Italy, England, Switzerland, India, Pakistan, Belgium, Spain, and the United States. Her first international course for teachers had students from all over the world: Europe, Australia, Africa, India, North America, the Philippines, and Panama. Maria was nominated for the Nobel Peace Prize and gave an address entitled "Education for Peace." She knew how her knowledge about children, who were the same all over the world, could foster international understanding.

Curriculum for a Global World

A global education curriculum includes "developing a better understanding of the world as a series of interrelated systems, paying more attention to the development of world civilizations as they relate to the history of the United States and devoting greater attention to the diversity of cultural patterns both around the world and within the United States."[4]

Multiculturalism is the interdisciplinary study of other cultures—their history, politics, economy, society, culture, art, music, and language. Advocates of multiculturalism or cultural

Map 12.1 Global World of Developing Nations

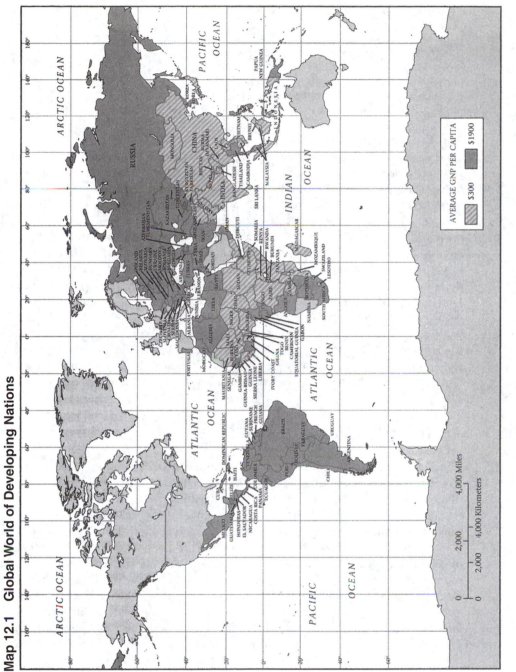

Source: From Anthony Esler, *The Human Venture, Combined Volume: From Prehistory to the Present*, 5th edition, 2004. Reprinted by permission of Pearson Education.

pluralism want to broaden the educational mainstream so that it reflects the diversity of the populations of the United States and their various cultures. We need to educate our young people so that they can take their place in the world. Their education has to have an international perspective so that they see we are globally interdependent and interconnected.[5]

Global Problem Solving

The work of Jean Piaget, the Swiss psychologist who made important contributions regarding the development of thought, cognition, and language in children, helps us today to improve learning in children by developing curriculum based on brain research. Piaget agreed with Montessori's insistence on allowing children to explore their own environment, as this process aided their cognitive development. Piaget suggested that human intelligence develops sequentially and the curriculum should be developed around these stages. Effective teaching is not transmitting information, but assisting children in their cognitive development, that is, to help them learn how to think. Piaget's principles of cognitive development inspired the method of developing higher order thinking skills in children by using higher order questioning, basing it on the child's cognitive level of development. Today brain research continues to help us coordinate curriculum to developmental levels. Critical thinking skills are necessary if young people are to be able to solve the kind of intricate problems we may globally encounter in the future. Piaget himself, as the President of the Swiss Commission of UNESCO, tried to solve some of these international problems of education by gathering researchers and educators from many different countries who were united by their interest in children and how they develop cognitively.

Education for Underdeveloped Countries

The demographics of the world are changing rapidly. Although it took 1800 years to reach a world population of one billion, it will take only a little over 200 years to reach a population of eight billion by 2012.[6] Three-quarters of these people live in countries that are underdeveloped; therefore almost seventy-five percent of the world's people may be undereducated, underemployed, and undernourished through lack of opportunity. We need to help these countries to develop educationally, economically, and socially. There is political unrest due to the lack of the necessities of life—jobs, food, and housing. There is an AIDS epidemic in some countries, especially in Africa, due to a lack of healthy conditions. Global trends include population expansion, economic interdependence, and technological connection; global problems include environmental pollution, inequitable distribution of resources, famine, drug abuse, and disease.[7] The plight of the world's poor and homeless is an urgent social and educational problem, a worldwide humanitarian issue of basic human rights and dignity. Global education has to deal with improving life for all people on this planet.

Education for Social Reconstruction

As an educational agency, the school can be used either to perpetuate the status quo of traditional knowledge and values or as an agency of social reconstruction. In other words, the curriculum can either reflect the status of what exists in society like a mirror or it can act as an agent of social change.[8]

Paulo Freire advocated an education that would act as an agent of social change and raise the consciousness of oppressed people in underdeveloped nations, a liberation pedagogy that involves learning for self-empowerment to secure basic political and social change. Freire's development education involves direct encounter in which people unite to discuss mutual problems. Freire's life illustrates the principles of international education articulated above. Freire was at Harvard during a time of political unrest in the United States over civil rights and the Vietnam War. This certainly influenced the positive reception of his revolutionary ideas. He lived through Chile's move toward socialism under Allende which culminated in the American-supported overthrow of the Chilean government in 1973.

"Liberation Theology" developed in the 1970s and 1980s, especially in Central and South America, as a movement to respond to political oppression. Freire used these ideas in his pedagogy of the oppressed. In exile in Geneva, Freire established the Institute for Cultural Action (IDAC) and worked with various third-world countries to establish literacy programs within the challenges of multi-lingualism.

Futuristic Trends

Global educators look for commonalities rather than differences among the earth's peoples and nations and are concerned with "emergent trends" that come from futuristic studies. For example, the technological advances of the computer have transformed life and education. In the past twenty years, some forty million Americans have learned how to use the personal computer and most learned this using informal avenues of education. Now we are able to connect with millions of people in other countries through the Internet. Web page counts are expected to double, growing by 7.3 million pages a day. By the year 2007, Chinese is expected to be the language most used on the World Wide Web.[9] Education for the future has to prepare students to learn how to solve problems for realities that have not yet been realized. Schools of the future will be very different from those of today. They will become resource centers where students will learn the inquiry, discovery, and problem-solving skills they will need for the international world of the future. Hopefully, these schools will teach people to use these skills in ethical and peaceful ways so that the future will see a better world for all people.

For Further Research on the Internet

Home page of the American Forum for Global Education, a site full of resources for learning and teaching about other cultures and countries. **http://www.globaled.org/**

The World Bank site on education with links to development projects in many different countries. **http://www1.worldbank.org/education/**

Notes

1. Gerald Gutek, *American Education in a Global Society: Internationalizing Teacher Education* (Prospect Heights, IL: Waveland Publishers, 1997), p. 29.
2. Ibid., p. 232.
3. Ibid., pp. 225–26.
4. Ibid., p. 30.
5. Ibid., p. 19.
6. John Pulliam and James Van Patten, *History of Education in America,* 8th ed. (Upper Saddle River, NJ: Merrill/Prentice Hall, 2003), p. 339.
7. Gutek, pp. 7, 29.
8. Ibid., p. 67.
9. Pulliam and Van Patten, pp. 339, 349.

Section 12.1: Maria Montessori (1870–1952)

Today, if you go into a preschool or kindergarten, you will see little sinks and tables at which the children work. Although we consider this common sense, it was not always so. It took Maria Montessori to point out that children love to work, taking care of their own life needs, if they are given an environment in which they can do this.

Maria Montessori's Life and Times

Maria Montessori was born on August 31, 1870 in Chiaravelli, Italy, the only child of a prosperous family. Her father, Alessandro, was a successful business manager and her mother, Renilde, encouraged her daughter in her every pursuit.[1]

Her Education

Her parents moved to Rome in 1875 and Maria enrolled in the first grade at the local public school when she was six. The crowded classroom was instructed through drill and exercises, i.e., recitation and dictation. Most girls did not go beyond elementary school instruction at that time, but Maria enjoyed math and went to study engineering at the Technical Institute, graduated in 1890, and entered the university to study medicine. Her father did not support her "outrageous" career decision, but her mother encouraged her daughter.[2] Originally, the university would not admit her, but she persisted and became the first female medical student in Italy. Forbidden to dissect with the male students, she had to enter the lab late at night to do her work. She won a scholarship each year and graduated as the first female Doctor of Medicine in Italy in 1896.[3]

Dr. Montessori

Dr. Montessori received a position as assistant doctor at the Psychiatric Clinic of the University of Rome to work with retarded children. Through observation and reading the works of Jean Itard and Edouard Sequin, she concluded that the children were more capable of learning than previously thought. She became convinced that retardation should be treated as a pedagogical, rather than a medical, problem and created the first Orthophrenic School in Rome to work with these children. The methods and materials she used with them were so successful that the children began to learn to read and write.[4] Maria lectured at the University of Rome and spoke at conferences. On her thirtieth birthday, her father, now proud of her career decision, gave her an album of over 200 newspaper articles that had been written about her in the past eight years.[5] A medical-pedagogical institute was set up in the spring of 1900 to train teachers in the care and education of deficient children. Montessori was appointed co-director of the school along with Dr. Giuseppe Montesano. Here Maria recommended diagnosis by a team consisting of a teacher, pediatrician, and psychiatrist, thus pioneering what is today called "multidisciplinary staffing."[6]

Casa del Bambini

Maria left the Orthophrenic School convinced that the educational principles she had developed while working with these children could be successfully employed with *all* children. She was able to try out her idea when the Association of Good Building in San Lorenzo asked her to work with children left unsupervised during the day by their working parents. She opened the Casa del Bambini on January 6, 1907 in one room with fifty children aged two to six. She brought in her teaching materials of three-dimensional shapes, objects of different colors, textures, and shapes, beads, and letters to be felt; she also had child-sized furniture and a washstand made.[7]

Maria observed how these sullen, withdrawn, and rebellious children became interested in working with these materials and soon became active, happy, and productive, learning to write and read with the sandpaper letters. A second Children's House was set up. A group of devoted followers began to gather around Montessori, finding in her a combination of mother and teacher.[8] Soon, visitors began to arrive from all over the world, due to press coverage, and five "houses" were set up, one outside Rome in Milan.

The Montessori Method

In the summer of 1909, Maria Montessori gave her first training course for about 100 teachers. She was encouraged to write down her method, so she wrote *The Montessori Method.* The heart of the book is the statement of her educational philosophy. Maria had discovered the world within the soul of the child, a discovery that made her famous. Her method is the consequence of this discovery. In the book, she defines the new science of pedagogy and explains her method in detail. What later became "the method" for doing things in every Montessori classroom around the world began as a way of doing things based on Maria's observations of the San Lorenzo children.[9] (See the timeline of Montessori's life in Figure 12.1.)

Anne George, an elementary teacher in Chicago, went to Italy in 1910 as the first American pupil enrolled in Montessori's training course. George opened the first Montessori school in America in New York. At the age of forty, Montessori decided to give up other work to devote herself to the schools and societies of the Montessori movement and to oversee the training of teachers in her method and the dissemination of her ideas. By the end of 1911, the Montessori Method had been officially adopted in the public schools

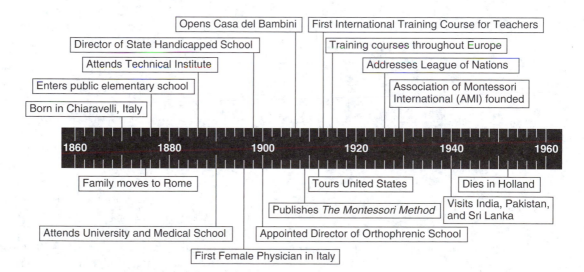

Figure 12.1   Montessori's Life and Times

of Italy and Switzerland, and model schools had been established in parts of England, China, India, Mexico, Argentina, and America.[10]

In January 1913, the first international course for teachers was given. Students came from all over the world, from Europe, Australia, Africa, India, North America, the Philippines, and Panama. Many found in the course not just an educational method, but also a philosophy of life. Maria lectured in a holistic and multidisciplinary way, speaking about medicine, psychology, education, and cultural anthropology.[11] In November, Maria went on a tour of the United States and was well received everywhere. She returned to the United States in 1915 under the auspices of the National Educational Association to give a training course in San Francisco. Unwilling to return to Italy due to the war, she settled in Barcelona with her son Mario and his new American wife, Helen Christie. Maria soon had four grandchildren. Mario assisted her in her work for the rest of her life.

Maria directed a course in Barcelona and one each year in locations across Europe and Latin America. In 1926, she gave an address to the League of Nations entitled "Education and Peace"; that same year, parents in Amsterdam established a secondary school based on her ideas. In 1929, the Association of Montessori International (AMI) was founded. It functioned as an organizer of the teacher training courses, a disseminator of information about the different schools, ideas and activities, and the controller of the rights for Montessori books and materials.[12] It was Maria's insistence that only she train teachers in her method that inhibited what could have been universal acceptance and implementation of this new way of educating young children.

At the age of 70, Maria flew to India to give a course to teachers. Due to the war, she was unable to return to Europe. During her stay in India and Pakistan, she lectured and wrote. She returned to Holland in 1946 and worked to reestablish the Montessori schools. The same activity and zeal she had shown throughout her career characterized the last days of her life. She was nominated for the Nobel Peace Prize and went to speak at the UNESCO conference in 1950. She died on May 6, 1952 in Noordwijk, Holland.

Montessori's Contribution to Educational Thought

Maria Montessori's most valuable contribution to education is the doctrine of the sensitive periods. (In 1917, she met the botanist Hugo de Vries, who suggested she use the term "sensitive periods" to describe her observations about children's growth and learning.)[13] According to Montessori, the essence of a sensitive period in human development is a burning intellectual love between the child and the environment. There are sensitive periods for language, order, sense refinement, and grammar.[14]

Stage of the Absorbent Mind

Montessori referred to the period from birth to age six as the "stage of the absorbent mind," a time when the child appears to almost absorb his environment. When he is given the freedom to explore, examine, experiment, and interact with the multitude of objects and situations in his environment, the child is stimulated and energized, and gains a sense of power in a period of literal self-creation. Montessori noted that a child would concentrate extremely hard, persistently repeat actions, and exhibit self-discipline as he worked diligently toward mastering a particular activity, thus developing character qualities. "Before six the child develops character and its qualities spontaneously. All know," Montessori said, "that the infant in arms cannot be influenced either by example or external pressure, so it must be nature herself who lays the foundation of character."[15] It was Montessori's conviction that, if children are to progress successfully through these sensitive periods of development, they must be free to act on objects or tasks in their environment when their interest arises. The power of a child's internal motivation is so intense that the need to reward or punish as a means of directing or motivating a child's educational efforts is not necessary.[16]

The second stage is from six years to twelve years and is a period of great stability of growth; the child begins to become conscious of right and wrong, not only in regard to his own actions, but also the actions of others. Problems of right and wrong are characteristic of this age; moral consciousness is being formed and this leads later to the social sense. It is during this period that the conscience begins to function in the child. The third stage, from twelve years to eighteen years, is a period of transformation from puberty to adolescence. In this period the love of country is born, the feeling of belonging to a national group and of concern for the honor of that group is fostered.[17] According to Montessori, the child is almost a different being at different stages of life and so there must be different educational methods for each stage.

Montessori's Philosophy of Education

Maria Montessori developed a complete philosophy of education based on her discovery of the child; it is actually a philosophy of early childhood education. The child and its development is something universal, common to all cultures, nations, societies, and religions, that is not culturally relative or culturally determined.[18]

Another crucial element of Montessori's philosophy of education is the role of the teacher. Maria presented an entirely new concept of the teacher's role. The directress was not to "teach"; she was to present, observe, and allow children to teach themselves as they worked with the materials that made up the properly prepared environment for their spontaneous activity.[19] Montessori believed that the essential instrument of effective teaching was observation; it was the tool that enabled teachers to determine the needs and interests of their students. The authority role of the instructor was replaced by that of the facilitator, whose major responsibility is to create a learning environment that, through careful observation of student movement and behavior, meets the needs and interests of the students and allows them to develop and achieve satisfaction.

Montessori defines the school as "a prepared environment in which the child, set free from undue adult intervention, can live its life according to the law of development."[20] Based on her theory of sensitive periods, Maria designed the curriculum that sought to develop the child's competencies in three areas—practical life skills, motor and sensory training, and more formal literary and computational skills—by preparing the learning environment of an effective classroom.[21] Preplanned didactic materials are provided for the children to manipulate in a self-directed manner, allowing them to attain mastery through individualized activity. The materials address, in a holistic nature, the child's physical, mental, and moral aspects. Certain materials promote competence in practical life skills that liberate the child by enabling him or her to independently handle ordinary tasks such as getting dressed and undressed, serving a meal, washing dishes, and displaying proper manners. Montessori presents a noble conception of work as something essential to the dignity of every human being; work gives joy to children and that is why they enjoy the Montessori school so much. The child achieves sensory development and muscular coordination through repetition of exercises. The child then proceeds at a rapid pace into the development of the formalized skills of reading, writing, and mathematics. In this method, Montessori explained, the "lesson" corresponds to an "experiment." The lessons are individual, brief, concise, simple and objective.[22]

The purpose of the school was to help the child self-develop his/her whole potential. All activity in her school was ordered to a definite end, helping the child to work well, and to engage in good productive things. Montessori considered herself a citizen of the world with a message for all humanity.

"When we see all these things ... which they have learned to enjoy so deeply, we are moved in spite of ourselves and feel that we have come in touch with the very souls of these little pupils."[23]

Notes

1. E. Mortimer Standing, *Maria Montessori, Her Life and Work* (New York: Plume, 1998), p. 21.
2. Rita Kramer, *Maria Montessori: A Biography* (New York: G.P. Putnam's Sons, 1976), p. 30.
3. Gerald Lee Gutek, "Introduction: A Biography of Montessori and an Analysis of the Montessori Method," in *The Montessori Method,* edited by G. L. Gutek. (Lanham, MD: Rowman & Littlefield Publishers, Inc., 2004), p. 5.
4. Standing, p. 28.
5. Kramer, p. 88.
6. Gutek, p. 7.
7. Maria Montessori, "The Montessori Method," in *The Montessori Method,* edited by G. L. Gutek (Lanham, MD: Rowman & Littlefield Publishers, 2004), p. 89.
8. Kramer, p. 133.
9. Maria Montessori, "Inaugural Address Delivered on the Occasion of the Opening of One of the 'Children's Houses,'" in *The Montessori Method,* edited by G. L. Gutek (Lanham, MD: Rowman & Littlefield Publishers, 2004), p. 101.
10. Kramer, p. 155ff.
11. Gutek, p. 13.
12. Kramer, p. 311.
13. Ibid., p. 252.
14. Maria Montessori, *The Secret of Childhood* (New York: Ballantine Books, Random House, 1974), p. 38.
15. Maria Montessori, *The Absorbent Mind* (New York: Holt, Reinhart and Winston, 1971), p. 196.
16. Ibid., p. 51.
17. Ibid., p. 194.
18. Gutek, p. 39.
19. Montessori, 2004, p. 73.
20. Ibid., p. 109.
21. Gutek, p. 17.
22. Montessori, 2004, p. 123ff, 162.
23. Ibid., p. 264.

Questions to Guide Your Reading

1. What did Maria learn from observing the little three-year-old girl in San Lorenzo, Rome?
2. What was Maria's "discovery"?
3. What is the basic problem or challenge of education according to Montessori?
4. What kinds of materials hold the attention of the child?

READING 12.1:
MY SYSTEM OF EDUCATION

My system is to be considered a system leading up, in a general way; to education. It can be followed not only in the education of little children from three to six years of age, but can be extended to children up to ten years of age. It is not simple theory, but has been experimented with and put into practice. Its results constitute a scientific proof of its value.

Although the first part of my experiment deals only with children between the ages of three and six years, nevertheless it must be considered as a directive system for the education of all children having attained the school age. In fact, my last experiments, not yet known to the public, have been made on children up to ten years of age, and the same directive system has proven satisfactory. The results were of still higher importance than in the first case with smaller children because it was richer in practical evidence both in the formation of character and in the attainment of knowledge.

The fact on which it was possible to establish my system is the psychological fact of the "attention" of the child, intensively chained to any exterior object or fact, which proves in the child a spontaneous, although complex activity of its entire little personality. It will be of some interest to relate here the episode that made me decide to plan out a special method for the education of children.

I was making the first experiments in San Lorenzo (Rome), trying to apply my principles and part of the material that I had previously used in the education of backward children.

A little girl, about three years of age, was deeply absorbed in the work of placing wooden blocks and cylinders in a frame for that purpose. The expression of her face was that of such intense attention, that it was almost a revelation to me. Never before had I seen a child look with such "fixedness" upon an object, and my conviction about the instability of attention which goes incessantly from one thing to another, a fact which is so characteristic in little children, made the phenomenon the more remarkable to me.

I watched the child without interrupting her, and counted how many times she would do her work over and over. It seemed that she was never going to stop. As I saw that it would take a very long time, I took the little armchair on which she was sitting and placed child and chair on the big table. Hastily she put the frame across the chair, gathered blocks and cylinders in her lap, and continued her work undisturbed. I invited the other children to sing, but the little girl went on with her work and continued even after the singing had ceased. I counted forty-four different exercises that she made, and when she finally stopped, and did so absolutely independently from an exterior cause that could disturb her, she looked around with an expression of great satisfaction, as if she were awakening from a deep and restful sleep.

The impression I received from the observation was that of a discovery. The same phenomenon became very common among those children, and it was noticed in every school in every country where my system was introduced; therefore it can be considered as a constant reaction that takes place in connection with certain exterior conditions that can be well established. Each time a similar "polarization" of the attention occurred, the child began to transmute itself completely; it became calmer, more expressive, more intelligent, and evidenced extraordinary interior qualities, which recalled the phenomena of the highest mentality. When the phenomenon of polarization of the attention had occurred, all that was confused and drifting in the conscience of the child seemed to assume a form, the marvelous characters of which were reproduced in each individual.

This reminded one of the life of a man that was scattered indiscriminately in a chaotic condition, until a special object attracts it and gives it a fixed form, and then only is man revealed unto himself and begins to live. This spiritual phenomenon, which

Source: Maria Montessori, "My System of Education" in the *Journal of Proceedings and Addresses of the Fifty-Third Annual Meeting and International Congress of Education, 4,* 1915.

may co-involve the whole conscience of the adult, is therefore but one of the ever-present aspects of the formation of the inner life." It is met with as a normal beginning of the inner life of children, and it follows the development so as to come within the reach of research as an experimental fact.

It was thus that the soul of the child gave its revelations and, guided by these revelations, there arose a method where spiritual liberty became demonstrated. The news of this fact rapidly spread throughout the world and it was received at first as a miracle. Then little by little, as the experiments were repeated among the most diverse races the simplicity and evidence of the principles of this spiritual treatment were recognized.

When you have solved the problem of controlling the attention of the child, you have solved the entire problem of its education. The importance of a scheme to concentrate the attention is self-evident. Professor William James, the renowned authority on psychology in America, points out to us how there exists in children that exterior variability of attention that makes it so difficult to give them the fast lessons. The reflective and passive character of the attention by which the child seems to belong less to itself than to any object that may attract its attention, is the first thing that each must conquer. The ability incessantly to recall a wandering and scattered attention, always ready to vanish, is the real root of judgment, character, and will; that system of education that succeeds in bringing this faculty to the highest degree should be the ideal and standard system.

To be able to choose objects that will interest and hold the attention of the child is to know the means of aiding it in its mental development. All things that naturally arise and hold the attention with considerable steadiness are those that represent a "necessity" for the child. Toward these things its attention is directed in a natural, almost instinctive way. All other things that attract its attention do so only lightly, transitorily, and for a very short period of time. Thus the newborn child has a series of uncoordinated movements, but the complex movement of sucking, which is in direct proportion to its need of food, is performed with regularity, coordination and steadiness. We must recognize that something like this is needed for its psychic development.

Consider the little girl only three years of age who performs the same exercise fifty times. A crowd is roaming about her, a piano is playing, a chorus is sung, and nothing can distract her from her deep concentration. In a similar way, the baby holds on to the breast of the mother without being interrupted by any exterior agent and lets go only after its need is satisfied.

How shall we choose the means of development by experiments? Since a constant and peculiar psychic reaction is an established fact, it is possible to determine some stimulating (reactive) agents or objects that can aid the spontaneous development. The character of this reaction itself must be the guide to the choice of these objects that are to constitute the implements or tools of this scientific work.

Each one of these instruments must be built with every detail to answer the purpose. As the lenses of the optician are made in accordance with the laws of refraction, the pedagogical instrument must be chosen to correspond exactly to the psychic manifestations of the child. Such an instrument could be compared to a systematized mental test. It is not, however, established as an external criterion of measurement with the purpose of estimating the instantaneous physical reaction.

Discussion Questions

1. How does Montessori's view of the child differ from other commonly held views?
2. How does the traditional conception of the classroom teacher differ from Montessori's directress?
3. Do you think that Montessori's "directive system" is too rigid and confining or is it too unstructured and lacking in control? Explain.
4. Do you feel that Montessori's claim of student self-discipline is realistic or overstated? Why?
5. Do you agree with Montessori that a child's character develops naturally as they proceed through each of the stages? How do you think she would explain the fact

that some children do not develop a good strong character whereas others (in the same neighborhood and family) do?

6. If you were to be appointed to a Montessori school, what objects would you bring to a productive learning environment? Do you think they would differ from the didactic materials Montessori developed?

For Further Research on the Internet

An interactive biography of Maria Montessori. **http://www.montessori.org/Resources/ Library/Educational/mariawho.htm**

The home page of the International Montessori Association. **http://www.montessori .edu**

The American Montessori Society home page. **http://www.amshq.org/**

Suggestions for Further Reading

Gutek, Gerald Lee. "Introduction: A Biography of Montessori and an Analysis of the Montessori Method." In *The Montessori Method*, edited by G. L. Gutek. Lanham, MD: Rowman & Littlefield Publishers, Inc., 2004.

Kramer, Rita. *Maria Montessori: A Biography*. New York: G. P. Putnam's Sons, 1976.

Montessori, Maria. *The Absorbent Mind*. New York: Holt, Reinhart and Winston, 1971.

Montessori, Maria. *The Secret of Childhood*. New York: Ballantine Books, Random House, 1974.

Montessori, Maria. "Inaugural Address Delivered on the Occasion of the Opening of One of the 'Children's Houses.'" In *The Montessori Method*, edited by G. L. Gutek. Lanham, MD: Rowman & Littlefield Publishers, Inc., 2004.

Montessori, Maria. "The Montessori Method." In *The Montessori Method*, edited by G. L. Gutek. Lanham, MD: Rowman & Littlefield Publishers, Inc., 2004.

Standing, E. Mortimer. *Maria Montessori, Her Life and Work*. New York: Plume, 1998.

Section 12.2: Jean Piaget (1896–1980)

Geometry is studied in the sophomore year of high school in most countries, certainly in the United States. You might ask why there is international agreement on this curricular item. We have Jean Piaget to thank for outlining the stages of cognitive development that define the kind of thinking students are able to do at different stages. Geometry involves the kind of abstract thought not developed until one is a teenager.

Jean Piaget's Life and Times

Jean Piaget was born on August 9, 1896, at Neuchatel in Switzerland, the only son of Arthur and Rebecca Piaget, who also had two younger daughters.[1]

In his autobiography, Piaget describes how his father taught him "the value of systematic work, even in small matters," and Piaget attributed his love of facts to his father's influence. His mother Rebecca was "very intelligent, energetic and kind" but her "rather neurotic temperament ... made family life troublesome" and Piaget's childhood unhappy. One of the "direct consequences of this situation was that I started to forego playing for serious work very early; this I obviously did as much to imitate my father as to take refuge in a private ... world."[2]

Jean's Education and Research

Rather precocious, as early as seven years old, Jean was studying mechanics, birds, fossils, and seashells. In 1907, Jean, a serious, inventive, and exceptionally intelligent ten-year-old, entered the Latin School. He sent a one-page article about a partly albino sparrow he saw in the park to a natural history magazine, where its publication launched young Piaget's career. Paul Godet, director of the Museum of Natural History, invited Jean to be his "volunteer assistant" working with the fossil and shell collection. Jean became an expert amateur malacologist and, over the next few years, published over twenty papers on the subject.[3]

In 1912, Jean entered the gymnasium, where he studied the college preparatory curriculum while continuing his investigations of scientific issues. He received intellectual encouragement and stimulus that assisted him in his development as a young scientist. During his adolescence, Jean also explored religion and philosophy under the guidance of his godfather, Samuel Cornut, who introduced him to the philosophy of Bergson. "The identification of God with life itself was an idea that stirred me almost to ecstasy because it now enabled me to see in biology the explanation of all things and of the mind itself."[4] As he matured, Piaget blended philosophy, religion, morality, and science in his work.

Piaget entered the University of Neuchatel in 1915, received his *licence,* or baccalaureate degree in natural sciences in July of 1918, and finished his doctoral dissertation a few months later.[5]

Dr. Piaget's Study of Children

Dr. Piaget then worked a short time in two different psychological laboratories in Zurich and spent two years at the Sorbonne in Paris studying and working in Binet's laboratory with Parisian schoolchildren. Here he developed expertise in the "clinical interview method"—questioning children, letting their responses direct the structure of the discourse; aiming at discovering the reasoning process underlying their answers. In Piaget's own words, "At last I had found my field of research ... This marked the end of my 'theoretical' period and the start of an inductive and experimental era in the psychological domain."[6]

In 1921, after publishing three papers in his new area of child psychology, Piaget was offered a position at the JJ Rousseau Institute in Geneva; he worked here for the rest of his life.[7] He married Valentine Chatenay, one of his students, and they had three children. Piaget and his wife spent considerable time observing and conducting various experiments with them.[8] (See the timeline of Piaget's life in Figure 12.2.)

Author of Books on Child Psychology

Some of Piaget's most important discoveries came from the study of his own children, and the results of this research became his first five books on child psychology, *The Language and Thought of the Child* (1924), *The Child's Conception of the World* (1926), *The Child's Conception of Causality* (1927), *Judgment and Reasoning in the Child* (1928) and *The Moral Judgment of the Child* (1932), which earned him international acclaim in the field. Piaget

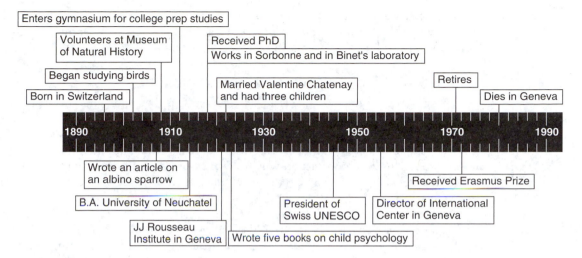

Figure 12.2   Piaget's Life and Times

outlines in these books, now a part of every teacher's studies in educational psychology, his discoveries of the following: Infants do not have the notion of permanence when an object disappears from view, children up to twelve years old do not believe in the constancy of material quantity, and abstract reasoning can only be done once a child is in adolescence.

Piaget maintained a heavy schedule most of his life, teaching as a professor at the Universities while conducting research at the JJ Rousseau Institute, traveling, and lecturing around the world. Piaget's collaborators, Barbara Inhelder and A. Szeminska, assisted him in the large scale of research they were able to produce at the Institute, which earned him many honors, including several honorary degrees as well as membership in the New York Academy of Sciences and the Erasmus Prize in 1972.

International Educator

In 1945, after World War II ended, Piaget was asked to be the President of the Swiss Commission of UNESCO, and was later appointed Director of the International Bureau of Education. In 1955, Piaget founded and became Director of the International Center for Genetic Epistemology at the University of Geneva, a center devoted to the scientific study of all aspects of knowledge and intellectual growth. Piaget continued to write books after his retirement in 1971. Including posthumous publications, Piaget produced some eighty books and 500 papers. He died on September 16, 1980 in Geneva, to the very end the grandfatherly humble sage, riding a bicycle with a beret on the head and a pipe in the mouth, immersed in the creative disorder of his study.[9]

Piaget's Importance for Educational Thought

Piaget is recognized as one of the most influential figures in modern psychology and education, and as the most important researcher in the field of child development, taking on, as the project of his life, to elaborate a "biological" explanation of knowledge.[10] Piaget moved epistemology, the study of knowledge, from the realm of philosophy to that of the science of psychology by studying, scientifically, the cognitive development of children. Piaget's theories have dramatically impacted teaching today. The contributions from his research have become essential content for every teacher's study of educational psychology and the teaching/learning process regarding the process of learning, cognitive development, and moral development.

Assimilation, Accommodation, Equilibration

Piaget stressed that learning is an active process, as the child is not just a passive recipient of knowledge. In order for a child to learn, he or she must *assimilate* or take information in from the world through his or her senses and then make a comparison of this new information to that already stored in the brain in the numerous schema of mental representation. This new information will either be more in-depth knowledge of what is already known, or it will be so new that new schema must be created to *accommodate* the new facts. Cognitive growth occurs as this new information is adapted to schema or new schema are created and *equilibration* is once again obtained. The current educational concept of *constructivism* is based on these ideas; that knowledge of the relationships among ideas, objects, and events is constructed by the active processes of assimilation, accommodation, and equilibration.[11] Piaget is also an advocate of discovery learning, seeing it as the fundamental basis of learning, for to understand is to discover, to produce, and create new knowledge. Piaget categorized knowledge into three types: the physical, which is knowledge of objects in external reality; the social, which is written and spoken languages; and the logico-mathematics, which is the relationships created by each individual.

Stages of Cognitive Development

Piaget found that children at different ages are able to accommodate new knowledge in different ways. He referred to this as a stage theory of cognitive development, with four major stages that all individuals pass through from birth to adolescence. Each child builds on the previous stage of cognitive development, increasing the child's ability to solve more complex problems. As you read the following text from Piaget, see if you can identify the four stages, their age level, and how Piaget explains the intellectual actions a child can perform at each level.

Theory of Moral Development

Piaget thought that moral development could also be explained using the same structural perspective, relating it to the levels of moral thinking possible at different ages. Very young children are amoral until around the age of three, when they are able to understand that rules must be followed, but are unable to distinguish subjective from objective aspects. They have an absolute morality, or a moral realism that sees rules as absolutes. Older children (starting around age eight) are able to reason more abstractly and to consider the situation and intention in judging morality.[12]

Piaget's Philosophy of Education

Although Piaget was an educational psychologist, his theories, if taken as a whole, create a very specific philosophy of education. Piaget saw the child as a social being who does not develop in cognitive isolation from others; however, Piaget was more concerned about the individual child—he was not interested in the child in a social context or as influenced culturally.

Teachers must, first of all, understand their children's way of understanding and that understanding must guide their teaching practice and evaluation. They need to individualize instruction in order to accommodate each child's readiness at different stages of development. Effective teachers will create learning centers in which children can experiment and manipulate objects and thus discover the structures in their environment.

Whether teaching in early childhood, elementary school, middle school, or high school classrooms, content that involves higher level thinking tasks needs to be introduced to students when they are cognitively ready for the level of abstraction involved in the study. That is why geometry is not studied formally until a child is around fourteen years of age and able to do formal operation. Middle school children who have difficulty with some classes are probably not yet intellectually at the appropriate level.

Piaget saw the purpose of schooling as helping children to learn to think, to discover, and create. Cooperation is a wonderful way for the achievement of mature thinking and mutual problem solving. Piaget saw no use for excessive nationalism and class warfare in a world that had become increasingly international and interdependent. Education would have both a psychological and political role as it helped people come out of their egocentricism with narrow ethnocentric positions so that they could coordinate their views with views held by others. "Cooperation among the children themselves ... is most apt to encourage real exchange of thought and discussion."[13]

Notes

1. Fernando Vidal, *Piaget before Piaget* (Cambridge: Harvard University Press, 1994), p. 13.
2. Jean Piaget, *An Autobiography* (New York: E.P. Dutton & Co., Inc., 1973), pp. 106–107.
3. Brian Rotman, *Jean Piaget: Psychologist of the Real* (Ithaca, NY: Cornell University Publishers, 1977), p. 9.
4. Piaget, p. 111.
5. Vidal, pp. 16–17.
6. Piaget, p. 111.
7. Vidal, p. 225.
8. Piaget, p. 127.
9. Leslie Smith, *Jean Piaget* (London: Routledge, 2001), p. 38; Vidal, p. 1; Leslie Smith, *General Introduction* (London: Routledge, 1992), p. xv.
10. Vidal, p. 1.
11. R. Oxford, "Constructivism: Shape-Shifting, Substance, and Teacher Education Applications," *Peabody Journal of Education* 72 (1997), p. 39.
12. Vidal, p. 1.
13. Jean Piaget, *Science of Education and the Psychology of the Child* (New York: Penguin Books, 1977), p. 180.

Questions to Guide Your Reading

1. Outline the four stages of cognitive development Piaget identifies. Include the age level of each stage and a description of the kind of cognitive ability at that level.

   a. Try some of the Piaget experiments with a young child with a watch as he suggests. Put the watch under something and see what the young child does.

   b. Question a middle school child and see if you can identify his or her cognitive level by their answers to your questions.

   c. Look through a set of math books: elementary, middle, and high school level. Can you identify word problems that are at the pre-operational, concrete operational, and formal operational level?

READING 12.2:
THE INTELLECTUAL DEVELOPMENT OF THE CHILD

Child development is a temporal operation par excellence. I will try to offer some data needed to understand this situation. More specifically, I will focus on two points. The first is the necessary role of time in the life cycle.... The second point is formulated in the questions: Does the life cycle express a basic biological rhythm, an ineluctable law? Does civilization modify this rhythm and to what extent? In other words, is it possible to increase or decrease this temporal development?

To discuss these two points I have in mind only the truly psychological development of the child as opposed to his school development or to his family development; that is, I will above all stress the spontaneous aspect of this development, though I will limit myself to the purely intellectual and cognitive development.

Actually we can distinguish two aspects in the child's intellectual development. On the one hand, we have what can be called the psychosocial aspect, that is, everything the child receives from without and learns in general by family, school, and educative transmission. On the other hand there is the development of the intelligence itself—what the child learns by himself, what none can teach him and he must discover alone; and it is essentially this development which takes time....

Thus what I am going to discuss is the spontaneous aspect of intelligence, and it is the only one I will mention because I am only a Psychologist and not an educator; also because from the viewpoint of time, it is precisely this spontaneous development which forms the obvious and necessary condition for the school development....

This brings us to the theory of the stages of development. Development is achieved by successive levels and stages. In this development that I am going to describe briefly, we distinguish four important stages.

First, we have a stage, before about eighteen months, which precedes speech and which we will call that of the sensorimotor intelligence. Secondly, we have a stage which begins with speech and lasts for about seven or eight years. We will call this the period of representation, but is preoperatory in the sense that I will soon define. Then, between about seven and twelve, we will distinguish a third period which we will call that of concrete operation. And finally, after twelve years, there is the stage of propositional or formal operations.

Thus we distinguish successive stages. Let us note that these stages are precisely characterized by their set order of succession. They are not stages which can be given a constant chronological date. On the contrary, the ages can vary from one society to another, as we will see at the close of this report. But there is a constant order of succession. It is always the same and for the reason we have just glimpsed; that is, in order to reach a certain stage, previous steps must be taken. The pre-structures and previous substructures that make for further advance must be constructed....

Let us rapidly describe these stages to show why time is necessary, and why so much time is required to reach these notions that are as obvious and simple as those I have used as examples.

Let us begin with the periods of sensorimotor intelligence. There is intelligence before speech, but there is not thought before speech. In this respect, let us distinguish intelligence and thought. Intelligence for the child is the solution of a new problem, in the coordination of the means to reach a certain goal which is not accessible in an immediate manner; whereas thought is interiorized intelligence no longer based on direct action but on a symbolism, and other means, which makes it possible to represent what the sensorimotor intelligence, on the contrary, is going to grasp directly....

...Let us give two examples. First, there is the notion of the permanent object.... Take an infant of five or six months after the coordination of vision and apprehension, that is, when he can begin to grasp the objects he sees. Offer him an object that interests him, for example a watch. Place it before him on the table and he reaches out to grasp the object.

Screen the object, for example, with a piece of cloth. You will see that the infant simply withdraws his hand as if the object is not important to him or becomes angry if the object has some special interest for him, for example if it is his feeding bottle. But he does not think of raising the cloth to find the object behind it. And this is not because he does not know how to move a cloth from an object. If you place the cloth on his face, he very well knows how to remove it at once, whereas he does not know how to look behind to find the object. Thus everything happens as though the object once it has disappeared from the field of perception, were reabsorbed, had lost all existence, had not yet acquired that substantiality which, as we have seen, requires eight years to reach its quantitative characteristic of conservation. The outer world is only a series of moving pictures which appear and disappear, the most interesting of which can reappear when one knows very well how to manage it (for example crying long enough if it is a question of someone whose return is desired). But these are only moving pictures without substantiality or permanence and, above all, without localization.

Second stage: You will see the infant raise the cloth to find the object hidden behind. But the following control shows that the entire notion has not really been acquired. Place the object on the infant's right, and then hide it; he is going to look for it. Then remove it from him, pass it slowly before his eyes, and place it at his left. (Here we are talking of an infant of nine or ten months.) After seeing the object disappear at his left, the infant will at once look for it at his right where he found it the first time. Thus here there is only semi-permanence without localization. The infant is going to look where the action of looking proved successful the first time and independently of the mobility of the object....

...I now come to the level of concrete operations, at an average age of about seven years in our civilizations. But we will see that there are delays or increases due to the action of social life. About the age of seven, a fundamental turning point is noted in a child's development. He becomes capable of certain logic; he becomes capable of coordinating operations in the sense of reversibility, in the sense of the total system of which I will soon give one or two examples. This period coincides with the beginning of

elementary schooling. Here again I believe that the psychological factor is a decisive one. If this level of the concrete operations came earlier, elementary schooling would begin earlier. This is not possible before a certain level of elaboration has been achieved, and I shall now try to give its characteristics.

Let us note at once that the operations of thought, on this level, are not identical to what is our own logic or to what adolescent logic will become. Adolescent logic—and our logic—is essentially a logic of speech. In other words, we are capable—and the adolescent becomes so as early as the age of twelve or fifteen—of reasoning on propositional, verbal statements. We are capable of manipulating propositions, of reasoning by placing ourselves in the viewpoints of others without believing the propositions on which we reason. We are capable of manipulating them in a formal and hypothetico-deductive manner.

As we will see, this logic requires much time to be constructed. Before this logic, a previous stage must be passed, and this is what I will call the periods of concrete operation. This precious period is that of a logic which is not based on verbal statements but only on the objects themselves, the manipulable objects. This will be a logic of classifications because objects can be collected all together or in classifications; or else it will be a logic of relations because objects can be combined according to their different relations; or else it will be a logic of numbers because objects can be materially counted by manipulating them. This will thus be a logic of classifications, relations, and numbers, and not yet a logic of propositions. Nevertheless, we are dealing with a logic, in the sense that, for the first time, we are in the presence of operations that can be reversed—for example addition, which is the same operation as subtraction but in a reversed way. It is a logic in the sense that the operations are coordinated, grouped in with systems that have their laws in terms of totalities. And we must very strongly insist on the necessity of these whole structures for the development of thought....

I come finally to the formal operations at about the age of twelve and with fourteen to fifteen years of age as equilibrium level. This concerns a final state during which the child not only becomes capable of reasoning and of deducting on manipulable objects, like sticks to arrange, numbers of objects to collect, etc. but he also becomes capable of logic and of deductive reasoning on theories and propositions. A new logic, a whole set of specific operations are superimposed on the preceding ones and this can be called the logic of propositions. Actually, this supposes two fundamental new characteristics. First there is the combinatory. Until now everything was done gradually by a series of interlockings; whereas the combinatory connect any element with any other. Here then is a new characteristic based on a kind of classification of all the classifications or seriation of all the seriations. The logic of propositions will suppose, moreover, the combination in a unique system of the different groupments, which until now were based either on reciprocity or on inversion, or, the different forms of reversibility (group of the four transformations: inversion, reciprocity, correlativity, identity). Thus we are in the presence of a completion that, in our societies, is not noted until about the age of fourteen or fifteen and which takes such a long time, because, to arrive at this point, the child must go though all kinds of stages, each being necessary to the achievement of the following one. . . .

If we compare to the young Greeks of the time when Socrates, Plato, and Aristotle invented the formal or propositional operations of our Western logic, our young contemporaries, who have to assimilate not only the logic of proportions but all the knowledge acquired by Descartes, Galileo, Newton, and others, a hypothesis must be made that there is a considerable increase in the course of childhood until the level of adolescence.

The ideal of education is not to teach the maximum, to maximize the results, but above all to learn to learn, to learn to develop, and to learn to continue to develop after leaving school.

Discussion Questions

1. Piaget distinguishes true psychological development from the development of the child in his family and school. Do you agree with his distinction? Do you think they can be separated or do they actually work together? Give examples to illustrate your answer.

2. Head Start is a program to give children from lower socioeconomic backgrounds a head start in school readiness activities. Do you think Piaget would support this program? Why or why not?

3. There is a movement in the schools to introduce more and more subjects at an earlier age. For instance, many seventh and eighth graders now study algebra for their math class. Do you think Piaget would support this movement? Why or why not?

4. Give some examples of how Piaget's psychological theories are still impacting educational practice today.

5. Discuss the moral implications of using your own children for your psychological research. Can you name some other authors who have also done this. If you are just observing your children and reporting on what you observe, is this more acceptable than actually experimenting on your children? What have you learned about teaching and learning from observing the children/students in your clinical experience?

For Further Research on the Internet

The Jean Piaget Society's home page, the Society for the Study of Knowledge and Development. http://www.piaget.org

A short biography of Piaget with links to his archives. http://www.piaget.org/biography/biog.html

The Jean Piaget archives with links to his writings and research. http://www.unige.ch/piaget/Presentations/Presentg.html

Suggestions for Further Reading

Oxford, R. "Constructivism: Shape-Shifting, Substance, and Teacher Education Applications." *Peabody Journal of Education* 72 (1977): 35–66.

Piaget, Jean. An Autobiography. In *Jean Piaget: The Man and His Ideas,* edited by S. R. I. Evan. New York: E. P. Dutton & Co., Inc., 1973.

Piaget, Jean. *Science of Education and the Psychology of the Child.* New York: Penguin Books, 1977.

Rotman, Brian. *Jean Piaget: Psychologist of the Real.* Ithaca, NY: Cornell University Publishers, 1977.

Smith, Leslie, ed. *General Introduction.* Edited by L. Smith. 4 vols. *Jean Piaget: Critical Assessments, Vol. I.* London: Routledge, 1992.

Smith, Leslie. "Jean Piaget." In *Fifty Modern Thinkers on Education: From Piaget to the Present,* edited by J. Palmer. London: Routledge, 2001.

Vidal, Fernando. *Piaget before Piaget.* Cambridge: Harvard University Press, 1994.

Section 12.3: Paulo Freire (1921–1997)

Do you remember the first word you learned to read? It may have been your name or Mom or Dad. For sure it was a word that had a lot of meaning for you. We have Paulo Freire to thank for emphasizing learning to read meaningful vocabulary.

Paulo Freire's Life and Times

Paulo Reglus Neves Freire was born on September 19, 1921 in Recife, Brazil, the youngest of four children. His father, Joaquin, and his mother, Edeltrudes, provided him with a happy, middle-class childhood giving him "mutual respect, dialogue, and free choice."[1]

Paulo's Education

Paulo first learned to read and write informally in the backyard under the trees "dialoguing" with his mother and father. Dialogue later became an important part of Paulo's teaching method. His first formal school was a small private school where he studied for one year, learning to "make sentences" by writing two or three words and orally using those words in a sentence. This strong oral tradition would stay with Paulo all his life; he was known to be a great storyteller.[2]

Paulo was eight when the world economic depression of 1929 hit. His family fell into abject poverty, and three years later Paulo's father died. Paulo did not enter high school until he was sixteen and even then he went poorly dressed and so hungry that he could not concentrate on his studies. This experience of poverty led him to dedicate his life to trying to improve life for the poor. He began to teach the rural children of Jaboatão the rudiments of literacy while still in high school.

Paulo's mother brought him up in the Catholic religion; he joined Catholic Action, an organization devoted to eliminating poverty and hunger in Northeast Brazil. Although Freire criticized the Catholic Church, calling it the Church of the Oppressors, he remained an active Catholic all his life and said his Christian upbringing influenced both his pedagogical theories and his practices.[3]

Teacher

Paulo started to study law at the University in Pernambuco when he was twenty, so that he could work "among the people of the slums" and help them understand their legal rights. To make money, he also taught Portuguese in a secondary school in Recife and became fascinated with language and syntax, finding teaching more rewarding than law.

After he graduated from college, he taught illiterate Brazilian peasants and developed a special interest in grammar, linguistics, and philology that became part of his theory of knowing, learning, and philosophy of education and of language.[4]

Family Man

The third important moment in his life was when he met Elza Maria Costa, a primary school teacher whom he married in 1944. They eventually had five children, three of whom became educators. Freire said that his marriage was a happy one and his wife was one of his close collaborators. His family life was a source of comfort, inspiration, and learning.

Circles of Culture

In 1946, Freire began to work at the Social Service of Industry where, as educational director, he coordinated the work of the teachers with the children while also working with the mostly illiterate families. Between 1947 and 1959, Paulo intensified his work with adult literacy, rejecting the traditional, authoritative methods of instruction and developing the "circles of culture." In a culture circle, the participants learned to read and write the words which were an important part of their lives and thus they were motivated to learn them. After just thirty to forty hours of meetings, about seventy-five percent of the participants could read the newspaper and write simple texts.[5]

Adult Literacy Teacher

Freire began doctoral studies at the University of Recife in the philosophy of education, reading the works of Marx, Hegel, Ortega y Gassett, Sarte, and other political philosophers. His dissertation criticized the Brazilian system of education and proposed radical revisions based on his work teaching the Brazilian peasants. He proposed that instead of following the current "banking method" of education in which the teacher "deposits" knowledge into the empty minds of the illiterate, a "pedagogy of the oppressed" be implemented in which students are enabled and empowered through education to transform the world in which they live by the knowledge they obtain.[6] He first piloted his new method in 1962 in the town of Angicos, where 300 rural farm workers were taught to read and write in 45 days. Paulo was invited to set up his adult literacy system for the entire country, but the military coup in 1964 established a dictatorship in Brazil and canceled his allegedly "subversive" work. Freire spent 70 days under house arrest before taking his family to Chile in exile from 1964 to 1969.[7] (See the timeline of Freire's life in Figure 12.3.)

Pedagogy of the Oppressed

In Santiago, Paulo worked for five years as a UNESCO consultant, directed the adult literacy program, and wrote *Education as a Practice of Freedom* and *The Pedagogy of the Oppressed* that established him as a leading figure in adult literacy and radical political education.

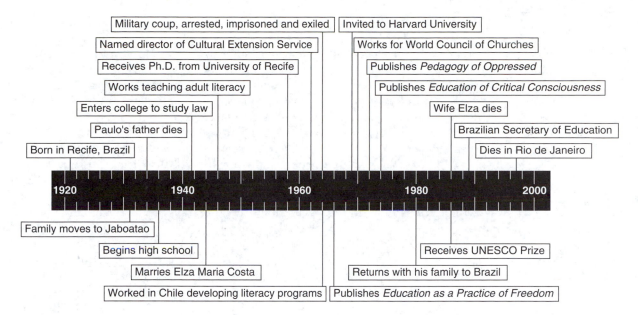

Figure 12.3   Freire's Life and Times

Freire was invited to Harvard University in 1969 to give seminars and conferences as a visiting professor and came in contact with many North American educators and scholars including Ivan Illich, another critic of schooling in industrialized countries. Here Freire published the most scholarly expositions of his theories, clearly delineating his Marxist interpretation of the situation of the illiterate in the third world while outlining the importance of dialogue as his methodology.[8] In 1970, Freire moved to Geneva, Switzerland and established the Institute for Cultural Action, working with various third-world countries to establish literacy programs encountering the challenges of multilingualism. A decade later, Freire, 57, was granted amnesty and was permitted to return to Brazil after fifteen years of exile. Accepting a position at the Pontifical Catholic University of São Paulo and the University of Campinas, he began immediately where he had left off, promoting political action that would support literacy programs for all Brazilians. His wife died after forty years of marriage in 1986, leaving him distraught, but two years later, Freire married an ex-pupil, Ana Maria Hasche, a widow.[9] From 1989 to 1991 he served as the Secretary of Education, which allowed him to implement adult literacy programs and work for the democratization of education in Brazil.[10]

Freire spent the last years of his life writing and speaking nationally and internationally about his ideas and his work. Central to understanding his work is his conviction that education is a political act; it involves policies and practices based on social relations and political choices. Freire died of a heart attack in Rio de Janeiro on May 2, 1997, at the age of 75, leaving behind a legacy of commitment, love, and hope for oppressed peoples throughout the world. His ideas continue to impact educators today.

Freire's Contribution to Educational Thought

Paulo Freire was truly a "citizen of the world" with an educational program that globally influenced teaching and learning. Freire made both practical and theoretical contributions to education as one of Latin America's most important intellectuals and adult educators and the best known literacy educator in the world. His literacy method is very successful, but for Freire, real education also promotes "political literacy," which is the process whereby men and women become liberated, a reality not yet realized.

Pedagogy of the Oppressed is Freire's classic text on education and politics and undoubtedly the best known. In it, he outlines his method for teaching adults to read: 1) studying the context to determine the common vocabulary and "generative themes"; 2) selection of the words to be used in instruction, i.e., the "vocabulary universe"; and 3) the actual literacy training in "culture circles" using the dialogue method.[11]

The central concepts in Freire's "pedagogy of the oppressed" are the concept of "conscientization," or as he describes it "the process in which men, not as recipients, but as knowing subjects, achieve a deepening awareness both of the sociocultural reality that shapes their lives, and of their capacity or 'praxis' to transform the reality through action upon it."[12] This awareness is developed using the dialogical method that powerfully engages the learners in a process of education that questions and evaluates all arguments and conclusions.

Some critique Freire for the language used in his books, saying that it is too difficult, elitist, arrogant, and sexist; and they contend that his explanation of oppression is only about class, not about race and gender.[13] Others say that Paulo Freire's greatest contribution is his ability to communicate and connect with so many people—different ages, races, religious beliefs, economic positions, ideologies … and to help them see that there is something called education, poverty, and oppression; and that there is a relationship among them and it is up to them to make this relationship liberating or to allow oppression to continue.[14]

Freire's Philosophy of Education

Paulo Freire's educational theories create a complete philosophy of education that answers the questions "What is the purpose of education? What are you teaching and how are you teaching it?" and "To whom are you teaching it?" central to any educational activity.

Education is for freedom. Freire does not see an intrinsic value in education for its own sake, he sees education as a political process; motivated by the realization that impoverished people live in many parts of the world, education is a way to help them to become empowered. He labels the authoritarian educational system as "banking education" with the role of the teacher as "depositing" content in the mind of the learners.

Accord to Freire's educational philosophy, reality is dynamic and changing, and knowledge is dynamic and changing. Human knowing is culturally and socially conditioned. For him, the quest for knowledge is a continuing one, especially since there are no absolutes.[15]

Freire's method of instruction is outlined in the following selection. It is a problem-based method using the dialogue. Magazine articles, newspapers, and books are read and discussed, along with problems. The dialogue method engages students and reduces teacher-talk.[16] Freire's method is especially helpful to teachers in America's schools faced with students from poverty backgrounds, with multicultural backgrounds and diverse linguistic needs. Freire addressed some of these problems in his *"Letter to North American Teachers."* He says that "a teacher must be fully cognizant of the political nature of his/her practice and assume responsibility for this," realizing that addressing issues of social class, gender, and race are the task of education.[17]

Like other educational philosophers, Freire believes that education is based on a theory of persons and the world. Humans are understood as beings of relationships, first to God and secondly to their fellow humans. They share a culture, reflect upon what they do, and have the freedom to do things differently. Freire sees religion and culture as one. Freire writes as if the oppressed will become different persons once liberated. He assumes that they will use their freedom wisely; however, experience shows that sometimes the oppressed, once freed, at times become the oppressors of others. Some critics argue that Freire's method emphasizes reflection over action without a clear conception of social change. His analysis is based on Hegelian dialects which see a constant tension of theses, antitheses, and syntheses; so education can only happen when the conflict between banking education, capitalistic development, and oppression is resolved.[18]

The view of human nature articulated by Freire can be aptly described as overly optimistic and utopian. His vision was fashioned upon the religious tradition in which he was raised and educated, but it is not in line with that tradition. Freire has a faulty view of human nature, for he fails to take into account the limitations of human freedom and the fact of human evil (the reality of original sin).[19]

Freire's educational principles are found in many of the contemporary ideas for education such as: (1) the responsibility for education is in the hands of the pupil himself, (2) the traditional school needs to be critiqued, (3) knowledge is the life of the local community, and (4) one learns by doing.[20]

Paulo Freire is one of the most significant educators of the later part of the twentieth century with a very unique and eclectic Christian, existential, and Marxist philosophy of education. His work makes a powerful statement about the power of education to address the social problems of the time. His message is that there is hope for humankind as long as people are free both to be educated and to educate. *"Citizenship is not obtained by chance: It is a construction that, never finished, demands we fight for it. It demands commitment, political clarity, coherence, decision. For this reason a democratic education cannot be realized apart from an education of and for citizenship."*[21]

Notes

1. L. Glenn Smith, and Joan K. Smith, *Lives in Education: A Narrative of People and Ideas,* 2nd ed. (New York: St. Martin's Press, 1994), p. 428.
2. Moacir Gadotti, *Reading Paulo Freire: His Life and Works,* translated by John Milton (Albany: State University of New York Press, 1994), pp. 1–2.
3. Gadotti, pp. 3–4.
4. John L. Elias, *Paulo Freire: Pedagogue of Liberation* (Malabar, FL: Krieger Publishing Company, 1994), pp. 2–3.
5. Elias, pp. 2–3; Smith and Smith, pp. 428–430.
6. Paulo Freire, *Pedagogy of the Oppressed,* translated by Myra Bergman Ramos (New York: Continuum, 1970), p. 8.
7. Elias, pp. 8–9.
8. Elias, p. 11.
9. Gadotti, p. 162.
10. Michal Apple, Luis Ganin, and Alvaro Hypolito, *Paulo Freire* (London: Routledge, 2001), p. 129.
11. Elias, p. 17.
12. Freire, 1970. p, 101.
13. Daniel Schugurensky, "The Legacy of Paulo Freire: A Critical Review of His Contributions," *Convergence* 31 (1/2) (1998), pp. 18, 21.
14. Rosa-Maria Torres, "The Million Paulo Freires," *Convergence* 31 (1/2) (1998), p. 116.
15. Elias, pp. 63, 69.
16. Ira Shor, "Educating the Educators: A Freirean Approach to the Crisis in Teacher Education," in *Freire for the Classroom: A Sourcebook for Liberatory Teaching,* edited by I. Shor (Portsmouth, NH: Boynton/Cook Publishers Inc., 1987), p. 23.
17. Paulo Freire, "Letter to North American Teachers," in *Freire for the Classroom: A Sourcebook of Liberatory Teaching,* edited by I. Shor (Portsmouth, NH: Boynton/Cook Publishers, Inc., 1987), p. 211.
18. Schugurensky, p. 21.
19. S. J. Dennis Collins, *Paulo Freire: His Life, Works and Thought* (New York: Paulist Press, 1977), p. 3.
20. Gadotti, pp. 55, 111–121.
21. Paulo Freire, *Teachers as Cultural Workers—Letters to Those Who Dare to Teach* (Boulder, CO: Westview Press, 1998), p. 90.

Questions to Guide Your Reading

1. What is the "banking" concept of education, according to Freire? Are there any subjects that are best taught using this method, or is this method always to be avoided?
2. What is "liberating" education, according to Freire? Can you give an example of this kind of education in today's classrooms?
3. Describe, in your own words, what Freire means by problem-posing education. (Be sure to mention the role and relationship of the teacher and of the student.)

READING 12.3:
PEDAGOGY OF THE OPPRESSED, EXCERPTS FROM CHAPTER 2

A careful analysis of the teacher-student relationship at any level, inside or outside the school, reveals its fundamentally *narrative* character. This relationship involves a narrating Subject (the teacher) and patient, listening objects (the students). The content, whether values or empirical dimensions of reality, tend in the process of being narrated to become lifeless and petrified. Education is suffering from narration sickness.

The teacher talks about reality as if it were motionless, static, compartmentalized, and predictable. Or else he expounds on a topic completely alien to the existential experience of the students. His task is to "fill" the students with the contents of his narration—contents that are detached from reality, disconnected from the totality that engendered them and could give them significance. Words are emptied of their concreteness and become a hollow, alienated, and alienating verbosity.

Narration (with the teacher as narrator) leads the students to memorize mechanically the narrated content. Worse yet, it turns them into "containers," into "receptacles" to be "filled" by the teacher. The more completely he fills the receptacles, the better a teacher he is. The more meekly the receptacles permit themselves to be filled, the better students they are.

Education thus becomes an act of depositing, in which the students are the depositories and the teacher is the depositor. Instead of communicating, the teacher issues communications and makes deposits which the students patiently receive, memorize, and repeat. This is the "banking" concept of education, in which the scope of action allowed to the students extends only as far as receiving, filling, and storing the deposits. They do, it is true, have the opportunity to become collectors or cataloguers of the things they store. But in the last analysis, it is men themselves who are filed away through the lack of creativity, transformation, and knowledge in this (at best) misguided system. For apart from inquiry, apart from the praxis, men cannot be truly human. Knowledge emerges only through invention and re-invention, through the restless, impatient, continuing, hopeful inquiry men pursue in the world, with the world, and with each other.

In the banking concept of education, knowledge is a gift bestowed by those who consider themselves knowledgeable upon those whom they consider to know nothing. Projecting an absolute ignorance onto others, a characteristic of the ideology of oppression, negates education and knowledge as processes of inquiry. The teacher presents himself to his students as their necessary opposite; by considering their ignorance absolute, he justifies his own existence. The

Source: By Paulo Freire, translated by Myra Bergman Ramos, copyright © 1970, 1993 by Paulo Freire. Reprinted by permission of The Continuum International Publishing Group.

students, alienated like the slave in the Hegelian dialectic, accept their ignorance as justifying the teacher's existence but, unlike the slave, they never discover that they educate the teacher....

This solution is not (nor can it be) found in the banking concept. On the contrary, banking education maintains and even stimulates the contradictions through the following attitudes and practices, which make for an oppressive society as a whole:

a. the teacher teaches and the students are taught;
b. the teacher knows everything and the students know nothing;
c. the teacher thinks and the students are thought about;
d. the teacher talks and the students listen—meekly;
e. the teacher disciplines and the students are disciplined;
f. the teacher chooses and enforces his choice, and the students comply;
g. the teacher acts and the students have the illusion of acting through the action of the teacher;
h. the teacher chooses the program content, and the students (who were not consulted) adapt to it;
i. the teacher confuses the authority of knowledge with his own professional authority, which he sets in opposition to the freedom of the students;
j. the teacher is the Subject of the learning process, while the pupils are mere objects....

...Those truly committed to liberation must reject the banking concept in its entirety, adopting instead a concept of men as conscious beings, and consciousness as consciousness intent upon the world. They must abandon the educational goal of deposit making and replace it with the posing of the problems of men in their relations with the world. "Problem-posing" education, responding to the essence of consciousness—*intentionality*—rejects communiqués and embodies communication. It epitomizes the special characteristic of consciousness: being *conscious of,* not only as intent on objects but as turned in upon itself in a Jasperian "split" consciousness as consciousness *of consciousness.*

Liberating education consists in acts of cognition, not transferals of information. It is a learning situation in which the cognizable object (far from being the end of the cognitive act) intermediates the cognitive actors—teacher on the one hand and students on the other. Accordingly, the practice of problem-posing education entails at the outset that the teacher-student Contradiction be resolved. Dialogical relations—indispensable to the capacity of cognitive actors to cooperate in perceiving the same cognizable object—are otherwise impossible.

Indeed, problem-posing education, which breaks with the vertical patterns characteristic of banking education, can fulfill its function as the practice of freedom only if it can overcome the above contradiction. Through dialogue, the teacher of the students and the students of the teacher cease to exist and a new term emerges: teacher-student with students-teachers. The teacher is no longer merely the one who teaches, but one who is himself taught in dialogue with the students, who in turn while being taught also teach. They become jointly responsible for a process in which all grow. In this process, arguments based on "authority" are no longer valid; in order to function, authority must be *on the side of* freedom, not *against* it. Here, no one teaches another, nor is anyone self taught. Men teach each other, mediated by the world, by the cognizable objects which in banking education are "owned" by the teacher.... The students, no longer docile listeners, are now critical co-investigators in dialogue with the teacher. The teacher presents the material to the students for their consideration, and reconsiders his earlier considerations as the students express their own...

...Students, as they are increasingly posed with problems relating to themselves in the world and with the world, will feel increasingly challenged and obliged to respond to that challenge. Because they apprehend the challenge as interrelated to other problems within a total context, not as a theoretical question, the resulting comprehension tends to be increasingly critical and thus constantly less alienated. Their response to the challenge evokes new challenges, followed by new understandings; and gradually the students come to regard themselves as committed.

...In problem-posing education, men develop their power to perceive critically *the way they exist* in the world *with which* and *in which* they find themselves; they come to see the world not as a static reality, but as a reality in process, in transformation. Hence, the teacher-student and the students-teachers reflect simultaneously on themselves and the world without dichotomizing this reflection from action, and thus establish an authentic form of thought and action. . . .

In sum:

Problem-posing education affirms men as beings in the process of *becoming*—as unfinished, uncompleted beings in and with a likewise unfinished reality. Indeed, in contrast to other animals who are unfinished, but not historical, men know themselves to be unfinished; they are aware of their incompletion. In this incompletion and this awareness lie the very roots of education as an exclusively human manifestation. The unfinished character of men and the transformational character of reality necessitate that education be an ongoing activity.

Education is thus constantly remade in the praxis. In order to *be*, it must *become*. Its "duration" (in the Bergsonian meaning of the word) is found in the interplay of the opposites *permanence* and *change*. The banking method emphasizes permanence and becomes reactionary; problem-posing education—which accepts neither a "well behaved" present nor a predetermined future—roots itself in the dynamic present and becomes revolutionary.

Discussion Questions

1. Compare and contrast the philosophy of education behind the "banking" concept of education with the "problem-posing" concept of education. How would Freire critique the current "back to basics movement" and the "standards-based" focus of education in the United States?

2. Do you think people are educationally "oppressed" in the United States, or is this only a reality in the third-world countries? What are the educational implications of current international problems such as terrorism and the violation of human rights?

3. Freire says that all education is inherently political. Do you agree? Why or why not?

4. In what ways do you think Freire has shaped educational discourse in the last half of the twentieth century? (You might want to consider his relationship to the "activity based" education of Dewey and Montessori, or to Piaget's constructivism.)

5. Consider how Freire's family's decline into poverty shaped his educational priorities. Speak with your classmates. How have your family backgrounds influenced your choice of education as a career? What are your goals and dreams as an educator?

6. Freire says in his *Letter to North American Teachers* that "since education is by nature social, historical, and political there is no way we can talk about some universal, unchanging role for the teacher." Now that we are at the end of this text, do you agree or disagree with Freire? Cite some of the other educational philosophers that we have read to support your position.

For Further Research on the Internet

A homepage on Paulo Freire with links to his works and criticisms of them. **http://www.infed.org/thinkers/et-freir.htm#critique**

Home page of the Paulo Freire Institute. **http://www.paulofreire.org**

A brief biography of Paulo Freire including links to his works. **http://fcis.oise.utoronto.ca/~daniel_schugurensky/freire/opp.htm**

Suggestions for Further Reading

Apple, Michael, Luis Armando Ganin, and Alvaro Moreira Hypolito. "Paulo Freire." In *Fifty Modern Thinkers on Education*, edited by J. Palmer. London: Routledge, 2001.

Collins, S. J. Dennis. *Paulo Freire: His Life, Works and Thought*, New York: Paulist Press, 1977.

Elias, John L. *Paulo Freire: Pedagogue of Liberation*. Malabar, FL: Krieger Publishing Company, 1994.

Freire, Paulo. *Pedagogy of the Oppressed*. Translated by Myra Bergman Ramos. New York: Continuum, 1970.

Freire, Paulo. *The Politics of Education*. Translated by Donaldo Macedo. Edited by P. Freire and H. Giroux, *Critical Studies in Education Series*. New York: Bergin & Garvey, 1985.

Freire, Paulo. "Letter to North American Teachers." In *Freire for the Classroom: A Sourcebook of Liberatory Teaching*, edited by I. Shor. Portsmouth, NH: Boynton/Cook Publishers, Inc., 1987.

Freire, Paulo. *Teachers as Cultural Workers—Letters to Those Who Dare to Teach*. Boulder, CO: Westview Press, 1998.

Freire, Paulo, and Ira Shor. *A Pedagogy for Liberation: Dialogues on Transforming Education*. South Hadley, MA: Bergin & Garvey Publishers, Inc., 1987.

Gadotti, Moacir. *Reading Paulo Freire: His Life and Works*. Translated by John Milton. Albany: State University of New York Press, 1994.

Lange, Elizabeth. "Fragmented Ethics of Justice: Freire, Liberation Theology and Pedagogies for the Non-poor." *Convergence* 31 (1/2) (1998): 81–101.

Schugurensky, Daniel. "The Legacy of Paulo Freire: A Critical Review of His Contributions." *Convergence* 31 (1/2) (1998): 17–29.

Shor, Ira. "Educating the Educators: A Freirean Approach to the Crisis in Teacher Education." In *Freire for the Classroom: A Sourcebook for Liberatory Teaching*, edited by I. Shor. Portsmouth, NH: Boynton/Cook Publishers, Inc., 1987.

Smith, L. Glenn, and Joan K. Smith. *Lives in Education: A Narrative of People and Ideas*, 2nd ed. New York: St. Martin's Press, 1994.

Torres, Rosa-Maria. "The Million Paulo Freires." *Convergence* 31 (1/2) (1998): 107–117.

CHAPTER ACTIVITIES

Linking the Past to the Present

Research contemporary living educators by using the Internet and journal articles. Circle up and use the critical dialogue method to discuss your educators and their contributions. Which do you think should be included in the next edition of this book? What is their main contribution to educational history and philosophy?

Developing Your Philosophy of Education

Now that you are at the end of this book, you want to finalize your philosophy of education paper. Begin the paper with an introductory paragraph in which you explain that this is your philosophy of education and how you will organize the paper. You may want to use a metaphor or a favorite quote to give your paper a unity.

Then develop separate paragraphs on each of the aspects of a philosophy of education upon which you would like to reflect. For instance, what role will you play as the teacher? What is your view of the student? What and how will you teach? What do you see as the purpose of education? You may cite ideas from some of the educators in this book.

Finally, write a concluding paragraph that is a summary of the main aspects of your paper. You will probably want to memorize this last paragraph in order to use it when you are interviewed for a teaching position and they ask you, "Can you explain your philosophy of education to us?"

Connecting Theory to Practice

Visit a Montessori school and observe the classroom. What is the role of the teacher/directress? What instruction is going on while you observe? Watch one student for fifteen minutes. What does the child do and learn in that time period?

Educators' Philosophies and Contributions to Education

TABLE 12.1 Philosophy and Contributions of International Educators

Educator	Role of Teacher & Learner	View of Curriculum & Methodology	Purpose or Goal of Education	Major Contribution
Montessori	The directress is a facilitator, preparing the environment so that the children can teach themselves as they interact with it according to their sensitive periods	Life skills, motor and sensory training, and formal literary and computational skills; this work gives joy to the child; spontaneous learning	Help the child to holistically develop his/her physical, moral, and mental potential	Transformed preschool education; view of the child as an absorbent mind
Piaget	Teachers organize instruction according to the cognitive level of the child, i.e., formal and concrete operations	Content is introduced when the child is at the appropriate cognitive level; learning centers; cooperative learning	Helping children to learn to think, discover, and create	Theory of stage of cognitive development in children
Freire	Teach reading by using generative words; education can help oppressed students become liberated	Dialogical method that engages learners in the process of education through culture circles	Real education is political; it should liberate	Foremost adult educator; problem-based method using dialogue

Index